JOHN BENSON'S A to Z BASEBALL PLAYER GUIDE 1997

DIAMOND LIBRARY

Executive Editor:
Marc Bowman

Associate Editors:
James Benson, Tony Blengino and Lawr Michaels

Layout and Design:
Stephen Wade Lunsford and Brian Weaver

Copyright (c) 1996 by John Chapman Benson with licenses to Diamond Analytics Corporation

All rights reserved under International and Pan-American Copyright Conventions

Library of Congress Catalog Data: Benson, John, *Baseball Player Guide A to Z 1997*
1. Baseball -- United States -- History
2. Baseball -- United States -- Records
I. Title

ISBN 1-880876-08-6

No part of this book may be reproduced or transmitted in any form by any means, electronic or mechanical, including photocopying, recording, electronic imaging or scanning, or by any information storage and retrieval system or method, unless expressly permitted in writing by the author and the publisher. For information contact Diamond Library Publishers.

Published by Diamond Library Publishers, a division of Diamond Analytics Corporation, with offices at 15 Cannon Road, Wilton, Connecticut, 06897. Telephone 203-834-1231.

PRINTED IN THE UNITED STATES OF AMERICA

Cover design by - Stephen Wade Lunsford
Production Manager - Brian Weaver
Editorial Consultant - James Benson

Statistics are provided by STATS, Inc. 8131 Monticello Ave. Skokie, IL 60076-3300
Telephone 847-676-3322.

This book is sold for entertainment purposes only. Neither the writers, nor the editors or publishers assume any liability beyond the purchase price for any reason.

Table of Contents

Credits   4

Introductions and acknowledgments   5

Draft Report Card by Jim Callis   7

Batters   11

Pitchers   153

Top 100 Prospects Now and for the Future   277

1997 Stat Projections   287

Resources   296

Credits:

James Benkard
James Benson
Tony Blengino
Marc Bowman
Darin Brown
Jason Brown
Lary Bump
Jim Callis
Greg Gajus
Bill Gilbert
Peter Graves
Bill Gray
Peter Keiser
David Luciani
Stephen Lunsford
Fred Matos
Lawr Michaels
Cole Pepper
John Perrotto
Brian Weaver
Alan Woodard

Introduction and Acknowledgments
by John Benson

As a baseball writer during the 1980's, I often found myself trying to find out what happened to a specific player who had disappeared from the usual reference books. In my office I have always had a library of the most recent annual guidebooks, but often I would have to call a major league front office to ask, "Do you know what happened to this guy who played in your system last year?" And sometimes, even the player's last major league team wouldn't know what happened to him.

The purpose of my A to Z Player Guide is to provide a book where "all" players appear in one volume, with information that goes beyond recent statistics. My intention is to answer the question: who is this guy? That job is much bigger than it sounds. Marc Bowman's acknowledgments, on the next page, help you understand what this simple goal requires in terms of work effort, which is somewhere beyond substantial.

It feels a little funny to hear people tell me, "You wrote this book," because there were so many other writers who did so much of the writing. Actually, what I did was to manage a project that produced this book. The writers whose names appear on the facing page are the core of a team of which I am just one guy on the field, if you know what I mean -- fairly useless without the others.

To all of the writers, I offer a hearty "thank-you" with a special appreciation for the splendid attention to timing, by everyone. In a book of this type, the pieces must fit together in the right place at exactly the right moment, or the team can't move along. Like the daylight play at second base, the run-and-hit, and the rotation play when executed perfectly, this year's teamwork was (again!) just right. Thanks and congratulations for a job well done.

While I am naturally reluctant to single out individual efforts in a teamwork project where everyone is indispensable, I have often used this space in past years to thank one person who made a special impression on me that year. In this 1997 edition, I want to say a special word of thanks to Bill Gilbert, who has been involved in my books since the very beginning, adding more knowledge and insight year after year. More than any other writer/analyst who helps me, Bill brings a widening perspective and joyful intensity to the subject of baseball player performance. Bill is blessed with a rare combination of historical context and personal knowledge of what happens in a major league front office and dugout. Bill's contributions would be excellent if that was all he offered, but in addition he is a fine writer of the English language. In any field, that combination of knowing a subject and being able to write about it means the reader gets the best possible product -- and that is what Bill brings to these pages. Simply stated (and I know Marc Bowman agrees with me) Bill offers an example that all other writers in the world of baseball would do well to emulate.

Marc Bowman always deserves extra thanks for his work as executive editor. Every year, I hope and pray that Marc will do a job about as good as he did the year before, and Marc consistently surpasses my hopes and prayers by surpassing himself. I honestly don't know how he does it.

Special thanks also go to John Dewan of STATS, Inc. for the many helpful and light-shedding statistics and wise counsel over the years. Whenever anyone asks (and sometimes before they ask) I recommend STATS as the best source for baseball factual information, and the fastest production of that information, and the sharpest presentation, and the most useful state-of-the-art media including their amazing on-line service. Beginning this year, my sales office at Diamond Library is proud to offer STATS books to all of our readers. The overwhelmingly visible presence of STATS books in press boxes, everywhere I go, is strong evidence of the books' value.

In conclusion, I urge all readers to take a long, hard look at the "credits" list on the facing page, and understand this book as springing from the hearts and minds of those individuals. I wish I could put all their names on the cover, because they deserve it.

John

Marc Bowman's Acknowledgments

Each fall we attempt to produce the best and most unique baseball book and each fall we try to do even more than the year before. This year we wanted to get this volume into your hands as quickly as possible. That meant doing the same voluminous work, but in about half as much time. Having seen the results, I'd say it was well worth the effort.

This year's edition covers more players than ever before (about 2800), does so in even more precise detail than in the past, and was accomplished much more quickly. The book you now hold in your hands is the best of its kind and is a tribute to the superb talents of the writers who produced it.

We ask each of our writers to cover specific teams and to write about any players who might appear in the major leagues in the next couple of seasons, providing a brief description of each players' strengths and weaknesses as well as what can be expected of him in the immediate future.

An easy way to think about this task is to pretend you are at a ballpark with a friend and are trying to describe an individual player as he strides to the plate or trots in from the bullpen (or saunters in, if you are describing Lee Smith). You have just a precious few seconds to describe the traits of the player before he actually performs. Try it some time and you'll discover how hard it really is to say something "insightful, clever, concise and comprehensive, quickly, now".

You'll find that the hardest part isn't finding enough to say about each of these players, but being relatively brief while still capturing their essential qualities. Bear in mind that several players in this volume have had entire books devoted exclusively to their exploits. Now multiply the singular task of writing about a specific player by approximately one hundred players for each major league organization, and then limiting the task at hand to a few weeks and you can get an appreciation for what these writers have accomplished.

Among the credited writers are many familiar names and a couple of new ones. I'm happy to say that several of these people have been involved with Benson's books for many years, and we have developed a nationwide network of friendship through this work. These writers have a great love for the game of baseball in addition to bringing their own special talents into these books. They are good people to know.

Of course, the usual gang is here. John Perrotto, Tony Blengino, Fred Matos, Greg Gajus, Bill Gray and James Benkard each covered more than one team and did so superbly. In particular, Tony helped out on several extra minor leaguers to provide even greater depth of coverage; I'm always amazed at Tony's wealth of knowledge when it comes to minor league talents.

Bill Gilbert, David Luciani, and Peter Graves each covered their own teams with acute precision. In his second year, Al Woodard did not suffer from a sophomore slump; his excellent work was even better this year.

Lawr Michaels and Cole Pepper were our rookies this year. One of the reasons this book is so good is because newcomers like Lawr and Cole stepped in with such fine work and both did it under very tight time constraints. Stephen Lunsford isn't new to Benson's books, but his contribution this year was even greater than in the past. Andy Bowman was instrumental in providing interesting details about minor league players

In the Diamond Libraries' office, Brian Weaver assisted with many details in a persistent, productive manner; this book wouldn't exist without his efforts. Of course, this book wouldn't be the same without John Benson's thoughtful musings. It was a pleasure to work with these people once again. A lot of effort went into producing what we believe is the very best baseball book of it's kind. We hope you enjoy it.

Marc Bowman - November, 1996

The 1996 Amateur Draft: REPORT CARDS
by Jim Callis, Managing Editor, Baseball America

The 1996 draft may have been the most unusual ever, as four of the first 12 picks were declared free agents because they weren't tendered proper contracts by the teams that selected them. First baseman Travis Lee, the number two overall pick, received a staggering $10 million deal from the expansion Arizona Diamondbacks, who also landed righthander John Patterson, the number five pick. Their expansion counterparts, the Devil Rays, snapped up lefthander Bobby Seay, the number 12 selection. And righthander Matt White, the number seven pick who had yet to sign by mid-November, may be the best high school pitching prospect of the draft era. Several first-round picks have yet to make their professional debuts because they spent the summer playing with the U.S. Olympic team.

AMERICAN LEAGUE DRAFT ALL-STARS

Catcher--A.J. Hinch, Athletics (third round). Drafted in the second round out of high school and the third round in 1995, Hinch drew scouts' ire for not signing either time. By his senior year at Stanford, most scouts were down on his arm strength and not excited by his lack of home run power. But the U.S. Olympic team catcher and the only player to be on Team USA for four straight years offers athleticism behind the plate, a decent bat, doubles power and above-average speed for a catcher. His upside is a poor man's Craig Biggio, which could make Hinch a rich man. ETA: Late 1999.

First Baseman--Gary LoCurto, Red Sox (second round). Boston took LoCurto with a compensation pick for the loss of free agent Erik Hanson, and seems to have come out ahead on the deal. LoCurto, a lefthanded hitter out of San Diego, can hit for both power (12 extra-base hits in 137 at-bats in the spacious parks of the Gulf Coast League) and average (.314). If Mo Vaughn becomes a Red Sox fixture, LoCurto will have to move to DH because he doesn't have outfield ability. ETA: Early 2000.

Second Baseman--Ryan Stromsborg, Blue Jays (fourth round). Stromsborg was pretty much a non-entity on Southern California's 1995 College World Series team, but came into his own last spring. A good all-around athlete, he runs a 6.6-second 60-yard dash and has begun to develop strength. His pro debut was solid, as he hit .310-8-38 in 216 at-bats and stole eight bases in the Pioneer League. ETA: Late 1999.

Third Baseman--Eric Chavez, Athletics (first round, number 10 overall). Considered the best pure hitter in the 1996 draft, Chavez could team with 1994 first-round pick Ben Grieve to form a formidable heart of the batting order for Oakland in the near future. Chavez has a short, compact stroke, already knows how to use the middle of the field and could be good for 20-plus home runs a year once he fills out. The San Diego native signed late, so has yet to make his pro debut. ETA: Mid-1999.

Shortstop--Joe Lawrence, Blue Jays (first round, number 16 overall). A compensation pick for the loss of free agent Robert Alomar, Lawrence probably won't approach Alomar's level of stardom but should be an offensive-minded middle infielder. A hamstring injury limited him to a .217 average in the New York-Penn League, a heady assignment for a high school player, but he should hit for average with some power. The Lake Charles, La., product could wind up at third base if he hit outgrows shortstop. ETA: Late 1999.

Outfielder--Chad Green, Brewers (first round, number eight overall). A reserve on the U.S. Olympic team, Green was a perfect fit for Milwaukee, which craved a center fielder and leadoff hitter. Green was the fastest player available in the draft, and was a star high school running back who attracted the interest of several college football powers before going to Kentucky. He has some pop, but needs to stop worrying about trying to go deep and let his speed carry him. ETA: Early 1999.

Outfielder--Dermal Brown, Royals (first round, number 14 overall). Like Green, Brown was a highly touted high school running back, and he could have gone from Marlboro, N.Y. to the University of Maryland had he wanted to stick with the gridiron. Kansas City scouting director Art Stewart says he has seen just three high school hitters who could hit a homer as quick and as far as Brown: Bo Jackson, Dave Kingman and Greg Luzinski. He went just one-for-20 in the Gulf Coast League after signing late, but should also hit for average and be a threat on the bases. ETA: Early 2000.

Outfielder--Jacque Jones, Twins (second round). Jones finished second on the U.S. Olympic team in most offensive categories, trailing only first baseman Travis Lee, Minnesota's first-round pick who signed with the Diamondbacks as a free agent. Jones doesn't have overwhelming tools, but he can hit and should add some homers and steals. A star at Southern California, he went two-for-three in the Florida State League before a minor knee injury ended his summer. ETA: Early 1999.

Designated Hitter--Danny Peoples, Indians (first round, number 28 overall). Even though Cleveland was swimming in money after selling out Jacobs Field for the entire season, the Tribe decided no player available when they picked warranted market value. So the Indians decided to take the first player on their draft list who would accept $400,000, and that turned out to be Peoples. The former Texas standout has impressive power and probably will wind up at first base despite playing third in his debut. He hit .239-3-26 in 117 New York-Penn League at-bats, then injured his shoulder and had surgery. ETA: Late 1999.

Starting Pitcher--Seth Greisinger, Tigers (first round, number six overall). Detroit really wanted John Patterson, but settled for Greisinger when Patterson went the pick before to Montreal. It couldn't have turned out better for the Tigers, who wound up with the pitcher who supplanted number one overall pick Kris Benson as the ace of the Olympic team and became the first Team USA pitcher ever to win nine games in a summer. Greisinger, a righthander who led Virginia to a surprising Atlantic Coast Conference championship, has a solid fastball to go with an outstanding curveball and changeup. He may start his pro career in Double-A and should reach Detroit in a hurry.

Starting Pitcher--Billy Koch, Blue Jays (first round, number four overall). Koch, who joined fellow Clemson ace Benson as the highest drafted pair of pitchers from one school, spent the summer in the U.S. Olympic starting rotation. A righthander, Koch should become a Toronto fan favorite, what with his 100-mph fastball (the hardest in the 1996 draft) and crazy antics (he's nicknamed "Captain Chaos" for good reason). How soon he helps Toronto and how big a star he becomes will depend on how well he can harness his command. ETA: Mid-1999.

Starting Pitcher--Eric Milton, Yankees (first round, number 20 overall). All three pitchers on this AL team starred in the ACC, though Milton did so for a dreadful Maryland program that plays in a hitter's paradise. A lefthander, he throws an ever-improving fastball and curveball and is fairly polished. He signed late, spending his summer pitching a no-hitter and setting a record with a 0.21 ERA in the Cape Cod League. ETA: Late 1998.

Closer--None. No frontline pitching prospect drafted by an AL team is slated for relief at this point.

NATIONAL LEAGUEE DRAFT ALL-STARS

Catcher-- Catcher--Lee Evans, Pirates (fourth round). Evans didn't receive a lot of attention as a high school player in Northport, Ala., but he reminds Pittsburgh of its incumbent catcher, Jason Kendall. Evans is a switch-hitter with the athletic ability to play just about anywhere on the diamond, and his best tool is his power. In his initial taste of pro ball, he batted .279--3-20 in 111 Gulf Coast League at-bats.

First Baseman--A.J. Zapp, Braves (first round, number 27 overall). Zapp, who hails from Greenwood, Ind., is an offensive machine. He had the best raw power of any player in the draft, and Atlanta says he's the best pure hitter it has drafted since taking Bob Horner number one overall in 1978.

Second Baseman--Brent Butler, Cardinals (third round). A shortstop out of Laurinburg, N.C., Butler is at second base on this team because scouts aren't convinced he can play short. But no one doubts his hitting ability after he batted .343-eight-50 in 248 at-bats and stole seven bases to win the Appalachian League MVP award. St. Louis, which believes he's one of the best hitters it has signed in years, responded by challenging him with an assignment in Hawaii Winter Baseball. ETA: Late 1999.

Third Baseman--Damian Rolls, Dodgers (first round, number 23 overall). The Kansas City, Kan. native improved his stock as much as anyone in the last weeks before the June draft. He's a good athlete who can run and throw and has untapped power. He batted .265-4-27 with 11 doubles in 257 at-bats and eight steals in the Northwest League, a good test for a high school player. ETA: Early 2000.

Shortstop--Mike Caruso, Giants (second round). San Francisco had a poor draft, but did find a keeper in Caruso. Like Rolls, he held his own in the Northwest League, batting .292-two-24 in 312 at-bats and swiping 24 bases. He's a switch-hitter with legitimate offensive ability and slightly above-average speed. ETA: Early 2000.

Outfielder--Mark Kotsay, Marlins (first round, number nine overall). Scouts still aren't excited about Kotsay's physical tools, but he went ninth in the draft on the basis of his hitting ability and his intangibles, which include unmatched desire, work ethic and will to win. After starring for the U.S. Olympic team, he stepped right into the Midwest League and easily adjusted to wood bats, hitting .283-2-8 in 60 at-bats. He led Cal State Fullerton to the College World Series title in 1995, when he won the Golden Spikes Award. ETA: Late 1998.

Outfielder--Robert Stratton, Mets (first round, number 13 overall). Coming out of Santa Barbara, Calif., Stratton is somewhat raw but shows plenty to like: power, decent speed and strong arm. His best tool is his longball ability, and he could grow into an above-average hitter as well. A minor elbow problem hampered him in his first pro summer, when he hit .254-two-nine in 59 Gulf Coast League at-bats. ETA: Early 2000.

Outfielder--Vernon Maxwell, Padres (second round). The best all-around athlete in the draft, Maxwell could have gone from Midwest City, Okla. to play safety at Tennessee. He has the total package, with six.five-second speed in the 60-yard dash, arm strength, defensive skills and hitting ability. He batted .253 with 10 extra-base hits in 194 at-bats and 15 steals in the Arizona Fall League after signing. ETA: Early 2000.

Starting Pitcher--Kris Benson, Pirates (first round, number one overall). Benson, Baseball America's 1996 College Player of the Year, dominated hitters while at Clemson and established a record for drafted players (non-free agent division) with a $two million bonus. Though the righthander spent the summer pitching for the U.S. Olympic team--he absorbed the upset loss to Japan in the semifinals--he should be the first player from the 1996 draft to reach the majors. Some scouts believe his 95-mph fastball, command of three pitches and professional approach could take him straight to Pittsburgh if the Pirates so desire. He'll probably debut in Double-A instead. ETA: Late 1997.

Starting Pitcher--Adam Eaton, Phillies (first round, number 11 overall). Eaton was part of a bumper crop of pitching talent in the state of Washington last spring, and the Snohomish native could solve Philadelphia's pitching problems in the near future. His fastball shot up from the mid-80s in 1995 to the 91-93 mph range in 1996, and as a teenager he could add even more velocity. He has yet to show his stuff as a pro because he signed late in the summer. ETA: Early 2000.

Starting Pitcher--Jake Westbrook, Rockies (first round, number 21 overall). Because Colorado has no trouble attracting quality hitters to Coors Field, it usually focuses on pitching in the draft. Westbrook was the latest example, coming out of Danielsville, Georgia, to earn top-prospect honors in the Arizona League (4-2, 2.87, 57 strikeouts in 63 innings) and star in the Northwest League (1-1, 2.55, 19 strikeouts in 25 innings). His fastball currently tops out at 92 mph and should improve as he grows into his six-foot-three, 180-pound frame. ETA: Late 1999.

Closer--Braden Looper, Cardinals (first round, number three overall). Looper easily was the best relief prospect in the draft after blowing away hitters for Wichita State and the U.S. Olympic team with a fastball that reaches 98 mph. He also throws a hard slider and has excellent command of both pitches. He also has a nasty changeup and could be a star as a starter, but his likely role will be to take over the St. Louis bullpen as soon as Dennis Eckersley falters, ETA: Early 1998.

EXPANSION TEAMS AND FREE AGENTS

Starting Pitcher--John Patterson, Diamondbacks (first round, number five overall, Expos). Patterson represented another coup for Arizona, which signed the Orange, Texas star as a free agent. The first high school player drafted in 1996, the righthander throws in the mid-90s and has ideal size (six-foot-five), a loose arm and good mechanics. His father Steve was a second-round pick of the Orioles in 1971 and reached Triple-A. ETA: Late 1999.

First Baseman--Travis Lee, Diamondbacks (first round, number two overall, Twins). A San Diego State star in the mold of former Aztec Mark Grace but with more power, Lee shook the foundation of baseball when he signed his unprecedented $10 million deal. He's a top-of-the-line athlete for a first baseman, combining hitting ability, plenty of power, decent speed and fine defense. He led the U.S. Olympic team in most offensive categories and won the Golden Spikes Award, amateur baseball's Heisman Trophy. He should be the Opening Day first baseman when Arizona begins play in 1998. ETA: Early 1998.

Starting Pitcher--Matt White, free agent (first round, number seven overall, Giants). Considered by some scouts to be the best high school pitcher since the draft began in 1965, White had yet to sign by mid-November but was expected to command Travis Lee money. The Waynesboro, Pa. righthander is a prototype power pitcher with a 94-96 mph fastball, command of three pitches, a fluid delivery, intelligence and size (six-foot-five, 230 pounds). He's so advanced that he survived the walk-on camp at the U.S. Olympic trials, though he failed to make the team and had to settle for winning the bronze-medal game at the World Junior (16-18) Championships. He should be the first high school pitcher to reach the major leagues, regardless of with whom he signs. ETA: Mid-1998.

Starting Pitcher--Bobby Seay, Devil Rays (first round, number 12 overall, White Sox). Seay was considered the top lefthander in the draft, and slid to number 12 only because of concerns about his bonus demands. After he was declared a free agent, he signed with Tampa Bay for $3 million. The third first-rounder from Sarasota (Fla.) High since 1993--following Doug Million and Matt Drews, Seay throws 90-91 mph and has an above-average curveball. ETA: Late 1999.

FIVE BEST DRAFTS

1. Red Sox. Boston has had the best series of drafts since Wayne Britton became scouting director in 1993, and this was no exception. The Red Sox landed a pair of power righthanders in first-round picks Josh Garrett and Chris Reitsma, and also picked up LoCurto while continuing their focus on young arms and athletes.

2. Padres. San Diego's first-round pick was solid shortstop Matt Halloran, but really scored by spending big money to land Maxwell ($425,000) and Jason Middlebrook, a power righthander who has bounced back from arm problems, in the ninth round. Middlebrook received $750,000, a record for a non-first-round selection.

3. Rangers. Texas had four picks in the first two rounds and used them to stock up on pitching with R.A. Dickey, Sam Marsonek, Corey Lee and Derrick Cook. The Rangers' next three picks, infielder Derek Baker, Kelly Dransfeldt and Warren Morris, also have potential.

4. Rockies. Colorado drafted pitchers with 14 of its first 15 picks, and scored with Westbrook, John Nicholson (second round) and Shawn Chacon (third) at the top. Also keep an eye on Alvin Rivera (eighth), Tom Stepka (10th) and Scott Schroeffel (15th).

5. Blue Jays. Besides Koch, Lawrence and Stromsborg, all of whom made our AL team of draft picks to watch, Toronto also landed the offensive potential of Pete Tucci (first round) and Brent Abernathy (second round). Fifth-round pick John Bale has exceptional potential for a lefthander if he can improve his command.

Honorable Mention: Diamondbacks. Lee and Patterson weren't selected by Arizona, but factor them in with lefthander Nick Bierbrodt (first round) and catcher Mark Osborne (third round), and the Diamondbacks signed plenty of talent in their first draft year.

DRAFT REPORT CARDS, 1993-96

A--Potential major league star.
B--Potential major league regular.
C--Potential major leaguer.
D--Disappointment thus far.
F--Failure; no chance to play in major leagues.

1993

1. Alex Rodriguez, ss, Mariners	A
2. Darren Dreifort, rhp, Dodgers	B
3. Brian Anderson, lhp, Angels (now with Indians)	C
4. Wayne Gomes, rhp, Phillies	C
5. Jeff Granger, lhp, Royals	C
6. Steve Soderstrom, rhp, Giants	C
7. Trot Nixon, of, Red Sox	B
8. Kirk Presley, rhp, Mets	D
9. Matt Brunson, ss, Tigers	F
10. Brooks Kieschnick, of, Cubs	B
11. Daron Kirkreit, rhp, Indians	D
12. Billy Wagner, lhp, Astros	A
13. Matt Drews, rhp, Yankees (now with Tigers)	B
14. Derrek Lee, 1b, Padres	A
15. Chris Carpenter, rhp, Blue Jays	B
16. Alan Benes, rhp, Cardinals	A
17. Scott Christman, lhp, White Sox	D
18. Chris Schwab, of, Expos	D
19. Jay Powell, rhp, Orioles (now with Marlins)	B

20. Torii Hunter, of, Twins — B
21. Jason Varitek, c, Twins — Did not sign
22. Charles Peterson, of, Pirates — B
23. Jeff D'Amico, rhp, Brewers — B
24. Jon Ratliff, rhp, Cubs — C
25. John Wasdin, rhp, Athletics — B
26. Kelly Wunsch, lhp, Brewers — D
27. Marc Valdes, rhp, Marlins — C
28. Jamey Wright, rhp, Rockies — B

1994

1. Paul Wilson, rhp, Mets — A
2. Ben Grieve, of, Athletics — A
3. Dustin Hermanson, rhp, Padres — B
4. Antone Williamson, 3b, Brewers — C
5. Josh Booty, ss, Marlins — C
6. McKay Christensen, of, Angels — C
7. Doug Million, lhp, Rockies — B
8. Todd Walker, 2b, Twins — A
9. C.J. Nitkowski, lhp, Reds (now with Tigers) — C
10. Jaret Wright, rhp, Indians — A
11. Mark Farriss, ss, Pirates — C
12. Nomar Garciaparra, ss, Red Sox — A
13. Paul Konerko, c, Dodgers — A
14. Jason Varitek, c, Mariners — B
15. Jayson Peterson, rhp, Cubs — C
16. Matt Smith, 1b, Royals — C
17. Ramon Castro, c, Astros — C
18. Cade Gaspar, rhp, Tigers (now with Padres) — C
19. Bret Wagner, lhp, Cardinals (now with Athletics) — C
20. Terrence Long, of-1b, Mets — B
21. Hiram Bocachica, ss, Expos — B
22. Dante Powell, of, Giants — B
23. Carlton Loewer, rhp, Phillies — C
24. Brian Buchanan, 1b-of, Yankees — C
25. Scott Elarton, rhp, Astros — B
26. Mark Johnson, c, White Sox — C
27. Jacob Shumate, rhp, Braves — D
28. Kevin Witt, ss, Blue Jays — B

1995

1. Darin Erstad, of, Angels — A
2. Ben Davis, c, Padres — C
3. Jose Cruz Jr., of, Mariners — A
4. Kerry Wood, rhp, Cubs — A
5. Ariel Prieto, rhp, Athletics — B
6. Jaime Jones, of, Marlins — B
7. Jonathan Johnson, rhp, Rangers — B
8. Todd Helton, 1b, Rockies — A
9. Geoff Jenkins, of, Brewers — A
10. Chad Hermansen, ss, Pirates — A
11. Mike Drumright, rhp, Tigers — B
12. Matt Morris, rhp, Cardinals — B
13. Mark Redman, lhp, Twins — B
14. Reggie Taylor, of, Phillies — C
15. Andy Yount, rhp, Red Sox — C
16. Joe Fontenot, rhp, Giants — B
17. Roy Halladay, rhp, Blue Jays — B
18. Ryan Jaroncyk, ss, Mets — C
19. Juan LeBron, of, Royals — C
20. David Yocum, lhp, Dodgers — C
21. Alvie Shepherd, rhp, Orioles — C
22. Tony McKnight, rhp, Astros — D
23. David Miller, 1b-of, Indians — C
24. Corey Jenkins, of, Red Sox — C
25. Jeff Liefer, 3b, White Sox — B
26. Chad Hutchinson, rhp, Braves — Did not sign
27. Shea Morenz, of, Yankees — C
28. Michael Barrett, ss, Expos — B

1996

These players have had very limited exposure to professional baseball, and thus these grades are not as accurate as the others.

1. Kris Benson, rhp, Pirates — A
2. Travis Lee, 1b, Twins (now with Diamondbacks) — A
3. Braden Looper, rhp, Cardinals — A
4. Billy Koch, rhp, Blue Jays — B
5. John Patterson, rhp, Expos — B
6. Seth Greisinger, rhp, Tigers — A
7. Matt White, rhp, Giants (unsigned free agent) — A
8. Chad Green, of, Brewers — B
9. Mark Kotsay, of, Marlins — A
10. Eric Chavez, 3b, Athletics — A
11. Adam Eaton, rhp, Phillies — B
12. Bobby Seay, lhp, White Sox (now with Devil Rays) — B
13. Robert Stratton, of, Mets — B
14. Dermal Brown, of, Royals — B
15. Matt Halloran, ss, Padres — B
16. Joe Lawrence, ss, Blue Jays — B
17. Todd Noel, rhp, Cubs — B
18. R.A. Dickey, rhp, Rangers — B
19. Mark Johnson, rhp, Astros — B
20. Eric Milton, lhp, Yankees — B
21. Jake Westbrook, rhp, Rockies — A
22. Gil Meche, rhp, Mariners — B
23. Damian Rolls, 3b, Dodgers — B
24. Sam Marsonek, rhp, Rangers — B
25. John Oliver, of, Reds — B
26. Josh Garrett, rhp, Red Sox — B
27. A.J. Zapp, 1b, Braves — B
28. Danny Peoples, 1b, Indians — B

ABAD, ANDY - OF/1B - BL - Age 24
In 1995 Abad went from Double-A back to Class A; last year he went the other way after hitting for average (.277) and power (22 doubles) with a reduction of strikeouts. Abad's poor outfield play has forced a move to first base, but he's really without a true position.

ABBOTT, JEFF - OF - BR - Age 24
His .325 average at Triple-A Nashville in 1996 actually caused his career pro batting average to go down. Abbott lines the ball to the gaps with consistency, but doesn't have the home run power nor blazing speed on the bases.

ABBOTT, KURT - SS/3B - BR - Age 27
Abbott's starting shortstop job was ended by phenom Edgar Renteria in 1996, and Abbott found himself reduced to caddying for Alex Arias at third base by season's end. Abbott is a wild swinger who has struck out in about 30% of his major league at-bats. He has above-average power but below-average defensive range for a middle infielder. His chief attribute is an ability to play three infield positions with competence.

	AB	R	HR	RBI	SB	BA	$
1995 Florida NL	420	60	17	60	4	.255	11
1996 Florida NL	320	37	8	33	3	.253	3

ABREU, BOB - OF - BL - Age 23
After six full seasons in the minor leagues, Abreu should have a good chance to be the starting leftfielder for the Astros in 1997. His second full year at Triple-A Tucson was less productive than his first year but he did make some progress in areas where he needed improvement. With gap power, he led the minor leagues in triples for the second straight year. Oddly, he had more triples than doubles in 1996. He should provide about the same production in left field that the Astros received from Luis Gonzalez in the early 1990s. However, Abreu possesses a stronger arm and more speed.

ADRIANA, SHARNOL - 3B/2B - BR - Age 26
Adriana played many of his games at third, but classify him as a utility infielder. He strikes out often (72 strikeouts in 292 at-bats with Triple-A Syracuse) though his power hitting improved to a career-high ten homers. If Ed Sprague is seriously injured, Adriana probably gets a chance. Otherwise, he's back at Syracuse to work on making contact.

AGBAYANI, BENNY - OF - BR - Age 25
After spending most of the year at Triple-A (.278-7-56 with 14 stolen bases for Norfolk) Agbayani finished the season rather deep in the Mets' outfield depth charts. His best chance at the majors in 1997 would be a defensive or pinch running bench role.

ALCANTARA, ISRAEL - 3B - TR - Age 24
Alcantara has a lightning quick bat, but his lack of plate discipline has made him an easy mark for Double-A hurlers in his two stints at that level. He's hit .211 both times, with a 143/35 strikeout/walk ratio in 455 at-bats.

ALDRETE, MIKE - 1B/OF - BL - Age 36
The poster player who got a second major league career as a result of expansion, Aldrete has faded back into a bench role. The Yankees thought enough of his ability to use him on their 1996 postseason roster.

	AB	R	HR	RBI	SB	BA	$
1995 California AL	149	19	4	24	0	.268	2
1996 New York AL	108	16	6	20	0	.213	-

ALEXANDER, MANNY - 2B - BR - Age 25
The experiment of moving Cal Ripken to third base was short lived last year, so Alexander continued to ride the bench. He's a fast base stealer, but he hasn't hit much in the minors, and would probably be a .200-220 hitter in the majors. Alexander has a hacking hitting style with poor plate discipline.

	AB	R	HR	RBI	SB	BA	$
1995 Baltimore AL	242	35	3	23	11	.236	6
1996 Baltimore AL	68	6	0	4	3	.103	-

ALFONZO, EDGAR - 3B - BR - Age 29
Not to be confused with the Mets' Edgardo Alfonzo, this Alfonzo has spent 12 years toiling in the minors, mostly in Double-A and below, in a number of organizations. He's not a prospect, and doesn't have much of a future.

ALFONZO, EDGARDO - 3B/2B - BR - Age 23
Once compared to Ryne Sandberg, Alfonzo actually had better Double-A numbers than Ryno, at a younger age. But Alfonzo didn't advance much, stat-wise, in 1996, after a good rookie season in 1995. Alfonzo is a sleeper, because so many people will forget how young he is. If he'd been in the minors the last two years, he would be at the top of everyone's 1997 rookie star list. Having been in the majors and learning for two years will only make him better.

	AB	R	HR	RBI	SB	BA	$
1995 New York NL	335	26	4	41	1	.278	6
1996 New York NL	368	36	4	40	2	.261	4

ALGUACIL, JOSE - 2B - BB - Age 24
Light hitting, but speedy, Alguacil spent a good portion of the year in Single-A San Jose, then was promoted more to fill holes created at higher levels due to San Francisco injuries. Stole 18 bases in the California League.

ALICEA, LUIS - 2B - BB - Age 31
Alicea returned to the Cardinals last season after a one-year hiatus in Boston and had an inconsistent year. He lost his starting job midway through the season then regained it down the stretch. Alicea is a better player in real life than on paper. His contributions, primarily defense and bat control, don't show up in the statistics.

	AB	R	HR	RBI	SB	BA	$
1995 Boston AL	419	64	6	44	13	.270	12
1996 St. Louis NL	380	54	5	42	11	.258	6

ALLENSWORTH, JERMAINE - OF - BR - Age 25
After getting off to a fine start at Calgary (.330 with 25 steals in 95 games) and playing in the Triple-A All-Star Game, Allensworth was summoned to Pittsburgh on July 23rd and installed as the starting centerfielder and leadoff hitter. Allensworth showed he is a first-rate defensive centerfielder but his minor league history before 1996 suggests he may not hit enough to be a regular in the major leagues.

	AB	R	HR	RBI	SB	BA	$
1996 Pittsburgh NL	229	32	4	31	11	.262	6

ALMANZAR, RICHARD - 2B - BR - Age 19
The top infield prospect in the Detroit system, Almanzar is a Dominican second baseman who will hit at the top of the order and play well defensively. He hit .306-1-36-53 for Class A Lakeland in '96.

ALOMAR, ROBERTO - 2B - BB - Age 29
Alomar had a hot bat for several months, hitting in the .400 range. He peaked at .410 on June 8th with a career-high 22-game hitting streak, and then went into a 22-for-97 (.227) tailspin in his next 25 games. Manager Davey Johnson was aware that Alomar was tired in September, failing to run out several grounders.

	AB	R	HR	RBI	SB	BA	$
1995 Toronto AL	517	71	13	66	30	.300	29
1996 Baltimore AL	588	132	22	94	17	.328	28

ALOMAR, SANDY - C - BR - Age 30
By Alomar's standards, he was quite healthy in 1996, amassing 418 at-bats; nearly a career high. However, the added durability only served to expose his weaknesses at the plate. He has never met a pitch he didn't like. He has all of 111 walks for his career (in 2237 plate appearances). Alomar is firmly entrenched as the Indians' catcher.

	AB	R	HR	RBI	SB	BA	$
1995 Cleveland AL	203	32	10	35	3	.300	8
1996 Cleveland AL	418	53	11	50	1	.263	5

ALOU, MOISES - OF - BR - Age 30
It is now becoming apparent that Alou will not become the superstar many predicted before his broken ankle late in the 1993 season. He is a good player but not a great one. If he leaves Montreal that might not be so bad as there is reportedly friction between him and his father Felipe, the Expos' manager.

	AB	R	HR	RBI	SB	BA	$
1995 Montreal NL	344	48	14	58	4	.273	12
1996 Montreal NL	540	87	21	96	9	.281	19

ALVAREZ, GABE - 3B - BR - Age 23
Alvarez had an excellent year in 1995, his first year as a pro, when he hit .344 in Single-A. He found Double-A much more difficult last year, so he's no longer on the fast track to the majors. With Ken Caminiti having great years with the Padres, they can afford to be patient and wait on Alvarez to develop.

AMADOR, MANNY - SS - BB - Age 21
Amador is a switch hitter who can provide quality defense at three infield positions, and more extra base power than is usually provided by a player his size (6'0", 160 lbs). His Double-A season was wasted as a backup, and then he battled minor injuries at High-A Clearwater. He's still a baby, and could make a quick upward progression. Look for him to move to another organization and thrive within the next two years.

AMARAL, RICH - OF - BR - Age 35
A potentially valuable sub with speed and a good batting average, Amaral played sparingly from August 1995 until Griffey was injured in 1996.

	AB	R	HR	RBI	SB	BA	$
1995 Seattle AL	238	45	2	19	21	.282	13
1996 Seattle AL	312	69	1	29	25	.292	14

AMARO, RUBEN - OF - BB - Age 32
Amaro was actually one of the Phils' few bright spots in 1996. He was a lethal pinch-hitter, and a competent defender capable of playing all three outfield positions. However, if you are the fifth outfielder for the second worst club in baseball, factoring in that they had already traded Pete Incaviglia and lost Jim Eisenreich to injury, your major league status is, at best, precarious.

	AB	R	HR	RBI	SB	BA	$
1995 Cleveland AL	60	5	1	7	1	.200	-
1996 Philadelphia NL	117	14	2	15	0	.316	4

ANDERSON, BRADY - OF - BL - Age 33
Anderson bashed 50 homers in 1996, one of the most surprising results of the year, and one that is frequently pointed to in discussions of the 1996 rabbit-ball year. He's had hot streaks before, usually lasting a month or so, but last year, he was in groove all season, hence the 50 dingers, many of which were long homers. He's not a big guy, but he has tremendous bat speed.

	AB	R	HR	RBI	SB	BA	$
1995 Baltimore AL	554	108	16	64	26	.262	23
1996 Baltimore AL	579	117	50	110	21	.297	33

ANDERSON, CLIFF - SS - BL - Age 26
Anderson got a double promotion in 1996, going from Class A San Bernardino to Double-A San Antonio, to Triple-A Albuquerque. But the bad news is that he needed four years spent almost exclusively in A-ball before he made that leap. Anderson is a relatively weak hitter whose glove is only fair.

ANDERSON, GARRET - OF - BL - Age 24
Looking at Anderson's record for 1996, one would think he had a good year. But considering it was a rabbit-ball year, the year looks disappointing. Anderson doesn't walk much, only 27 times in 1996. He's a free swinger with a lack of patience.

	AB	R	HR	RBI	SB	BA	$
1995 California AL	374	50	16	69	6	.321	18
1996 California AL	607	79	12	72	7	.285	13

ANDERSON, MARLON - 2B - BL - Age 23
The Phils' 1995 second round draftee jumped all the way to Double-A Reading by the midpoint of his first full pro season. Unlike most minor league second sackers, he is not a converted shortstop. He has played second for years. He has excellent range afield and great speed on the bases, but is prone to careless errors.

ANDREWS, SHANE - 3B/1B - BR - Age 25
Andrews is a perplexing player who looks great at times and bad at other times. He has decent power for a third baseman and time is still on his side.

Benson's Baseball Player Guide: 1997

	AB	R	HR	RBI	SB	BA	$
1995 Montreal AL	220	27	8	31	1	.214	2
1996 Montreal NL	375	43	19	64	3	.227	3

ANGELI, DOUG - SS - BR - Age 26
The Phils' 1993 16th round draftee is a journeyman who finally made it to Double-A at the ripe age of 25 in 1996. He missed significant time with a broken wrist, but actually showed extra base pop for the first time ever - after his return. He is surehanded defensively though he has only average range.

ANTHONY, ERIC - OF/1B - BL - Age 29
Anthony joined the Rockies late in 1996 and saw moderate playing time due to Larry Walker's injury. Decent bat speed, power and defensive ability should assure this former Astros prospect of at least a back-up job in 1997.

	AB	R	HR	RBI	SB	BA	$
1995 Cincinnati NL	134	19	5	23	2	.269	4
1996 Colorado NL	185	32	12	22	0	.243	2

ARIAS, ALEX - SS/3B - BR - Age 29
Each year, Arias plays a larger role than was intended in the team's master plan. Arias is a competent, versatile defender who handles the bat well and makes consistent contact, but with no better than singles power. He has now produced all of eight homers and four steals in 901 major league at-bats.

	AB	R	HR	RBI	SB	BA	$
1995 Florida NL	216	22	3	26	1	.269	3
1996 Florida NL	224	27	3	26	2	.277	4

ARIAS, DAVID - 1B - BL - Age 21
The Twins traded Dave Hollins for Arias last August. Arias was one of the best hitters in the Midwest league and can be expected to improve.

ARIAS, GEORGE - 3B - BR - Age 25
Rookie power hitter George Arias was the Angels starting third baseman at the start of 1996, but he struggled at the plate (hitting .184) and was sent to Triple-A. He hit better when recalled in late July, and is expected to be the Angels third baseman of the future. His hitting should improve in 1997 and in future years.

	AB	R	HR	RBI	SB	BA	$
1996 California AL	252	19	6	28	2	.238	1

ASHLEY, BILLY - OF - BR - Age 26
Ashley lost any chance of a regular job with the Dodgers when Todd Hollandsworth developed. Ashley struck out 40% of his at-bats, but his on-base and slugging averages were comparable to Raul Mondesi. Ashley ended the season typecast as a pinch hitter after hitting five homers off the bench.

	AB	R	HR	RBI	SB	BA	$
1995 Los Angeles NL	215	17	8	27	0	.237	3
1996 Los Angeles NL	110	18	9	25	0	.200	-

AUDE, RICH - 1B - BR - Age 25
Once upon a time, the Pirates figured Aude would eventually turn into their cleanup hitter. However, he has fallen out of favor in the organization and wasn't even recalled in September. He's a big guy who reminds you of Dick Stuart or Dave Kingman and he is still an intriguing first base prospect, though he will probably have to move on to another club to ever get a major league chance.

AURILIA, RICH - SS - BR - Age 25
Aurilia clobbered the ball over 10 games in Triple-A, then was called up to fill in for Robby Thompson, and then Shawon Dunston. Aurilia has excellent range, a good glove and a fair bat. Though he is not really All-Star material, he is a serviceable day-to-day shortstop who will improve with experience.

	AB	R	HR	RBI	SB	BA	$
1995 San Francisco NL	19	4	2	4	1	.474	1
1996 San Francisco NL	318	27	3	26	4	.239	0

AUSMUS, BRAD - C - BR - Age 27
Ausmus played every day in Detroit after he arrived from San Diego via trade. Young Raul Casanova will pose a challenge to his job in a year. Ausmus falls in that group of catchers who have no outstanding weakness or strength.

	AB	R	HR	RBI	SB	BA	$
1995 San Diego NL	328	44	5	34	16	.293	13
1996 San Diego NL	149	16	1	13	1	.181	-
1996 Detroit AL	226	30	4	22	3	.248	1

AVEN, BRUCE - OF - BR - Age 25
Aven has done a solid job for a 30th round draft pick, averaging 24 homers and 19 steals in his first two full pro campaigns. However and the Indians' major league outfield depth will prevent him from starting in the bigs. He'll spend 1997 at Triple-A, and could be a future backup in the majors.

AVERSA, JOE - SS/2B - BB - Age 28
Aversa is a steady and sometimes spectacular defender at multiple infield positions, but he flat out can't hit. His .234 mark at Double-A Portland in the Marlins' chain matched his career high. This guy actually has a .252 career slugging percentage over seven pro seasons, with one career homer.

AVILA, ROLO - OF - BR - Age 23
The Orioles promoted Avila from Single-A to Double-A at mid-year. He didn't exactly burn up the tough Double-A Eastern League, but he made good progress, enough to get promoted to Triple-A where he hit for a good average in only 47 at-bats. Avila has good base-stealing speed and will probably develop more power as he matures. He's young and learning.

AYRAULT, JOE - C - BR - Age 25
A superior defensive catcher, Ayrault has never been a good hitter in seven pro years. Above A-ball, he's a career .234 hitter with a strikeout-to-walk ratio of 3.5 to 1 and just marginal power. Ayrault got to the big leagues for the first time in 1996 on the strength of his defense.

AZUAJE, JESUS - 2B - BR - Age 24
Azuaje looked better two years ago, when he was hitting for good average and stealing bases in the low minors. He hit just .239 in high A-ball in 1995 and then .237 at Double-A in 1996, fading out of the Mets' major league plans.

BAERGA, CARLOS - 2B - BB - Age 28
Mets management looked darned clever when they traded Jeff Kent and Jose Vizcaino to Cleveland, for three-time All-Star Baerga plus Alvaro Espinoza; but after the trade, it turned out that Espinoza was the only reliable asset New York had obtained. Baerga came down with a pulled abdominal muscle, unable to play the field or run the bases. He will obviously come back some distance in 1997, but how far is another question.

	AB	R	HR	RBI	SB	BA	$
1995 Cleveland AL	557	87	15	90	11	.314	25
1996 Cleveland AL	424	54	10	55	1	.267	5
1996 New York NL	83	5	2	11	0	.193	-

BAEZ, KEVIN - SS - BR - Age 30
Baez is a veteran minor league infielder who surfaced with the Mets as a good-field no-hit shortstop in 1990-1993. He is not a prospect.

BAGWELL, JEFF - 1B - BR - Age 28
Bagwell has established himself as one of the best players in the major leagues, hitting for both power and average. Last year, in this book, he was projected at .320-30-120-15 and he delivered .315-31-120-21. Bagwell's complex batting stance and swing can sometimes get out of kilter and it appeared to be that way at times in 1996, particularly in July. Bagwell is a hard worker who can be expected to maintain his current level of production for another decade. However, he is not likely to repeat his spectacular 1994 season.

	AB	R	HR	RBI	SB	BA	$
1995 Houston NL	448	88	21	87	12	.290	22
1996 Houston NL	568	111	31	120	21	.315	35

BAINES, HAROLD - DH - BL - Age 38
The White Sox had to unretire his number after signing him as a free agent in the off-season. The front office was hoping the signing of Baines would stimulate the waning interest in the ballclub and sell some tickets. He played in 143 of the clubs games and doesn't seem to be wearing down a bit. Should he be in a Sox uniform in 1997 look for more of the same.

	AB	R	HR	RBI	SB	BA	$
1995 Baltimore AL	385	60	24	63	0	.299	15
1996 Chicago AL	495	80	22	95	3	.311	17

BAKO, PAUL - C - BL - Age 24
Previously considered a marginal prospect at best, Bako made major strides offensively in 1996. At Double-A Chattanooga in a pitcher's park, he matched his 1996 performance in A ball (in hitter's heaven Winston-Salem) showing some power and decent strike zone judgment. He isn't a great prospect due to his age, but lefthanded hitting catchers are a rare enough commodity to usually get a chance.

BALFE, RYAN - 3B - BB - Age 21
A third baseman in the Tigers' system, Balfe hit .280-11-66-3 at high Class A in '96 and is a potential big league regular.

BALL, JEFF - 1B/3B - BR - Age 27
Ball is a capable Triple-A hitter (.324-19-73 in 1996) who has had trouble finding a defensive position. The best he can hope for is to be a utility player in the majors.

BANKS, BRIAN - OF - BB - Age 26
Banks is a hard-swinging, hard-running type of player, not too old for a shot at the majors. In 1996 at Triple-A New Orleans on the Brewers farm, he hit .271 with 16 home runs and 17 stolen bases.

BARBERIE, BRET - 2B - BB - Age 29
Barberie looked like a good prospect several years ago with the Expos and Marlins, but he has become a journeyman infielder. He spent most of 1996 playing second and third with the Iowa Cubs. He has a decent glove, but Barberie lost the stick that he showed when he hit .301 with Florida in 1994.

BARGER, MIKE - OF - BR - Age 25
This speedster lost over a hundred points off his batting average in a move up the ladder to Double-A Port City in 1996. He has little power; his age and a .205 average in 1996 will keep him from being considered for major league duty in the near future.

BARKER, GLEN - OF - BR - Age 25
Chronic low batting averages will limit this young outfielder to a career in the minor leagues.

BARKER, TIM - IF/OF - BR - Age 28
A veteran of the Expos and Brewers farm systems, Barker finished 1996 with the Yankee Clippers at Triple-A Columbus, where he hit .266-2-45, one of his better seasons. Barker has good speed (41 steals in 1994 at Triple-A) but is long past the prospect stage. For the majors he is, at best, a depth chart filler for pinch running and utility defense.

BARNES, LARRY - 1B - BL - Age 22
Power-hitting Angels farmhand Larry Barnes had a terrific season in Class-A last year, one of the best in the minor leagues. He was tested against tougher competition in the Arizona Fall League. He will probably begin 1997 in Double-A, with a possible promotion to Triple-A or even the big time.

BARRETT, MICHAEL - C - BR - Age 20
The Expos' 1995 first round pick was moved from shortstop to catcher in his first full pro season in 1996. Though he burned out offensively in the second half, Barrett impressed with his athleticism and his quick adjustment to the game's most difficult position. At 6'3", 185, the Expos' expect him to fill out and develop extra base power - many of the 29 doubles he hit in 1996 should become homers later.

BARRON, TONY - OF - BR - Age 30
A veteran minor league outfielder, Barron finally got a brief major league stint in 1996, with the Expos.

BARRY, JEFF - OF/3B - BB - Age 28
Barry got 15 at-bats with the Mets in 1995. He was traded to the Padres where he spent most of last year in Double-A and his .243 didn't excite anybody. Barry will likely play in Triple-A in 1997, and could get called up as a reserve outfielder.

BARTEE, KIMERA - OF - BB - Age 24
Bartee arrived in Detroit after bouncing around between the Twins and Orioles. He is a speedy outfielder who impressed the Tigers in '96.

	AB	R	HR	RBI	SB	BA	$
1996 Detroit AL	217	32	1	14	20	.253	8

BATES, JASON - 2B/3B/SS - BB - Age 26
Bates had a chance to challenge for the starting second base job due to Eric Young's injury, but faltered. He never found his stroke in 1996. He's a scrappy utility man who is likely to improve in 1997.

	AB	R	HR	RBI	SB	BA	$
1995 Colorado NL	322	42	8	46	3	.267	8
1996 Colorado NL	160	19	1	9	2	.206	-

BATISTA, TONY - SS - BR - Age 23
After putting up excellent numbers at Edmonton, Batista was brought up. With Brent Gates injured, and Rafael Bournigal unable to hit with authority, Batista claimed the second base spot, probably at the expense of Gates. As a former shortstop, Batista has the skill to play second. He still needs to work on his selectivity at the plate.

	AB	R	HR	RBI	SB	BA	$
1996 Oakland AL	238	38	6	25	7	.298	7

BATISTE, KIM - 3B/SS - BR - Age 29
Former Philly Kim Batiste went up and down with San Francisco last year, playing with the Giants, with Triple-A Phoenix, and with Single-A San Jose. He's likely to remain in the minors, despite his speed and versatility.

	AB	R	HR	RBI	SB	BA	$
1996 San Francisco NL	130	17	3	11	3	.208	-

BATTLE, ALLEN - OF - BR - Age 28
1996 was supposed to be Battle's chance to show what he could do at the big league level. Unfortunately, the results suggest a career minor leaguer.

	AB	R	HR	RBI	SB	BA	$
1995 St. Louis NL	118	13	0	2	3	.271	1
1996 Oakland AL	130	20	1	5	10	.192	1

BATTLE, HOWARD - 3B - BR - Age 25
How bad were the Phils in 1996? When Battle was called into the manager's office at Triple-A Scranton-Wilkes Barre while he was flirting with the Mendoza Line, he figured he was being released. He has clearly regressed as a prospect. His swing looks slower, his foot speed has diminished, and he seemed disinterested at times during last season.

BAUTISTA, DANNY - OF - BR - Age 24
A changing of the guard in Tigertown left Bautista with an unclear future, and he was dealt to Atlanta. He got 20 at-bats for the Braves, then got hurt, wiping out the rest of his season. 1996 was a major disappointment and Bautista's chances to play regularly in Atlanta are considerably dimmer than they would have been in Detroit.

	AB	R	HR	RBI	SB	BA	$
1995 Detroit AL	271	28	7	27	4	.203	1
1996 Detroit AL	64	12	2	8	1	.250	-

BAUTISTA, JUAN - SS - BR - Age 21
Although Bautista hit only .234 in Double-A last year, he's only 21 and has great potential. He's making excellent progress, and could be Baltimore's future shortstop, but he needs more experience and maturity.

BAUXBAUM, DANNY - 1B - BR - Age 24
Buxbaum is an Angels prospect who had a good season in Single-A last year, but he needs to prove himself in tougher competition.

BEAMON, TREY - OF - BL - Age 23
Beamon regressed last season (.288 in 111 games at Triple-A Calgary) after winning the Double-A Southern League batting title in 1994 at the ripe old age of 20, then finishing third in the Triple-A Pacific Coast League in 1995. The Pirates told Beamon to start hitting for more power and his swing got fouled up. He planned to stay in Pittsburgh during the offseason for an extensive weight room program which he hoped would add pop without having to change his swing again. He's still young enough to blossom into a .300 hitter in the majors but will need to add at least a little power if he is to be a true impact player.

	AB	R	HR	RBI	SB	BA	$
1996 Pittsburgh NL	51	7	0	6	1	.216	-

BEASLEY, TONY - OF/2B - BR - Age 30
Beasley has had quite a comeback. He was released by the Pirates during minor league spring training in 1994 and started working for his father's logging company in Virginia. He resurfaced as a replacement player in the spring of 1995, stuck at Double-A Carolina after the strike ended and wound up making the Southern League's post-season All-Star team last season as a utility player. He's still a longshot to make it to the majors.

BECKER, RICH - OF - BL - Age 25
Becker established himself as a major league hitter with a bang in '96, as he posted solid totals while recording an amazing 18 assists from center field. Becker has given up switch hitting and now bats lefthanded only; hitting southpaws could take him a few years (.171 in '96). He's a good young player.

	AB	R	HR	RBI	SB	BA	$
1995 Minnesota AL	392	45	2	33	8	.237	4
1996 Minnesota AL	525	92	12	71	19	.291	19

BELK, TIM - 1B - BR - Age 26
Bouncing back from a serious beaning in 1995, Belk turned in a decent year and set a career high for homers at Triple-A Indianapolis. Despite the improvement, his power is marginal for a first baseman and after he displayed good strike zone judgment in previous years, his walks were down and strikeouts were up. At best, he could make the Reds as a pinch-hitter/ platoon first baseman, but he's too old to be considered a serious prospect.

BELL, DAVID - 2B/3B - BR - Age 24
The Cardinals went into spring training hoping Bell could be their second baseman but then signed Luis Alicea as a free agent midway through the exhibition season. Bell went on to have a rather miserable season, including a .176 batting average in 136 at bats at Triple-A Louisville. Bell is caught in a predicament. He hasn't developed enough power to be a third baseman, his natural position, and he isn't good enough defensively to play second base. It's starting to look like he will wind up as a career utility player.

	AB	R	HR	RBI	SB	BA	$
1995 St. Louis NL	144	13	2	19	1	.250	1
1996 St. Louis NL	145	12	1	9	1	.214	-

BELL, DEREK - OF - BR - Age 28
Bell is an aggressive player who is hard to figure. After hitting .334 in 1995, he tailed off to .263 in 1996. Bell drove in a career high 113 runs but batted only .229 after the All-Star break and .233 with runners in scoring position. He has all the tools and could put it all together for a monster season. Bell is a strong defensive player with a good arm and enough speed to consistently steal 25 bases. He hit 21 home runs in 1993 but has failed to top 17 in the last three years.

	AB	R	HR	RBI	SB	BA	$
1995 Houston NL	452	63	8	86	27	.334	29
1996 Houston NL	627	84	17	113	29	.263	20

BELL, JAY - SS - BR - Age 31
Yes, he had a career high in RBI and his batting average wasn't bad. But it took a big September surge for Bell to wind up with below-average numbers. Bell seemed disinterested during much of the Pirates' march to a second straight last-place finish in the National League Central. The Pirates wanted to dump his $4.8 million salary by the start of the season and he should do better if he is traded.

	AB	R	HR	RBI	SB	BA	$
1995 Pittsburgh NL	530	79	13	55	2	.262	10
1996 Pittsburgh NL	527	65	13	71	6	.250	7

BELL, JUAN - 2B/SS - BB - Age 29
For the first time in five seasons, Bell managed to stay with the same organization for two straight seasons. Playing primarily when Bill Selby wasn't in the lineup, Bell showed little major league potential and stayed out of the majors for the first time since 1988. He was released in August and will have to look hard for a job this spring.

BELL, MIKE - 3B - BR - Age 22
Buddy's other son made good progress toward the majors in his first Double-A season, improving his power stats and his fielding. Bell was slated for the Arizona Fall League and should get a shot at Triple-A this year. Don't look for him in the majors before 1998.

BELLE, ALBERT - OF - BR - Age 30
Lost in all the uproar about Belle's off-field problems is the fact that he has improved many facets of his game gradually over the years. Everyone knows about the long balls, but Belle continues to reduce his strikeout rate and increase his walk rate, and has worked hard to become a quite passable defensive leftfielder.

	AB	R	HR	RBI	SB	BA	$
1995 Cleveland AL	546	121	50	126	5	.317	35
1996 Cleveland AL	602	124	48	148	11	.311	32

BELLHORN, MARK - 2B/SS - BB - Age 22
Bellhorn turned in a creditable second professional season at Double-Huntsville. He does strike out a lot, but his walks increased last year as did his steals and general power numbers. A former number two pick, he is worth keeping an eye on.

BELLIARD, RAFAEL - SS/2B - BR - Age 35
This slick fielder gives the Braves fine substitute infield defense, but he can't hit at all. In the year of the hitter, Belliard established new career lows in batting average, OBP (.179) and slugging average (.218). He hasn't recorded double-digit RBI since 1992 and hasn't homered since the Reagan administration. Belliard faces a challenge from other good glove men who are better hitters, like Mike Mordecai.

	AB	R	HR	RBI	SB	BA	$
1995 Atlanta NL	180	12	0	7	2	.222	-
1996 Atlanta NL	142	9	0	3	3	.169	-

BELLIARD, RONNIE - 2B - BR - Age 21
Belliard is a genuine prospect with a bright future. At Double-A El Paso in 1996, he hit .279. Belliard has outstanding strike zone judgment and patience to work the count and draw a walk, and outstanding speed to use when he gets on base.

BELLINGER, CLAY - SS - BR - Age 28
Formerly in the Giants farm system, Bellinger played for the Orioles Triple-A team last year. He made the International League post-season all-star team, and the .301 and 78 RBI were career-highs for him. He improved a great deal, and could be a good alternative to Manny Alexander at shortstop should Cal Ripken move to third base.

BELTRE, ADRIAN - 3B - BR - Age 18
Beltre is a well-rounded player who hits for both average and power, and also has a good glove and strong arm. He was the youngest player in the California League, but the league's best third baseman.

BELTRE, ESTEBAN - SS - BR - Age 29
This journeyman infield backup latched on with the Phils as a Triple-A reserve late in 1996. He is an OK-field, no-hit utility player who can get a major league reprieve from the this round of expansion.

	AB	R	HR	RBI	SB	BA	$
1995 Texas AL	92	7	0	7	0	.217	-
1996 Boston AL	62	6	0	6	1	.258	-

BENARD, MARVIN - OF - BL - Age 27
Called up during the Giants spate of injuries, Benard, a speedster, was given the centerfield job. He was in over his head. Benard doesn't have a lot of plate patience and he loses concentration from time-to-time. Strictly a fourth outfielder.

	AB	R	HR	RBI	SB	BA	$
1995 San Francisco NL	34	5	1	4	1	.382	1
1996 San Francisco NL	488	89	5	27	25	.248	7

BENBOW, LOU - 3B - BR - Age 25
Formerly with Blue Jays and Mets farm clubs, Benbou reached Triple-A for the first time in 1996, although that's likely his peak. He has a decent glove at shortstop, but little power or speed and is a lifetime .200 hitter. Benbow is a minor league version of Rafael Belliard.

BENAVIDES, FREDDIE - SS - BR - Age 30
After surfacing with the Reds and Expos as a backup infielder from 1991-4, Benavides spent 1995 as the regular shortstop for the Triple-A Iowa (Cubs), and played little in 1996. It now looks like his career is over.

BENITEZ, YAMIL - OF - BR - Age 24
Benitez has had two straight good years at Triple-A Ottawa. However, the Expos do not project him as a starting outfielder in the major leagues. The guy has some ability, though.

BENJAMIN, MIKE - 2B/SS - BR - Age 31
Benjamin found his way onto the disabled list in mid-1996 at the exact moment he raised his career batting average to a perfectly even .200. Virtually all of his 1996 hits took place in a torrid stretch against the Cubs, the team he victimized in a record three-game span in 1995. Benjamin is a versatile utilityman who struggles with the bat against righties. He does have a remarkable career 24 for 26 mark (92%) stealing bases. A neck injury ended his 1996 season.

	AB	R	HR	RBI	SB	BA	$
1995 San Francisco NL	186	19	3	12	11	.220	4
1996 Philadelphia NL	103	13	4	13	3	.223	-

BENNETT, GARY - C - BR - Age 24
A decent defensive catcher, Bennett has endured for seven minor league seasons, with September callups the last two years. He did manage to reach humble career highs last year in doubles (15), homers (eight) and walks (24). He's caught in a big time squeeze for 1997, with Mike Lieberthal projected as the big league backup and top prospect Bobby Estalella penciled in for Triple-A duty.

BERBLINGER, JEFF - 2B - BR - Age 26
The best all-around player for Arkansas in 1996, Berblinger has good pop for a second baseman. He has been an overachiever since being drafted out of the University of Kansas. He runs well and has good range defensively, but he only plays one position, second base, and that's a position the Cardinals are well stocked with Luis Alicea, David Bell, and, to a lesser extent, Darrell Deak. Berblinger was a Double-A All-Star for the second straight season in 1996.

BERG, DAVE - SS/2B - BR - Age 26
The Marlins' 1993 38th round draft pick is fundamentally sound at bat and in the field, with solid plate discipline, above-average speed and decent gap power. He has a chance to get a major league cameo as a multi-positional backup, but seems destined to be a Triple-A fixture for years to come.

BERNHARDT, STEVE - 3B - BR - Age 26
After starting the season at Class A Salem and seeing limited duty at Double-A New Haven in 1996, Bernhardt ended the year with a career best batting average. 1997 will be his fifth year in the minors with little likelihood of progress above the Double-A level.

BERRIOS, HARRY - OF - BR - Age 25
Berrios was the Orioles minor league player of the year in 1994 after an outstanding year in Single-A. But he struggles every time he gets up to Double-A, and at age 25, he must get his act together quickly as he will soon run out of chances. Last year, Berrios was released by the Orioles during the season, and signed by the Indians who sent him back to Single-A ball.

BERROA, GERONIMO - OF - BR - Age 32
Mixed in amongst a myriad of wild swings were good stats. There does seem to be a method to his madness. He certainly can hit, but in the field, well, that is another story.

	AB	R	HR	RBI	SB	BA	$
1995 Oakland AL	546	87	22	88	7	.278	19
1996 Oakland AL	586	101	36	106	0	.290	18

BERRY, MIKE - 3B - BR - Age 26
Berry was formerly an Expo farmhand, but he's now in the Orioles system where he won the Single-A California League batting title last year. His .354 in Double-A and Single-A combined was the overall third best in the minors in 1996, his 116 RBI ranked fourth, and even more impressive, his exceptional .471 on-base-percentage was the best in the minors.

BERRY, SEAN - 3B - BR - Age 31
Berry injured his throwing shoulder in the first week of the season, causing him to miss 30 games during the season when it was too painful for him to play. Nevertheless, he set career highs in most offensive categories including home runs and runs batted in. After off-season surgery he should get more playing time in 1997 which should give him a good chance for 25 home runs and 100 runs batted in.

	AB	R	HR	RBI	SB	BA	$
1995 Montreal NL	314	38	14	55	3	.318	15
1996 Houston NL	431	55	17	95	12	.281	17

BESS, JOHNNY - C - BB - Age 26
Bess certainly did his job in Double-A Shreveport. Nothing fancy, nothing to be embarrassed about either. He is stuck behind a couple of real catching prospects in the Giants organization is probably not going too much farther.

BETTS, TODD - 3B - BL - Age 23
Betts' Double-A debut was a disappointment, and delayed his chances for a major league career, especially in the deep Indians' chain. He is a patient singles hitter who showed less patience against the tougher pitching, and who eventually lost playing time to journeyman Luis Raven.

BETZSOLD, JAMES - OF - BR - Age 24
Betzsold showed power potential at High-A Kinston in 1995, but was done in by injuries and his relatively slow bat at Double-A in 1996. The 1994 20th round pick will likely need to repeat at that level, the kiss of death in the plentiful Indians' organization.

BICHETTE, DANTE - OF - BR - Age 33
A 30-30 year with an average over .300 is nothing to scoff at, but Bichette must prove he can come back from reconstructive knee surgery in 1997. In spite of his defensive liabilities, he's likely to be the starting leftfielder for the Rockies in 1997 unless an AL team believes Bichette can make a top-notch DH.

	AB	R	HR	RBI	SB	BA	$
1995 Colorado NL	579	102	40	128	13	.340	42
1996 Colorado NL	633	114	31	141	31	.313	41

BIESER, STEVE - C/OF - BB - Age 29
Bieser is a true survivor. The 1989 32nd round Phils' draft pick has endured despite notching only four homers in 1,853 career minor league at bats. He moved to the Expos' chain in 1996, and had his best year ever, batting .322 with 27 steals at Triple-A Ottawa. As a contact hitter with baserunning savvy and the ability to catch, Bieser has a chance to make the majors as a 25th man.

BIGGIO, CRAIG - 2B - BR - Age 31
Biggio had another strong season in 1996 but fell short of his outstanding 1995 performance. He entered the 1996 season as the top second baseman in the National League but may have yielded that honor to Eric Young. Biggio remains an aggressive player who excels in every phase of the game and should continue to produce at a high level for several years.

	AB	R	HR	RBI	SB	BA	$
1995 Houston NL	553	123	22	77	33	.302	33
1996 Houston NL	605	113	15	75	25	.288	24

BLAIR, BRIAN - OF - BL - Age 24
Blair is a spray-hitting outfielder who likely would have had a hard time securing a full-time job in almost any organization other than the weak Rangers' chain. The lefty has little power or speed, though he lines the ball to the gaps.

BLANCO, HENRY - C - BR - Age 26
Despite being an above-average defensive third baseman, Blanco switched to catcher at Double-A San Antonio in 1996. His hitting is more in line with a catcher's, but his .267-5-40 line in the Texas League is still pretty weak. Blanco's versatility will certainly help his career, but he's only going to be a reserve in the majors.

BLAUSER, JEFF - SS - BR - Age 31
Injuries cost Blauser about half the season, but he managed to regain some of his batting stroke after a dreadful 1995. When healthy, Blauser will hit for a little power and get on base regularly. His below-average defense means he's easily replaced by the next big superstar, or if the Braves open up their deep pocketbook to purchase a big name shortstop. Blauser can hit, and had better start doing it again before he's out of a regular job.

	AB	R	HR	RBI	SB	BA	$
1995 Atlanta NL	431	60	12	31	8	.211	4
1996 Atlanta NL	265	48	10	35	6	.245	4

BLOSSER, GREG - OF - BL - Age 25
Although he was a 1989 first-round draft pick, the Red Sox gave up on Blosser because he didn't hit consistently. He's a typical Triple-A low-average slugger. He played for the Orioles Triple-A club in 1996, but the new set of coaches didn't help. Blosser can hit the ball a mile, when he hits it.

BLOWERS, MIKE - 3B - BR - Age 31
Blower's struggles in the National League should have been no surprise to anyone who studies park effects. By the time he started adjusting to the NL, he blew out a knee and was finished for the year. The competition to regain his starting role is not exactly intense, but don't be surprised to see the Dodgers import a free agent third baseman. Blowers best case is around .265-15-70, but given his age, less production is more likely.

	AB	R	HR	RBI	SB	BA	$
1995 Seattle AL	439	59	23	96	2	.257	14
1996 Los Angeles NL	317	31	6	38	0	.265	4

BLUM, GEOFF - 2B - BB - Age 24
The Expos' 1994 seventh round pick does enough little things to make himself a valuable minor leaguer. He makes contact and will take a walk, but has little power or speed, and only average defensive ability. Second base is not well-stocked in the Expos' upper minors, so Blum remains a prime candidate to start at Triple-A in 1997, leaving him a heartbeat away from the majors.

BOCACHICA, HIRAM - SS - BR - Age 21
The Expos' 1995 first round pick is an offensive machine, combining a lively line drive bat with power to the gaps, excellent plate discipline and blazing speed on the bases. This package earned him the number five prospect ranking in the High-A Florida State League. His defense has been the rub. He missed much of his 1996 High-A season with elbow trouble, and was relegated to DH duty upon his return.

BOGAR, TIM - SS - BR - Age 30
Strictly an off-the-bench utility player, Bogar is hard-working over-achiever. Though short on raw talent compared to other major leaguers, he is a good role model, and that's what has kept him in the majors.

	AB	R	HR	RBI	SB	BA	$
1995 New York NL	145	17	1	21	1	.290	3
1996 New York NL	89	17	0	6	1	.213	-

BOGGS, WADE - 3B - BL - Age 38
A stiff back limiting Boggs' ability to turn on the ball prompted the Yankees to reacquire righty hitter Charlie Hayes. Boggs was once a career .356 hitter; now he is just a tough out with excellent strike zone judgment and good hands.

	AB	R	HR	RBI	SB	BA	$
1995 New York AL	460	76	5	63	1	.324	14
1996 New York AL	501	80	2	41	1	.311	8

BOGLE, BRYAN - OF - BR - Age 23
Bogle was formerly a Cubs minor leaguer, but was released in 1995 and claimed by the Orioles. After struggling earlier in his career, he hit well in Single-A last year, showing good power and some speed.

BONDS, BARRY - OF - BL - Age 32
Attitude or not, in a year of great performances Bonds' 42 homers, 129 RBI, .308 average and record 155 walks are pretty much run-of-the-mill for him. Even his 40-40 accomplishment of last year seemed lost within the myriad of great stats around the majors. There doesn't seem to be any question about his skills, but there is a question in which city they will be displayed.

	AB	R	HR	RBI	SB	BA	$
1995 San Francisco NL	506	109	33	104	31	.294	37
1996 San Francisco NL	517	122	42	129	40	.308	40

BONIFAY, KEN - 3B - BL - Age 26
There is doubt that this guy would still be playing professional baseball if it wasn't for the fact his uncle, Cam Bonifay, is the Pirates' General Manager. He hit .243-6-42 in 95 games at Double-A Carolina in 1996.

BONNICI, JAMES - 1B - BR - Age 25
A late round draft pick in 1991, Bonnici has made very steady progress through the Mariners' farm system, producing extremely consistent results at each stop. In 1996, he hit .292-26-74 for Triple-A Tacoma.

BONILLA, BOBBY - OF/3B - BB - Age 34
Bonilla had a rough start in 1996 hitting a weak .217 as a DH, and was complaining about it in the newspapers. He just doesn't have the mental make-up to be a DH, and must be in the game as a fielder to be a productive hitter. Once moved to the outfield, he had a very good year, breaking 100 RBI for the first time since 1991. A free-agent, Bonilla endeared himself to Oriole management during the Orioles stretch run, and he may be with them in 1997.

	AB	R	HR	RBI	SB	BA	$
1995 Two Teams	554	96	28	99	0	.329	26
1996 Baltimore AL	595	107	28	116	1	.287	17

BOONE, AARON - 3B - BR - Age 24
Bret's brother and the Reds' third round selection in 1994, Aaron is developing into an interesting power/speed combination with 44 doubles, 17 homers, and 21 steals at Double-A Chattanooga. His minuses at this point are strike zone judgment and age, but he should be contending for the Reds' third base job by 1998.

BOONE, BRET - 2B - BR - Age 27
1996 should be considered an off year for Boone, who brought many of the problems on himself by rushing back two weeks after surgery removed bone spurs from his elbow in April. His 1996 batting, slugging, and on-base averages were all career lows. Healthy, Boone is one of the best second basemen in the league, combining good power and defense and, would be a good bet for a comeback in 1997, but probably not with the Reds.

	AB	R	HR	RBI	SB	BA	$
1995 Cincinnati NL	513	63	15	68	5	.267	14
1996 Cincinnati NL	520	56	12	69	3	.233	1

BOOTY, JOSH - 3B - BR - Age 21
The Marlins' 1994 first round pick made slight progress at Low-A Kane County in 1996, lacing 21 home runs, but striking out 195 times in 475 at bats. He was called to the majors late in the season but hardly got into a game.

BORDERS, PAT - C - BR - Age 33
The Angels acquired veteran catcher Borders in a June trade with the Cardinals, and he was later acquired by the White Sox. Once a starter with the Blue Jays in their championship years, he's been with five teams in two years, not an encouraging sign. Borders' role is now backup catcher where he can hit around .250, his career average.

	AB	R	HR	RBI	SB	BA	$
1995 Two Teams	178	15	4	13	0	.208	-
1996 St. Louis NL	69	3	0	4	0	.319	1
1996 Chicago AL	151	12	5	14	0	.258	-

BORDICK, MIKE - SS - BR - Age 31
One of the smoothest defensive shortstops around, Bordick is both durable and dependable. And, he also contributes at the plate with a little pop.

	AB	R	HR	RBI	SB	BA	$
1995 Oakland AL	428	46	8	44	11	.264	11
1996 Oakland AL	525	46	5	54	5	.240	3

BORRERO, RITCHIE - C - BR - Age 24
Borrero spent the first half of the year in extended spring training, then rose quickly to Double-A Trenton by showing good power at three levels. He hit for a decent average for the first time in his seven year pro career (.310 at Trenton), but Borrero strikes out too much and his defense is below par, so he'll have to keep up the power stroke at higher levels. Borrero appears to be headed for a reserve role in the big leagues at best.

BOSTON, D.J. - 1B - BL - Age 25
The Pirates acquired Boston in mid-May from Toronto in a trade for Jacob Brumfield. The Pirates felt they could unlock the power in Boston's 6'7" frame. They couldn't (eight homers in 93 games at Double-A Carolina) and his chances of ever reaching the major leagues like his brother Daryl did are miniscule.

BOURNIGAL, RAFAEL - 2B/SS - BR - Age 30
The quintessential utility infielder, Bournigal surprised all around him by actually flirting with the .300 mark for a few weeks. His final numbers are more what is to be expected. But he has a great glove, and for that alone he'll be around the majors for a while.

	AB	R	HR	RBI	SB	BA	$
1996 Oakland AL	252	33	0	18	4	.242	-

BOWERS, BRENT - OF - BL - Age 25
The Orioles signed ex-Blue Jay farmhand Bowers as a free agent in November 1995. He was once considered a good prospect, but his star faded in recent years. Given a new life, he hustled and hit well in Double-A and Triple-A, even earning a surprise promotion to the majors where he got into 21 games. His likeliest major league role looks like a reserve outfielder, but he may continue to surprise people with his good hitting and overall hustling play.

BOYKIN, TYRONE - 1B/OF - BR - Age 28
Boykin has now spent three years and part of a fourth in Double-A without showing much improvement in his hitting.

BRADSHAW, TERRY - OF - BL - Age 28
Bradshaw has some power and speed but no chance of cracking the Cardinals' strong outfield. He will be 28 by opening day, meaning his window of opportunity for becoming a starter is just about shut. However, he could still become a productive player in the right situation. The Pirates should trade for him; after all, wouldn't Pittsburgh fans embrace a guy named Terry Bradshaw?

BRADY, DOUG - 2B - BB - Age 27
White Sox farm hand Brady is a good fielder and has excellent speed, but probably won't hit enough to survive in the majors. In 1996 he hit .241 with 20 steals at Triple-A

BRAGG, DARREN - OF - BL - Age 27
Bragg struggled through four months with the Mariners before his trade to Boston. His good batting eye returned and he blossomed into a good leadoff hitter and centerfielder without too many defensive problems.

	AB	R	HR	RBI	SB	BA	$
1995 Seattle AL	145	20	3	12	9	.234	4
1996 Seattle-Boston AL	417	74	10	47	14	.261	10

BRAGGS, GLENN - OF - BR - Age 34
After 2,336 at-bats with the Brewers and Reds, Braggs went to Japan. In 1996 he was playing for Yokohama, hitting .273 with 11 home runs.

BRANSON, JEFF - 3B/SS - BL - Age 30
Branson was effective under Davey Johnson in 1995 but was downgraded to one of Ray Knight's constantly rotating band of four players sharing third base in 1996. Branson is a useful reserve, with good power for a middle infielder, the versatility to play three infield positions, and left handed bat, but his playing time is likely to be curtailed in 1996 due to the development of Willie Greene.

	AB	R	HR	RBI	SB	BA	$
1995 Cincinnati NL	331	43	12	45	2	.260	8
1996 Cincinnati NL	311	34	9	37	2	.244	2

BRANYAN, RUSSELL - 3B - BB - Age 21
The Indians' 1994 seventh round pick is a home run machine. His total of 40 at Low-A Columbus ranked second in the minors in 1996. He has a huge swing that is conducive to mammoth whiff totals - 166 in 1996 - but his strikeouts per at bat decreased while his walks dramatically increased. Look for a major step forward from this potential future major league power stud. 1997 is a pivotal year for this high risk, high reward prospect.

BREAM, SCOTT - 2B/OF - BB - Age 26
Bream can steal some bases, but it's doubtful that he can beat out established veterans, so his best opportunity for major league playing time is as a utility man or a replacement.

BREDE, BRENT - OF - BL - Age 25
Brede should have a major league career after finishing second in the Triple-A Pacific Coast League in batting (.348) in '96. He doesn't have power or speed but can hit .270 in the majors.

BRIDGES, KARY - 2B - BL - Age 25
Bridges has hit for average but not power in each of his four seasons in the Astro system (.322-5-54-5 split between Triple-A and Double-A in 1996). He is a contact hitter who rarely strikes out (22 times in 478 at-bats in 1996). Bridges is a marginal prospect who will have difficulty getting a major league opportunity.

BRIGGS, STONEY - OF - BR - Age 25
A marginal power hitter, Briggs strikes out in bunches. In two years above A-ball, Briggs has twenty homers, but has amassed 256 whiffs, more than 30% of his at-bats.

BRINKLEY, DARRYL - OF - BR - Age 28
Brinkley tore up the Class A California League last year earning a mid-season promotion to Double-A where he continued his outstanding play. He's been an offensive force so far, hitting for a good average with power and stealing bases. Previously, he was in the Toronto organization and played in Mexico where he was successful. Brinkley could be in the Padres outfield sometime in 1997, probably as a reserve fourth or fifth outfielder.

BRITO, BERNARDO - DH/OF - BR - Age 33
Brito got five at-bats for the Twins before going to Japan in 1995. He had good power as a minor leaguer; it might be interesting to see what he could do in the majors full-time.

BRITO, JORGE - C - BR - Age 30
A season of injuries and the signing of Jeff Reed (and later Steve Decker) by the parent Rockies limited Brito to fewer than 200 at bats in 1996, all at the Triple-A level. Brito was released by the Rockies at season's end. He'll need his health, a strong offensive performance and a lot of luck to move up to the show in 1997.

BRITO, LUIS - SS - BB - Age 26
A six-year minor league free agent from the Phillies, Brito spent 1996 shuttling between Class A Durham, Double-A Greenville and the Mexico City Tigers of the Mexican League. He has some speed, but poor plate discipline, especially for guy with little power. Brito can field the position well enough.

BRITO, TILSON - SS - BR - Age 24
Brito had a chance to succeed Roberto Alomar at second base but ultimately gave way to Domingo Cedeno followed by Tomas Perez. A natural shortstop, he could get another look this spring but needs to work on his defense (32 errors at Triple-A last year). Alex Gonzalez is younger so Brito may need a position change. With Cedeno gone, Brito may open 1997 as Gonzalez's backup.

	AB	R	HR	RBI	SB	BA	$
1996 Toronto AL	80	10	1	7	1	.238	-

BROACH, DONALD - OF - BR - Age 25
The Reds' 1993 26th round pick is a speedy outfielder who stole 20 bases playing two thirds of the time at Double-A Chattanooga in 1996. He has a little too much uppercut in his swing, and was a little old to just be establishing himself at the Double-A.

BROGNA, RICO - 1B - BL - Age 26
When he got away from the Tigers, where he was coached to be a pull hitter and then labeled a failure, Brogna blossomed in New York. Asked to hit the ball wherever it was pitched, he showed that his best power is to straightaway centerfield, left-center, and right-center. He was starting another productive season when a labral tear in his right shoulder sidelined him in June, 1996.

	AB	R	HR	RBI	SB	BA	$
1995 New York NL	495	72	22	76	0	.289	17
1996 New York NL	188	18	7	30	0	.255	2

BROOKS, JERRY - OF - BR - Age 30
Why hasn't this guy gotten a full season chance as a major league backup? He has consistently hit for average and power throughout his minor league career, most recently blasting 34 homers at Triple-A Charlotte in the Marlins' chain. If not in 1997, Brooks could finally get a chance as a 25th man with 1998 expansion.

BROSIUS, SCOTT - 3B/OF - BR - Age 30
Given a chance to play regularly, including the chance to play through the slumps which had plagued him, Brosius turned in a fine year at the plate and in the field. He bested career highs all around despite missing six weeks with a broken elbow. Brosius is now among the best defensive third sackers in the league.

	AB	R	HR	RBI	SB	BA	$
1995 Oakland AL	388	69	17	46	4	.262	10
1996 Oakland AL	428	73	22	71	7	.304	16

BROWN, ADRIAN - OF - BR - Age 23
A lightly regarded minor leaguer in the Pirates' farm system, Brown was a revelation last season. He had his best season at the plate (.321 at Class A Lynchburg, .296 at Double-A Carolina with a combined 45 steals) and finally learned to take advantage of his outstanding speed. Jermaine Allensworth is the Pirates' centerfielder/leadoff man of the future but Brown will be putting pressure on him by 1998.

BROWN, BRANT - 1B - BL - Age 26
Brown possesses a good-looking stroke from the left side with gap power. He hit double figures in home runs for the first time in his professional career with ten in 94 games at Iowa in 1996. Brown has a tremendous glove. He might have been the best defensive player in the American Association regardless of position in '96. Brown runs well for a first baseman. The Cubs sent him to the instructional league to play outfield because they want to get his bat into the lineup. Overall, Brown's tools mirror Mark Grace closely.

	AB	R	HR	RBI	SB	BA	$
1996 Chicago NL	69	11	5	9	3	.304	3

BROWN, JARVIS - OF - BR - Age 29
Brown is a speedy little outfielder who has played mostly in Triple-A for the past six years getting some major league playing time here and there, enough to accumulate 227 at-bats. He doesn't hit much, but he can steal a base or two, once stealing 72 in Single-A. The Orioles released Brown from Triple-A in June when they wanted to give their younger prospects more playing time.

BROWN, KEVIN - C - BR - Age 23
Brown the catcher is a 1994 first-round pick with good power and decent skills behind the plate. He is tall and athletic, somewhat reminiscent of Carlton Fisk in his physical attributes. He got a cup of coffee with Texas in September and was scheduled to play in the Arizona Fall League. Only two years younger than Ivan Rodriguez, Brown may need a position or organizational change, but should be ready for duty in the majors by 1998.

BROWN, RANDY - SS - BR - Age 26
1996 was Brown's most successful season despite time spent on the DL. His .298 average and 11 homers for Double-A Trenton were easily career highs and earned Brown a promotion to Pawtucket. He's a good athlete who may be getting a little long in the tooth to be playing regularly at Double-A. Brown has a chance to earn a major league reserve infielder role.

BROWN, RAY - 1B - BL - Age 24
A 28th-round draft choice in 1994, Brown turned in a good year at Double-A Chattanooga with a .413 on-base percentage and a .519 slugging average. A bit old to be considered a great prospect, Brown combines decent power with good strike zone judgment, and has more upside potential than other first basemen in the organization.

BROWN, RON - OF - BR - Age 27
As the Marlins' 24th round pick in 1993, Brown was one of the older college players drafted to stock the chain's Class A rosters. His offensive skills (power, average, speed) were below average across the board, but he served his purpose - filling time until the younger prospects developed. He was released in 1996, with only 10 Double-A at bats on his resume.

BROWN, ROOSEVELT - OF - BL - Age 21
A young power/speed combination, Brown was traded to Florida in the Terry Pendleton trade. He has a lot of tools and can move up the Marlins' chain quickly.

BRUMFIELD, JACOB - OF - BR - Age 31
Brumfield played like a new man after being traded from the Pirates, even taking playing time from John Olerud and Shawn Green. At thirty-two years of age, he's obviously not a prospect by the usual standards but has a shot at landing at least a platoon job in the outfield.

	AB	R	HR	RBI	SB	BA	$
1995 Pittsburgh NL	402	64	4	26	22	.271	13
1996 Pittsburgh NL	80	11	2	8	3	.250	1
1996 Toronto AL	308	52	12	52	12	.256	10

BRUMLEY, MIKE - SS - BB - Age 33
Brumley is a veteran utility player who has appeared in the major leagues with six different teams. After hitting only .234 at Triple-A Tucson in 1996, he may be at the end of the line.

BRUNO, JULIO - 2B - BR - Age 24
Although Bruno spent most of 1994 in Triple-A, he started last year in Double-A. He was promoted to Triple-A when prospect Homer Bush broke his leg. Bruno hit decently in Triple-A in 1996, but thus far, he hasn't shown much power or a strong bat.

BRYANT, PAT - OF - BR - Age 24
The Indians' have been exceedingly patient with their 1990 second round draft pick, but despite brief glimpses of power and speed, they have been rewarded with consistent mediocrity. Bryant split 1996 between Double-A and Triple-A, and couldn't make contact at either level. He may have reached the end of the line.

BRYANT, RALPH - OF - BL - Age 35
Bryant spent 1988-1995 with the Kinetsu Buffaloes of the Japanese Pacific League. He returned to the United States and was a player-coach in Double-A for the Angels last year, hitting a poor .208. Bryant was released as a player in July.

BRYANT, SCOTT - OF - BR - Age 29
Bryant has bounced around Triple-A for the last five years without a sniff of the big leagues. He usually hits for a high average and a little power, but 1996 was a down year for him. Bryant's .266-2-19 performance in the hitting-haven of the Pacific Coast League will not impress the Mariners. Look for Bryant to continue his Triple-A travels in 1997.

BUCCHERI, JIM - OF - BR - Age 28
Most recently an Expos' farmhand, Buccheri is now up to 3,278 minor league at bats without a single major league opportunity. Buccheri has been a solid minor league leadoff man for years, making contact, drawing walks and stealing

bases easily despite unspectacular speed. Triple-A International league managers voted him the circuit's top baserunner in 1996. He has an unimpressive .322 career slugging percentage.

BUCHANAN, BRIAN - OF - BR - Age 23
The Yankees first round pick in 1994, Buchanan hit .260 with 23 steals at Class-A Tampa in 1996.

BUFORD, DAMON - OF - BR - Age 26
Buford hit 70 points over his previous career average in 1996 as an extra outfielder with Texas. He has speed, but is a low-percentage base stealer (20 for 35 in the majors). Buford's defensive skills, versatility and speed should keep him in the majors, but a starting job is likely out of reach.

	AB	R	HR	RBI	SB	BA	$
1995 New York NL	136	24	4	12	7	.235	3
1996 Texas AL	145	30	6	20	8	.283	5

BUHNER, JAY - OF - BR - Age 32
Although he reached forty homers for the second year in a row, his home run rate fell a bit. In 1995, Bone went yard once every 11.75 at-bats; in 1996 it was once every 12.82. He's a true power hitter; no matter how juiced the ball it won't make a bit of difference in his output.

	AB	R	HR	RBI	SB	BA	$
1995 Seattle AL	470	86	40	121	0	.262	21
1996 Seattle AL	564	107	44	138	0	.271	19

BULLETT, SCOTT - OF - BL - Age 28
A free swinger with some pop, Bullett qualifies as a reserve outfielder but no better, right now. He runs well for a big man (220 lbs.), has an average glove and a decent arm. Bullett collected his first major league hit on a bunt against Greg Maddux in 1993. With all of the young outfielders the Cubs have to choose from, Bullett's major league experience may set him apart.

	AB	R	HR	RBI	SB	BA	$
1995 Chicago NL	150	19	3	22	8	.273	5
1996 Chicago NL	165	26	3	16	7	.212	-

BURKE, JAMIE - 3B - BR - Age 25
Burke hit .319 in Double-A, but found the going much tougher in Triple-A. He doesn't have any power or speed, and it's doubtful that he can make the Angels in 1997, even as a bench player.

BURKS, ELLIS - OF - BR - Age 32
In his first injury-free season in three years, this free agent became the only player other than Henry Aaron to have at least 40 homers, 30 steals and 200 hits. He was also in the top ten in almost every NL offensive category. Look for Burks to move to centerfield in 1997 if he re-signs with the Rockies. If he signs elsewhere, expect a significant drop in homers, RBI and other power categories, despite the fact that Burks was the Rocks' most consistent hitter on the road in 1996.

	AB	R	HR	RBI	SB	BA	$
1995 Colorado NL	278	41	14	49	7	.266	11
1996 Colorado NL	613	142	40	128	32	.344	51

BURNITZ, JEROMY - OF - BL - Age 27
The Indians were loaded in the outfield, but reportedly didn't want to give up Burnitz in the Seitzer trade. Burnitz has a legitimate chance to earn a starting job with the retooling Brewers. He offers above-average power in a hitters' ballpark. After the trade, he was in the Brewers' lineup nearly every day in September.

	AB	R	HR	RBI	SB	BA	$
1996 Clev-Milwaukee AL	200	38	9	40	4	.265	5

BURTON, DARREN - OF - BB - Age 24
1996 was a calm year for Burton compared to 1995 when he was let go three times in five months. It was a watershed season as he had to prove himself all over again. Back with the Royals, Burton showed unusual power; his 28 doubles led Omaha and his 15 homers and 67 RBI were second on the club. He has always possessed a good arm and above-average speed. Being a switch-hitter and adding power to his arsenal increase Burton's chances of sticking with the big club this spring. He will surprise in 1997.

BURTON, ESSEX - 2B - BR - Age 27
Burton is the type of player who sells minor league tickets, but has little chance of ever reaching the majors. He steals at will, but with no regard for game situation, and has only average range, poor technique and a weak throwing arm on defense, despite his plus speed. Assuming he is retained by the Phillies, his 1997 home will be determined by better prospect Marlon Anderson's progress, not his own.

BUSCH, MIKE - 1B/3B - BR - Age 28
Busch did not receive much of a chance at the third base job after Mike Blowers struggled and eventually went down for the year, and the late-season signing of Tim Wallach would have to be considered a vote of no confidence by the organization. Busch hit well in a short stint at Albuquerque (.303 with 12 homers in 142 at-bats) but in the majors he was another Billy Ashley, striking out 40% of the time while hitting a few home runs and not much else. Busch is too old to be considered a prospect and he is not likely to get a chance at regular play with the Dodgers.

	AB	R	HR	RBI	SB	BA	$
1995 Los Angeles NL	17	3	3	6	0	.235	0
1996 Los Angeles NL	83	8	4	17	0	.217	-

BUSH, HOMER - 2B - BR - Age 24
Padres prospect Bush got the call for the promotion to the Padres, but he broke his leg sliding into second and was lost for the season. He was hitting .362 in Triple-A at the time. He was a fast base stealer, but it remains to be seen if he comes all the way back. The Padres see Bush as their future second baseman.

BUTLER, BRETT - OF - BL - Age 39
After his remarkable comeback from throat cancer, he wants to return in 1997. It would be extremely difficult for the Dodgers to say no, and Butler is the type of player (slap hitter with good strike zone judgment) that can play effectively until he is in his forties.

	AB	R	HR	RBI	SB	BA	$
1995 Two Teams	513	78	1	38	32	.300	22
1996 Los Angeles NL	131	22	0	8	8	.267	3

BUTLER, ROB - OF - BL - Age 26
Butler is another Phillie farmhand whose falling stock is underlined by the fact that he was not one of the 54 players used by the club at the major league level. Butler is a slap hitter whose formerly above-average speed has deteriorated rapidly, making him a less attractive extra outfielder than Ricky Otero. His lack of power and insistence on swinging at nearly every pitch also make him an unattractive option as a pinch hitter.

CABRERA, JOLBERT - SS - BR - Age 24
Cabrera is an above average defensive shortstop without much offensive skill. He is an undisciplined hitter with little power and has never learned to incorporate his above average speed into his offensive game. Hiram Bocachica is about ready to leapfrog over him in the Expos' chain.

CABRERA, ORLANDO - SS - BR - Age 23
Cabrera had an eye-catching initial year in a full-season league, as he was named the best defensive shortstop and baserunner in the Low-A South Atlantic League. He stole 51 bases, drew 54 walks, and lashed 28 doubles and 14 homers, solid pop for a smallish (5'11", 165 pound) middle infielder.

CAIRO, MIGUEL - 2B - BR - Age 22
Coming over from the Mariners in the Bill Risley deal, Cairo spent most of 1996 with Triple-A Syracuse and quietly posted good numbers. He played most of his games at second base (with some at third) and his defense showed moderate improvement. He doesn't hit for power but he runs quickly and has good range. Cairo will compete for a major league spot this spring.

CAMERON, MIKE - OF - BR - Age 24
Cameron is a typical "tools guy" who finally got all of the components of his game into sync in 1996, showing a combination of power, speed and patience unmatched in the upper minor leagues. He was tabbed as the best baserunner and most exciting player.

CAMINITI, KEN - 3B - BB - Age 33
Caminiti had an MVP-type year leading the Padres to the western division crown. He won another Gold Glove in 1996, and his team leadership is outstanding. One of the best baseball stories of 1996 occurred when Caminiti became ill and severely dehydrated during the Padres games in Mexico City. He was unable to eat or drink and was taking fluids intravenously when he pulled the IV out of his arm and announced he was able to play. He promptly hit two home runs. Caminiti had shoulder surgery after the season, and although the rehab time is long, he's expected to be ready for spring training.

	AB	R	HR	RBI	SB	BA	$
1995 San Diego NL	526	74	26	94	12	.302	27
1996 San Diego NL	546	109	40	130	11	.326	37

CAMPOS, JESUS - OF - BR - Age 23
Signed by the Expos out of the Dominican Republic at age 17, Campos is a diminutive (5'9", 145 lbs) outfielder with no extra base power at all. He has all of 19 extra base hits (16 doubles, three triples) in 681 at bats over the past two seasons, most recently at Double-A Harrisburg.

CANDAELE, CASEY - 2B/OF - BB - Age 36
Yes, it was the same old Casey Candaele you saw bridging the gap between Carlos Baerga and Jose Vizcaino for the Indians. Did a pretty darn good job, too. He will continue to be a light-hitting Triple-A insurance policy until he decides to begin his coaching career.

	AB	R	HR	RBI	SB	BA	$
1996 Cleveland AL	44	8	1	4	0	.250	-

CANDELARIA, BENJAMIN - OF - BL - Age 21
Splitting 1996 between Class A Dunedin and Double-A Knoxville, Candelaria ironically performed better at the higher level. He isn't very fast and strikes out a lot considering his lack of power.

CANGELOSI, JOHN - OF - BB - Age 34
Cangelosi had a productive year with Houston in 1996 in his tenth major league season. He should be able to stay in the majors for at least one more year as a fourth outfielder. He is especially valuable for his ability to get on base (.378 on-base percentage) and steal bases.

	AB	R	HR	RBI	SB	BA	$
1995 Houston NL	201	46	2	18	21	.318	13
1996 Houston NL	262	49	1	16	17	.263	6

CANIZARO, JAY - 2B - BR - Age 23
Canizaro is progressing well through the Giants system, having played three-fourths of the year at Triple-A Phoenix and the remainder with the big club. He was a little over matched at Phoenix, and seriously so in the majors. Since Mueller and Aurilia will be the guys up the middle for the next year or so, Canizaro can take it slow at Triple-A for at least another year. Once he gets the hang of major league pitching he could be a good hitting middle infielder.

	AB	R	HR	RBI	SB	BA	$
1996 San Francisco NL	120	11	2	8	0	.200	-

CANSECO, JOSE - DH - BR - Age 32
He had to sit out a month or so with his usual assortment of injuries, but when healthy Canseco was the most feared right-handed bat in the Red Sox lineup. He started out in rightfield - and was dreadful- but returned to his accustomed DH role after just a few weeks. Canseco can definitely hit for power. He is a big supporter of Kevin Kennedy and he'll likely remain a regular DH as long as Kennedy is managing in Boston.

	AB	R	HR	RBI	SB	BA	$
1995 Boston AL	396	64	24	81	4	.306	19
1996 Boston AL	360	68	28	82	3	.289	14

CAPPUCCIO, CARMINE - OF - BL - Age 27
Cappuccio is the stereotypical minor league journeyman outfielder. He is impatient at the plate though he makes consistent contact.

CARABALLO, GARY - 3B - BR - Age 25
Caraballo is an adequate defensive player who needs to improve his hitting in all phases to become a real prospect. Caraballo's production at Double-A was substandard even for an infielder in a terrible hitter's park.

CAREY, TODD - 3B - BL - Age 25
Considered a marginal prospect before 1996, Carey was one of the Red Sox' most pleasant surprises. He had shown power in the past, but stepped his game up to a new level last year, hitting 20 homers with 78 RBI while playing a solid third base. Carey also has the defense to reach the majors and will get the chance if he can only cut his strikeouts while playing at Triple-A Pawtucket in 1997.

CARPENTER, BUBBA - OF - BL - Age 28
After six years on the Yankee farm, Carpenter has been stuck at Triple-A for two and a half seasons. He was no closer to a major league role at the end of 1996 than he was in 1993. Carpenter has noticeable power and speed but is not outstanding in any aspect.

CARR, CHUCK - OF - BR - Age 28
Carr blew out his knee after appearing in only 27 games in 1996. As the injury came early in the year, he's had a long time to rehab, but remains a question mark at this point. His strength was his defense, and the Brewers wanted him in centerfield every day. He was doing well in the field and at the plate when he went down. The Brewers acquired Gerald Williams who can play center, and is a better hitter than Carr.

	AB	R	H	RBI	SB	BA	$
1995 Florida NL	308	54	2	20	25	.227	9
1996 Milwaukee AL	106	18	1	11	5	.274	1

CARR, JEREMY - 2B - BR - Age 26
Carr's terrific speed (175 steals in four pro seasons) and lively bat added some excitement to Wichita Wrangler's games in 1996. In his first year above A-ball, he moved to the outfield. However, the Royals are also loaded with speedy outfield prospects, so his fate will hinge on continuing to show some discipline at the plate.

CARREON, MARK - 1B/OF - BR - Age 33
Carreon had people believing he was a first-rate starting first sacker with a solid 1995 campaign, but was then traded by the Giants to the Indians for Jim Poole last season. Carreon is a useful bench player and spot starter who can roll out of bed and hit line drives. As a starting first baseman, however, he is below average in all areas, due in part to his impatience at the plate and lack of defensive skills. Look for him to amass around 300 at bats as a part-timer in 1997, with ten homer potential.

	AB	R	HR	RBI	SB	BA	$
1995 San Francisco NL	396	53	17	65	0	.301	15
1996 San Francisco NL	292	40	9	51	2	.260	5
1996 Cleveland AL	142	16	2	14	1	.324	2

CARTER, JEFF - OF - BB - Age 33
Here's a guy who deserved to spend at least a little while in a major league uniform, but never got the chance. Carter has now spent seven years as a Triple-A second baseman, posting excellent on-base percentages all along - twice exceeding .420.

CARTER, JOE - OF - BR - Age 37
After Carter signed a contract extension in late summer, his bat weakened. The front office said in October that Carter would shift to first base full-time this year if the club moved John Olerud in a deal. Despite Carter's late-season collapse, he still topped the 100 RBI mark for the ninth time in the past eleven years.

	AB	R	HR	RBI	SB	BA	$
1995 Toronto AL	558	70	25	76	12	.253	18
1996 Toronto AL	625	84	30	107	7	.253	15

CARTER, MIKE - SS/OF - BR - Age 27
After leading the American Association in hitting with a .325 average in 1995, Carter dropped off considerably in '96. Some, not all, of his dropoff can be attributed to nagging injuries he fought most of the season. Carter has averaged 19 walks per year in his professional career. He has good speed but doesn't run the bases well. After committing 71

errors in his first two years of pro ball at shortstop, Carter has developed into an above-average outfielder, mostly due to his speed. Many of the Cubs younger outfielders have vaulted past him.

CARVAJAL, JOVINO - OF - BB - Age 28
Although older than his minor league peers, Angel prospect Carvajal was making good progress through the minors until he reached Triple-A last year and had a setback, hitting a weak .239. He doesn't have much power, but he can steal bases. Unfortunately, he can't steal first.

CARVER, STEVE - 1B - BL - Age 24
The Phils' 1995 fourth-round draftee is 6'3", 215 pounds and showed consistent gap power and occasional flashes of long ball ability in his first full pro season at High-A Clearwater. It is hard to get too excited about a player of his age who has yet to play at Double-A, but Carver could ratchet up the homer total in 1997 and move up the ladder quickly.

CASANOVA, RAUL - C - BB - Age 24
Casanova, a good catching prospect, came to Detroit from San Diego in the spring of '96 and is the organization's future backstop. He battled nagging injuries in '96 yet managed a decent year between Triple-A (.273) and Detroit (.188 with four homers). Casanova projects as a .265 hitter with twenty home runs per season in three to four years. He'll play regularly by '99.

	AB	R	HR	RBI	SB	BA	$
1996 Detroit AL	85	6	4	9	0	.188	-

CASEY, SEAN - 1B - BL - Age 22
Casey has a sweet lefthanded swing, and has posted a .330 average with gap power in his first two pro season. At 6'4", 215 pounds, he is a candidate to turn those doubles into homers. If he does so, he will be a dynamite all-around offensive performer, as he rarely strikes out. A big year in 1997 could propel him ahead of Richie Sexson and into a major league job in 1998.

CASTELLANO, PEDRO - 3B - BR - Age 27
Castellano had another solid year at Triple-A, but is unlikely to see much playing time with the Rockies so long as Castilla stays healthy and Jason Bates, who can play all infield positions, remains the primary utility man.

CASTILLA, VINNY - 3B - BR - Age 29
Everyone expected Castilla's numbers to drop significantly after his career year in 1995. Everyone was wrong. If anything, Castilla showed more power in 1996. In 1997, he'll no doubt continue starting for the Rockies at third base.

	AB	R	HR	RBI	SB	BA	$
1995 Colorado NL	527	82	32	90	2	.309	26
1996 Colorado NL	629	97	40	113	7	.304	32

CASTILLO, ALBERTO - C - BR - Age 27
A mature minor leaguer, Castillo has been praised by new manager Bobby Valentine for helping young pitchers to develop on the Mets farm. That factor might get Castillo a major league backup job, but he will never hit well enough to play regularly in New York, especially not with Todd Hundley around. Castillo finished with a .208 average at Triple-A in 1996.

CASTILLO, LUIS - 2B - BB - Age 21
Castillo's speed and defense drive his game. He was recognized as the best and fastest baserunner and as the best defensive second baseman in the Double-A Eastern League prior to his recall. A patient slap hitter of small proportions (5'11", 155 pounds), Castillo was at times overmatched by major league fastballs. His 46/14 major league strikeout/walk ratio was well below his minor league norms. He underwent offseason shoulder surgery, but is the frontrunner to win the job in 1997. He will be a perennial stolen base championship candidate, and could one day steal 100 in a season.

	AB	R	HR	RBI	SB	BA	$
1996 Florida NL	164	26	1	8	17	.262	5

CASTLEBERRY, KEVIN - 2B - BL - Age 28
The typical minor league journeyman, Castleberry didn't reach Triple-A until age 27, but he has established himself as a scrappy player at that level for the Expos over the past two seasons. Defense is his forte. His range isn't remarkable, but he is extremely surehanded. A rare lefthanded bat at second base, he is patient and hits line drives to all fields. He will likely serve as Triple-A injury insurance yet again.

CASTRO, JUAN - SS/2B/3B - BR - Age 24
Castro is a defensive specialist who got to play some due to injuries to Greg Gagne and the ineffectiveness of Delino DeShields. Castro has little power or speed and little chance to expand his role with the Dodgers.

	AB	R	HR	RBI	SB	BA	$
1996 Los Angeles NL	132	16	0	5	1	.197	-

CASTRO, RAMON - C - BR - Age 21
Castro was Houston's number one draft choice in 1994. He has played three years with little progress. His primary asset is power but he hit only seven homers while batting .248 at Class A Quad Cities. Castro has a lot of work ahead of him to reach the majors, but he has plenty of time.

CATALANOTTO, FRANK - 2B - BL - Age 22
Catalanotto raised his average 72 points in his second Double-A season (.298-17-67-15). He will have a major league career as either a decent regular or a great backup.

CEDENO, ANDUJAR - SS - BR - Age 27
Once a bright power-hitting middle-infield prospect in the Astros' system, Cedeno has been traded twice in the last two years and has essentially hit bottom as a potential major league regular. Cedeno's inability to distinguish between strikes and balls has caught up to him; his wild-swinging approach at the plate and porous defense in the field leave him with no proven position or role. He'll have to start all over again in 1997, probably with yet another team.

	AB	R	HR	RBI	SB	BA	$
1995 San Diego NL	390	42	6	31	5	.210	1
1996 Houston NL	153	11	3	18	3	.231	-
1996 Detroit AL	179	19	7	20	2	.196	-

CEDENO, DOMINGO - SS/2B - BB - Age 28
Cedeno landed an everyday job early in the year but his light bat and the improving play of Tomas Perez allowed the Blue Jays to ship him off to the White Sox. Cedeno turned twenty-eight in November and he reverts to being a utility infielder.

	AB	R	HR	RBI	SB	BA	$
1995 Toronto AL	161	18	4	14	0	.236	0
1996 Toronto-Chicago AL	301	46	2	20	6	.272	3

CEDENO, ROGER - OF - BB - Age 22
A slashing switch-hitter, Cedeno spent a good portion of the year in Los Angeles. It was a poor showing for the young prospect, though, and he saw his playing time decrease during the pennant drive. The Dodgers brought in Chad Curtis and Wayne Kirby to serve their immediate needs. Cedeno can be a good leadoff hitter and centerfielder if the Dodgers give him time to develop.

	AB	R	HR	RBI	SB	BA	$
1995 Los Angeles NL	42	4	0	3	1	.238	-
1996 Los Angeles NL	211	26	2	18	5	.246	1

CEPEDA, JOSE - 3B - BR - Age 22
Orlando's nephew Jose is a contact hitter who also has a decent glove at the hot corner. He hits well enough for average, but doesn't have much power.

CHAMBERLAIN, WES - OF - BR - Age 30
With the Chiba Lotte Marines in Japan in 1996, ex-Phillie Chamberlain hit .259 with 10 home runs.

CHARLES, FRANK - C/1B - BR - Age 27
Charles is a catcher-DH who is unlikely to hit or field well enough to advance beyond Triple-A.

CHAVEZ, RAUL - C - BR - Age 24
The Expos like the defensive skills Chavez possesses. However, he won't hit enough to be more than a second or third string catcher in the major leagues.

CHIMELIS, JOEL - SS/3B - BR - Age 29
Chimelis was a classic career minor leaguer stuck in the Giants' farm system since 1988 until a brief callup in 1995. The Mets took a quick look at him in 1996 (76 at-bats for Triple-A Norfolk) and decided they could get along without him.

CHOLOWSKY, DAN - OF/3B - BR - Age 26
Cholowsky was demoted from Triple-A Iowa to Double-A Orlando when Kevin Orie was called up to Iowa.

CHRISTENSEN, McKAY - OF - BL - Age 21
The Angels selected the speedy Christensen in the first round of the 1994 draft, even though he went on a mission for the Mormon church until 1996.

CHRISTOPHERSON, ERIC - C - BR - Age 27
Christopherson was a second round draft choice by the Giants in 1990 and was signed to a minor league contract by the Astros in 1996. He has played the last two seasons at the Triple-A level where he appears to have topped out.

CIANFROCCO, ARCHI - 1B/SS - BR - Age 30
Cianfrocco proved that he was a valuable all-around utility man last year, playing all of the positions except center field and pitching. He played 31 games at first base, capably filling in for the injured Wally Joyner. His solid .281 was a career high for him.

	AB	R	HR	RBI	SB	BA	$
1995 San Diego NL	118	22	5	31	0	.263	
1996 San Diego NL	192	21	2	32	1	.281	4

CIRILLO, JEFF - 3B/2B - BR - Age 27
Cirillo's development enabled the Brewers to move Kevin Seitzer, and remove any doubt that Cirillo is capable of handling a starting role at third. He hit over .300 against everything. He also hit over 40 doubles, and that suggests he may be in the 20-25 homer range in 1997. While he's not a great base stealing threat, he attempted to run often, failing twice as often as he succeeded. If he remains aggressive, that could yield 10-15 thefts in 1997.

	AB	R	HR	RBI	SB	BA	$
1995 Milwaukee AL	328	57	9	39	7	.277	10
1996 Milwaukee AL	566	101	15	83	4	.325	18

CLAPINSKI, CHRIS - SS/3B - BB - Age 25
Clapinski has defied his marginal ability, and has parlayed patience at the plate, excellent bat handling ability and defensive versatility into a viable upper minor league career, most recently at Triple-A Charlotte in the Marlins chain. However, the Marlins glut of middle infielders made Kurt Abbott the major league utilityman.

CLARK, DAVE - OF - BL - Age 34
An excellent platoon outfielder who was acquired by the Dodgers for the stretch run during the Pirates latest fire sale, Clark features a good batting average, decent power and good strike zone judgment and could have a shot at a role if the Dodgers decide that Roger Cedeno is not ready for centerfield and move Todd Hollandsworth there. Jim Leyland always found Clark plenty of at-bats.

	AB	R	HR	RBI	SB	BA	$
1995 Pittsburgh NL	196	30	4	24	3	.281	5
1996 Los Angeles NL	226	28	8	36	2	.270	5

CLARK, HOWIE - 2B - BL - Age 22
Clark doesn't have much power or speed, but he hit for a decent average in Double-A last year. He's a second baseman and utility infielder who usually makes good contributions to whatever team he's with. He was voted co-MVP of the Bowie Double-A club last year. Clark played all nine positions for Bowie in the last game of last season.

CLARK, JERALD - OF/1B - BR - Age 33
Clark has bounced around the majors, minors, Japan and the disabled list over the last few years; 1996 marked his fifth organization in as many years. He's a righthanded bat off of the bench at this point in his career and can provide an occasional homer.

CLARK, PHIL - OF/3B - BR - Age 28
While Clark is a jack of all trades, he's a master of none. He can play first, third, catcher or in the outfield and contributes power hitting. The problem for Clark is that he isn't skilled enough with the glove to play regularly in the majors at catcher or third and he doesn't hit quite enough to be a big-league regular at first or in the outfield. Clark's true abilities lie somewhere in the middle of the .325-12-69 season he posted at Pawtucket and his recent struggles in the big leagues. His immediate future will resemble his immediate past: major league fringe player and Triple-A insurance.

CLARK, TONY - 1B - BB - Age 24
Clark had a good rookie year as he showed his tremendous power and played a decent first base. On the negative side, the former college basketball star struck out too often, and lefthanders gave the switch hitter problems.

	AB	R	HR	RBI	SB	BA	$
1995 Detroit AL	101	10	3	11	0	.238	0
1996 Detroit AL	376	56	27	72	0	.250	8

CLARK, WILL - 1B - BL - Age 33
Clark's season was nearly a duplicate of 1993, his last (and least productive) year with the Giants. Particularly toward the end of the season, Clark was struggling at the plate. Some observers believed that his chronic elbow problems were affecting his hitting, particularly for power; of the Ranger regulars, only Mark McLemore had fewer extra-base hits. Still, Clark has never hit less than .282 or 11 homers in the majors and those numbers are probably reasonable projections for him in 1997. Never particularly durable, Clark made three trips to the disabled list in the last two months of the season.

	AB	R	HR	RBI	SB	BA	$
1995 Texas AL	454	85	16	92	0	.302	16
1996 Texas AL	436	69	13	72	2	.284	9

CLAYTON, ROYCE - SS - BR - Age 27
Clayton was thrust into a most difficult situation last season with the Cardinals after being acquired in a winter trade from San Francisco. He was asked to replace a legend in Ozzie Smith when the legend was still around. Clayton handled the situation well and had a solid season. It's doubtful he will become the superstar some people once predicted but he has a long and productive career ahead of him.

	AB	R	HR	RBI	SB	BA	$
1995 San Francisco NL	509	56	5	58	24	.244	14
1996 St. Louis NL	491	64	6	35	33	.277	17

CLINE, PAT - C - BR - Age 21
Cline set the Daytona Cubs record for home runs with 17 last year. Cline is showing improvement defensively, and can hit for average and power.

CLYBURN, DANNY - OF - BR - Age 22
Formerly a top prospect in the Pirates and Reds organizations, power hitting outfielder Clyburn played with the Orioles Double-A team last year, being acquired in the Brad Pennington trade in mid-1995. He was on his way to a great year, when he went down with a severe hamstring injury. Although Clyburn has shown good power in the minors, he's very raw.

COCKRELL, ALAN - OF - BR - Age 34
This career minor leaguer (and outstanding college QB at Tennessee), a productive regular at Triple-A Colorado Springs, got his first cup of coffee in the bigs after a September call-up. His first major league hit at Coors Field drew a standing ovation. He may be more likely to return to the Rockies organization as a coach than a player in 1997.

COFFEE, GARY - 1B - BR - Age 22
At 6'3", 230 pounds, Coffee can hit the ball a long way - when he hits it. He struck out 141 times in 393 at-bats, or 50 times more than he hit safely. Still, the Royals love Coffee's power potential; he's still a long ways from Kauffman Stadium, but has time to advance.

COLBERT, CRAIG - C - BR - Age 32
For the most part, Colbert has been in Triple-A for the past seven years, making it to the show with the Giants for 163 at-bats in 1992 and '93 where he hit a career .215. He played for the Padres Triple-A club last year.

COLBRUNN, GREG - 1B - BR - Age 27
Colbrunn's 1996 season was somewhat of a disappointment. He has been plagued by overaggressiveness at the plate. He posted only 25 walks, and has but 68 free passes in 1,608 career plate appearances. Since he is often behind in the count, he rarely gets fat fastballs to drive, dropping his home run totals to below average levels for a first sacker. Expect Colbrunn's batting average to remain in the .285-.305 range in the intermediate term, but he will have trouble taking the next step to stardom until he learns the value of taking a pitch.

	AB	R	HR	RBI	SB	BA	$
1995 Florida NL	528	70	23	89	11	.277	22
1996 Florida NL	511	60	16	69	4	.286	16

COLE, ALEX - OF - BL - Age 31
Cole had a chance to win the Red Sox' leadoff hitter/centerfielder job early in 1996. He hit and fielded poorly and was considered a contributing factor to Boston's early-season woes. Yet another leg injury virtually ended his season early in May. Cole's future is uncertain; he'll hook on as an extra outfielder in the majors in 1997, but a return to full-time duty is a long shot at best.

	AB	R	HR	RBI	SB	BA	$
1995 Minnesota AL	79	10	1	14	1	.342	2
1996 Boston AL	72	13	0	7	5	.222	-

COLEMAN, VINCE - OF - BB - Age 35
Coleman was released by the Reds, and the Angels signed him to a minor league contract in June simply because they needed a Triple-A outfielder. He hit a weak .207 in Triple-A, a sudden decline from his usually steady .240-280 in the majors in recent years.

	AB	R	HR	RBI	SB	BA	$
1995 Two Teams	455	66	5	29	42	.288	28
1996 Cincinnati NL	84	10	1	4	12	.155	-

COLES, DARNELL - OF - BR - Age 34
Coles peaked in 1986 with the Tigers, hitting .273 with 20 homers. In 1996 he was in Japan, producing a .313 average and 28 home runs for Chunichi.

COLLIER, LOUIS - SS - BR - Age 23
Injuries caused Collier to have a somewhat disappointing year at Double-A Carolina (.280 with three homers in 119 games), though he did start in the Double-A All-Star Game. He has a live bat, good speed and outstanding arm, though the time is nearing when he must learn to start using those tools better. Jay Bell was a free agent at the end of last season and Collier will put himself in position to be the replacement as the Pirates' shortstop in 1998 with a good season at Triple-A Calgary.

COLON, DENNIS - 1B - BB - Age 23
Colon hit .280-12-58 in his second year at Double-A in 1996. He does not appear to have a major league future.

CONGER, JEFF - OF - BL - Age 25
Conger has some speed and is pretty good defensively, but his lack of hitting (.232 last year at Double-A Carolina) has kept him from becoming the top centerfield prospect the Pirates had hoped he'd be.

CONINE, JEFF - 1B/OF - BR - Age 30
The Marlins have been happy with Conine, one of their expansion draft selections. He has crushed lefthanded pitching (.393 in 1996), played nearly every day and has served as a more than adequate protector for Gary Sheffield in the lineup. His last three seasons are virtually indistinguishable. He can be counted upon for a .290-.310 average with 20-25 homers.

	AB	R	HR	RBI	SB	BA	$
1995 Florida NL	483	72	25	105	2	.302	23
1996 Florida NL	597	84	26	95	1	.293	22

CONNER, DECOMBA - OF - BR - Age 23
Conner was traded by the Reds to the Tigers following the 1996 season in exchange for Ruben Sierra. Conner has an intriguing power/speed combination. He hit 20 homers and stole 33 bases in 1996 at High-A Winston-Salem.

COOK, HAYWARD - OF - BR - Age 24
Cook is a free-swinging, line-drive gap hitter with above-average speed. The 1994 ninth-round draftee has a number of drawbacks. He does not walk enough to be a top of the order hitter, and it took him until after his 24th birthday to reach Double-A, for 46 at-bats. His chances of cracking the major leagues appear slim.

COOKSON, BRENT - OF - BR - Age 27
Cookson played for the Orioles Triple-A club in 1996 showing good power. But it's significant that he was passed over when the Orioles needed outfield help. He was formerly in the Giants, Royals and Red Sox organizations where he had some good minor league years. Some observers believe he could hit 25 homers given a full shot in the majors.

COOLBAUGH, SCOTT - 3B - BR - Age 30
Coolbaugh returned from Japan to play at Triple-A Ottawa in the Expos' chain. Once a power threat with no plate discipline, Coolbaugh has evolved into a former power threat with a little plate discipline.

COOMER, RON - 3B - BR - Age 30
Coomer had a nice first full season in the major leagues as he played mostly first base against lefthanders.

	AB	R	HR	RBI	SB	BA	$
1995 Minnesota AL	101	15	5	19	0	.257	1
1996 Minnesota AL	233	34	12	41	3	.296	7

COOPER, SCOTT - 3B - BL - Age 29
Sometimes the best laid plans go awry. The Cardinals needed a third baseman going into 1995 and Cooper appeared to be the perfect fit when they acquired him in a trade with Boston. He had played in the previous two All-Star games and was a hometown boy from St. Louis. However, Cooper struggled miserably, then played in Japan in 1996.

CORA, JOEY - 2B - BB - Age 31
Cora's speed isn't gone despite just five stolen bases after swiping 18 in 1995. With all of the big boppers in Seattle, it just was not, and will not be necessary for him to run much.

	AB	R	HR	RBI	SB	BA	$
1995 Seattle AL	427	64	3	39	18	.297	17
1996 Seattle AL	530	90	6	45	5	.291	9

CORDERO, WILFREDO - 2B/OF - BR - Age 25
The almost constant injuries that Cordero battled in 1996 made him one of the Red Sox' biggest disappointments. He wasn't up to playing second base as they had hoped and he barely managed 200 at-bats, with little power or speed. The bright side is that Cordero is only 25 years old in 1997 and is clearly capable of much better things. He can be a .300 hitter with power if he can only stay in the lineup.

	AB	R	HR	RBI	SB	BA	$
1995 Montreal NL	514	64	10	49	9	.286	15
1996 Boston AL	198	29	3	37	2	.288	3

CORDOVA, MARTY - OF - BR - Age 27
There was no sophomore jinx for Cordova, as he followed up his Rookie of the Year season with an even better year. He led the Twins in home runs and was second in RBI to Paul Molitor. Being a spray hitter helps in the Metrodome, and Cordova fits perfectly into the Twins "doubles happy" offense.

	AB	R	HR	RBI	SB	BA	$
1995 Minnesota AL	512	81	24	84	20	.277	26
1996 Minnesota AL	569	97	16	111	11	.309	21

CORREA, MIGUEL - OF - BB - Age 25
Correa has now failed twice in trials at Double-A Greenville, posting a combined .215 average over the last two seasons. That's not going to cut it.

CORREIA, ROD - OF/IF - BR - Age 29
Former Angels' middle-infielder Correia fell out of favor in California and was traded to the Cardinals over the previous winter. He had a bad year at Triple-A Louisville, where he switched to the outfield. As a shortstop he was a weak hitter with an average glove. As an outfielder he's a weak hitter whose defensive skills are misused.

COSTO, TIM - 1B/OF - BR - Age 28
Mr. Aluminum Bat Power has not had a major league at-bat since 1993, and showed a slow bat and vastly diminished long ball power at Triple-A Buffalo in 1996.

COTTON, JOHN - OF - BL - Age 26
Cotton joined the Tigers as a six-year, minor league free agent over the winter. He's got a little pop in his bat, but is just far too impatient to be a successful hitter, even in the high minors.

COUGHLIN, KEVIN - 1B - BL - Age 26
Formerly of the White Sox farm system, Coughlin is an aging first baseman and outfielder who just doesn't hit enough for average to justify his lack of power; he has six professional homers in eight minor league seasons - none above Double-A. He has almost no chance to reach the bigs.

COUNSELL, CRAIG - SS - BL - Age 26
The outstanding improvement in Eric Young's fielding, the crowded infield situation at Triple-A and a series of injuries limited this converted shortstop's playing time in 1996. The rapid emergence of Neifi Perez further limits Counsell's upside potential as a utility man for the Rocks in 1997.

COX, DARRON - C - BR - Age 29
A six-year minor league free agent signee, Cox got as far as a spring training invitation to the major league camp. He has little offensive potential but owns a good arm and is an above-average defensive catcher.

COX, STEVE - 1B - BL - Age 22
His numbers dropped a little with the promotion to Double-A, but not much. Cox is big and strong, is a choosy swinger, and has big time potential. He should move up and his biggest roadblocks are McGwire and Giambi, not his abilities.

CRADLE, RICKEY - OF - BR - Age 24
Cradle runs fast but gets caught too often when trying to steal. The power numbers could move up more and he can take a walk. He is good enough to be at Triple-A but is behind a number of outfield prospects in the Toronto organization.

CRANFORD, JAY - 3B - BR - Age 25
Once considered a marginal prospect, the Pirates released Cranford in spring training and then re-signed him a few weeks into the minor league season. He didn't show anything to merit getting a third chance, hitting .269 with two homers in 90 games with Double-A Carolina.

CRESPO, FELIPE - 2B - BB - Age 24
Crespo came out of spring training as the Jays' backup second baseman but a late-spring hamstring injury combined with a fast start by Domingo Cedeno saw him lose the job he had won in spring training. Crespo is better at making contact than any young hitter in the organization and has a bit of speed, even though it hasn't shown up in his stolen base numbers. He is very close and could open 1997 as Toronto's everyday second baseman if he shows improved defense this spring.

CROMER, BRANDON - SS - BL - Age 24
Cromer has an excellent batting eye, yet has trouble making contact when he gets his pitch. His future may be at shortstop (where he played the majority of his games last year) but some suggest he's better-suited to be a third baseman. He could use another year at Double-A to work on being more aggressive early in the count.

CROMER, D.T. - DH - BL - Age 25
The California League MVP led all minor leagues with 130 RBI. 1996 was his fourth year in the Athletics' farm system at single A, and he has established himself as a lefthanded power prospect.

CROMER, TRIPP - SS - BR - Age 29
For the better part of three years, Cromer was injury insurance stored at Triple-A Louisville. That insurance policy was needed in 1995 when Ozzie Smith missed a significant chunk of playing time. But, with Royce Clayton on the scene, Cromer wasn't needed in St. Louis. Cromer is not a particularly good hitter or fielder.

CRUZ, DEIVE - SS - BR - Age 20
Cruz set a Midwest League fielding percentage for a shortstop at .980 in 1996. He also has a strong arm, and hit well for a shortstop last year.

CRUZ, FAUSTO - SS - BR - Age 24
A middle infielder who came to Detroit in 1996 from Oakland. The Tigers may keep Travis Fryman at shortstop in 1997 but Cruz will get his shot and might develop into a regular.

CRUZ, IVAN - 1B - BL - Age 28
An outstanding Double-A season in 1995 (31 homers and 93 RBI to place among the leaders in the Southern League) and a good winter as the cleanup hitter for a strong Ponce team in Puerto Rico added some life to Cruz' career. On the Tigers farm he had been passed by Tony Clark. With the Yankee organization he became a deep reserve as a lefty bat off the bench, although he didn't get much time in New York.

CRUZ, JACOB - OF - BL - Age 24
Cruz got his first crack at the majors in 1996 after three consecutive seasons of steady progress up the Giants farm ladder. He has a good eye and the patience to benefit from it, plus fair speed and a little power. He hit .285 at Triple-A Phoenix in 1996.

	AB	R	HR	RBI	SB	BA	$
1996 San Francisco NL	77	10	3	10	0	.234	-

CRUZ, JOSE Jr. - OF - BR - Age 22
One of the most coveted amateur players taken in the 1995 draft, Cruz is the Mariners' best young hitting prospect. He blazed his way from Class A Lancaster (.325-6-43-7) through Double-A Port City (.282-3-31-5) to make a late season appearance at Triple-A Tacoma (.237-6-15-1). He's going to be a good hitter - just like his father. Leftfield in the Kingdome awaits young Mr. Cruz.

CUMMINGS, MIDRE - OF - BL - Age 25
Cummings' days in the Pirates' organization appear to be over after he wasn't recalled in September. He has been blessed with incredible talent, including a quick bat and good speed, but has never been inclined to use his gifts. He actually showed some renewed interest when called up for a one-month stretch in the first half of last season but sulked again after being sent down to Triple-A Calgary. Once upon a time, scouts predicted Cummings as a future winner of batting titles.

	AB	R	HR	RBI	SB	BA	$
1995 Pittsburgh NL	152	13	2	15	1	.243	1
1996 Pittsburgh NL	85	11	3	7	0	.224	-

CURTIS, CHAD - OF - BR - Age 28
Curtis was acquired from the Tigers to help patch up the mess in centerfield for the Dodgers, and he did not perform well in Los Angeles in 1996. Curtis does have some secondary skills, notably decent power, speed and strike zone judgment. He would contribute double-digit homers and steals if he gets an opportunity.

	AB	R	HR	RBI	SB	BA	$
1995 Detroit AL	586	96	21	67	27	.268	26
1996 Detroit AL	400	65	10	37	16	.263	11
1996 Los Angeles NL	104	20	2	9	2	.212	-

CURTIS, KEVIN - OF - BR - Age 24
Oriole farmhand Curtis hit 18 homers in the pitching-tough Double-A Eastern League last year, but his .246 average was disappointing. For 1997, it looks like Triple-A, with a possible call-up to the Orioles as a fifth outfielder.

CUYLER, MILT - OF - BB - Age 28
As expected, Cuyler changed organizations in 1996; but he had the same old results. He just can't hit enough to play regularly or even platoon. He's still a good defensive outfielder with above average speed. A role as a fifth outfielder is Cuyler's most likely situation for 1997.

	AB	R	HR	RBI	SB	BA	$
1995 Detroit AL	88	15	0	5	2	.205	-
1996 Boston AL	110	19	2	12	7	.200	1

DALESANDRO, MARK - 3B/OF - BR - Age 28
A high-average, high-OBP type of batter in the minors, Dalesandro never had much speed and didn't develop any power. Even at the minor league level, his career is on the downside.

DALTON, DEE - 3B - BR - Age 24
Dalton had a forgettable year at Double-A Arkansas in 1996. He doesn't have enough power as a third baseman to overcome his strikeout tendencies and he's not a wizard with the glove, either. Dalton needs to improve in a number of different areas to get noticed.

DAMON, JOHNNY - OF - BL - Age 23
1996 was a disappointing year for Damon watchers. He was expected to take a leadership role for a young club but finished the season looking overmatched and confused. But, keep in mind how young Damon is and that his first full season in the majors wasn't all bad. Damon is at the stage of his career where he will make tremendous strides all at once. When everyone stops trying to make Damon into the next George Brett and just lets him play his own game he'll finally become everything his fans want him to be.

	AB	R	HR	RBI	SB	BA	$
1995 Kansas City AL	188	32	3	23	7	.282	6
1996 Kansas City AL	517	61	6	50	25	.271	16

DANAPILIS, ERIC - OF/DH - BR - Age 25
Danapilis made a bit of a splash coming out of Notre Dame when he batted .341 in the New York-Penn League, then followed it up with 23 homers in the Sally League. When he moved up to Double-A in 1995, he found the going tougher. Danapilis has little speed.

DANDRIDGE, BRAD - OF - BR - Age 25
The prognosis for a player moving from catcher, one of the Dodgers' leanest minor league positions, to outfield, where they boast a stable of baseball's finest youngsters...not a bright future.

DASCENZO, DOUG - OF - BB - Age 32
Dascenzo spent five years with the Cubs and one with the Rangers with a career record of .235-5-90 in 1,216 at-bats, showing that he's a weak hitter. He played for the Padres Triple-A club last year, hoping to get back to the majors as a reserve outfielder.

DAULTON, DARREN - OF - BL - Age 35
1996 likely marked the end of Daulton's courageous and productive career with the Phils. He began it as a sore-kneed, immobile major league leftfielder, and had to shut it down only one game into a rehab assignment in Single-A ball.

DAVALILLO, DAVID - 2B - BR - Age 22
Davalillo had a good year in Single-A last year. Moved up to Double-A, he struggled hitting .171, in only 82 at-bats.

DAVIS, BEN - C - BB - Age 20
In 1995, Baseball America tabbed catcher Davis as their High School Player of the Year. The Padres also ranked him highly, and selected him in the first round and as the number two overall draft pick. He had a good first year in 1995, but elbow injuries slowed his growth last year. Davis has tremendous potential.

DAVIS, CHILI - DH - BB - Age 37
Angels' power hitter Davis quietly had another outstanding season in 1996 showing no signs of slowing down. He stayed healthy and appeared in 145 games, the most since 1993.

	AB	R	HR	RBI	SB	BA	$
1995 California AL	424	81	20	86	3	.318	20
1996 California AL	530	73	28	95	5	.292	18

DAVIS, ERIC - OF - BR - Age 34
Davis had a brilliant (and unlikely) comeback season that was one of the keys for the Reds staying in contention as long as they did. Davis is still fragile and slowing down (his 72 percent stolen base rate was the lowest of his career) but he displayed the multi-faceted offensive skills not seen since his prime from 1986-1990. He was a free agent and despite his great season, his return to the Reds was questionable.

	AB	R	HR	RBI	SB	BA	$
1996 Cincinnati NL	415	81	26	83	23	.287	22

DAVIS, JAMES - C - BR - Age 24
Davis is a defensive specialist. He was selected as the best defensive catcher in the Low-A South Atlantic League by its managers in 1996. He has little extra-base power despite his 6'4", 210, frame.

DAVIS, RUSSELL - 3B - BR - Age 27
For the second straight year, Davis suffered a severe, season ending injury. One of the more intriguing prospects at the beginning of 1996, Davis was finally going to get a chance to play on a regular basis. He batted only .234 in 167 at-bats with five homers, then the leg injury took him out.

	AB	R	HR	RBI	SB	BA	$
1995 New York AL	98	14	2	12	0	.276	-
1996 Seattle AL	167	24	5	18	2	.234	0

DAVIS, TOMMY - 1B/3B - BR - Age 23
Oriole farmhand Davis was a third baseman in his first two years as a pro, but he was moved to first in 1996 because of his poor defense. He has shown some power in the minors, usually hitting in the .260-270 range.

DAWKINS, WALTER - OF - BR - Age 24
The Phils' 1995 15th round draftee was a regular Double-A outfielder by season's end. Dawkins is a poor man's version of late season callup Wendell Magee - an athletic outfielder with slightly above average speed and doubles power. He is willing to take a walk, and can play all three outfield positions. Drafted after his senior season, he needs another year of improvement to be in the hunt for a backup major league role in 1998.

DAWSON, ANDRE - DH/OF - BR - Age 42
Now that Dawson's career has officially ended, all that's left is the handicapping of his Hall of Fame chances. By most standards, Dawson should be elected, although possibly on a second or third ballot.

	AB	R	HR	RBI	SB	BA	$
1995 Florida NL	226	30	8	37	0	.257	5
1996 Florida NL	58	6	2	14	0	.276	1

DEAK, DARREL - 2B - BB - Age 27
Formerly, Deak was considered a big-time secondbase prospect. At Double-A in 1994, Deak showed terrific power, hit for average and made tough plays defensively. He and John Mabry came through the Cardinals' system together and both looked like outstanding prospects. Mabry made it, Deak has not and it doesn't look like he will.

DeBOER, ROB - C - BR - Age 25
A solid (5'10", 205 pounds) guy who can hit. If Steinbach chooses to finish his career at home in Minnesota, DeBoer very well could be the heir apparent. 12 homers over 249 at-bats speaks some, but 74 walks compared to 75 strikeouts over the same period. His improvement in 1996 was very good.

DECKER, STEVE - C - BR - Age 31
Decker caught on with his old team, the Giants, for the start of 1996, but was traded to Colorado and assigned to the Triple-A Sky Sox late in the season. He was called up to the Rocks in September, endeared himself to Baylor by pushing the pace of the pitching staff, and got most of the catching duties in the final month.

	AB	R	HR	RBI	SB	BA	$
1995 Florida NL	133	12	3	13	1	.226	0
1996 Colorado NL	147	24	2	20	1	.245	0

DEER, ROB - OF - BR - Age 36
Deer was released last spring so he signed a Padres Triple-A contract, and he made it back to the big leagues. He's still the same old Rob Deer that we remember from the American League: a low-average power hitter with lots of strikeouts, some home runs and doubles, and very few singles.

	AB	R	HR	RBI	SB	BA	$
1996 San Diego NL	50	9	4	9	0	.180	-

DE LA CRUZ, LORENZO - OF - BR - Age 24
One of the developing sluggers in the Toronto farm system, he is blessed with perhaps the best bat speed behind Chris Weinke and Tom Evans. Of course, he swings at too many pitches.

DELEON, ROBERTO - 2B/3B - BR - Age 26
Former Padre, former shortstop, Deleon has become a utility player in the minors. He split time between Shreveport where he played second base and hit .236 and Phoenix, where he played third and hit .194.

DELGADO, ALEX - C - BR - Age 26
Delgado made three separate trips to the majors to fill a reserve catcher role when injuries struck in Boston. He supplied steady defense, but little else. Delgado is no better or worse than many of the reserve catchers shuttling between teams in any given year.

DELGADO, CARLOS - 1B/OF - BL - Age 24
In Puerto Rico playing winter ball, Delgado mastered the art of adjusting to breaking pitches. The result was a very successful spring training, followed by a breakthrough year in the majors. This slugger has arrived.

	AB	R	HR	RBI	SB	BA	$
1995 Toronto AL	91	7	3	11	0	.165	-
1996 Toronto AL	488	68	25	92	0	.270	11

DELGADO, WILSON - SS - BB - Age 21
Delgado will eventually learn how to hit, but he's not there yet. He got 22 at-bats for the Giants, but will start 1997 in the minors. His .364 average in San Francisco was a fluke.

DELLUCCI, DAVID - OF - BL - Age 23
Orioles minor league outfielder Dellucci was an All-American at the University of Mississippi. Last year, he hit well in the pitching-tough Double-A Eastern League. Dellucci is reported to be a favorite of Syd Thrift, Orioles farm system director, but even if he is a favorite, the competition for an Orioles outfield slot is tough.

DEMETRAL, CHRIS - 2B - BL - Age 27
Demetral is a scrappy, useful minor league performer who doesn't have a singular outstanding tool that would propel him to the majors. He is average in the field, is a sub-50% basestealer for his career, and has little extra-base power.

DENSON, DREW - 1B - BR - Age 31
Denson has spent 12 years in the minors, and six in Triple-A. He's shown some good home run power in Triple-A, where he usually hits .270-280. His DH-only limitation hinders his progress, and he is no longer considered a prospect despite his good Triple-A years.

DESHIELDS, DELINO - 2B - BL - Age 28
In 1993, DeShields was a 25 year old rising star at second base, hitting .295 with excellent speed and strike zone judgment. In 1996, when his career should have been peaking, it has instead bottomed out, with speed as his only remaining skill. DeShields was a free agent and went to Cincinnati as their 1997 starter, so don't write him off just yet.

	AB	R	HR	RBI	SB	BA	$
1995 Los Angeles NL	425	66	8	37	39	.256	21
1996 Los Angeles NL	581	75	5	41	48	.224	7

DEVAREZ, CESAR - C - BR - Age 27
For the most part, catcher Cesar Devarez has struggled at the plate in the minors. If he gets any major league playing time, it will be as a back-up catcher, called up when one of the other catchers is injured.

DEVEREAUX, MIKE - OF - BR - Age 33
Devereaux got over 300 at-bats in 1996 because of injuries to other Oriole outfielders. Although he hit a weak .229, he came through with some clutch hits. Devereaux is now limited to reserve outfielder and pinch-hitting roles.

	AB	R	HR	RBI	SB	BA	$
1995 Atlanta NL	55	7	1	8	2	.255	16
1996 Baltimore AL	323	49	8	34	8	.229	3

DIAZ, ALEX - OF - BB - Age 28
Injured nearly all year in 1996, Diaz is a backup outfielder who may only bat 100-135 times. The diminishing importance of stolen bases in this power laden lineup reduces Diaz role even further.

	AB	R	HR	RBI	SB	BA	$
1995 Seattle AL	270	44	3	27	18	.248	10
1996 Seattle AL	79	11	1	5	6	.241	1

DIAZ, EDWIN - 2B - BR - Age 22
Diaz, a second-round 1993 draft pick, is steadily improving at the plate. If he can cut down on his strikeouts, he has a chance at a major league job by 1998. His glove is a question mark, so a switch to the outfield is a possibility.

DIAZ, EINAR - C - BR - Age 24
Diaz has an amazing record of making contact in over 90% of his at-bats in all of his minor league seasons; he struck out only 22 times and walked 12 times in 407 plate appearances at Double-A last season. He is a consistent line drive gap hitter with solid defensive skills who probably isn't big enough (5'10", 165 pounds) to ever play every day in the majors, but projects as a solid backup beginning in 1997.

DIAZ, LINO - 3B - BR - Age 26
Diaz has hit well enough at every level as he has gradually advanced through the Royals chain. 1996 offered a reversal for Diaz as he started at Triple-A Omaha, hit .271-3-28, and was demoted to Wichita where he posted his lowest batting average since his pro debut. Diaz has never been a highly regarded prospect; the midseason demotion may be a signal that his luck has finally run out.

DIAZ, MARIO - 2B - BR - Age 35
Diaz' main attributes are his abilities to play multiple infield positions and handle the bat well. He also functions as a mentor for young Latin ballplayers.

DiFELICE, MIKE - C - BR - Age 27
DiFelice got his first crack at the majors last September when the Cardinals called him up to serve as the third catcher in their march to the National League Central title. He hit .285 with nine homers in 246 at-bats at Triple-A Louisville and has the reputation of being above average defensively. He should be able to stick around for a few years in the majors as a decent backup catcher.

DIGGS, TONY - OF - BB - Age 29
Diggs has begun to add a little power to his game. He's always had decent speed and the ability to put the ball in play. However, he's now 29 years old - far too late to just be developing as a hitter. Triple-A is the best that Diggs can hope for.

DiSARCINA, GARY - SS - BR - Age 29
The Angels signed DiSarcina to a four-year contract in June 1996, so he's obviously in their long-range plans. He hit .307 in 1995, and appeared to have arrived as a hitter. But 1996 saw him get off to a slow start in April and May, he hit .315 in June and finished strong. DiSarcina is a team leader, and Manager John McNamara appointed him as team co-captain.

	AB	R	HR	RBI	SB	BA	$
1995 California AL	362	61	5	41	7	.307	12
1996 California AL	536	62	5	48	2	.256	3

DiSARCINA, GLENN - SS - BL - Age 26
The wild swinging brother of Gary made a successful return from injury after missing virtually all of the 1996 season, once again proving himself a capable defensive shortstop.

DODSON, BO - 1B - BL - Age 26
After seven years in the Brewers' minor league system, Dodson joined Triple-A Pawtucket where he platooned and battled injuries. Although he turned in a successful year with the bat - hitting .344 with eleven homers - Dodson is not a good prospect for the Red Sox. To have a better chance he'll probably move to another organization in 1997, but Dodson is just Triple-A injury insurance at this point.

DONATO, DAN - 3B - BL - Age 26
A Sally League All-Star in 1995 when he hit .318 with 69 RBI, Donato is a good all-around athlete (a college hockey star) making average progress up the Yankees farm ladder. At Double-A Norwich in 1996 he hit .285-2-48 with five stolen bases.

DONNELS, CHRIS - 3B/1B - BL - Age 30
Donnels is a below average hitter in every respect and is a fringe major leaguer who took his act to Japan in 1996. He was last seen in the states in 1995 with Boston.

DORSETT, BRIAN - C/1B - BR - Age 35
A veteran catcher playing in the minor leagues, getting by on guile, fighting injuries, Dorsett helped the young pitchers at Iowa, but was broken down most of the season. If he's healthy, Dorsett could be a second or third catcher for the Cubs.

DOSTER, DAVID - 2B - BR - Age 26
Doster has excited fans with his aggressive style of play, and his ability to drive the ball well. He is capable of playing only second base, and his bat and foot speed are both a shade slow. Kevin Sefcik's versatility gives him an edge over Doster for the deep utility role likely to be available on the major league club in 1997.

	AB	R	HR	RBI	SB	BA	$
1996 Philadelphia NL	105	14	1	8	0	.267	0

DOWLER, DEMITRIUS - OF - BR - Age 25
"Dee" has good speed and is solid defensively. Dowler won't hit for much of an average, but gets a high percentage of doubles due to his speed. He's the cousin of Green Bay Packer Boyd Dowler.

DRINKWATER, SEAN - 3B - BR - Age 25
Drinkwater's relatively weak hitting was good enough when he was a shortstop, but it's not enough now that he's playing third base. He's not a great glove man and his singles hitting won't help him reach the majors.

DUCEY, ROB - OF - BL - Age 31
Ducey could never earn more than a reserve outfield role in the U.S., so he left for Japan in 1995 where he became a good power hitter for the Nippon Ham Fighters and continued his international act in 1996.

DUNCAN, ANDRES - SS - BB - Age 25
Duncan didn't fare much better with the Giants farm teams in '96 than he did with the Twins teams of '95. Mariano Duncan's younger brother hasn't had even Andres Thomas' success. Duncan the Younger hasn't stuck in two brief Triple-A trials.

DUNCAN, MARIANO - 2B/SS - BR - Age 34
New manager Joe Torre wanted a National League type of infield utility player for the Yankee bench, and thus Duncan came to New York. An injury to Pat Kelly elevated Duncan into a starter's role at second base, and the veteran became an unlikely star. On paper he is still a utility player, but Duncan deserves another long look as a starter (at least a platooner) based on what he did in 1996.

	AB	R	HR	RBI	SB	BA	$
1995 Cincinnati NL	265	36	6	36	1	.287	7
1996 New York AL	400	62	8	56	4	.340	13

DUNN, STEVE - 1B - BL - Age 26
Dunn has all of 41 major league at-bats to show for his nine year pro career, and that won't change any time soon. He has shown a penchant for swinging wildly in the minors that would doom him in the majors. Being marooned in the Indians' system in 1996 didn't help either.

DUNN, TODD - OF - BR - Age 26
The third of Milwaukee's four first-round draft picks in '93, and the most successful to date. Drafted out of the University of North Florida, where he had transferred after first attending Georgia Tech on a football scholarship. Played center field at Helena.

DUNSTON, SHAWON - SS - BR - Age 34
Dunston actually improved his on base percentage by a significant margin. His career mark of .296 was topped by a '96 seasonal mark of .331. He still refuses to walk and scores way too few runs for a .300 hitter out of the number two slot. The Giants wanted to keep him and make him a center fielder in 1997.

	AB	R	HR	RBI	SB	BA	$
1995 Chicago NL	477	58	14	69	10	.296	19
1996 San Francisco NL	287	27	5	25	8	.300	10

DUNWOODY, TODD - OF - BL - Age 22
The Marlins boldly advanced their 1993 seventh round draftee from Low-A to Double-A Portland in 1996, and he responded with an All-Star performance. He is a power/speed prospect, compiling 14 homers and 39 steals in 1995, and 24 homers and 24 steals in 1996. He is also an above-average defender in center field with a plus arm. He still strikes out too much (149 whiffs in 1996), often on bad pitches.

DURANT, MIKE - C/DH - BR - Age 27
Durant is not a particularly good defensive catcher. He can hit, and can run a bit.

	AB	R	HR	RBI	SB	BA	$
1996 Minnesota AL	81	15	0	5	3	.210	-

DURHAM, RAY - 2B - BB - Age 25
Durham continues to impress offensively for the Sox. The speedy second baseman has a solid hold on his position. Look for continued improvement as he continues to settle in at the major league level.

	AB	R	HR	RBI	SB	BA	$
1995 Chicago AL	471	68	7	51	18	.257	15
1996 Chicago AL	557	79	10	65	30	.275	21

DYE, JERMAINE - OF - BR - Age 23
When David Justice was lost for the season, Dye stepped forward. Dye isn't the hitter Justice is - not yet, at least. Dye will have to reign in his aggressiveness at the plate and learn to take a pitch; Dye does have Justice's rightfield arm and, if Justice isn't re-signed, he may have his job in 1997.

	AB	R	HR	RBI	SB	BA	$
1996 Atlanta NL	292	32	12	37	1	.281	8

DYKSTRA, LENNY - OF - BL - Age 34
Dykstra was a force in 1996 - for about two weeks, before a recurrence of the chronic back problems (spinal stenosis, to be exact) sent him to the sidelines for the season, and quite possibly forever.

	AB	R	HR	RBI	SB	BA	$
1995 Philadelphia NL	254	37	2	18	10	.264	6
1996 Philadelphia NL	134	21	3	13	3	.261	2

EASLEY, DAMION - 3B/2B - BR - Age 27
Easley came to Detroit from the Angels in '96 and had a brief shot at shortstop before getting hurt. Easley can swipe a few bases and he will compete with Fausto Cruz for the job if Fryman plays third.

	AB	R	HR	RBI	SB	BA	$
1995 California AL	357	35	4	35	5	.216	2
1996 Detroit AL	112	14	4	17	3	.268	1

ECHEVARRIA, ANGEL - OF - BR - Age 25
Echevarria had another productive year at hitter-friendly Triple-A Colorado Springs, and got a couple of cups of coffee with the Rockies over the course of the season. The outfield is where the Rockies have the most depth, however, so absent the departure of Burks or Bichette, or a sophomore slump by the promising Quinton McCracken, most of Echevarria's playing time is likely to be at the Triple-A level.

EDGE, TIM - C - BR - Age 28
He is the ultimate organizational player, a good defensive catcher with outstanding intelligence. He is willing to go wherever the Pirates tell him and he'll probably get to the big leagues some day - as a coach or manager.

EDMONDS, JIM - OF - BL - Age 26
Edmonds broke out with a tremendous year in 1995. In 1996, a sprained thumb sent him to the disabled list, and for the season, he had 127 fewer at-bats than in 1995. He really didn't take advantage of the rabbit ball, homering around six percent of his at-bats, about the same as in 1995. Edmonds is 26 years old with three full years of major league experience, a profile that frequently means that a monstrous career year is ahead.

	AB	R	HR	RBI	SB	BA	$
1995 California AL	558	120	33	107	1	.290	23
1996 California AL	431	73	27	66	4	.304	16

EENHOORN, ROBERT - SS - BR - Age 29
A great athlete from the Netherlands, Eenhoorn could have been a European soccer pro but chose the international route and pursued baseball. His skills fell a bit short of major league material, however. Eenhoorn finally hit over .300 as a part-timer at Triple-A, but he was on waivers from the Yankees in September 1996 when he got picked up by the Angels.

EISENREICH, JIM - OF - BL - Age 37
All this guy has done is bat .318, .300, .316 and most recently, a lusty .361, in his four stellar seasons with the Phils. He rips the ball to the gaps, is an above-average defensive outfielder, and has been successful in an amazing 32 for 35 (91%) basestealing attempts as a Phillie.

	AB	R	HR	RBI	SB	BA	$
1995 Philadelphia NL	377	46	10	55	10	.316	17
1996 Philadelphia NL	338	45	3	41	11	.361	23

ELLIS, PAUL - C - BL - Age 28
Ellis has a reputation as an adept handler of pitchers, which is his main reason for being in uniform. He's a weak contact hitter with little power and no speed. Ellis is at Double-A for one reason only; to help develop young Cards' pitchers. Perhaps he'll reach the majors as a coach.

ELSTER, KEVIN - SS - BR - Age 32
Elster's has to be the most improbable comeback story in recent memory. Prior to 1996, he had 108 major league at-bats in four years, and a .220 lifetime batting average with one homer every 48 at-bats. The rest, of course, is history. Most of his hits and RBI were accumulated in the first half of the season; pitchers eventually figured out how to handle him. Regardless, though, Elster has emerged from rehab a much more powerful hitter than before, and he should have a major league job sewn up for the foreseeable future.

	AB	R	HR	RBI	SB	BA	$
1995 New York AL	17	1	0	0	0	.118	
1995 Philadelphia NL	53	10	1	9	0	.208	-
1996 Texas AL	515	79	24	99	4	.252	11

ENCARNACION, ANGELO - C - BR - Age 23
Encarnacion's defense has never been questioned as he has a strong arm and outstanding mobility behind the plate. He answered the questions about his bat with a good season at Calgary (.319 in 75 games), starting in the Triple-A All-Star Game. Encarnacion now appears capable of being a starting catcher in the major leagues. The problem is the Pirates had two rookie catchers turn in solid years in 1996, Jason Kendall and Keith Osik. Encarnacion can be valuable as trade bait.

ERSTAD, DARIN - OF - BL - Age 22
To people who have seen Erstad play, his rapid rise to the majors is not surprising. He was the Angels top draft pick in 1995, out of the University of Nebraska. There was no adjustment period for him, as he came out hitting like a veteran. He was called up to the Angels in June and impressed everybody with his hitting, speed, and outstanding defense. Erstad has a bright future, and the Angels may trade an outfielder to make a starting spot for him.

	AB	R	HR	RBI	SB	BA	$
1996 California AL	208	34	4	20	3	.284	3

ESPINOSA, RAMON - OF - BR - Age 25
Any future this outfielder had with the Pirates was tied to his speed. However, he lost that after undergoing knee surgery in 1995 and is now nothing more than a Triple-A singles-hitting reserve outfielder.

ESPINOZA, ALVARO - 3B/SS - BR - Age 35
Although he is really a weak hitter, Espinoza had some fun in the National League in 1996, as over-optimistic pitchers threw him too many fastballs out over the plate, when the right approach is hard stuff inside and offspeed pitches away. Espinoza looked like a bench player going into 1997.

	AB	R	HR	RBI	SB	BA	$
1995 Cleveland AL	143	15	2	17	0	.252	0
1996 Cleveland AL	112	12	4	11	1	.223	-
1996 New York NL	134	19	4	16	0	.306	4

ESTALELLA, BOBBY - C - BR - Age 22
Estalella established himself as a power threat and a durable defensive receiver with a fine Double-A season in 1996. He still has major improvements to make. He needs to stop trying to hit every ball 500 feet, and begin slapping breaking pitches the other way for singles. He also needs to take more control when handling a pitching staff. Estalella will contend for a share of the big league job in 1998, and eventually be a 25+ homer threat.

ESTRADA, OSMANI - 3B - BR - Age 28
Estrada is a Cuban defector whose versatility will probably land him a utility infield role in the majors.

EUSEBIO, TONY - C - BR - Age 29
Eusebio had a disappointing season in 1996 when he was hampered by injuries. He should have a more productive year in 1997 if he is injury free. He is just average defensively and will probably not have an opportunity to be a full time starter.

	AB	R	HR	RBI	SB	BA	$
1995 Houston NL	368	46	6	58	0	.299	10
1996 Houston NL	152	15	1	19	0	.270	2

EVANS, TOM - 3B - BR - Age 22
Evans has become better at taking a walk than almost any hitter in the minor leagues. He has developed more pure power than any hitter in the Toronto organization not named Chris Weinke. Despite past knee problems, he has great range and a strong throwing arm. If he starts making consistent contact, he'll become a thirty homer threat.

EVERETT, CARL - OF - BB - Age 25
Everett went to spring training a year ago penciled in as the Mets everyday right fielder. But then he spent the month of March flailing at offspeed junk and looking helpless, while Butch Huskey spent March setting the Mets' all-time record for home runs in the Grapefruit League. By opening day Everett had become a backup, and he stayed in that role until Alex Ochoa came up and seized the right field starter's job. Everett remains young and talented, and new manager Bobby Valentine did take another long look at Everett in September.

	AB	R	HR	RBI	SB	BA	$
1995 New York NL	289	48	12	54	2	.260	9
1996 New York NL	192	29	1	16	6	.240	1

FABREGAS, JORGE - C - BL - Age 27
Fabregas got much more playing time under Managers John McMamara and Joe Maddon than he did under Marcel Lachemann, and he responded with his career-best year. But he may be destined for a backup role if slugging prospect Todd Greene develops as the Angels expect. It helps that Fabregas bats lefthanded because he could get additional at-bats in a platoon role or as a pinch hitter.

	AB	R	HR	RBI	SB	BA	$
1995 California AL	227	24	1	22	0	.247	0
1996 California AL	254	18	2	26	0	.287	2

FANEYTE, RIKKERT - OF - BR - Age 27
Apart from a brief stint with the Rangers, Faneyte once again toiled at Triple-A in 1996. He would be a serviceable backup outfielder, but doesn't quite have the speed or bat to play a significant role for a major league team.

FARIES, PAUL - 2B - BR - Age 32
This ten-year pro who toiled in the Indians' chain last season once had 65 steals in a season; speed was his chief weapon then, and it has largely abandoned him. His ability to play multiple positions and handle the bat well will enable him to linger a while longer as a Triple-A insurance policy, his role for the last seven seasons.

FARRELL, JON - OF - BR - Age 25
The Pirates chose Farrell as a catcher in the first round of the 1991 draft and he was a bust. He never hit much and he was moved from behind to the plate to the outfield before the end of his first professional season. The Pirates finally gave up on Farrell last year and sent him to the New York Mets in a minor league deal at midseason. Mets farm director Jack Zduriencik was the Pirates' scouting director when Pittsburgh made Farrell its top pick.

FASANO, SAL - C - BR - Age 25
The Royals began to bury Fasano in 1996. He started slowly, gradually gained momentum and started hitting homers. Then Fasano got on Manager Bob Boone's bad side and they benched, then demoted him to Triple-A Omaha, saying they wanted to send him a message. It went undelivered as Fasano struggled at Omaha, too. Fasano has about as much chance of earning a regular job in Kansas City as ... Bob Hamelin.

	AB	R	HR	RBI	SB	BA	$
1996 Kansas City AL	143	20	6	19	1	.203	-

FEBLES, CARLOS - 2B - BR - Age 20
Yet another slick-fielding second sacker in the Royals chain, Febles can hit some, too. He has above-average speed (his 30 steals were second best for Class A Lansing) and he walks as often as he strikes out. The Royals are grooming him as a top-of-the-order hitter. This Dominican is just 20 years old and has time to develop further.

FELDER, MIKE - OF - BB - Age 34
Felder spent most of the season playing in an independent league before the Pirates came up short on outfielders at Triple-A Calgary in August.

FERGUSON, JEFF - 2B - BR - Age 23
Ferguson lost all of 1995 to injury, so his 1996 campaign at Double-A New Britain was his first full season as a pro. He can hit for average, but doesn't have much power or speed. He's still unproven as a prospect.

FERMIN, FELIX - SS - BR - Age 33
Fermin was the Mariners' regular shortstop before Alex Rodriguez. He was released by Seattle and caught on with the Cubs. He didn't show much at the plate in Iowa but managed to hit a respectable .286 in 33 games with the I-Cubs. He will swing at anything close, and usually make contact, but he'll never be a regular big leaguer again because of his age.

FERNANDEZ, ANTONIO - 3B - BR - Age 23
Padres prospect Antonio Fernandez was hitting .371 in Single-A in July, but he slumped badly the rest of the season finishing at .308. He showed a little power with nine homers last year, but he could grow into a power hitter as he matures. He was slated for the Arizona Fall League.

FERNANDEZ, TONY - SS - BB - Age 34
The arrival of Derek Jeter as the Yankee shortstop for the next six years was enough to push Fernandez into obscurity in 1996. Even if he had been healthy, which he wasn't, Fernandez would have been just a caddy for Jeter. For 1997 Fernandez has no clear role.

	AB	R	HR	RBI	SB	BA	$
1995 New York AL	384	57	5	45	6	.245	6

FICK, CHRIS - OF - BL - Age 27
Fick has a ton of power potential, but has been inconsistent at Double-A Arkansas. He showed a lot of power, with 25 doubles and 19 home runs. A classic big swinger, Fick struck out 93 times at Arkansas.

FIELDER, CECIL - 1B/DH - BR - Age 33
The Yankees wanted a big righty bat to counter the southpaws being thrown at them during the pennant stretch of 1996, and Fielder fit the bill. He is a tad heavy for a professional athlete, but he still has quick wrists that can surprise any overoptimistic pitcher who thinks Fielder can no longer pull an outside fastball.

	AB	R	HR	RBI	SB	BA	$
1995 Detroit AL	494	70	31	82	0	.243	13
1996 Detroit-New York AL	591	85	39	117	2	.252	15

FIGUEROA, BIEN - 2B/SS - BR - Age 33
Figueroa is a veteran of 11 years in the minor leagues mostly with the Cardinals and Rangers. He played in Triple-A with the Orioles organization last year.

FINLEY, STEVE - OF - BL - Age 32
Finley resurrected his career in San Diego in 1995, and continued playing outstanding ball in 1996. He hit 45 doubles, tying for second in the league, and his 126 runs scored ranked second in the National League, and set a new Padres team record. He batted third in the order, indicating the high respect that the Padres have for his hitting. Finley's defense won him another Gold Glove in 1996, making him even more valuable.

	AB	R	HR	RBI	SB	BA	$
1995 San Diego NL	562	104	10	44	36	.297	27
1996 San Diego NL	655	126	30	95	22	.298	31

FINN, JOHN - 2B - BR - Age 29
Finn is a journeyman minor league utility man. Iowa picked him up late in the season when they needed bodies.

FISHER, DAVID - 2B - BR - Age 27
The Phils' 1992 29th round draft pick spent his second consecutive season as a deep infield reserve at Double-A Reading. He's fundamentally sound but has no particular skill that would allow him to succeed at the next level.

FLAHERTY, JOHN - C - BR - Age 29
Traded to the Padres in midseason, catcher Flaherty took an immediate liking to National League pitching and promptly went on a hitting tear with a 27-game hitting streak, good for second longest in the National League last year. "The difference in leagues is that people throw more strikes here," he said. Flaherty was a streaky hitter with the Tigers, and National League pitchers will likely find his weaknesses in 1997.

	AB	R	HR	RBI	SB	BA	$
1995 Detroit AL	354	39	11	40	0	.243	4
1996 Detroit AL	152	18	4	23	1	.250	0
1996 San Diego NL	264	22	9	41	2	.303	10

FLETCHER, DARRIN - C - BL - Age 30
Fletcher has quietly become one of the more consistent offensive catchers in the National League. However, his defense has always been suspect and the Expos were not expected to exercise the option year on his contract. He'll land somewhere and hit his usual .270 with 10 homers and a fair number of RBIs.

	AB	R	HR	RBI	SB	BA	$
1995 Montreal NL	350	42	11	45	0	.286	9
1996 Montreal NL	394	41	12	57	0	.266	7

FLORA, KEVIN - OF - BR - Age 27
Once an exciting, speedy middle infielder in the Angels' system, Flora suffered through leg miseries and personal grief over a family loss, bouncing around and getting a callup with the Phillies in 1995. His speed was again visible in 1996 playing at Triple-A for the Mets (nine steals in 135 at-bats) but he hit just .222 and is now a faded prospect.

FLORES, JOSE - 2B/SS - BR - Age 23
Flores is a no-hit, decent-field middle infielder who got an unexpected promotion to Triple-A when the Phils recalled several players from their Triple-A club in late summer. He catches the ball, makes consistent - albeit weak - contact, and steals the occasional base.

FLOREZ, TIM - 2B - BR - Age 27
Florez hit well at both Shreveport and Phoenix, but there are a number of players ahead of him and he's getting on in years.

FLOYD, CLIFF - 1B - BL - Age 24
Floyd has yet to justify all the hype that surrounded his arrival in the major leagues back in 1994. Granted, he had the shattered wrist in 1995 but Floyd just hasn't done a whole lot for the Expos. Yet he did improve late in the summer.

	AB	R	HR	RBI	SB	BA	$
1995 Montreal NL	69	6	1	8	3	.130	-
1996 Montreal NL	227	29	6	26	7	.242	2

FONVILLE, CHAD - SS - BB - Age 26
A Tommy LaSorda favorite, Fonville failed to make much offensive contribution to the Dodgers in 1996. Fonville is versatile (playing five positions) and has some speed, but his .234 (not a typo) slugging average and .266 on base average in 201 at-bats make him an offensive liability.

	AB	R	HR	RBI	SB	BA	$
1995 Two Teams	320	43	0	16	20	.278	11
1996 Los Angeles NL	201	34	0	13	7	.204	-

FORBES, P. J. - 2B - BR - Age 29
Forbes spent the past two years in Triple-A where he hit .274 in both years. He doesn't have any power, and is not regarded as a prospect. Forbes looks like a career minor leaguer.

FORDYCE, BROOK - C - BR - Age 26
A good defensive catcher, Fordyce posted a decent offensive year at Triple-A Indianapolis, setting career highs in homers and RBI. He is not likely to grab a significant role at the major league level, but could catch on as a third catcher.

FORKNER, TIM - 3B - BL - Age 24
Forkner has made modest progress in his four year minor league career. He hit .293 in his first full season at Double-A in 1996. With only 17 career homers, he does not have the power desired in a third baseman.

FOX, ANDY - 3B - BL - Age 26
This Arizona Fall League alumnus broke through to the utility role the Yankees wanted him to grow into. Then with the injury to Pat Kelly in 1996, Fox was a platooner at second base for much of the season, sharing with Mariano Duncan. For 1997 Fox can expect to be a useful off-the-bench multi-position infield backup.

	AB	R	HR	RBI	SB	BA	$
1996 New York AL	189	26	3	13	11	.196	2

FOX, ERIC - OF - BB - Age 33
The embodiment of Triple-A bat speed - Fox has ripped the ball to all fields everywhere he has played in the minors, but has been overmatched in four major league trials, with a composite batting average of .198.

FRANCISCO, DAVID - OF - BR - Age 25
He has a great glove, stole 30 bases at Double-A in 1995, but has no power and way too many strikeouts. He's two years away at the least and unlikely to be anything more than a fifth outfielder at the major league level.

FRANCO, JULIO - DH - BR - Age 35
Franco returned from Japan with a flourish in 1996, showing the consistent line drive bat for which he has always been known. However, trouble signs abound. Franco missed an abundance of time with an assortment of nagging injuries last season, and was the oldest regular first baseman in the American League.

	AB	R	HR	RBI	SB	BA	$
1996 Cleveland AL	432	72	14	76	8	.322	17

FRANCO, MATT - 1B - BL - Age 27
A line drive singles/doubles hitter who had no hope of displacing Mark Grace from first base for the Chicago Cubs, Franco moved on to another organization, the Mets, and tried to learn another position. He has appeared at second base, catcher, and even as a pitcher, but now he's working on third. The results have been only fair.

FRANKLIN, MICAH - OF - BB - Age 24
Once an up-and-comer with the Pirates, Franklin's rise has stalled as much due to a perceived attitude problem as with his sometimes spotty play. He is now with his third organization in as many years and displayed good power at Triple-A Louisville in 1996 (36 extra-base hits in just 289 at-bats). Franklin continues to whiff at a high rate - about a quarter of his at-bats - and is never going to challenge for a batting title. Franklin still has time to make it in the majors, although he'll probably have to lower his sights and settle for a role as a fourth outfielder.

FRAZIER, LOU - OF - BB - Age 32
Frazier is a one-dimensional player whose speed alone isn't enough to keep him in the majors on a consistent basis. And he's not getting any younger.

	AB	R	HR	RBI	SB	BA	$
1995 Montreal NL	63	6	0	3	4	.190	-
1995 Texas AL	99	19	0	8	9	.212	4
1996 Texas AL	50	5	0	5	4	.260	-

FREEMAN, SEAN - 1B - BL - Age 25
Freeman has already surpassed expectations for someone drafted in the 43rd round ('94) by hitting 25 homers at Double-A in '96. He will develop into a good Triple-A player who might have a few callups to the majors.

FRENCH, ANTON - OF - BB - Age 20
French is a young outfield prospect who was traded from Atlanta to Detroit in '96. He can steal a lot of bases (47 in '96) but needs three more years in the minors to develop some offensive punch.

FRIAS, HANLEY - SS - BB - Age 23
In the last two years, Frias has played his way into prospect status -- middle infielders who can hit can generally find work. Frias has advanced rapidly and should get a full season at Triple-A in 1997.

FRIEDMAN, JASON - 1B - BL - Age 27
With his third organization, Friedman has the look of a career minor leaguer. Hitting under .200 at two high-minors stops in 1996 isn't going to help him as he looks for a job with yet another club in 1997.

FRYE, JEFF - 2B - BR - Age 30
Frye escaped being "Triple-A insurance" for the Rangers with a midseason trade to the Red Sox. A passable defensive player, Frye gave the Red Sox what they had hoped to get from Wil Cordero; a hitter who could get on base (.372 OBP) and he had enough speed to hit near the top of the order. The addition of Frye to the regular lineup was one of the things that helped turn Boston's season around. Because he's not a sharp fielder, Frye will have to battle for a regular job in 1997, although he appears to have the inside track.

	AB	R	HR	RBI	SB	BA	$
1995 Texas AL	313	38	4	29	3	.278	6
1996 Boston AL	419	74	4	41	18	.286	13

FRYMAN, TRAVIS - 3B - BR - Age 28
The steady and methodical Fryman churned out another good year in '96, causing speculation that a breakout season could be in store. He drove in a hundred runs for the first time in his career in '96. Buddy Bell moved Fryman back to shortstop for the last six weeks of the season. Fryman will hit wherever he is but clearly is more of a third baseman than a shortstop.

	AB	R	HR	RBI	SB	BA	$
1995 Detroit AL	567	79	15	81	4	.275	15
1996 Detroit AL	616	90	22	100	4	.268	13

FRYMAN, TROY - 1B - BL - Age 26
Travis' younger brother bounced from Birmingham (White Sox) to Orlando (Cubs) to Greenville (Braves) before announcing his retirement in August. He never could hit above Class A.

FULLMER, BRAD - OF - BL - Age 21
The Expos' 1993 second round pick has shown a consistent line drive bat with doubles power in his short pro career, but has not generated the expected power. However, he did respond with career-best production after being summoned to Double-A Harrisburg for the stretch run in 1996, where he helped Vladimir Guerrero carry the club to the Eastern League championship. You don't hear the comparisons to George Brett as much anymore, but Fullmer still has a batting title caliber swing with 20 homer potential, and rarely strikes out. He's less valuable in left field than at third base, but still looks like a major league starter, circa 1998.

GAETTI, GARY - 3B/1B - BR - Age 38
It looked like the Cardinals were taking a gamble when they signed the 37-year-old third baseman as a free agent prior to the 1996 season. However, he had a fine year and was a big reason why the Cardinals won the division. Gaetti is playing better now than he did five years ago.

	AB	R	HR	RBI	SB	BA	$
1995 Kansas City AL	514	76	35	96	3	.261	19
1996 St. Louis NL	522	71	23	80	2	.274	14

GAGNE, GREG - SS - BR - Age 35
1996 was a pretty typical year for Gagne, who has hit between .255 and .259 the last three years, and totaled between six and 10 home runs the last eight years. He has reached the age when any season might be his last. His slightly above average offense for a middle infielder and okay defense is still valuable to the Dodgers, who had only one potential replacement (Wilton Guerrero) for two potential free agent middle infielders (Gagne and Delino DeShields).

	AB	R	HR	RBI	SB	BA	$
1995 Kansas City AL	430	58	6	49	3	.256	6
1996 Los Angeles NL	428	48	10	55	4	.255	6

GAINER, JAY - 1B - BL - Age 30
Gainer had the distinction of hitting a homer in his first major league at bat in 1993, but that was almost four years ago. He has remained at the Triple-A level because of a perceived weakness in hitting breaking balls. Since Gainer was unlikely to challenge either Andres Galarraga or phenom Todd Helton (who leap-frogged Gainer in only two seasons), the Rockies released him at the end of the 1996 campaign.

GALARRAGA, ANDRES - 1B - BR - Age 35
The Big Cat continued to hit for power in the clutch for the Rockies . He's now both the single-season Venezuelan and Latino home run leader - but he also got back over .300 for the first time since 1994. Cat's one-in-four strikeout ratio is high, but is not appreciably different from his career average. Expect more Coors Field fireworks from Galarraga in 1997.

	AB	R	HR	RBI	SB	BA	$
1995 Colorado NL	554	89	31	106	12	.280	27
1996 Colorado NL	626	119	47	150	18	.304	38

GALLEGO, MIKE - SS/2B/3B - BR - Age 36
Leg injuries kept Gallego out for the first half of last season and he didn't do much for the Cardinals once he got healthy. Once one of the game's top utility players, Gallego is really starting to slow down.

	AB	R	HR	RBI	SB	BA	$
1995 Oakland AL	120	11	0	8	0	.233	-
1996 St. Louis NL	143	12	0	4	0	.210	-

GANT, RON - OF - BR - Age 32
Hamstring problems sidelined Gant for five weeks or his numbers would have been better. Gant proved during his one-year stint in Cincinnati in 1995 that he has come all the way back from his broken leg and he's got more big seasons ahead of him.

	AB	R	HR	RBI	SB	BA	$
1995 Cincinnati NL	410	79	39	88	23	.276	28
1996 St. Louis NL	419	74	30	82	13	.246	12

GARCIA, CARLOS - 2B - BR - Age 29
Garcia's window of opportunity for developing into a star player was re-opened by his move to Toronto. He was primed for a big year in 1996 but missed a large chunk of time with hamstring problems. He has played second base for the Pirates because of the presence of shortstop Jay Bell, then shifted to third base in September after Charlie Hayes was traded. Garcia has a lot of skills but needs to stay healthy.

	AB	R	HR	RBI	SB	BA	$
1995 Pittsburgh NL	367	41	6	50	8	.294	12
1996 Pittsburgh NL	390	66	6	44	16	.285	13

GARCIA, GUILLERMO - C - BR - Age 25
Garcia was a pleasant surprise to Reds' brass in 1996, going from a .237 High-A hitter the previous season to a .315 Double-A mark with solid extra-base power.

GARCIA, KARIM - OF - BL - Age 21
This prospect suffered two setbacks in 1996. He did not play particularly well at Albuquerque, sulked, and was sent to San Antonio for an attitude adjustment. More importantly, the development of Todd Hollandsworth means the Dodgers can be patient with their still young prospect. Garcia is still a good prospect in Raul Mondesi mold (power, strong arm, and poor strike zone judgment) but his arrival in the majors could easily be delayed to 1998.

GARCIA, LUIS - SS - BR - Age 21
One of many Dominican shortstops in the pros, Garcia handles the glove pretty well, but lacks enough bat to reach the majors for a lengthy career. He has shown a little power and speed in the low minors, although it isn't likely to be sustained through the high minors.

GARCIA, OMAR - 1B - BR - Age 25
A smallish first baseman, Garcia hits for a decent average and wields a good glove. However, his lack of power limits his upside potential. Garcia is injury insurance.

GARCIA, VINCENTE - 2B - BR - Age 22
An early season shoulder injury slowed Garcia's start in 1996 at Double-A New Haven. He has never hit above .243 in his three years with the Rockies organization, but occasionally exhibits some extra-base pop in his bat. His primary value is on the defensive side.

GARCIAPARRA, NOMAR - SS - BR - Age 23
After beginning the year on the DL with a knee injury at Double-A Trenton, Garciaparra quickly jumped to Triple-A Pawtucket, then to the big club in September. Garciaparra will be a good young hitter in the majors soon; but the Red Sox will first have to make some choices about what to do with their existing major league infielders. The most likely scenario is a shift of John Valentin to third base.

	AB	R	HR	RBI	SB	BA	$
1996 Boston AL	87	11	4	16	5	.241	2

GARRISON, WEBSTER - 1B - BR - Age 31
Had Garrison not elected to play replacement ball, at least one writer believes he would have had an excellent chance to stick as a utility man on the Rockies' major league roster in 1995. As it was, he wasn't even called up in September 1995 after a solid Triple-A season. The career minor leaguer's opportunities are dwindling.

GATES, BRENT - 2B - BB - Age 27
After finally knowing he was going to get his chance to get 500 at-bats, and enduring his usual slow start, Gates was just getting his game together when he broke his leg, lost the rest of his season and lost his position to Tony Batista. A new start with a new team would do him a world of good.

	AB	R	HR	RBI	SB	BA	$
1995 Oakland AL	524	60	5	56	3	.254	7
1996 Oakland AL	247	26	2	30	1	.263	1

GEISLER, PHIL - OF/1B - BL - Age 27
Geisler's career peaked in March 1994 when he had a hot month of spring training with the Phillies major leaguers. For the Mets at Double-A in 1996, he hit .251 with 11 homers and 59 RBI.

GIAMBI, JASON - 3B - BL - Age 26
No one doubted that Giambi could hit, but no one dreamed he would hit as well, with the added bonus of power, so soon after reaching the majors. Giambi suffered some endurance difficulties over the long season, and had to adjust to playing the outfield. He has a beautiful swing, and is one of those guys who gets hot and hits everything hard and where they ain't.

	AB	R	HR	RBI	SB	BA	$
1995 Oakland AL	176	27	6	25	2	.256	3
1996 Oakland AL	536	84	20	79	0	.291	12

GIANNELLI, RAY - 1B - BL - Age 31
Gianelli has proven he can hit minor league pitching, but appears to have Triple-A bat speed. Hitting double-digits in homers and nearly .300 over the last five years in the upper minors has earned Gianelli two trips to the big leagues, where he has gotten 35 at-bats. He's an extra bat stored at Triple-A and will probably be looking for his fourth organization in as many years in 1997.

GIBRALTER, DAVID - OF - BR - Age 21
A big (6'3", 215 pound) power prospect, Gibralter continued to amass extra base hits in 1996 - and strikeouts. His batting average rose to a career best .285 as he had a solid season in the "High" Class A Florida State League, a tough hitters league. Gibralter is a good long-range prospect.

GIBRALTER, STEVE - OF - BR - Age 24
Gibralter regressed in 1996. At his best, Gibralter is a broad based talent with above-average power, speed, average, and defense. His only weakness is strike zone judgment (114 K's and 26 walks in 126 games last year at Triple-A) and he is unlikely to make the jump to the majors until he improves in that crucial area. He is young enough to come back and make an impact on the major league level.

GIBSON, DERRICK - OF - BR - Age 22
Gibson has power, speed (32 homers and 31 steals in 1995 at Low A Asheville), and tremendous baseball instincts, and is justifiably the Rockies number one long-term outfield prospect. In 1996 at Double-A New Haven, he also demonstrated that he has a long way to go to become a mature and complete ballplayer. He led the Ravens in RBI and was second in hits and home runs, but also struck out better than one in four times at bat. If Gibson succeeds in improving his discipline at the plate and in the field in 1997, he may advance to Triple-A Colorado Springs by season's end.

GIL, BENJI - SS - BR - Age 24
A back injury sidelined Gil in spring training, and Kevin Elster's improbable comeback kept Gil in the minors until mid-September. Gil didn't exactly give the Rangers much of a reason to recall him, hitting in the low .200's and striking out once in every three trips. Gil has a better chance of improving at the major league level than with another year at Triple-A, and still has a bright future, with a breakout season by 1998 a distinct possibility.

	AB	R	HR	RBI	SB	BA	$
1995 Texas AL	415	36	9	46	2	.219	3

GILBERT, SHAWN - 2B/SS - BR - Age 32
A stereotypical career minor leaguer, Gilbert has a .254 lifetime average in various farm systems. For the Mets at Triple-A in 1996, he hit .256 with nine home runs and 17 stolen bases.

GILES, BRIAN - OF - BL - Age 26
Giles was an offensive force after being summoned by the Indians from the minors midway through the 1996 season. He swings at strikes, takes balls, and hits the ball where it's pitched with above average power. He is versatile, if unspectacular defensively, and parlays his average speed into a weapon with his above-average baserunning instincts. Obviously, there is no room at the inn in the Indians' outfield (if Belle stays).

	AB	R	HR	RBI	SB	BA	$
1996 Cleveland AL	121	26	5	27	3	.355	5

GILKEY, BERNARD - OF - BR - Age 30
Gilkey lifted his game to a higher level when he was installed as the Mets' number three hitter in 1996. He made a run at franchise records for extra base hits, RBI and runs scored. Not tiring as the season wore on, he hit .358 over a three-week stretch into mid-September.

	AB	R	HR	RBI	SB	BA	$
1995 St. Louis NL	480	73	17	69	12	.298	21
1996 New York NL	571	108	30	117	17	.317	35

GIOVANOLA, ED - SS - BL - Age 28
Following up his career year in 1995 with a more average performance in 1996, Giovanola is a relatively weak hitter who succeeds by slapping the ball through the infield. He's not a flashy gloveman, either, so Giovanola doesn't figure

to pressure Jeff Blauser for playing time in Atlanta; a utility role is the best Giovanola can hope for.

	AB	R	HR	RBI	SB	BA	$
1996 Atlanta NL	82	10	0	7	1	.232	-

GIPSON, CHARLES - OF - BR - Age 24
Double-A centerfielder Gipson is a slap-hitting speedster. He wields a good glove and stole 26 bases for Port City in 1996. He'll get a chance to move up in 1997 and appears to have a future as a fourth outfield in the majors.

GIRARDI, JOE - C - BR - Age 32
Fans surprised by the dismissal of Mike Stanley and the arrival of Girardi were initially skeptical. Manager Joe Torre knew what he was doing, however. Girardi has defensive skills that don't get into box scores. He is a fine pitcher-handler and game-caller. The hitting was a pleasant surprise. For 1997 he appears set as the starter.

	AB	R	HR	RBI	SB	BA	$
1995 Colorado NL	462	63	8	55	3	.262	9
1996 New York AL	422	55	2	45	13	.294	11

GIUDICE, JOHN - OF - BR - Age 25
After an impressive start at Class A Salem in 1996 (where he tied for the team lead in homers and RBI), Giudice finished the year at Double-A New Haven. For the first time in his pro career, he's starting to show more consistent power. Giudice will likely start 1997 at Double-A, with a good chance to move up to Triple-A Colorado Springs by season's end.

GLANVILLE, DOUG - OF - BR - Age 26
Glanville is the reason the Cubs could stand to lose Brian McRae. Glanville is a leadoff man who hits well and uses his speed to get on base. He is a good, not great, base-stealer. To be a productive leadoff man in the majors, Glanville must cut down on his strikeouts and take more walks. He earned his degree in science and engineering from Penn.

	AB	R	HR	RBI	SB	BA	$
1996 Chicago NL	83	10	1	10	2	.241	-

GLENN, LEON - 1B - BL - Age 27
Glenn hit a poor .213 in the hitter-friendly Texas League last season. He spent six years in rookie and Class-A ball, and at age 27 with his record, he's far behind the progress curve.

GOFF, JERRY - C - BL - Age 32
Goff is a veteran Triple-A player who made a brief appearance for Houston in 1996 as an injury replacement. With six passed balls in the only game he caught, he probably won't be back.

GOMEZ, CHRIS - SS/2B - BR - Age 25
Tigers' GM Randy Smith covets Padre prospects, and he gave up Chris Gomez and others to acquire them. Gomez adjusted well to the National League and had a solid season for the Padres, improving in many areas. Gomez is on the verge of a good breakout season.

	AB	R	HR	RBI	SB	BA	$
1995 Detroit AL	431	49	11	50	4	.223	5
1996 Detroit AL	128	21	1	16	1	.242	-
1996 San Diego NL	328	32	3	29	2	.262	3

GOMEZ, LEO - 3B - BR - Age 30
Gomez spent most of the season at third base for Chicago, but struggled with the bat. A career .245 hitter with Baltimore, Gomez didn't reach that height with Chicago. The Cubs will be patient with Gomez but perhaps not for more that a year or so. Regardless of who is at third, they will just hold down the position until the arrival of one of the Cubs' better prospects, Kevin Orie.

	AB	R	HR	RBI	SB	BA	$
1995 Baltimore AL	127	16	4	12	0	.236	0
1996 Chicago NL	362	44	17	56	1	.238	3

GONZALES, RENE - 3B/1B - BR - Age 35
Gonzales is a versatile and experienced utilityman who could have another year or so on a major league bench.

	AB	R	HR	RBI	SB	BA	$
1995 California AL	18	1	1	3	0	.333	-
1996 Texas AL	92	19	2	5	0	.217	-

GONZALEZ, ALEX - SS - BR - Age 23
Gonzalez improved his defensive skills dramatically in 1996 but his hitting hasn't come around the way some expected. The power was there but the batting average remained in the .230's Clearly, he is the shortstop of the present and will remain an everyday player for a long time.

	AB	R	HR	RBI	SB	BA	$
1995 Toronto AL	367	51	10	42	4	.243	6
1996 Toronto AL	527	64	14	64	16	.235	10

GONZALEZ, ALEXANDER - SS - BR - Age 20
Gonzalez is yet another in the long line of Marlins' middle infield prospects considered to be a potential future major league starter. However, 1996 was a lost season, limited to ten Low-A at-bats by injury. He is a defensive wizard who must pack on pounds (he's 6'0", 170 pounds) to become a credible offensive force. He could make the jump to High-A Brevard County in 1997 as the teammate of bonus babies Jaime Jones, Nate Rolison, Josh Booty and Mark Kotsay. He is a breakout prospect for 1997.

GONZALEZ, JIMMY - C - BR - Age 24
Gonzalez was a first round compensation pick by the Astros in 1991. However, he has not developed at all as a hitter and hasn't been able to stick above the Class-A level.

GONZALEZ, JUAN - DH/OF - BR - Age 27
In the 1995-96 offseason, Gonzalez discontinued the weight training that had robbed him of flexibility and left him susceptible to back problems. The result? A career year -- Gonzalez was behind only Mark McGwire in slugging and Albert Belle in RBI. For the combination of power and average, Gonzalez and Belle stand alone in the American League. Gonzalez was moved to right field, and acquitted himself well with the glove. He murders lefthanded pitching, hitting at a .376 clip. Gonzalez should remain at or near his peak level for the next couple of years.

	AB	R	HR	RBI	SB	BA	$
1995 Texas AL	352	57	27	82	0	.295	17
1996 Texas AL	541	89	47	144	2	.314	27

GONZALEZ, LUIS - OF - BL - Age 29
Gonzalez looked like a sure-bet star his rookie year when he lost out to Houston teammate Jeff Bagwell for Rookie of the Year honors. He hit .300 in 1993 but hasn't lived up to expectations in Chicago. Gonzalez hit well at Wrigley Field as a member of the Astros, but has struggled at home as a Cub. Gonzalez didn't have a terrible 1996, but he'll have to get back on the right track in order to keep his outfield job for much longer.

	AB	R	HR	RBI	SB	BA	$
1995 Chicago NL	471	69	13	69	6	.276	14
1996 Chicago NL	483	70	15	79	9	.271	13

GONZALEZ, PETE - C - BR - Age 27
Gonzalez was acquired by the Rockies from the Tigers and was initially assigned to Double-A New Haven. He moved up to the Triple-A level due primarily to a rash of injuries at the catcher position. His good defensive skills are overshadowed by his poor offensive talent, which should keep him in the minors in 1997.

GOODWIN, CURTIS - OF - BL - Age 24
Goodwin is an extremely fast, no power outfielder who showed signs of turning his tools into skills in 1996. He led the American Association in steals and was voted best baserunner in the league. by Baseball America. More importantly, he improved his strike zone judgment, with career highs in walks and on-base average. Shuttled between Indianapolis and Cincinnati in 1996, Goodwin will get the first shot at the Reds centerfield job in 1997 and will be good for at least 40 steals if he can hold it.

	AB	R	HR	RBI	SB	BA	$
1995 Baltimore AL	289	40	1	24	22	.263	13
1996 Cincinnati NL	136	20	0	5	15	.228	2

GOODWIN, TOM - OF - BL - Age 28
The fastest man in baseball. Goodwin can also hit a little, too, but it's his startling speed that catches your eye. A ribcage injury kept him on the bench the final two weeks, preventing a head-to-head showdown for the AL stolen base crown when Kenny Lofton and the Indians visited Kauffman Stadium the final weekend in 1996. Goodwin has 70-steal speed and a proven track record of .280+ hitting in the majors. He's in his prime.

	AB	R	HR	RBI	SB	BA	$
1995 Kansas City AL	480	72	4	28	50	.288	32
1996 Kansas City AL	524	80	1	35	66	.282	35

GORDON, KEITH - OF - BR - Age 28
Formerly in the Reds farm system, Gordon played in the Orioles organization last year. He's had some below-average years in the minors. The Reds second round draft pick in 1990, Gordon had a good year at Triple-A in 1995.

GRACE, MARK - 1B - BL - Age 32
Grace turned in one of the most impressive defensive seasons for a first baseman. In over 1000 chances, Grace committed just four errors. He also recorded one of his best years at the plate. Grace is already 32 years old, but he's the best of a group of good-fielding, low-power first basemen that includes Wally Joyner, David Segui, Hal Morris and others. Grace exercised his player option for 1997. He'll probably finish his career in Chicago.

	AB	R	HR	RBI	SB	BA	$
1995 Chicago NL	552	97	16	92	6	.326	25
1996 Chicago NL	547	88	9	75	2	.331	27

GRAFFANINO, TONY - 2B - BR - Age 24
His 1995 season was such a setback that Graffanino lost his "top prospect" label in most forums. 1996 saw him get right back on track with good hitting and solid defense, while earning his first cup of coffee in the majors. It won't be his last. Graffanino is now in a position to challenge Mark Lemke for playing time, although that will probably wait one more year. The Braves are unlikely to break up a winning combination to insert an unproven rookie in place of a known, solid regular. If Graffanino can continue on this same pace, he'll reach the majors for good late in 1997.

GREBECK, BRIAN - 3B/SS - BR - Age 29
Grebeck hit well in the lower minors, but found things much tougher in Triple-A. Even when he hit over .300 in the lower levels, he didn't produce many runs. His chances of getting substantial time, even as a reserve bench player in the majors, are slim.

GREBECK, CRAIG - SS - BR - Age 32
Grebeck was a deep infield reserve for the Marlins in 1996, and lasted the season only because of injuries to other infielders as well as the trade of Terry Pendleton, which slid Kurt Abbott and Alex Arias to the other side of the infield. Grebeck holds his own against lefties, but that's it. Defensively he is surehanded, but not spectacular enough to stand out. The Marlins have more talented players to assume his role, so Grebeck will likely move on, and split his time between Triple-A and the majors.

	AB	R	HR	RBI	SB	BA	$
1995 Chicago AL	154	19	1	18	0	.260	0
1996 Florida NL	95	8	1	9	0	.211	-

GREEN, BERT - OF - BR - Age 22
Drafted as a speedy shortstop in 1993, Green has instead developed into a speedy outfielder. He's stole 13 bases a Class A St. Petersburg, then 21 more at Double-A Arkansas in 1996, but he's still a weak hitter who must dramatically improve his contact hitting and bump his average up several notches to earn an advance above his present level. Green's first trip above A-ball was a disappointment.

GREEN, SHAWN - OF - BL - Age 24
A bad first half and a strong finish added up to a disappointing season and Green's immediate future is not as promising as it looked a year ago. His quick bat will result in a lot of doubles and some homers but he still has occasional mental lapses in the field. He opens 1997 at least as a platoon right fielder.

	AB	R	HR	RBI	SB	BA	$
1995 Totonto AL	379	52	15	54	1	.288	11
1996 Toronto AL	422	52	11	45	5	.280	8

GREENE, CHARLIE - C - BR - Age 26
Greene got a September callup from the Mets, mainly for the purpose of providing an extra catcher to warm-up the many pitchers who were being evaluated by new manager Bobby Valentine and his new pitching coach Bob Apodaca. Greene hit .244-2-27 for Double-A Binghamton. He is not in the major league picture for 1997.

GREENE, TODD - C - BR - Age 25
Angels catching prospect Greene hit 40 home runs in 1995 in Single and Double-A ball, and was named Baseball Weekly's Minor League Player of the Year. But his power stroke deserted him last year in Triple-A, and as a converted outfielder, his catching skills are still a little raw. He has a good work ethic and he's determined to succeed. Last year, his progress was slowed by a broken bone in his hand that caused him to miss almost two months. Greene may still develop into a first-rate catcher and a big power hitter.

	AB	R	HR	RBI	SB	BA	$
1996 California AL	79	9	2	9	2	.190	-

GREENE, WILLIE - 3B - BL - Age 25
A strong September (including six homers in the last week) may have finally convinced Reds management that Greene can play in the majors. The first half of the season had been a rerun of previous years, when Greene pulled a hamstring just as he was establishing himself as the regular third baseman. He didn't really get the full time job back until September as Ray Knight played Lenny Harris and others at third base instead of the best power prospect in the organization. Per 500 at-bats, his season worked out to 33 homers, 110 RBI and 63 walks. Greene did struggle against lefties (.159 batting average in 44 at-bats) and defensively (.927 fielding average) so a platoon or move to left field is possible in 1997.

	AB	R	HR	RBI	SB	BA	$
1995 Cincinnati NL	19	1	0	0	0	.105	-
1996 Cincinnati NL	287	48	19	63	0	.244	5

GREENWELL, MIKE - OF - BL - Age 33
Nine RBI in one game! Greenwell set a major-league record with his early September outburst, driving in all nine runs in a 9-8 victory over Seattle. He spent nearly all year on the disabled list or otherwise hurt; he was a non-factor for the first five months of the year. Greenwell's on a downturn at this phase of his career. While he's not as bad as he looked the first five months, he's also not as good as he looked in September.

	AB	R	HR	RBI	SB	BA	$
1995 Boston AL	481	67	15	76	9	.297	19
1996 Boston AL	295	35	7	44	4	.295	7

GREER, RUSTY - OF - BL - Age 28
Greer established himself firmly as an everyday player, setting career highs in virtually every offensive category despite missing almost three weeks down the stretch with bruised ribs. He has also become one of the best defensive leftfielders in the American League. Although 1996 was likely his career year, Greer is fully capable of remaining around the .300 level, with double-digit home run power and occasional speed. He has a knack for hitting in the clutch.

	AB	R	HR	RBI	SB	BA	$
1995 Texas AL	417	58	13	61	3	.271	11
1996 Texas AL	542	96	18	100	9	.332	23

GREGG, TOMMY - OF - BL - Age 33
Gregg has thrashed Triple-A pitching for a decade now, but has not exhibited the bat speed to do similar damage in the majors during his many trials. He is basically a Triple-A insurance policy. The smart money says that Gregg, a line drive hitter with occasional longball power, has another handful of major league at-bats left in him.

GRESHAM, KRIS - C - BR - Age 26
Last year Gresham was a catcher with Double-A Bowie in the Orioles organization. In June, he was demoted to Single-A to make room for a better prospect, and at age 26, Gresham opted to retire rather than go back to Single-A ball.

GRIEVE, BEN - OF - BL - Age 20
Former first round pick, Grieve ripped through the California League earning a promotion to Double-A Huntsville. He had some adjustment problems, but if his improvement from 1995 to 1996 was indicative of how he learns, he should again explode on Southern League pitchers in 1997 and move on to Edmonton before long.

GRIFFEY, CRAIG - OF - BR - Age 25
It looks like Ken Jr. got the lion's share of the hitting genes. Craig's .222 average at Double-A Port City was his best mark in the last three years. Obviously, he'll get a longer look than most 25-year-olds who hit at the Mendoza line in Double-A. But, eventually, the courtesy will wear off and Craig will have to look for a job outside of baseball.

GRIFFEY, KEN JR - OF - BL - Age 27
He didn't win the MVP and didn't get elected President, but otherwise Griffey had a very successful season in 1996. Fans wondering when he's going to have a really big year need to look closer. He just had one. And if you missed it, he will have another in 1997.

	AB	R	HR	RBI	SB	BA	$
1995 Seattle AL	260	52	17	42	4	.258	9
1996 Seattle AL	545	125	49	140	16	.303	33

GRIFOL, PEDRO - C - BR - Age 27
The Mets have maintained a healthy mixture of mature farmhands to help their kids develop. Grifol is defense-oriented backstop who handled about half of the catching chores for Double-A Binghamton in 1996, batting .236

GRIJAK, KEVIN - 1B - BL - Age 26
Grijak can hit, but that's about it. He is a career .300 hitter over the course of his six minor league seasons, with some power. However, he is a defensive liability at first base and in the outfield. Grijak's best chance is to leave the Braves as a minor league free agent and hook on with an AL team that can use an extra bat off the bench; then he'd be able to DH in the majors.

GRISSOM, MARQUIS - OF - BR - Age 29
The speed, defense and high-average hitting were all in evidence again for Grissom as he added another element: power. Grissom rebounded from an off year in 1995 with career highs in most offensive categories, including hits, triples, homers, runs scored and batting average. It was a big year for Grissom, who was a big part of the Braves' repeat as pennant winners.

	AB	R	HR	RBI	SB	BA	$
1995 Atlanta NL	551	80	12	42	29	.258	19
1996 Atlanta NL	671	106	23	74	28	.308	34

GROPPUSO, MIKE - 3B - BR - Age 27
Groppuso was a first round compensation pick in the Astros' 1991 draft. He is prone to strikeouts and, although he received some playing time at the Triple-A level in 1996, he appears to have topped out at Double-A.

GROTEWOLD, JEFF - 1B - BL - Age 31
The definition of the Triple-A extension of the bench, Grotewold filled a role for Omaha in 1996, giving them a consistent power bat in the middle of the order. He has gone as far as his one-dimensional play will take him.

GRUDZIELANEK, MARK - 2B/SS - BR - Age 26
There's a lot to like about the Expos' young infielder. He knows how to hit, he looks like he'll develop some pop and he hustles. He is going to have a long career and make his share of All-Star Games before his career is over.

	AB	R	HR	RBI	SB	BA	$
1995 Montreal NL	269	27	1	20	8	.245	4
1996 Montreal NL	657	99	6	49	33	.306	29

GRUNEWALD, KEITH - 3B - BB - Age 25
Following his promotion from Class A Salem after a solid 1995 campaign, Grunewald had a disappointing 1996 offensively at Double-A New Haven, posting a career low .227 average. More seasoning in the middle minors is probable for 1997.

GUERRERO, VLADIMIR - OF - BR - Age 21
Guerrero went on a rampage at two levels in 1996, being named by Baseball America as the best batting prospect, power prospect, defensive outfielder, outfield arm, and overall prospect in the Double-A Eastern League, as well as the most exciting player in both that league and the High-A Carolina League. He bulked up to 6'2", 175 pounds, and littered Eastern League diamonds with powerful line drives all season. He flirted with .400 for much of the year.

GUERRERO, WILTON - 2B/SS - BR - Age 22
1996 was a breakthrough year for the Dodgers heir apparent at second base. Formerly a shortstop, Guerrero was third in the PCL in batting average and demonstrated good speed (26 steals and 12 triples). Strike zone judgment and power are his major weaknesses. Guerrero would probably hit .270 and provide good defense at second base for the Dodgers, and he has no real competition for the second base job unless the Dodgers sign someone in the off season.

GUEVARA, GIOMAR - SS/2B - BB - Age 24
Guevara runs pretty well and slings a lot of leather; he has won several low-minors fielding awards. At the plate he strikes out too much for a non-power hitter. If he learns to take more advantage of his speed by getting on base at a better rate, Guevara could have a shot at the majors. Otherwise, he's got an outside shot at a utility role.

GUIEL, AARON - 3B - BL - Age 24
Guiel has shown a little power and hitting smarts in the minors, and could make the Angels as a reserve infielder. He was shifted from second to third base to increase his promotability. It helps that he bats left.

GUILIANO, MATT - SS - BR - Age 24
Guiliano is a scrapper drafted in the 20th round by the Phillies in 1994.

GUILLEN, JOSE - OF - BR - Age 20
The Carolina League MVP led the league in homers and RBI. He's a driven player, who combines speed and power and a strong outfield arm.

GUILLEN, OZZIE - SS - BL - Age 33
The man who never saw a pitch he didn't like. His batting average was .263 and on base average only 10 points higher. In other words without a hit he wasn't getting on. He fielded his position well enough to keep him in the lineup and the disappointing offense of Chris Snopek didn't hurt either.

	AB	R	HR	RBI	SB	BA	$
1995 Chicago AL	415	50	1	41	6	.248	5
1996 Chicago AL	499	62	4	45	6	.263	5

GULAN, MIKE - 3B - BR - Age 26
The best offensive player in 1995 at Arkansas, Gulan is a third baseman with good power. Gulan is an above-average defensive player with a cannon arm. His weakness is striking out a lot, as in 119 times in 419 at-bats last year.

GUTIERREZ, RICKY - 2B - BR - Age 27
Not to be confused with the Astros' major leaguer of the same name, this is the Ricky Gutierrez that has served as a big brother and role model for the younger Hispanic players in the Indians' chain, most notably pitching phenom Bartolo Colon. It's hard to envision a player of his age with only one plus skill - speed - enduring much longer.

GUTIERREZ, RICKY - SS - BR - Age 26
Gutierrez solidified his status as a capable major league utility infielder in 1996 by hitting .284 as a reserve at shortstop and third base. He can be expected to fill the same role in 1997.

	AB	R	HR	RBI	SB	BA	$
1995 Houston NL	156	22	0	12	5	.276	3
1996 Houston NL	218	28	1	15	6	.284	5

GWYNN, CHRIS - OF - BL - Age 32
Gwynn is a reserve outfielder and pinch hitter who usually gets 80-100 at-bats every year. He doesn't have any big power or offensive talents to speak of, but he's a good team player who fills his reserve role adequately. Gwynn can come through with an occasional key clutch hit like he did against the Dodgers last year in the season-ending showdown for the Western Division pennant.

	AB	R	HR	RBI	SB	BA	$
1995 Los Angeles NL	84	8	1	10	0	.214	-
1996 San Diego NL	90	8	1	10	0	.178	-

GWYNN, TONY - OF - BL - Age 36
Gwynn missed a great deal of last season because of a partially torn Achilles tendon, but nevertheless, he won his

seventh batting championship even though he didn't have enough official at-bats. A little used rule permitting him to add sufficient at-bats without base hits to qualify gave him the title, another notch towards Cooperstown.

	AB	R	HR	RBI	SB	BA	$
1995 San Diego NL	535	82	9	90	17	.368	33
1996 San Diego NL	451	67	3	50	11	.353	28

GYSELMAN, JEFF - C - BR - Age 26
The Phils' 1993 19th round pick has been little more than top prospect Bobby Estalella's caddy during the last two seasons, in which he has amassed a total of 192 at-bats, 33 hits (.172 average), and two extra base hits - both doubles.

HAJEK, DAVE - 2B - BR - Age 29
Hajek has put together three almost identical seasons at Triple-A, (.317-4-64-9 in 1996). He had two stints in the majors in 1996 but his playing time was limited. He is the type of player who has to be seen every day to be appreciated. A fundamentally sound contact hitter who rarely strikes out, Hajek should be able to play in the majors if given the opportunity.

HALE, CHIP - 2B - BL - Age 32
Hale continued to fill his role as a pinch hitter deluxe in '96, as he appeared in fifty five games as a pinch hitter and is not an easy out.

	AB	R	HR	RBI	SB	BA	$
1995 Minnesota AL	103	10	2	18	0	.262	1
1996 Minnesota AL	87	8	1	16	0	.276	-

HALL, BILLY 2B - BB - Age 28
Hall's career is in reverse, as he dropped back a level to Double-A in the Reds' chain after spending five years with the Padres' organization. He's scrapper with a .295 career average and 193 career steals.

HALL, JOE - OF - BR - Age 31
Veteran minor leaguer Joe Hall had another solid season in Triple-A last year, and his 95 RBI were tops for his Rochester club. Except for a total of 43 at-bats in the majors with the White Sox and Tigers in 1994 and 1995, Hall has been in the minors for nine years. In past years, in addition to the outfield, Hall has also played first, second, third and caught.

HALL, MEL - OF - BL - Age 36
Why exactly did the Giants see fit to grant a roster spot to Mr. Happy for part of the 1996 season? He scratched out three singles in 25 at-bats before being released.

HALTER, SHANE - SS - BR - Age 27
The definition of an organizational player, Halter was loaned by the Royals to the Marlins' Triple-A club to fill a middle-infield gap caused by injuries - and played centerfield. He remained in the outfield when he returned, but continued to hit like a shortstop, showing little power and a marginal batting average. Halter is a fine fielder, but just doesn't hit enough to make it to the big leagues for more than a cup of coffee.

HAMELIN, BOB - 1B - BL - Age 29
Big Bob's train departed the KC station about three months before the end of the 1996 season. He slumped to start the year, then got hurt and, despite hitting .294 over the second half of the season, his name was rarely called by Manager Bob Boone in September, even when platoon advantages fairly screamed for the "Hammer" to play. Hamelin and the Royals gladly parted ways during the off-season. He can still hit, and that may come back to haunt the Royals.

	AB	R	HR	RBI	SB	BA	$
1995 Kansas City AL	208	20	7	25	0	.168	-
1996 Kansas City AL	239	31	9	40	5	.255	5

HAMILTON, DARRYL - OF - BL - Age 32
Let go by the Brewers, his talent and durability disparaged in the process, Hamilton signed with the Rangers and promptly had one of his best years. Hamilton consistently hits for a high average and has moderate speed. As a leadoff hitter in a powerful lineup, Hamilton should continue to post high run totals. He played 147 games in centerfield without committing an error.

Benson's Baseball Player Guide: 1997

	AB	R	HR	RBI	SB	BA	$
1995 Milwaukee AL	398	54	5	44	11	.271	11
1996 Texas AL	627	94	6	51	15	.293	15

HAMMONDS, JEFFREY - OF - BR - Age 26
Hammonds began last season starting in the Orioles outfield. But he had a disappointingly weak bat, not delivering in clutch situations, and was sent to Triple-A to improve his hitting and learn to play centerfield. A leg injury then caused him to miss some time. The Orioles have concluded that he will never be a big impact player ala Rickey Henderson, but he could be a solid contributor if he gets his swing and plate discipline together. Orioles management is running out of patience, and he was the subject of numerous trades during the season and nearly traded to Cleveland at mid-year.

	AB	R	HR	RBI	SB	BA	$
1995 Baltimore AL	178	18	4	23	4	.242	3
1996 Baltimore AL	248	38	9	27	3	.226	1

HANEL, MARCUS - C - BR - Age 25
Hanel was always a favorite of Pittsburgh manager Jim Leyland. Primarily it's because Hanel is the same kind of player Leyland was in Detroit's farm system: Good behind the plate but weaker when standing at it.

HANEY, TODD - 2B - BR - Age 31
Haney spent some time with the Chicago Cubs the past three seasons. He's a utility infielder who makes good contact. He hit .411 in 25 games for Chicago in '95. By doing so, he became the fifth major leaguer to finish over .400 with at least 50 at-bats since Ted Williams' .406 season in 1941.

	AB	R	HR	RBI	SB	BA	$
1995 Chicago NL	73	11	2	6	0	.411	3
1996 Chicago NL	82	11	0	3	1	.134	-

HANSEN, DAVE - 3B - BL - Age 28
Hansen does not appear to have much of a future in Los Angeles. The Dodgers signed Mike Blowers for the third base job rather than give Hansen a chance as a platoon regular, then brought back the ancient Tim Wallach when Blowers went down for the year. To add insult to injury, the Dodgers made Billy Ashley their primary pinch hitter, reducing Hansen's main role over the last few seasons. If Hansen got a legitimate chance he wouldn't be great, but his .270 or so average and 10 home runs would be a marked improvement over Juan Castro or Mike Busch.

	AB	R	HR	RBI	SB	BA	$
1995 Los Angeles NL	181	19	1	14	0	.287	2
1996 Los Angeles NL	104	7	0	6	0	.221	-

HANSEN, JED - 2B - BR - Age 24
Shortly after appearing in the Double-A All-Star game, Hansen earned a promotion to Triple-A Omaha. He's one of the few good prospects remaining in the Royals high minors - the rest have already joined the big league club. Hansen's .286-12-50 showing at Wichita, including 14 steals, have pushed him ahead of Sergio Nunez in the Royals' second base pecking order. Despite the high strikeout rate, Hansen produced better than expected in 1996 and should be in the majors after a year of seasoning at Omaha in 1997.

HANSEN, TERREL - OF/1B - BR - Age 30
As a ten-year minor league veteran, Hansen knows how to hit a mistake pitch a long way; he was one of Jacksonville's leading power threats in 1996. However, his tendencies to swing at bad pitches have prevented Hansen from getting beyond the high minors. He's a career minor leaguer.

HARDTKE, JASON - 2B - BB - Age 25
Known as an extremely hard worker, Hardtke explained his September callup with the Mets as being attributable to defensive improvement. For Triple-A Norfolk he hit .300 with nine home runs in 1996.

	AB	R	HR	RBI	SB	BA	$
1996 New York NL	57	3	0	6	0	.193	-

HARKRIDER, TIM - SS - BB - Age 25
Harkrider is a scrappy contact-hitting Angels prospect who has hit for a decent average in the minors. He missed all of 1996 with an ankle injury. He's fast and a decent fielder, and he could make the Angels as a utility man.

HARMES, KRIS - C - BL - Age 25
Back-to-back disappointing Double-A campaigns promise little. Harmes continued to play catcher and didn't hit. He has little power and is a slow baserunner, only a little better than the .213 average he posted last year. He turns twenty-six in June and is running out of time.

HARRIS, LENNY - 3B/2B - BL - Age 32
Harris may have extended his career another year or two with a fine 1996 season, accumulating 302 at-bats as a semi-regular at second base, third base, and right field. Batting average, surprising speed (14 of 20 in steals in 1996), and versatility are his strengths.

	AB	R	HR	RBI	SB	BA	$
1995 Cincinnati NL	197	32	2	16	10	.208	2
1996 Cincinnati NL	302	33	5	32	14	.285	10

HARVEY, RAY - OF - BL - Age 28
Harvey's career is clearly stuck in reverse. After spending two full seasons at Double-A, he finished 1996 at High-A Kinston. He has always hit for a decent average, but hasn't reached double figures in homers since his first pro season in 1991. There is no compelling reason for the Indians to employ him any longer.

HASELMAN, BILL - C - BR - Age 30
As the Red Sox' primary reserve catcher, Haselman turned in his best season yet. He reached career highs in nearly every offensive category while he filled in well in Mike Stanley's brief absence. His skills are on a par with most other second-line catchers: occasional power, but below-average in most aspects. Haselman is good enough with the glove to be a backup backstop in the big leagues, but he would not be a good long-term catcher.

	AB	R	HR	RBI	SB	BA	$
1995 Boston AL	152	22	5	23	0	.243	1
1996 Boston AL	237	33	8	34	4	.274	5

HASTINGS, LIONEL - 3B - BR - Age 24
The Marlins' 1996 Double-A third sacker is an undersized (5'9", 165 pounds) scrapper who was overmatched at the plate. His two chief offensive skills are bunting and getting hit by pitches. His ability to also play second base could allow him to endure another season or two in a similar role.

HATCHER, CHRIS - OF - BR - Age 28
Hatcher is a power hitter who has been in the Astro system for seven years. After being hampered by injuries and excessive strikeouts through his career, he had by far his best season in 1996. He split time between Double-A and Triple-A, hitting .304 with 31 home runs and 97 runs batted in. However, he also struck out in 25 % of his at-bats. He should get a look in a major league camp in 1997 and it will probably be his last chance.

HATTEBERG, SCOTT - C - BL - Age 27
Long considered the Red Sox' catcher of the future, Hatteberg is a respectable power threat with on-base ability. However, his catching skills haven't develop as expected. With Mike Stanley under contract for another year, Hatteberg won't be a regular in Boston in 1997. By 1998, better prospects may be on the scene. Hatteberg can be a useful reserve catcher and extra bat off the bench, but a larger role is unlikely.

HAWS, SCOTT - C - BL - Age 25
After missing virtually all of 1995 due to reconstructive elbow surgery - not a great operation for a catching prospect - Haws became a little-used, light-hitting High-A backup in the Phils' chain in 1996.

HAYES, CHARLIE - 3B - BR - Age 31
Just a steady player who will never be an All-Star, Hayes tends to be overlooked even on a championship team. He helped the Yankees when they needed it in 1996, however (Wade Boggs had a stiff back and a general slump in RBI production). Hayes can be useful in 1997 as a platooner or everyday player as needed.

	AB	R	HR	RBI	SB	BA	$
1995 Philadelphia NL	529	58	11	85	5	.276	15
1996 Pittsburgh NL	459	51	10	62	6	.248	5
1996 New York AL	67	7	2	13	0	.284	-

HAZLETT, STEVE - OF - BR - Age 27
Hazlett lost nearly a hundred points off his batting average in his second Triple-A season, not the type of performance employers desire.

HEFFERNAN, BERT - C - BL - Age 31
The erstwhile backup catcher hasn't batted 200 times in a minor league season since 1990. A reliable line drive hitter who handles young pitchers well, he is a decent platoon option in the minors because of his lefty bat.

HELD, DAN - 1B - BR - Age 26
Held has come quite a long way for a 1993 42nd round - and last Phils' draftee. He simply cranks for the fences on each at bat - his homers have increased from 18 to 22 to 26, while his whiffs have increased from 119 to 128 to 141 over the past three seasons. However, it is a major negative that he has yet to reach Triple-A at his advanced age. In the mold of the legendary Pork Chop Pough, Held could linger indefinitely as a minor league masher with little upward mobility.

HELFAND, ERIC - C - BL - Age 28
Helfand is a good-field, no-hit catcher who served as a Triple-A insurance policy for the Indians in 1996. With Einar Diaz as the heir apparent to the backup job in the majors, Helfand will, at best, assume the same role in 1997. Offensively, his most notable skill is getting hit by pitches (10 HBP in 1996).

HELMS, WESLEY - 3B - BR - Age 20
Young Helms, Robert Smith, Rob Sasser and Danny Magee give the Braves a lot of depth at the hot corner. Helms has power, hits for average and has a gun for an arm; he was among the league leaders in several offensive categories when he was promoted from Class A Durham to Greenville in July. Helms' new conditioning program helped him lose weight while gaining strength. Should he continue to produce as he has over his first three pro years, Helms will be in Atlanta before the end of the year - perhaps Chipper Jones' move to shortstop will become more permanent.

HELTON, TODD - 1B - BL - Age 23
In only his second season as a pro, this Rockies phenom jumped from Double-A New Haven (where he was named Rockies Player of the Year) to the parent team at the end of the season. After tearing up the Eastern League in several offensive categories for most of 1996, Helton was sent up to Triple-A Colorado Springs, where he will likely be the starting first baseman in 1997. His willingness to play the outfield may hasten his route to the Rockies.

HEMOND, SCOTT - IF/C - BR - Age 31
Hemond had fashioned a respectable fringe major league career as a third catcher/reserve infielder with three teams over the previous seven seasons. He took a step back in 1996, to Triple-A Louisville, where he served the same role and gave the Cardinals some organizational depth. Hemond can still play, but he's going to have to work hard to find a major league job that fits his specialized skills.

HENDERSON, RICKEY - OF - BR - Age 38
Although Henderson hit only .241 last year in his first year in the National League, his OBP was an excellent .410, and he scored 110 runs. It took Henderson a couple of months to adjust to the National League, explaining his .241 down year. He had a good attitude when sharing playing time with Greg Vaughn.

	AB	R	HR	RBI	SB	BA	$
1995 Oakland AL	407	67	9	54	32	.300	27
1996 San Diego NL	465	110	9	29	37	.241	10

HENLEY, BOB - C - BR - Age 23
Henley skipped a level to Double-A in 1996, showcasing excellent plate discipline (70 walks in 359 plate appearances) and little else. Only two years removed from a 20 homer season, Henley has misplaced his power swing, only hitting three homers in 1996. The bat speed to hit with authority at higher levels simply isn't there.

HENRY, SANTIAGO - SS/2B - BR - Age 24
Henry flipped between shortstop and second base last year and made thirty errors in the process. After posting mediocre seasons in 1994 and 1995, his average improved to .270 but the rest of the necessary numbers weren't there.

HERMANSEN, CHAD - SS - BR - Age 19
How good is the Pirates' first-round draft pick in 1995? So good that managers in both the short-season Class A New York-Penn League and Rookie-level Gulf Coast League selected him as their leagues' best prospect - and he was only 17 years old. He may eventually move to third base but the ultra-poised Hermansen figures to be a power-hitting threat in the big leagues - perhaps in the not-to-distant future.

HERNANDEZ, CARLOS - C - BR - Age 29
Several years ago, Hernandez was a good hitting catching prospect trapped behind Mike Piazza. Long time defensive specialist Tom Prince has since taken the number two job behind Piazza and Hernandez spent most of the year at Albuquerque, where he hit a rather empty .240. He won't get a chance behind Piazza, and if he keeps hitting .240 at Albuquerque, he won't get a chance anywhere.

HERNANDEZ, JOSE M. - SS/2B - BR - Age 27
If you look at Hernandez's numbers, you'd think he was a light-hitting middle infielder who doesn't run much. You'd be right. Hernandez isn't a long term answer at shortstop, but there are a lot of teams that would love to have a player like him on their roster. Hernandez can make some spectacular plays in the field, but is best relegated to a platoon or utility role.

	AB	R	HR	RBI	SB	BA	$
1995 Chicago NL	245	37	13	40	1	.245	6
1996 Chicago NL	331	52	10	41	4	.242	3

HERNANDEZ, RAMON - C - BR - Age 20
The Arizona League MVP and batting champion in 1995, he was also great behind the plate last year. While in 1996, he did not hit for high average, he had a lot of extra base hits.

HERRERA, JOSE - OF - BL - Age 24
His hitting improved but his fielding deteriorated in 1996. Herrera spent the year in the majors and probably wasn't ready. He has never played at Triple-A, and a year there would do his confidence wonders. He is still young, has a lot of talent, and he wants to improve. The A's like his attitude, and baserunners fear his arm.

	AB	R	HR	RBI	SB	BA	$
1995 Oakland AL	70	9	0	2	1	.243	-
1996 Oakland AL	320	44	6	30	8	.269	6

HERRICK, JASON - OF - BL - Age 23
Herrick hit .319 last year, showing some power, but he struck out about 25 percent of the time. The Angels regard him highly, sending him to the Arizona Fall League to face tougher competition.

HIATT, PHIL - 3B/OF - BR - Age 27
Hiatt had an excellent year (.261-42-119-17) playing third base for Triple-A Toledo in '96. He's not likely to develop into a regular player at twenty-seven but can help a major league club with a few seasons of fifteen home runs between thirdbase and the outfield.

HICKEY, MIKE - 2B - BR - Age 26
Hickey is a passable second sacker with a good batting eye. He supplemented a .255 batting average at Double-A Port City in 1996 with 58 walks in 305 plate appearances; almost as many walks as hits. He lacks any real pop, so the challenge for Hickey will be at Triple-A when they start throwing him more strikes.

HIDALGO, RICHARD - OF - BR - Age 21
Rushed to Double-A at age 20 in 1995, Hidalgo improved significantly in his second year at that level (.294-14-78-11). Hidalgo is one of the Astros' top prospects and could be in the major leagues as the starting right fielder by 1998. He has exceptional tools and just needs more time to refine his skills.

HIGGINSON, BOB - OF - BL - Age 26
Higginson had a great second major league season in '96 and gave more than a hint that he could become an impact player. He punished righthanders (.335) and posted an astounding .577 slugging percentage; not bad for someone the scouts never considered a top prospect when he was in the minors. Higginson will likely play a lot of centerfield in 1997.

	AB	R	HR	RBI	SB	BA	$
1995 Detroit AL	410	61	14	43	6	.224	6
1996 Detroit AL	440	75	26	81	6	.320	19

HILL, GLENALLEN - OF - BR - Age 32
Injured with a broken wrist for a good part of 1996, Hill continues to improve nearly every aspect of his game. He was on a pace to eclipse personal highs of walks, homers, RBI, runs and slugging had he not been injured. Only his speed was down from '95. His defense, as always, was good.

	AB	R	HR	RBI	SB	BA	$
1995 San Francisco NL	497	71	24	86	25	.264	26
1996 San Francisco NL	379	56	19	67	6	.280	14

HOCKING, DENNY - SS/OF - BB - Age 26
Hocking is a young utility infielder who played some in the outfield in '96 for Minnesota. He needs to start hitting for average since he lacks power and speed.

	AB	R	HR	RBI	SB	BA	$
1995 Minnesota AL	25	4	0	3	1	.200	-
1996 Minnesota AL	127	16	1	10	3	.197	-

HOILES, CHRIS - C - BR - Age 32
Last season, Hoiles had a poor first half (.224-12-30) followed by a solid second half (.294-13-43), and since it was his second consecutive year of such production, it may become a long term trend. Oddly enough, he also hit the same .294 in the second half of 1995. The Orioles were unhappy with Hoiles at mid-year, and placed him on waivers, but no one claimed him because of his large salary. Runners are also taking advantage of his poor throwing arm.

	AB	R	HR	RBI	SB	BA	$
1995 Baltimore AL	352	53	19	58	1	.250	9
1996 Baltimore AL	407	64	25	73	0	.258	9

HOLBERT, AARON - SS - BR - Age 24
Holbert was long considered the heir apparent to Ozzie Smith with the Cardinals. However, with Royce Clayton around, Holbert can forget about becoming the starter in St. Louis. His lack of offense forced the Cardinals to trade for Clayton, though Holbert's speed and defense could make him a good major-league utility man.

HOLBERT, RAY - SS - BR - Age 26
Holbert spent the entire 1995 season with San Diego except for a short rehab stint at Triple-A. After a trade to Houston, he failed to make the major league team in 1996. At Triple-A Tucson, he was injured and missed most of the season, batting .247 in 97 at-bats. He has speed but his career batting average is under .250. He needs a strong comeback in 1997 to have even a remote shot for a return to the majors.

HOLDREN, NATE - 1B - BR - Age 25
This former Michigan football player has good power in his bat, but faces a host of talent ahead of him in Helton and Kennedy. Cutting down on his strikeouts could help Holdren to the Triple-A level in 1997.

HOLIFIELD, RICK - OF - BL - Age 27
Nine minor league seasons have turned this once-promising power/speed candidate into just another minor league outfielder. Holifield led Double-A Trenton with 35 steals, but struck out more than once out of every four at-bats, then hit .069 in a brief trial at Pawtucket. Holifield is running short of time; he's old to just be reaching Triple-A.

HOLLANDSWORTH, TODD - OF - BL - Age 23
Hollandsworth made the most of the Dodgers left field vacancy. His real strength was his batting average - his speed was a little above average and his power and strike zone judgment are below average. His .437 slugging average is not good for a left fielder and his .348 on base average is inadequate for a leadoff hitter, where he batted much of the year. He is young enough to continue to develop, but a likely candidate for a sophomore slump if he does not widen his skills. The Dodgers have several good outfield prospects, and center field is also an option if Brett Butler does not return.

	AB	R	HR	RBI	SB	BA	$
1995 Los Angeles NL	103	16	5	13	2	.233	2
1996 Los Angeles NL	478	64	12	59	21	.291	20

HOLLINS, DAMON - OF - BR - Age 22
The Braves are still high on their fourth round pick from 1992, having advanced him one level each year to Triple-A Richmond in 1996. Re-aggravating an old high school injury forced Hollins to the DL midway through the season, though; he'll have to start over at Richmond again in 1997. Hollins has excellent power and is a superb fielder. Once he cuts his strikeouts he'll challenge for a role with Atlanta (rightfield?), possibly by the end of 1997.

HOLLINS, DAVE - 3B/1B - BB - Age 30
Hollins hadn't seen 400 at-bats since he was with Philadelphia in 1993. While he struggled in Minnesota, his trade to Seattle and his typical September hot streak made his stats respectable. If he stays in Seattle he could do OK sharing third with Russ Davis and helping out at first base.

	AB	R	HR	RBI	SB	BA	$
1995 Philadelphia NL	205	46	7	25	1	.229	2
1995 Boston AL	13	2	0	1	0	.154	-
1996 Seattle AL	516	88	16	78	6	.262	10

HORN, JEFF - C - BR - Age 26
Horn has hit for a good average as he has advanced in the Twins' minor league system, especially at the higher levels. However, he hasn't shown much power and his defensive skills are just average. Horn could get to the majors in a reserve role.

HORNE, TYRONE - OF - BL - Age 26
Horne looked better a year ago, when he was coming off a 16-homer year at the Double-A level. He reached Triple-A in 1996 but hit only .230 while up there. He did a little better in 125 at-bats with Double-A Binghamton in the Mets' system.

HOSEY, DWAYNE - OF - BB - Age 30
The Hosey-in-centerfield experiment was a bust; he drew a lot of heat for the Red Sox' poor start, then finished the year back at Triple-A where his old hitting returned. His 1996 hitting line for Pawtucket is interchangeable with any of his last four Triple-A seasons. Hosey hits for average and power and has above-average speed (his 20 stolen bases led Pawtucket) but it appears that he's one of those players that just can't make the adjustment to big-league pitching. Perhaps another round of expansion - or a trip to Japan - can get Hosey another chance in the majors.

	AB	R	HR	RBI	SB	BA	$
1995 Boston AL	68	20	3	7	6	.338	3
1996 Boston AL	78	13	1	3	6	.218	0

HOSEY, STEVE - OF - BR - Age 27
Hosey spent most of his pro baseball career in the Giants organization where he had two good years in Triple-A hitting around .290, with 15 homers, and stealing a few bases, but that was a long time ago. He was hanging on in Independent ball in 1996.

HOUSTON, TYLER - 1B - BL - Age 26
Houston was the first pick in the 1989 draft by the Braves. He was traded by the Braves in midseason 1996 to the Cubs. It's no longer realistic to consider Houston a full-time catcher. Houston spent some time as a second baseman, but he's not exactly Ryne Sandberg with the glove. Houston should be in the mix for the utility spot with the Cubs.

	AB	R	HR	RBI	SB	BA	$
1996 Atlanta-Chicago NL	142	21	3	27	3	.317	6

HOWARD, CHRIS - C - BR - Age 31
A .160 performance in a part-time trial with the Mets' Triple-A farm team looked like the end for Howard, who had surfaced briefly with the Mariners in 1994. Not to be confused with Chris Howard the pitcher.

HOWARD, DAVID - SS/2B - BB - Age 30
After a "career year" of hitting .243 in 1995, Howard dropped back to his usual low-power, low-average, low-everything output with the bat. Because no one else on the club could play shortstop well enough, and because Howard plays it extremely well, he was the regular shortstop over the last four months of 1996 and enters 1997 with the job.

	AB	R	HR	RBI	SB	BA	$
1995 Kansas City AL	255	23	0	19	6	.243	3
1996 Kansas City AL	420	51	4	48	5	.219	0

HOWARD, MATT - SS/2B - BR - Age 29
Howard hit for high average as a part-timer for Triple-A Columbus in 1996 (.347-2-16 with nine stolen bases) but he didn't look prominent in the Yankees plans at any time during the season. He once stole 50 bases in a minor league season and would be a pinch runner if he had a major league role.

	AB	R	HR	RBI	SB	BA	$
1996 New York AL	54	9	1	9	1	.204	-

HOWARD, THOMAS - OF - BB - Age 32
Howard's playing time was boosted by the numerous injuries in the Reds outfield in 1996, but his performance level dropped from his fine 1995 season. Howard gives you a decent batting average, and a little power and speed, but his defense is no longer adequate in centerfield, he won't take a walk, and he cannot hit lefties at all. He's a useful reserve/platoon outfielder, but that is the limit of his ability.

	AB	R	HR	RBI	SB	BA	$
1995 Cincinnati NL	281	42	3	26	17	.302	13
1996 Cincinnati NL	360	50	6	42	6	.272	8

HOWELL, JACK - 3B - BL - Age 35
Howell was signed by the Angels as insurance in case rookie George Arias wasn't ready for the majors. That proved to be the case early in the season, and Howell responded well in a platoon role. Prior to 1995, he played in Japan for four years where he was a home run slugger, once bashing 38 homers in only 387 at-bats. Last year was Howell's second tour of duty with the Angels, having been with them in 1985-91 for 2,108 at-bats and a composite .238 batting average. Arias appears to be ready, so Howell's playing time may decline.

	AB	R	HR	RBI	SB	BA	$
1996 California AL	126	20	8	21	0	.270	1

HOWITT, DANN - OF/1B - BL - Age 33
This minor league journeyman power hitter was once Mark McGwire's chief minor league competition in the A's chain. He's now a certified nomad who had appeared in the majors in six straight seasons before falling short in 1995, when he toiled at Triple-A in the Indians' system.

HUBBARD, MIKE - C - BR - Age 26
This ex-Cub was at Triple-A in 1996, hitting .293 for Iowa.

HUBBARD, TRENIDAD - OF - BR - Age 32
Hubbard had high hopes to stick with the Rockies when 1996 began, but he was outshone by teammate Quinton McCracken. As a consequence, he had another productive year at Triple-A Colorado Springs, until he was made part of a late-season trade to the Giants. Hubbard is a fiery, scrappy player with decent power, but age is beginning to limit his options.

	AB	R	HR	RBI	SB	BA	$
1995 Colorado NL	58	13	3	9	2	.310	2
1996 San Francisco NL	89	15	2	14	2	.213	-

HUCKABY, KEN - C - BR - Age 26
The Dodgers' second-round draft pick in 1991, Huckaby displays fine catching skills. He's not a terrible hitter, although his .275-3-41 season at Triple-A Albuquerque in 1996 is relatively weak considering the hitting conditions at that park. He'll challenge for a reserve role in Los Angeles in 1997.

HUDLER, REX - OF/IF - BR - Age 36
At age 35, the hustling Rex Hudler had his career-best year in 1996 setting all sorts of personal records. His hustling play is a throw back to the old days of iron men and baggy cotton uniforms, and his playing style even got some national media attention when he was the subject of a "Sports Illustrated" article. Hudler is certainly capable of having another .300 season.

	AB	R	HR	RBI	SB	BA	$
1995 California AL	223	30	6	27	13	.265	10
1996 California AL	302	60	16	40	14	.311	15

HUFF, MICHAEL - OF - BR - Age 33
Huff tried first base and third base in addition to playing the outfield with Syracuse and earned a brief return to the big team. At thirty-three years old, he's obviously no longer a prospect but could hang on as a role-player. His best bet is to try landing a bench role somewhere.

HUGHES, BOBBY - C - BR - Age 26
Hughes hit just .200 at Triple-A, although he did better at Double-A on the Brewers farm.

HULSE, DAVID - OF - BL - Age 29
Team injuries and front office friends provided Hulse more opportunity than his performance warranted. The acquisitions of Burnitz, Newfield and Williams and the return of Chuck Carr will impact Hulse in Milwaukee, and may lead to a spell in the minors.

	AB	R	HR	RBI	SB	BA	$
1995 Milwaukee AL	339	46	3	47	15	.251	11
1996 Milwaukee AL	117	18	0	6	4	.222	-

HUNDLEY, TODD - C - BB - Age 27
In a season noted for the successful assault on Roy Campanella's all-time record for home runs by a catcher, Hundley established himself as the best all-around catcher in the game. He even played much of the year with an ailing wrist.

	AB	R	HR	RBI	SB	BA	$
1995 New York NL	275	39	15	51	1	.280	10
1996 New York NL	540	85	41	112	1	.259	16

HUNTER, BRIAN L. - OF - BR - Age 26
After an impressive debut as a rookie in 1995, Hunter did not progress as much as had been hoped in 1996. His strongest asset is speed but he needs work on his defense in center field. Hunter has good tools and is young enough to have a productive major league career if he is able to improve his defense and plate discipline.

	AB	R	HR	RBI	SB	BA	$
1995 Houston NL	321	52	2	28	24	.302	16
1996 Houston NL	526	74	5	35	35	.276	18

HUNTER, BRIAN R. - 1B - BR - Age 29
Hunter gave the Mariners an effective platoon with Paul Sorrento; he also appeared in 29 games last year. A lifetime .231 hitter going into 1996, Hunter hit a career best .268 and poked seven home runs in 198 at-bats. He is destined to remain in the first base platoon, but could see more playing time with a full year under his belt. A former Atlanta prospect who never reached his potential in the NL, Hunter may be a modest surprise in 1997.

	AB	R	HR	RBI	SB	BA	$
1995 Cincinnati NL	79	9	1	9	2	.215	0
1996 Seattle AL	198	21	7	28	0	.268	2

HUNTER, SCOTT - OF - BR - Age 21
Hunter is a speedy outfielder obtained by the Mets from the Dodgers for Brett Butler. At Port St. Lucie in 1996 (high Class A) Hunter hit .257 with 49 stolen bases. His project for 1997 is to show progress with his hitting while moving up to Double-A.

HUNTER, TORII - OF - BR - Age 21
Hunter had a decent season (.263, seven homers) at Double-A and hit well in the second half. A first-round pick in '93, he'll be at least a fourth outfielder in the big leagues but needs to produce more in '97.

HURST, JIMMY - OF - BR - Age 25
Hurst, a 6-6, 225-pound package of power, had trouble making contact in Class A, but moved up to Double-A anyway. He hit .265 with 19 stolen bases on the Brewers farm in 1996.

HUSKEY, BUTCH - 3B - BR - Age 25
The much-heralded Huskey finally spent a full year in the majors in 1996, playing some rightfield before Alex Ochoa came up, and filling in for the injured Rico Brogna at firstbase.

	AB	R	HR	RBI	SB	BA	$
1995 New York NL	90	8	3	11	1	.189	-
1996 New York NL	414	43	15	60	1	.278	11

HUSON, JEFF - SS/2B - BL - Age 32
Huson was released by the Orioles in 1996 and spent the final weeks of the minor league season with Triple-A Colorado Springs. He signed a minor league contract with the Rockies at the end of the 1996 season which includes an invitation to big-league spring training. Huson is likely to challenge for a job as a utility infielder for the Rockies in 1997.

HYERS, TIM - 1B - BL - Age 25
Hyers has played in three organizations. He probably won't do more than pinch hit and spot duty in the major leagues.

HYZDU, ADAM - OF - BR - Age 25
Hyzdu had his best season yet for Double-A Trenton, finally showing the power that was expected when the Giants drafted him number one in 1990. He hit .337 with a team-leading 25 homers and 80 RBI. He's not a highly regarded prospect within the Red Sox organization, but Hyzdu could draw some attention with a fast start at Triple-A Pawtucket in 1997.

IBANEZ, RAUL - OF - BL - Age 24
A converted catcher, Ibanez got a double promotion in 1996, reaching the majors for a cup of coffee in 1996. After hitting .368 in a short stint in Double-A, Ibanez showed power for Tacoma. He hit 20 homers with 108 RBI in A-ball in 1995. Ibanez is not a good outfielder and wasn't a good catcher, either. His bat will carry him back to the majors, but how much playing time he'll get may depend upon his finding a position he can handle.

INCAVIGLIA, PETE - OF - BR - Age 32
Incaviglia was traded to the Orioles by the Phillies late in 1996 as they went on a youth movement. He provided bench strength for the Orioles in their pennant drive, and he did not disappoint them, delivering several clutch homers. He may not be in the Orioles plans for 1997, so it's likely that he will sign with another team needing a power hitting left fielder or DH. Inky's still capable of hitting 20 homers in a season, but his average will be around .250.

	AB	R	HR	RBI	SB	BA	$
1996 Philadelphia NL	269	33	16	42	2	.234	3
1996 Baltimore AL	33	4	2	8	0	.303	-

INGRAM, GAREY - 3B - BR - Age 26
Triple-A roster filler, Ingram managed two brief trials for the Dodgers in 1994 and 1995. His role of emergency infield reserve has be taken over by Chad Fonville. He hasn't hit over .270 in the minors since 1992.

INGRAM, RICCARDO - OF - BR - Age 30
Once a power-hitting prospect with the Tigers, Ingram's star faded and it appears that Triple-A is the highest level he will achieve. He's been in the Twins organization, and he played with the Padres Triple-A club last year hitting a poor .249.

ISON, JOHNNY - OF - BR - Age 23
In only his second pro season, Oriole prospect Isom was named to the Single-A Carolina League post-season all-star team last year, one of the tougher Single-A leagues. His 104 RBI led the league. Isom hit for a good average for the second year in a row, and he showed some power. Isom's power should improve as he matures.

JACKSON, DAMIAN - SS - BR - Age 23
Once a premium prospect who started in Double-A at age 20, Jackson has shown minimal progress since. He still envisions himself as a power hitter despite his size (5'10", 160 pounds), his stolen base total was the lowest of his five-year career, and he is still prone to careless errors despite excellent range at shortstop. Enrique Wilson is ready to pass him, and Omar Vizquel is entrenched in the majors, so Jackson needs a change of scenery to get a major league opportunity.

JACKSON, DARRIN - OF - BR - Age 33
Jackson spent 1995 and 1996 as one of the Seibu Lions' better power threats. He has expressed an interest in returning to the U.S. and would be a fine platoon player who can hit .280 with occasional power.

JACKSON, GAVIN - SS - BR - Age 23
A decent prospect who advanced two levels to Triple-A in 1996, Jackson handles the glove well enough although he's a little weak with the bat. He has almost no power and not enough speed to be a successful base thief in the majors. Jackson is young enough to advance, but has better prospects in front of him with the Red Sox.

JACKSON, JEFF - OF - BR - Age 25
The legend of the "Guy Picked Before Frank Thomas" continued to grow. He has struck out once every three at-bats in his six-year pro career. Jackson fell to Class A and independent ball in 1996.

JACKSON, RYAN - 1B/OF - BL - Age 25
Jackson missed all but the last week of the 1996 season after knee surgery. This was the last thing that a guy who was slated to skip a level to Double-A needed. He is now 25 years old, and has yet to play at that level.

JAHA, JOHN - 1B - BR - Age 30
A poor man's Mark McGwire, Jaha was in some danger of being cut loose after the 1994 season, but posted a career year in 1995, despite playing in only 88 games. He remained healthy in 1996, and gave the Brewers what they asked: back to back good seasons. Will he stay at his 1996 level? Injuries and slumps have enabled Jaha to have but two full major league seasons. A late arrival in the majors, he's now 30 and 1996 was only his second season with more than 500 AB. Other negatives: Jaha had a career high number of strikeouts and his average against right handed pitching was significantly below his 1995 performance, so it may be foolish to expect improvement.

	AB	R	HR	RBI	SB	BA	$
1995 Milwaukee AL	316	59	20	65	2	.313	15
1996 Milwaukee AL	543	108	34	118	3	.300	21

JAMES, DION - OF - BL - Age 34
James quietly became important after the Yankees jettisoned Luis Polonia in late 1995. In 1996 James appeared just briefly in the minors.

JARRETT, LINK - 2B - BB - Age 25
This former Florida State All-American spent 1996 as a back-up infielder at Class A Salem and Double-A New Haven in the Rockies organization. He is competent defensively, but has posted weak offensive numbers in his three-year pro career.

JAVIER, STAN - OF - BB - Age 33
Another of the Giants walking wounded of 1996, Javier pulled a hamstring at the end of the pre season and never fully recovered. He is a good fourth outfielder but not a full-fledged starter, and he'll fill that role in San Francisco in 1997.

	AB	R	HR	RBI	SB	BA	$
1995 Oakland AL	442	81	8	56	36	.278	26
1996 San Francisco NL	274	44	2	22	14	.270	7

JEFFERIES, GREGG - 1B - BB - Age 29
Jefferies spent two months on the disabled list in 1996, but a late surge gave him respectable numbers. Though he had a solid batting average and was aggressive on the bases, he had the lowest slugging percentage (.401) among regular NL first basemen. He is an ideal number two hitter who can be an excellent complementary player on a good club.

	AB	R	HR	RBI	SB	BA	$
1995 Philadelphia AL	480	69	11	56	9	.306	18
1996 Philadelphia NL	404	59	7	51	20	.292	17

JEFFERSON, REGGIE - 1B - BB - Age 28

Can this guy hit or what? Jefferson started slowly in 1996 due to injury, then settled in to hit for average and power in a platoon role. He was used as a DH, first baseman and outfielder, but he's a weak outfielder and Mo Vaughn has first base covered. So, the Red Sox will have to find a way to get his bat in the lineup without compromising their defense (remember: Jose Canseco also plays for this team).

	AB	R	HR	RBI	SB	BA	$
1995 Boston AL	121	21	5	26	0	.289	3
1996 Boston AL	386	67	19	74	0	.347	16

JENNINGS, DOUG - 1B - BL - Age 32

After trials with the Cubs, Athletics and Reds, Jennings went to Japan. He slumped to a .220 average in 1996, but poked 14 home runs for the Blue Wave.

JENNINGS, ROBIN - OF - BL - Age 24

A pretty lefthanded swinger with good natural pop, Jennings hardly runs at all and doesn't have much range in the outfield but has a good arm. Jennings, who was born in the Republic of Singapore, led the Arizona Fall league in hitting in 1995. The Cubs would like to get him into the majors, but if they sign a big name free agent to play left field, Jennings would most likely return to Iowa.

	AB	R	HR	RBI	SB	BA	$
1996 Chicago NL	58	7	0	4	1	.224	-

JENSEN, MARCUS - C - BB - Age 24

Jensen will be the number two catcher for San Francisco this year after putting up respectable numbers over a full season at Triple-A last year. He even got a September call-up, getting a taste of the future. He has patience, a little pop and good defense. He'll be the man behind the plate full time in 1998.

JETER, DEREK - SS - BR - Age 22

If he had arrived in any other year (i.e. without Alex Rodriguez in Seattle), Jeter would be drawing comparisons to Barry Larkin and Ernie Banks. After just one year in the majors, it's obvious that Jeter compares favorably to all-time Yankee shortstops going back through Tony Kubek and Phil Rizzuto. Jeter is better than steady on defense, and his hitting stats don't fully reflect an unusual ability to get big hits in critical situations.

	AB	R	HR	RBI	SB	BA	$
1995 New York AL	48	5	0	7	0	.250	-
1996 New York AL	582	104	10	78	14	.314	20

JIMENEZ, MANNY - SS - BR - Age 25

A seven-year pro from the Dominican Republic, Jiminez has advanced slowly through the Braves chain to reach Double-A Greenville last year. Although he has great speed (71 stolen bases in 1995), he isn't a good hitter and is not a dominant defensive shortstop, either. Jiminez is a long shot to reach the majors as a reserve.

JOHNS, KEITH - SS - BR - Age 25

Johns' second year at Double-A Arkansas was less impressive than his first. He's a super fielder whose hitting has always been suspect. Unless he can show more with the bat, his only chance will be as a utility infielder.

JOHNSON, BRIAN D. - C - BR - Age 29

Johnson is one of the better hitting back-up catchers in the majors. He got more playing time last year, and had his career-best year. Johnson could probably be a starter on other clubs, and he could even take over the Padres catching job if incumbent John Flaherty goes into a bad hitting slump.

	AB	R	HR	RBI	SB	BA	$
1995 San Diego NL	207	20	3	29	0	.251	2
1996 San Diego NL	243	18	8	35	0	.272	5

JOHNSON, CHARLES - C - BR - Age 25
Johnson is arguably the most devastating defensive force behind the plate since Johnny Bench. Johnson threw out 47.6% of would-be basestealers, and allowed only .40 baserunners per nine innings to successfully steal - both figures led the NL by wide margins. Offensively, well, he's got some work to do. He has battled through sub-.200 first halves in both of his seasons as a starter, but has shown above-average pop for a receiver. He has the tools to be a .250 average, 20 homer producer - such performance would raise him near the Piazza/Rodriguez level in terms of overall value to his club.

	AB	R	HR	RBI	SB	BA	$
1995 Florida NL	315	40	11	39	0	.251	6
1996 Florida NL	386	34	13	37	1	.218	-

JOHNSON, EARL - OF - BB - Age 25
The Padres have high expectations for Johnson, a fast outfielder who stole 94 bases back in 1994 in Single-A. His stolen base production has declined in recent years, and he hit a weak .252 last year in Double-A. He's a Lance Johnson-type player, but he needs to improve his hitting to make progress towards the majors. His defense is excellent, a plus in his favor.

JOHNSON, ERIK - 2B - BR - Age 31
Johnson is a ten-year minor league journeyman who has bounced through the Giants, Pirates, and now the Marlins' chains, accumulating 18 major league at-bats along the way. He was a Triple-A backup in 1996, and was a non-factor with the bat, compiling a .209 on-base percentage and .211 slugging percentage. He can play multiple positions, but that's the only attraction at this point.

JOHNSON, J.J. - OF - BR - Age 23
Johnson regained his status as a minor prospect in '96 at Double-A after he came across from Boston via trade. He is a corner outfielder who can provide ten homers a year for the Twins if he continues to progress.

JOHNSON, LANCE - OF - BL - Age 33
At an age when many speed-oriented offensive players are beginning to fade, Johnson soared to new heights. He shattered Mets' franchise records for hits, triples and multi-hit games. Also impressive was his RBI total compiled in a season when he started every game by coming to the plate with the bases empty, and when he didn't hit a ton of home runs.

	AB	R	HR	RBI	SB	BA	$
1995 Chicago AL	607	98	10	57	40	.306	35
1996 Chicago AL	682	117	9	69	50	.333	45

JOHNSON, MARK - C - BL - Age 21
The White Sox' 1994 first round pick has been a disappointment with the bat thus far in his pro career, generally batting in the low-.200's with little extra-base power, though he has shown extreme patience, consistently laying off bad pitches. Defensively, he is durable with an above average throwing arm and solid defensive mechanics. With a lack of catching prospects ahead of him, Johnson will advance once his bat catches up to his glove.

JOHNSON, MARK - 1B - BL - Age 29
After he got off to a good start last season, the Pirates were fooled into thinking he could solve their problems at first base and cleanup. However, he hit just one homer while playing regularly in the season's final two months. He's now 29 and spent three straight years at Double-A before making his major league debut in 1995. It was quite silly of the Pirates to think he could suddenly turn into the next Willie Stargell.

	AB	R	HR	RBI	SB	BA	$
1995 Pittsburgh NL	221	32	13	28	5	.208	5
1996 Pittsburgh NL	343	55	13	47	6	.274	10

JOHNSON, RUSS - SS - BR - Age 24
Johnson was the Southeastern Conference Player of the Year as Todd Walker's double play partner at LSU in 1994. He began his professional career at Double-A Jackson in 1995. In his second year at Double-A in 1996, he was an All Star (.310-15-74-9). He is the top shortstop prospect in the Astro organization and should play at the Triple-A level in 1997. He could be a major league regular in 1998.

JOHNSON, TODD - C - BR - Age 26
The Indians think so highly of Johnson that they have loaned him out to independent High-A Bakersfield of the California League both of the last two seasons. No wonder - Johnson hit for one of the lowest averages (.238) with virtually no power in a hitters' park in a hitters' league.

JONES, ANDRUW - OF - BR - Age 20
As an 18-year-old, Jones tore through the low minors in 1995. As a 19-year-old, he did the same in the high minors in 1996. Jones was named Baseball America's minor league player of the year both years, just the second repeat winner in the sixteen year history of the award (Gregg Jefferies in 1986-7 was the first). Jones advanced from Class A Durham, to Double-A Greenville, to make a cursory stop at Triple-A Richmond before finally joining the big Braves in Atlanta for the stretch drive and the post season. His season totals - .316-39-105-33 with a .612 slugging average - are enough to make any pitcher gag. As we said last year, it's too early even to guess at a limit of Jones' potential; he can do it all.

	AB	R	HR	RBI	SB	BA	$
1996 Atlanta NL	106	11	5	13	3	.217	-

JONES, CHIPPER - 3B - BB - Age 24
Thirty homers, a hundred RBI and a .300 average are perennial possibilities for Jones. His defense improved in 1996 and he stole a few bases, too. Jones was the hitter that drove the Braves offense last year. He's the best player on the best team in the NL; and he's just 24 years old. Jones is on the verge of some big years.

	AB	R	HR	RBI	SB	BA	$
1995 Atlanta NL	524	87	23	86	8	.265	19
1996 Atlanta NL	598	114	30	110	14	.309	32

JONES, CHRIS - OF - BR - Age 31
Jones has successfully kept a major league role as an off-the-bench player, by providing good pinch hitting against southpaws and by offering passable defense in leftfield, rightfield and at first base. His days as a starter are long gone, however, and even for injury replacements the Mets had better and younger players at the end of 1996.

	AB	R	HR	RBI	SB	BA	$
1995 New York NL	182	33	8	31	2	.280	
1996 New York NL	149	22	4	18	1	.242	0

JONES, DAX - OF - BR - Age 26
Solid at Triple-A, weak in the bigs all the way around. The Giants wasted little time releasing him at the end of '96, and for a reason.

	AB	R	HR	RBI	SB	BA	$
1996 San Francisco NL	58	7	1	7	2	.172	-

JONES, JAIME - OF - BL - Age 20
The Marlins 1995 first round draftee suffered through an injury plagued and erratic first full pro season at Low-A Kane County. He did show flashes of a textbook lefthanded swing, with over 40% of his hits going for extra bases. However, he got himself out constantly, rarely walking and striking out in almost a third of his at-bats. At 6'4", 195 pounds, the Marlins expect him to develop into a .300 hitter with 25 homer power.

JONES, RYAN - 1B - BR - Age 22
Although he showed good power numbers, he has trouble laying off the high fastball. Defensively, he's improved dramatically and still has lots of time to learn. Jones could see action at Triple-A this year and is one of the top prospects in the Toronto organization.

JONES, TERRY - OF - BB - Age 26
Jones was the everyday center fielder for Triple-A Colorado Springs in 1996, leading the team in stolen bases, and improving his discipline at the plate. Because of the crowded outfield situation on the parent club, and the presence of the Jones-like Quinton McCracken, Jones will likely spend most of 1997 at the Triple-A level.

JORDAN, BRIAN - OF - BR - Age 30
The former Atlanta Falcons safety continued to make huge strides last season with the Cardinals. Now with five full years of baseball under his belt, Jordan is on the cusp of becoming one of the top players in the National League. He

hits for average and steal bases. The next step is becoming a 30-homer guy, which he'll do this year if he can put last season's wrist injury behind him.

	AB	R	HR	RBI	SB	BA	$
1995 St. Louis NL	490	83	22	81	24	.296	28
1996 St. Louis NL	513	82	17	104	22	.310	29

JORDAN, KEVIN - 2B - BR - Age 27
Shortly after earning a material major league role for the first time as a result of an injury to Gregg Jefferies, Jordan injured his knee and was lost for the bulk of the 1996 season. Jordan is an offensive force against lefties. He is an aggressive (to a fault) hitter who makes consistent contact with longball potential. Defensively, he was only average before his knee injury, but is valuable because of his ability to play middle and corner infield positions. Expect him to be a top Phils' reserve in 1997, earning 250 at-bats, with six-eight homers a distinct possibility.

	AB	R	HR	RBI	SB	BA	$
1995 Philadelphia NL	54	6	2	6	0	.185	-
1996 Philadelphia NL	131	15	3	12	2	.282	3

JORDAN, RICKY - 1B - BR - Age 31
Jordan reappeared briefly in a first base platoon experiment with Paul Sorrento in Seattle. The experiment ended before it had a chance to fail as Jordan went on the DL for the season with a knee injury after playing just 15 games.

JORGENSEN, RANDY - 1B - BL - Age 24
Jorgensen has hit for a good average in his four-year pro career, but not much power. He's an exceptional fielder, too. Jorgensen's slow bat will keep him from getting to the majors.

JOSE, FELIX - OF - BB - Age 31
This ex-star came to the Royals spring training camp overweight and out of shape in 1995 and has gone downhill ever since. He was at Triple-A on the Jays farm in 1996, hitting .257

JOYNER, WALLY - 1B - BL - Age 34
Joyner got off to a torrid start in his first National League stint, hitting .321 when he had the bad luck of fracturing his thumb sliding into second in early June causing him to miss six weeks. He's still a good .290-310 hitter, but the strong power stroke is gone. The power didn't appear last year, even though it was a rabbit-ball year.

	AB	R	HR	RBI	SB	BA	$
1995 Kansas City AL	465	69	12	83	3	.310	17
1996 San Diego NL	433	59	8	65	5	.277	11

JUSTICE, DAVID - OF - BL - Age 30
Surgery ended Justice's season after just 40 games in 1996, but the Braves filled rightfield nicely with Mark Whiten, Jermaine Dye and others. There was much speculation entering the off-season that Justice wouldn't be back with Atlanta in 1997; the Braves are deep in the outfield with Andruw Jones now ready to become a big-league regular. Justice is a good RBI hitter who is still in his prime; he'll produce wherever he plays.

	AB	R	HR	RBI	SB	BA	$
1995 Atlanta NL	411	73	24	78	4	.253	15
1996 Atlanta NL	140	23	6	25	1	.321	7

KARKOVICE, RON - C - BR - Age 33
Still has great defensive assets including a strong arm. He can still pop the occasional home run but is past his prime.

	AB	R	HR	RBI	SB	BA	$
1995 Chicago AL	323	44	13	51	2	.217	4
1996 Chicago AL	355	44	10	38	0	.220	-

KARROS, ERIC - 1B - BR - Age 29
Karros declined some from his peak of 1995, but his power and durability make him a valuable player for the Dodgers, who have a lineup full of players who are neither. Probably the biggest surprise of his season was his eight steals, after totaling eight steals in five previous seasons. Expect Karros to maintain this level of performance for a few more seasons, but he will be pushed by Paul Konerko (or possibly Mike Piazza) by 1998.

	AB	R	HR	RBI	SB	BA	$
1995 Los Angeles NL	551	83	32	105	4	.298	27
1996 Los Angeles NL	608	84	34	111	8	.260	17

KEEFE, JAMIE - 2B - BR - Age 23
Padres minor leaguer Keefe hit okay in the lower level Class A Midwest League last year, but struggled in the higher level Class A California League and in Double-A. He will probably start 1997 in Double-A.

KELLNER, FRANK - SS - BB - Age 30
Kellner spent all of 1996 at Triple-A Tucson after splitting time between Triple-A and Double-A for the previous four years. He is an organization player who is not considered a major league prospect.

KELLY, MIKE - OF - BR - Age 26
The top draft pick of the Braves in 1991, Kelly is all tools (good size, speed, and power) and few skills. He was handed the Reds center field job to start the season, but failed and then hit .209 in Triple-A. Until his strike zone judgment improves he will never hold a major league job, but his tools will continue to give him opportunities. The Reds do not have a shortage of outfield candidates, so Kelly will have to raise his level of play significantly to win a job.

	AB	R	HR	RBI	SB	BA	$
1995 Atlanta NL	137	26	3	17	7	.190	2
1996 Cincinnati NL	49	5	1	7	4	.184	-

KELLY, PAT - 2B - BR - Age 29
A truly superior athlete once projected to hit .280 with 15 homers and 15 steals per year, Kelly has never been healthy long enough to show much of anything. He still has a marvelous package of skills hidden by all those nagging injuries, and is still young enough to merit a starting role.

	AB	R	HR	RBI	SB	BA	$
1995 New York AL	270	32	4	29	8	.237	5
1996 New York AL	21	4	0	2	0	.143	-

KELLY, ROBERTO - OF - BR - Age 32
Have you noticed how players such as Kelly always succeed on a team such as the Twins? Perhaps it's because the blue collar Twins have a good atmosphere, and Tom Kelly knows how to use a bench. Kelly hit .406 against lefties in '96.

	AB	R	HR	RBI	SB	BA	$
1995 Two Teams	504	58	7	57	19	.278	17
1996 Minnesota AL	322	41	6	47	10	.323	12

KENDALL, JASON - C - BR - Age 22
Kendall had quite a rookie season, hitting .300, making excellent contact and playing in the All-Star Game after making the jump from Double-A. However, don't punch his ticket to Cooperstown yet. It was a weak .300 and Kendall has never exhibited much power in his whole career. Furthermore, his throwing mechanics are poor and the Pirates have considered the possibility of eventually moving him to second base, a la Craig Biggio.

	AB	R	HR	RBI	SB	BA	$
1996 Pittsburgh NL	414	54	3	42	5	.300	13

KENDALL, JEREMY - OF - BR - Age 25
A speedster who stole 62 bases in 1994, Kendall was dealt a severe blow by a badly broken arm in 1995 which cost him a crucial developmental year. After being overmatched at Double-A Reading in the Phils' chain, Kendall continued his struggles with the bat in A-ball. A leadoff man needing plate discipline is not a desirable commodity - only his ability to go get the ball in center field and his basestealing ability will keep him gainfully employed in the baseball business for another season or two.

KENNEDY, DAVE - 1B - BR - Age 26
This Northern League veteran's power production fell off somewhat in 1996, possibly due in part to the fact that he was platooned rather than an everyday player. Due to the wealth of 1B talent in the Rockies system, he may be more valuable as a 1B/DH elsewhere in 1997.

KENNEDY, DARRYL - C - BR - Age 28
Surprisingly, Kennedy got the hang of Triple-A pitching last year, batting .307 over 192 at-bats for Phoenix. At 28 he's probably not ever going to be much more than a back up, but hey, who among us wouldn't sell our soul for a chance to be even that?

KENNEDY, JUSTIN - OF - BL - Age 19
The Phils' 1995 38th round pick was impressive enough early last spring to earn the starting left field job at Low-A Piedmont, but he was overmatched. The Phils envision him as a speedy, slashing gap hitter, but he has shown an urge to swing at nearly every pitch with home run intentions. He is extremely raw, and the possibility that the burst that earned him the job in the first place was a fluke, but Kennedy will get another chance at the same level in 1997. Even league-average performance will stamp him as a player to watch.

KENT, JEFF - 2B - BR - Age 29
Getting a second chance in the National League, Kent went from an above-average offensive second baseman in the NL in to a little-used backup corner infielder in the AL in 1996. Kent is a free swinger with decent power for a middle infielder. He has poor defensive mechanics at every position he has played - witness the great "scoop" at first base in the AL playoffs. He's still young enough to have a productive major league future. Now he won't have to wait for expansion to be a starter again.

	AB	R	HR	RBI	SB	BA	$
1995 New York NL	472	65	20	65	3	.278	15
1996 New York NL	335	45	9	39	4	.290	10
1996 Cleveland AL	102	16	3	16	2	.265	1

KESSINGER, KEITH - SS - BB - Age 30
Kessinger retired to be an assistant coach at his alma mater, Ole Miss.

KIESCHNICK, BROOKS - OF - BL - Age 24
A power hitting lefthanded batter, Kieschnick was the Cubs first pick in the 1993 draft. He played leftfield and firstbase in '96. He doesn't run well at all and has an average glove and a strong arm. He still strikes out too much for his power output, but he is one of the few true power prospects in the Cubs chain. Because the Cubs have a wealth of outfielders and Brant Brown and Mark Grace at first, Kieschnick is one of the few tradable Cubs prospects with some value.

KILLEEN, TIM - C - BL - Age 26
Although Killeen hit only .259 last year, it was in the tough Double-A Southern League. He also showed a little power, another plus for him. But he has a big swing, striking out 25-30 percent of the time, an area he needs to improve. Lefthanded hitting catchers are a rarity, giving Killeen an advantage.

KING, BRETT - SS - BR - Age 24
A little power (34 extra-base hits), a little speed (19 steals) and a lot of strikeouts (119). King is improving, but he has an awful long way to go.

KING, JEFF - 3B/1B - BR - Age 32
If King hadn't played on a last-place team, he would have been considered one of the most valuable players in the National League last season. He had career-best numbers and also spent a majority of the season at second base, where he played well despite limited experience. At age 31, last year was likely the season of his life but he is a solid run producer.

	AB	R	HR	RBI	SB	BA	$
1995 Pittsburgh NL	445	61	18	87	7	.265	16
1996 Pittsburgh NL	591	91	30	111	15	.271	21

KINGERY, MIKE - OF - BL - Age 36
Kingery was a major bust last season after the Pirates signed him as a free agent in the offseason with hopes he could fill their holes at center field and leadoff. He got off to a difficult start. Though he rebounded somewhat, he was long gone from the starting lineup, having lost his job in early May. He is a terrific person who was asked to be something he's not. He would still make a good bench player, though the 36-year-old went into the offseason contemplating retirement.

	AB	R	HR	RBI	SB	BA	$
1995 Colorado NL	350	66	8	37	13	.269	11
1996 Pittsburgh NL	276	32	3	27	2	.246	1

KINGSALE, GENE - OF - BB - Age 20
The speedy Kingsale was added to the Orioles major league roster in September in case they needed a pinch runner. Previously, he was in Single-A. In 1997, to get more experience, it's likely that he will start in Double-A with a possible promotion to Triple-A, followed by the majors. Kingsale has the distinction of being the first native of Aruba to play in the majors.

KINGSTON, MARK - 3B - BR - Age 27
A switch-hitting third baseman, Kingston struggled at the plate in '96. He didn't show any power and struck out far too much.

KIRBY, WAYNE - OF - BL - Age 33
An aging platoon outfielder whose only real strengths are defense and above average speed, Kirby was acquired to help plug the hole in center field when Brett Butler and Roger Cedeno went down. He could grab a piece of the center field job in 1997, but don't expect much offensive production if he did.

	AB	R	HR	RBI	SB	BA	$
1995 Cleveland AL	188	29	1	14	10	.207	3
1996 Cleveland AL	16	3	0	1	0	.250	-
1996 Los Angeles NL	188	23	1	11	4	.271	3

KIRGAN, CHRIS - 1B - BL - Age 23
Kirgan is a distant relative of Ty Cobb, but he didn't inherit the Hall-of-Famer's genes, at least when it comes to stolen bases because he's a big lumbering power-hitter. Although he played all year in Single-A, he won the minors overall RBI crown in 1996 with 131, and he ranked third with 35 homers. All of his hitting was in the California League, a hitter's paradise, but such statistics are still worth noting. The bad news is that he struck out about 30 percent of the time.

KIRKPATRICK, JAY - 1B - BL - Age 27
Kirkpatrick missed most of 1996 with an injury, then played primarily at DH after his return. He has a little pop in his bat, but he's far too old to be playing at Double-A. Kirkpatrick is no prospect.

KLESKO, RYAN - OF - BL - Age 25
A streaky hitter, Klesko is quickly becoming one of the NL's most feared power hitters. He hits the ball a long way, when he makes contact. Klesko still has some holes in his swing, although they aren't as large as they once were. Now entering his "growth" years as a hitter, Klesko could put up some truly huge numbers over the next few seasons.

	AB	R	HR	RBI	SB	BA	$
1995 Atlanta NL	329	48	23	70	5	.310	19
1996 Atlanta NL	528	90	34	93	6	.282	21

KMAK, JOE - C - BR - Age 33
The poster child for the word journeyman. He didn't make his major league debut until age 30, and three years later was no better than a Triple-A backup in the Reds' chain. Kmak has middling defensive skills and swings a powerless bat.

KNAPP, MIKE - C - BR - Age 32
Knapp has been in the minors for eleven years, most of the last seven in Triple-A. His job is to help develop the pitching prospects in an organization, so his .190 batting average in 1996 can be ignored. Knapp has no hope of getting to the majors as a player.

KNOBLAUCH, CHUCK - 2B - BR - Age 28
Knoblauch raised his game yet another notch to the MVP level in '96. The future of the Twins rested to a large degree on signing him to a long term contract, and this was accomplished. In the battle for the best second baseman in the game; Roberto Alomar may be a little better hitter than Knoblauch, and Craig Biggio does just about everything Knoblauch does. But no GM in baseball would trade Knoblauch for any other second baseman.

	AB	R	HR	RBI	SB	BA	$
1995 Minnesota AL	538	107	11	63	46	.333	41
1996 Minnesota AL	578	140	13	72	45	.341	39

KNOWLES, ERIC - SS - BR - Age 23
An error-prone shortstop early in his pro career, Knowles has grown steadier in the field and hits just enough (.245-7-42 at Double-A Norwich in 1996) to remain a candidate for advancement to the majors.

KNORR, RANDY - C - BR - Age 28
Knorr's contract was purchased from Toronto by Houston in May 1996. He finished the season as the third catcher. A .230 hitter with limited power, Knorr is a major league backup catcher, at best.

	AB	R	HR	RBI	SB	BA	$
1995 Toronto AL	132	18	3	16	0	.212	-
1996 Houston NL	87	7	1	7	0	.195	-

KOELLING, BRIAN - 2B - BR - Age 27
Koelling spent the season on the Triple-A Scranton-Wilkes Barre (Phillies) disabled list after being obtained from the Reds in exchange for Mariano Duncan late in 1995. His spot is far from secure for 1997 as second base is one of the few well-fortified positions in the Phils' chain. Koelling is a speedy spray hitter with acceptable defensive skills, but has no singular ability which will return him to the bigs.

KONERKO, PAUL - 1B/C - BR - Age 21
Like most of the Dodgers' catching prospects, Konerko shifted positions in 1996, playing primarily at first base while leading Double-A San Antonio in most hitting categories. His 29 homers were more than twice as many as the second-best slugger had on that team. The Dodgers' top pick in the 1994 draft, this guy has real power; it's rare to see so many homers from someone so young, despite the Texas League's high-offense tendencies. Konerko will be a good power hitter in the majors; the only real questions are when he'll get there and where he'll play.

KOSCO, BRYN - 3B - BL - Age 30
While suffering through knee problems and surgery, Kosco missed all but 26 games in '96. The Cubs released the 30-year-old late in the season.

KOSLOFSKI, KEVIN - OF - BL - Age 30
Long-time Royals prospect Koslofski platooned at Triple-A New Orleans in 1995, hitting just .212 with 100 strikeouts in 312 at-bats. He has "career minor leaguer" written all over him, after hitting .231 in 1996.

KOTSAY, MARK - OF - BR - Age 21
The Marlins drafted Kotsay with the ninth pick in the first round of the 1996 draft. His lack of raw tools has prejudiced scouts against him at every turn, but all he does is produce. He adjusted easily to the wooden bat, driving the ball consistently to the gaps and showing extreme patience in his brief Low-A trial at the end of 1996. Whatever it takes, Kotsay will get it done. He will eventually be a productive, Mike Greenwell-like number two hitter in the majors, likely by the end of 1998.

KOWITZ, BRIAN - OF - BL - Age 27
Kowitz has on-base ability but had a difficult season in 1996. His playing time evaporated as he spiraled down to a .222-1-22 season. Kowitz is barely twelve months removed from his ten at-bat trial with the Braves in 1995. Kowitz will probably try to hook on with another organization in 1997, but he is beginning to look like a career minor leaguer.

KREUTER, CHAD - C - BB - Age 32
The pitching staff just loves this guy. When he went down with a season ending injury many of the players wore Chad's number on their caps in honor of him. You might think he was the everyday catcher but he wasn't. He's not a good hitter and doesn't have much power.

	AB	R	HR	RBI	SB	BA	$
1995 Seattle AL	75	12	1	8	0	.227	-
1996 Chicago AL	114	14	3	18	0	.219	-

LADELL, CLEVELAND - OF - BR - Age 26
Ladell is a five year minor league veteran of the Reds' system with one marketable tool - speed. He has poor plate discipline, little power for an outfielder, and an inconsistent uppercut swing, but has averaged 26 steals per season.

LADJEVICH, RICK - 3B - BR - Age 25
Ladjevich has always hit for a high average. His limitation is a lack of power. He's an above-average fielder, but, at age 25 and still in Double-A, Ladjevich is not on track for major league stardom.

LAKER, TIM - C - BR - Age 27
Laker, a favorite of Expos manager Felipe Alou, missed the 1996 season after undergoing reconstructive elbow surgery. Laker has never established much of a track record as a hitter in the majors and now he is coming off major surgery. Despite all the question marks, Montreal planned not to pick up the option year on Darrin Fletcher's contract and go into 1997 with Laker as its starting catcher. It's an interesting decision.

LAMPKIN, TOM - C - BL - Age 33
Lampkin, is a serviceable back-up catcher, but his San Francisco days are numbered because starter Rick Wilkins is a lefthanded hitter and of the existence of Marcus Jensen.

	AB	R	HR	RBI	SB	BA	$
1995 San Francisco NL	76	8	1	9	2	.276	1
1996 San Francisco NL	177	26	6	29	1	.232	0

LANE, RYAN - SS/2B - BR - Age 22
Lane emerged as one of the best prospects in the Twins system in '96 as he hit .272-9-62-21 at high Class A. He is a second baseman who rates a bit above average in each area without having a dominant tool. Lane projects as a good regular player after he spends another two years in the minors.

LANKFORD, RAY - OF - BL - Age 29
Lankford quietly had another fine season in 1996 and played a bigger role in the Cardinals winning their first division title in nine years than he got credit for. Lankford has never turned into the type of player that hits .300 with 30 homers, 100 RBIs and 30 steals, causing some to term him an underachiever. That's not fair. He'll be good for .280-20-90-20 for many years to come.

	AB	R	HR	RBI	SB	BA	$
1995 St. Louis NL	483	81	25	82	24	.277	27
1996 St. Louis NL	545	100	21	86	35	.275	24

LANSING, MIKE - 2B - BR - Age 28
Lansing is an underrated player. He is one of the better second basemen in the National League with good power and speed. In a lot of ways, he is the heart and soul of the Expos. He figures to have many more good years ahead of him.

	AB	R	HR	RBI	SB	BA	$
1995 Montreal NL	467	47	10	62	27	.255	19
1996 Montreal NL	641	99	11	53	23	.285	21

LARKIN, BARRY - SS - BR - Age 32
If the MVP means "most indispensable player on a pennant contender" Larkin would win every year. The only thing surprising about Larkin's season was his home run total, which exceeded his last three seasons combined. He may be slowing a little (his stolen base rate of 78% was his lowest since 1989) but the increased power more than compensates. His only weakness used to be staying healthy, but in the last three seasons he has missed only 25 games. Larkin probably needs four more good seasons to merit Hall of Fame consideration.

	AB	R	HR	RBI	SB	BA	$
1995 Cincinnati NL	496	98	15	66	51	.319	39
1996 Cincinnati NL	517	117	33	89	36	.298	32

LAROCCA, GREG - 2B - BR - Age 24
LaRocca had a solid but unspectacular season in Double-A last year. He hasn't shown much power or speed, just solid play with an occasional homer. He can also play shortstop, enhancing his promotion potential, and he could make the majors as a utility infielder.

LATHAM, CHRIS - OF - BB - Age 23
Latham is a decent prospect who came to Minnesota from Los Angeles in '95. His '96 season in Triple-A (.274-9-50-26) was good considering he was in A-ball in '95. Expect Latham to be a solid fourth outfielder.

LAWTON, MATT - OF - BL - Age 25
Lawton had a decent rookie year playing mainly rightfield for the retired Kirby Puckett. Lawton can steal 15 bases and hit .280, and he's solid defensively.

	AB	R	HR	RBI	SB	BA	$
1995 Minnesota AL	60	11	1	12	1	.317	1
1996 Minnesota AL	252	34	6	42	4	.258	4

LEACH, JALAL - OF - BL - Age 28
The former Yankees' farmhand moved over to the Expos' system in 1996, and had a fine season split between Double and Triple-A, batting a career-high .325. He has line drive power to the gaps, but his speed has deteriorated over the years, and he has shown little defensive aptitude or plate discipline.

LEARY, ROB - 1B - BL - Age 25
The Pirates thought they might have found a power-hitting first baseman in the rough after signing Leary out of the Northern League following the 1994 season. However, Leary couldn't cut it at Double-A and was released last June. He headed back to the Northern League and likely oblivion.

LeBRON, JUAN - OF - BR - Age 19
The Royals' top pick of 1995, LeBron came from a Puerto Rican high school. The Royals believe he's a pure hitter, but are worried about his defense.

LEDEE, RICKY - OF - BL - Age 23
Although he still has trouble with lefty pitchers, Ledee took a big step forward as a hitter in 1996, earning a midseason promotion. In the field he has fair range and a better-than-average arm.

LEDESMA, AARON - SS - BR - Age 25
Ledesma had a solid year in Triple-A last season, and he could be called up to the Angels when an injury occurs. He doesn't have any power or speed.

	AB	R	HR	RBI	SB	BA	$
1995 New York NL	33	4	0	3	0	.242	-

LEE, CARLOS - 3B - BR - Age 21
Lee is an intriguing offensive prospect with a natural swing that has only produced power to the gaps to date, though his 6'2", 205, frame should eventually produce 20 homers annually. He also has excellent raw speed, though he is still harnessing it. He is undisciplined at the plate, but is young enough to make the needed adjustments. Defensively, he is erratic, and may need to change positions down the road. The White Sox will eventually have to find a spot for his bat, however.

LEE, DEREK - OF - BL - Age 30
Don't let the name fool you: you want the one who plays for the Padres. Lee is a good minor league hitter with a little speed. His age should be a major deterrent to further advancement.

LEE, DERREK - 1B - BR - Age 21
The Padres' Derrek Lee is one of the top prospects in baseball. He had a great year in the Double-A Southern League last year, and was named the league MVP while also having the distinction at age 20 of being its youngest player. He showed tremendous power, but he also struck out 170 times in 500 at-bats, an area where improvement is needed. He is always in demand in trade talks, but the Padres have resisted all offers thus far. His growth is on track, and he should be in San Diego in 1997 for some playing time to gain experience. Lee's talented and there's a 30-homer year somewhere in his future.

LEIUS, SCOTT - 3B/SS - BR - Age 31
Leius evolved from a versatile utilityman on a weak team (Twins) in 1995 to a rarely used spare part on a great team (Indians) in 1996. Leius is a hard-working veteran who always gives you a professional at-bat, but his skills are

obviously slipping, especially at the plate. He will likely play everyday at third base in Triple-A for someone in 1997, and will be ready to help out in the bigs in the event of injuries.

	AB	R	HR	RBI	SB	BA	$
1995 Minnesota AL	372	51	4	45	2	.247	4
1996 Cleveland AL	43	3	1	3	0	.140	-

LEMKE, MARK - 2B - BB - Age 31
The defensive glue of the Braves' infield, Lemke plays the game the way it was meant to be played. He does all of the little things well and has a knack for the big play, especially in the post season. Tony Graffanino will eventually press Lemke for playing time, but 1997 should belong exclusively to Lemke.

	AB	R	HR	RBI	SB	BA	$
1995 Atlanta NL	399	42	5	38	2	.253	5
1996 Atlanta NL	498	64	5	37	5	.255	4

LENNON, PATRICK - OF - BR - Age 28
A speedy former first round picked who has now bounced around more than a super ball. Lennon had a good year in Edmonton in many ways, but he still swings at too many bad pitches.

LEONARD, MARK - OF - BL - Age 32
Leonard is a decent hitter, but can't do any one thing well enough to earn even a major league bench role. Every year is about the same for Leonard; he bides his time in Triple-A, awaiting the inevitable injury that gives him a chance for a few more major league at-bats. He can pop an occasional homer in a reserve role. Leonard is Triple-A injury insurance.

LESHER, BRIAN - OF - BR - Age 26
A first baseman in Edmonton who played in the outfield for Oakland after his call-up, Lesher has good power and has been a reliable RBI man. But, like so many young power hitters he swings too much and makes contact too little.

	AB	R	HR	RBI	SB	BA	$
1996 Oakland AL	82	11	5	16	0	.232	-

LeVANGIE, DANA - C - BR - Age 27
Three separate trips to the DL limited this organizational catcher to just 59 at-bats in 1996. LeVangie is no prospect.

LEVIS, JESSE - C - BL - Age 28
A lefthanded hitting backup catcher with a groundball stroke, Levis is no lock for a big league job. Despite clearly demonstrating that he can hit for average, with excellent patience, at the major league level, doubts about his defense and size (5'9", 180 lbs.) have reduced him to an afterthought in the system's eyes. He could fit in somewhere as a third catcher/lefthanded bat off the bench. It's at least as likely that he will settle in for the long haul at the Triple-A level.

	AB	R	HR	RBI	SB	BA	$
1995 Cleveland AL	18	1	0	3	0	.333	-
1996 Milwaukee AL	233	27	1	21	0	.236	-

LEWIS, ANTHONY - DH/OF - BL - Age 26
Signed away from the Cardinals as a minor league free agent, Lewis has pretty good power despite his diminutive stature (5'11", 185 lbs.) Lewis led Double-A New Britain with 95 RBI and was second with 24 homers in 1996. He'll make a try for his second appearance at Triple-A in 1997.

LEWIS, DARREN - OF - BR - Age 29
Not a banner year offensively for Lewis. He went from being the everyday centerfielder to a reserve role. His primary use by seasons end was as a pinch runner or defensive replacement in the outfield. The Sox had hoped to use him in the one or two spot in the batting order but his inability to hit for average or get on base put an end to that plan. He now sits in a crowded outfield situation with the likes of Dave Martinez and minor leaguers Jeff Abbott and Mike Cameron looking to take his roster spot.

	AB	R	HR	RBI	SB	BA	$
1995 Two Teams	472	66	1	24	32	.250	14
1996 Chicago AL	337	55	4	53	21	.228	10

LEWIS, MARC - OF - BR - 21
Obtained in the Mike Stanton deal late in 1995, Lewis made an immediate impression by hitting .315-5-28 with 25 steals for Class A Macon, earning a promotion to Durham. He already hits for average and has good speed; now he's adding power to his game. A versatile young outfielder, Lewis should start 1996 at Durham with a chance to move higher quickly.

LEWIS, MARK - 3B - BR - Age 27
Lewis played well in his first season as a major league regular since '92. He improved his defense at second as the season went on and showed some power. Lewis hits lefthanders well (.351 in '96) and slowed down with the bat in the second half.

	AB	R	HR	RBI	SB	BA	$
1995 Cincinnati NL	171	25	3	30	0	.339	6
1996 Detroit AL	545	69	11	55	6	.270	9

LEWIS, T.R. - OF/DH - BR - Age 25
Nearly a .300 hitter throughout his eight year minor league career (the first seven years on Orioles' farm clubs), Lewis had his best power season yet for Triple-A Pawtucket in 1996, hitting 14 homers and driving in 52 runs. Lewis has a decent batting eye; he could be a useful fourth outfielder in the majors. Boston's muddled outfield picture may allow him to break through to the bigs for the first time in 1997, perhaps in a reserve role. Lewis' bat has to carry him; he's a defensive liability.

LEYRITZ, JIM - 1B/C - BR - Age 33
A gritty competitor who became the longevity king in the Yankee clubhouse in 1996, Leyritz offers a variety of skills on offense and defense. He is good under pressure and is worth more than his stats would indicate.

	AB	R	HR	RBI	SB	BA	$
1995 New York AL	264	37	7	37	1	.269	5
1996 New York AL	265	23	7	40	2	.264	3

LIEBERTHAL, MIKE - C - BR - Age 25
Lieberthal established himself as a legitimate major league backup in 1996, as he was a positive surprise with the bat and a slight negative surprise with the glove and arm. The Phils are considering him as their everyday receiver for 1997. Bobby Estalella, not Lieberthal, is their catcher of the future.

	AB	R	HR	RBI	SB	BA	$
1995 Philadelphia NL	47	1	0	4	0	.255	-
1996 Philadelphia NL	166	21	7	23	0	.253	2

LIEFER, JEFF - 3B - BL - Age 22
Liefer showed excellent longball potential, as he was ranked the number two overall prospect and the best batting and power prospect in the Low-A Midwest League by Baseball America in 1996. The White Sox' 1995 first round pick then struggled mightily at High-A after being promoted. That struggle plus his defensive deficiencies are two reasons to not yet assume future major league dominance for Liefer. He will likely be a firstbaseman or leftfielder due to his erratic throwing arm, and he has yet to prove he possesses the consistent offensive punch necessary to play either position.

LINIAK, COLE - 3B - BR - Age 20
In just his second pro season Liniak showed a good batting eye and emerging power. Liniak is a good fielding third baseman, too. He was among the younger players in the Midwest League, so he has plenty of time to develop even further.

LIRIANO, NELSON - 2B - BB - Age 32
Liriano has become an outstanding pinch hitter in the latter stages of his career and is a competent utility player, though he can't really be trusted in the field anywhere other than second base. However, his value would lie more with a contending team than a rebuilding club like the Pirates. He was under contract with the Pirates for 1997 but will likely land elsewhere.

	AB	R	HR	RBI	SB	BA	$
1995 Pittsburgh NL	259	29	5	38	2	.286	7
1996 Pittsburgh NL	217	23	3	30	2	.267	3

LIS, JOE - 2B - BR - Age 28
Every organization needs a few guys like Lis - a versatile backup infielder at many positions who will take a pitch and hit the occasional longball. He is a prime candidate to bounce from chain to chain in similar roles in the coming seasons.

LISTACH, PAT - SS - BB - Age 29
After stealing 54 bases and hitting .290 as a rookie in 1992, Listach has spent the rest of his career just wishing his knees would stop aching. A perennial spring training success, Listach explains the situation better than anyone else can: "It's easy to feel healthy playing in 80-degree weather, but when you get off the plane up north in April, you never know what to expect."

	AB	R	HR	RBI	SB	BA	$
1995 Milwaukee AL	334	35	0	25	13	.219	4
1996 Milw-New York AL	317	51	1	33	25	.240	11

LITTLE, MARK - OF - BR - Age 24
Little is a genuine prospect following a nice year at Double-A. He was one of the few Rangers minor leaguers to attract trade interest in the 1995-96 offseason, and should eventually hit for average, with good power and decent speed.

LIVINGSTONE, SCOTT - 3B/DH - BL - Age 31
Livingstone was valuable to the Padres last season when he filled in at first base for the injured Wally Joyner. He's a reserve at first and third, and also a good pinch hitter. Livingstone doesn't have much power, but he usually hits for a solid average in the .280-300 range, with a lot of singles and numerous clutch hits.

	AB	R	HR	RBI	SB	BA	$
1995 San Diego NL	196	26	5	32	2	.337	8
1996 San Diego NL	172	20	2	20	0	.297	4

LOCKHART, KEITH - 2B/3B - BL - Age 32
The Lockhart-for-All-Star bandwagon careened off the road at midseason and hasn't been seen since. With no outstanding Kansas City candidates for the All-Star game and Lockhart hitting .313 at the break, there was speculation in that he would be the Royals' lone representative. Jeff Montgomery was selected instead and Lockhart proceeded to hit .227 in the second half. Lockhart has lost his regular role and will now have to platoon or serve as a reserve infielder.

	AB	R	HR	RBI	SB	BA	$
1995 Kansas City AL	274	41	6	33	8	.321	12
1996 Kansas City AL	433	49	7	55	11	.273	10

LOFTON, KENNY - OF - BL - Age 29
No one can quibble with his basestealing ability and excellence in the field, but his on-base percentage has hovered not far above the average of AL regulars in both of the past two seasons. He was only sixth on his own club in that department in 1996. He probably only has another season or two as the bulletproof league leader in steals, and his value will dissipate after that point.

	AB	R	HR	RBI	SB	BA	$
1995 Cleveland AL	481	93	7	53	54	.310	39
1996 Cleveland AL	662	132	14	67	75	.317	51

LOMBARD, GEORGE - OF - BL - Age 21
Lombard slumped early last year and did not start to blossom until July. He's got speed and power, but still hit for low average last year.

LONG, KEVIN - OF - BL - Age 30
Talked out of retirement after 1995, Long provided stability, a good batting eye and defense in the midst of the youthful Double-A Wichita lineup. Since none of his skills are of major league quality, Long can either continue in a teaching role in the high minors, or retire as planned.

LONG, RYAN - 3B - BR - Age 24
Long supplied a large portion of Double-A Wichita's power over the last half of the season, finishing with 20 homers and 78 RBI; both totals were second best on the team. Despite his power, Long's upward path probably goes no higher than Triple-A, since his fielding skills are merely average, he lacks good speed, and his batting eye is below average. Long is not in the Royals' long-range plans.

LONG, TERRENCE - OF - BR - Age 21
Long had a good year in the low Class A Sally League, hitting .288-12-78 with 32 stolen bases. He has been highly touted as a prospect but still has a lot to learn about the strike zone before being projected as a major leaguer.

LONGMIRE, TONY - OF - BL - Age 28
Longmire missed all of 1996 after surgery on the navicular bone in his right (throwing) wrist. This is the single slowest healing bone in the body, and has ended the careers of a few professional athletes, most recently hockey player Jeff Chychrun. At best, he will return without the power he exhibited in his breakout 1995 campaign as a Phils' backup. His career may be over, if so future Total Baseball readers will be intrigued by the mystery of the player who ended his career with a season in which he batted .356 with a .419 OBP and .510 SLG.

LOPEZ, JAVIER - C - BR - Age 26
As expected, Lopez added more power in 1996. The unexpected was his improvement behind the plate. The whole package is a high-average, moderate power catcher whose defense is now above average. His strike zone judgment improved, albeit slightly; Lopez's high strikeout rate remains his most obvious weak spot. Still, Lopez is one of the top five catchers in the game right now and is just 26 years old.

	AB	R	HR	RBI	SB	BA	$
1995 Atlanta NL	333	37	14	51	0	.315	13
1996 Atlanta NL	489	56	23	69	1	.282	15

LOPEZ, LUIS - 2B - BB - Age 26
After a solid 1994 season, Lopez was tabbed as the Padres starting second baseman at the beginning of 1995, but he tore a ligament in his elbow missing the entire season. Jody Reed took over, and did a good job. Lopez's role is now utility infielder, and he's a .250 hitter, at best.

	AB	R	HR	RBI	SB	BA	$
1995 San Diego NL	Did Not Play - Injured						
1996 San Diego NL	139	10	2	11	0	.180	-

LOPEZ, LUIS - OF - BR - Age 32
Lopez finally found success in Japan. He hit .315 with 22 home runs and 99 RBI for Hiroshima in 1996. He's a free swinger with extra-base power.

LOPEZ, MENDY - 3B - BR - Age 22
Defense and speed are Lopez's claim to fame. He passed an important test by hitting for average with Double-A Wichita in 1996 and will get another challenge when he moves to Omaha in 1997. Although he hasn't shown much pop in his bat, he is just 22 years old and beginning to fill out his 6'2" frame. Lopez is already skilled enough to play the hot corner in the big leagues and may soon get a chance should he turn in another good year in 1997.

LOPEZ, RENE - C - BR - Age 25
Lopez is a pretty good defensive catcher, but a relatively weak hitter. He has never hit more than seven homers or higher than .264 in his four years as a pro; his .237-3-30 season in 1996, split between Double-A and Triple-A is very much in line with his career numbers. Lopez is an organizational catcher.

LORETTA, MARK - SS - BR - Age 25
Loretta may evolve into a starter at short or second, but if he makes the club it'll be as the fifth infielder. At the plate Loretta can give the Brewers the same thing as Kevin Seitzer did for years; hitting close to .300, and performing well in the clutch. He has not shown much power, and any long ball he gets is a bonus.

	AB	R	HR	RBI	SB	BA	$
1995 Milwaukee AL	50	13	1	3	1	.260	-
1996 Milwaukee AL	154	20	1	13	2	.279	1

LOTT, BILLY - OF - BR - Age 26
Free-swinging Lott led Triple-A Albuquerque with 19 homers, but also led with 124 strikeouts. It was his fourth year out of the last five with 100+ whiffs and his career strikeout-to-walk ratio is nearly four to one. Lott could get to the majors, but he'd be strictly a one-shot bench jockey.

The curse of Sparky Anderson lies heavy on Torey. He has had his chances, and it looks like he has used them all up.

	AB	R	HR	RBI	SB	BA	$
1996 Oakland AL	82	15	3	9	1	.220	-

LOWERY, TERRELL - OF - BR - Age 26
Lowery never got back on track after an Achilles tendon injury ruined his 1995 season. In 1994 he stole 33 bases in a season, but collected only 11 in 1996, while hitting .233 in 195 at-bats for the Mets at Triple-A, and .275 in 211 at-bats at Double-A.

LUCCA, LOU - 3B - BR - Age 26
This 32nd round draftee rode a combination of a line drive, gap power bat and defensive steadiness to an improbable rise through the Marlins' chain. He crashed with a thud in 1996, as he compromised the patient hitting style he had previously used to his advantage and became overaggressive, walking only 11 times.

LUCE, ROGER - C - BR - Age 27
Luce has played six years in the minor leagues, splitting the last three between Double-A and Triple-A. He has not consistently hit for power or average and is not considered a prospect.

LUKACHYK, ROB - OF - BL - Age 28
Lukachyk's journey to the major leagues last season was interesting. Detroit released him from its minor league camp in spring training and he was working out at his home in Sarasota, Fla., hoping for a chance. The Expos signed him to a Triple-A Ottawa contract and he wound up spending a few days in the big leagues. He hit just .264 at Ottawa and chances are he'll be back in Sarasota for good before long.

LUKE, MATT - OF - BL - Age 26
An exciting power hitter three years ago in the Florida State League, Luke continues to impress with the home runs (19 in just 264 at-bats in 1996 for Triple-A Columbus) but age is becoming a factor in the outlook for his career.

LUULOA, KEITH - 2B - BR - Age 22
Angel prospect Luuloa needs to improve his hitting as .260 in the hitter-friendly Texas League shows his weakness. Even .350 averages in the Texas League are not truly reflective of a hitter's ability.

LUZINSKI, RYAN - C - BR - Age 23
A first round pick in 1992, Luzinski played at all three minor league levels in 1996. He has not yet developed the power shown by his dad Greg (or for that matter, the power shown by Greg Gagne) with 33 homers in 1503 minor league at-bats. His only five homers in 1996 were in Class-A. Luzinski could still develop, but right now he is not a prospect.

LYDY, SCOTT - OF - BR - Age 28
Lydy didn't hit during his first trip to the majors in 1993, and will apparently never get a second chance. He's a fourth outfielder at best, although he would be a good one. He was in Japan in 1996.

Got a Question? Ask John Benson

LIVE - Not a tape

1-900-773-7526

(900-PRE-PLAN)

Just $2.49 per minute 1PM - 11PM Eastern Time

MAAS, KEVIN - DH/1B - BL - Age 32
The man who got his first 11 major league home runs faster than any other player in major league history, Maas finally succumbed to breaking junk and went to Japan. In 1996 he was with the Hanshin Tigers, hitting .250 with seven home runs in 208 at-bats.

MABRY, JOHN - OF - BL - Age 26
Mabry slumped in the second half of last season but is ready to blossom into one of the best pure hitters in the National League. A long string of seasons in which he hits .330 or better is quite possible. Mabry doesn't have the power one looks for in a first baseman but he will move over to third or back to right field, where the Cardinals can take better advantage of his great arm, once an opening occurs.

	AB	R	HR	RBI	SB	BA	$
1995 St. Louis NL	388	35	5	41	0	.307	10
1996 St. Louis NL	543	63	13	74	3	.297	18

MACFARLANE, MIKE - C - BR - Age 32
Missing Macfarlane's hard-nosed defense and power bat, the Royals re-acquired him after he spent a year in Boston. They got exactly what they bargained for as Macfarlane had a 1996 campaign identical to his last four in Kansas City. Macfarlane is signed through 1997 and is expected to be an on-the-job tutor for young catching prospects Mike Sweeney and Sal Fasano before stepping out of their way in 1998.

	AB	R	HR	RBI	SB	BA	$
1995 Boston AL	364	45	15	51	2	.225	6
1996 Kansas City AL	379	58	19	54	3	.274	9

MACHADO, ROBERT - C - BR - Age 23
Still some distance from a job with the White Sox, Machado was at Double-A in 1996. The smallish defensive specialist hit .239 with six homers.

MACK, QUINN - OF - BL - Age 31
Mack is a ten-year minor league journeyman who has somehow endured seven years at Triple-A, mostly as a regular, never hitting more than seven homers or stealing more than 11 bases.

MACK, SHANE - OF - BR - Age 33
Mack was a good hitting Twins outfielder who opted to play in Japan in 1995 rather than go through a major league strike. He usually hit around .300 in the majors, and last year in Japan, he hit .293-19-67 for the Yomiuri Giants.

MAGADAN, DAVE - 3B/1B - BL - Age 34
If there is one thing that Dave Magadan can do, it is hit righthanded pitching (.301 vs righties over the past three seasons). But he didn't do that in 1996. Although he compiled only 169 at-bats in '96, (161 against righthanded pitchers) Magadan hit .248 against righties. At times, Magadan can be painful to watch on defense. He has never found a home in his 11-year career and he can't run. But he is a valuable commodity to have on the bench. He should fill a similar role for some team in '97.

	AB	R	HR	RBI	SB	BA	$
1995 Houston NL	348	44	2	51	2	.313	10
1996 Chicago NL	169	23	3	17	0	.254	1

MAGEE, DANNY - 3B - BR - Age 22
Scouts love Magee's arm and his versatility as a hitter. He hits for average and power, has some speed and a good glove, too. The only concern may be his propensity for striking out, although Magee reduced his whiffs in 1996. In his second season at Durham, he hit .299-12-40 with 17 steals after moving to third base from shortstop. Magee may have a better chance back at shortstop, though, because third base is already well stocked with Chipper Jones, Bobby Smith and Wes Helms in front of him in the Braves' system.

MAGEE, WENDELL - OF - BR - Age 24
Magee is a exceptional all-around athlete who is just getting the hang of this baseball thing. The 6'0", 220 pounder, outfielder showed flashes of power and speed ability in Double-A and Triple-A, though his offensive skills weren't ready for prime time in the majors. He must learn to stay back on the breaking ball and line it the other way. Defensively, he plays all three outfield positions extremely well, and with reckless abandon. He doesn't have the offensive upside

to be a productive major league starter, but could make a great fourth outfielder.

	AB	R	HR	RBI	SB	BA	$
1996 Philadelphia NL	142	9	2	14	0	.204	-

MAKAREWICZ, SCOTT - C - BR - Age 30
After seven years on the Astros' farm (the last five in the high minors), Makarewicz joined the Tigers as minor league free agent. It was his best season as a hitter (.314-14-49), but Makarewicz has almost no chance to play ball in the majors; he's minor league roster filler.

MALAVE, JOSE - OF - BR - Age 25
An early-season stint on the DL kept Malave from being at the forefront when the Red Sox were looking for outfield help from their farm club. He eventually got his chance and did as well as can be expected. Malave is a good power prospect but lacking in most other aspects: defense, batting eye, speed. Once considered among Boston's better outfield prospects, Malave now looks more like a major league reserve or Triple-A regular.

	AB	R	HR	RBI	SB	BA	$
1996 Boston AL	102	12	4	17	0	.235	-

MALLOY, MARTY - 2B - BL - Age 24
An overachiever who wasn't drafted (signed as a free agent), Malloy spent all of 1996 at Double-A Greenville except for a short stint in Richmond. He impressed Braves' brass with his .312 average and keen batting eye; Malloy drew more walks than he struck out last year. But, most impressive to the scouts was his growth as a fielder. Already a good glove man, Malloy was named the Southern League's best defensive second baseman in 1996 by Baseball America. Malloy is behind Tony Graffanino in the Braves chain, but not by much.

MANAHAN, TONY - 3B - BR - Age 28
A former Mariners' first round pick, Manahan's opportunity for playing time in the Phils' organization was ended by injury and by the explosive progress of phenom Scott Rolen. Manahan has been a pesky singles hitter throughout his seven year minor league career, and will likely have little trouble finding a new minor league home in 1997, though he has practically no chance of ever reaching the majors.

MANESS, DWIGHT - OF - BR - Age 22
A gifted athlete with excellent speed, Maness is young enough to develop more patience at the plate and eventually to become a major league leadoff hitter, a job filled for the Mets by Lance Johnson in 1996.

MANTO, JEFF - 3B/1B - BR - Age 32
Give Manto credit for perseverance. He has spent all or parts of the last ten years in the high minors only to get brief trials in the majors. At least he got a taste of a pennant chase when the Red Sox dealt him to Seattle for the stretch drive. Manto can play either infield corner, but isn't a good glove man. His best role is as a part-time/platoon DH and extra power bat on the bench. In between his erstwhile major league appearances, Manto will remain at Triple-A, waiting for yet another brief major league trial.

	AB	R	HR	RBI	SB	BA	$
1995 Baltimore AL	254	31	17	38	0	.256	7
1996 Boston AL	102	15	3	10	0	.196	-

MANWARING, KIRT - C - BR - Age 31
Manwaring had a career year in 1993 with a .275 batting average and a gold glove. His hitting has declined since then and, with no power or speed, his only asset is his defense.

	AB	R	HR	RBI	SB	BA	$
1995 San Francisco NL	379	21	4	36	1	.251	4
1996 Houston NL	227	14	1	18	0	.229	-

MARINI, MARC - OF - BL - Age 27
Stuck in a Cleveland system overloaded with outfield talent, Marini finally got a chance with another organization in 1996. But he was unimpressive in 135 at-bats (.267 with two home runs) and faded out of the picture.

MARRERO, ELIESER - C - BR - Age 23
Marrero shows good power and may be the best defensive catcher in the Cardinals' chain. He showed a cannon for

an arm and above-average movement behind the plate. Marrero runs well for a catcher, stealing nine bases in fifteen tries. He needs to be a little more patient at the plate, but is a legitimate big-league prospect with legitimate power.

MARRERO, ORESTE - 1B - BL - Age 27
A 10 year minor league veteran, Marrero posted an okay year at Triple-A Albuquerque and was rewarded with a September callup to the Dodgers. His age, mediocre power for a first baseman and almost four-to-one strikeout to walk ratio suggest he is not much of a prospect.

MARSH, TOM - OF - BR - Age 31
You might remember then-Phillie Marsh ramming his head into Orlando Miller's knee in a nationally televised game in 1995 - Marsh was knocked cold for an extended period, and was initially thought to be seriously hurt. He wound up returning to play weeks before Miller. This latter-day Crash Davis is a gamer with some power, but his inability to lay off a pitch will keep him on the wrong side of the major league fringe.

MARTIN, AL - OF - BL - Age 29
Martin emerged into a star player last season, though no one outside of Pittsburgh really notices. Finally given the chance to play every day after sitting against lefthanders during his first three full seasons, Martin had good power and speed numbers. He is now in the prime of his career and his statistics will continue to get better for the next few years. While the Pirates figure to trade most of their veterans for prospect in the offseason, Martin is one guy they will keep and build around.

	AB	R	HR	RBI	SB	BA	$
1995 Pittsburgh NL	439	70	13	41	20	.282	18
1996 Pittsburgh NL	630	101	18	72	38	.300	32

MARTIN, CHRIS - SS/2B - BR - Age 29
The Expos' 1991 second round pick hasn't developed into the caliber of player one desires in such a high draft pick, but he has stood out as a defensive stalwart at shortstop. Triple-A International League managers rated him the circuit's best defensive shortstop, and he also showed career best offensive pop with 30 doubles. He has stolen 55 bases over the past two seasons, and has proven himself capable of playing second base, shortstop, and third base over the years.

MARTIN, JIM - OF - BL - Age 26
Martin had the worst year of his five pro seasons, splitting time between Double-A San Antonio and Class A San Bernardino. He hit poorly at both locations, posting a low batting average, little power and displaying a tendency to strike out in bunches. Martin is fading out as a prospect.

MARTIN, NORBERTO - 2B/SS - BR - Age 30
The utility infielder hit .350 in 1996. Unfortunately for him he missed over two months with a fractured jaw. His role had increased in the off-season with Craig Grebeck going to Florida. Paco made the most of the time he had though. Nobody is ready in the minors to compete with him for playing time in 1997 unless the club makes a move in the free agent market.

	AB	R	HR	RBI	SB	BA	$
1995 Chicago AL	160	17	2	17	5	.269	4
1996 Chicago AL	140	30	1	14	10	.350	7

MARTINDALE, RYAN - C - BR - Age 28
A perennial injury casualty, Martindale got only 19 at-bats in 1996 and has faded out of the prospect picture.

MARTINEZ, DAVE - OF - BL - Age 34
Martinez had a terrific year. He hit for average (.318), with a little power (10 HR's), and even stole 15 bases. He played center field when Darren Lewis was struggling and even spelled Frank Thomas at first base from time to time. Look for his flexibility to keep him in a Sox uniform in 1997 and beyond.

	AB	R	HR	RBI	SB	BA	$
1995 Chicago AL	303	49	5	37	8	.307	11
1996 Chicago AL	440	85	10	53	15	.318	17

MARTINEZ, DOMINGO - 1B - BR - Age 29
Last July, the Orioles signed Martinez out of the Mexican League to a Triple-A contract. He's an ex-Blue Jay, Cardinal,

and White Sox farmhand who spent five years in Triple-A where he showed some good power in tough-to-hit ballparks. He was also known for his many strikeouts. The Orioles are solid at first base and at DH, so Martinez's best shot may be with another organization.

MARTINEZ, EDDY - SS - BR - Age 19
Orioles prospect Martinez could be the man to take over shortstop from Cal Ripken in a few years. At age 18, Martinez was the youngest player in the Single-A Carolina League last year, a tough league. Martinez has a great deal of potential.

MARTINEZ, EDGAR - 1B - BR - Age 34
If Russ Davis goes down again, Piniella should play third before allowing Edgar to. Martinez broke a rib in his first appearance at 3B after Davis' injury. He remains a tremendous hitter, but fell off a bit when he returned as his bad rib affected his stroke. Fully recovered, he should have another great season.

	AB	R	HR	RBI	SB	BA	$
1995 Seattle AL	511	121	29	113	4	.356	31
1996 Seattle AL	499	121	26	103	3	.327	21

MARTINEZ, FELIX - SS - BB - Age 22
Volatile Martinez has great tools, but poor discipline both in the field and at the plate. Spotty mechanics and a combative nature have overshadowed his natural talents thus far. He's still young, though, and once he learns to keep his head in the game. Martinez can realize his potential.

MARTINEZ, MANNY - OF - BR - Age 26
The Phillies became the fourth club in the last three years to take a look-see at Martinez, and were not impressed. Martinez is an aggressive hitter who is looking for excuses to swing the bat, even in must-take situations. He has exhibited gap power and decent speed in the minors, but was so overmatched in the majors that none of those abilities surfaced. Defensively he has poor instincts which more than offset his decent speed. The Phils now have no illusions about his ability to play at the major league level.

MARTINEZ, RAMON - 2B - BR - Age 24
Injuries prevented Martinez from building on his career best season of the previous year. He flashes a lot of leather but doesn't hit enough to earn a regular major league job. Martinez can get to the majors in a reserve role.

MARTINEZ, PABLO - SS - BB - Age 27
Martinez is a slap-hitter who can steal a base but has no idea of the strike zone. He once led a rookie league in stolen bases (1989) and swiped 14 last year at Triple-A Richmond. Martinez isn't a particularly slick fielder and he has little power.

MARTINEZ, RAY - SS/3B - BR - Age 28
Martinez spent five years in A-ball, and another four in Double-A and Triple-A. Other than hitting .302 in Triple-A in 1992, his bat has been weak. He got some playing time with the Angels Triple-A club in 1996, but didn't show much.

MARTINEZ, SANDY - C - BL - Age 24
Despite his rocket of a throwing arm, he isn't hitting enough and doesn't show signs that he's about to. Things got so bad that Charlie O'Brien, who was signed to teach more than to play, ended up as the Blue Jays' regular catcher. A sprained ankle in August made his 1996 season even worse and he must show something in spring training.

	AB	R	HR	RBI	SB	BA	$
1995 Toronto AL	191	12	2	25	0	.241	
1996 Toronto AL	229	17	3	18	0	.227	-

MARTINEZ, TINO - 1B - BL - Age 29
After his big season in Seattle in 1995, the only question was whether Tino's new-found ability to hit lefty pitching was a temporary illusion or lasting reality. In 1996 the American League's southpaws tried to make adjustments and treat Martinez with more respect, but he proved himself again.

	AB	R	HR	RBI	SB	BA	$
1995 Seattle AL	519	92	31	111	0	.293	22
1996 New York AL	595	82	25	117	2	.292	18

MARTINS, ERIC - 3B - BR - Age 24
Think Ron Cey without the power, Martins stands 5'9" but had good stints at Southern Oregon and Modesto. In a little over his head at Huntsville, his OBP and average dropped off according. Worth watching to see how he adjusts this year.

MARX, TIM - C - BR - Age 28
He is a solid if unspectacular catcher who has little future in the Pirates' organization with Jason Kendall, Keith Osik and Angelo Encarnacion ahead of him.

MARZANO, JOHN - C - BR - Age 34
In 1996, Marzano reached 100 at-bats for only the third time in his major league career which began in 1987. He hasn't hit a home run since 1989.

	AB	R	HR	RBI	SB	BA	$
1996 Seattle AL	106	8	0	6	0	.245	-

MASHORE, DAMON - OF - BB - Age 27
Heralded years ago by Baseball America as a future center fielder for the A's, Mashore finally did arrive in the majors last year, but the results, though not bad, portend little more than fourth outfielder.

	AB	R	HR	RBI	SB	BA	$
1996 Oakland AL	105	20	3	12	4	.267	1

MASHORE, JUSTIN - OF - BR - Age 25
The twenty-five-year-old Mashore changed his hopes of making the major leagues in '96 from "none" to "slim" with a decent (.285, 17 steals) season in Double-A.

MASSARELLI, JOHN - OF - BR - Age 31
Massarelli is a veteran of 10 minor league seasons, rising as high as Triple-A in 1991-95. He took a step backwards last year, playing in Double-A. At age 31, he's much older than his peers, and doesn't appear to be making much progress. He's had a below-average minor league record, and it may be time to hang 'em up.

MASTELLER, DAN - 1B/OF - BL - Age 29
Masteller made a major move backward in 1996, going from a major league platoon in Minnesota in 1995 to a the Double-A first baseman's job in the Expos' chain. Though he has batted .300 in four consecutive minor league seasons, he has never hit more than 10 homers in a season - not good news for a first sacker.

MATEO, AMAURY - OF - BR - Age 19
Rangers prospect Mateo has fine raw speed (30 stolen bases at Class A Charleston in 1996) and developing power.

MATEO, RUBEN - OF - BR - Age 18
Mateo's biggest strength is his speed, but his overall power may go up this year since he is adding some muscle to his slender frame.

MATHENY, MIKE - C - BR - Age 26
A right handed batter, the Brewers number one catcher hit under .200 against lefties. Good defensive tools are his meal ticket.

	AB	R	HR	RBI	SB	BA	$
1995 Milwaukee AL	166	13	0	21	2	.247	1
1996 Milwaukee AL	313	31	8	46	3	.204	-

MATOS, FRANCISCO - 2B/SS - BR - Age 27
The proud owner of 28 major league at bats (with the A's in 1994) continued his decline into mediocrity with a subpar Triple-A season in the Expos' chain in 1996. A versatile infielder with above average defensive skills, Matos has little power or speed, and is a indiscriminate swinger at the plate.

MATTINGLY, DON - 1B - BL - Age 35
Back problems (which Mattingly will never use as an excuse, and won't even mention unless pressed to admit they

have existed) changed this .330, 30-homer hitter into a mere .300 hitter who is also a defensive gem and one of the last great team leaders. He was talking comeback late in the 1996 season.

	AB	R	HR	RBI	SB	BA	$
1995 New York AL	458	59	7	49	0	.288	9
1996			Did Not Play				

MAURER, RON - SS/C - BR - Age 28
Maurer's versatility is a plus, but it's not going to be enough to get him to the majors. He's a marginal hitter, even in the Pacific Coast League, and he doesn't do any one thing well enough to advance any farther.

MAXWELL, PAT - 2B - BL - Age 27
Maxwell is a survivor, a 1991 29th round Indians' pick who has endured five nondescript minor league seasons. Maxwell makes consistent contact, but hits for a mediocre average with no power. He is surehanded defensively, and can play second base, shortstop and third base.

MAY, DERRICK - OF - BL - Age 28
One of Houston's biggest needs is a left handed outfielder with power. This would appear to be a perfect opportunity for May but he failed to capitalize on it. Without any outstanding attributes, he appears destined for a career as a spare outfielder and a pinch hitter.

	AB	R	HR	RBI	SB	BA	$
1995 Milwaukee AL	113	15	1	9	0	.248	-
1995 Houston NL	206	29	8	41	5	.301	10
1996 Houston NL	259	24	5	33	2	.251	2

MAYNE, BRENT - C - BL - Age 28
Mayne is good enough with the bat and glove to be a starting catcher for most teams, but being on the same roster with Todd Hundley reduces him to a backup role.

	AB	R	HR	RBI	SB	BA	$
1995 Kansas City AL	307	23	1	27	0	.251	1
1996 New York AL	99	9	1	6	0	.263	0

McBRIDE, CHARLIE - OF - BR - Age 23
"Gator" McBride advanced to Double-A Greenville after starting the year at Durham. He wasn't overly impressive, posting a .268-4-50 season but continuing to strike out at a high rate - more than once every four at-bats last year and for his entire career. McBride doesn't really have any great tools, so he's not a great prospect, despite the great nickname.

McCALL, ROD - 1B - BL - Age 25
This 1990 ninth round Indians' draftee emerged from independent Bakersfield in 1995 to become a lethal power force at Double-A Canton-Akron in 1996. This 6'7", 220 pound, hulk has only one marketable skill - power. Be cautious - men of his age who have yet to play at Triple-A rarely produce much in the majors. An eventual major league bit role is his greatest hope.

McCARTY, DAVID - OF/1B - BR - Age 27
Clearly able to master Triple-A pitching, McCarty needs yet another chance to show what he can do in the majors. He had a lot of opportunities with two successive teams who really needed someone to establish himself as the first baseman.

	AB	R	HR	RBI	SB	BA	$
1995 Minnesota AL	55	10	0	4	0	.218	-
1995 San Francisco NL	20	1	0	2	1	.250	-
1996 San Francisco NL	175	16	6	24	2	.217	-

McCLAIN, SCOTT - 3B - BR - Age 24
McClain's a mid-level prospect who can play third or first base. He's got decent power (17 homers, 23 doubles in 1996) and hit for a pretty good average (.281) in his first year at Triple-A. McClain's got an above-average glove although he strikes out a little bit too much. He'll challenge for a bench role in the majors in 1997.

McCONNELL, CHAD - OF - BR - Age 26
A hard-working player who has been beset by chronic shoulder injuries, McConnell has shown little home run power, plate discipline or speed, and has been marooned at Double-A for the better part of three seasons. He might be able to get by one more year, but that will be it.

McCRACKEN, QUINTON - OF - BB - Age 27
McCracken won a back-up job with the Rocks in 1996, and became almost an every day player when Larry Walker injured his collar bone. It took awhile for "Q" to warm up to major league pitching, but the speedy, switch-hitting rookie raised his average almost 100 points after he started playing regularly. Look for more playing time (and definitely more steals) in 1997, particularly if the Rockies lose Burks or deal Bichette.

	AB	R	HR	RBI	SB	BA	$
1996 Colorado NL	283	50	3	40	17	.290	12

MAGDALENO, RICKY - SS - BR - Age 22
The Reds' 1992 second round pick has stagnated as a prospect over the past two seasons, as he has been operating under the misconception that he is a power hitter.

McCLAIN, SCOTT - 3B - BR - Age 24
Orioles Triple-A third baseman McClain is excellent defensively with a strong and accurate arm, but he needs to improve on his hitting, especially the power, if he is to make the Orioles or another major league team.

McDAVID, RAY - OF - BL - Age 25
The former blue-chip Padres' prospect has now suffered through two injury-ravaged seasons, the last one in the Expos' chain. He hasn't truly dominated in the minors since 1992 at High-A High Desert, the best hitters' park around. He retains his blazing speed and willingness to draw walks, but the two lost seasons might be too much for him to conquer.

McDONALD, JASON - SS/2B - BB - Age 25
After his breakthrough year with Modesto in 1995, McDonald moved all the way up to Triple-A last year and found the going just a little tougher. All-in-all, he weathered the experience well. He does have Tony Batista ahead of him, but McDonald has what it takes to be a good lead off or number two hitter. Since he is a second baseman, has patience at the plate and good speed, he is much worth keeping an eye on.

McEWING, JOE - OF - BR - Age 24
Two straight sub-par years with the bat have seriously dimmed McEwing's major league chances. He hit just .208 at Double-A Arkansas, rendering him unable to take advantage of his above-average speed.

McFARLIN, JASON - OF - BL - Age 26
1996 was McFarlin's fifth year spent mostly at Double-A. With his third organization in two years, he served as a reserve outfielder for Greenville and he proved his .337 average from 1995 was a fluke by going .230-4-21. McFarlin is no prospect and will likely move on to another venue in 1997.

McGEE, WILLIE - OF - BB - Age 38
Left for dead in 1994 after tearing his Achilles tendon while playing for San Francisco, McGee was reborn last season in his return to St. Louis. He had a fine year in the fourth outfielder role.

	AB	R	HR	RBI	SB	BA	$
1995 Boston AL	200	32	2	15	5	.285	4
1996 St. Louis NL	309	52	5	41	5	.307	12

McGRIFF, FRED - 1B - BL - Age 33
It would be hard to name a steadier hitter over the last decade. Since 1988, the following are season lows for McGriff: .269-27-82. Most seasons are like the one he had in 1996: high-power, high-average, solid RBI production. McGriff has an expensive, long-term contract through 1999. He'll continue to produce big numbers for Atlanta for three more years.

	AB	R	HR	RBI	SB	BA	$
1995 Atlanta NL	528	85	27	93	3	.280	21
1996 Atlanta NL	617	81	28	107	7	.295	26

McGUIRE, RYAN - 1B - BL - Age 25
Acquired by the Expos from the Red Sox in the Wil Cordero deal, McGuire bounced back from a poor start to post respectable numbers (.257, 12 homers, 60 RBI, 11 steals) at Triple-A Ottawa. He hits line drives to all fields, will take a walk, is a smooth fielder around the bag, and can also play adequate outfield defense.

McGWIRE, MARK - 1B - BR - Age 33
Probably the most exciting power hitter in the game, if McGwire ever gets to play a full season of games it is scary to think of how he will do. For the record, McGwire slugged to the tune of .730, turned 55% of hits into extra-base ones, and managed a record home run every 8.13 at bat. Give him 100 more at-bats (or 32 more games) than he garnered in 1996 and you have 64 home runs.

	AB	R	HR	RBI	SB	BA	$
1995 Oakland AL	317	75	39	90	1	.274	19
1996 Oakland AL	423	104	52	113	0	.312	24

McINTOSH, TIM - C - BR - Age 32
At one time McIntosh offered two exciting features: a high batting average and the ability to handle catching chores. Both aspects have faded with age. McIntosh hit .277 with 10 home runs at Triple-A Columbus in 1996. He was passed by Jorge Posada on the New York depth charts.

McKEEL, WALT - C - BR - Age 25
Hard work and perseverance paid off for this 1990 third-round draftee when he got a September callup last year. McKeel posted career bests in many offensive categories, including 16 homers and 78 RBI (more than twice as many RBI as his previous career best), while hitting .302 and drawing 60 walks. The best defensive catcher in the Red Sox' organization, McKeel looks like he'll soon be ready to challenge for a major league reserve role.

McLEMORE, MARK - 2B - BB - Age 32
McLemore quietly went about having a career year in his second season with Texas. Underrated defensively, he makes up for limited range with steady play, and turns the double play well. Even in the power-oriented Ranger offense, McLemore finished seventh in steals in the AL. He probably will never hit .290 again, but should remain a productive regular for the foreseeable future.

	AB	R	HR	RBI	SB	BA	$
1995 Texas AL	467	73	5	41	21	.261	15
1996 Texas AL	517	84	5	46	27	.290	19

McMILLON, BILL - OF - BL - Age 25
McMillon was born to hit. He is a line drive machine who hits rockets into the gaps consistently, with decent longball ability despite his 5'11", 172 pound, frame. However, the Marlins were content to let him sit on the major league bench for a sizeable portion of the 1996 season, indicating that they do not consider him a future starter. McMillon looks like a fourth outfielder or platooner at the major league level, beginning in 1997.

	AB	R	HR	RBI	SB	BA	$
1996 Florida NL	51	4	0	4	0	.216	-

McMULLEN, JON - 1B - BL - Age 23
This once-promising Phils' prospect has been severely hindered by shoulder problems which have cost him the bulk of the past two seasons. The Phils have yet to give up, but it appears that irreparable damage has been done to his swing. 1997 is likely his last chance to impress.

MCNABB, BUCK - OF - BL - Age 24
A speedy outfielder with no power, McNabb has not advanced above the Double-A level in his six year career. He hasn't hit for a high enough average to receive attention as a prospect.

McNEELY, JEFF - OF - BR - Age 27
Once a top Red Sox prospect, the blazing fast McNeely has swiped as many as 40 bases in a Triple-A season. But the best he could hit in Triple-A was a weak .236, and he lacks power. He was with Midland in the hitter-friendly Double-A Texas League last year where he hit a weak .240, and the Angels released him in August. He also got a handful of at-bats for the Cardinals' Triple-A club.

McRAE, BRIAN - OF - BB - Age 29
The Cubs re-signed McRae to a three year contract. Although he has made himself into a pretty good leadoff man, McRae still must cut down on his strikeouts. His 73 walks were 19 more that his previous career high. McRae may never be a .300 hitter, but he can score some runs, steal some bases and makes spectacular catches weekly in centerfield. McRae is a good player, but hasn't gotten any closer than the fringe of stardom.

	AB	R	HR	RBI	SB	BA	$
1995 Chicago NL	580	92	12	48	27	.288	24
1996 Chicago NL	624	111	17	66	37	.276	24

MEARES, PAT - SS - BR - Age 28
Meares continued his slow and steady progress in '96 as he set career highs in at-bats, runs, hits, and RBI. His plate discipline is still poor, leading to low on base percentages.

	AB	R	HR	RBI	SB	BA	$
1995 Minnesota AL	390	57	12	49	10	.269	13
1996 Minnesota AL	517	66	8	67	9	.267	10

MEDRANO, TONY - SS - BR - Age 22
Acquired from Toronto in the David Cone trade after the 1994 season, Medrano is a go-go shortstop who is aggressive in the field and at bat. His already good glove work improved in his first year at Double-A Wichita, although he remained the same free-swinger at the plate. Medrano has gap power and above-average speed. He's still younger than most of the players at his level, so there is room for improvement. Medrano has some big-league potential.

MEJIA, MIGUEL - OF - BR - Age 21
The Cardinals had to keep the speedy outfielder on the roster all season after selecting him from Baltimore via the Rule Five Draft. Mejia had never played above Class A and Cardinals manager Tony La Russa used him sparingly. It's hard to tell if Mejia is capable of playing in the majors as he'll need at least a year at both the Double-A and Triple-A level before being ready.

MEJIA, ROBERTO - 2B - BR - Age 24
The former Rockie phenom posted a fine year at Indianapolis before being dealt to the Red Sox for Kevin Mitchell. Mejia has decent speed and power for a middle infielder, but suffers from below average strike zone judgment. He is still young enough to make an impact for a major league team.

MELENDEZ, DAN - 1B - BL - Age 26
Melendez has had about two good months at Double-A as a hitter and has otherwise struggled to hit anything as a pro. He's an excellent fielder, but he's going to have to hit a whole lot more to advance.

MELHUSE, ADAM - C - BB - Age 25
He will be twenty-five this year and needs to post a strong season to continue moving up the ranks. There are at least six catchers ahead of him in the farm system and he looked overmatched at Double-A.

MELO, JUAN - SS - BB - Age 20
Padre prospect Melo is young and improving. He's learning and could emerge as a good prospect and solid major leaguer.

MELUSKEY, MITCH - C - BB - Age 23
Meluskey had a breakout season in 1996, hitting .333 at Class A Kissimmee before a promotion to Double-A Jackson where he hit .313. He had not hit above .246 in his first four years. With limited power, he needs to follow it up with another strong year to gain status as a prospect.

MENECHINO, FRANKIE - 2B - BR - Age 26
Too old to be a prospect, Menechino played at Double-A in the White Sox chain in 1996, .292 with 12 home runs in 415 at-bats.

MERCED, ORLANDO - 1B/OF - BL - Age 30
Merced was the Pirates' cleanup hitter and reached a career-high in homers last season despite three trips to the disabled list with hamstring and groin pulls. Merced is what he is, he'll hit around .285 with homer totals in the teens

and a decent number of RBI. He isn't going to get any better and he doesn't figure to get appreciably worse for a few years. The Pirates, though, will look to dump his $2.7-million salary as they go with young players.

	AB	R	HR	RBI	SB	BA	$
1995 Pittsburgh NL	487	75	15	83	7	.300	20
1996 Pittsburgh NL	453	69	17	80	8	.287	17

MERCEDES, HENRY - C - BR - Age 27
If the Mendoza line is .215 it should be the Mercedes line. It's what he has hit at Triple-A each of the last two seasons and is a true measure of his hitting abilities. Mercedes is a fine defensive catcher who can't hit a lick. He's injury insurance stored at Triple-A.

MERCHANT, MARK - DH - BL - Age 28
Ten years ago he was the Florida State High School player of the year and the Pirates first round pick (1987). Now, after three injury-shortened seasons, Merchant is with his fourth organization (third in three years). His speed is gone and his power hasn't developed as expected. Merchant will be fortunate to remain in professional baseball much longer.

MERLONI, LOU - 3B - BR - Age 25
A fine athlete, Merloni can play almost anywhere on the infield. However, he doesn't hit enough to be a true prospect. If he makes it at all, it will be as a reserve infielder. Merloni's versatility will help him advance.

MERULLO, MATT - DH/C - BL - Age 31
Merullo retired early in the season, then resurfaced with the Lake Elsinore Storm. He gave up seven stolen bases in one game while with the Storm.

MEULENS, HENSLEY - OF - BR - Age 29
The Yankees "Bam Bam" who never made it with New York, Meulens went to Japan. The native of Curacao now speaks English, Dutch, Spanish, Antillean and Japanese. In 1996 he hit 25 home runs for Yakult.

MIESKE, MATT - OF - BR - Age 29
Mieske showed some pop last year, but is in danger of losing playing time due to his continuing inability to hit righties. If Jeromy Burnitz and Marc Newfield falter, Mieske may benefit, but without showing significant improvement against righties, it's just a matter of time until he's a spare. He has benefited by a high number of injuries to Brewer outfield the last few years.

	AB	R	HR	RBI	SB	BA	$
1995 Milwaukee AL	267	42	12	48	2	.251	7
1996 Milwaukee AL	374	46	14	64	1	.278	8

MILLAR, KEVIN - 1B - BR - Age 25
Millar has been a consistent offensive performer throughout his pro career with the Marlins, hitting for average and solid power, and making excellent contact. However, he is regularly shoved aside to make room for younger prospects with higher upsides. In 1996, he performed designated hitter duty quite often to clear room for converted catcher John Roskos at first base. Millar should have no problem excelling with the bat at Triple-A, but he will likely earn no better than a cameo role in the majors.

MILLARES, JOSE - 2B - BR - Age 29
Oriole farmhand Millares got some playing time for Double-A Bowie last year hitting a poor .186. It was his third year for Bowie, and he appears to be a career minor leaguer.

MILLER, DAMIAN - C - BR - Age 27
It took a while to show, but Miller is turning out to be a reasonably good hitter. He had good campaigns in '94 and '95, but '96 was his best season yet. Miller hit .286-7-55 as Triple-A Salt Lake City's primary catcher. He is already an above-average defensive receiver; he'll soon challenge for a major league reserve role.

MILLER, DAVID - OF - BL - Age 23
The Indians 1995 first round pick was somewhat of a disappointment in his first pro season, at High-A Kinston. His bat is slow compared to his teammate and 1995 number two pick Sean Casey. Miller must develop more consistent

power (he's 6'3", 185 pounds) and must become more selective. Miller could have trouble against Double-A pitching in 1997 - not good news for a number one pick of his age.

MILLER, ORLANDO - SS - BR - Age 28
Miller provides some power for a shortstop but tends to be erratic and has limited range. He could be moved to third base at some point. With 14 walks and 116 strikeouts in 1996, he will have difficulty hitting for average unless he improves his plate discipline.

	AB	R	HR	RBI	SB	BA	$
1995 Houston NL	324	36	5	36	3	.262	6
1996 Houston NL	468	43	15	58	3	.256	7

MILLER, ROGER - C - BR - Age 29
Signed as a minor league free agent from the Giants, Miller spent most of 1996 at Double-A New Haven in the Rockies organization. A decent defensive catcher who has a mid-.200 career average, Miller is not likely to reach the parent club in 1997, even with all the uncertainty at the position.

MILLETTE, JOE - SS - BR - Age 30
Total Baseball and The Baseball Encyclopedia - take your pick as the official source - both list Millette as having played 33 career major league games with Philadelphia in 1992. Those statistics will never have to updated as he barely hit his weight last season in a reserve role with the Pirates' Triple-A Calgary farm club.

MILLIARD, RALPH - 2B - BR - Age 23
Milliard did nothing in 1996 to diminish his standing as one of the finest second base prospects in baseball - but still found himself demoted to Double-A Portland late in 1996 to make room for even better prospect Luis Castillo with the Marlins, and still youthful Quilvio Veras at Triple-A. Milliard is a patient hitter with surprising pop in his bat for someone his size (5'11", 165 pounds), and a smooth and sometimes spectacular glove. Milliard is likely to be traded in the offseason, and if he falls into the right opportunity, could start in the bigs in 1997.

	AB	R	HR	RBI	SB	BA	$
1996 Florida NL	62	7	0	1	2	.161	-

MIRABELLI, DOUG - C - BR - Age 26
Mirabelli was the man behind the plate for Shreveport last year. He hit for average and power, and performed well even when promoted to Phoenix. His main problems are that he is only a couple of years younger than incumbent Rick Wilkins, and then he must pass Marcus Jensen. If he keeps up the stick, he could become a good number two guy with the Giants.

MITCHELL, DONOVAN - 2B - BL - Age 27
Mitchell has spent five years in the minors reaching Double-A for the first time in 1996. He does not project above that level based on his age and a mediocre .252-3-32-11 season.

MITCHELL, KEITH - OF - BR - Age 27
Kevin Mitchell's cousin has shown signs of developing some power (27 homers in 570 at-bats the last two seasons at Triple-A), and his fine year at Indianapolis suggests he could help a major league team as a fourth outfielder. He's not likely to get the chance with Cincinnati, who have about a thousand candidates for outfield positions, most of whom are younger than Mitchell (but not necessarily any better).

MITCHELL, KEVIN - OF - BR - Age 35
A Hall of Fame hitter when healthy and interested, Mitchell hit well for the Reds, but was suspended the last two weeks when he did not show up for a series in Pittsburgh. He can still hit, is useless in the outfield, makes Eric Davis look durable, and is about the biggest longshot gamble around.

	AB	R	HR	RBI	SB	BA	$
1996 Boston AL	92	9	2	13	0	.304	0
1996 Cincinnati NL	114	18	6	26	0	.325	6

MITCHELL, TONY - OF - BB - Age 26
In his eighth minor league season, Mitchell rode a .312-11-41 performance at Double-A Jacksonville to reach Triple-A for the first time. He continued to hit for power at Toledo and has an outside shot for a major league bench role in 1997.

MOEDER, TONY - 1B - BR - Age 25
After having a solid season in Class-A, Angel minor leaguer Moeder was promoted to Double-A last year. He didn't get much of a chance to prove himself.

MOLER, JASON - 3B/C - BR - Age 27
The Phils' 1992 fourth round pick was once a solid catching prospect, but was moved to third base despite an excellent defensive track record as a receiver because of his awkward throwing motion. A power threat who has a good eye and rarely strikes out, he has not been promoted to Triple-A during the past two seasons. He is a fiery type who was the unquestioned leader of his club over that period, but has likely run out of time to make it to the bigs.

MOLINA, BEN - C - BR - Age 22
Young Angels farmhand Molina hit decently in Class A in 1994 and '95, and last year in Double-A. He's making good progress through the minors, and he's beginning to show some power as he matures. He doesn't strike out much, another positive sign. He should spend 1997 in Triple-A, getting a tougher test.

MOLINA, IZZY - C - BR - Age 25
Former California League All-Star, Molina wields a good glove and his hitting did improve last year, but he still has a ways to go before he will be a major leaguer.

MOLITOR, PAUL - DH - BR - Age 40
The amazing Molitor had a season for the ages in '96 as he led the majors in hits on his way to collecting his 3,000th hit in September. Perhaps the most astounding statistic of Molitor's year was that he did not score 100 runs despite being on base over 280 times! The Twins don't have power down in their order, but if Molitor is around in 1997, they'll have a number three hitter.

	AB	R	HR	RBI	SB	BA	$
1995 Toronto AL	525	63	15	60	12	.270	17
1996 Minnesota AL	660	99	9	113	18	.341	30

MONDESI, RAUL - OF - BR - Age 26
Sammy Sosa Jr. basically matched his fine 1995 season in every area except steals, which dropped from 27 to 14. Like Sosa, Mondesi has great power, an excellent arm in right field, and hits for a good average despite poor strike zone judgment. Mondesi is a prime candidate for a breakout season in 1997, given his age and experience level.

	AB	R	HR	RBI	SB	BA	$
1995 Los Angeles NL	536	91	26	88	27	.285	30
1996 Los Angeles NL	634	98	24	88	14	.297	27

MONDS, WONDERFUL - OF - BR - Age 24
Yes, that's his real name - actually, it's Wonderful Terrific Monds the third. Monds was on the Braves 40-man roster to start the season, then got in just 110 at-bats for Double-A Greenville before a broken hand ended his season; it was his second straight injury-shortened season. When healthy, Monds can deliver speed, but not much else. He has some talent, but his power won't carry to the majors and he needs to cut his strikeouts before he'll get a second look. Until he proves otherwise, Monds is wonderful in name only.

MONTGOMERY, RAY - OF - BR - Age 27
Montgomery had his second straight strong year at Triple-A in 1996 and had three separate stints in the majors. In his seven year career in the Astro system, he has developed some power and could stay in the major leagues as a reserve outfielder.

MONTOYO, CHARLIE - 3B - BR - Age 32
The clock finally is about to strike midnight for Montoyo, one of the more interesting minor league players of the last decade. He only earned five major league at bats, but they included two key pennant race hits for the Expos in 1993. He has played all infield positions, and has quietly posted an amazing career .400 on-base percentage.

MONZON, JOSE - C - BR - Age 28
Playing at age 27 in Double-A, Angels farmhand Monzon is getting passed over by younger and better prospects. His major weakness is hitting, and his role is back-up catcher in the minors.

MOORE, BOBBY - OF - BR - Age 31
In his sixth year at Triple-A, Moore's season was cut short by injury. His ten years as a pro have produced 14 major league at-bats. Moore is a career minor leaguer who is in the organization to help develop young Braves outfielders like Jermaine Dye, Andruw Jones and Damon Hollins.

MOORE, KERWIN - OF - BB - Age 26
Moore can run, but he can't hit. After several minor league seasons with eye-popping steals and walks totals, Moore slipped at Triple-A last season in 1995. A football player in high school, Moore will never hit for average. After last year, his prospects have dimmed, following a shoulder injury.

MOORE, MIKE - OF - BR - Age 26
The Dodgers got Moore in the first round of the 1992 draft and he hasn't developed, primarily due to serious knee injuries. He lost part of 1994 and all of 1995, then hit just .240 at Double-A San Antonio in 1996 while striking out a third of the time. It doesn't look like he'll be able to overcome the injury setback.

MOORE, VINCE - OF - BL - Age 25
Padre farmhand Moore is one of the proceeds of the Fred McGriff trade. He has problems hitting, has little power, but can steal a few bases.

MORA, MELVIN - OF/3B - BR - Age 25
Mora is one of the many young players signed by the Astros out of Venezuela. Speed was his biggest asset through 1995 but he had only seven stolen bases in 1996. His combined numbers in 483 at-bats at Triple-A and Double-A in 1996 (.284-8-49) do not project him as a prospect.

MORALES, WILLIE - C - BR - Age 24
The A's brought Morales along slowly, but the move may have paid off. Morales had an excellent first season at Double-A Huntsville. Morales is ready to move to Triple-A Edmonton and see what he can do.

MORANDINI, MICKEY - 2B - BL - Age 30
Morandini is a surehanded, if unspectacular second baseman who has improved upon his shortcomings throughout his career. He no longer is overmatched by lefties, and has bulked up enough to drive the ball to the gaps regularly.

	AB	R	HR	RBI	SB	BA	$
1995 Philadelphia NL	494	65	6	49	9	.283	13
1996 Philadelphia NL	539	64	3	32	26	.250	8

MORDECAI, MIKE - SS/2B - BR - Age 29
The Braves' solid regular lineup accords Mordecai a role well-suited to his talents: defensive replacement and sometime pinch-hitter. He doesn't sling the leather like his counterpart, Rafael Belliard (few do), but he's a far better hitter. Look for Mordecai's role to continue to grow as Belliard's fades.

	AB	R	HR	RBI	SB	BA	$
1995 Atlanta NL	75	10	3	11	0	.280	1
1996 Atlanta NL	108	12	2	8	1	.241	-

MORGAN, KEVIN - 2B - BR - Age 27
A journeyman infielder, Morgan spent most of 1996 at Double-A in the Mets system, hitting .252 with 13 stolen bases. He exemplifies the Mets method of mixing in mature farmhands with their budding youngsters.

MORGAN, SCOTT - OF - BR - Age 23
The Indians 1995 seventh round pick who hit for average and excellent power at Low-A Columbus in 1996. Morgan was one of the older starters in his league, and needs to make a successful two-level jump to Double-A in 1997 to truly certify himself as a prospect. A large target at 6'7", 230 pounds, he must continually work on refining his mechanics to shrink the weak spots in the strike zone.

MORILLO, CESAR - SS - BB - Age 23
Morillo returned to the Royals after spending 1995 on load to co-op Bakersfield in 1995. He hit a little better, but is still a weak-hitting glove man with little major league future.

MORMAN, RUSS - OF - BR - Age 33
Morman remains a dominant Triple-A force, hitting for high average with extreme power, and making excellent contact despite iffy plate discipline. However, his bat is a tad slow for him to perform similar feats in a sizeable major league role. He will likely fill a similar role at Triple-A for someone in 1997, and won't embarrass himself if he graduates to the majors as an injury replacement.

MORRIS, BOBBY - 1B - BL - Age 24
Bobby hits like his brother Hal. He has a fair glove but his arm is erratic. He can't produce enough power to play firstbase for most major league teams, but his arm limits him at secondbase, his natural position. He should be a DH but again, doesn't have the power.

MORRIS, HAL - 1B - BL - Age 31
Morris finished the season with a 29 game hitting streak and career highs in runs, RBI, and home runs. He has three career homers in over 600 at-bats against southpaws, and his career high .273 average against them in 1996 was completely empty (.341 slugging and .322 on base percentage in 132 at-bats). Morris is a decent player, but in the context of the offensive explosion of 1996 his high average barely offsets his mediocre power for a first baseman.

	AB	R	HR	RBI	SB	BA	$
1995 Cincinnati NL	359	53	11	51	1	.279	10
1996 Cincinnati NL	528	82	16	80	7	.313	24

MOSQUERA, JULIO - C - BR - Age 25
A late-season injury to Sandy Martinez earned Mosquera his first shot at the big leagues. Mosquera has little power and has trouble blocking pitches. Although his arm has improved, his bat looked overmatched in the majors. Depending on Sandy Martinez's role, Mosquera could find himself in the majors in 1997 as a second or third catcher.

MOTA, GARY - OF - BR - Age 26
Once one of the top prospects in the Astro organization after a big year at Class A in 1992, Mota has never performed well above that level. He has spent most of the last four years at Double-A but has not hit above .240. Manny's fourth son does not appear to have a major league future.

MOTA, JOSE - 2B - BB - Age 32
Having played for six different organizations in his twelve-year pro career, Mota has collected 38 major league at-bats. He's a versatile, capable infielder who can serve as a guide for younger players on a farm team. Mota has no future in the big leagues.

MOTTOLA, CHAD - OF - BR - Age 25
The Reds first round pick in 1992, Mottola is a prospect in the Mike Kelly mold, with more tools than skills at this point in his career. Mottola is 6-3, 220 and has a great arm, but his power hasn't developed and he strikes out too much. He will compete for a reserve role with the Reds in 1997.

	AB	R	HR	RBI	SB	BA	$
1996 Cincinnati NL	79	10	3	6	2	.215	-

MOUTON, JAMES - OF - BR - Age 28
Mouton's 1996 numbers, which were nearly identical to 1995 established a performance level which is good enough to play in the major leagues but not strong enough to claim a regular job. His biggest asset is his speed which is good for around 20 stolen bases as a part time player.

	AB	R	HR	RBI	SB	BA	$
1995 Houston NL	298	42	4	27	25	.262	13
1996 Houston NL	300	40	3	34	21	.263	9

MOUTON, LYLE - OF - BR - Age 27
The superb season turned in by Dave Martinez squeezed Mouton out of some playing time. He made good use out of the time he got, hitting nearly .300 over 214 at-bats. If the Sox pass on a second season with Tartabull then Mouton could see more playing time. Of course Jeff Abbott and Mike Cameron are coming up the pike as well.

	AB	R	HR	RBI	SB	BA	$
1995 Chicago AL	179	23	5	27	1	.302	5
1996 Chicago AL	214	25	7	39	3	.294	5

MUELLER, BILL - 3B - BB - Age 26
Mueller had a fabulous three-quarters of a season in Triple-A and then continued his great contact hitting and plate discipline with the Giants, subbing for the injured Matt Williams. A perfect number two hitter, Mueller spent the early post-season learning to play second base in the Arizona Fall League. That is where he will play this year.

	AB	R	HR	RBI	SB	BA	$
1996 San Francisco NL	200	31	0	19	0	.330	8

MULLIGAN, SEAN - C - BR - Age 26
Mulligan matured into a power hitter in 1996, and had a good year in Triple-A. With John Flaherty and Brad Johnson, the Padres are solid at catching, so he has an uphill battle to win a roster spot in 1997. A major hitting slump by starter John Flaherty or an injury could provide an opportunity for Mulligan.

MUMMAU, BOB - 2B/SS - BR - Age 25
Mummau took a step up the organizational ladder and posted decent numbers over limited work with Double-A Knoxville. If Tom Evans moves up the ladder, there may be room for Mummau to take over as the Double-A third baseman.

MUNOZ, OMER - 2B - BR - Age 31
Munoz has bounced around the minor leagues since 1985 without ever getting a call to the big leagues, though he once really had enough talent to be a decent utility infielder. Early last season, the Pirates gave up on his as a player and made him a coach in their farm system.

MUNOZ, PEDRO - OF - BR - Age 28
Munoz came out of the blocks with a hot bat, as a free-agent veteran outfielder on a team with little in the way of a set lineup, and an outfield with a lot of questions. He promptly got hurt. He missed 400 at-bats and lost the rest of the year.

	AB	R	HR	RBI	SB	BA	$
1995 Minnesota AL	376	45	18	58	0	.301	13
1996 Oakland AL	121	17	6	18	0	.256	0

MURPHY, MIKE - OF - BR - Age 25
A 1990 sixth round pick, Murphy abandoned switch hitting in 1992, with positive results. He has excellent speed (33 steals in 1993) and hit 29 doubles at Single-A Spartanburg, but he needs to improve his discipline at the plate (only 35 walks in 544 plate appearances). He dropped back to Class A, slowing his progress.

MURRAY, CALVIN - OF - BR - Age 25
The Giants, and probably everyone else in the universe are waiting for Murray to do something to confirm how highly thought of he was as a draft pick. He's got some speed, and a glove, but he can't hit well.

MURRAY, EDDIE - DH - BB - Age 41
The Indians believed that Murray's bat had slowed considerably, and traded him to the Orioles. The bat speed came to life with the Orioles as he hit home run number 500 for his career, and delivered numerous clutch hits. Overall he looked good hitting for the Orioles, and he was a good clubhouse presence. Murray is now strictly a DH, being too slow to play first base, but the Orioles may bring him back for another season.

	AB	R	HR	RBI	SB	BA	$
1995 Cleveland AL	436	68	21	82	5	.323	22
1996 Clev-Baltimore AL	566	69	22	79	4	.260	11

MURRAY, GLENN - OF - BR - Age 26
This career .234 minor league hitter fooled the Phils into believing he was major league timber on the strength of 142 excellent Triple-A at-bats in 1996. He is a wild swinger with longball potential who got himself out constantly on bad pitches in his major league trial. He is also a weak defender with a below average arm. He lost the last half of the season to wrist surgery, and will likely find himself left out of the major league outfield derby.

	AB	R	HR	RBI	SB	BA	$
1996 Philadelphia NL	97	8	2	6	1	.196	-

MYERS, GREG - C - BL - Age 30
This platoon catcher had a good season for the Twins in '96 and is capable of holding down the fort until Jose Valentin arrives. Myers should play even more in '97 than he did in '96.

	AB	R	HR	RBI	SB	BA	$
1995 California AL	273	35	9	38	0	.260	
1996 Minnesota AL	329	37	6	47	0	.286	5

MYERS, RODERICK - OF - BL - Age 24
He is a fleet-footed outfielder with growing power potential. If he didn't bat lefthanded he would already be a regular in Kansas City, but the Royals are loaded with lefty outfielders. Myers led Triple-A Omaha with 37 steals while also bashing 44 extra-base hits; he slugged .479 for Omaha. If the Royals move Michael Tucker to first base as expected, Myers and Jon Nunnally will duke it out for the vacant rightfield job.

	AB	R	HR	RBI	SB	BA	$
1996 Kansas City AL	63	9	1	11	3	.286	0

MYROW, JOHN - OF - BR - Age 25
Myrow is a slap-hitting speedy guy in an organization with the likes of Quinton McCracken and Terry Jones. He was a regular at Double-A New Haven in 1996, leading the team in steals.

NAEHRING, TIM - 3B - BR - Age 30
The oft-injured Naehring had another good year with the bat in 1996, adding more power to his already high batting average. The knocks against Naehring haven't changed: defensive limitations and continual injuries. What has changed is a new threat from Nomar Garciaparra. Garciaparra will soon be in Boston and could force John Valentin over to the hot corner, leaving Naehring out on a limb. Naehring's days in Beantown may be numbered.

	AB	R	HR	RBI	SB	BA	$
1995 Boston AL	433	61	10	57	0	.307	12
1996 Boston AL	430	77	17	65	2	.288	10

NATAL, BOB - C - BR - Age 31
Natal was the Marlins' second or third catcher for the fourth consecutive season in 1996. He is a decent defensive receiver who has well below average bat speed. He was outrighted off of the 40-man roster at season's end, and will likely have to be content with a Triple-A job in another organization in 1997.

	AB	R	HR	RBI	SB	BA	$
1995 Florida NL	43	2	2	6	0	.233	-
1996 Florida NL	90	4	0	2	0	.133	-

NEAL, MIKE - 2B - BR - Age 25
The Indians' 1993 16th round pick from LSU, Neal has a chance to reach the majors as a utilityman, but doesn't have nearly enough tools to be a regular. Second base is one of the least fortified positions in the Indians' system, which should enable Neal to start in Triple-A, where he will be only a heartbeat away from a major league audition.

NEEL, TROY - 1B - BL - Age 31
Neel has been in Japan since 1995. Should Neel return to the States, he would best serve a team in a platoon role and would hit for a low batting average, but decent power.

NELSON, BRYANT - SS - BB - Age 23
A 44th round draft choice in 1993, Nelson moved close to the head of his class after two solid seasons. He achieved prospect status by being selected to play in the Arizona Fall League. However, he failed to progress in 1996, batting only .252 at Class-A Kissimmee. He needs a breakout season in 1997 to have any chance of reaching the major leagues.

NEVERS, TOM - SS - BR - Age 25
A former top draft pick by the Astros (1990), Nevers just hasn't developed. He was at Double-A New Britain in 1996 where he hit .264-7-44 - much in line with his career norms. Nevers looks like a first-round bust.

NEVIN, PHIL - 3B - BR - Age 26
Nevin impressed in a big league audition in '96 (.292 with eight home runs) after playing at Double-A (.294 with 24

homers) while learning how to catch. Nevin will share time at third with Phil Hiatt in '97 or spend the year filling in the outfield.

	AB	R	HR	RBI	SB	BA	$
1995 Houston NL	60	4	0	1	1	.117	
1995 Detroit AL	96	9	2	12	0	.219	-
1996 Detroit AL	120	15	8	19	1	.292	2

NEWELL, BRETT - SS - BR - Age 24
Newell isn't a good hitter in any respect; he's advanced this far (Double-A Greenville) on the strength of his glove alone. Unfortunately for Newell, it's not enough for him to get to the big leagues.

NEWFIELD, MARC - OF/1B - BR - Age 24
Coming back to the AL in the Greg Vaughn deal. Newfield is even money to be the Brewers regular leftfielder in 1997. There is stiff competition for left field time on the Brewers. Jeromy Burnitz, and Gerald Williams won't make it easy. If Newfield is the man, he is capable of hitting 20 homers or more.

	AB	R	HR	RBI	SB	BA	$
1995 Seattle AL	85	7	3	14	0	.188	
1995 San Diego NL	55	6	1	7	0	.309	
1996 San Diego NL	191	27	5	26	1	.251	2
1996 Milwaukee AL	179	21	7	31	0	.307	4

NEWSON, WARREN - OF - BL - Age 32
Newson has generally posted good numbers as a part-time player, and 1996 was no exception. He has almost no chance of ever becoming a regular, but should be able to remain in the majors as a reserve. Newson posted double-digit figures in homers for the first time, but also struck out at an alarming rate (more than once in every three at-bats).

	AB	R	HR	RBI	SB	BA	$
1995 Chicago-Seattle AL	157	34	5	15	2	.261	2
1996 Texas AL	235	34	10	31	3	.255	3

NEWSTROM, DOUG - 3B - BL - Age 25
Newstrom was a Dodger farmhand for three years, and was drafted by the Orioles in the Triple-A phase of the Rule Five draft. He has hit for a decent average in his minor league career, but doesn't have much power. At age 25, and just completing a year in Single-A, the clock is running out on Newstrom.

NIEVES, MELVIN - OF - BB - Age 25
Nieves was streaky in his first full major league season, dominating a handful of games with home runs while striking out repeatedly in others. Nieves is a young Pete Incaviglia; he can produce 25 home runs a year with a decent average, but is a poor outfielder with little speed.

	AB	R	HR	RBI	SB	BA	$
1995 San Diego NL	234	32	14	38	2	.205	4
1996 Detroit AL	431	71	24	60	1	.246	7

NILSSON, DAVE - OF - BL - Age 27
Relatively healthy in 1996, Nilsson produced disappointing home run totals, but his overall improvement is right on target and he'll be more of a force in 1997. He will hit lefthanded pitching better in 1997 which should enable him to reach 520 at-bats and move him close to the 30 homer, 100 RBI range. It may well shave some points from his batting average, but he should stay near .300.

	AB	R	HR	RBI	SB	BA	$
1995 Milwaukee AL	263	41	12	53	2	.278	9
1996 Milwaukee AL	453	81	17	84	2	.331	17

NIXON, OTIS - OF - BB - Age 38
Nixon was expected to be a regular player but has never played 140 games in a season. A sore hamstring forced him to the disabled list for the first time in his career. Otis retains his great running speed and is always a threat to steal but the Blue Jays were concerned about a lack of overall run production from the center field position. With Shannon Stewart knocking on the door, Nixon's future in Toronto looked uncertain at the end of the 1996 season.

	AB	R	HR	RBI	SB	BA	$
1995 Texas AL	589	87	0	45	50	.295	34
1996 Toronto AL	496	87	1	29	54	.286	29

NIXON, TROT - OF - BL - Age 22
Since his selection in the first round of the 1993 draft (seventh overall), Nixon has been slowed by a back injury. While he's no longer the Red Sox best overall prospect, Nixon is still among their top five after an injury-free year at Double-A Trenton where he went .251-11-63-7. As a rightfielder, Nixon is above average and he can play centerfield. Look for him to start 1997 at Triple-A Pawtucket as a 22-year old; the Red Sox still expect big things from Nixon.

NORMAN, LES - OF - BR - Age 28
The only righthanded outfielder on the Royals' roster in 1996, Norman nonetheless got to play mostly with his glove. He's a decent fielder, but not a major league hitter, so he's a fifth outfielder at this point.

	AB	R	HR	RBI	SB	BA	$
1995 Kansas City AL	40	6	0	4	0	.225	-
1996 Kansas City AL	49	9	0	0	1	.122	-

NORTHRUP, KEVIN - OF - BR - Age 27
Northrup is a line-drive hitter with gap power. He is a good-looking player but was held back by the glut of outstanding outfield prospects in the Expos' farm system.

NORTON, GREG - SS - BB - Age 24
Norton split his time between Double-A and Triple-A on the White Sox farm, where he is being converted to shortstop. Norton has fair power (15 home runs and 70 RBI totals in 1996) and a little speed. The only question now is defense. He did well in the Arizona Fall League after the 1995 season.

	AB	R	HR	RBI	SB	BA	$
1996 Chicago AL	23	4	2	3	0	.217	-

NUNEVILLER, TOM - OF - BR - Age 27
Once a bonafide offensive prospect, Nuneviller first injured his knee almost five years ago. His latest problems have cost him all but 12 games of the last two seasons. The pro career of the Phils' 1990 fifth round pick has likely reached its end.

NUNEZ, RAMON - 1B/OF - BR - Age 24
Nunez shifted from shortstop to first base in 1995, then started last year at third base. It was a disappointing season all the way around as he hit and fielded poorly at Double-A Greenville and got demoted after going .201-4-26 with five times as many strikeouts as walks. He hit much better back at Durham - his 55 RBI were second on the club - but it isn't encouraging for a 24-year old to be sent back to Class A.

NUNEZ, SERGIO - 2B - BR - Age 22
Speedy Nunez spent his second straight year at Class A Wilmington and again led the club in steals. His hitting improved some and he had a steadier glove in 1996. He has been passed by Jed Hansen in the Royals' second base race; Nunez will have to do more than outrun everyone to reach the majors.

NUNNALLY JON - OF - BL - Age 25
A year after his phenomenal leap from Class A to the majors as a Rule Five selection, Nunnally spent most of 1996 in Triple-A where he led Omaha in homers, RBI and slugging average. A good outfielder with a strong arm, Nunnally's faults are a strikeout every 3.5 at-bats and batting lefthanded; there are just too many lefties in the Royals' outfield already. But, if Michael Tucker shifts to first base, Nunnally and Roderick Myers will fight for the rightfield job.

	AB	R	HR	RBI	SB	BA	$
1995 Kansas City AL	303	51	14	42	6	.244	8
1996 Kansas City AL	90	16	5	17	0	.211	-

OBANDO, SHERMAN - OF/DH - BR - Age 27
The Expos have had so much success in turning other organization's spare parts into fine major league players over the years that it seemed the same thing would happen last year when they got Obando from Baltimore in spring training. It looks like Montreal struck out this time. Obando is an impressive physical specimen but won't be anything more than a part-time outfielder in the majors.

	AB	R	HR	RBI	SB	BA	$
1995 Baltimore AL	38	0	0	3	1	.263	-
1996 Montreal NL	178	30	8	22	2	.247	2

O'BRIEN, CHARLIE - C - BR - Age 35
A career .219 hitter going into 1996, O'Brien took advantage of Sandy Martinez's struggles to post his best season in the majors. He calls an excellent game and the Blue Jays wanted him to return for 1997.

	AB	R	HR	RBI	SB	BA	$
1995 Atlanta NL	198	18	9	23	0	.227	2
1996 Toronto AL	324	33	13	44	0	.238	2

OCHOA, ALEX - OF - BR - Age 25
In a year of phenomenal progress, Ochoa came up and took over the Mets' right field job after Carl Everett and then Butch Huskey failed to click. Ochoa's season peaked with a five-hit, for-the-cycle performance, and he finished the year strong.

	AB	R	HR	RBI	SB	BA	$
1995 New York NL	37	7	0	0	1	.297	-
1996 New York NL	282	37	4	33	4	.294	8

OFFERMAN, JOSE - 2B/SS - BB - Age 28
Last year we said he'd need a trade and position change to reach his potential. He got both the trade and defensive shift and had his best season yet. The usual defensive headaches forced Offerman away from shortstop early in the year, but a funny thing happened on the way to Offerman's demise. He began to hit again. As expected, Offerman's base-stealing returned in the Royals' slash-and-dash offense. He finished the year on fire as a leadoff hitter and regular second baseman; Manager Bob Boone believes he has found his 1997 starting second baseman.

	AB	R	HR	RBI	SB	BA	$
1995 Los Angeles NL	429	69	4	33	2	.287	8
1996 Kansas City AL	561	85	5	47	24	.303	20

OGDEN, JAMIE - 1B/OF - BL - Age 26
It took Ogden five years to get out of A-ball, but once he did he has quickly improved his standing as a prospect. Ogden followed up his '95 performance at Double-A New Britain (.284-13-61) with a .263-18-74 showing at Triple-A Salt Lake City. He still strikes out too much (105 Ks in 448 at-bats in 1996) and isn't a good glove man. Ogden has a chance to be a major league reserve, on the strength of a marginal power bat.

O'LEARY, TROY - OF - BL - Age 27
Perhaps O'Leary's season was a disappointment for some Boston fans, but his offensive numbers rank among the team's best in most power categories; he was one of the steadier hitters for the BoSox in 1996. The major stumbling block for O'Leary has been an inability to play centerfield. He may not have to worry about it as Mike Greenwell should move on to another venue in 1997, opening up leftfield to O'Leary and others. Don't be surprised to see O'Leary in a platoon in right or leftfield; he regularly rips righthanded pitching.

	AB	R	HR	RBI	SB	BA	$
1995 Boston AL	399	60	10	49	5	.308	14
1996 Boston AL	497	68	15	81	3	.260	8

OLERUD, JOHN - 1B - BL - Age 28
The Toronto organization officially lost patience with John Olerud and announced in October that they would make every effort to deal him during the winter. Olerud's "disappointing" numbers were partially the result of him sitting on the bench much of the time and he remains a threat to win another batting title. He's entering the final year of an expensive contract and could disprove the arguments of those who say he has lost it.

	AB	R	HR	RBI	SB	BA	$
1995 Toronto AL	492	72	8	54	0	.291	10
1996 Toronto AL	398	59	18	61	1	.274	8

OLIVA, JOSE - 3B - BR - Age 26
Oliva put up huge numbers in 1996. He needs to find a spot soon as he's not getting younger. Oliva led the Cardinals organization, minors and majors, with 31 home runs. He drove in 86 runs to lead all Cards minor leaguers. Mostly a DH, can play a little 3B and a little 1B. The Cards hope he is another Geronimo Berroa-type - a late bloomer.

OLIVER, JOE - C - BR - Age 31
A decent platoon catcher, Oliver received more playing time than expected when Ray Knight decided that he called a better game than Eddie Taubensee. He needs a reality check after demanding a guarantee of 120 starts in 1997 to sign with the Reds, after a .242-11-46 season. Brook Fordyce (who had a decent year in Triple-A) and Taubensee (a much superior hitter) will probably deliver the reality check. If Oliver lands a full time job, his performance would plummet, as he struggles against right handed pitching.

	AB	R	HR	RBI	SB	BA	$
1995 Milwaukee AL	337	43	12	51	2	.273	9
1996 Cincinnati NL	289	31	11	46	2	.242	3

OLMEDA, JOSE - 2B - BB - Age 28
The eight-year minor league veteran can play second base, shortstop, third base and the outfield and had his best offensive season in 1996, his first year in the Marlins' system. However, he has only doubles power and little speed, and is one of the more undisciplined hitters in the upper minors. He could linger for a while at Triple-A, but is a longshot to ever earn a major league at bat.

O'MALLEY, TOM - OF - BL - Age 36
After spending parts of nine seasons in the majors with half a dozen different teams, O'Malley went to Japan. He hit .319 with 18 home runs and 94 RBI for the Yakult Swallows in 1996.

O'NEILL, PAUL - OF - BL - Age 34
Although he had a late season slump brought on by nagging little aches and pains, O'Neill remained one of the American League's most dangerous hitters, and with a winter of rest he should be rejuvenated and ready for a big 1997 season.

	AB	R	HR	RBI	SB	BA	$
1995 New York AL	460	82	22	96	1	.300	19
1996 New York AL	546	89	19	91	0	.302	14

OQUENDO, JOSE - SS/2B - BB - Age 33
Oquendo last appeared with the Cards in 1995. Injuries took him out in 1996.

ORDONEZ, REY - SS - BB - Age 25
Brought to the majors for his superb defense, Ordonez got off to a good start at the plate and, although he slumped a little in midsummer, he finished strong as well. Ordonez is a good contact hitter who will eventually become a prolific RBI producer. And the defense? This is a unique player. The high number of errors will diminish as official scorers learn: if Ordonez can't get it, it's a hit.

	AB	R	HR	RBI	SB	BA	$
1996 New York NL	502	51	1	30	1	.257	2

ORIE, KEVIN - 3B - BR - Age 24
A good-looking young third base prospect with a live bat, Orie hit home runs to both fields in his first game at Triple-A Iowa. He didn't hit another homer the rest of the year. He suffered a cartilage tear in his right wrist in '94 and his throwing has been erratic since. Orie played with injuries most of his Triple-A season in '96.

ORSULAK, JOE - OF - BL - Age 34
One of the good guys of the game, Orsulak is an above-average defender at all three outfield positions, but both his wheels and his bat have slowed over the years, making his presence on a 1997 major league roster quite uncertain. A frequent platooner over the years, Orsulak batted a paltry .215 against righties in 1996 - not a good sign.

	AB	R	HR	RBI	SB	BA	$
1995 New York NL	290	41	1	37	1	.283	5
1996 Florida NL	217	23	2	19	1	.221	-

ORTIZ, BO - OF - BR - Age 26
Ortiz is an Angel minor leaguer who had a good season in the Double-A Texas League last year, even getting named to the post-season All-Star team. The bad news is that it was his second year in the league. At age 26, and just completing Double-A, he's playing against younger guys. Time is running out on him.

ORTIZ, HECTOR - C - BR - Age 27
Ortiz is a journeyman minor league catcher. Ortiz will be 27 when the season begins and he hasn't shown anything that would make anyone believe he would be a major leaguer. Ortiz throws pretty well, but has just two home runs in his professional career.

ORTIZ, LUIS - 3B - BR - Age 26
Ortiz has nothing left to prove in the minors, but still awaits the chance to play regularly in the majors. If he ever gets the chance, he'll probably be a high average hitter with occasional power. He can't play third base, so he spent the year successfully learning to play first base. Unfortunately, there aren't many teams for whom a high-average first baseman with moderate power would be a marked improvement, so there are legitimate questions as to Ortiz' major league future.

ORTIZ, NICK - 2B - BR - Age 23
A career-best .302 season for Class-A Michigan helped Ortiz jump to Double-A for the first time in his six-year pro career. Having been tried at third base and at shortstop in past seasons, he is now settling in as a second baseman. Ortiz has the look of a reserve infielder due to his versatility and lack of power or speed.

ORTON, JOHN - C - BR - Age 31
Orton has accumulated over 400 major league at-bats spread over five years. He has a career batting average of .200, four homers, and 29 RBI, weak hitting that indicates that his usefulness to a major league team is as a backup catcher. The Angels released Orton from their Triple-A team in June 1996.

OSIK, KEITH - C/3B - BR - Age 28
Osik had a solid rookie season with the Pirates as backup catcher to Jason Kendall in 1996. He'll probably never be a starter in the big leagues but he's a decent hitter and his ability to play the corners of the infield and outfield only enhance his value.

	AB	R	HR	RBI	SB	BA	$
1996 Pittsburgh NL	140	18	1	14	1	.293	3

OTANEZ, WILLIS - 3B - BR - Age 23
Formerly a Dodger minor leaguer, Otanez was traded to the Mariners, then waived and claimed by the Orioles. He showed good power in the pitching-tough Double-A Eastern League last year, and he plays good defense. He hit six homers in one stretch of 15 at-bats. Otanez needs to develop a more consistent bat to get serious consideration for a major league job.

OTERO, RICKY - OF - BB - Age 24
Otero is a scrappy hustler who makes consistent contact, but has several nagging flaws. He constantly dives for balls in the outfield, costing his club extra bases more often than it gains outs, and has a poor throwing arm. His decisions on the basepaths generally don't take the game situation into account, and he swings at too many bad pitches when ahead in the count. He is a useful extra outfielder candidate, but will never again accumulate as much playing time as he did in 1996.

	AB	R	HR	RBI	SB	BA	$
1995 New York NL	51	5	0	1	2	.137	-
1996 Philadelphia NL	411	54	2	32	16	.273	10

O'TOOLE, BOBBY - C - BR - Age 22
O'Toole's in the Orioles farm system, and last year was his first in pro ball. He saw a lot of the country, playing in the Rookie League, two different levels of Class A, and Double-A. He got some at-bats at each stop, but he didn't hit much as he had difficulty adjusting to wooden bats. O'Toole is out of Providence University where he was Big East Conference MVP, and a third-team All-American.

OWEN, SPIKE - SS - BB - Age 35
Owen's career ended with a brief stint at Triple-A.

OWENS, BILLY - 1B - BB - Age 25
Owens appeared to be maturing into a decent power hitter and run producer with his solid .269-17-91 in the tough Double-A Eastern League in 1995. He had a much harder time hitting when promoted to Triple-A last year, and knee

surgery slowed his progress. Owens could come around in 1997, but he's not going to dislodge Rafael Palmeiro.

OWENS, ERIC - SS - BR - Age 26
The American Association MVP in 1995, Owens had a rough year in 1996. As a player with strong on base skills, extra base power, and speed, you would think he would be an excellent candidate for the vacant role of lead off hitter. The Reds instead brought in Vince Coleman and Mike Kelly, shuttled Owens between second base, third base, and left field (putting Owens in the impossible position of learning a new position at the major league level) and sent Owens to Triple-A at every opportunity (he was sent down and recalled a total of four times). Owens can play, and a smart organization would steal him away while his value is down.

	AB	R	HR	RBI	SB	BA	$
1996 Cincinnati NL	205	26	0	9	16	.200	-

OWENS, JAYHAWK - C - BR - Age 28
Owens lost his chance to become the Rockies' starting catcher out of spring training when he injured his wrist with a head-first slide. The wrist never really healed, and Owens underwent surgery at the end of the 1996 season. He is a big question-mark for 1997.

	AB	R	HR	RBI	SB	BA	$
1995 Colorado NL	45	7	4	12	0	.244	1
1996 Colorado NL	180	31	4	17	4	.239	1

Do You Surf The NET?

Visit John Benson's Web Site:

hhtp://www.johnbenson.com

For the latest news on products and services.

Download Benson's
Draft Software DEMO - FREE !!

View a FREE copy of the on-line magazine
John Benson on Baseball

PADILLA, ROY - OF - BL - Age 21
Padilla used the instructional league in 1995 to shift from the pitching mound to the outfield. The transition was a success as he hit .280 and led Class A Michigan with 21 steals. He has an overpowering arm and is a fine all-around athlete; watch for this youngster at Sarasota in 1997.

PAGANO, SCOTT - OF - BB - Age 25
Speed is Pagano's main asset (26 stolen bases for the Mets Double-A Binghamton team in 1996). He can draw a walk and provide adequate defense, but he is past the prospect stage.

PAGNOZZI, TOM - C - BR - Age 34
Pagnozzi had the best year of his career for the Cardinals last season at age 34, proving that he shouldn't be written off. At his age, with his chronic bad knees, it's unlikely he will duplicate 1996 again.

	AB	R	HR	RBI	SB	BA	$
1995 St. Louis NL	219	17	2	15	0	.215	-
1996 St. Louis NL	407	48	13	55	4	.270	9

PALMEIRO, ORLANDO - OF - BL - Age 28
With the exception of 1991, his first pro year, Palmeiro has hit over .300 every year in the minors, peaking at .328 in Triple-A in 1994. Last year was his third in Triple-A. He's a steady and productive singles hitter without much power, so he doesn't get a lot of publicity or attention. Given a long trial in the majors, he would probably hit around .300, but the Angels are loaded with good young outfielders, so his future doesn't look bright with them.

	AB	R	HR	RBI	SB	BA	$
1995 California AL	20	3	0	1	0	.350	-
1996 California AL	87	6	0	6	0	.287	-

PALMEIRO, RAFAEL - 1B - BL - Age 32
For the Orioles, Palmeiro's outstanding 1996 season was overshadowed by Brady Anderson's 50 home runs, and Eddie Murray hitting career homer number 500. But his 142 RBI set a new Orioles record. Palmeiro is one of the best hitters in baseball, and he is a consistent and steady producer. Only 32, he still could put up a career-best year.

	AB	R	HR	RBI	SB	BA	$
1995 Baltimore AL	554	89	39	104	3	.310	28
1996 Baltimore AL	626	110	39	142	8	.289	25

PALMER, DEAN - 3B - BR - Age 28
Palmer made enough progress defensively to remain at the hot corner for the time being, although his future could be at first base. He continues to strike out a lot. Only four American League hitters struck out more times last season. He is also a notoriously streaky hitter, and can carry a team with one of his hot streaks. Palmer should be able to stay around the .270-30-90 level for the next couple of years.

	AB	R	HR	RBI	SB	BA	$
1995 Texas AL	119	30	9	24	1	.336	6
1996 Texas AL	582	98	38	107	2	.280	18

PAPPAS, ERIK - C - BR - Age 30
Pappas is a Triple-A catcher with solid minor league credentials. He had a fine year, ending it as the MVP in the American Association championship series.

PAQUETTE, CRAIG - 3B - BR - Age 28
He was released during spring training by Oakland and ended up at Triple-A for Kansas City before joining the Royals in May. Paquette never saw a pitch he didn't like; at least he hit enough of them to lead the team in homers and RBI. Manager Bob Boone loves Paquette and will play him at every opportunity; so he's probably the Royals' starting third baseman going into 1997.

	AB	R	HR	RBI	SB	BA	$
1995 Oakland AL	283	42	13	49	5	.226	7
1996 Kansas City AL	429	61	22	67	5	.259	10

PARENT, MARK - C - BR - Age 35
Parent had a burst of power in 1995 when he hit 18 home runs, surprising because he had never before hit more than

seven in a season. Detroit signed him for 1996, but the power disappeared, even in the rabbit-ball year. He was waived in late August and signed by the Orioles with whom he had played in 1992 and '93. He was a backup to Chris Hoiles and late-inning defensive replacement. One reason for the Orioles to sign him for 1997 is that he's become Scott Erickson's personal catcher.

	AB	R	HR	RBI	SB	BA	$
1995 Two Teams	265	30	18	38	0	.234	7
1996 Baltimore AL	137	17	9	23	0	.226	0

PARKER, RICK - OF - BR - Age 34
A journeyman outfielder who hits for average and not much else, Parker managed to get another cup of coffee (his sixth) in the majors in 1996, pinch hitting for the Dodgers.

PATEL, MANNY - 2B - BL - Age 24
Patel's first year above A-ball resulted in a weak .220 season at Double-A Port City. He's not a flashy glove man, so his lack of power and average speed will keep him from advancing much farther.

PATTON, GREG - 3B - BR - Age 25
Formerly a shortstop, Patton has shown an adequate glove at the hot corner while hitting for power. However, he swings at far too many bad pitches resulting in increasingly lower batting averages and higher strikeout totals at each successively higher level. Patton is already 25 years old but has little time above Class A ball; he's a marginal prospect, at best.

PATZKE, JEFF - 2B - BB - Age 23
Patzke showed remarkable improvement making the move to Double-A. He can take a close pitch and will eventually make better contact. Not blessed with much power or speed, he is reliable defensively. Patzke could be the dark horse of the 1997 second baseman candidates.

PAUL, JOSH - OF/C - BR - Age 21
The White Sox' 1996 third round pick was immediately inserted into the lineup at Low-A Hickory in the South Atlantic League, bypassing Rookie ball. He showed excellent power/speed ability, hitting eight homers and stealing 13 bases in 226 at-bats. He made a seamless transition to the wooden bat, foreshadowed by a solid Cape Cod League season back in 1995. His catcher's arm is an asset in right field, which is likely his long term home.

PAYTON, JAY - OF - BR - Age 24
A year ago, Payton looked like a viable candidate for a Mets outfield job in 1996 (he hit .345 at Double-A in 1995) but elbow surgery slowed his advance. Payton remains an exciting upward-bound prospect. Gerry Hunsicker's three-word scouting report: born to hit.

PEARSON, EDDIE - 1B - BL - Age 23
An injury laid waste Pearson's 1995 season, but he did come back in 1996, hitting .223 with eight homers at Double-A Birmingham on the White Sox farm.

PECORILLI, ALDO - 1B - BR - Age 26
Pecorilli can certainly hit. In his first full year at Triple-A, he batted .290 and led the club with 15 homers and 62 RBI. The downside is that he lacks a true position and has been stuck at first base despite a trial as a catcher.

PEGUES, STEVE - OF - BR - Age 28
Persevering through eight years in the minors got Pegues a shot as a reserve outfielder with Pittsburgh in 1995. It was his peak as he kept the same role in 1996, but fell back a level to Triple-A Richmond. Pegues can hit a little and has some power and speed.

PEGUERO, JULIO - OF - BB - Age 28
Peguero got to the majors for fourteen games with the Phillies back in 1992. Since then he's bounced from the Mexican League through every minor league level. In 1996 he was Triple-A Tacoma's fourth outfielder, hitting .280-1-21-7. Peguero has decent speed, but it's really his only asset, and not enough to get him back to the bigs.

PELTIER, DAN - OF - BL - Age 28
Like former teammate McCarty, Peltier had a chance to establish himself both at first and in the outfield for the Giants last year. He didn't do either.

	AB	R	HR	RBI	SB	BA	$
1996 San Francisco NL	59	3	0	9	0	.254	-

PEMBERTON, RUDY - OF - BR - Age 27
Acquired at the end of May for pitcher Bryan Eversgerd, former Tigers' prospect Pemberton led Pawtucket with triple crown totals of .326-27-92. By placing among the top five in all three categories, he was an International League All-Star and MVP candidate. Power has always been his forte, but Pemberton's strikeout woes continued last year; he did nothing to improve on his career strikeout-to-walk ratio of nearly 3 to 1. Pemberton has good speed but is still a below average outfielder. He can serve as a reserve outfielder in the majors and provide power off the bench.

	AB	R	HR	RBI	SB	BA	$
1995 Detroit AL	30	3	0	3	0	.300	-
1996 Boston AL	41	11	1	10	3	.512	3

PENA, GERONIMO - 2B - BB - Age 30
The speed is gone, but he consistently drives the ball hard to the gaps from both sides of the plate. A club giving him 250 strategically placed at-bats will be handsomely rewarded with a .290 average and 20 extra base hits.

	AB	R	HR	RBI	SB	BA	$
1995 St. Louis NL	101	20	1	8	3	.267	1
1996 Cleveland AL	9	1	1	2	0	.111	-

PENA, TONY - C - BR - Age 39
Pena remained a valuable defensive asset and clubhouse leader as a backup with the Indians last season. Rookie Einar Diaz is no more than a half-season from being ready, so Pena's days as a major leaguer appear numbered.

	AB	R	HR	RBI	SB	BA	$
1995 Cleveland AL	263	25	5	28	1	.262	3
1996 Cleveland AL	174	14	1	27	0	.195	-

PENDLETON, TERRY - 3B - BB - Age 36
In what may have been Pendleton's last full big-league season, he returned to the Braves in time for the stretch drive and the playoffs. Pendleton is a sentimental favorite in Atlanta; his arrival in Georgia marked his MVP season in 1991 and the rise of the Braves' juggernaut. He's not the feared hitter and spectacular fielder he once was, but can still help a team in a pinch. This intelligent, multi-talented player just might make a good coach when he retires.

	AB	R	HR	RBI	SB	BA	$
1995 Florida NL	513	70	14	78	1	.290	16
1996 Florida-Atlanta NL	568	51	11	75	2	.238	2

PENN, SHANNON - OF/2B - BB - Age 27
Formerly a promising second-base prospect with the Tigers, Penn has stalled at Triple-A and has now shifted to the outfield. He led Toledo with 22 steals, but it was his fourth lowest steal total in the last five years.

PENNYFEATHER, WILLIAM - OF - BR - Age 28
Pennyfeather had three short looks by the Pirates in 1992-94, but came up short each time. He began 1996 with the Reds, and was traded to the Angels for Eduardo Perez. He can hit .270-285 in Triple-A, but he's not considered a major league prospect. Last year was his best minor league season. Pennyfeather could latch on somewhere as a reserve outfielder.

PEOPLES, DANNY - 1B/3B - BR - Age 22
The normally dead-on Indians' organization reached for Peoples, only Baseball America's 88th-ranked prospect, on the first round of the 1996 draft. Considered a power prospect with below average defensive skills, Peoples moved from first to third base in Rookie Ball - and he prompted injured his throwing shoulder. It's early, but things could be better.

PEREZ, DANNY - OF - BR - Age 26
Perez didn't generate much power last season playing in his hometown, El Paso, but he did hit .351 in his 154 at-bats.

Benson's Baseball Player Guide: 1997

PEREZ, EDDIE - C - BR - Age 28
One of the things that makes the Braves so tough to beat is having reserves like Perez. He gives Atlanta respectable defense and can pop an occasional homer. The Braves hardly miss a beat when Perez is behind the plate, although he wouldn't be nearly as valuable in a starting role.

	AB	R	HR	RBI	SB	BA	$
1995 Atlanta NL	13	1	1	4	0	.308	-
1996 Atlanta NL	156	19	4	17	0	.256	1

PEREZ, EDUARDO - 3B/1B - BR - Age 27
Tony's son is a little old to be considered a serious prospect, but he posted an excellent year at Indianapolis after the Reds acquired him from the Angels, with 21 homers, 84 RBI and 11 steals in 122 games. Unlike most of the other Reds prospects, Perez has demonstrated decent strike zone judgment throughout his minor league career. Perez would make an excellent platoon partner for Hal Morris, and he may get that chance in 1997.

	AB	R	HR	RBI	SB	BA	$
1995 California AL	71	9	1	7	0	.169	-
1996 Cincinnati NL	36	8	3	5	0	.222	-

PEREZ, JHONNY - SS - BR - Age 20
Perez (yes he does spell his first name that way) is a genuine prospect on the Astros farm. In his second year at high Class A, he lifted his power output, from four homers in 1995 to 12 in 1996. Anyone in double digits in the Florida State League at age 21 has major league power potential. And Perez has speed, too (16 stolen bases last year).

PEREZ, NEIFI - SS - BB - Age 22
Perez was named the Rockies Player of the Year for 1996 at Triple-A Colorado Springs, and made his way to the parent club even before the September call-ups. He is unparalleled defensively, but he now hits more consistently and with more power than earlier in his (brief) career. If the Rockies lose Weiss or Young during the off-season, Perez will likely be a starter in 1997.

PEREZ, ROBERT - OF - BR - Age 27
Perez won the International League batting title in 1995 and went on to hit .327 in just over 200 at-bats with the Jays last year. Although he makes good contact, he swings at far too many pitches and his power leaves something to be desired. Therefore, the Toronto organization asked him to spend the off-season working with instructors to alter his swing. His average could drop in favor of some homers and he stands an excellent chance of platooning this year.

	AB	R	HR	RBI	SB	BA	$
1996 Toronto AL	202	30	2	21	3	.327	4

PEREZ, TOMAS - SS - BB - Age 23
Perez returned from Syracuse in midseason to steal the second base job from three other candidates. He is superior defensively to Felipe Crespo and Miguel Cairo but his hitting leaves much to be desired. Perez entered the winter as the most likely candidate to take over at second base but the Jays were in the market for a veteran at that position.

	AB	R	HR	RBI	SB	BA	$
1995 Toronto AL	98	12	1	8	0	.245	-
1996 Toronto AL	295	24	1	19	1	.251	-

PERRY, HERBERT - 1B/3B - BR - Age 27
This natural line drive hitter could compete for his old platoon role in 1997, and could be a early draftee of one of the 1998 expansion clubs.

PETAGINE, ROBERTO - 1B - BL - Age 25
Once regarded as a future batting champ stuck behind Jeff Bagwell in the Houston depth charts, Petagine's career drifted sideways in San Diego where he couldn't win the starting first base job, and then he had an OK but unspectacular season at Triple-A in 1996. As Petagine put it himself in September, he has "about one more chance" to make it as a major leaguer.

	AB	R	HR	RBI	SB	BA	$
1995 San Diego NL	124	15	3	17	0	.234	1
1996 New York NL	99	10	4	17	0	.232	-

PETERSEN, CHRIS - 2B - BR - Age 26
Peterson is a slick-fielding shortstop with no stick. If you've seen David Howard play, you might as well have seen Peterson. Peterson did turn in his best professional year at the plate, hitting .284 while splitting time between Orlando and Iowa. Peterson could be a defensive replacement for a team with an open roster spot, but he won't be Alex Rodriguez or even Marc Belanger.

PETERSON, CHARLES - OF - BR - Age 22
Peterson, the Pirates' top draft pick in 1993, is the poster boy for the organization's fascination with "tools" players. His 6-foot-3, 203-pound body looks great in a uniform and he was a legend as a high school quarterback in South Carolina. If the Pirates were trying to beat Florida and Tennessee for the SEC football title, he'd be a great help. But like so many of the Pirates' "tools" guys, he can't play baseball.

PETERSON, NATE - OF - BL - Age 25
Peterson is an Australian who has moved up a level in each of his four years in the Astro organization. He hits about .280 with three homers and three stolen bases wherever he plays. That won't get him to the majors.

PETRICK, BEN - C - BR - Age 19
This young prospect spent his first professional season at Low-A Asheville, leading the Rockies affiliate in runs scored. Although his hitting was inconsistent at best, he showed discipline at the plate and led the team in walks. Because the Rockies are relatively weak at catcher organization-wide, offensive improvement could make Petrick's progress swift.

PHILLIPS, GARY - 3B - BR - Age 25
Phillips possesses a good enough glove and strong arm, but doesn't do enough at the plate to merit moving much further up the ladder.

PHILLIPS, J.R. - 1B - BL - Age 26
The Giants' longball prospect moved to the Phils' chain in 1996, but that's all about him that changed. He's still a wild swinging, occasional long ball threat that enables him to dominate in the minors and struggle mightily in the majors.

	AB	R	HR	RBI	SB	BA	$
1995 San Francisco NL	231	27	9	28	1	.195	1
1996 Philadelphia NL	104	12	7	15	0	.163	-

PHILLIPS, TONY - 3B/OF - BB - Age 37
Finally the White Sox have a leadoff hitter. He almost retired in spring training but changed his mind after less than a week. His on-base percentage was over .400 and he played in 153 games. He didn't get as many hits as Lance Johnson did or steal as many bases, but did add stability to the top of the batting order. He also played well defensively.

	AB	R	HR	RBI	SB	BA	$
1995 California AL	525	119	27	61	13	.261	19
1996 Chicago AL	581	119	12	63	13	.277	14

PIAZZA, MIKE - C - BR - Age 28
It was a great season by a great player at his peak, but as anyone who saw the last few games of the season and the playoffs knows, the price was high. If the Dodgers persist in working him into the ground (146 games at catcher in 1996) he isn't going to last long enough to be considered for the Hall of Fame. Sparky Anderson used to rest Johnny Bench 15 games a season in the outfield, and the Dodgers would be well advised to consider the same for Piazza. There is no reason to expect a lesser performance in 1997, keeping in mind the caution that catchers (particularly catchers that catch 145 games a year) are as injury prone as starting pitchers.

	AB	R	HR	RBI	SB	BA	$
1995 Los Angeles NL	434	82	32	93	1	.346	28
1996 Los Angeles NL	547	87	36	105	0	.336	35

PIERZYNSKI, A.J. - C - BL - Age 19
A catcher with a strong arm and quick release, Pierzynski was also a fairly good hitter in the Midwest Class A league.

PIRKL, GREG - 1B - BR - Age 26
Unable to crack the Mariners' lineup in three previous tries, Pirkl had his best chance in 1996. But, instead of platooning at first base with Paul Sorrento, he lost the job to Brian Hunter and wound up back in Triple-A again. The trade to Boston

won't help Pirkl's chance at regular big-league play, either. Pirkl can hit for power, but is below-average in most every other respect.

PLANTIER, PHIL - OF - BL - Age 28
Talk about riddles, once one of the most promising power hitters in baseball has become an overswinging afterthought. He'll catch on with someone, but Plantier has become little more than an extra outfielder, and even that is questionable.

	AB	R	HR	RBI	SB	BA	$
1995 San Diego NL	216	33	9	34	1	.255	5
1996 Oakland AL	231	29	7	31	2	.212	-

PLEDGER, KINNIS - OF - BL - Age 28
If he was five years younger, Pledger would be an exciting combination of speed, power, and defensive savvy (19 homers and 20 steals at Double-A Norwich in 1996). Given his birth certificate, he's now just a deep extension of the major league bench.

PODSEDNIK, SCOTT - OF - BL - Age 21
The 1994 Rangers' number three pick was acquired by the Marlins prior to the 1996 season, and made consistent contact with no power and decent speed as one of the younger starters in the High-A Florida State League. Podsednik does not have any one overwhelming skill that will put him on the fast track to the majors, but he appears to have the defensive skills and bat-handling ability to eventually (late 1998?) develop into a serviceable extra outfielder at the big league level.

POE, CHARLES - OF - BR - Age 25
Just the acquisition of Poe has to be considered a triumph as he was paired with Andrew Lorraine in exchange for Danny Tartabull. Poe's numbers have remained almost the same over his last three years.

POLCOVICH, KEVIN - SS - BR - Age 26
Polcovich's value lies in the fact he is an above-average defensive player at second base, shortstop and third base.

POLONIA, LUIS - OF - BL - Age 32
This much-travelled, singles-hitting speedster was used sparingly in Baltimore before joining the Braves for the post-season roster. It was the second year in a row that Polonia joined Atlanta for the pennant race. Polonia is a one-dimensional player whose value is directly tied to how he is used. On a team that values speed, Polonia can be a deadly weapon. For just about any other team he's more valuable as a reserve than as a starter; he can't help a team unless he can run.

	AB	R	HR	RBI	SB	BA	$
1995 NY AL - Atlanta NL	291	43	2	17	13	.261	7
1996 Baltimore AL	175	25	2	14	8	.240	2
1996 Atlanta NL	31	3	0	2	1	.419	2

POSADA, JORGE - C - BB - Age 25
After a solid season at Triple-A in 1996, Posada got a callup to New York and earned a place as the number two catcher for 1997. He can do everything well: hit for some power, draw a walk, and handle pitchers.

POSE, SCOTT - OF - BL - Age 30
He remains a good defensive outfielder with no power. For pure running speed, he is one of the fastest runners in the organization. It wasn't enough with Florida and likely won't be enough with Toronto to qualify him as a major leaguer.

POUGH, PORK CHOP - 3B/1B - BR - Age 27
Tom Gordon's cousin, Clyde Pough - a.k.a. "Pork Chop" - had a dismal year sharing third base at Triple-A Pawtucket in 1996. His power evaporated and his average plummeted as he led the team in strikeouts; Pough was eventually released by the Red Sox. He's not a good fielder and hasn't made the adjustments necessary to succeed above Double-A ball. Pough has the look of a career minor leaguer.

POWELL, ALONZO - OF - BR - Age 32
After surfacing briefly with the Expos and Mariners, Powell went to Japan. He likes it there, hitting .349 for the Chunichi Dragons in 1996.

POWELL, DANTE - OF - BR - Age 23
Powell is a solid a prospect as the Giants own-he has good power and tremendous speed. At 23 he played well at Double-A in 1996.

POZO, ARQUIMEDEZ - 2B - BR - Age 23
Unlike Tacoma teammate Greg Pirkl, Pozo's late-season trade to Boston will improve his chances at big-league play. He hits for power and average, can run a little, and wields a good glove. A shift from second base to third in 1996 can be reversed should Pozo need to play second to get to the majors. Questions have recently arisen over Pozo's true age; he may be two years older than previously stated. If he's really 25 years old entering 1997 then it may limit his upward mobility.

	AB	R	HR	RBI	SB	BA	$
1996 Boston AL	58	4	1	11	1	.172	-

POZO, YOHEL - C - BR - Age 23
This weak-hitting catcher saw playing time at Triple-A Colorado Springs due to a rash of injuries on the club, then was himself a victim. He's unlikely to stick with or rise above Triple-A level absent offensive improvement.

PRIDE, CURTIS - OF - BL - Age 28
One of the nicer stories of '96 was the good season Pride, who is deaf, put together as a reserve outfielder.

	AB	R	HR	RBI	SB	BA	$
1995 Montreal NL	63	10	0	2	3	.175	
1996 Detroit AL	267	52	10	31	11	.300	10

PRIETO, ALEJANDRO - SS - BB - Age 21
Prieto is a fine fielder who can run well. More importantly, he made great strides as a hitter in 1996, reaching a career-high .284 average in a tough hitters' park at Class A Wilmington. Young Prieto will pressure the Royals' older prospects at higher levels soon.

PRIETO, CHRIS - OF - BL - Age 24
Padre farmhand Prieto is a small outfielder with no power to speak of, but he has hit for a decent .270-280 average in the minors. He can also steal a base occasionally.

PRINCE, TOM - C - BR - Age 32
Prince replaced Carlos Hernandez as Mike Piazza's primary backup and he actually hit well in 64 at-bats, a first for the former Pirate who had a career average of .181 entering the season. As long as Piazza catches 145 games a year, Prince is an adequate backup thanks to strong defensive skills, but the Dodgers will need to upgrade if they are going to give Piazza some rest playing other positions.

	AB	R	HR	RBI	SB	BA	$
1996 Los Angeles NL	64	6	1	11	0	.297	1

PRITCHETT, CHRIS - 1B - BL - Age 27
Pritchett was a Triple-A All-Star last year. It was his second full year in Triple-A, and he improved all of his major statistics, and showed more power while hitting with authority. His path to the Angels is blocked by incumbent J.T. Snow, and Jim Edmonds, who can also play first base.

PUCKETT, KIRBY - OF - BR - Age 36
Puckett retired in the middle of the '96 season with an early form of glaucoma in one of his eyes. The ten-time All Star retired with 2,304 hits, a .318 average, and millions of fans who felt privileged to see one of the game's most graceful performers.

PULLIAM, HARVEY - OF - BR - Age 29
Injuries derailed Pulliam in 1996 after a productive comeback year in 1995. This power-hitter needs some help from off-season moves to have a realistic shot at a job with the Rockies in 1997.

PYE, EDDIE - 2B - BR - Age 30
Pye had cups of coffee with the Dodgers in 1994 and 1995 and averaged over .320 in the Pacific Coast League from 1991 through 1995. Pye batted .257 for Triple-A Tucson in 1996 before becoming disenchanted with his playing time and leaving the team in midseason. His career may be over.

Benson's Baseball Player Guide: 1997

QUINLAN, TOM - 3B - BR - Age 29
Quinlan has gotten four visits to the majors as the result of bashing Triple-A pitching for the last six years. Unfortunately, he has never learned any plate discipline, so the visits have been brief. Quinlan was one of Triple-A Salt Lake City's better power hitters in 1996, batting .283-15-81, but he also led the club with 121 strikeouts in 491 at-bats.

QUINN, MARK - OF - BR - Age 22
Quinn's first full season as a pro was an unqualified success as he showed power (nine homers, 71 RBI), speed (14 steals) and a good batting eye (one walk per ten at-bats) while hitting .302 and playing well in the outfield. Quinn was older than most of his counterparts in the Midwest League, though, so he'll need to have similar success at higher levels to be a true prospect.

RAABE, BRIAN - 2B - BR - Age 29
Raabe is a Jody Reed/Jeff Frye type of player who had an excellent year (.351, 18 homers) at Triple-A Salt Lake in '96. Raabe is just as good as many big leaguers and someone should give him a shot in '97.

RADMANOVICH, RYAN - OF - BL - Age 25
After missing almost all of 1995 with a serious knee injury, Radmanovich put together his best season as a pro, hitting .280-25-86 for Double-A New Britain. His 25 homers led the club - but so did his 122 strikeouts. He can play centerfield and should eventually reach the majors as a reserve outfielder.

RAINES, TIM - OF - BB - Age 37
After a slow spring and summer characterized by hamstring problems, Raines came on strong late in 1996. He was instrumental in the Yankees championship campaign with on-field leadership and exciting baserunning. Among the all-time leaders in stolen bases, he is still a threat to run any time.

	AB	R	HR	RBI	SB	BA	$
1995 Chicago AL	502	81	12	67	13	.285	18
1996 New York AL	201	45	9	33	10	.284	8

RAMIREZ, ALEX - OF - BR - Age 22
Ramirez was arguably the most improved player in the Indians' chain in 1996, showing a consistent line drive bat with gap power and above-average speed at Double-A Canton-Akron as one of the younger regulars in the Eastern League. However, the Indians' organizational outfield depth and Ramirez' career 365/91 strikeout/walk ratio could limit him to an extra outfield role in the majors, possibly beginning in 1998.

RAMIREZ, ANGEL - OF - BR - Age 23
Ramirez moved up to Double-A and posted similar results as a year earlier at Dunedin. He needs to take more walks to be of value and he has little power.

RAMIREZ, MANNY - OF - BR - Age 24
Quietly, Ramirez has developed into one of the most devastating all-around offensive forces in all of baseball. He hits for average (his mark vs. righties was .304 in 1996, two years removed from a sub-Mendoza Line number) and has extreme power to all fields, but has only scratched the surface of his immense potential. The Indians are slowly being transformed from the Belle/Lofton edition to the Thome/Ramirez edition - the latter will be the one that snags a World Series title. Ramirez is on the verge of challenging for a Triple Crown amid one of the greatest arrays of sluggers ever assembled in one league at the same time.

	AB	R	HR	RBI	SB	BA	$
1995 Cleveland AL	484	85	31	107	6	.308	26
1996 Cleveland AL	550	94	33	112	8	.309	24

RAMOS, JOHN - DH - BR - Age 31
Ramos continued to hang on to his precarious career in 1996. He can catch, play first base or the outfield and could become someone's pinch-hitter and emergency catcher. After a great 1995 season that saw him club twenty homers with Syracuse, he came back to his normal level.

RAMOS, KEN - OF - BL - Age 29
Ramos is a veteran minor league outfielder who has consistently hit for average and stolen some bases. However, his performance declined in 1996 (.270-4-34-6 at Triple-A) and he may be at the end of the line.

RAMSEY, FERNANDO - OF - BR - Age 31
A great defensive outfielder with good speed, Ramsey has never been able to hit enough to stick in the majors with the White Sox. He hit just .217 at Triple-A in 1996.

RANDA, JOE - 3B - BR - Age 27
Randa quietly had one of the year's best rookie seasons. His .303 average was a career best since his first pro season (hitting .338 at low-A Eugene in 1991). He's a marvelous defensive player and useful all-around offensive player, but, unfortunately, Manager Bob Boone would rather play Craig Paquette everyday.

	AB	R	HR	RBI	SB	BA	$
1995 Kansas City AL	70	6	1	5	0	.171	-
1996 Kansas City AL	337	36	6	47	13	.303	12

RAPPOLI, PAUL - OF - BL - Age 25
An elbow injury knocked Rappoli out for the entire 1995 season, then he played sparingly for Double-A Trenton in 1996, batting just .212 with little of his former speed. Time appears to be running out for Rappoli;

RAVEN, LUIS - 3B - BR - Age 28
A solid minor league journeyman. Raven has minor league power numbers. His total of 38 walks in 1996 was easily the highest mark of his eight-year pro career. Raven could make it back to Triple-A in 1997, but no higher.

RAYNOR, MARK - SS - BR - Age 24
The Phils' 1995 13th round pick is a scrapper whose zest for the game overcomes a lack of raw tools. He slaps singles to all fields, makes contact, draws walks and manages to steal bases on guile rather than speed. However, a 24-year-old with only 55 High-A at-bats under his belt is not exactly on the express train to the majors. With the shortstop position wide open ahead of him in the Phils' system, Raynor needs to have a big year and advance two levels in 1997 to have a chance to eventually be a backup in the bigs.

READY, RANDY - 3B - BR - Age 37
Veteran Randy Ready spent all or parts of 13 years in the majors, peaking with a .309 season in 1987 with the Padres. He was released by the Phillies in 1995, and retired. But he signed a minor league contract with the Padres in 1996 where he played in Triple-A, trying to get back to the majors. Ready will make an excellent coach.

REBOULET, JEFF - SS/3B - BR - Age 32
The Twins' jack-of-all-trades had a dismal season with the bat in 1996. He played almost every position on the field last year, but never did get his bat going. He's the kind of player that managers love to have because he can do so many different things. He can hit better than he did last year and his versatility is a big plus. Reboulet will again be a useful major league reserve in 1997.

	AB	R	HR	RBI	SB	BA	$
1995 Minnesota AL	216	39	4	23	1	.292	4
1996 Minnesota AL	234	20	0	23	4	.222	-

REDMOND, MIKE - C - BR - Age 25
Redmond has adequate defensive skills, and was much improved in his second tour of the Double-A Eastern League. Most impressive was his durability.

REED, JEFF - C - BL - Age 34
Reed was signed by the Rockies as a lefty backup, but he ended the season with most of the playing time at catcher. Coors Field inflated his average and power numbers; increased playing time had an adverse effect on his defense.

	AB	R	HR	RBI	SB	BA	$
1995 San Francisco NL	113	12	0	9	0	.265	0
1996 Colorado NL	341	34	8	37	2	.284	9

REED, JODY - 2B - BR - Age 34
Veteran Reed slumped late in the season, actually losing his job to Craig Shipley. Reed had been a steady performer for the Padres, but his hitting productivity declined last year. Rookie prospect Homer Bush, the heir apparent, missed much of last season in the minors, so he may not be ready.

	AB	R	HR	RBI	SB	BA	$
1995 San Diego NL	445	58	4	40	6	.256	7
1996 San Diego NL	495	45	2	49	2	.244	1

REESE, CALVIN - SS - BR - Age 23
Reese used to be an extremely well regarded prospect (rated as the number one prospect in the Reds organization by Baseball America). Defensively, Reese is a major league shortstop now but Rey Ordonez is a better hitter. Reese showed gap power in the past, but he slugged only .300 in 1996 at Indianapolis. He is still young enough to develop, but Barry Larkin isn't going anywhere,

REID, DEREK - OF - BR - Age 27
Both his power numbers and average have improved recently, but he's playing against guys three plus years younger.

REIMER, KEVIN - OF/DH - BL - Age 32
Back in the U.S. after two years in Japan, Reimer is strictly a lefty power hitter. He is a poor outfielder with a career .258 major league batting average and a lot of strikeouts. If Reimer gets back to the majors it'll be as a lefty bench bat.

RELAFORD, DESI - SS - BB - Age 23
The Phils acquired Relaford from the Mariners for Terry Mulholland before the 1996 trading deadline. The presence of Alex Rodriguez in Seattle caused Relaford to be shifted from his more comfortable shortstop position to second base at Triple-A in 1996, and he let it negatively affect his offense. He is a rangy but at times erratic defender with a cannon arm and good speed who must learn to hit fewer fly balls to be a passable offensive player in the majors. He is a likely Phils' utilityman in 1997, who could unseat Kevin Stocker by season's end.

	AB	R	HR	RBI	SB	BA	$
1996 Philadelphia NL	40	2	0	1	1	.175	-

RENTERIA, EDGAR - SS - BR - Age 21
Renteria was a revelation in his rookie season, dazzling with both his acrobatics and consistency afield, and showing much more consistency than expected at the plate. Most impressive was his .326 average against righties - this guy should be a perennial .300 hitter with 30 steal speed and eventual 10-15 homer power. Defensively, he's a greyhound who might not get the headlines of a Rey Ordonez, though he is more consistent. Most players his age are still toiling in the low minors - Renteria is a worthy member of the Rodriguez/Jeter/Garciaparra/Ordonez etc. Era of the Shortstop club. Think Barry Larkin.

	AB	R	HR	RBI	SB	BA	$
1996 Florida NL	431	68	5	31	16	.309	18

RHODES, KARL - OF - BL - Age 28
"Tuffy" hit little in brief major league stints for the Cubs and Red Sox, but could never find his place and left for Japan in 1996.

RICE, LANCE - C - BB - Age 30
Rice is a 30-year-old catcher who has spent about seven years in Double-A with a number of organizations. Like Earl Weaver and other successful major league managers who spent many years in the minors, maybe Rice's future is in managing.

RICHARDSON, BRIAN - 3B - BR - Age 21
Richardson is a strong defensive player who is starting to hit for power. He's already skilled enough with the glove to play in the big leagues. As he matures and becomes a better hitter, he'll get a chance to play third base regularly for Los Angeles.

RIGGS, ADAM - 2B - BR - Age 24
Riggs advanced to Double-A for the first time and had a fine season at the plate, batting .283-14-66 with 16 stolen bases. But, he's a below-average glove man, so he may have to move elsewhere to get an extended shot above Double-A.

RIGGS, KEVIN - 2B - BL - Age 28
Part of the Yankees' player development program includes keeping mature players scattered around the system to provide stable teammates for up-and-coming youngsters. Riggs may be nowhere on the major league depth chart, but he's a career .302 minor league hitter with a job at Double-A if he wants one.

RILEY, MARQUIS - OF - BR - Age 26
Riley has only one marketable tool - raw speed, enabling him to excel defensively. He ranks among the least powerful hitters in the minor leagues. He has never exceeded the humble totals of 12 doubles, six triples, or one homer in any of his five pro seasons.

RIOS, ARMANDO - OF - BL - Age 25
Rios' speed numbers fell off a little after his promotion to Double-A last year, but he turned in a good year hitting for power and showing great plate discipline (44 walks to 42 strikeouts). He should play in Phoenix in 1997 with teammate Dante Powell.

RIOS, EDDIE - 2B - BR - Age 24
A contact-hitting glove man, Rios switched from second base to third base in 1996. He's a below-average hitter who could someday be a big-league utility player.

RIPKEN, BILLY - 2B - BR - Age 32
Utility infielder Ripken will never get to play much as long as the Orioles have solid regulars like Roberto Alomar and Cal Ripken who can play day-in and day-out. Even if he somehow manages to get 400 at-bats, he would probably hit .230. Ripken hit .291 in 1990, so he could get lucky again, but it's a reach.

	AB	R	HR	RBI	SB	BA	$
1995 Cleveland AL	17	4	2	3	0	.412	-
1996 Baltimore AL	135	19	2	12	0	.230	-

RIPKEN, CAL - SS - BR - Age 36
When Ripken gets into slumps, and he tinkers with his batting stance, especially how he holds his bat waiting for the pitch. He changes his stance about once a week. Thus far, the process is working as he doesn't get into prolonged slumps, and he usually has his solid year. He may have lost a step in the field, and there is renewed talk about moving him to third base. On the other hand, the "Baseball America" poll of managers rated him as the second-best defensive shortstop in the American League.

	AB	R	HR	RBI	SB	BA	$
1995 Baltimore AL	550	71	17	88	0	.262	12
1996 Baltimore AL	640	94	26	102	1	.278	15

RIVERA, LUIS - 2B/SS - BR - Age 33
The former Red Sox regular is one more case where the Mets have made some effort to enrich their farm teams with experienced personnel. Having hit just .225 at Triple-A and being only a fair fielder, Rivera is long past his major league prime, a .258-8-40 season with Boston in 1991.

RIVERA, RUBEN - OF - BR - Age 23
Although he didn't exactly blossom as a hitter in 1996, Rivera showed some patience and go-with-the-pitch ability during his September callup, and he was in New York mainly to provide solid right field defensive support. Rivera remains a major prospect for the long term.

	AB	R	HR	RBI	SB	BA	$
1996 New York AL	88	17	2	16	6	.284	3

ROBERGE, JOHN - 3B - BR - Age 24
Roberge hit for a good average in his first Double-A duty, earning a trip to Triple-A with his .293-6-27 showing at San Antonio. He continued to hit for average at Albuquerque (.321), but Roberge is a distant prospect. He lacks a true position and his hitting is one-dimensional; all batting average, low power and poor strike-zone judgment. Roberge is not a good prospect.

ROBERSON, KEVIN - OF - BB - Age 29
Still young enough to advance and possessing fair power, Roberson has already missed some opportunities when he was called up with the Cubs in 1993, 1994 and 1995. The Mets have a number of better outfield prospects, and they didn't use Roberson as an everyday player, even at Triple-A.

	AB	R	HR	RBI	SB	BA	$
1995 Chicago NL	38	5	4	6	0	.184	0
1996 New York NL	36	8	3	9	0	.222	-

ROBERTS, BIP - 2B - BB - Age 33
Multiple injuries again dimmed Roberts performance; first he tore a hamstring and later injured his ribcage. The injuries kept him from getting the 500 at-bats necessary to roll his contract over to 1997; he was a free agent over the off-season. Roberts still turned in a respectable year with the bat and managed 52 RBI without a homer. Roberts will help his new team by giving them good batting average and excellent speed - at least until he gets hurt again.

	AB	R	HR	RBI	SB	BA	$
1995 San Diego NL	296	40	2	25	20	.304	14
1996 Kansas City AL	339	39	0	52	12	.283	9

ROBERTS, LONELL - OF - BB - Age 25
He missed much of 1996 but remains the second-highest center fielder prospect in the organization, behind Shannon Stewart. Roberts is the fastest pure runner the Jays have and his fourteen times caught stealing were a mirage. Possibly superior to Stewart defensively, Roberts is likely ticketed for a comeback season in the minors. He is capable of pulling off an upset by becoming the Jays' center fielder in spring training.

ROBERTSON, JASON - OF - BL - Age 26
After seven years in the Yankees' chain, Robertson became a Double-A Marlin in 1996, his fifth straight campaign at that level. He has some gap power and decent speed, but is a wild swinger who consistently strikes out in about one quarter of his at-bats. He has clearly found his plateau, and might linger for another couple of years, with uninspiring results.

ROBERTSON, MIKE - 1B - BL - Age 26
Stuck behind Frank Thomas on the White Sox roster, Robertson has spent two years at Triple-A Nashville, collecting 19 homers in 1995 and 21 more in 1996.

ROCHA, JUAN - OF - BR - Age 23
A late round draft pick in 1994 (67th round), Rocha had a breakout year in 1996, batting .268 and leading Class A Lansing with 14 homers and 83 RBI. However, he also struck out 116 times.

RODARTE, RAUL - OF - BR - Age 27
A good all-around athlete, Rodarte developed slowly in the Mariners' system before having his best pro season in 1996. His .306-6-34 showing for Double-A Greenville helped him move up to Richmond where he led the club with a .338 average as an outfielder. Rodarte is an aging prospect who has greatly improved his chances of reaching the majors in a reserve role, although he'll have a better chance with an organization less well-stocked than the Braves.

RODRIGUEZ, ALEX - SS - BR - Age 21
All the fans not old enough to remember Honus Wagner can now see what a great hitting shortstop looks like.

	AB	R	HR	RBI	SB	BA	$
1995 Seattle AL	142	15	5	19	4	.232	3
1996 Seattle AL	601	141	36	123	15	.358	37

RODRIGUEZ, HENRY - OF - BL - Age 29
Rodriguez's final numbers are certainly nice. However, he crashed after a surprising first half and Expos manager Felipe Alou frequently benched him down the stretch because of Rodriguez's lack of plate discipline. Quite simply, Rodriguez's 1996 season was a fluke. He'll never approach those numbers again. He's a part-time player who found lightning in a bottle. That is why Montreal went into the offseason actively shopping Rodriguez.

	AB	R	HR	RBI	SB	BA	$
1995 Montreal NL	138	13	2	15	0	.239	0
1996 Montreal NL	532	81	36	103	2	.276	19

RODRIGUEZ, IVAN - C - BR - Age 25
The premier catcher in the American League, Rodriguez established career highs in runs, hits, homers, RBI and walks while displaying a new level of durability. Rodriguez caught 147 games, and amassed 125 more at-bats than any other AL catcher. Oh, did we mention that he also threw out 50% of opposing basestealers? If he can stay healthy over the long haul (and one has to be concerned about such a heavy workload), Rodriguez could be one of the greatest players ever at his position.

	AB	R	HR	RBI	SB	BA	$
1995 Texas AL	492	56	12	67	0	.303	14
1996 Texas AL	639	116	19	86	5	.300	17

RODRIGUEZ, LIU - 2B - BB - Age 20
Rodriguez lacks awesome raw tools, but was a solid defender and difficult out at Low-A Hickory in the White Sox' chain. He has a small strike zone (5'9", 170), makes pitchers throw strikes, and has above average baserunning instincts despite a lack of overwhelming speed. He hit .249 with 15 steals as one of the few teenagers starting in a full season minor league.

RODRIGUEZ, STEVE - SS - BR - Age 26
Rodriguez hit well enough at Triple-A in 1996 (.285, 18 steals) to give him hope of having a few seasons as a backup infielder in the majors.

RODRIGUEZ, TONY - SS - BR - Age 26
A fine all-around athlete, Rodriguez is a utility infielder in the making. He has played all over the diamond during his six years as a pro, finally reaching the majors for the first time in 1996. Rodriguez doesn't have enough of a bat to be a regular at any position and doesn't show enough glove to play shortstop regularly, either. Still, he's versatile enough to be a major league reserve infielder.

	AB	R	HR	RBI	SB	BA	$
1996 Boston AL	67	7	1	9	0	.239	-

RODRIGUEZ, VICTOR - SS - BR - Age 20
The Marlins' 1994 number two pick is another in a long line of slick fielding Marlins' middle infielders ranking among the youngest regulars in their respective minor leagues. Rodriguez is a contact hitter with little extra base power, though that could change as his 6'1", 175 pound, frame develops. He also has above average speed. He's no Edgar Renteria, but is a potential future big league starter who will toil at Double-A in 1997.

ROHRMEIER, DAN - OF/DH - BR - Age 31
Rohrmeier has spent ten years in the minors, including all of 1993 and parts of 1992 and 1995 in Triple-A. He played in the Double-A Southern League in the Padres organization last year where he won the batting championship while showing good power. The problem is that he was 30 years old last year, and he looks more and more like a career minor leaguer. In fact, "Baseball America" referred to him as a "Double-A Lifer." Following the 1996 season, Rohrmeier announced that he will either play in Triple-A in 1997, or play overseas.

ROLEN, SCOTT - 3B - BR - Age 21
Rolen served notice that he is ready to be a premium performer in the majors with a stellar 1996 minor league season followed by an impressive all around major league debut, interrupted by a broken arm. Rolen is comparable to Mike Schmidt. That means if you live in Philadelphia, maybe he'll be the best third baseman ever, and if you live anywhere else in the country maybe he'll be the second best Phillies thirdbaseman ever. Offensively, he's a .300 hitter candidate who showed signs of being able to lift the ball for power against quality pitching just before he was injured. He is a frontrunner for the Rookie of the Year Award, and should be a perennial All Star and team leader.

	AB	R	HR	RBI	SB	BA	$
1996 Philadelphia NL	130	10	4	18	0	.254	1

ROLISON, NATE - 1B - BL - Age 20
The Marlins' 1995 second round pick is a massive (6'5", 210 pounds) prospect who struck out in over a third of his at-bats as one of the younger regulars in the Low-A Midwest League. However, nearly 40% of his hits went for extra bases, and some were tape measure homers. Despite the strikeout totals, Rolison was well enough respected by hurlers that he ranked among league walk leaders. If he can whittle down his whiffs by 20 per year without sacrificing power, he'll contend for the Marlins first base job in 1999.

ROLLINS, JIMMY - SS - BB- Age 18
The Phils' 1996 second round draft pick is an exciting bundle of raw talent who will be one of the few 18-year-olds playing regularly in Low-A ball in 1997. Despite his 5'8", 160 pound, frame, Rollins has gap power potential and the plate discipline of a veteran (28 walks in 200 Rookie Ball plate appearances). Despite unremarkable speed, Rollins will steal bases because of his technique and solid instincts. Defensively, he might not have the arm to play shortstop

at higher levels, but he is certainly consistent enough with the glove to remain in the infield as a second baseman. He's a kid to watch in 1997.

ROMERO, MANDY - C - BB - Age 29
Padre farmhand Romero had a disappointing year in Double-A last year, his second year in Double-A, and unfortunately, a much worse year than he had in 1995. He's shown a little power, but needs to hit more consistently to move up. Romero is also three to four years older than his minor league peers, not a favorable sign, especially after posting a so-so year.

ROMERO, WILLIE - OF - BR - Age 22
Romero has good defensive tools (range, arm) and can steal a base. He hit for a good average in 1996 (.295 at Double-A San Antonio), but scouts question whether he can hit in the majors. A full year at Triple-A Albuquerque could answer that question.

RONAN, MARC - C - BL - Age 27
Do not be fooled by his fine offensive performance in the Marlins' chain in 1996. This man cannot hit. He's a .230 career hitter in seven pro seasons, with a career slugging percentage barely over .300. He is a fine defensive receiver who was among the most unlikely Rule 5 draftee selections ever (by the Yankees) following the 1995 season.

ROPER, CHAD - 3B - BR - Age 23
It has taken Roper a couple of years to master each minor league level, and he had a respectable season at Double-A New Britain in 1996. He's a fine fielder who has a little pop in his bat. Triple-A Salt Lake City will be his next stop.

ROSARIO, MEL - C - BB - Age 22
Orioles minor league catcher Rosario was promoted from Single-A to Double-A at mid-year last season. He hit well in Single-A, but he had trouble hitting in the pitching-tough Double-A Eastern League. He was formerly in the White Sox and Padres farm systems. The Orioles are high on Rosario, but he's got to hit better to move up to the majors; he's still young and learning.

ROSE, BOBBY - IF/OF - BR - Age 30
After spending parts of several seasons with the Angels, Rose went to Japan. In 1996 he was in Yokohama, where he hit .305 with 14 home runs.

ROSE, PETE Jr. - 3B - BL - Age 27
Son of the former great Red, this Pete has yet to play above Double-A and probably never will. If his name was John Smith Jr. he'd never attract attention.

ROSKOS, JOHN - 1B - BR - Age 22
Along with fellow top prospects Luis Castillo and Todd Dunwoody, Roskos was skipped over a level to Double-A Portland in the Marlins' organization. To further complicate matters, Roskos also underwent a position change, from catcher to first base. All things considered, he did quite well. He remains a batting practice threat capable of gargantuan drives, and also has above average plate discipline.

ROSS, TONY - OF - BR - Age 21
Ross was overmatched when he reached the Double-A level for a brief time in his fifth minor league season in 1996. He has some speed but no power and will have to hit for a much higher average to have a chance to move up.

ROSSY, RICO - SS - BR - Age 33
Rossy is a good Triple-A player, a veteran of 12 minor league seasons. He has 236 major league at-bats with a career .216 batting average, and he would have a longer major league career if he had hit better. Triple-A is about what he can expect in 1997.

ROWLAND, RICH - C - BR - Age 33
Rowland will turn thirty-three in February and can't hang on much longer. He has always had good power but at his age, hitting .226 at Triple-A doesn't promise much of a future. He should hope for nothing more than the same chance he had last year.

ROYSTER, AARON - OF - BR - Age 24
The Phils' 1994 35th round draftee showed a live bat with gap power at High-A Clearwater, and then held his own after a promotion to Double-A in 1996. He does not have the power or speed one looks for in a starting major league outfielder, and likely does not have the defensive ability to be a top backup. He has made substantial progress for such a low draftee, but as of now projects as no better than a future Triple-A regular who could get a brief call to the majors as an injury replacement.

RUMFIELD, TOBY - 1B - BR - Age 24
The Reds' 1991 second round pick has made only plodding offensive progress, consistently hitting line drives but with below average power (nine homers) for a corner infielder. He played his second season at Double-A Chattanooga.

RUPP, BRIAN - 1B - BR - Age 25
Rupp played third most of the season at Double-A Arkansas with Mike Gulan and Jose Oliva sharing at third in Louisville. Lacking pop for a corner infielder, Rupp is a decent fielder who is caught in a numbers game. Most likely, Rupp will be relegated to Double-A in 1997 due to the talent at third base ahead of him.

RUPP, CHAD - 1B - BR - Age 25
Not considered a good prospect, Rupp has advanced slowly, reaching Double-A for the first time last year. He isn't a particularly good hitter, but he has some power; Rupp hit 18 homers in just 278 at-bats for New Britain in 1996. He needs to have a similar homer rate for a full season to rate a longer look as a prospect.

RUSSO, PAUL - 3B - BR - Age 27
Russo was formerly in the Twins organization where he had some good years in Triple-A, but he was never called up even though the Twins had big holes at third, and he was never considered to be a prospect. He played for the Padres Triple-A club last year, his fourth year in Triple-A, and unfortunately, his worst.

STATS, INC.
Minor League Handbook - 1997

The most complete career minor league statistics

Bill James' major league equivalencies

Minor league leader board

Stadium pitching and hitting data

See order form inside the back cover for more details

SABO, CHRIS - 3B/1B - BR - Age 36
It looks like the end of the line for the 1990 World Series hero. Sabo didn't hit that badly in limited playing time in 1996, but about the only things he accomplished was getting suspended for using a corked bat and taking playing time away from Willie Greene and Eric Owens. With the development of Greene, Sabo has no role with the Reds in 1997.

	AB	R	HR	RBI	SB	BA	$
1995 Two Teams	84	10	1	11	3	.238	1
1996 Cincinnati NL	125	15	3	16	2	.256	1

SADLER, DONNIE - SS - BR - Age 21
Young Sadler was a highly touted prospect in many spring publications. Fans fell in love with his speed, cannon arm, and batting eye. In his third pro season, Sadler was shifted from shortstop to centerfield, then back again as the experiment was a bust. Through the turmoil Sadler continued to display gap power and good speed; his 34 steals were second best for Double-A Trenton. Considering his relative youth and being shifted all over the playing field last year, his season was a success. Sadler and Nomar Garciaparra give the Red Sox great depth at shortstop.

SAENZ, OLMEDO - 3B - BR - Age 26
Saenz is a little too good for the minors, but he remained blocked by Robin Ventura on the White Sox roster. Saenz hit .261 with 18 home runs at Triple-A.

SAFFER, JON - OF - BL - Age 22
The Expos' 1992 fifth round draftee is a latter-day Greg Gross. He lines singles and doubles to all fields, rarely strikes out, has a great eye and below average speed for a top of the order hitter. The Expos were pleased to see him drive the ball more consistently to the gaps and beyond (26 doubles, 10 homers) in 1996, finally putting his 6'2", 200 pound, frame to better use. Saffer is a year away from competing for a fourth outfielder role in the major leagues. A tough out at any level.

SAGMOEN, MARC - OF - BL - Age 25
After a poor 1995, Sagmoen got back on track, ending with a strong showing at Triple-A. Sagmoen should start 1997 at Triple-A, and has an chance to appear in the majors sometime during the season. He's a moderately high-average hitter with power that should continue to develop.

SALMON, TIM - OF - BR - Age 28
Salmon had a slow start last year, but later came on strong but quietly. Overall, his 1996 season was somewhat below 1995. He admitted that he was swinging for the fences during a stretch of 45 games in the first two months, only to fail, hitting only three homers. He did much better after cutting down on his swing. Salmon is a young All-Star outfielder who can be counted on to hit 30 homers and drive in 100 runs every year in the near future, with a career-best year still possible.

	AB	R	HR	RBI	SB	BA	$
1995 California AL	537	111	34	105	5	.330	30
1996 California AL	581	90	30	98	4	.286	18

SAMUEL, JUAN - 1B/OF - BR - Age 36
Samuel entered the offseason as the only potential free agent on the Blue Jays' roster and was anxious to stay for 1997. He still runs well and can fill the gaps caused by injuries. His numbers say that he can still be useful to someone.

	AB	R	HR	RBI	SB	BA	$
1995 Kansas City AL	205	31	12	39	6	.263	9
1996 Toronto AL	188	34	8	26	9	.255	5

SANCHEZ, REY - SS - BR - Age 29
Sanchez has been fighting a problem in his left wrist since 1995. He'd been on and off the disabled list until the problem was a broken hamate bone. Thanks to the hamate, the same injury suffered by Ken Griffey, Jr., Sanchez played in just 95 games. The Cubs need Sanchez to be healthy. They are thin on middle infield prospects throughout their system. Sanchez with a healthy hamate makes the Cubs a much deeper team, allowing them to have Todd Haney and Jose Hernandez on the bench instead of in the starting lineup.

	AB	R	HR	RBI	SB	BA	$
1995 Chicago NL	428	57	3	27	6	.278	8
1996 Chicago NL	289	28	1	12	7	.211	-

SANCHEZ, VICTOR - 1B - BR - Age 25
Sanchez is a strikeout-prone first baseman who has some power. He struggled in his first season at Double-A and will have trouble getting beyond that level.

SANDBERG, RYNE - 2B - BR - Age 37
In his return season, Sandberg did exactly the opposite of what many expected him to do at the plate. He hit for a low average, but collected a high number of homers. Sandberg is no longer the top defensive player at his position (he wasn't when he first retired either) but he is still fundamentally solid and knows how to play those tricky Wrigley Field pop ups as well as anyone. Sandberg could play for one more season, or three or four more. His body held up well during the season, another surprise. Sandberg should break Joe Morgan's record of 266 homers by a second baseman in 1997. He needs two more to break the record.

	AB	R	HR	RBI	SB	BA	$
1995			Did Not Play				
1996 Chicago NL	554	85	25	92	12	.244	10

SANDERS, ANTHONY - OF - BR - Age 24
Sanders has been ordinary defensively, doesn't run fast, doesn't hit for power, doesn't take walks and strikes out a lot. He needs a lot of time to develop and probably will do so as a regular outfielder at Double-A.

SANDERS, REGGIE - OF - BR - Age 29
Injuries (back, ribcage, and thumb) wrecked Sanders' season after an MVP candidate performance in 1995. His decline in strike zone judgment (which was never great) is of major concern - Reggie struck out 86 times in only 287 at-bats in 1996. He is still an intriguing power/speed combination, but if he doesn't regain control of the strike zone, it is unlikely that he will return to his 1995 level of production.

	AB	R	HR	RBI	SB	BA	$
1995 Cincinnati NL	484	91	28	99	36	.306	38
1996 Cincinnati NL	287	49	14	33	24	.251	10

SANFORD, CHANCE - 2B - BL - Age 24
Sanford once projected to be a Mike Gallego-type, a little guy with some pop who could play competently at second base, third base and shortstop. However, a knee injury ruined his 1995 season and he had a poor season at Double-A for the Pirates last year. The Pirates have two players with the first name of Chance at their Carolina farm club last season - Sanford and Reynolds, a reserve catcher.

SANTANA, RUBEN - 3B - BR - Age 27
Santana spent his fourth straight season at Double-A in 1996, his first in the Reds' chain. Marooned at that level behind Alex Rodriguez, Desi Relaford, Arquimedez Pozo and company in the middle infield, key developmental years went by in the Mariners' system.

SANTANGELO, F.P. - 3B/OF - BB - Age 29
Santangelo is the ultimate Expo. He wasn't heralded in the minor leagues and looked like nothing but a spare part in the majors. Nobody gets more out of these kinds of players than Felipe Alou, though, and Santangelo had a fine rookie season. He can play in the infield and outfield while doing a lot of things well. He's going to stick around for a long time as a productive player.

	AB	R	HR	RBI	SB	BA	$
1995 Montreal NL	98	11	1	9	1	.296	1
1996 Montreal NL	393	54	7	56	5	.277	10

SANTIAGO, BENITO - C - BR - Age 32
After a checkered first decade in the majors, Santiago has finally matured as a player. He will never be a patient hitter, but he no longer gets himself out on bad pitches when ahead in the count. He throws from his knees less often, and no longer does so just to show off. Plus, he really does block the plate now - no more sweep tags. Most impressively, he has matured into a legitimate power hitter and a true club leader who knows how to handle a pitching staff.

	AB	R	HR	RBI	SB	BA	$
1995 Cincinnati NL	266	40	11	44	2	.286	9
1996 Philadelphia NL	481	71	30	85	2	.264	13

SASSER, ROB - 3B - BR - Age 22
Sasser is one of several Braves prospects at the hot corner, and is the farthest away from the majors. He has excellent speed (38 steals in 1996) and emerging power; his eight homers and 64 RBI were well more than he'd produced in his previous three pro years combined. The major concerns about Sasser are his strikeout frequency and the heavy load of prospects ahead of him in the Braves' system.

SAUNDERS, CHRIS - 3B - BR - Age 26
Looking like a late Bloomer, Saunders just had his best year ever, in his second try at the Double-A level. His .298 average, 17 home runs and 105 RBI were all career bests. He is good enough to merit a trial with the Mets major leaguers at spring training in 1997.

SAUNDERS, DOUG - 3B - BR - Age 27
Long-time Mets' farmhand Saunders reached the majors for 28 games with New York back in 1993. Since then he has served as a reserve infielder in the high minors for the Mets, Athletics and Mariners. Saunders is now a Triple-A roster filler.

SBROCCO, JON - 2B - BL - Age 26
Since he was older than most of his Single-A league mates in 1995, it was understandable that Sbrocco should hold his own in that milieu. Not so in '96 in Double-A. He isn't going much further.

SCALZITTI, WILL - C - BR - Age 24
After a mediocre 1996, Scalzitti starts his sixth season as a pro, never having risen above the Double-A level. He's just never been able to hit with any degree of consistency at any level of play.

SCARSONE, STEVE - 3B/1B - BR - Age 30
Scarsone dropped off significantly over all major offensive categories in 1996 despite having a similar number of plate appearances. He plays all the infield positions well enough, and has a little power. The Giants released him but someone will pick him up.

	AB	R	HR	RBI	SB	BA	$
1995 San Francisco NL	233	33	11	29	3	.266	7
1996 San Francisco NL	283	28	5	23	2	.219	-

SCHALL, GENE - OF/1B - BR - Age 26
Schall has proven that he can hit minor league pitching of any kind for average and power. He was marginally better with the bat in his second crack at the bigs in 1996, but still didn't show the expected home run power. At first glance, he would appear to be a viable platoon candidate at first base for the Phils in 1997 should they not sign an expensive free agent or move Gregg Jefferies there. However, Schall has consistently hit righties better than lefties throughout his career. He is likely to remain an unexciting major league bench option for the foreseeable future.

	AB	R	HR	RBI	SB	BA	$
1995 Philadelphia NL	65	2	0	5	0	.231	-
1996 Philadelphia NL	66	7	2	10	0	.273	1

SCHOFIELD, DICK - SS - BR - Age 34
Veteran Schofield got a few at-bats with the Angels in 1996. He's at the tail end of his career, and over his 14-year career, he's been the prototypical poor-hitting shortstop. His career batting average is .230, but he did hit 13 homers back in 1986, an aberration.

SCHU, RICK - 3B - BR - Age 35
Old failed phenoms never die. Schu returned from the baseball dead to play in one game for the Expos last season. It will certainly be his last game in the major leagues.

SCHWAB, CHRIS - OF - BR - Age 22
The Expos envisioned Schwab as a big-time power prospect when they made him their top draft pick in 1993. However, he has struggled in making the conversion from the aluminum to wood bat and is years away from the big leagues.

SCOTT, GARY - 3B - BR - Age 28
Scott was once a top Cub prospect, but he had trouble with major league pitching and they eventually gave up on him. He played for the Padres Triple-A club last year, hitting .272. He's no longer a prospect.

SCUTARO, MARCO - 2B - BR - Age 21
Scutaro dazzled in the 1995 Dominican Summer League, batting .393 and showing great speed on the bases. He moved from third base to second base at Low-A Columbus in 1996 and showed a quick bat with power potential. He must shorten his swing and learn to lay off bad pitches. He's one to watch.

SECRIST, REED - 3B - BL - Age 26
A non-drafted free agent from Briar Cliff (Iowa) University, an NAIA school, Secrist spent four seasons at the Class A level or lower before suddenly becoming a first-half revelation at Triple-A Calgary last season. Secrist hit 15 homers in the first half and looked like the heir apparent to Charlie Hayes at third base for the Pirates. However, he hit only two homers in the second half, clouding his major league future.

SEEFRIED, TATE - 1B - BL - Age 24
Seefried's career has been moving slowly since 1993 when he hit .265 with 21 home runs and 89 RBI at Class A. He was still at Double-A in 1996, still striking out too much (128 whiffs), and his average slipped to .208, lowering his career mark to .228 as a pro.

SEFCIK, KEVIN - SS/2B - BR - Age 26
Sefcik acquitted himself quite well in a utility role with the Phils in 1996. Sefcik is a spray hitter who makes consistent contact at the plate, and makes all of the plays that his limited range allows him to reach. His lack of raw tools, especially in the field, will prevent him from ever gaining a more substantial major league role. He could find himself losing his spot to newly acquired Desi Relaford, who has a much higher upside.

	AB	R	HR	RBI	SB	BA	$
1996 Philadelphia NL	116	10	0	9	3	.284	2

SEGUI, DAVID - 1B - BB - Age 30
Segui is a solid hitter, though he doesn't provide the power one would like in a first baseman. A wrist injury slowed him last season but he's capable of hitting .300 with a decent number of RBI when healthy.

	AB	R	HR	RBI	SB	BA	$
1995 NY - Montreal NL	456	68	12	68	2	.309	16
1996 Montreal NL	416	69	11	58	4	.286	12

SEITZER, BRAD - 3B - BR - Age 27
Kevin's brother performed well in his first season at Double-A El Paso, but is too old to be considered a prospect.

SEITZER, KEVIN - 1B/3B - BR - Age 35
Seitzer possesses remarkable patience at the plate, and routinely laces line drives to the gaps. He is becoming little more than a DH option at this point, and will likely see his playing time reduced if he remains with the Indians in 1997 due to the presence of lefthanded options like Brian Giles. He will linger as a productive hitter in the AL for years in a gradually diminishing role. Look for another .300 average in 400 at-bats, with diminished power and less speed.

	AB	R	HR	RBI	SB	BA	$
1995 Milwaukee AL	492	56	5	69	2	.311	14
1996 Milw-Cleveland AL	573	85	13	78	6	.326	19

SELBY, BILL - 2B - BL - Age 26
A versatile infielder with some pop in his bat, Selby got his first shot at the big leagues and was an immediate success in a limited role. He was among team leaders in power categories for Triple-A Pawtucket at the time of his call-up and he showed a little of that power for Boston, too. A late-blossoming prospect, Selby can play anywhere on the infield except shortstop. He'll challenge for a reserve infield role for the Red Sox.

	AB	R	HR	RBI	SB	BA	$
1996 Boston AL	95	12	3	6	1	.270	-

SERVAIS, SCOTT - C - BR - Age 29
Servais got off to a hot start in '96 but finished with just 11 home runs. Servais is a reliable receiver, but will never

win a gold glove. Servais is the most reliable and skilled catcher the Cubs have so he's the guy. The Cubs hope Pat Cline can mature and take over the spot in a couple of seasons, but that won't be for at least another year.

	AB	R	HR	RBI	SB	BA	$
1995 Houston - Chicago NL	264	38	13	47	2	.265	9
1996 Chicago NL	445	42	11	63	0	.265	7

SEXSON, RICHIE - 1B - BR - Age 22
Sexson took some baby steps backward developmentally in 1996, swinging at too many bad pitches. He was one of the younger Double-A Eastern League regulars. Sexson has prodigious power and an excellent work ethic, but has many holes in his swing. 1997 will be a pivotal year - if he does not produce while cutting down his whiffs and increasing his walks, he could be bypassed by Sean Casey as the heir apparent to the Franco/Carreon/Seitzer/Perry mixture in Cleveland.

SEXTON, CHRIS - SS - BR - Age 25
This former Reds prospect was the everyday shortstop for the Rockies' Double-A New Haven team. Sexton is a good glove man with a strong arm, but his batting average reached a career low in 1996, and must improve for him to move up in 1997.

SHARPERSON, MIKE - 2B - BR - Age 35
Sharperson was a veteran of all or parts of eight major league seasons, and was the Dodgers' lone All-Star representative in 1992. He was serving as an extra infielder at Triple-A Las Vegas when he was called up by the Padres last August. Unfortunately, he died in a car wreck before he could get to the airport for a trip to San Diego. He was considered a leader both on and off the field and would have made a good coach. Sharperson will be missed.

SHAVE, JON - 2B - BR - Age 29
Shave is a reasonably good Triple-A player with a slight chance of making the majors as a utility player. He has a little power and speed, but would not be likely to hit for average at the major league level.

SHEAFFER, DANNY - C - BR - Age 35
Sheaffer is a valuable guy for the Cardinals. In addition to being a reliable second catcher, he can play every other position on the field.

	AB	R	HR	RBI	SB	BA	$
1995 St. Louis NL	208	24	5	30	0	.231	2
1996 St. Louis NL	198	10	2	20	3	.227	-

SHEETS, ANDY - SS/2B - BR - Age 25
Injuries to Alex Rodriguez and other Mariners' infielders helped Sheets get to the majors for the first time in 1996. He's a singles hitter who had a fine season at Triple-A Tacoma last year, hitting .358. Sheets lacks power or substantial speed and strikes out with regularity. Still, he can serve a big-league club as a utility player.

	AB	R	HR	RBI	SB	BA	$
1996 Seattle AL	110	18	0	9	2	.191	-

SHEFF, CHRIS - OF - BR - Age 26
Sheff was at Double-A for the third consecutive season. He excelled there, and became a Triple-A regular. He has above average defensive ability, power to the gaps and average speed. For an outfield prospect of his age, that's not enough to get you to the bigs. What could be a long Triple-A odyssey should continue in 1997.

SHEFFIELD, GARY - OF - BR - Age 28
Sheffield finally exhibited what he is capable of doing in a full season unencumbered by injury. He showed spectacular power to all fields, nudged his career average towards .300, refused to swing at bad pitches, and continued to strike out much less than other prolific longball mashers. Sheffield's style of play in right field will continue to make him vulnerable to injury, but he is the closest thing to a Triple Crown threat in major league baseball today.

	AB	R	HR	RBI	SB	BA	$
1995 Florida NL	213	46	16	46	19	.324	19
1996 Florida NL	519	118	42	120	16	.314	35

SHIPLEY, CRAIG - 3B/SS - BR - Age 34
Shipley is a veteran utility infielder who missed a lot of playing time last year with hamstring and tendon injuries. He has little power, but in 1994, he hit .333 in 240 at-bats, his career-best season. His hitting makes him more valuable than the typical utility man.

	AB	R	HR	RBI	SB	BA	$
1995 Houston NL	232	23	3	24	6	.263	5
1996 San Diego NL	92	13	1	7	7	.315	4

SHOCKEY, GREG - OF - BL - Age 26
Angels minor leaguer Shockey has hit over .300 at almost every minor league level. There's not much home run power, but he hits lots of doubles. He should get a bigger test in Triple-A in 1997, and he could be called up sometime during the season as a reserve outfielder.

SHORES, SCOTT - OF - BR - Age 25
The Phils' 1994 fifth round pick is an aggressive player with the bat and on the bases. He drives the ball consistently to the gaps, but he does so with an uppercut swing that results in an inordinate number of strikeouts and relatively few walks. He is always looking to steal a base, but has not had a particularly good success rate (66% over the last two seasons). A Double-A fourth outfielder for much of 1996, Shores is too unrefined at too advanced an age to be considered any more than a fringe major league prospect.

SHUMPERT, TERRY - 2B - BR - Age 30
Shumpert shuttled back and forth between the Cubs and Triple-A Iowa in '96. Exclusively a second baseman early in his career, Shumpert was once considered the heir to Frank White in Kansas City. KC rushed him and it took Shumpert several seasons to recover. Shumpert has learned to play third base and has even spent a little time in the outfield. His best chance to stick on a major league roster is as a utility player. He can still run, he stole 13 bases in 72 games for Iowa, and Shumpert is an adept hit-and-run man despite his 44 strikeouts in 246 Triple-A at-bats.

	AB	R	HR	RBI	SB	BA	$
1995 Boston AL	47	6	0	3	3	.234	0
1996 Chicago NL	31	5	2	6	0	.226	-

SIDDALL, JOE - C - BL - Age 29
After eight years in the Expos' chain, Siddall moved to the Marlins' chain and actually functioned as their part-time starter while Charles Johnson was on the disabled list. His respectable 1996 Triple-A stats aside, Siddall had never hit above .236 prior to last season, and has never shown power or patience at the plate. His defense is solid, but it won't get him back to the majors.

	AB	R	HR	RBI	SB	BA	$
1995 Montreal NL	10	4	0	1	0	.300	-
1996 Florida NL	47	0	0	3	0	.149	-

SIERRA, RUBEN - OF/DH - BB - Age 31
Sierra played his way out of New York in '96 as the Yankees insisted Detroit take him in the Cecil Fielder trade. Sierra is still a major league hitter, but his demands to play the outfield, where he isn't good, have created problems wherever he has gone, now Cincinnati.

	AB	R	HR	RBI	SB	BA	$
1995 Oakland - NY AL	479	73	19	86	5	.263	15
1996 New York-Detroit AL	518	61	12	72	4	.247	6

SILVESTRI, DAVE - 2B - BR - Age 29
Once a top Yankees' shortstop, Silvestri's star fell last season, his first full year with the Expos. He doesn't play any of three infield positions particularly well, so he has to hit to be an effective utility player. He didn't hit last year and he's not getting any younger.

	AB	R	HR	RBI	SB	BA	$
1995 NY AL - Montreal NL	93	16	3	11	2	.226	1
1996 Montreal NL	162	16	1	17	2	.204	-

SIMMONS, BRIAN - OF - BB - Age 23
The White Sox' 1995 second round pick broke through with a huge first full pro season, in which he was named the

number three prospect in the Low-A Midwest League on the strength of his 52 extra base hits (out of 106 hits) and 14 steals. But wait a minute...... Simmons, at 22, was one of his league's older starters, and should have been expected to dominate that league. To certify his newfound pedigree, Simmons needs to jump to Double-A in 1997 and showcase his skills similarly. There should be little organizational resistance, so it is all in Simmons' hands.

SIMMS, MIKE - 1B - BR - Age 30
Simms finally showed that he could hit major league pitching in his fifth trial with the Astros in 1995. However, he failed to repeat in 1996 and was demoted to Triple-A. Simms is a good Triple-A power hitter but only a fringe major leaguer.

	AB	R	HR	RBI	SB	BA	$
1995 Houston NL	121	14	9	24	1	.256	4
1996 Houston NL	68	6	1	8	1	.176	-

SIMON, RANDELL - 1B - BL - Age 21
Simon is progressing steadily through the Braves' chain. At age 21, he led Double-A Greenville with 18 homers and 77 RBI last year. He needs to improve his defense and keep up the steady hitting when he advances to Richmond in 1997; Simon is the best first base prospect in the Braves' system.

SIMONS, MITCH - 2B - BR - Age 28
Simons' second try at Triple-A Salt Lake City was a big step backwards. After hitting .325 with more walks than strikeouts in 1995, Simons fell back to a .264-5-59 year in 1996. He's an average second baseman, but has pretty good speed (67 steals in the last two years). Simons' path to the majors is blocked with the Twins, but he could earn a shot elsewhere if he can get his hitting back on track in 1997.

SIMONTON, BENJI - 1B - BR - Age 24
The Giants could use a first baseman, and Simonton is just that, with good power. He could use a little more time in the minors to work on his mechanics. His low average (.248) and strikeouts (144) need some help. But, he did walk 101 times last year showing he has a good idea of what to do.

SINGLETON, CHRIS - OF - BL - Age 24
Singleton improved considerably last year, hitting close to .300 and swiping 27 at Shreveport. With fellow Captains Dante Powell and Armando Rios, the troika of outfielders could move up together and give the Giants a real boost in a couple of years.

SINGLETON, DUANE - OF - BL - Age 24
Singleton was once one of the Brewers' better outfield prospects. They soured on him after two marginal seasons at Triple-A New Orleans and dealt him to the Tigers in the off-season. He's got pretty good speed, but the knock against Singleton is that he can't hit enough in the majors to use that speed. He's still young enough to improve; Singleton will challenge for playing time in the majors soon.

	AB	R	HR	RBI	SB	BA	$
1996 Detroit AL	56	5	0	3	0	.161	-

SISCO, STEVE - OF/2B - BR - Age 27
Sisco just keeps on hitting, turning in a .297-13-74 season for Wichita, his second season at Double-A. Despite his versatility in the field, Sisco is lackluster with the glove. He also doesn't run the bases particularly well and hasn't shown a keen batting eye above A-ball. Time is running out for Sisco; at age 27, he's on the verge of becoming an organizational player who has little chance for big-league success.

SLAUGHT, DON - C - BR - Age 38
Veteran National Leaguer Slaught was signed by the Angels as a stop-gap measure until prospect Todd Greene was ready. It was a good move, and Slaught made some good contributions. He was traded to the White Sox in September. Slaught is a good-hitting catcher, but at age 38, his best chance of getting a major league job is as a backup catcher.

	AB	R	HR	RBI	SB	BA	$
1995 Pittsburgh NL	112	13	0	13	0	.304	1
1996 Cal-Chicago AL	243	25	6	36	0	.313	5

SMITH, BOBBY - 3B - BR - Age 22
Of Baseball America's pre-season 1996 top ten prospects for the Braves, Smith is the highest ranked prospect who

has yet to reach the majors. He's a multi-faceted hitter and a good fielder at third base; his versatility in the field may allow a shift elsewhere as other third base prospects push up the Braves chain. He was slated to try a move to the outfield in the fall instructional league. Smith still must cut his whiffs (over 100 each of the last three seasons) to get an extended shot in the bigs.

SMITH, BUBBA - 1B - BR - Age 27
Smith had a tremendous offensive season at Double-A, and was voted the Texas League MVP. However, he was one of the older players at that level. Smith made progress with the glove as well, but is not generally regarded as a prospect.

SMITH, DESMOND - OF - BB - Age 24
Formerly with the Angels, Smith has good speed. He has a little promise but he looks more like a fourth outfielder if that.

SMITH, DWIGHT - OF - BL - Age 33
The Braves' primary lefty pinch-hitter for the last two years, Smith has a large platoon differential, making him a fine fit for the role. It's a job he does well, but he'd be a detriment to his team if he plays regularly in the outfield. Smith will remain among the majors best pinch-hitters in 1997.

	AB	R	HR	RBI	SB	BA	$
1995 Atlanta NL	131	16	3	21	0	.252	1
1996 Atlanta NL	153	16	3	16	1	.203	-

SMITH, IRA - OF - BR - Age 29
Smith has had some excellent minor league seasons with the Padres, once stealing 46 bases. He struggled, hitting .242 in Triple-A last year, his worst minor league season, and he hasn't stolen many bases in the past three years.

SMITH, MARK - OF - BR - Age 26
Smith hit well for the Orioles Triple-A club last year, but it was his fourth year with the team. He was with the Orioles and finally playing well when he had the bad luck of severely bruising his leg causing him to miss more than a month. The Orioles have a number of talented veteran outfielders, so Smith will have another uphill battle to win a roster spot in 1997. His best opportunity may be with another organization.

	AB	R	HR	RBI	SB	BA	$
1995 Baltimore AL	104	11	3	15	3	.231	1
1996 Baltimore AL	78	9	4	10	0	.244	-

SMITH, MATT - 1B - BL - Age 20
The Royals first round pick of 1994, Smith was also an accomplished pitcher in high school. He hasn't shown much with the bat, yet, hitting a combined .228 in his first two pro seasons. Then in 1996 he hit .248 with five homers at Class A Wilmington.

SMITH, OZZIE - SS - BB - Age 42
1996 was Smith's last hurrah, but he gave hints that his retirement might not be permanent. Should his career be over, he went out on a good note. He handled the passing of the Cardinals' shortstop torch to Royce Clayton better than Tony La Russa did and performed well in his limited role. He is a wonderful man, the type of person baseball can ill afford to lose

	AB	R	HR	RBI	SB	BA	$
1995 St. Louis NL	156	16	0	11	4	.199	-
1996 St. Louis NL	227	36	2	18	7	.282	6

SNOPEK, CHRIS - 3B - BR - Age 26
After showing the club what he could do in 1995, Snopek's 1996 campaign can only be described as a setback. He appeared in only 46 games at the major league level and struggled to maintain a .260 average. In 40 games at Triple-A Nashville he only hit .248. He needs to find that hitting stroke again and he'll be just fine. The shortstop job will be coming open soon as Guillen won't last much longer.

	AB	R	HR	RBI	SB	BA	$
1995 Chicago AL	68	12	1	7	1	.324	1
1996 Chicago AL	104	18	6	18	0	.260	0

Benson's Baseball Player Guide: 1997

SNOW, J.T. - 1B - BL - Age 29
Considering that 1996 was a lively ball year, Snow didn't take advantage of it and had a disappointing season. It was particularly disappointing when compared to his outstanding .289-24-102 in 1995 after which many people believed that Snow had finally realized his potential. Last year, he hit a weak .199 vs. lefties, causing him to reconsider his switch-hitting.

	AB	R	HR	RBI	SB	BA	$
1995 California AL	544	80	24	102	2	.289	20
1996 California AL	575	69	17	67	1	.257	7

SOJO, LUIS - 2B/SS - BR - Age 31
Whenever he gets to play, Sojo shows bat and glove skills that make fans wonder why he doesn't have an everyday job. Part of the reason is that he has never been in the right place at the right time for a full year, and another reason is that managers love to have his diverse skills on the bench, to insert him at the moment he is most needed.

	AB	R	HR	RBI	SB	BA	$
1995 Seattle AL	339	50	7	39	4	.289	9
1996 Seattle-New York AL	287	23	1	21	2	.220	-

SOLIZ, STEVE - C - BR - Age 26
The Indians' 1993 13th round draftee is a solid defensive receiver with modest offensive skills. He has been unable to secure a full-time role at any point in his career to date, and is likely nearing the end of the line.

SORRENTO, PAUL - 1B - BL - Age 31
Sorrento has always struggled against lefties. 1996 was no exception but he was effective enough against righties. In a platoon he'll continue to be a fairly productive hitter.

	AB	R	HR	RBI	SB	BA	$
1995 Cleveland AL	323	50	25	79	1	.235	11
1996 Seattle AL	471	67	23	93	0	.289	13

SOSA, SAMMY - OF - BR - Age 28
Sammy Sosa has power. Plain and simple. When Sosa settles into a groove, he hits homers in bunches. Despite missing 38 games during the season, due to a broken bone in his hand, Sosa became the eighth Cub to reach the 40-homer plateau. The Cubs will play Sosa in the outfield, but depending on personnel moves and performance, Sammy may be in right or left. He's more valuable in rightfield because of his strong arm.

	AB	R	HR	RBI	SB	BA	$
1995 Chicago NL	564	89	36	119	34	.268	37
1996 Chicago NL	498	84	40	100	18	.273	23

SPARKS, DON - 3B - BR - Age 30
This nine-year minor league veteran has consistently sprayed line drives around minor league ballparks with doubles power. He is quite slow, and not a particularly good fielder, but would not embarrass himself should Jim Thome pull a muscle or something, thereby allowing Sparks to inherit the job for a short time. He's a nice Triple-A insurance policy.

SPEARMAN, VERN - OF - BL - Age 27
Spearman has been stuck at Double-A San Antonio for nearly five years. He has been passed by most of the better prospects and is not a prospect himself.

SPEHR, TIM - C - BR - Age 30
Spehr is the ultimate third string catcher. He is good behind the plate, moves well enough to pinch run but can't hit much. Few guys have stuck around the majors as long as a third catcher.

	AB	R	HR	RBI	SB	BA	$
1995 Montreal NL	35	4	1	3	0	.257	-
1996 Montreal NL	44	4	1	3	1	.091	-

SPENCER, SHANE - OF - BR - Age 25
With a total of 32 home runs and 95 RBI at Double-A and Triple-A in 1996, Spencer hung on to the prospect label, but he's getting up there in years. He did spend a long time at the Rookie and Class A levels and then stepped up the rate of progress in 1996.

SPIERS, BILL - 2B - BL - Age 30
Spiers was a useful utility infielder for Houston in 1996 and should fill that role again this year. He played primarily at third base but looked good at his old position of shortstop late in the season and may see more action there in 1997. He also had some success as a pinch hitter with two home runs.

	AB	R	HR	RBI	SB	BA	$
1995 New York NL	72	5	0	11	0	.208	-
1996 Houston NL	218	27	6	26	7	.252	4

SPIEZIO, SCOTT - 3B - BB - Age 24
Son of former major leaguer Ed Spiezio, Scott has excellent power, a good eye, and a good glove. Spiezio's biggest problem is the number of quality corner players ahead of him.

SPRAGUE, ED - 3B - BR - Age 29
Sprague finally had his breakthrough year and established himself as a team leader. His defense has consistently improved and his power has finally arrived. Clearly, he is the everyday third baseman.

	AB	R	HR	RBI	SB	BA	$
1995 Toronto AL	521	77	18	74	0	.244	9
1996 Toronto AL	591	88	36	101	0	.247	12

STAHOVIAK, SCOTT - 3B/1B - BL - Age 27
In the '96 A-Z we forecasted Stahoviak to produce ".270-20-75" totals after a couple of years, and he is heading for this. A highly regarded amateur player, Stahoviak is starting to show respectable power totals for a first baseman.

	AB	R	HR	RBI	SB	BA	$
1995 Minnesota AL	263	28	3	23	5	.266	3
1996 Minnesota AL	405	72	13	61	3	.284	9

STAIRS, MATT - OF - BL - Age 28
Stairs played well in a limited role with Oakland through the stretch. His offense can be scary, but so can his defense. Not a bad guy to have coming off the bench.

	AB	R	HR	RBI	SB	BA	$
1995 Boston AL	88	8	1	17	0	.261	-
1996 Oakland AL	137	21	10	23	1	.277	3

STANKIEWICZ, ANDY - 2B - BR - Age 32
He had a good 1996 season in a limited role with the Expos. He has enough skills to hang around for a while as a utility infielder but he'll never be a starter again.

	AB	R	HR	RBI	SB	BA	$
1995 Houston NL	52	6	0	7	4	.115	-
1996 Montreal NL	77	12	0	9	1	.286	1

STANLEY, MIKE - C - BR - Age 33
Joining the Red Sox as a free agent over the winter, Stanley took some of the heat for the team's slow start but still turned in a good year in 1996. The nicks and dings acquired from catching every day wore him down by season's end. Stanley needs a respite from catching duties more often, but his bat is too valuable and the Red Sox are crowded at the only other logical positions for Stanley to play: first base and DH.

	AB	R	HR	RBI	SB	BA	$
1995 New York AL	399	63	18	83	1	.268	12
1996 Boston AL	397	73	24	69	2	.270	10

STATON, T.J. - OF - BL - Age 22
Stanton jumped from low Class A to Double-A last season; the 22-year-old outfielder suddenly emerged as a prospect for the Pirates with 15 homers and 17 steals. Staton has good power and speed but the real test will be this season when he is sent to Triple-A Calgary.

STEFANSKI, MIKE - C - BR - Age 27
The Cardinals traded for Stefanski over the previous winter, then installed him at Triple-A Louisville as a backup catcher. He's got a strong arm, but is no more than an extra catcher stored in the high minors in case of emergency.

STEINBACH, TERRY - C - BR - Age 35
Steinbach, who as much as anyone in the league epitomizes class and loyalty, put together a dream year in 1996. He has always been good with runners in scoring position and in pressure situations. And Steinbach has also shown some power, but never a hint of what he did in '96.

	AB	R	HR	RBI	SB	BA	$
1995 Oakland AL	406	43	15	65	1	.278	11
1996 Oakland AL	514	79	35	100	0	.272	15

STEVENS, LEE - OF - BL - Age 29
Stevens returned from Japan a different player than he had been with the Angels. A shorter swing and a more controlled response to adversity were Stevens' new attributes. An American Association MVP season resulted, followed by a late-season callup by the Rangers. He still has enough pop in his bat and is young enough to have a major league career as a bench player.

	AB	R	HR	RBI	SB	BA	$
1996 Texas AL	78	6	3	12	0	.231	-

STEVERSON, TODD - OF - BR - Age 25
The Padres acquired outfielder Steverson from the Tigers in a trade. He has shown a little power and speed in the minors, and the Padres hope that he will mature into a major league power hitter.

STEWART, ANDY - 1B/C - BR - Age 26
In his second try at Triple-A, Stewart didn't hit much and was demoted to Wichita. He got a recall back to Omaha, but as a replacement for career minor leaguer Scooter Tucker - which doesn't bode well for his major league future. He's not skilled enough to play regularly behind the plate and doesn't hit enough to hold down a job at first base. Stewart's only hope for a major league role is as a reserve.

STEWART, SHANNON - OF - BR - Age 23
Named the Blue Jays' Triple-A player of the year, Stewart is ready for the major leagues and is waiting for an opportunity to play. The Blue Jays entered the winter determined to revive a slumping offence and one possibility was to play Stewart in center field in place of Otis Nixon. Stewart has great speed and better power than Nixon. Stewart is frequently compared to a young Rickey Henderson.

STILLWELL, KURT - 2B/SS - BB - Age 31
Stillwell managed to stay in the majors for a full season in 1996, although he didn't play much. Since he doesn't offer much more than a decent bat and some versatility this may have been his last extended tour in the bigs.

	AB	R	HR	RBI	SB	BA	$
1996 Texas AL	77	12	1	4	0	.273	-

STINNETT, KELLY - C - BR - Age 27
Mike Matheny is a better defensive catcher and for the moment, a more reliable hitter. It's not too late for Stinnett to improve.

STOCKER, KEVIN - SS - BB - Age 27
After spending one and a half seasons in a funk both at the plate and in the field, Stocker closed out 1996 with a second-half surge that likely saved his starting job for 1997. Stocker finished third on the club with 33 extra-base hits. Though he strikes out often, he draws many walks, turning over the lineup. Defensively, his confidence is back, and he again routinely converts most plays within his limited range. Look for a .250 average with little power or speed from Stocker in 1997.

	AB	R	HR	RBI	SB	BA	$
1995 Philadelphia NL	412	42	1	32	6	.218	1
1996 Philadelphia NL	394	46	5	41	6	.254	4

STOVALL, DAROND - OF - BB - Age 24
The Cards' 1991 fifth round draftee was obtained by the Expos in 1995, and has continued to struggle to realize his power/speed potential. An impressive athlete who hits occasional tape measure bombs, Stovall has continually struggled to make contact throughout his career, producing batting averages in the low-.220's with low walk totals.

STRANGE, DOUG - 3B - BB - Age 33
The numbers game reduced Strange to a bit part in the Mariners pennant drive. He gave them good pinch-hitting and versatile defensive play. Strange is no more than a reserve, but a good one.

	AB	R	HR	RBI	SB	BA	$
1995 Seattle AL	155	19	2	21	0	.271	1
1996 Seattle AL	183	19	3	23	1	.235	-

STRAWBERRY, DARRYL - OF - BL - Age 35
After falling a long way from stardom with the Mets to near unemployment, Strawberry put together a decent comeback season with a championship team in 1996. Although his defensive skills have waned, and his batting is now best suited to a platoon role and pinch hitting, he has regained his status as a viable major leaguer.

	AB	R	HR	RBI	SB	BA	$
1995 New York AL	87	15	3	13	0	.276	1
1996 New York AL	202	35	11	36	6	.262	6

STRICKLAND, CHAD - C - BR - Age 25
Poor hitting continues to hold Strickland back. He has made slow, steady progress through the Royals farm system due to outstanding defensive skills behind the plate and a great arm. But, in three full seasons above A-ball, Strickland is a .223 hitter with little power. It's hard to imagine him passing better prospects like Sal Fasano and Mike Sweeney to reach Kansas City.

STRICKLIN, SCOTT - C - BL - Age 25
A minor league free agent formerly of the Twins, Stricklin again struggled with the bat. No matter how good his defense is, he has no chance unless he becomes a much better hitter.

STRITTMATTER, MARK - C - BR - Age 27
Stritty jumped to the Rockies' Triple-A Colorado Springs team in 1996, but struggled at the plate. Absent substantial improvement in the offensive area, Strittmatter is unlikely to challenge for a shot with the Rockies in 1997.

STURDIVANT, MARCUS - OF - BL - Age 23
Sturdivant's first year above A-ball produced his usual good batting average and above-average speed. He's an aggressive hitter who needs to become more patient in order to take advantage of his speed. Sturdivant can play any outfield position but lacks sufficient power to become a regular at the major league level. Versatility should help Sturdivant reach the bigs as a fifth outfielder.

STYNES, CHRIS - 2B/3B - BR - Age 24
A switch to the outfield was much to Stynes' liking in 1996. Between trips to Kansas City to ride the bench, he lit up American Association pitching for a .356 average and a .553 slugging average. He also has some speed; Stynes stole three bases in one game for Kansas City in 1996 and has recently stolen as many as 28 in a single minor league season. He had previously bounced between second and third base in six minor league seasons; now Stynes has a chance to stick with the major league club as their only righthanded outfielder.

	AB	R	HR	RBI	SB	BA	$
1995 Kansas City AL	35	7	0	2	0	.171	-
1996 Kansas City AL	92	8	0	6	5	.293	1

SURHOFF, B.J. - 3B/OF - BL - Age 32
The Baltimore fans and the Orioles love Surhoff's hustling and intense "blue-collar" playing style. He had a good year with the Orioles, although he went into a bad slump late in the season. The outlook for 1997 is another solid season, and hitting at the .320 level where he has hit in the past is possible and would not be a surprise.

	AB	R	HR	RBI	SB	BA	$
1995 Milwaukee AL	415	72	13	73	7	.320	19
1996 Baltimore AL	537	74	21	82	0	.292	13

SUTTON, LARRY - 1B - BL - Age 26
A fractured elbow shortened Sutton's first try at Double-A in 1995, but he made the most of his return to Wichita, leading the club with 22 homers and 84 RBI. That's not the whole story for Sutton, though, as he also led the club in OBP by walking more often than he struck out. He's also a wizard with the glove; Sutton was named the best defensive

first baseman in the Texas League, his second such fielding honor in three years. A member of the Royals' 40-man roster, Sutton can do everything except run; watch for him at Triple-A Omaha in 1997.

SVEUM, DALE - 1B - BB - Age 33
Sveum got a surprise September callup to the Pirates last season after having been out of the majors since 1994 and having not spent a full season in the big leagues since 1992. He played well and, suddenly, is in the Pirates' plan for 1996. At worst, he will be a switch-hitting utility player. This probably says more about the Pirates' talent level than Sveum's ability.

SWANN, PEDRO - OF - BL - Age 26
In his sixth pro season, Swann got his first extensive shot at Triple-A Richmond, turning in a .250-4-35 performance there after hitting .310 for Greenville. Swann is a decent hitter that is overshadowed by the other, better prospects in the Braves' system. He has a better chance elsewhere and may go that route as a six-year minor league free agent. Swann can get to the majors in a reserve role in 1997.

SWEENEY, MARK - 1B - BL - Age 27
Sweeney provides a solid lefthanded bat off the bench for the Cardinals. As a first baseman-outfielder, his opportunities to advance are limited in St. Louis and he will always struggle to get at-bats.

	AB	R	HR	RBI	SB	BA	$
1995 St. Louis NL	77	5	2	13	1	.273	1
1996 St. Louis NL	170	32	3	22	3	.265	3

SWEENEY, MIKE - C - BR - Age 23
What a good looking hitter! After jumping from Class A directly to the majors in 1995, Sweeney made the more regular route of going from Double-A to Triple-A back to the majors in 1996. But, he did it in about two months and he wasn't fazed much by big league pitching once he arrived. Sweeney has a sweet swing and emerging power, but needs work defensively. He'll get lots of teaching instruction from Mike Macfarlane in 1997 before likely taking over the full-time catching chores in 1998.

	AB	R	HR	RBI	SB	BA	$
1996 Kansas City AL	165	23	4	24	1	.279	2

SWEET, JOHN - C - BL - Age 26
Sweet is in the Pirates' farm system. Jason Kendall, Keith Osik, Angelo Encarnacion and Tim Marx stand between him and the major leagues.

TACKETT, JEFF - C - BR - Age 31
Tackett reached his peak as an Orioles' major league reserve catcher early in the 1990's. He doesn't hit for average or power and his defensive skills are average. The whole package adds up to a Triple-A catcher who could get another big-league chance, but only as a reserve.

TAKAYOSHI, TODD - C - BL - Age 26
Last year was Takayoshi's third year in Class A. He's improving his hitting, and should be tested more in Double-A in 1997. The Angels have a number of good minor league catchers, so the competition is tough.

TALANOA, SCOTT - OF - BR - Age 27
The massive (6'5", 240 pound) first sacker has one tool - raw power. However, his subpar bat speed has been exposed at higher levels, most recently at Double-A Harrisburg in the Expos' chain in 1996. Though he is willing to take a walk, his vulnerability to strikeouts and his below average defensive ability has made him an overall liability to his more recent clubs.

TARASCO, TONY - OF - BL - Age 26
The Orioles obtained outfielder Tarasco from the Expos in exchange for Sherman Obando. They had great expectations that he would develop into a multi-dimensional impact player, but he was inconsistent and quickly landed in the minors. Furthermore, it was soon discovered that he had a serious shoulder problem requiring surgery and several months on the disabled list. He has some power and speed, and he could still develop into a good outfielder. There will be great competition for an Orioles outfield job in 1997, so Tarasco will have an uphill battle on his hands.

	AB	R	HR	RBI	SB	BA	$
1995 Montreal NL	438	64	14	40	24	.249	16
1996 Baltimore AL	84	14	1	9	5	.238	0

TARTABULL, DANNY - OF/DH - BR - Age 34
The latest reclamation project for the Sox training staff. One of the key features in Tartabull's season was his lack of time on the disabled list. Although his full season figures are only average at best, he finished the season strong. In September he hit .298 with 8 home runs. Moving him into the 6th spot in the order and out of the 4th and 5th spot sparked this second half surge. He could be considered the comeback player of the year.

	AB	R	HR	RBI	SB	BA	$
1995 NY - Oakland AL	280	34	8	35	0	.236	3
1996 Chicago AL	472	58	27	101	1	.254	11

TATIS, FERNANDO - 3B - BB - Age 22
This 6'1", 175 pound switch-hitting third baseman has the size to develop into a power hitter. He can contribute an occasional stolen base, and is the Rangers best hitting prospect. Look for him at Tulsa this year.

TATUM, JIM - 1B/3B/C - BR - Age 29
If they considered Triple-A records, Jim Tatum would be a candidate for the Hall-of-Fame. In Triple-A, he usually hits over .300 with good power, but he's failed in numerous major league trials. The Padres are his fifth organization, and even his willingness to learn other positions such as catching and first base hasn't earned him a major league job.

TAUBENSEE, EDDIE - C - BL - Age 28
The Reds refuse to give Taubensee the full time catching job, and it is hard to see why. Taubensee outhit Joe Oliver by 50 points, outslugged him by almost 60 points and had a better on-base average, but Ray Knight gave Oliver half of the starts despite a shortage of left handed power in the Reds lineup. Taubensee has 20 home run potential if he ever gets a chance (and he actually hit better against lefties in 1996 in limited at-bats).

	AB	R	HR	RBI	SB	BA	$
1995 Cincinnati NL	218	32	9	44	2	.284	8
1996 Cincinnati NL	327	46	12	48	3	.291	11

TAVAREZ, JESUS - OF - BB - Age 26
Tavarez has proven to be no better than a fifth outfielder at the major league level, showing an excellent glove and good speed, but modest offensive skills. He is overaggressive at the plate, and doesn't hit the ball on the ground often enough to properly utilize his wheels. With prospects like Billy McMillon, Todd Dunwoody and Mark Kotsay all within two years of him, Tavarez' window of opportunity for material playing time is closing.

	AB	R	HR	RBI	SB	BA	$
1995 Florida NL	190	31	2	13	7	.289	4
1996 Florida NL	114	14	0	6	5	.219	-

TAYLOR, JAMIE - 3B - BL - Age 26
This Northern League refugee was the everyday third baseman at the Rockies' Double-A New Haven club in 1996. Taylor was impressive enough both in the field and at the plate to make a jump to Triple-A likely for 1997.

TAYLOR, REGGIE - OF - BL - Age 20
The Phils' 1995 first round pick's natural ability was evident in his full season debut as one of the youngest Low-A South Atlantic League regulars, but so were his flaws. He has blazing speed and terrific range in center field, but swings at too many bad pitches, in the process giving away countless at-bats. He should make significant progress over the next two seasons, and be ready for a major league job by the turn of the century. Think Lance Johnson.

TEJADA, MIGUEL - SS - BR - Age 20
Tejada of the Modesto A's is both strong in the field as well at the plate. His manager praised him as versatile, player with good tools. He's young and improving.

TEJERO, FAUSTO - C - BR - Age 28
Tejero is a weak-hitting reserve catcher in Triple-A. The Angels have too much talent ahead of him.

TETTLETON, MICKEY - C/1B/OF - BB - Age 36
Tettleton's knees are in bad shape. He needed offseason surgery to repair a torn ligament in one, and both are chronically sore. As a DH, Tettleton can probably continue to play for a while, but he's slowing down. His slugging and on base percentages were their lowest since 1990, his last season in Baltimore. And, as always, Tettleton strikes out frequently (137 times last year). You know what you get with Tettleton: low average, lots of strikeouts and good power. But one gets the feeling that Tettleton isn't too far away from a dramatic decline in performance.

	AB	R	HR	RBI	SB	BA	$
1995 Texas AL	429	76	32	78	0	.238	13
1996 Texas AL	491	78	24	83	2	.246	9

THOMAS, BRIAN - OF - BL - Age 25
The former Texas A&M standout was a crowd favorite at Oklahoma City, but didn't distinguish himself in his first Triple-A season. The Rangers like him, though, and he'll get another season to try to improve his hitting.

THOMAS, FRANK - 1B - BR - Age 28
For the first time, The Big Hurt actually did get hurt. A broken foot cost him nearly a month at the all-star break and was a crucial blow to a team in the pennant race at the time. To make matters worse the pressure of supporting his team finally got the better of him. In a much publicized scene he had to be restrained from fighting with teammate Robin Ventura. He did appear to put all the year's frustrations behind him though with a solid September.

	AB	R	HR	RBI	SB	BA	$
1995 Chicago AL	493	102	40	111	3	.308	28
1996 Chicago AL	527	110	40	134	1	.349	29

THOMAS, GREG - OF - BL - Age 24
After a dreadful High-A season in 1995, the Indians' 1993 ninth round draftee mashed righties in a platoon role at Double-A Canton-Akron. In this organization, where Herbert Perry hits over .300 in the majors and can't stick, intermittent bursts of longball power are not good enough. Thomas' best bet for an eventual promotion to the majors as a backup will be with the thinning of talent during the 1998 expansion season.

THOME, JIM - 3B - BL - Age 26
Among third basemen, there is no surer thing at the plate than Thome. He combines on-base and slugging ability like few players have at a similar stage of development.

	AB	R	HR	RBI	SB	BA	$
1995 Cleveland AL	452	92	25	73	4	.314	21
1996 Cleveland AL	505	122	38	116	2	.311	22

THOMPSON, FLETCHER - 2B - BL - Age 28
Base-stealing is Thompson's strength. The Orioles signed him following his outstanding 1995 year with Alexandria in the independent Texas-Louisiana League where he swiped 43 bases, while hitting .343 with 15 homers. But Thompson found the going much tougher last year in the Double-A Eastern League, even though he was a year or two older than his peers.

THOMPSON, JASON - 1B - BL - Age 25
The Padres gave Thompson a chance when Wally Joyner was injured. But he didn't hit well, and was returned to Triple-A. He had his second solid season in the minors, again showing some power, but he strikes out 25 percent of the time. He plays excellent defense, and could win the Padres first base job in a few years. But top prospect Derrek Lee is also a first baseman, so the competition for playing time will be fierce.

THOMPSON, MILT - OF - BL - Age 38
After being turned loose by Cincinnati, this aging veteran spent a few weeks in spot duty for the Rockies, where his batting eye just never focused. His release from Colorado may be the end of a long and productive road.

	AB	R	HR	RBI	SB	BA	$
1996 Colorado NL	66	3	0	3	1	.106	-

THOMPSON, ROBBY - 2B - BR - Age 34
Injured more often than not over the past three years, this scrappy former Giant star looks pretty much like a former major league star. He just can't stay healthy long enough.

	AB	R	HR	RBI	SB	BA	$
1995 San Francisco NL	336	51	8	23	1	.223	1
1996 San Francisco NL	227	35	5	21	2	.211	-

THOMPSON, RYAN - OF - BR - Age 29
The cycle continues year after year: Thompson a learns a compact swing, generates more power, hits home runs, and then begins making the wildly looping undisciplined swings again. And now he's gone through elbow ligament and hamstring woes. Thompson still has speed and power, but he looked about done as a major leaguer when last season ended.

	AB	R	HR	RBI	SB	BA	$
1995 New York NL	267	39	7	31	3	.251	5
1996 Cleveland AL	22	2	1	5	0	.318	-

THURMAN, GARY - OF - BR - Age 32
Having spent part or all of eight years in the major leagues (although he never won a regular job) Thurman is one more case of the Mets' method of mixing genuine veterans with their budding youngsters on the farm. Thurman still has speed (25 stolen bases at Triple-A in 1996).

TIMMONS, OZZIE - OF - BR - Age 26
Timmons showed a ton of power at Iowa. He hit 17 homers in 213 at-bats. The Cubs gave him the everyday rightfield job in September after using him as a reserve in April and May. He showed power in the majors as well. Between Triple-A and the majors, Timmons hit 24 home runs in 353 at-bats. Timmons is an average defensive player who doesn't possess the arm to play rightfield. Still, Timmons was one of the dozen outfielders the Cubs were looking at for 1997.

	AB	R	HR	RBI	SB	BA	$
1995 Chicago NL	171	30	8	28	3	.263	5
1996 Chicago NL	140	18	7	16	1	.200	-

TINGLEY, RON - C - BR - Age 37
Veteran Ron Tingley played with the Angels Class-A Lake Elsinore club only because he could commute from home. He served as insurance in case one of the Angels major league catchers went down.

TINSLEY, LEE - OF - BB - Age 28
Tinsley undoubtedly knows the highways between Philadelphia and Boston by heart. Traded from the Red Sox to the Phillies over the previous winter in the Heathcliff Slocumb deal, Tinsley wound up back in Boston after just 31 games for the Phillies in 1996. He had a more substantive role for the Red Sox as they tried desperately to find a centerfielder. Tinsley wasn't the answer and wound up on Boston's bench. He offers decent speed and a little pop, but Tinsley will never again be a major league regular.

	AB	R	HR	RBI	SB	BA	$
1995 Boston AL	341	61	7	41	18	.284	16
1996 Philadelphia NL	52	1	0	2	2	.135	-
1996 Boston AL	192	28	3	14	6	.245	2

TOKHEIM, DAVE - OF - BL - Age 27
Drafted at age 22, Tokheim excelled at Class A against competition two and three years his junior, and was heralded as a prospect. Once he reached the upper minors, however, true prospects of a more recent vintage made him an extra Triple-A outfielder. Tokheim has never exceeded 18 doubles, 13 homers or 12 steals in any season.

TOMBERLIN, ANDY - OF - BL - Age 30
Once noted for moving from the regular minor league season into the major league spring training season (after the strike ended in April 1995), Tomberlin become a productive pinch hitter and spot starter in right field for the 1996 Mets. He is a good clubhouse personality, the type to stick around the majors for reasons other than box score accomplishments.

	AB	R	HR	RBI	SB	BA	$
1995 Oakland AL	85	15	4	10	4	.212	1
1996 New York NL	66	12	3	10	0	.258	0

TORRES, JAIME - C - BR - Age 26
A .265 career hitter in the minors, Torres offers enough defense to remain a candidate for a major league backup role. The Yankees finished 1996 with a fairly strong depth chart at catcher, but this position does get more than its fair share of injuries, and those can lead to promotions.

TORRES, PAUL - OF/1B - BR - Age 26
Torres' 1996 campaign was somewhat better than his first year at Double-A Arkansas in 1995. He hit .262-11-44 for the Travelers to reach Triple-A for the first time (just two at-bats). Torres has a little pop, but not much speed; he is a distant hope for major league playing time.

TORRES, TONY - 2B/3B - BR - Age 26
Torres is one of the all-around good guys of the minor leagues, a versatile, multi-positional backup who despite marginal tools and size (5'9", 170 pounds) has always been useful largely due to his zest for the game. He is surehanded defensively, sprays the ball around and is an efficient basestealer. He was also a solid veteran presence for the Marlins' youthful middle infield prospects.

TOTH, DAVE - C - BR - Age 27
Toth played extensively at Double-A Greenville in 1996, but was uninspiring despite showing rare power (10 homers, 55 RBI). Now 27 years old, Toth is merely an organizational catcher who won't challenge for big league time.

TOWLE, JUSTIN - C - BR - Age 23
The Reds' 1992 12th round pick has an intriguing bundle of talents. He combines above average power (16 homers in 1996) and speed (17 steals) for a catcher with extreme patience (93 walks) and excellent defensive skills.

TRAMMELL, ALAN - SS/3B - BR - Age 39
Trammell retired with a base hit in his last at-bat, a similar looking single to the one which opened his career in '77. He was a great player in his time and the Tigers will miss him.

	AB	R	HR	RBI	SB	BA	$
1995 Detroit AL	223	28	2	23	3	.269	3
1996 Detroit AL	193	16	1	16	6	.233	1

TRAMMELL, BUBBA - OF - BR - Age 25
Trammell had an outstanding season on the Tigers farm, hitting well over .300 between Double-A and Triple-A while swatting 33 home runs. A corner outfielder, Trammell was the Tigers 11th-round selection in the '94 draft. He will be ready for Detroit in a year and is regarded as a hard worker.

TREANOR, MATT - C - BR - Age 21
Treanor showed improved bat speed and power for Class A Lansing. He's a good defensive catcher who should soon pass Chad Strickland on the Royals' catching depth charts.

TREDAWAY, CHAD - 2B - BB - Age 24
Padre farmhand Tredaway struggled at the plate in Triple-A, and was returned to Double-A in June, and later to Single-A. He worked his way back to Triple-A where he showed some hitting improvement. Tredaway has no power or speed, but he makes good contact and plays good defense, and those skills and talents point to "utility man" as his role if he makes it to the majors.

TUCKER, MICHAEL - OF - BL - Age 25
He has now shown excellent power in two brief second halves after struggling in two first halves. Tucker has a beautiful, quick power stroke and will be a 25 homer guy with a good batting average once he gains just a little more experience. He's nearly there now. The Mike Tucker who slugged .550 in the second half last year is the one most likely to make his mark in 1997.

	AB	R	HR	RBI	SB	BA	$
1995 Kansas City AL	177	23	4	17	2	.260	2
1996 Kansas City AL	339	55	12	53	10	.260	9

TUCKER, SCOOTER - C - BR - Age 30
Tucker had an outside shot to be Mike Macfarlane's backup in the big leagues and was instead relegated to part-time

duty for Triple-A Omaha. A groin injury shortened his season before he was released mid-year. He can catch, but can't hit; Tucker is the epitome of a career minor leaguer.

TURANG, BRIAN - OF - BR - Age 29
The end may be near for this one-time Seattle Mariner. Turang hit just .172 with limited work at Syracuse and he tried to play the infield. He can take a walk and makes better contact than the average implies but there isn't much work for thirty year old utility players coming off disappointing minor league seasons. He's still good enough to be someone's twenty-fifth player but not much more than that.

TURNER, BRIAN - 1B - BL - Age 25
After spending five years in A-ball, Turner has developed a little power recently. He's still a relatively low-average, high-strikeout first baseman who won't hit the ball out of the park enough to get to the big leagues.

TURNER, CHRIS - C - BR - Age 28
Turner played much of 1996 in Triple-A, but he has 237 at-bats in the majors, mostly in 1993 and '94, with a career batting average of .249. He has little power, and his best chance of staying in the majors is as a back-up catcher.

TYLER, BRAD - 2B - BL - Age 28
Taylor is a Triple-A infielder, primarily a second baseman, in the Orioles farm system who had a few decent years in the minors showing some power and speed. His best shot at the majors is as a utility infielder.

UNROE, TIM - 3B - BR - Age 26
Exposed to the majors in 1995, Unroe spent 1996 at Triple-A New Orleans on the Brewers farm, hitting .270 with 25 homers.

VALDEZ, MARIO - 1B - BL - Age 22
Valdez earned an aggressive in-season promotion from Low-A to Double-A in 1996 on the strength of a .376 average with power and patience at Low-A South Bend. Valdez is not a typical first baseman offensively. He does not possess prodigious longball power, but like Frank Thomas, he makes himself into a .300 hitter by never swinging at bad pitches. Valdez is one to two strong minor league seasons away from settling into a productive 300 at bat per season role in the majors, with David Segui-like numbers in the short-term.

VALDEZ, PEDRO - OF - BL - Age 23
His smooth, powerful swing is similar to Rafael Palmeiro's. For some reason, when Valdez struggled, Iowa played well and vice versa. Valdez makes some tough plays in the outfield, but he isn't a stand out defensively. Valdez turned 23 during the season and he hit .295 at Triple-A with 15 home runs. His bat is his ticket to the majors.

VALENTIN, JOHN - SS - BR - Age 30
In 1996, Valentin hit for about half the power he had demonstrated during his phenomenal 1995 campaign. While it has to be considered a major disappointment for Red Sox' fans, Valentin's hitting is still among the elite for AL shortstops. Nomar Garciaparra looms large on the horizon, so a shift to third base for Valentin is a likely course. The offensive stakes are higher for a third baseman, though, so Valentin will need to at least approach his watershed '95 numbers to remain in the league's upper half.

	AB	R	HR	RBI	SB	BA	$
1995 Boston AL	520	108	27	102	20	.298	31
1996 Boston AL	527	84	13	59	9	.296	14

VALENTIN, JOSE - C - BB - Age 21
Valentin had an unremarkable season offensively in '96 but solidified his status as a top catching prospect. He stayed healthy and made progress defensively, and held his own at high Class A (.263) before a late promotion to Double-A. Valentin needs two more years in the minors before becoming a regular big leaguer.

VALENTIN, JOSE - SS - BB - Age 27
Valentin has always had good power for a shortstop, but until last year he was badly overmatched by lefties, carrying a career .149 average against southpaw pitching. In 1996 Valentin improved vs lefties by nearly 100 points and exceeded 20 homers for the first time in his career. The power is no fluke. In the field he made a pile of errors, and an equal number of spectacular plays. He faded offensively in September.

	AB	R	HR	RBI	SB	BA	$
1995 Milwaukee AL	338	62	11	49	16	.219	11
1996 Milwaukee AL	552	90	24	95	17	.259	18

VALLE, DAVE - C - BR - Age 36
Valle is the catcher's version of the Maytag Repairman. As Ivan Rodriguez' backup, Valle performed well in limited duty. He handles pitchers well, and can handle long stretches of inactivity without a noticeable falloff in performance. Valle has a couple more years in him as a backup, if he wants them.

	AB	R	HR	RBI	SB	BA	$
1995 Two Teams	75	7	0	5	1	.240	-
1996 Texas AL	86	14	3	17	0	.302	0

VALRIE, KERRY - OF - BR - Age 28
A career minor leaguer, Valrie was at Triple-A Nashville for the White Sox in 1996, hitting .273 with 13 homers and 10 stolen bases.

VAN BURKLEO, TY - 1B - BL - Age 33
When Van Burkleo returned from Japan in 1991, some observers expected another Cecil Fielder. Plus Van Burkleo also stole bases. But the observers were wrong, and he's been moving through various organizations playing at various minor league levels. He was in Single-A with the Angels last year.

VANDER WAL, JOHN - 1B/OF - BL - Age 30
Vander Wal was again the top pinch-hitter for the Rockies, being the only real off-the-bench power threat the team possessed most of the 1996 season. His ability to play the outfield may result in more playing time in 1997.

	AB	R	HR	RBI	SB	BA	$
1995 Colorado NL	101	15	5	21	1	.347	5
1996 Colorado NL	151	20	5	31	2	.252	2

VARITEK, JASON - C - BB - Age 25
Varitek's slow progress as a pro makes you wonder what all the fuss was about. He wrangled with the Mariners after being a high draft pick and eventually signed a contract. After a poor first year at Double-A Port City in 1995, Varitek hit for a better average and more power at the same level in 1996. But, he's still whiffing at a high rate. When Varitek cuts his strikeouts he'll get promoted quickly.

VAUGHN, GREG - OF/DH - BR - Age 31
The Padres obtained slugger Vaughn from the Brewers in late July to bolster their hitting for the stretch run. But he struggled and had difficulty adjusting to National League pitching. He was a free agent. Over an injury-free full season, Vaughn is capable of hitting 30-plus homers while driving in 120 runs.

	AB	R	HR	RBI	SB	BA	$
1995 Milwaukee AL	392	67	17	59	10	.224	10
1996 Milwaukee AL	375	78	31	95	5	.280	16
1996 San Diego NL	141	20	10	22	4	.206	0

VAUGHN, MO - 1B - BL - Age 29
Coming off of an MVP season in 1995, the Hit Dog started slowly, then came on strong down the stretch. He was the most reliable hitter over the second half of the season for the Red Sox as they made a late-season charge at the Yankees. A highly respected leader on and off the field, Vaughn is a superstar in every sense of the word.

	AB	R	HR	RBI	SB	BA	$
1995 Boston AL	550	98	39	126	11	.300	32
1996 Boston AL	635	118	44	143	2	.326	30

VELANDIA, JORGE - SS - BR - Age 22
Padres farmhand Velandia had a solid, but below-average, year in Double-A last year. But it was a step backwards as he spent most of 1995 in Triple-A. He's a small guy who hits mostly singles, and once had a reputation as a good glove man.

VELARDE, RANDY - OF/SS - BR - Age 34
Veteran Velarde had more than 412 at-bats for the first time in his career, and given the opportunity, he responded with his career-best year. His solid play should continue into 1997, although the home runs may decline if they quit using rabbit-balls.

	AB	R	HR	RBI	SB	BA	$
1995 New York AL	367	60	7	46	5	.278	9
1996 California AL	530	82	14	54	7	.285	12

VELASQUEZ, EDGARD - OF - BR - Age 21
This youngster from Puerto Rico is becoming a phenom in the Rockies organization, having led his Double-A New Haven team in homers, hits, runs and RBI (tied for lead with teammate Derrick Gibson). His strong arm and defensive skills make a move up to Triple-A Colorado Springs likely in 1997.

VELEZ, JOSE - OF - BB - Age 23
As expected, Velez returned to Double-A Arkansas in 1996, but didn't make much improvement. He's an aggressive hitter with some speed. He doesn't make effective use of his tools, though, because he won't take a pitch and he doesn't have enough power to be such a free swinger.

VENTURA, ROBIN - 3B - BL - Age 29
Another solid season from the veteran third sacker. Ventura continues to hit for average with power numbers that are impressive for his position. He emerged as a team leader too.

	AB	R	HR	RBI	SB	BA	$
1995 Chicago AL	492	79	26	93	4	.295	21
1996 Chicago AL	586	96	34	105	1	.287	18

VENTURA, WILFREDO - C - BR - Age 20
It is always worth watching a professional ball player who is under 21 and has had a couple of seasons under his belt. Ventura struck out almost five times for each walk he earned, but if you are going to look for future stars, he is the kind of guy you seek.

VERAS, QUILVIO - 2B - BB - Age 25
Something funny happened to Veras on the road to surefire stardom. The reigning NL stolen base champ suffered from a pulled hamstring early in the season, and never hit his basestealing stride. The even faster Luis Castillo stole his job and never looked back. Veras is a prime candidate for a move elsewhere in 1997. He draws lots of walks, and will soon return to the upper echelon among leadoff hitters.

	AB	R	HR	RBI	SB	BA	$
1995 Florida NL	440	86	5	32	56	.261	27
1996 Florida NL	253	40	4	14	8	.253	3

VESSEL, ANDREW - OF - BR - Age 22
Vessel was one of the bigger disappointments for the Rangers this year. This 6'3" 210 pound outfielder hasn't displayed much power at any level. He has a long way to go to live up to Texas' expectations.

VIDRO, JOSE - 3B - BB - Age 22
Quietly, the Expos' 1992 sixth round draftee has performed admirably with the bat and glove while consistently ranking among his leagues' youngest regulars. Though only 5'11", 185, he generates solid bat speed and extra base power (25 doubles, 18 homers at Double-A in 1996). He has below average speed for a second baseman, but is surehanded at both and second and third base. He is overaggressive at the plate, but generally makes contact.

VINA, FERNANDO - 2B - BL - Age 27
His hard-nosed style sits well with his manager and some teammates, but not with Albert Belle. Vina's talents include his speed and defense.

	AB	R	HR	RBI	SB	BA	$
1995 Milwaukee AL	288	46	3	29	6	.257	5
1996 Milwaukee AL	554	94	7	46	16	.283	14

VINAS, JULIO - C - BR - Age 23
Vinas has moved steadily up the White Sox farm ladder, advancing about one level per year. Offensively he offers some pop in the bat (11 homers at Triple-A in 1996) but will be a low-.200's hitter if and when he reaches the majors.

VITIELLO, JOE - 1B/OF - BR - Age 26
When Bob Hamelin failed, Vitiello had a chance to secure a platoon job at first base or as a DH. Instead he went into a slump and was demoted to Omaha. He hit better after his recall, but the damage has been done. Even with Jose Offerman moving off of first base to second base, Vitiello is not the most likely candidate for a regular job in the Royals' 1997 lineup. He's not done yet, but Vitiello will have to regain his 1994 American Association batting champ swing before he'll get another big chance.

	AB	R	HR	RBI	SB	BA	$
1995 Kansas City AL	130	13	7	21	0	.254	2
1996 Kansas City AL	257	29	8	40	2	.241	2

VIZCAINO, JOSE - SS/3B/2B - BB - Age 29
Vizcaino earned a starting job with the Mets in 1996, on the strength of his surprising 1995 campaign, but with Rey Ordonez ready for the majors, Vizcaino had to slide over to second base. Then with Edgardo Alfonzo maturing and Jason Hardtke coming behind him, Vizcaino slid over to Cleveland. He can hit for average and play all three infield skill positions, making a good fit for an off-the-bench role in 1997.

	AB	R	HR	RBI	SB	BA	$
1995 New York NL	509	66	3	56	8	.287	13
1996 New York NL	363	47	1	32	9	.303	12
1996 Cleveland AL	179	23	0	13	6	.285	3

VIZQUEL, OMAR - SS - BB - Age 29
Though his thunder was stolen by the dramatic rise to power of youngsters Alex Rodriguez and Derek Jeter as the premier players at his position last season, Vizquel continued turning into one of the best all-around shortstops in baseball in 1996. Always a defensive standout, Vizquel has improved the rest of his game since his move from Seattle to Cleveland in 1994. Though he doesn't have Lofton-like speed, he has improved from a 50% to an 80% basestealing success rate over the past three seasons. He has also become a bat control specialist with a knack for yanking doubles down the line. 1996 will go down as his career year with the bat, but pencil him in for a .270, 25 steal year in 1997.

	AB	R	HR	RBI	SB	BA	$
1995 Cleveland AL	542	87	6	56	29	.266	22
1996 Cleveland AL	542	98	9	64	35	.297	26

VOIGT, JACK - OF - BR - Age 30
Voigt is a versatile player who can really handle Triple-A pitching but can't seem to stay in the majors. He had a cup of coffee in September, and still could stick as a utility player with the right team, but age is beginning to hurt his chances.

**GOT A QUESTION?
CALL JOHN BENSON LIVE**

Your Question - Your Roster - Your Situation

Let the top analyst in the business help you!!

1-900-773-7526

$2.49/minute

1 pm to 11 pm Eastern Time - 7 days a Week

WALBECK, MATT - C - BB - Age 27
It is fairly certain, after almost 1000 major league at-bats and an average under .230, that Walbeck will not be a regular player. He has enough skills to be a good backup catcher.

	AB	R	HR	RBI	SB	BA	$
1995 Minnesota AL	393	40	1	44	3	.257	4
1996 Minnesota AL	215	25	2	24	3	.223	-

WALKER, LARRY - OF - BL - Age 30
Walker broke his collarbone crashing into the center field wall in midseason, and never made it all the way back. He'll be healthy and return to right field in 1997, where his strong arm and quick bat should produce outstanding results.

	AB	R	HR	RBI	SB	BA	$
1995 Colorado NL	494	96	36	101	16	.306	33
1996 Colorado NL	272	58	18	58	18	.276	14

WALKER, SHON - OF - BL - Age 22
Walker was a supplemental first-round draft pick of the Pirates. In 1996 he hit .303 with 14 homers at Class A Lynchburg.

WALKER, TODD - 3B/2B - BL - Age 23
Walker dominated Triple-A pitching in '96 (.339-28-111-13) before being called up to Minnesota for his first big-league experience (.256). The former LSU star took only two years to race through the minor leagues. Walker will need a couple of years to hit his full stride, which will be impressive. He has arrived.

	AB	R	HR	RBI	SB	BA	$
1996 Minnesota AL	82	8	0	6	2	.256	-

WALLACH, TIM - 3B/1B - BR - Age 39
The Rasputin of third basemen, one would assume Wallach would retire after a dismal season with the Angels and Dodgers. The Dodgers brought him back for the stretch run, but a .333 slugging average and .286 on base average are not likely to earn an invitation to spring training. With the exception of his stunning 1994 season, he hasn't really had a good year since 1990.

	AB	R	HR	RBI	SB	BA	$
1995 Los Angeles NL	327	24	9	38	0	.266	6
1996 California AL	190	23	8	20	1	.237	0
1996 Los Angeles NL	162	14	4	22	0	.228	-

WALTON, JEROME - OF - BR - Age 31
Walton hurt himself in spring training, then never really won back his super-sub role once he got to Atlanta. With far better outfield prospects already on the scene, Walton became a fifth wheel instead of a fifth outfielder; he was not included on the club's post-season roster and will have to latch on with yet another team in 1997. He can hit (a little) and run (a little) and play some defense, too. He was the NL's Rookie of the Year just seven years ago.

	AB	R	HR	RBI	SB	BA	$
1995 Cincinnati NL	162	32	8	22	10	.290	9
1996 Atlanta NL	47	9	1	4	0	.340	1

WARD, DARYLE - 1B - BR - Age 22
Daryle Ward, the son of former major leaguer Gary, is a minor prospect in Detroit's system. A lefty swinging first baseman, he can hit for average but lacks the power required of a regular. Ward is two years away from the major leagues.

WARD, TURNER - OF - BB - Age 31
Ward is just a fringe player with limited opportunities at best. If he sticks, he usually has one early hot streak in him.

	AB	R	HR	RBI	SB	BA	$
1995 Milwaukee AL	129	19	4	16	6	.264	4
1996 Milwaukee AL	67	7	2	10	3	.179	-

WARNER, MIKE - OF - BL - Age 25
After getting midseason promotions in each of his first four pro seasons, Warner was a big disappointment in 1996, falling all the way back to Class A Durham. He simply hasn't improved over the last two years after showing a lot of

promise early in his career. Warner is a distant hope for the majors.

WARNER, RON - 1B/3B/SS - BR - Age 28
A good defensive player, Warner can play first, third, and short. He showed some pop with 22 doubles, and also hit .300. But, Warner is old to still be biding time in Double-A.

WASZGIS, BJ - C - BR - Age 26
Waszgis' weakness is defense, but he has a decent bat with some power. The poor defense prevented him from getting called up last summer when the Orioles needed catching help.

WATKINS, PAT - OF - BR - Age 24
Watkins appeared to be an interesting power/speed combination after a 27 home run, 31 steal season at Class-A Winston-Salem, a hitters haven. Since then, he has stalled at Double-A, where he has made good contact, hit for a decent but not great average, and shown a little power and speed, but not enough to get excited about. Watkins should start the 1997 season in Indianapolis.

WAWRUCK, JIM - OF - BL - Age 26
Wawruck is a singles hitter who has hit for good averages in Triple-A the past two years. He's a good leadoff or number two hitter, but his weak arm limits his major league opportunities because he can't play all the outfield positions.

WEBSTER, LENNY - C - BR - Age 32
Webster is always on the major league bubble. He needs to hit to stick in the majors, at least better than his .230 average of last season. He's likely to get squeezed out in Montreal where Tim Laker figures to be the starting catcher and rookie Raul Chavez and veteran Tim Spehr are in reserve.

	AB	R	HR	RBI	SB	BA	$
1995 Philadelphia NL	150	18	4	14	0	.267	2
1996 Montreal NL	174	18	2	17	0	.230	-

WEDGE, ERIC - 1B/C - BR - Age 29
The definition of fringe major leaguer, Wedge has spent the last six years bouncing between Triple-A and spot duty in the majors with three different organizations. Wedge can provide good power, but little else. He's a defensive liability with no real position.

WEHNER, JOHN - 3B - BR - Age 29
He is a classic case of a player who adds more value to his team than his stats show. He can play six positions (first, second, third and all three outfield spots) well, can catch in a pinch and has decent speed.

	AB	R	HR	RBI	SB	BA	$
1995 Pittsburgh NL	107	13	0	5	3	.308	-
1996 Pittsburgh NL	139	19	2	13	1	.259	1

WEINKE, CHRIS - 1B - BL - Age 24
He split 1996 between Double-A and Triple-A with mixed results. At Knoxville, Weinke dominated power-wise. At Syracuse, he struggled to a .186 clip and clubbed only three homers. He has perhaps the best bat speed in the organization and can take a walk with the best of them. With no rush from the parent club, he will likely start the year as Syracuse's regular first baseman.

WEISS, WALT - SS - BB - Age 33
This quiet veteran and clubhouse leader made more errors in 1996 than Rockies fans expected, but continued to set the table offensively by leading the swing-happy team in walks. The emergence of Neifi Perez may make Weiss expendable for 1997, but he remains a solid, if not flashy, middle infielder, whose value to a team goes far beyond his stats.

	AB	R	HR	RBI	SB	BA	$
1995 Colorado NL	427	65	1	25	15	.260	8
1996 Colorado NL	517	89	8	48	10	.282	14

WELLS, FORRY - OF - BL - Age 26
Wells platooned in the Double-A New Haven outfield in 1996, getting occasional clutch hits but hitting for a disappointing average.

WHITAKER, CHAD - OF - BL - Age 20
The Indians' 1995 third round pick is extremely raw, but he did show a smooth lefthanded stroke with significant power potential at Low-A Columbus. He swings at bad pitches too often, but he nailed over 40% of his hits for extra bases. He might need another season at the same level, but should show dramatic improvement. He's a prime candidate for a breakthrough season in 1997.

WHITE, BILLY - 2B - BR - Age 28
This career minor leaguer and 1995 replacement player served primarily as a utility man at Triple-A Colorado Springs in 1996. With the Rockies' infield personnel being staffed by players with stronger skills, White is unlikely to make the jump to the show.

WHITE, DEVON - OF - BB - Age 34
White has neatly made the transition from a table-setter to a legitimate extra-base power threat with the bat. He is primarily a threat from the right side of the plate now, and is no longer a leadoff candidate, but may have just now peaked as an all-around offensive performer.

	AB	R	HR	RBI	SB	BA	$
1995 Toronto AL	427	61	10	53	11	.283	15
1996 Florida NL	552	77	17	84	22	.274	19

WHITE, RONDELL - OF - BR - Age 25
His horrific crash into the outfield fence at Coors Field cost him two months and effectively ruined his season. He is a much better player than last year's numbers show. He has all the tools to become a superstar and a perennial 30-30 man.

	AB	R	HR	RBI	SB	BA	$
1995 Montreal NL	474	87	13	57	25	.295	24
1996 Montreal NL	334	35	6	41	14	.293	13

WHITEN, MARK - OF - BB - Age 30
Seattle was Whiten's third team in 1996, and his locale could change again. He struggled in Philadelphia and was in Atlanta only briefly, but he came on at the plate in Seattle. Whiten is not a tremendously savvy ballplayer - he will swing at pitches early in the count when his team is behind in the late innings, and is infatuated with his strong throwing arm, more errors than assists. However, if you throw him a mistake, he will hit it nine miles.

	AB	R	HR	RBI	SB	BA	$
1995 Two Teams	320	51	12	47	8	.241	9
1996 Atlanta NL	272	45	10	38	15	.243	6
1996 Seattle AL	140	31	12	33	2	.300	5

WHITMORE, DARRELL - OF - BL - Age 28
Long heralded by the mainstream baseball media as an offensive force-in-waiting, Whitmore effectively admitted he couldn't make the grade in the majors when he accepted a contract offer from the Japanese League in 1996. Whitmore is a wild swinger who consistently tasted success at the Triple-A level, hitting for average and power. He then got himself out on a regular basis against the superior major league pitching.

	AB	R	HR	RBI	SB	BA	$
1995 Florida NL	58	6	1	2	0	.190	-

WIDGER, CHRIS - C - BR - Age 25
The luckless Widger is stuck between Dan Wilson, who has put two solid seasons together, and Jason Varitek, a recent number one draft choice. Over the last two years, Widger has batted only 56 times in Seattle.

	AB	R	HR	RBI	SB	BA	$
1995 Seattle AL	45	2	1	2	0	.200	-

WILKINS, RICK - C - BL - Age 29
Acquired from the Astros midseason last year, Wilkins showed the signs of power he displayed in Chicago during the 1994 season. The Giants can use a veteran to help their pitchers and be a mentor to young Marcus Jensen. Wilkins is probably that man.

	AB	R	HR	RBI	SB	BA	$
1995 Houston NL	202	30	7	19	0	.203	0
1996 San Francisco NL	411	53	14	59	0	.243	3

WILLIAMS, BERNIE - OF - BB - Age 28
Nothing could be sweeter than coming of age as a superstar in the New York media glare. For years our books have been telling you that Williams had untapped power potential. This year we will just say that he's headed upward and hasn't yet had his career year.

	AB	R	HR	RBI	SB	BA	$
1995 New York AL	563	93	18	82	8	.307	23
1996 New York AL	551	108	29	102	17	.305	26

WILLIAMS, EDDIE - 1B - BR - Age 32
Williams never got on track in '96 in his first season with Detroit. He may have to swat some home runs in Triple-A to get back to the major leagues. He could be finished.

	AB	R	HR	RBI	SB	BA	$
1995 San Diego NL	296	35	12	47	0	.260	7
1996 Detroit AL	215	22	6	26	0	.200	-

WILLIAMS, GEORGE - C - BB - Age 27
Williams is a former Pacific Coast League All-Star. Switch-hitting catchers who can hit for average and power, with walks, are rare. If he gets at-bats, Williams will hit.

	AB	R	HR	RBI	SB	BA	$
1995 Oakland AL	79	13	3	14	0	.291	1
1996 Oakland AL	132	17	3	10	0	.152	-

WILLIAMS, GERALD - OF - BR - Age 30
Williams is getting a late start at being a regular after spending his prime years on the Yankees bench. After the Brewers acquired him, he started in center nearly every game but didn't exactly light it up at the plate. He has 20-20 power and speed and is a bona fide sleeper for 1997.

	AB	R	HR	RBI	SB	BA	$
1995 New York AL	182	33	6	28	4	.247	4
1996 NY-Milwaukee AL	325	43	5	34	10	.252	5

WILLIAMS, JUAN - OF - BL - Age 24
Williams potential may be greater than first appears when looking at his .272-15-52 line from Triple-A Richmond in 1996. Because he's a patient hitter, Williams hasn't always produced astounding numbers. He runs and throws well enough to play anywhere in the outfield. As a potential minor league free agent, keep an eye on Williams should he go somewhere else; he would no longer have to compete with the likes of Andruw Jones or Jermaine Dye for major league opportunities.

WILLIAMS, KEITH - OF - BR - Age 24
Williams played well enough in 1995 for Phoenix, though his average dropped some. There must be some reason the Giants didn't bring him up during their spate of injuries in 1996. He might get a look in 1997. He isn't a bad ballplayer at all and could be a good number four outfielder.

WILLIAMS, MATT - 3B - BR - Age 31
In 1994 it was the strike. In 1995 it was a broken foot. In 1996 it was a bad shoulder, which has since been surgically corrected. If he could play for a full season, it would great to see what he could do. Maybe 1997 is the year. Just a terrific all-around third sacker and hitter, now in the small-ballpark American League.

	AB	R	HR	RBI	SB	BA	$
1995 San Francisco NL	283	53	23	65	2	.336	19
1996 San Francisco NL	404	69	22	85	1	.302	18

WILLIAMS, REGGIE - OF - BB - Age 30
Williams is a good average, low power hitter who has shown good speed in the past, but is clearly not a prospect. He is not likely to get a serious chance with the Dodgers.

WILLIAMS, RICKY - OF - BR - Age 20
The Texas Longhorn halfback just completed his sophomore football season, and his first full pro baseball season. He struck out nearly every third at bat, and his flawed mechanics wouldn't allow his solid 6'0", 215 pound, body to

generate consistent longball power, but he showed excellent basestealing ability, and would occasionally induce gasps with feats which can be performed only by world-class athletes. He can excel at whichever sport he chooses.

WILLIAMSON, ANTONE - 3B - BL - Age 23
The Brewers first round draft pick in 1994. Went to Triple-A New Orleans, where he was limited to 199 at-bats in 1996.

WILSON, BRANDON - SS - BR - Age 28
The longtime White Sox' prospect dropped off with the bat in his first year in the Reds' chain, in which he received substantial Triple-A playing time due only to an injury to top prospect Pokey Reese. Wilson is a surehanded if unspectacular defender, and has a winning attitude.

WILSON, CRAIG - SS - BR - Age 26
This Craig Wilson, not to be confused with the one who once played for St. Louis and Kansas City has little power or speed, but can field well. He hit .282 at Double-A Birmingham on the White Sox farm.

WILSON, DAN - C - BR - Age 28
Wilson has become one of the better catchers in the AL. His strong defense and ability to manage the pitching staff is reason enough to be a starter. In the past two years, he has added some power, and improved a .220 stroke into the .280 range.

	AB	R	HR	RBI	SB	BA	$
1995 Seattle AL	399	40	9	51	2	.278	9
1996 Seattle AL	491	51	18	83	1	.285	11

WILSON, DESI - OF - BL - Age 28
Wilson is a solid, if not powerful first baseman. He was called up in August and did well enough, but he has little power. Wilson might be fine off the bench, but he is probably not much of a long term solution.

	AB	R	HR	RBI	SB	BA	$
1996 San Francisco NL	118	10	2	12	0	.271	1

WILSON, ENRIQUE - SS - BB - Age 21
Simply one of the finest shortstop prospects in baseball, Wilson was voted the best defensive infielder with the best infield throwing arm in the Double-A Eastern League as one of its youngest regulars. The .300 hitter is no slouch with the bat either. After one more year of seasoning, he will settle in as the Indians' starting shortstop, or as their second baseman.

WILSON, NIGEL - OF - BL - Age 27
The former number one expansion draft pick of the Marlins had to go out and ruin his perfect major league batting record (0-23 with no walks) with a massive September home run on national TV following his 1996 callup. A below average fielder, Wilson has unquestionable tools at the plate, with a powerful, fluid swing. However, he is only now learning the value of taking a pitch

WILSON, POOKIE - OF - BL - Age 27
Wilson is the perfect example of the kind of player which an expansion team initially stocks its minor league rosters. He once possessed good speed, but has only stolen 16 bases in 29 attempts over the past two seasons. He is also a wild swinger with little power or plate discipline.

WILSON, TOM - C - BR - Age 26
Wilson is a six-year veteran journeyman who had a .230 career batting average before he went on an offensive rampage at Triple-A Buffalo. He was acquired by the Indians from the Yankees' chain during the 1996 season. 1996 will likely go down as the apex of his career.

WIMMER, CHRIS - OF - BR - Age 26
The former Wichita State star was unproductive at Louisville in 1996, hitting a soft .249 (just two homers and 23 RBI). Wimmer should get comfortable in the minors; he's likely to stay there.

WINN, RANDY - OF - BR - Age 22
Winn, the Marlins' 1995 third round draftee, possibly has the greatest pure speed of any Marlins' prospect, but remains

a raw offensive player. Despite his rangy 6'2", 175 pound frame, he has developed no extra base power, and is too eager to swing at bad pitches to be successful near the top of the order at higher levels. The fact that he was in the older third of the Low-A Midwest League's starters makes it unlikely that he can correct his flaws in time to contend for a material major league role.

WITT, KEVIN - 3B/SS - BL - Age 21
Witt was the final player chosen in the 1994 draft's first round, by the Blue Jays. He's a former tennis player who was a high school star in Jacksonville. Witt hit .271 with 13 homers at Class A Dunedin in 1996.

WOLFE, JOEL - 1B/OF - BR - Age 26
A shift to first base in 1996 did nothing to improve Wolfe's hitting. He has now spent three and a half years at Double-A with disappointing results to show for it. Serious improvements are necessary for Wolfe's pro career to have much chance for advancement.

WOLFF, MIKE - OF - BR - Age 26
After two years in Double-A, Wolff played in Triple-A last year, hitting a weak .250, hurting his progress. He's got a rifle arm, but needs to improve his bat to get to the Angels.

WOMACK, TONY - SS - BL - Age 27
He rose from the dead in the Pirates' organization last year, getting back to Pittsburgh in September after a solid year at Triple-A Calgary (.298, 37 steals). He was the Pirates' minor league player of the year in 1993 but was taken off the 40-man roster after the 1995 season and considered out of the plans. He has great speed and has finally learned to use it by bunting and chopping down on the ball. The fact that Womack, a middle infielder by trade, added center field to his resume in 1996 makes him a serious major league utility candidate.

WOODS, KEN - OF/3B - BR - Age 26
Woods did okay playing third base for Shreveport and then outfield for Phoenix, but he is down there on the depth chart, and doesn't do any one thing better than any of the superior outfielders in the system. Might be a fourth outfielder somewhere, but it better be soon.

WOODS, TYRONE - OF - BR - Age 27
Woods has a good power stroke, but has topped out at Double-A. Being a defensive liability probably won't help him advance, either.

WOODSON, TRACY - 3B - BR - Age 34
If he was ten years younger, Woodson's performance at Triple-A Columbus (.288-21-81) in 1996 would have been exciting. Given his age, however, he is another one of those deep extensions of the major league bench, waiting for multiple injuries to create an opening in the majors.

WORTHINGTON, CRAIG - 3B - BR - Age 31
In June, Ex-Orioles, Reds, Indians and Rangers third baseman Worthington signed with the Hanshin Tigers of Japan's Central League, but he didn't hit well in Japan. He spent all or parts of seven years in the majors with 1989, his rookie year, being his best.

WRIGHT, RON - 1B - BR - Age 21
Considered the best power hitter in the Braves farm system, Wright was part of the take the Pirates received in the Denny Neagle trade. Before the deal Wright smashed 36 homers and drove in 114 runs at two different levels in 1996, giving him 68 homers and 218 RBI in his first two full seasons as a pro. Wright can make rapid progress through the relatively thin Pirates system; he could reach the majors in 1997, at the tender age of 21.

WRONA, RICK - C - BR - Age 33
Wrona is an awful offensive player who backed up for Triple-A Scranton-Wilkes Barre in the Phils' chain in 1996. He can't hit for average or power and swings at everything, but is an adequate defensive player and positive veteran influence to younger players. He is likely to latch on somewhere in a similar role in 1997.

YAN, JULIAN - 1B - BR - Age 31
The eleven-year minor league veteran hit the wall suddenly in 1996, playing himself out of a Triple-A job in the Expos'

chain in short order. He posted a 238/48 strikeout/walk ratio over his last 867 major league at bats - pitchers refused to throw Yan strikes in 1996, and he couldn't resist. Yan had shown occasional home run power over the years, but nothing special for a first baseman.

YARD, BRUCE - SS - BL - Age 25
A late-round draft pick in 1993, Yard has hit for a high average at Double-A San Antonio the last two years. But he's a weak singles hitter whose defensive skills are rudimentary.

YOUNG, DMITRI - 3B - BB - Age 23
Young showed in 1996 why the Cardinals used the fourth overall pick in the 1991 draft on him. Finally. It's been an uphill climb for Young but he finally got to the majors last August after a .333-15-64 year at Triple-A Louisville. Young's future depends on what the Cardinals do with Gary Gaetti. If Gaetti returns, then Young either goes back to Louisville or sits on the bench. If Gaetti retires or isn't re-signed, then Young becomes the starting first baseman with John Mabry moving to third.

YOUNG, ERIC - 2B - BR - Age 29
Surprisingly, Young played almost Gold Glove defense in 1996, while leading the NL in steals and sporting an OBP of almost .400. He'll be looking for a big raise in 1997, and the Rockies aren't sure whether to sign Young or move phenom Neifi Perez to second base and pass on the talented "EY."

	AB	R	HR	RBI	SB	BA	$
1995 Colorado NL	366	68	6	36	35	.317	24
1996 Colorado NL	568	113	8	74	53	.324	39

YOUNG, ERNIE - OF - BR - Age 27
Young finally got a season's worth of at-bats, giving him a chance to show what he is capable of. Young has always fared better during a second season at a given level, so 1997 will be his year to excel. He is capable of 25 homers and a .280 average at the major league level. He played a lot of center in 1996, but Oakland really sees him as a left fielder.

	AB	R	HR	RBI	SB	BA	$
1995 Oakland AL	50	9	2	5	0	.200	-
1996 Oakland AL	462	72	19	64	7	.242	8

YOUNG, KEVIN - 1B - BR - Age 27
Young was on the Pirates' trading block in spring training and many people speculated he'd be dealt to the Royals. He eventually joined Kansas City, but not before the Pirates waived him and he hit 13 homers in just 186 at-bats at Triple-A Omaha. A Kansas City native, Young continued his power stroke once recalled to the bigs. For the year, he had 21 homers in 318 at-bats. He can also play decent defense at third or first base and fill in as an outfielder, too. Young has earned another chance in the majors and he'd prefer to do it in Kansas City, although their roster may just be too crowded to accommodate him.

	AB	R	HR	RBI	SB	BA	$
1995 Pittsburgh NL	181	13	6	22	1	.232	2
1996 Kansas City AL	132	20	8	23	3	.242	2

ZAMBRANO, EDDIE - 1B/OF - BR - Age 31
Originally a Red Sox' farm talent, Zambrano climbed through the Indians' and Cubs' chains to reach the majors in 1993. That was the pinnacle, however, as he came back to earth quickly; Zambrano has batted .134 over the last two seasons, spent largely at Double-A.

ZAUN, GREG - C - BB - Age 25
Zaun was acquired by the Marlins from the Orioles late in 1996 in a move which should provide a greater benefit to the Fish in the long run. He is a smallish (5'10", 170 pounds) singles hitter who makes consistent contact and has solid defensive skills, though he wears down easily when he has to catch several games in a row. He has the ideal mentality to be a productive backup, and his ability to switch-hit is a plus.

	AB	R	HR	RBI	SB	BA	$
1995 Baltimore AL	104	18	3	14	1	.260	1
1996 Baltimore AL	108	16	1	13	0	.231	-
1996 Florida NL	31	4	1	2	1	.290	0

ZEILE, TODD - 3B - BR - Age 31
Ziele came over from the Phillies in a late-season trade when the Orioles needed additional hitting strength in the stretch drive. He played a decent third base and came through with a number of clutch hits. Overall, the Orioles were impressed with his hitting, adequate defense, hustle and good attitude. The problem is that Ripken may be moved to third base, limiting the number of available positions.

	AB	R	HR	RBI	SB	BA	$
1995 Chicago NL	426	50	14	52	1	.246	8
1996 Philadelphia NL	500	61	20	80	1	.268	12
1996 Baltimore AL	117	17	5	19	0	.239	-

ZINTER, ALAN - C/1B - BB - Age 28
Zinter was once traded to the Tigers for Rico Brogna before signing with the Red Sox as a minor league free agent last winter. A 1988 member of Team USA, Zinter was originally drafted as a catcher by the Mets in the first round. He has since spent eight pro seasons searching for a position and for a way to cut his strikeout totals. He's still searching for both. Zinter offers power and nothing else.

ZOSKY, EDDIE - SS - BR - Age 29
Back in 1991 and '92, the Blue Jays gave Zosky a chance to be their starting shortstop, but he didn't hit so it was more Triple-A for him. He was with Florida in 1995, and last year he played for the Orioles Triple-A club where he still didn't hit well. He may make the majors again, but as a utility infielder.

ZUBER, JON - 1B/OF - BL - Age 27
Zuber is a line drive machine who makes contact and will take a walk, but was one of the least powerful first sackers to play regularly in the upper minors in 1996. He is a solid defensive player, but only has a chance to stick as a major league reserve. He should be entrenched at the Triple-A level for years to come.

	AB	R	HR	RBI	SB	BA	$
1996 Philadelphia NL	91	7	1	10	1	.253	0

ZUPCIC, BOB - OF - BR - Age 30
The one-time Red Sox' fourth outfielder was reduced to being a Triple-A backup in the Phils' chain in 1996. Never an offensive force, Zupcic's bat and legs have slowed, leaving his defensive ability and a knack for making contact as his only attractive capabilities. Zupcic has not been a regular at any level since 1991.

GOT A QUESTION?
CALL JOHN BENSON LIVE

Your Question - Your Roster - Your Situation

Let the top analyst in the business help you!!

1-900-773-7526

$2.49/minute

1 pm to 11 pm Eastern Time - 7 days a Week

ABBOTT, JIM - TL - Age 29
Abbott is not the pitcher he was a few years ago. His fastball velocity was in the low 80's last year, making him easily hittable, and he even spent time in Triple-A trying to get things together. Abbott has pitched over 1,500 innings in his eight major league seasons, and they have taken their toll on his arm.

	W	SV	ERA	IP	H	BB	SO	B/I	$
1995 Two Teams	11	0	3.70	197	209	64	86	1.39	12
1996 California AL	2	0	7.48	142	171	78	58	1.75	-

ABBOTT, KYLE - TL - Age 29
Abbott has pitched in 54 major league games for the Angels and Phillies, making 22 starts. But he hit bottom in 1992 with a 1-14 record with the Phils. He even spent some time in 1994 pitching in Japan, and last June, he was signed to a minor league contract by the Angels. Abbott had a decent year with the Angels Double-A team trying to prove himself and get back to the big time.

ABBOTT, PAUL - TR - Age 29
This Padres Triple-A reliever is a veteran of 12 minor league seasons, appeared in 33 major league games during that interval. The Twins and Indians used him as a starter, but he just didn't make it. Now he's a reliever, and he had a good season in Triple-A last year. He may come back to the majors somewhere as a middle reliever, but he's got Triple-A talent.

ACEVEDO, JUAN - TR - Age 26
In 1994 at Double-A New Haven, Acevedo looked like a superprospect, using his 93 MPH fastball and sharp forkball to fan 161 batters while walking only 38 and compiling a 2.37 ERA. Since then he has gone through a series of shocks including a rushed promotion to the majors in 1995 when spring training was too short for the returning veterans. Then pitching in Denver was a shock. Tendinitis and elbow stiffness have been problems, but Acevedo still has the velocity and pitches to make a career.

ACRE, MARK - TR - Age 28
Acre lost confidence in his forkball, and the A's have lost confidence in him. This "former future closer" is barely in the major leagues.

	W	SV	ERA	IP	H	BB	SO	B/I	$
1995 Oakland AL	1	0	5.71	52	52	28	47	1.54	-
1996 Oakland AL	1	2	6.12	25	38	9	18	1.88	-

ADAMS, TERRY - TR - Age 24
The Cubs think of Adams as their closer of the future. He may still need another year to learn the league. Adams' fastball tops out around 94 or 95 and he complements it with a hard slider. Look for Adams to begin the 1997 season as the Cubs' setup man, but he could finish the season as the closer.

	W	SV	ERA	IP	H	BB	SO	B/I	$
1995 Chicago NL	1	1	6.50	18	22	10	15	1.78	-
1996 Chicago NL	3	4	2.94	101	84	49	78	1.32	7

ADAMS, WILLIE - TR - Age 24
A former number one pick and Stanford grad, Adams arrived on the scene and pitched well over twelve starts. He has a good fastball in the high 80's a killer sinker and excellent control. Watch him blossom.

	W	SV	ERA	IP	H	BB	SO	B/I	$
1996 Oakland AL	3	0	4.01	76	76	23	68	1.30	3

ADAMSON, JOEL - TL - Age 25
Adamson is a lefty with average stuff and solid control who got a brief look-see with the Marlins in 1996. He has routinely given up more than a hit per inning throughout his seven year pro career. The only reason he remains in the hunt for a big league role is his status as a southpaw.

AGOSTO, JUAN - TL - Age 39
The fact that this war horse was still playing professional baseball last season at Triple-A Calgary tells you something about the general dearth of pitching in the sport and the limited talent in the Pirates' organization.

AGUILERA, RICK - TR - Age 35
The Twins re-signed Aguilera and then announced he would move into their rotation. Arm troubles delayed the start of his season until July and he was inconsistent thereafter. Aguilera is not likely to succeed as a starter.

	W	SV	ERA	IP	H	BB	SO	B/I	$
1995 Minnesota - Boston AL	3	32	2.60	55	46	13	52	1.08	37
1996 Minnesota AL	8	0	5.42	111	124	27	83	1.36	3

AHEARNE, PAT - TR - Age 27
Ahearne has bounced through three organizations in the last two years. He has marginal big-league stuff and is edging towards a career in the minors.

ALBERRO, JOSE - TR - Age 27
Alberro continued to make good progress in 1996. He has a live arm and good presence on the mound; like many young pitchers, though, he suffers from inconsistency when facing major league hitters. A reliever for most of his career, Alberro was used mostly as a starter, with good results. He'll contend for a big league roster spot in the spring. Alberro has also worked as a closer.

ALDRED, SCOTT - TL - Age 28
The Tigers and then the Twins both decided in '96 that Aldred, only a year removed from major arm surgery, was capable of a starting job. Aldred can succeed in a spot role out of the bullpen.

	W	SV	ERA	IP	H	BB	SO	B/I	$
1996 Minnesota AL	6	0	6.21	165	194	68	111	1.59	-

ALFONSECA, ANTONIO - TR - Age 24
Alfonseca is a righty with solid control who stepped backwards with a poor Triple-A season in 1996. His strikes caught too much of the plate, and his fastball was not lively enough to bail him out of the resulting jams.

ALKIRE, JEFF - TL - Age 27
The Cards' 1992 fifth round pick bounced to the independent Northern League in 1995, and got a short, unsuccessful opportunity as a middle reliever at Double-A Portland in the Marlins' chain last season. His repertoire has earned him nothing but success at the High-A level, and nothing but failure above. His mid-to-upper 80's fastball is enough at the lower levels, but he does not locate it effectively enough to overmatch better hitters.

ALMANZAR, CARLOS - TR - Age 23
He completed his transition from starting pitcher to reliever and spent much of his time as Knoxville's backup closer behind Brian Smith. Almanzar's control is better than any of the prospects at this level. He could use another year at Double-A, and with some work, could become closer material.

ALSTON, GARVIN - TR - Age 25
Alston may turn into a decent closer or setup man someday, but he's got to develop more control over his 90+ MPH heater. He led the Triple-A Sky Sox in saves, but saw only limited duty with the parent Rockies in 1996.

ALVAREZ, TAVO - TR - Age 25
In 1996 Alvarez finally started justifying all the hype he has received over the years. He got his weight under control and started taking the game more seriously. He is only 25 and is poised to blossom into a solid starter for the Expos.

	W	SV	ERA	IP	H	BB	SO	B/I	$
1995 Montreal NL	1	0	6.75	37	46	14	17	1.62	-
1996 Montreal NL	2	0	3.00	21	19	12	9	1.48	-

ALVAREZ, WILSON - TL - Age 27
Although his 1996 season looks good on paper, it could have been much better. Alvarez pitched extremely well in Venezuelan winter ball, had a good spring training, but then became tired after the '96 season was underway. He is capable of having some really big years in his career, and has not yet delivered the best of them. Alvarez features a 90+ fastball and a good curve. His changeup has improved, too.

	W	SV	ERA	IP	H	BB	SO	B/I	$
1995 Chicago AL	8	0	4.32	175	171	93	118	1.51	4
1996 Chicago AL	15	0	4.22	217	216	97	181	1.44	13

ANDERSON, BRIAN - TL - Age 24
Anderson is a finesse lefty with a diverse repertoire who needs pinpoint precision to be effective. He has four major league pitches but can't get the key strikeout with any of them. The Angels' first round pick has been used as a starter throughout his pro career, but the Indians might be best served if he narrowed his repertoire to his two best pitches and became an Assenmacher-like bullpen specialist used to retire lefties.

	W	SV	ERA	IP	H	BB	SO	B/I	$
1995 California AL	6	0	5.87	99	110	30	45	1.40	0
1996 Cleveland AL	3	0	4.91	51	58	14	21	1.41	-

ANDERSON, JIMMY - TL - Age 21
Anderson led the Class A Carolina League in ERA (1.93 in 11 starts at Lynchburg) before a mid-June promotion to the Double-A Southern League, where he still pitched well despite being the youngest starter in the league. He was 8-3, 3.34 in 17 games at Carolina. He has the ability and confidence to be a front-line starter in the major leagues. With the Pirates rebuilding, he could get a chance in the big leagues by the middle of this season.

ANDERSON, MIKE - TR - Age 30
Former Cub farmhand Anderson was hittable in a brief trial with Oklahoma City; he's a longshot to make it to the majors.

ANDUJAR, LUIS - TR - Age 24
Andujar has a 90 MPH fastball, with a good slider and straight change. The Blue Jays were planning to try their new acquisition in the starting rotation in 1997.

	W	SV	ERA	IP	H	BB	SO	B/I	$
1995 Chicago AL	2	0	3.26	30	26	14	9	1.33	1
1996 Chicago-Toronto AL	1	0	6.99	37	46	16	11	1.67	-

APANA, MATT - TR - Age 26
Apana's 5.33 ERA was the highest among Double-A Port City starters in 1996. He walked 69 batters in 96 innings; he has always struggled with his control throughout his four pro seasons. Apana won't go far pitching like he did last year.

APPIER, KEVIN - TR - Age 29
The hard-throwing ace of a good Royals' pitching staff, Appier had shoulder problems for a third straight season, although it only cost him two starts in 1996. Still, he's been one of the winningest pitcher of the 1990's, going 94-61 in seven straight winning campaigns. His exaggerated, overhand delivery puts a strain on his shoulder; the Royals' high-dollar, two-year contract with Appier was a big risk on their part.

	W	SV	ERA	IP	H	BB	SO	B/I	$
1995 Kansas City AL	15	0	3.89	201	163	80	185	1.21	19
1996 Kansas City AL	14	0	3.62	211	192	75	207	1.26	19

AQUINO, LUIS - TR - Age 31
Competent when healthy, but often hurt, Aquino hit the DL almost immediately after coming to the Giants in 1995. Aquino spent 1996 playing overseas in Japan.

ARNOLD, JAMIE - TR - Age 23
The Braves' first-round pick in 1992 has not developed as expected. In his first full-season above A-ball, Arnold went 7-7 with a 4.92 ERA in 23 starts. In four-plus seasons, he has yet to post a record over .500, his strikeout rate is getting weaker every year and he continues to allow homers at a frightening pace. Arnold is beginning to look like a first-round bust.

AROCHA, RENE - TR - Age 31
After doing a decent job as the Cardinals' closer in 1994, Arocha was bumped to a setup role in 1995 as Tom Henke became the bullpen ace. Though he has an assortment of about eight pitches which would seemingly make him a better starter, he likes closing. Arocha was out of baseball in 1996 after an injury-filled 1995 season.

ARRANDALE, MATT - TR - Age 26
As Triple-A Louisville's primary right-handed setup man, Arrandale did what he has always done - throw strikes and

put the ball in play. He led the club in appearances (63) and even managed three saves. Arrandale is a candidate for a St. Louis bullpen job, although he's not a hot prospect and would just be an 11th man on the staff.

ASHBY, ANDY - TR - Age 29
Shoulder tendinitis put Andy Ashby on the disabled list twice last year. He's a talented pitcher with good stuff and command, and with good health, he could go 15-6 with an ERA below 3.00.

	W	SV	ERA	IP	H	BB	SO	B/I	$
1995 San Diego NL	12	0	2.94	192	180	62	150	1.26	15
1996 San Diego NL	9	0	3.23	150	147	34	85	1.21	10

ASSENMACHER, PAUL - TL - Age 36
With the trade of Jim Poole and the struggles of Alan Embree, Assenmacher was the only viable lefthanded relief option for the Indians for much of 1996. He continued to be effective in short spurts, throwing his overhand curves for strikes anywhere in the count.

	W	SV	ERA	IP	H	BB	SO	B/I	$
1995 Cleveland AL	6	0	2.82	38	32	12	40	1.15	5
1996 Cleveland AL	4	1	3.09	46	46	14	44	1.30	3

ASTACIO, PEDRO - TR - Age 27
So much attention is focused on Nomo, Martinez, and Valdes that Pedro Astacio is easily forgotten in the Dodger rotation. He quietly posted a good season in 1996, with an excellent 3.44 ERA and a decent ratio in 32 starts. His 9-8 record was due entirely to a lack of run support (only 4.0 runs per game). Astacio is often overlooked. He is quite effective compared to most starters in the league, his performance is protected by Dodger Stadium, and he is nearly unknown compared to the hype surrounding the other Dodger starters.

	W	SV	ERA	IP	H	BB	SO	B/I	$
1995 Los Angeles NL	7	0	4.24	104	103	29	80	1.27	4
1996 Los Angeles NL	9	0	3.44	211	207	67	130	1.30	11

AUCOIN, DEREK - TR - Age 27
Aucoin looks like a good pitcher at 6'7". The Expos certainly hope he blossoms into a good reliever because he's French-Canadian, which would help attract a few more fans. However, nothing in Aucoin's numbers at the Double-A and Triple-A levels really suggest he'll be anything more than a middle or mop-man man.

AUSANIO, JOE - TR - Age 31
This aging reliever joined the Rockies Triple-A Colorado Springs team as a setup man in late 1996, and demonstrated improved control in limited duty. He's no prospect, but with the Rockies' pitching a perpetual question mark, a trip to the show isn't out of the question in 1997.

AUSTIN, JAMES - TR - Age 33
Austin is a former Brewers' bullpen denizen who hasn't been an effective pitcher for about three years. He relies primarily on a hard slider and was last seen at Triple-A Pawtucket in 1996.

AVERY, STEVE - TL - Age 26
Make it three straight disappointing years. A nagging injury and poor control led to Avery's downfall. He is still a young lefthander with the potential to be a quality pitcher, however, so Avery is far from being finished as a major league pitcher.

	W	SV	ERA	IP	H	BB	SO	B/I	$
1995 Atlanta NL	7	0	4.67	173	165	52	141	1.25	4
1996 Atlanta NL	7	0	4.47	131	146	40	86	1.42	1

AYALA, BOBBY - TR - Age 27
Ayala still overthrows and pays the price with poor control. His three saves were his fewest in the past three years. He is now a setup man, and any hopes of regaining his closer role is slight. Norm Charlton was quickly re-signed and will again close.

	W	SV	ERA	IP	H	BB	SO	B/I	$
1995 Seattle AL	6	19	4.44	71	73	30	77	1.45	21
1996 Seattle AL	6	3	5.88	67	65	25	61	1.34	3

AYBAR, MANUEL - TR - Age 22
Aybar, a Dominican, was drafted as a shortstop, but his hitting lacked so the Cardinals put him on the mound. He's just 22 years old and needs to learn to pitch, but he has time and the Cardinals like his arm. He posted a solid year at Double-A Arkansas and Triple-A Louisville. His combined 3.09 ERA was the sixth best in the Cards minor league system.

AYRAULT, BOB - TR - Age 30
Ayrault briefly looked good in a trial with the Phillies, but since 1990 he has generally struggled in repeated shots at the majors. Last seen playing out the string in independent ball in 1996.

BACKLUND, BRETT - TR - Age 27
In 1993, the righthander went to the Pirates' spring training camp as a phenom and the favorite to win the number five starter's job less than a year after being drafted from the University of Iowa. Backlund bombed that spring and has yet to recover. It now seems his chances of even pitching in the major leagues are slim.

BADOREK, MIKE - TR - Age 27
A 1995 elbow injury has damaged Badorek's future. He had just average stuff before the injury and now is below average in most aspects. He was a swingman at Triple-A Louisville in 1996, going 0-4 with a 5.29 ERA.

BAILEY, CORY - TR - Age 26
Bailey was an unsung hero last season in middle relief for the Cardinals. The Red Sox once thought he could become a closer when he was coming up through their farm system. That probably won't happen in St. Louis where T.J. Mathews is the heir apparent to closer Dennis Eckersley but Bailey has the stuff to be a good setup man for many years.

	W	SV	ERA	IP	H	BB	SO	B/I	$
1995 St. Louis NL	0	0	7.36	3	2	2	5	1.09	-
1996 St. Louis NL	5	0	3.00	57	57	30	38	1.53	1

BAILEY, ROGER - TR - Age 26
Bailey got the opportunity to be a starter for the Rockies in 1996 not so much because of his talent, but because of a pitching staff decimated by injuries. His pitch placement was better at times than prior years, but his strikeout ratio was still weak.

	W	SV	ERA	IP	H	BB	SO	B/I	$
1995 Colorado NL	7	0	4.98	81	88	39	33	1.57	-
1996 Colorado NL	2	1	6.24	83.2	94	52	45	1.75	-
	4	0	4.94	84	90	39	50	1.53	-

BAKKUM, SCOTT - TR - Age 27
After struggling as a starter for four seasons in the Red Sox' chain, he became an excellent finesse setup man in 1995 under the tutelage of pitching coach Al Nipper. Just as he became comfortable, he was traded to the Phils' chain, where his Triple-A pitching coach was called up to the majors and his manager was fired for cocaine use. Bakkum's strikes caught too much of the plate and were waxed, and he became a mopup reliever by season's end. His prospects for a major league future are bleak.

BALDWIN, JAMES - TR - Age 25
A hard thrower with a good career ahead of him, Baldwin stuck for a full year in the majors in 1996, after struggling and returning to the minors in '95. He is still improving.

	W	SV	ERA	IP	H	BB	SO	B/I	$
1995 Chicago AL	0	0	12.89	14	32	9	10	2.80	-
1996 Chicago AL	11	0	4.42	169	168	57	127	1.33	10

BANKS, WILLIE - TR - Age 28
This former Twins' number one pick bounced around the National League (Cubs, Dodgers and Marlins) in 1995. Banks has tantalized all of his employers with glimpses of his hard fastball and deceptive straight change.

BAPTIST, TRAVIS - TL - Age 25
A sore arm has slowed Baptist the last two years. In a pitcher's league (the International League) in 1996, Baptist had a poor 5.43 ERA while allowing 187 hits in just 141 innings. Baptist may need to switch to the bullpen to revive his prospect status.

BARBER, BRIAN - TR - Age 24
The Cardinals have had high hopes for the lefthander since making him a first-round pick in 1991. However, arm and leg injuries have continually hampered Barber to the point where it now looks like he won't turn into a front-line starter in the majors. He was 0-6 in 11 starts at Double-A Louisville last season and was hammered in his lone start with the Cardinals.

BARCELO, MARC - TR - Age 25
Barcelo was a first round pick by Minnesota's back in '93, and the righthander had a great year at Double-A in '94. Inconsistency and shoulder troubles at Triple-A the past two years have reduced expectations for him.

BARK, BRIAN - TL - Age 28
A crafty lefty who wasn't good enough to make it with the Braves, Bark got a second chance with the Red Sox and then a third chance with Mets, who weren't impressed and released him.

BARKLEY, BRIAN - TL - Age 21
A lefty control pitcher, Barkley was one of several highly-regarded prospects drafted by the Red Sox in 1994. He struggled early in his first year at Double-A Trenton, but came on strong by season's end. At age 21, Barkley has time on his side; look for a 1998 major league arrival.

BARNES, BRIAN - TL - Age 30
Barnes, a lefthander, made progress toward reaching the majors again in '96 while pitching for Detroit's Double-A and Triple-A teams. He struck out 144 batters in 163 innings and should be in someone's bullpen in '97.

BARRIOS, MANUEL - TR - Age 22
Barrios made a successful jump from low Class-A to Double-A in 1996. He had 23 saves in both 1995 and 1996 and in each year struck out more than one batter per inning. This performance rated an appearance in the Arizona Fall League after which he should be a candidate for the closer job at Triple-A in 1997.

BARTON, SHAWN - TL - Age 33
Can you spell "career minor league mop-up specialist?" Barton is beginning to look like the George Brunet of the minor leagues. He did pitch in the majors enough last year to get completely clobbered (19 hits over 8.1 innings).

BATCHELOR, RICHARD - TR - Age 29
Batchelor was once considered a closer prospect. However, he has now reached the stage of his career where he bounces back and forth between the majors and Triple-A. If he gets a break, he could stick as the 11th man on the Cardinals' staff.

BATISTA, MIGUEL - TR - Age 26
Somehow, despite retiring virtually no one at the Triple-A level over the past two seasons, Batista was given his second major league opportunity by the Marlins in 1996, with predictably mediocre results. Batista had always possessed an above average fastball, though he has lost velocity of late, and has never located it well. He might have a hard time finding a minor league job in 1997.

BAUTISTA, JOSE - TR - Age 32
Bautista really did improve his numbers a lot in 1996 from those of 1995. And, though he reduced the number of homers he gave up from 24 to 10, his innings pitched totals were reduced from 100 to 69.2. He was released by the Giants at the end of 1996.

	W	SV	ERA	IP	H	BB	SO	B/I	$
1995 San Francisco NL	3	0	6.44	100	120	26	45	1.46	-
1996 San Francisco NL	3	0	3.36	69	66	15	28	1.17	3

BAXTER, BOB - TL - Age 28
This Harvard-bred southpaw would no longer be in baseball if he was righthanded. He is a finesse hurler who has walked just over two batters per nine innings over his seven year pro career, but his pitches caught way too much of the plate in 1996, when he allowed 104 hits in 82 innings in his second Triple-A season in the Expos' chain. He is no better than a decent Double-A pitcher.

BEATTY, BLAINE - TL - Age 32
Beatty, once a New York Mets' pitching prospect, is still hanging around because he has developed a knuckleball. He has no hopes of getting back to the major leagues and keeps playing for the Pirates' Double-A Carolina farm club only because it is close to his home.

BEAUMONT, MATT - TL - Age 23
Midland in the Double-A Texas League is tough on pitchers, and Angels starter prospect Matt Beaumont took his lumps there, giving up 198 hits in 162 innings. But he also struck out 132. He needs to improve his breaking ball or learn how to change speeds.

BECK, ROD - TR - Age 28
Though he is still the "man" for the Giants, his velocity is fading which is a bad sign for a 28 year old. He got off to a hot streak, allowing nothing over his first nine appearances. From then on, he was often toast. He needs to learn both another pitch, and how to pitch now that he cannot blow it by hitters at will.

	W	SV	ERA	IP	H	BB	SO	B/I	$
1995 San Francisco NL	5	33	4.45	58	60	21	42	1.39	29
1996 San Francisco NL	0	35	3.34	62	56	10	48	1.06	30

BECKETT, ROBBIE - TL - Age 24
Beckett has an overpowering fastball, but poor control. He would remain at the Double or Triple-A level for further seasoning in most organizations, but with the dearth of lefties in the Rockies' system, spot duty with the parent club a possibility in 1997.

BEECH, MATT - TL - Age 25
The Phils' 1994 seventh round pick dominated at Double-A Reading, mixing a sinking fastball, curveball and changeup with great precision. He is particularly lethal against lefthanded hitters, but didn't see many of them in his major league trial, where he struggled after an excellent first start. He is also vulnerable to the gopher ball.

	W	SV	ERA	IP	H	BB	SO	B/I	$
1996 Philadelphia NL	1	0	6.97	41	49	11	33	1.46	-

BELCHER, TIM - TR - Age 35
Belcher was the Royals' most consistent hurler in 1996; he matched his career high in victories. Except for a six-game spell in June Belcher never went more than three starts without a victory. He is making a successful transition from power to finesse pitching and was rewarded with a two-year contract extension in September.

	W	SV	ERA	IP	H	BB	SO	B/I	$
1995 Seattle AL	10	0	4.52	179	188	88	96	1.55	4
1996 Kansas City AL	15	0	3.92	238	262	68	113	1.39	17

BELINDA, STAN - TR - Age 30
Belinda spent most of the 1996 season battling arm miseries, and struggled in his sporadic major league outings. He couldn't finish his delivery, leaving his fastball weak and high in the strike zone; the results speak for themselves. Belinda was expected to be ready for spring training in 1997 and challenge for a setup role once again.

	W	SV	ERA	IP	H	BB	SO	B/I	$
1995 Boston AL	8	10	3.10	69	51	28	57	1.13	19
1996 Boston AL	2	2	6.59	28	31	20	18	1.81	-

BELL, ERIC - TL - Age 33
Bell has spent parts of six seasons in the major leagues. However, in 1996 he was hit so hard at Triple-A Tucson (4-14, 5.65 ERA, 177 hits in 127 innings).

BELL, JASON - TR - Age 22
Bell, a Twins starting prospect, is on the fast track to the major leagues after leading the organization in strikeouts with 177 in his first full pro season. Minnesota's second round pick out of Oklahoma State U. in '95, Bell dominated the Class A Florida State League in '96 (6-3, 1.69) and spent the second half at Double-A (2-6, 4.40).

BELTRAN, RIGO - TL - Age 27
His numbers were excellent in '96. In 130.1 innings, Beltran struck out 132 batters and walked just 24. He started 16

games, working half the season out of the bullpen. At age 27, he can't be considered a real prospect but because of his numbers at Louisville, he should get a look in 1997.

BENES, ALAN - TR - Age 25
Benes was the best rookie starter in the National League last year, though he did tail off in the second half. With big brother Andy Benes, Todd Stottlemyre and Donovan Osborne around, the Cardinals have the luxury of slowly breaking this fine young pitcher into the majors.

	W	SV	ERA	IP	H	BB	SO	B/I	$
1995 St. Louis NL	1	0	8.44	16	24	4	20	1.75	-
1996 St. Louis NL	13	0	4.90	191	192	87	131	1.46	2

BENES, ANDY - TR - Age 29
Benes finally shed the underachiever tag last year in his first year with the Cardinals. He won 17 of his last 20 decisions to turn a 1-7 disaster into an 18-10 success. Benes now has an air of confidence that he never exhibited in San Diego or Seattle. Cardinals pitching coach Dave Duncan is the reason Benes has finally emerged into a premier starting pitcher.

	W	SV	ERA	IP	H	BB	SO	B/I	$
1995 San Diego NL	4	0	4.17	118	121	45	126	1.40	
1995 Seattle AL	7	0	5.86	63	72	33	45	1.67	4
1996 St. Louis NL	18	1	3.83	230	215	77	160	1.27	15

BENITEZ, ARMANDO - TR - Age 24
Benitez has an outstanding fastball occasionally hitting 100 MPH and a wicked slider. Immaturity has slowed his progress toward becoming the Orioles closer, and an elbow injury caused him to miss a large part of 1996. He has to overcome getting rattled when somebody hits a home run or gets a key hit off him, but he's getting better at it as he came around late in the season and in playoff pressure situations. The playoffs also showed that he was a little home run prone.

	W	SV	ERA	IP	H	BB	SO	B/I	$
1995 Baltimore AL	1	2	5.66	47	37	37	56	1.55	0
1996 Baltimore NL	1	4	3.77	14	7	6	20	0.92	3

BENNETT, ERIK - TR - Age 28
Bennett is a righthander who saw spot duty with the Twins in '96 after spending most of his career with California. He can be effective if healthy in a limited bullpen role.

BENNETT, JOEL - TR - Age 27
Orioles Farm Director Syd Thrift finds players in the most obscure places. The Orioles signed righthander Joel Bennett from the Newburgh (N.Y.) Nighthawks in the independent Northeast League where he had an outstanding record as a starter. Prior to that he had a few relief appearances in the Red Sox organization with Trenton in the Double-A Eastern League, but was released. The Orioles let him start with Bowie, also in the Eastern League, where he had some good outings.

BENNETT, SHAYNE - TR - Age 25
Bennett is a hard-throwing righthander acquired by the Expos from the Red Sox in the Wil Cordero deal following the 1995 season. He has a durable two-inning arm, has greatly improved his control, and might add another inch or two to his fastball as his 6'5", 200, body fills out. He has struck out 164 batters in 163 innings over the past two seasons. He could be the Expos' Triple-A closer in 1997, and could fit in as a middleman in the bigs shortly thereafter.

BENZ, JAKE - TL - Age 25
The Expos' 1994 13th round pick is a diminutive (5'9", 162) southpaw who, like many finesse hurlers, confidently worked the black of the plate in Class A ball, only to nibble at the Double-A level and struggle with his control. After posting 22 saves and a 1.17 ERA at High-A in 1995, Benz walked 27 hitters in only 38 innings in 1996 at Double-A. Since he's a lefty, he will get many more chances to prove he can succeed in a specialty role, but it is highly unlikely that he will ever make it to the majors.

BERE, JASON - TR - Age 25
With a big fastball and big problems, Bere struggled again in 1996, but this time he had a good reason: elbow tendinitis.

Going on the 60-day DL April 22nd, he missed almost the entire season. Bere did appear at Triple-A Nashville for three brilliant starts as rehab work in late August, but he hurt his arm again and had surgery.

	W	SV	ERA	IP	H	BB	SO	B/I	$
1995 Chicago AL	8	0	7.19	137	151	106	110	1.88	-
1996 Chicago AL	0	0	10.26	16	26	18	19	2.72	-

BERGMAN, SEAN - TR - Age 26
Bergman's 4.37 ERA with the Padres in a rabbit-ball year looks magnificent when compared with his 5.12 ERA in his rookie 1995 year with the Tigers. He improved and should be even better in 1997. He's a sinker-baller who gets a lot of ground balls, and it helps that he has good glove men like Ken Caminiti and Wally Joyner behind him. Bergman should be a number four or five starter in 1997.

	W	SV	ERA	IP	H	BB	SO	B/I	$
1995 Detroit AL	7	0	5.12	135	169	67	86	1.75	-
1996 San Diego NL	6	0	4.37	113	119	33	85	1.34	2

BERTOTTI, MIKE - TL - Age 27
Bertotti was forced along from Double-A Birmingham to Triple-A Nashville and up to the big leagues despite relatively poor performances at each level; he got worse with each promotion, too. The White Sox once had high hopes for this strikeout pitcher.

	W	SV	ERA	IP	H	BB	SO	B/I	$
1995 Chicago AL	1	0	12.56	14	23	11	15	2.37	-
1996 Chicago AL	2	0	5.14	28	28	20	19	1.71	-

BERUMEN, ANDRES - TR - Age 25
Padres middle reliever Andres Berumen had a rough time in Triple-A last year, essentially his second full year in the league. His ERA in Double-A and Triple-A is usually around 6.00, and he walks as many as he strikes out. But he has a good arm, and was promoted to the Padres. Berumen will likely spend much of 1997 in Triple-A.

BETTI, RICH - TL - Age 23
New England native Betti earned his way onto the Red Sox' 40-man roster with a fine 1995 season split between three Class A venues. He continued his improbable advance with a fine season in relief for Class A Springfield and Double-A Trenton. Betti was a middle-round, 1993 draft pick by Atlanta, but was released after just one pro season. He has added some size and improved his breaking ball.

BEVIL, BRIAN - TR - Age 25
Bevil anchored the Double-A Wrangler's rotation. After he was promoted to Omaha, the Wranglers fell apart. A hard-thrower with good control, Bevil's power pitching returned in 1996 after an off-season in 1995; he fanned more than a batter per inning with a strikeout-to-walk ratio better than 3-to-1. The crowded rotation in Kansas City means he'll probably start 1997 at Triple-A Omaha, but major league teams always need more pitching, so Bevil will be in KC sometime during 1997.

BIELECKI, MIKE - TR - Age 37
Basically, all this guy does is succeed. Bielecki has to rely on good control because he can't throw the ball past anyone. He's now 37 years old, so it would be easy to write him off. But, he's hit bad times before and come back and he's coming off of one of his best seasons ever. Bielecki should be back with the Braves in 1997, although it would be a surprise if he enjoys the same level of success.

	W	SV	ERA	IP	H	BB	SO	B/I	$
1995 California AL	4	0	5.97	75	80	31	45	1.48	-
1996 Atlanta NL	4	2	2.63	75	63	33	71	1.28	6

BLAIR, WILLIE - TR - Age 31
The well-travelled Willie Blair had a good season as a middle reliever for the Padres. He held opposing hitters to a .240 batting average.

	W	SV	ERA	IP	H	BB	SO	B/I	$
1995 San Diego NL	7	0	4.34	114	112	45	83	1.38	2
1996 San Diego NL	2	1	4.60	88	80	29	67	1.24	1

BLAIS, MIKE - TR - Age 25
Double-A Trenton's predominant middle-innings righthander, Blais is nothing special, despite his 10-3, 3.94 showing in 1996. He doesn't have closer-type stuff and has too much competition to succeed in a middle-relief role in the majors.

BLAZIER, RON - TR - Age 25
It took Blazier until his sixth pro season to finally make it to Double-A in 1995. After starting for five seasons, Blazier comfortably settled into his role as Eastern League champion Reading's setup man. He averaged two innings per outing, striking out a batter per inning with a strikeout/walk ratio better than three to one. His high 80's fastball retains its velocity much better when it only travels once around the batting order.

	W	SV	ERA	IP	H	BB	SO	B/I	$
1996 Philadelphia NL	3	0	5.87	38	49	10	25	1.55	-

BLOMDAHL, BEN - TR - Age 26
The Tigers hoped to resurrect Blomdahl's career by converting him to a long relief role in 1995. It hasn't worked; Blomdahl had his worst season as a pro last year, going 2-6 with a 6.22 ERA. Moreover, his strikeout rate continues to deteriorate, raising questions about his ability to pitch on short rest.

BLUMA, JAIME - TR - Age 24
Bluma has followed his script after being drafted third in 1994. He has 70 professional saves and has moved steadily up the Royals' chain to lead Triple-A Omaha with 25 saves in 1996. Given a September callup to gain experience, he was suddenly thrust into the closer role when Jeff Montgomery had season-ending shoulder surgery. He was perfect, saving five games in five tries. Bluma is ready to pitch in the majors and will get the chance as Montgomery's setup man in 1997.

	W	SV	ERA	IP	H	BB	SO	B/I	$
1996 Kansas City AL	0	5	3.60	20	18	4	14	1.10	3

BOCHTLER, DOUG - TR - Age 26
Bochtler had an outstanding year setting up ace closer Trevor Hoffman. He held lefthanded batters to a .189 average and righthanded hitters to .200, and he's one reason why the Padres have one of the best bullpens in baseball. He throws a fastball, slider and changeup.

	W	SV	ERA	IP	H	BB	SO	B/I	$
1995 San Diego NL	4	1	3.57	45	38	19	45	1.26	3
1996 San Diego NL	2	3	3.02	65	45	39	68	1.29	4

BOCK, JEFF - TR - Age 25
Late-season arm trouble ended Bock's season after a 6-5, 5.35 showing for Double-A Greenville. It was his first season above A-ball and not especially impressive. He doesn't throw hard and lacks the good control needed for a finesse pitcher to succeed.

BOEHRINGER, BRIAN - TR - Age 27
Boehringer was one of the better starters at Triple-A Columbus before the Yankees brought him up to help with their bullpen. Boehringer has a decent fastball/slider repertoire that worked well in relief stints, after he got over some early bumps upon arriving in the majors.

	W	SV	ERA	IP	H	BB	SO	B/I	$
1996 New York AL	2	0	5.44	46	46	21	37	1.45	-

BOEVER, JOE - TR - Age 36
Boever had a strange 1996, being released by Detroit, the worst team in baseball, on the last day of spring training then going 12-1 at Triple-A Calgary and finishing the season by saving games for Pittsburgh, one of the worst teams in the National League. Boever is still a solid innings-eating reliever who will wind up adding some veteran presence to a young Pirates bullpen this season.

	W	SV	ERA	IP	H	BB	SO	BP	$
1995 Detroit AL	5	3	6.39	98	128	44	71	1.74	-
1996 Pittsburgh NL	0	2	5.40	15	17	6	6	1.53	-

BOGLE, SHAWN - TR - Age 23
Bogle pitched in just 4 games in 1996 due to injury. The 23-year-old righthander has pitched out of the bullpen the past two and a half seasons. The Indiana State product must regain health and should spend another season at Double-A.

BOGOTT, KURTISS - TL - Age 24
Only his mediocre control is holding him back from landing at least a promotion to Triple-A. He struck out fifty-six batters in fifty-four innings at Double-A but recorded twelve wild pitches, something a major league roster won't tolerate from a situational lefty.

BOHANON, BRIAN - TL - Age 28
After starting the year in the Blue Jays' bullpen, Bohanon was sent to Triple-A Syracuse at the end of May and quietly posted a decent minor league season.

	W	SV	ERA	IP	H	BB	SO	B/I	$
1995 Detroit AL	1	1	5.54	105	121	41	63	1.54	-
1996 Toronto AL	0	1	7.77	22	27	19	17	2.09	-

BOLTON, RODNEY - TR - Age 28
Bolton is one of those great minor league pitchers who simply can't make the jump to the bigs. Compare his minor league career record of 67-30 and 2.41 ERA to his big league record of 2-8, 7.69 ERA. Bolton's finesse style just doesn't fool major league hitters so he went to Japan in 1996.

BOLTON, TOM - TL - Age 34
The veteran lefthander had a good 1996 (12-5, 4.02) as a swingman for Triple-A Calgary. He didn't get a callup by the Pirates last season. Given the fact Bolton is left handed and still breathing, there's always a chance he could still resurface somewhere in the big leagues.

BONES, RICKY - TR - Age 27
Bones is a durable worker with a mediocre fastball and a curve. When he succeeds, he depends on his defense catching the ball, which is almost always put in play. Bones' role depends on the strength of the team that has him. With the Brewers he was among the top starters in the rotation; with the Yankees he was relegated to the bullpen.

	W	SV	ERA	IP	H	BB	SO	B/I	$
1995 Milwaukee AL	10	0	4.63	200	218	83	77	1.51	4
1996 Milw-New York AL	7	0	6.22	152	184	68	63	1.66	-

BONANNO, ROB - TR - Age 26
Bonanno pitched for the Angels Single-A and Double-A clubs last year, mostly as a reliever, also starting eight games. He found Double-A ball much tougher, although the Texas League can be tough on pitchers.

BORBON, PEDRO - TL - Age 29
Adding a little extra hop to his fastball made Borbon the Braves' best lefty reliever. It was the best year of his career and he should be able to succeed in a lefthanded setup role by working almost exclusively with his fastball. Watch for Borbon to have an important bullpen role for Atlanta in 1997.

	W	SV	ERA	IP	H	BB	SO	B/I	$
1995 Atlanta NL	2	2	3.09	32	29	17	33	1.44	2
1996 Atlanta NL	3	1	2.75	36	26	7	31	0.92	3

BORLAND, TOBY - TR - Age 27
Borland is a durable sidearming righty who ranked third in the National League in relief innings pitched in 1996. Borland is quite tough on righties, whom he held to a .210 average in 1996 with his sinker/slider combination. However, he is prone to mental lapses on the mound - for example, forgetting to cover first base - and has thrown 22 wild pitches over the past two seasons.

	W	SV	ERA	IP	H	BB	SO	B/I	$
1995 Philadelphia NL	1	6	3.77	74	81	37	59	1.59	3
1996 Philadelphia NL	7	0	4.07	90	83	43	76	1.40	2

BOROWSKI, JOE - TR - Age 25
Obtained in the off-season Kent Mercker deal, Borowski spent 1996 shuttling between Richmond and Atlanta. He doesn't have overpowering stuff; he just gets people out. A sinker/slider pitcher, Borowski is not a closer candidate, but could do the job as a middle reliever for Atlanta.

	W	SV	ERA	IP	H	BB	SO	B/I	$
1995 Baltimore AL	0	0	1.23	7	5	4	3	1.23	0
1996 Atlanta NL	2	0	4.85	26	33	13	15	1.77	-

BOSIO, CHRIS - TR - Age 33
Bosio was DL'd for much of 1996 with a bad knee. He made only nine starts and by the end of the year was working out of the bullpen. He's been in decline for three straight years.

	W	SV	ERA	IP	H	BB	SO	B/I	$
1995 Seattle AL	10	0	4.92	170	211	69	85	1.65	0
1996 Seattle AL	4	0	5.93	60	72	24	39	1.59	-

BOSKIE, SHAWN - TR - Age 30
After starting last season in the Angels bullpen, Boskie was pressed into service as a starter, and he turned out to be a good workhorse, starting 26 games. And in mid-July, Boskie was carrying the Angels pitching load. His best pitch is a sinking fastball, and he walks few, but he is homer prone, giving up 40 dingers last year, tying for first in the American League. His good 1996 season caught peoples' attention and should help him lock up a starter's slot in 1997.

	W	SV	ERA	IP	H	BB	SO	B/I	$
1995 California AL	7	0	5.64	111	127	25	51	1.36	2
1996 California AL	12	0	5.32	189	226	67	133	1.55	3

BOTTALICO, RICKY - TR - Age 27
Bottalico established himself as one of baseball's premier closers in his first full major league season in that role. He combines a mid-90's fastball with an excellent overhand curve, both of which he throws consistently for strikes. He also possesses the gunslinger mentality so vital in a closer.

	W	SV	ERA	IP	H	BB	SO	B/I	$
1995 Philadelphia NL	5	1	2.46	87	50	42	87	1.05	11
1996 Philadelphia NL	4	34	3.19	67	47	23	74	1.04	31

BOTTENFIELD, KENT - TR - Age 28
After posting 18 saves with a 2.19 ERA with Iowa, Bottenfield got the call to Chicago. Bottenfield could find himself as a long man with the Cubs in '97, depending on the development of some of the younger pitchers in the Cubs chain.

	W	SV	ERA	IP	H	BB	SO	B/I	$
1996 Chicago NL	3	1	2.63	61	59	19	33	1.27	3

BOUCHER, DENIS - TL - Age 29
The Expos had better give up on their hopes that the French Canadian Boucher will ever enter their starting rotation. Once a crafty lefty who would frustrate high minor league hitters with his offspeed repertoire, Boucher's stuff has dissipated gradually over the last five seasons, and he is now virtually incapable of getting a strikeout, and has also lost his confidence to challenge hitters. His 9.30 Triple-A ERA and 130 baserunners allowed in 61 innings in 1996 was likely the final straw.

BOURGEOIS, STEVE - TR - Age 24
Showing that he was clearly not ready to face major league hitters during his short stint with the Giants, Bourgeois turned in good numbers with Phoenix. He isn't any kind of a strikeout pitcher, but he is generally around the plate.

	W	SV	ERA	IP	H	BB	SO	B/I	$
1996 San Francisco NL	1	0	6.30	40	60	21	17	2.02	-

BOVEE, MIKE - TR - Age 23
Curveball specialist Bovee was the workhorse of the Wichita staff, leading the club in starts, innings, wins and strikeouts. However, he was also among Texas League leaders in hits allowed. Bovee's fastball isn't strong enough for him to succeed in the majors as a starter; his long-range future is in long relief.

BOWEN, RYAN - TR - Age 29
The charter member of the expansion Marlins got a trial at Triple-A New Orleans in the Brewers' chain. It was the same old story - good stuff, especially his heater, but poor command and a penchant for every type of injury imaginable.

BOWERS, SHANE - TR - Age 25
A control specialist, Bowers probably doesn't have the depth of repertoire to make it as a starting pitcher. But his good control should help him eventually win a major league bullpen job.

BOYD, DENNIS - TR - Age 37
Last year, Oil Can pitched and doubled as a pitching coach for the Bangor Blue Ox in the independent Northeast League. He's also been seen in the Northern League and Mexican League in recent years.

BOZE, MARSHALL - TR - Age 25
Boze lacks velocity, and in 1996 at Triple-A New Orleans on the Brewers farm, he nibbled too much, walking 29 batters in 39 innings.

	W	SV	ERA	IP	H	BB	SO	B/I	$
1996 Milwaukee AL	0	1	7.79	32	47	25	19	2.24	-

BRANDENBURG, MARK - TR - Age 26
Boston's return on their trade of Mike Stanton to Texas, Brandenburg is a side-armer who got fine results with a sinker/slider combination, especially after he joined the Red Sox. The righthander probably doesn't throw hard enough to be a closer or setup man, but could become a valuable two-inning reliever as long as his control stays as sharp as it was in the second half of 1996.

	W	SV	ERA	IP	H	BB	SO	B/I	$
1995 Texas AL	0	0	5.93	27	36	7	21	1.57	-
1996 Boston AL	5	0	3.43	76	76	33	66	1.43	4

BRANTLEY, JEFF - TR - Age 33
The former Giant has developed into one of the most reliable closers in the National League, turning in his third straight good year for the Reds. Brantley set a team record with 44 saves in 49 opportunities, and has saved 72 games (in only 81 opportunities) in the last two years. Brantley relies on an excellent splitter and gives up very few hits and has decent control. He signed a three year contract at the end of 1995 (at considerably under his market value) to stay in Cincinnati, guaranteeing he will be the Reds closer for the foreseeable future.

	W	SV	ERA	IP	H	BB	SO	B/I	$
1995 Cincinnati NL	3	28	2.82	70	53	20	62	1.04	31
1996 Cincinnati NL	1	44	2.41	71	54	28	76	1.15	39

BREWER, BILLY - TL - Age 28
A top lefty setup man with the Royals in 1994 (producing a 2.56 ERA) Brewer ran into trouble in 1995 when his pitches got up in the strike zone too often. In 1995-1996 he didn't have the touch and feel that made him successful; if he ever finds those qualities again, he can still be an effective reliever.

BREWER, BRIAN - TL - Age 25
Oriole farm hand Brian Brewer started 24 games for their Single-A and Double-A clubs last year, struggling with so-so years in both levels. Nevertheless, he's making progress.

BREWINGTON, JAMIE - TR - Age 25
Whatever he seemed to be doing right in 1995 unraveled completely in 1996 for Brewington. He was moved from the rotation in Phoenix to the bull pen, but was pretty much ineffective in all roles. He is still young but he has to do better.

BRISCOE, JOHN - TR - Age 29
A hard thrower, Briscoe suffers from classic "wildness." When he is on, he is devastating, but he isn't on very often. Briscoe is one of those pitchers who could just put it all together, step into a closer role and amaze. Since the job is open with Oakland, he is worth the watch just for that. Just the same, he is a longshot.

	W	SV	ERA	IP	H	BB	SO	B/I	$
1995 Oakland AL	0	0	8.35	18	25	21	19	2.51	-
1996 Oakland AL	0	1	3.76	26	18	24	14	1.61	-

BRITO, MARIO - TR - Age 30
Brito spent 1995 with Brother of the Taiwanese League, opened the season as the Marlins' Triple-A closer with four dominating saves, then was allowed out of his contract to sign with the Yomiuri Giants of the Japanese League.

BROCAIL, DOUG - TR - Age 29
Brocail has been a spot starter and long reliever in his two years with Houston but hasn't achieved consistent success in either role. He is not a hard thrower despite his impressive size. He has had shoulder problems and is not likely to have a major role in 1997.

	W	SV	ERA	IP	H	BB	SO	B/I	$
1995 Houston NL	6	1	4.19	77	87	22	39	1.41	2
1996 Houston NL	1	0	4.58	53	58	23	34	1.53	-

BROCK, CHRIS - TR - Age 27
Removed from the Braves' 40-man roster going into 1996, Brock earned an invitation to Spring Training with a strong winter performance in Puerto Rico. In his second stint at Triple-A Richmond, he improved to 10-11 with a 4.67 ERA after a poor 1995 showing. Brock is not an overpowering pitcher, getting by on a good curveball; he is Triple-A injury insurance for the Braves, although he might get a longer look with a club that isn't so well stocked with pitching.

BROHAWN, TROY - TL - Age 24
Brohawn had some trouble after his promotion to Double-A in 1996. He showed some durability, but the level of competition moved up a notch for him and he hasn't learned to adjust yet. He is young, so the jury will be out for another year or so.

BROSNAN, JASON - TL - Age 29
Brosnan spent his eight pro seasons moving around from one team to another, often getting promoted or demoted during the season. Formerly with the Dodgers, Brosnan moved to the Mariners in 1996 and, to no one's surprise, split the year between Double-A and Triple-A. Being lefthanded will keep Brosnan in pro baseball, but his marginal stuff will keep him in the minors.

BROW, SCOTT - TR - Age 28
Called up to the Blue Jays late in 1996, in one game against the Orioles he walked in two runs and then served up a grand slam fastball to Eddie Murray. Although he has a reputation for good control and an ability to get the ball in play, it hasn't translated to favorable results. To his credit, he has recovered nicely from arthroscopic surgery a year and a half ago.

	W	SV	ERA	IP	H	BB	SO	B/I	$
1996 Toronto AL	1	0	5.59	38	45	25	23	1.83	-

BROWN, CHAD - TL - Age 24
Brown keeps the ball down in the strike zone better than any prospect in the Jays organization, protecting him from the long ball. He struck out nearly a batter an inning with Double-A Knoxville and if he earns another ticket to Syracuse this year, he needs to show better control than his brief collapse of 1995 (17 unintentional walks in 22 innings with the Chiefs).

BROWN, DICKIE - TR - Age 26
Brown didn't last long at Double-A in his seventh year in the Indians' chain. Brown is an undersized righty (5'9", 170 pounds) who has generally been a fourth or fifth starter or middle reliever throughout his minor league career.

BROWN, J. KEVIN - TR - Age 32
Brown's first National League season was truly superb; he posted a sub-2.00 ERA in a season featuring record-setting offense. Brown moved his fastball/slider combination from corner to corner with amazing efficiency, allowing well under a baserunner per inning. It must be noted that his campaign was well out of line with his career norms, and that he is at about the age where finesse pitchers begin to lose their edge.

	W	SV	ERA	IP	H	BB	SO	B/I	$
1995 Baltimore AL	10	0	3.60	172	155	48	117	1.18	16
1996 Florida NL	17	0	1.89	233	187	33	159	0.94	33

BROWN, WILLARD - TR - Age 24
Brown spent last year in Double-A, his second year in the league. He was also hit pretty hard in 1995, and only got into nine games last season. He had an excellent record in Single-A, but found it much tougher in Double-A ball.

BROWNE, BYRON - TR - Age 26
A tall, hard-thrower, Browne looked better a year ago when he was 10-4 with a 3.43 ERA at Double-A El Paso on the Brewers' farm. At the Triple-A level in 1996, batters wouldn't swing at Browne's pitches out of the strike zone. He walked 73 in 107 inning and was 3-9 with a 6.20 ERA.

BROWNSON, MARK - TR - Age 21
Brownson has two qualities the Rockies desperately need: he's a strikeout pitcher with excellent control. After starting 1996 in the bullpen for Double-A New Haven, Brownson ended up in the starting rotation and led the team in innings pitched and strikeouts. More seasoning at the Double or Triple-A level is likely for 1997.

BRUNER, CLAY - TR - Age 20
The righthanded Bruner was the Tigers' fourth round pick in the '95 draft and he had a good '96 season at low Class A (14-5, 2.59).

BRUNSON, WILLIAM - TL - Age 27
Brunson has made steady progress in the Dodgers' farm system since they acquired him from the Reds in trade. He's not a highly regarded prospect. His repertoire is relatively weak, but he could make the majors as a long-relief specialist.

BRUSKE, JIM - TR - Age 32
A late blooming relief prospect, Bruske is a converted outfielder who received brief trials with the Dodgers in 1995 and 1996. He could pitch in the majors as a middle reliever, but the Dodgers have no shortage of younger candidates for those roles.

BUCKLEY, TRAVIS - TR - Age 26
Buckley has taken major steps backward as a prospect since joining the Reds' chain in mid-1994. He throws strikes, but relies on a mediocre fastball/slider combination which yielded only 58 strikeouts in 122 innings at Triple-A Indianapolis in 1996.

BULLARD, JASON - TR - Age 28
After spending the better part of two seasons with St. Paul in the independent Northern League, Bullard came out of nowhere to be an effective setup reliever for Double-A Canton-Akron in the Eastern League. He only got around the league (and the batting order) once, however.

BULLINGER, JIM - TR - Age 31
Bullinger, a former minor league shortstop, is one of the best defensive pitchers in the league. That's a good thing because he has given up a ton of hits recently. Bullinger features a good curve, a sinking fastball and will occasionally throw a cutter to lefthanded batters. After putting up the highest ERA of his professional career in '96, Bullinger may be on the bubble to stay with the Cubs. At age 31, his durability is also a question.

	W	SV	ERA	IP	H	BB	SO	B/I	$
1995 Chicago NL	12	0	4.14	150	152	65	93	1.45	4
1996 Chicago NL	6	1	6.54	129	144	68	90	1.64	-

BULLINGER, KIRK - TR - Age 27
The brother of Cubs' pitcher Jim, Bullinger is a crafty righthanded reliever who has enjoyed success throughout his minor league career despite a lack of raw stuff. He has posted a 1.82 ERA in four pro seasons, and earned the Expos' Double-A closer role in 1996 ahead of the more talented Shayne Bennett.

BUNCH, MELVIN - TR - Age 25
It's hard to see why Bunch is still considered one of the Royals' best and brightest. In two years above A-ball, Bunch is 10-19 with a 5.61 ERA. His strikeout rate isn't particularly impressive and he doesn't have great velocity. Bunch has displayed good control, but he looks like a marginal major leaguer at best.

BURBA, DAVE - TR - Age 30
In his first full season as a starter, Burba struggled early in the season with his control, and by the time he rounded into form, the Reds quit scoring runs for him. He was 3-9 despite a 4.05 ERA at the break, and a strong second half (8-4, 3.57) suggests that Burba is a decent gamble to improve in 1997. Burba will not be a rotation workhouse, but he is a decent number three starter who will usually give you six good innings.

	W	SV	ERA	IP	H	BB	SO	B/I	$
1995 Two Teams	10	0	3.97	106	90	51	96	1.32	6
1996 Cincinnati NL	11	0	3.83	195	179	97	148	1.42	7

BURGER, ROB - TR - Age 21
The Phils' 1994 tenth round draftee pitched in the shadows of more heralded hurlers Randy Knoll and David Coggin at Low-A Piedmont. He doesn't have Coggin's raw stuff or Knoll's precision or the pitcher's body of both of them, but he throws a high-80's fastball with great movement and above average control.

BURKE, JOHN - TR - Age 27
Burke's 1996 season began dismally as a starter at Triple-A Colorado Springs, where his acute control problems from two years ago re-emerged. He was finally sent down to Class A Salem and banished to the bullpen, where - surprise - Burke's confidence and control returned. This first-ever Rockies draft pick earned his first appearance with the parent club late in the season, and has a good shot of starting 1997 on the big league roster.

BURKETT, JOHN - TR - Age 32
Burkett is an inning-eating control specialist who can be successful nibbling at the corners of the strike zone and changing speeds. He's a less extreme form of Bob Tewksbury: you can hit him, but he won't walk many. Burkett isn't a staff ace, but he can be a reliable second or third starter, particularly for a team who will make the defensive plays behind him.

	W	SV	ERA	IP	H	BB	SO	B/I	$
1995 Florida NL	14	0	4.30	188	208	57	126	1.41	5
1996 Florida NL	6	0	4.32	154	154	42	108	1.27	4
1996 Texas AL	5	0	4.06	68	75	16	47	1.33	3

BURLINGAME, BEN - TR - Age 27
Burlingame is a tall righthander who fit in with many of the Iowa Cubs' starters in '96. He's nothing special, but like most of the I-Cubs staff, he had a few performances that make it hard to give up on him. Burlingame spent most of the season as a reliever, but started 11 games, most of them late in the season for Iowa.

BURROWS, TERRY - TL - Age 28
A hot prospect when he was with the Rangers organization (he had a composite 2.14 ERA at three minor league levels in 1992) Burrows ran into trouble at the Triple-A level and has generally struggled in the majors. He keeps getting chances, mainly because he's lefthanded.

BUSBY, MIKE - TR - Age 24
Busby was the Cardinals' minor league pitcher of the year in 1995 and began last season in the major league rotation. However, big-league hitters mauled him and he went 2-5 in 14 starts at Triple-A Louisville before undergoing arm surgery. Busby, who relies on finesse and location, was not a great prospect to begin with and the arm problems only cloud his future.

BUSTILLOS, ALBERT - TR - Age 29
This former replacement player and Dodger prospect led Triple-A Colorado Springs in innings pitched and strikeouts, but Bustillos' stuff is neither overpowering nor crafty enough to enable him to be consistently effective on the major league level.

BUTCHER, MIKE - TR - Age 30
Once considered a major league closer candidate with the Angels, Butcher has deteriorated into a mediocre Triple-A middle reliever with below average control and velocity. If he were lefthanded, he might get another major league shot, but he is quite likely finished.

BUTLER, ADAM - TL - Age 23
Butler blazed his way from Macon, through High-A Durham, to Double-A Greenville in 1996, saving 30 games in 59 appearances. It was his first full season as a pro and was impressive; he led Greenville with 17 saves and was second best for both Macon and Durham. Butler works primarily with a fastball set up by a curve and changeup. Overlooked twice in June drafts, Butler was signed as an undrafted free agent in 1995 and now has the attention of Braves' brass.

BYRD, MATT - TR - Age 25
In his first year above A-ball, Byrd had a poor season, going 4-9 with a 6.97 ERA as a spot starter and middle reliever for Double-A Greenville. Now 25 years old and lacking overpowering stuff, Byrd's chances are slim.

BYRD, PAUL - TR - Age 26
After a successful 1995 season rising through the Mets bullpen to do critical setup work, Byrd started 1996 on the DL with a herniated disc. He finally joined the Mets on June 9th, but his control wasn't as sharp as it had been before the injury. When he's right, Byrd's curve, sinker, slurve and straight change can tantalize hitters, but he needs to hit precise spots.

	W	SV	ERA	IP	H	BB	SO	B/I	$
1995 New York NL	2	0	2.05	22	18	7	26	1.14	2
1996 New York NL	1	0	4.24	46.2	48	21	31	1.49	-

BYRDAK, TIM - TL - Age 23
This lefty curveballer struggled at Double-A Wichita before being sidelined for the season with an elbow problem. 1996 represented a big step back for Byrdak after a phenomenal 11-5, 2.16 season at Class A Wilmington in 1995. Assuming he's healthy in the spring, Byrdak should get another shot at Wichita in 1997.

BYRNE, EARL - TL - Age 24
Byrne, a lefthander, split time between A-ball and Double-A while working out of the bullpen and spot starting. Byrne is a wiry Australian whom the Cubs signed as a 21-year old in 1994. He's not a strikeout pitcher and he struggled with his control at times in 1996. But he's lefthanded and everybody loves the southpaws.

CABRERA, JOSE - TR - Age 25
Cabrera is the perfect example of the effective Class A pitcher with average velocity and good control who is then victimized by the superior Double-A hitters because of his inability to get the ball past them. Cabrera has been unable to maintain a spot in the Indian's Double-A rotation for two seasons.

CADARET, GREG - TL - Age 35
Veteran lefty reliever Cadaret has bounced around in seven organizations. Since there are always places for a lefty reliever, Cadaret may get another job in the majors, probably as a lefty setup man and situational reliever.

CAFARO, ROCCO - TR - Age 24
Cafaro was a starter and reliever for the Orioles Double-A club last year. He had a rough year, giving up 130 hits in 103 innings, but he's young with time to improve and move up.

CAIN, TIM - TR - Age 27
An aging middleman, Cain left Triple-A Pawtucket in midseason and retired.

CAMPBELL, MIKE - TR - Age 33
The experienced Campbell simply outfoxed Triple-A hitters at the start of the season in Iowa. The 32-year-old righthander went 8-2 before his call up. Campbell underwent elbow surgery shortly after his call up and had his innings limited. Campbell doesn't throw hard, but he worked both sides of the plate well enough to post an 11-3 combined record in 1996.

	W	SV	ERA	IP	H	BB	SO	B/I	$
1996 Chicago NL	3	0	4.46	36	29	10	19	1.08	0

CANDIOTTI, TOM - TR - Age 39
After four years of non-support from the Dodgers, Tom Candiotti finally got some runs to work with (5.1 per game) in 1996.

Unfortunately, he posted his worst year in the majors since 1987, and was touched up for a 5.58 ERA at Dodger Stadium. Given his age, Candiotti may be considered expendable by the Dodgers to create room in the rotation for Chan Ho Park.

	W	SV	ERA	IP	H	BB	SO	B/I	$
1995 Los Angeles NL	7	0	3.50	190	187	58	141	1.29	9
1996 Los Angeles NL	9	0	4.49	152	172	43	79	1.41	2

CARIDAD, RON - TR - Age 25
The Twins' second-round draft pick in 1990, Caridad hasn't developed as expected. He lost all of 1994 to an injury and has been used in light relief work since. He can still get a strikeout, but Caridad's good control needs to return for him to have a real shot at the big leagues.

CARLSON, DAN - TR - Age 27
Carlson completed his third year in Triple-A with solid reductions in his ERA and ratio, and a big improvement in his strikeout-to-walk ratio as well. He really has mastered this level, so you must wonder why the injury laden Giants did not bring him up.

CARLYLE, KENNY - TR - Age 27
In his fifth pro season, Carlyle took a step backwards, to Double-A Jacksonville where he went 8-5 with a 4.05 ERA. His results have been about the same for the last three years. Carlyle appears to have topped out in the high minors.

CARMONA, RAFAEL - TR - Age 24
A pitcher to watch, Carmona had a rather strong debut, ringing up eight wins and a save. This former top prospect could earn a spot in the rotation.

	W	SV	ERA	IP	H	BB	SO	B/I	$
1995 Seattle AL	2	1	5.66	47	55	34	28	1.87	-
1996 Seattle AL	8	1	4.28	90	95	55	62	1.66	2

CARPENTER, BRIAN - TR - Age 26
An aging swingman at Arkansas, Carpenter had a good year in his second season in Double-A. He lacks major league stuff, so Carpenter will have to settle for besting hitters several years younger than himself in the high minors.

CARPENTER, CHRIS - TR - Age 22
Carpenter has a fastball that's been clocked in the mid-90's and a good curve. He needs to develop an offspeed pitch that he can control but is close to the majors without it.

CARPENTER, CRIS - TR - Age 31
This veteran showed good control pitching on the Brewers farm in 1996, collecting eight saves with a 2.52 ERA for Triple-A New Orleans.

CARPER, MARK - TR - Age 28
A midseason acquisition from the Yankees, Carper has struggled with his control throughout his six pro seasons. He doesn't throw especially hard and appears to be a career minor leaguer.

CARRARA, GIAVANNI - TR - Age 29
Lacking a big fastball, Carrara is the type of pitcher who frequently gets trapped in the minors. He has been consistent with good control of several pitches though out his minor league career. The Reds claimed him off waivers from Toronto to replenish their Triple-A staff, but when Carrara went 4-0 with an 0.76 ERA and 45 strikeouts and 9 walks in 47.2 innings, he got the call to the majors. He made a handful of starts but suffered from control problems with the Reds. He has an outside shot a job as a fifth starter in 1997.

CARRASCO, HECTOR - TR - Age 27
Carrasco suffered from a horrendous start, earning a return to Triple-A Indianapolis, but generally pitched well after his return. His control (5.4 walks per game) is still a problem, and his strikeout rate has been declining. Any chance of an early shot at the Cincinnati closer role has been eliminated by Jeff Brantley's performance and Carrasco's own erratic performance. In 1997, it is likely he will share the primary setup role with Jeff Shaw.

	W	SV	ERA	IP	H	BB	SO	B/I	$
1995 Cincinnati NL	2	5	4.12	87	86	46	64	1.51	3
1996 Cincinnati NL	4	0	3.75	74	58	45	59	1.39	1

CARRASCO, TONY - TL - Age 22
Carrasco's first year above A-ball was a disappointment. He failed in a starting role, then wasn't much better in long relief. Carrasco has some ability, but it didn't show in 1996. He'll be back at Double-A New Britain for another try in 1997.

CARTER, JOHN - TR - Age 25
After a big year at Class A in 1993, Carter ran into arm trouble and had Tommy John surgery in 1995. He's making a valiant try to get back on the prospect track, but isn't there yet. He went to the Arizona Fall League at the end of '96.

CASIAN, LARRY - TL - Age 31
Although he's not exactly Tony Fossas, Casian is a good situational lefthander out of the bullpen. He simply overmatched hitters, especially lefthanders, at the Triple-A level. When Casian gets his breaking ball over, there are few lefthanded hitters who want to face him.

	W	SV	ERA	IP	H	BB	SO	B/I	$
1995 Chicago NL	1	0	1.93	23	23	15	11	1.63	0
1996 Chicago NL	1	0	1.88	24	14	11	15	1.04	0

CASTILLO, FRANK - TR - Age 28
Castillo is not a hard thrower but knows how to pitch and how to set up hitters. Castillo is an intelligent control pitcher who can be a ten or twelve game winner in the big leagues, if he just keeps the ball down.

	W	SV	ERA	IP	H	BB	SO	B/I	$
1995 Chicago NL	11	0	3.21	188	179	52	135	1.23	14
1996 Chicago NL	7	0	5.28	182	209	46	139	1.40	-

CASTILLO, MARINO - TR - Age 26
Castillo pitched well in relief at San Jose (19 strikeouts to 0 walks over 11 innings) but the league caught up with him a little when he was promoted to Shreveport. He does have good control but he is not a closer. He could turn into an effective set up man, though.

CASTILLO, TONY - TL - Age 34
Everyone, including his manager, said that he was getting saves because there wasn't anyone else. Castillo will be a lefty setup man not likely to be used in many save situations in 1997.

	W	SV	ERA	IP	H	BB	SO	B/I	$
1995 Toronto AL	1	13	3.22	72	64	24	38	1.21	17
1996 Toronto-Chicago AL	5	2	3.60	95	95	24	57	1.25	8

CASTRO, NELSON - TR - Age 25
Primarily a setup man, Castro has the rubber arm to log a lot of bullpen innings.

CATHER, MIKE - TR - Age 26
Formerly in the Rangers' farm system, Cather joined the Braves as a minor league free agent. He had a decent year for Double-A Greenville, saving five games while posting a 3.70 ERA and a strikeout-to-walk ratio better than 2-to-1. Still, Cather has the appearance of a organizational pitcher who will not stand in the way of better prospects.

CEDERBLAD, BRETT - TR - Age 23
This Australian righthander earned a midseason promotion from Double-A Trenton to Pawtucket, where he continued to enjoy remarkable success. He lacks overpowering stuff, but throws strikes and has succeeded at every level. Cederblad will challenge for a relief role in Boston's pen in 1997.

CENSALE, SILVIO - TL - Age 25
He is a hard thrower who has regained most of his velocity and possesses solid control for a power pitcher.

CHARLTON, NORM - TL - Age 34
Charlton is always an injury risk. He will get his saves, but wears down in the second half. He is the ultimate team player and won't conceal an injury. Think of him as the head of the committee, not the sole closer.

	W	SV	ERA	IP	H	BB	SO	B/I	$
1995 Philadelphia NL	2	0	7.36	22	23	15	12	1.73	
1995 Seattle AL	2	14	1.51	47	23	16	58	0.83	20
1996 Seattle AL	4	20	4.04	75	68	38	73	1.41	21

CHAVES, RAFAEL - TR - Age 28
Chaves would have been the Pirates' closer if replacement ball came to fruition in 1995. That saved his career and he has come back to have two fine minor league seasons. However, most of that has come at the Class A level.

CHAVEZ, CARLOS - TR - Age 24
Chavez was the only pitcher to spend all season on the Orioles' Bowie Double-A club. He has good control and strikes out a lot of batters, and he should move up to Triple-A or even the Orioles in 1997.

CHAVEZ, TONY - TR - Age 26
Chavez is a mediocre middle reliever in the Angels farm system. He did okay in Single-A ball, but he's having difficulty in Double-A.

CHERGEY, DAN - TR - Age 26
The Marlins 1993 22nd round pick is your typical journeyman - a reliever who, despite a history of good control, has never been entrusted with a minor role in a minor league bullpen.

CHITREN, STEVE - TR - Age 29
Once the heir apparent to Dennis Eckersley, Chitren hurt his arm and lost something off his fastball. He tried to comeback in 1994 with Bowie, the Orioles Double-A club where he pitched well, but the fastball velocity didn't return. He was last seen in 1995 with Amarillo, an independent team.

CHOUINARD, BOB - TR - Age 24
Chouinard mastered the ever-difficult-for-pitchers PCL, but didn't fare as well in the majors, where he seemed more overwhelmed than overmatched. Given a little time and experience, Chouinard could be a solid starter.

	W	SV	ERA	IP	H	BB	SO	B/I	$
1996 Oakland AL	4	0	6.10	59	75	32	32	1.81	-

CHRISTIANSEN, JASON - TL - Age 27
The lefthander debuted with the Pirates in the 1995 opener and had a good first half as a reliever. Christiansen then had a poor second half and didn't do any better in 1996 before the Pirates decided to send him to Triple-A Calgary in mid-July and turn him into a starter. He had two good starts then underwent elbow surgery. He has some ability but the arm problems and lack of a role make his future cloudy.

	W	SV	ERA	IP	H	BB	SO	B/I	$
1995 Pittsburgh NL	1	0	4.15	56	49	34	53	1.48	-
1996 Pittsburgh NL	3	0	6.70	44	56	19	38	1.70	-

CHRISTOPHER, MIKE - TR - Age 33
The Tigers' most consistent reliever in '95, Christopher was shelled back to Triple-A with 12 homers in 30 innings against him in the first half of '96.

	W	SV	ERA	IP	H	BB	SO	B/I	$
1995 Detroit AL	4	1	3.82	61	71	14	34	1.40	4
1996 Detroit AL	1	0	9.30	30	47	11	19	1.93	-

CLARK, DERA - TR - Age 31
Pitching in Double-A, Clark is much older than his peers, in his 10th season in the minors. He got into nine games for the Padres Double-A club last year, and his career appears to be over.

CLARK, MARK - TR - Age 28
Clark has real major league stuff: a high 80's fastball and good offspeed pitches. He was held back mainly by injuries,

not lack of talent, before 1996. When the Mets needed help in their rotation, Clark really stepped forward, raising his stock for 1997.

	W	SV	ERA	IP	H	BB	SO	B/I	$
1995 Cleveland AL	9	0	5.27	124	143	42	68	1.48	2
1996 New York NL	14	0	3.43	212	217	48	142	1.25	14

CLARK, TERRY - TR - Age 36
Clark surfaced briefly with the Astros in 1996 before becoming disabled with ligament damage in his left knee. He probably won't get another opportunity.

CLEMENS, ROGER - TR - Age 34
Despite the losing record, Clemens was again the Red Sox ace. He placed among league leaders in most pitching categories, including easily leading the A.L. in strikeouts. He was especially sharp down the stretch as the Red Sox made a stretch-drive run for the playoffs. The Rocket was back in full force as he had a record-tying (his own record) 20 K performance in September. Clemens wants a World Series ring and is determined to stick around long enough to get one.

	W	SV	ERA	IP	H	BB	SO	B/I	$
1995 Boston AL	10	0	4.18	140	141	60	132	1.44	7
1996 Boston AL	10	0	3.63	242	216	106	257	1.33	18

CLEMENT, MATT - TR - Age 22
Padre farm hand Matt Clement pitched in two Class-A leagues last year. He's worth following because he struck out 184 in 152 innings.

CLONTZ, BRAD - TR - Age 25
Hard-throwing Clontz led the National League with 81 appearances in 1996, helping set the table for closer Mark Wohlers. He has a good fastball, but little else and got into occasional trouble when he went through brief periods of getting the fastball too high, both in and out of the strike zone.

	W	SV	ERA	IP	H	BB	SO	B/I	$
1995 Atlanta NL	8	4	3.65	69	71	22	55	1.35	8
1996 Atlanta NL	6	1	5.69	80	78	33	49	1.38	-

COGGIN, DAVE - TR - Age 20
Coggin has the classic pitchers' body (6'4", 195 pounds), a 90 MPH fastball and diversified offspeed repertoire, along with good control. However, he is prone to the big inning and has not fine-tuned his mechanics for maximum performance.

COLON, BARTOLO - TR - Age 21
Though he remains one of the foremost pitching prospects in baseball, Colon has missed significant portions of the last two seasons with minor elbow trouble. Colon has a 96 MPH fastball, and a biting slider. Double-A Eastern League managers voted him the circuit's best pitching prospect, with its best fastball. To lessen the strain on his elbow, he will likely be transformed into a lethal two-pitch closer.

COLON, JULIO - TR - Age 24
After a year spent sharing a closer role at Class A San Bernardino, Colon went back to the starting rotation and finished the year with six starts at Double-A San Antonio. He walks too many hitters to be considered a good prospect at this point.

CONE, DAVID - TR - Age 34
Cone has long been among the top pitchers in all of baseball. He was at his career peak in early 1996 when he was suddenly sidelined with an aneurysm requiring surgery. He came back later in the year, pitched well, and looked ready to pick up in 1997 where he left off in '96.

	W	SV	ERA	IP	H	BB	SO	B/I	$
1995 Toronto - New York AL	18	0	3.57	229	195	88	191	1.24	23
1996 New York AL	7	0	2.88	72	50	34	71	1.17	7

CONNER, SCOTT - TR - Age 25
Reliever and starter Scott Conner had a rough year last season with the Double-A Bowie BaySox in the Orioles farm system. It was his second year with the club, and he posted a worse record.

CONNOLLY, MATT - TR - Age 28
Connolly is a big, righthanded power pitcher. To look at his numbers, you'd think he was ready for a look at the majors. But he's done most of his damage playing against much younger players. Connolly finished 7-3 with two saves and a 3.31 ERA while splitting time as a starter and reliever. He still posted good strikeout numbers, 80 in 87 innings, but he was a 27-year-old pitcher throwing to 22-year olds.

CONVERSE, JIM - TR - Age 25
Converse lost all of 1996 to surgery. He wasn't an especially good pitcher before the surgery.

COOK, DENNIS - TL - Age 34
Cook had a nice year with Texas, mostly in middle relief. In a marked contrast to 1995, Cook allowed only two home runs in more than 70 innings. He has a few more years as a bullpen lefty ahead of him.

	W	SV	ERA	IP	H	BB	SO	B/I	$
1995 Two Teams	0	2	4.53	57	63	26	53	1.54	1
1996 Texas AL	5	0	4.09	70	53	35	64	1.26	4

COOKE, STEVE - TL - Age 27
After a promising 10-10 rookie season in 1993, Cooke has had three wasted seasons while battling nerve problems in his shoulder. He was awful in his brief major league stint last year and not much better at Double-A Carolina (1-5, 4.36 ERA in 12 starts). He could have been a top-flight starter in the majors but it now looks like that's not going to happen.

COOPER, BRIAN - TR - Age 22
Cooper is an Angels prospect who had an excellent record in the California League last year. He strikes out an average of almost one hitter per inning.

COPPINGER, ROCKY - TR - Age 23
Coppinger is a big hard thrower with a good fastball with movement and a power slider. The Orioles brought him up in early June, and considering all the factors such as his age, 23, and that the Orioles later were in many pressure packed games in a pennant race, he pitched well overall. The downside was that he showed some inconsistencies that are typical of rookie pitchers. Coppinger has a bright future.

	W	SV	ERA	IP	H	BB	SO	B/I	$
1996 Baltimore AL	10	0	5.18	125	126	60	104	1.49	3

CORBIN, ARCHIE - TR - Age 29
"I can't believe I'm here," said Archie Corbin as he won a game for the Orioles last year. He labored 11 years in the minor leagues with the Mets, Royals, Expos and Pirates, first reaching the show by pitching two innings with the Royals in 1991. His career hit rock bottom, and he was actually unemployed last year, finally hooking with the Reynoso Broncos in the Mexican League who also later released him. But in July, Baltimore signed him to a Triple-A contract where he proved himself, and his fastball was rated the best in the league by a "Baseball America" poll of managers. He got the big promotion to the majors when the Orioles were in dire need for bullpen help. Corbin throws hard with a 95 MPH fastball, and he was a big help to the O's bullpen.

CORDOVA, FRANCISCO - TR - Age 24
Cordova came out of the Mexican League and saved a career-high 12 games as a rookie with the Pirates last season. He moved to the rotation in September and pitched even better. He is a little guy but has nasty movement on his pitches and has the chance to develop into a good major league starter.

	W	SV	ERA	IP	H	BB	SO	B/I	$
1996 Pittsburgh NL	4	12	4.09	99	103	20	95	1.24	12

CORMIER, RHEAL - TL - Age 29
The Expos are always desperately looking for a French-Canadian to become a hero for the Montreal fans. They acquired Cormier from Boston prior to last season and he was so-so as a starter before being sidelined by elbow

tendinitis in September. Cormier seems to have the makings of a decent lefthanded starter but he's now spent all or parts of the last six seasons in the majors without doing a whole lot.

	W	SV	ERA	IP	H	BB	SO	B/I	$
1995 Boston AL	7	0	4.07	115	131	31	69	1.41	6
1996 Montreal NL	7	0	4.17	159	165	41	100	1.29	5

CORNELIUS, REID - TR - Age 26
At Triple-A Buffalo in the Indians' chain, Cornelius has never been able to locate his average stuff on the corners of the strike zone. After making Team USA in 1998, Cornelius has had a career featuring mainly arm problems.

CORPS, EDWIN - TR - Age 24
Becoming a career Double-A set up guy, Corps won thirteen games for Double-A Shreveport in 1995, but didn't pitch well.

CORREA, RAMSER - TR - Age 26
Correa has never gotten consistent control of his good fastball. Correa was the closer at Double-A San Antonio in 1995 and 1996 but was inconsistent. The big guy throws heat, but often has control problems. He needs a reliable breaking pitch.

CORSI, JIM - TR - Age 35
Corsi is at the end of the line with the A's. A longtime Tony LaRussa/Dave Duncan associate, Corsi could catch on with St. Louis, but probably not anywhere else.

	W	SV	ERA	IP	H	BB	SO	B/I	$
1995 Oakland AL	2	2	2.20	45	31	26	26	1.27	6
1996 Oakland AL	6	3	4.03	73	71	34	43	1.43	6

COSTA, TONY - TR - Age 26
It took the Phils' 1992 16th round draft pick until his fifth pro season to reach Double-A, and his once solid control escaped him as he turned into a cautious nibbler against the more seasoned hitters. The 6'4", 210 pounds, Costa has honed his mechanics through the years and become more of a strikeout threat.

COURTRIGHT, JOHN - TL - Age 26
A 26 year old lefty who was not much of a prospect, Courtright went 8-0 with the best ERA of his career at Double-A Chattanooga after being required by the Reds. He will not be major league pitcher unless he learns some new tricks.

CRABTREE, TIM - TR - Age 27
Crabtree spent the last month of the season on the disabled list but arrived as the setup man the Blue Jays have been searching for. A Mike Timlin/Tim Crabtree combination is the best the Blue Jays have had since Duane Ward and Tom Henke pitched back-to-back in 1992. With the exception of saves, his numbers were better than Timlin's.

	W	SV	ERA	IP	H	BB	SO	B/I	$
1995 Toronto AL	0	0	3.09	32	30	13	21	1.34	1
1996 Toronto AL	5	1	2.54	67	59	22	57	1.21	7

CRAWFORD, JOE - TL - Age 26
A Rule Five draftee taken by Boston but returned to the Mets, Crawford fittingly threw a no-hitter in his first 1996 start, against the Red Sox Eastern Leaguers. He has an adequate fastball and excellent control.

CREEK, DOUG - TL - Age 28
Creek got into a lot of games last year and didn't perform well in most of them. On the good side, the Giants were usually so far behind when he came in that it really didn't matter.

	W	SV	ERA	IP	H	BB	SO	B/I	$
1996 San Francisco NL	0	0	6.52	48	45	32	38	1.60	-

CREEK, RYAN - TR - Age 24
In Creek's second year at Double-A Jackson, he led the staff with fifteen losses and had a career-high 5.26 ERA. His strikeout ability remains, but Creek walked 121 batters in 142 innings, twice his walk rate from the previous year. Creek wasn't an especially hot prospect before 1996; now he's definitely on the cold side.

CROGHAN, ANDY - TR - Age 27
Croghan looked better in 1994 when he got 16 saves at Double-A. He got 22 innings at Triple-A in 1996 but had an ERA of 8.46. Croghan had surgery on his non-pitching elbow in 1995, and the time off made him rusty.

CROUSHORE, RICK - TR - Age 26
The fifth starter and long reliever for Double-A Arkansas, Croushore had a dismal season. He was 5-10 with a 4.92 ERA. He's not a highly regarded prospect.

CROW, DEAN - TR - Age 24
The Double-A Port City closer in 1996, Crow sports a 90+ MPH fastball and good control. He saved 26 games last year and had a 3.04 ERA. He should get a shot at the Mariners' bullpen this spring. Remember, minor league saves mean little; Crow would be a middle-innings man when he first gets to the bigs.

CROWTHER, BRENT - TR - Age 24
After outstanding success at the Class A level in 1995, 1996 was a disappointment for Crowther, as he gave up better than a hit per inning and his ratio soared to over 1.5. He'll start 1997 at Double-A New Haven.

CUMBERLAND, CHRIS - TL - Age 24
Cumberland was a top prospect before elbow trouble sidelined him in 1995, when he had ERA's below 2.00 at two levels in the low minors.

CUMMINGS, JOHN - TL - Age 27
Cummings pitched in relief for Detroit after he came from Los Angeles via trade. He is in his correct role, but this doesn't mean he'll succeed in '97.

	W	SV	ERA	IP	H	BB	SO	B/I	$
1995 Seattle AL	0	0	11.81	5	8	7	4	2.81	
1995 Los Angeles NL	3	0	3.00	39	38	10	21	1.23	0
1996 Los Angeles NL	0	0	6.75	5	12	2	5	2.75	-
1996 Detroit AL	3	0	5.12	31	36	20	24	1.79	-

CUNNANE, WILL - TR - Age 22
Cunnane is a finesse pitcher who was surprisingly left at Double-A Portland in the Marlins' chain for a second consecutive season. He recovered from a poor start and was one of the Eastern League's most effective starters by season's end. There are many Marlins' starting pitcher prospects with better raw stuff, but Cunnane's career 354/95 strikeout/walk ratio in 475 innings can't be ignored. Look for Cunnane to reach the majors as a spot starter/middle reliever, possibly by the end of 1997.

CURTIS, CHRIS - TR - Age 25
Curtis has been less than impressive both as a starter and a reliever, and doesn't appear to have good enough stuff to progress further.

CZAJKOWSKI, JIM - TR - Age 33
Don't be fooled by his good year at Syracuse. He's just a crafty veteran. Czajkowski led Triple-A Colorado Springs with 17 saves in 1995. He's not an especially hard thrower, though, and walks too many batters to be successful in a setup role.

DAAL, OMAR - TL - Age 25
The Expos moved Daal into the starting rotation and he did OK. Expos manager Felipe Alou is convinced the lefthander is much better suited to starting and he's probably right. Daal has a good feel for pitching and he's just 25. He has many good seasons ahead.

	W	SV	ERA	IP	H	BB	SO	B/I	$
1995 Los Angeles NL	4	0	7.20	20	29	15	11	2.20	-
1996 Montreal NL	4	0	4.02	87	74	37	82	1.27	2

DABNEY, FRED - TL - Age 29
Dabney was the do-it-all pitcher for Iowa in 1996. Pitching mostly out of the bullpen, Dabney typically put in solid work. He's a minor league veteran with little chance of making the majors.

DACE, DEREK - TL - Age 21
Dace pitched at three levels in 1996, finishing with a start at Double-A Jackson. His overall 9-4 record with an ERA of 3.18 suggests he will bear watching for the future.

D'AMICO, JEFF - TR - Age 21
He was the only real prospect in the Brewers farm system, and he appears to be set in their rotation, but he's still pretty raw, and just 21 years old. Some fine tuning in the minors is not unlikely.

	W	SV	ERA	IP	H	BB	SO	B/I	$
1996 Milwaukee AL	6	0	5.44	86	88	31	53	1.38	1

DANIELS, LEE - TR - Age 26
Injuries continue to plague Daniels; it was the second time in two years that he lost time due to shoulder problems. In 1996, he was leading Double-A Greenville with nine saves when he underwent surgery in June. Drafted by the Blue Jays as an outfielder, Daniels has shown some promise in a relief role. The biggest question for him is whether or not he can overcome his recurring shoulder problems.

DARENSBOURG, VIC - TL - Age 26
Darensbourg was a blue-chip closer prospect prior to losing the entire 1995 season to elbow surgery. He appeared to have regained most of his velocity at Triple-A Charlotte in the Marlins' chain in 1996, and was particularly effective against lefties. No longer a closer candidate, he will have to be content with contending for the lefty specialist role held for so long in South Florida by Yorkis Perez.

DARWIN, DANNY - TR - Age 41
After two unproductive years in the American League, Darwin returned to the National League with Pittsburgh in 1996 and returned to his old form before wearing down later in the year. After being traded to Houston in July, he worked as both a starter and in relief with mixed results. Darwin is still a fierce competitor but he has lost considerable velocity.

	W	SV	ERA	IP	H	BB	SO	B/I	$
1995 Two Teams	3	0	7.45	99	131	31	58	1.64	-
1996 Houston NL	10	0	3.77	164	160	27	96	1.14	11

DARWIN, JEFF - TR - Age 27
Another one of the White Sox tall relievers, Darwin was the righthanded closer for Triple-A Tacoma in 1995, his second straight year in that role.

	W	SV	ERA	IP	H	BB	SO	B/I	$
1996 Chicago AL	0	0	2.93	30	26	9	15	1.16	-

DASPIT, JAMIE - TR - Age 27
Daspit completed a seventh professional season in Triple-A middle relief.

DAULT, DONNIE - TR - Age 24
Dault spread his 31 relief innings over three levels in 1996, finishing with two appearances at Triple-A. With only six wins and 10 saves in a career beginning in 1991, he hasn't done enough to attract attention as a prospect.

DAVIS, TIM - TL - Age 26
A crafty lefty with only a so-so fastball but many pitches including a curve, slider, sinker and changeup, Davis has had some success in a starter's role where he gets to use his many pitches and give a different look the second and third time through a lineup. Unfortunately for Davis, the Mariners have usually wanted to use him in short relief situations where he must rely heavily on his mediocre fastball, never getting to use his full repertoire.

	W	SV	ERA	IP	H	BB	SO	B/I	$
1995 Seattle AL	2	0	6.38	24	30	18	19	2.00	-
1996 Seattle AL	2	0	4.01	42	43	17	34	1.42	-

DAVISON, SCOTT - TR - Age 26
Davis had nine saves for Seattle's Triple-A Tacoma franchise. He fanned twenty three batters in twenty three innings while issuing six walks. His ERA was a tiny 0.39. Obviously he's a prospect to watch.

DEAN, GREG - TR - Age 22
Dean is from Oklahoma State where he pitched in the College World Series. In 1996, he struggled in the Class-A California League, but that's a pitchers' snake pit. He walked a lot of hitters and had almost as many walks as strikeouts. Nevertheless, he was promoted to Double-A where he found things even tougher.

DeCLUE, JOHN - TL - Age 26
DeClue had a rough season last year starting and relieving in the tough Texas League. Being a lefty helps him, as they are always in demand. He could make it to the majors as a situational reliever.

DEDRICK, JIM - TR - Age 28
Normally a reliever, Dedrick was pressed into service as a starter for some games in Triple-A last year because the starters were either promoted to Baltimore or on the disabled list. Overall he had a rough time as both a starter and reliever last year, somewhat surprising because he had an excellent minor league record prior to 1996.

DEHART, RICK - TL - Age 27
DeHart is a lefty who has never held a big role on any minor league club during his five year pro career. Most recently, he has been a middle reliever in the Expos' chain, posting a respectable 2.68 ERA, but allowing 65 baserunners in 44 Double-A innings in 1996.

DeJEAN, MIKE - TR - Age 26
This former Yankees prospect started his 1996 season as the primary closer at Double-A New Haven and finished the year as a middle reliever at Triple-A Colorado Springs. Absent only serious injury problems to the Rockies' pitching staff in 1997, DeJean will stay at the Triple-A level.

DEJESUS, JOSE - TR - Age 32
This tall, lanky righty once had velocity in the high 90's, but he never had good control, and in 1992 he suffered a torn rotator cuff. The velocity is back to major league caliber, but he is still searching for that control.

DE LA MAZA, ROLAND - TR - Age 25
De La Maza possesses average velocity and excellent control, but he is not as good a prospect as his 40-13 minor league record would indicate. He tends to give up runs in bunches, and is generally much more effective the first time around the batting order. For that reason, his best hope of reaching the majors is as a middle reliever.

De La ROSA, MAXIMO - TR - Age 25
De La Rosa and Rolando De La Maza both pitched at Double-A in the Cleveland organization, both are righthanders who both started and relieved, and they are the same age. De La Rosa has less ability, however. He has decent velocity, but relatively poor command.

DE LOS SANTOS, MARIANO - TR - Age 26
Once a top starting pitching prospect in the Pirates' farm system, De Los Santos pitched middle relief at Double-A last season. He doesn't throw hard enough to set up his changeup.

DeLUCIA, RICH - TR - Age 32
DeLucia signed a two-year deal with the Giants at the beginning of last year, and it is a good thing for him. He can function well as a set up pitcher when he is on. When he is off, the ball flies out of the park.

	W	SV	ERA	IP	H	BB	SO	B/I	$
1995 St. Louis NL	8	0	3.39	82	63	36	76	1.21	7
1996 San Francisco NL	3	0	5.84	61	62	31	55	1.52	-

DEMPSTER, RYAN - TR - Age 19
He has a plus fastball and solid breaking stuff, though he needs to establish more consistent command. He is considered to have one of the highest upsides among Marlin pitching prospects, and could advance to Double-A by the end of 1997.

DENNIS, SHANE - TL - Age 25
Southpaw starter Shane Dennis won the ERA title in the Southern League last year, striking out more than one hitter per inning while walking comparatively few. His promotion potential is enhanced because he's a lefty, and he could make the Padres staff in 1997 as a middle reliever or setup man.

DESILVA, JOHN - TR - Age 29
DeSilva was a non-roster invitee to the Royals' spring camp, then was released outright at the beginning of the minor league season. He hooked on with Triple-A Pawtucket and had a forgettable season in their rotation. DeSilva was once a marginal major leaguer; now he's marginal in the high minors.

DESSENS, ELMER - TR - Age 25
Another one of the Mexican pitchers the Pirates have tried as part of their working agreement with the Mexico City Reds, Dessens has struck out less than four batters per nine innings in his professional career. He showed little hope of ever developing into a major league pitcher during his major league trial last season.

DETMERS, KRIS - TL - Age 22
Detmers has a big time curveball. That, coupled with his 6'5" frame, can give hitters fits. He's not a flamethrower, but has above-average velocity. A tall, Graeme Lloyd type, Detmers walks a lot of batters, but that's due mostly to the movement on his pitches. One of four good major league prospects as pitchers at Arkansas last season, Detmers is just 22 years old and he's big and lefthanded, both big pluses.

DETTMER, JOHN - TR - Age 27
Fastball/slider pitcher Dettmer joined the Braves as a minor league free agent, then spent part of the season pitching for the Mexico City Tigers before pitching for both Greenville and Richmond. Used occasionally as a starter, but primarily in long relief, Dettmer showed uncanny control. He walked just 15 against 54 strikeouts in 101 innings. Formerly with the Rangers, Dettmer will get a chance to earn a relief role for Atlanta in the spring.

DEWEY, MARK - TR - Age 32
Amazingly, Dewey led the pitching staff in appearances and all-in-all fared pretty well. He must keep the ball down as he is not a strikeout pitcher. He can get wild when his sinker isn't sinking.

	W	SV	ERA	IP	H	BB	SO	B/I	$
1995 San Francisco NL	1	0	3.13	31	30	17	32	1.48	0
1996 San Francisco NL	6	0	4.21	83	79	41	57	1.44	1

DICKSON, JASON - TR - Age 24
Dickson made eight starts in Double-A, and was promoted to Triple-A where he held his own by posting an excellent 3.80 ERA in the tough Pacific Coast League. He was promoted to the Angels where he made five starts, getting hit pretty hard, but you can write it off to rookie jitters. He has a live fastball with good movement, and has good command.

	W	SV	ERA	IP	H	BB	SO	B/I	$
1996 California AL	1	0	4.57	43	52	18	20	1.62	-

DICKSON, LANCE - TL - Age 27
Dickson was the Cubs top draft pick and the 23rd pick overall in the 1990 draft. He's talented but has been beset with ailments over the years, spending time on the disabled list. When healthy, Dickson can be an effective pitcher.

DIPOTO, JERRY - TR - Age 28
With a heavy, sinking fastball that's hard to get into the air, DiPoto generally stays out of trouble. He is no longer considered as a possible closer candidate, but DiPoto can obviously get an occasional win by keeping things under control in a close or tied game.

	W	SV	ERA	IP	H	BB	SO	B/I	$
1995 New York NL	4	2	3.78	78	77	29	49	1.36	4
1996 New York NL	7	0	4.19	77	91	45	52	1.76	-

DISHMAN, GLENN - TL - Age 26
Lefty starter Glen Dishman had a rough year in Triple-A last season, trying to perfect a breaking ball to go with his good fastball. He started 16 games for the Padres in 1995, going 4-8 with a 5.01 ERA. With a little improvement, Dishman could be a solid fourth or fifth starter in the majors.

DIXON, BUBBA - TL - Age 25
Southpaw reliever Bubba Dixon has some impressive minor league statistics. His strikeout rate is excellent as he whiffed 77 in 63 innings in Double-A last year while walking 28 and giving up only 53 hits. Dixon will soon be pitching for the Padres if he keeps it up.

DIXON, STEVE - TL - Age 27
Dixon got into six major league games in 1993 and '94 with the Cardinals. Otherwise he's been relieving in Triple-A for five years. He pitched for the Orioles Triple-A club last year, never getting a call-up when they were desperate for bullpen help. That's a significant point, taken together with the fact that he's also been toiling in Triple-A for the Cards and Cubs without much major league time.

DODD, ROBERT - TL - Age 24
The Phils' 1994 14th round pick suffered through a poor season in his first full season as a reliever. The Phils lack viable lefthanded relief prospects in their system, and had hoped that the 6'3", 195 pounds, Dodd could excel against lefthanded hitters. He battled control problems, and actually fared worse against lefties than righties at Double-A Reading.

DOHERTY, JOHN - TR - Age 29
Once the Tigers' top pitcher, Doherty has slipped off the edge of being a fringe major league pitcher. Spending most of the season on the DL or getting lit up at Triple-A Pawtucket, Doherty's combined ERA for the last three full seasons is 5.91, including Triple-A.

DOOLAN, BLAKE - TR - Age 28
As expected, the Phils' 1992 33rd round pick proved that his 11 win, 16 save season as Double-A closer in 1995 was a fluke. He battled arm trouble, couldn't get the ball past Triple-A batters whom he was facing for the first time at age 27, and caught too much of the plate with his average stuff.

DOORNEWEERD, DAVID - TR - Age 24
Doorneweerd is an ex-Twins farm hand who pitched in the Angels system last year. He didn't pitch much, but he was hittable when he did.

DORLARQUE, AARON - TR - Age 27
Dorlarque posted ERA's of 1.79 and 1.46 in his two A-ball seasons in 1992 and 1993, but allowed 89 baserunners in 44 innings in a 1996 season split between Double and Triple-A, posting 9.41 ERA. His control has been his strength throughout his career, but his strikes catch too much of the plate and are eminently hittable by higher classification hitters.

DOUGHERTY, JIM - TR - Age 29
Dougherty is a sidewheeling righthander who was a successful closer in his first four minor league seasons. He is not overpowering and has trouble with lefthanded batters. After spending most of the 1995 season in Houston, he failed to stick in 1996 and had a mediocre year as a middle reliever at Triple-A Tucson (4-3, 3.50 ERA, one save). He is not likely to be a serious candidate for a major league job.

DRABEK, DOUG - TR - Age 34
Drabek had his second straight disappointing season in 1996 in the final year of a four-year contract. Without an overpowering fastball, he must rely on changing speeds and pinpoint control to be effective. At times he was able to do this but, more often than not, he was hit hard. His best years are behind him.

	W	SV	ERA	IP	H	BB	SO	B/I	$
1995 Houston NL	10	0	4.77	185	205	54	143	1.40	1
1996 Houston NL	7	0	4.57	175	208	60	137	1.53	-

DRAHMAN, BRIAN - TR - Age 30
At age 29 last year, Drahman got into only nine games for the Padres Triple-A club, and his career may be over. He spent almost all of 11 years in the minors, relieving in 47 games in the majors in 1991-94 with a 3-2 record.

DREIFORT, DARREN - TR - Age 24
A first round pick in 1993, Dreifort recorded six saves for the Dodgers in 1994 before blowing out an elbow. His velocity has recovered (75 strikeouts in 86 innings) but his command has not (52 walks). The Dodgers brought him back up in September anyway, where he exhibited the same pattern. When Dreifort regains his command, he will be serious candidate for a closer or setup role for the Dodgers.

	W	SV	ERA	IP	H	BB	SO	B/I	$
1996 Los Angeles NL	1	0	4.94	23	23	12	24	1.51	-

DREWS, MATT - TR - Age 22
Drews, a tall (6'8") starting pitcher, came to Detroit from New York for Cecil Fielder in '96. He instantly became the Tigers' top prospect despite struggling in '96 as the Yankees tried to skip him past Double-A. Drews is a power pitcher who went 15-7, 2.27 at Class A in '95, his first full pro season. He has star potential.

DREYER, STEVE - TR - Age 27
A finesse righty, Dreyer had a respectable season at Triple-A. His stuff is nothing special, so he'll have to be impressive to make it back to the majors.

DRISKILL, TRAVIS - TR - Age 25
The Indians' 1993 fourth round draftee made an impressive conversion from short reliever to starter at Double-A Canton-Akron in 1996. He keeps the ball down and throws hard strikes, generally to quality locations.

DRUMRIGHT, MIKE - TR - Age 22
Drumright is a good young starting pitcher in the Tiger system who threw well in '96, his first full pro year. A minor arm problem limited him to 100 innings, but he should be fine in '97. Drumright will need a full year in Triple-A before entering the lion's den of Tiger Stadium.

DUNBAR, MATT - TL - Age 28
Dunbar finally had success at Triple-A in 1996. In fact he pitched at three levels on the Yankees farm and kept his ERA under 2.00 at all of them. As a lefty who can throw strikes, Dunbar could have reached the majors sooner in an organization with less pitching talent than the Yankees have.

DURAN, ROBERTO - TL - Age 22
Duran throws exceptionally hard, but doesn't have a clue where it's going. In 1996 he walked 61 batters in 81 innings while fanning 74. Don't dig in against this guy. If he can find the plate, Duran will advance quickly.

DUROCHER, JAYSON - TR - Age 22
The Expos' 1993 ninth round pick has made steady progress, emerging as their best starter at High-A West Palm Beach in 1996. He has adequate stuff with above average control. Questions remain. He averaged less than six innings per start. Double-A will be a key test in 1997.

DYER, MIKE - TR - Age 30
Dyer has a great arm and throws 90+ MPH. However, he has little control and grooves too many pitches in tight situations. The Expos claimed him off waivers from Pittsburgh late in spring training last year and he was a major disappointment after a good start. His days in the big leagues are numbered.

	W	SV	ERA	IP	H	BB	SO	B/I	$
1995 Pittsburgh NL	4	0	4.34	74	81	30	53	1.49	0
1996 Montreal NL	5	2	4.40	75	79	34	51	1.50	1

EATON, ADAM - TR - Age 19
Eaton was the 11th overall selection in the 1996 draft. He hurt his arm playing second base in an American Legion game after the draft. He is apparently fine, but missed the rest of 1996. He has few innings under his belt, but has a 95 MPH heater. The Phils would love Eaton to follow in the footsteps of their 1995 draftees who pitched well at Low-A Piedmont in their first full pro season.

ECKERSLEY, DENNIS - TR - Age 42
Many thought the Cardinals made a mistake by trading for Eckersley prior to last season. Tony La Russa and Dave Duncan had the last laugh, though, as Eckersley had a fine season. He's no longer the unhittable Eck that dominated in Oakland in the early part of this decade. He's also 42 but he stays in excellent shape, which should allow him one more big year before T.J. Mathews takes over as St. Louis' closer.

	W	SV	ERA	IP	H	BB	SO	B/I	$
1995 Oakland AL	4	29	4.83	50	53	11	40	1.27	30
1996 St. Louis NL	0	30	3.30	60	65	6	49	1.18	25

EDDY, CHRIS - TL - Age 27
Eddy came up through the Royals farm system before being taken as a Rule Five draft pick by Oakland in 1995. He was unsuccessful in a few major league outings and was returned to the Royals. In 1996, he got a short trial at Triple-A New Orleans, posting a 9.72 ERA in 12 games, while allowing 24 baserunners in his eight innings pitched. Eddy returned to the Royals' Double-A franchise and had better results, but he's going to be a career minor leaguer.

EDENFIELD, KEN - TR - Age 30
Edenfield is a middle reliever and setup man who pitched well in Triple-A in 1996, for the third year in a row. He's a sinker/slider pitcher who could probably fill a role in a major league bullpen, but his only shot came in 1995 in seven games with the Angels. Edenfield was traded to the Yankees in July.

EDENS, TOM - TR - Age 35
Veteran reliever Tom Edens has a 19-12 career record with a 3.86 ERA in the majors spread over seven years. He was cut by the Royals in 1996 spring training, and signed by the Orioles for whom he pitched in Triple-A. The Orioles were desperate for quality relievers at mid-year, but Edens never got the call.

EDMONDSON, BRIAN - TR - Age 24
Lacking a big fastball and surviving with good location and changing speeds, Edmondson never made it as a starter in the minors (best year was at Class A in 1993). The Mets tried him as a reliever in 1996 and got some noticeable improvement as Edmondson didn't have to give hitters a second and third look at him (his 4.25 ERA at Double-A was his best since '93). He is still some distance from the majors.

EDROS, TODD - TR - Age 23
Edros was the ace closer of the Padres Single-A Rancho Cucamonga club in the California League. His 3.74 ERA is excellent for a league that is known for its easy hitting, and he struck out an eye-popping 82 in 67 innings. The Padres slated him for the Arizona Fall League.

EDSELL, GEOFF - TR - Age 25
Edsell led all of the minors with 193 innings pitched last year. He had a good record, but he walks almost as many as he strikes out, and he doesn't strikeout many. He tries to be too fine a pitcher, and has some difficulty. He was promoted from Single-A to Triple-A last July, and pitched well at the higher level. Edsell is from Montoursville, PA, Mike Mussina's hometown.

EHLER, DAN - TR - Age 22
Ehler, the Marlins' 1993 third round pick, is a control specialist who has been unable to blow the ball past Class-A hitters at this point in his pro career. The Marlins envisioned a power pitcher when they drafted him out of high school. At this point, he has not established himself as a major league prospect.

EICHHORN, MARK - TR - Age 36
Veteran Mark Eichhorn is a sidearming reliever who had some good years with Toronto, Atlanta, Baltimore and California as a setup man and situational reliever. He missed all of 1995 following rotator cuff surgery, returning to action with the Angels in 1996. He experienced some shoulder discomfort in June, so he is not all the way back.

	W	SV	ERA	IP	H	BB	SO	B / I	$
1995			Did Not Play						
1996 California AL	1	0	5.04	30	36	11	24	1.56	-

EILAND, DAVE - TR - Age 30
Getting chances as a major league starter every year from 1988 through 1995, Eiland never had any real success except for five good starts in 1990. He has been able to hang on around the fringe of the major leagues, mainly because he can throw strikes.

EISCHEN, JOEY - TL - Age 26
Eischen has posted steady and useful numbers wherever he has pitched. In 1996, he came to the Tigers in the Chad Curtis trade and became Detroit's most reliable situational lefty in the bullpen. Eischen is a groundball pitcher who rarely gives up the longball, but also doesn't strikeout many hitters. His role in a major league bullpen is secure.

	W	SV	ERA	IP	H	BB	SO	B/I	$
1995 Los Angeles NL	0	0	3.10	20	19	11	15	1.48	-
1996 Los Angeles NL	0	0	4.78	43	48	20	36	1.58	-
1996 Detroit AL	1	0	3.24	25	27	14	15	1.64	-

ELARTON, SCOTT - TR - Age 21
Elarton was a first round draft choice by Houston in 1994 and was impressive in his first professional season. After a mediocre second season in 1995, he posted a 12-7 record with a 2.92 ERA at Class A Kissimmee in 1996. He joined Double-A Jackson for the Texas League playoffs and pitched and won the clinching games in both rounds. He has a plus 90 MPH fastball, a curve, a straight change and great makeup. At 6'7" and 225 pounds, Elarton is an imposing figure on the mound. He should pitch at Double-A in 1997 and remains one of the top pitching prospects in the Astro system.

ELDRED, CAL - TR - Age 29
Eldred returned from a serious injury a bit sooner than expected. He was effective in his Triple-A rehab with New Orleans and added a few wins when recalled to the Brewers late in the season. Once a 200+ inning workhorse, he'll be on a pitch count which may enable him produce a better ERA and ratio if limited to six innings.

	W	SV	ERA	IP	H	BB	SO	B/I	$
1995 Milwaukee AL	1	0	3.42	23	24	10	18	1.44	0
1996 Milwaukee AL	4	0	4.46	84	82	38	50	1.43	2

ELLIOTT, DON - TR - Age 28
In his second tour of the Phils' system, Elliott is not the promising prospect he was the first time around. He still possesses an above average fastball, though it is not the 90 MPH force that he possessed as a teenager. He has never been able to throw strike one consistently, and that has been his undoing. It has left him unable to pitch deeply into games as a starter, and has made managers reluctant to call him into a game with runners on base as a reliever. He has also battled arm trouble.

ELLIS, ROBERT - TR - Age 26
Ellis was traded by the White Sox to the Angels in July, and he pitched for the Angels briefly in a September call-up. He was once a top prospect for the White Sox, but had a poor year in Triple-A in 1994, and missed most of 1995 due to an injury. Last season, he had a poor record for the White Sox in Triple-A, but he turned it around and had a good record for the Angels in Triple-A earning his promotion.

EMBREE, ALAN - TL - Age 27
Don't be misled by Embree's poor mainstream stats in 1996 - a deeper look reveals a flamethrower ready to come into his own. Embree allowed only five of 17 inherited baserunners to score, and his ERA was inflated by his successors' allowance of an above average number of Embree's baserunners to score. The lefty boasts a mid-90's fastball, but needs to show more consistent command to excel at the major league level. Still, he held lefties to a .186 average, and was certainly one of the most uncomfortable hurlers for a lefty batter to face.

	W	SV	ERA	IP	H	BB	SO	B/I	$
1995 Cleveland AL	3	1	5.11	24	23	16	23	1.58	1
1996 Cleveland AL	1	0	6.39	31	30	21	33	1.65	-

EMERSON, SCOTT - TL - Age 25
Emerson's slow progress through the Orioles and Red Sox farm systems slowed even further in 1996, primarily due to arm miseries. He was on the DL three different times during the season, managing just 39 innings with two clubs. He walks too many batters to be a good prospect.

ERICKS, JOHN - TR - Age 29
Ericks finished last season as the Pirates' closer after failing as a starter. He has the arm and mentality to be a closer but his command and control have to improve. He'll get a chance to close this spring and the exhibition boxscores will give an indication of if he can win the job.

	W	SV	ERA	IP	H	BB	SO	B/I	$
1995 Pittsburgh NL	3	0	4.58	106	108	50	80	1.49	-
1996 Pittsburgh NL	4	8	5.79	46	56	19	46	1.62	3

ERICKSON, SCOTT - TR - Age 29
Erickson can be tough to hit when his sinking fastball is working. Otherwise, he can be hittable. His sinker works better when he's pitching on three days' rest as in a four-man rotation, which is a rarity these days. Taken all together, Erickson usually has his ups-and-downs during the season, resulting in a .500 record.

	W	SV	ERA	IP	H	BB	SO	B/I	$
1995 Two Teams	13	0	4.81	196	213	67	106	1.43	7
1996 Baltimore AL	13	0	5.02	222	262	66	100	1.48	7

ESCOBAR, KELVIM - TR - Age 21
Escobar remained a starter but allowed too many hits. A strikeout pitcher, he is in danger of being rushed and needs at least another year or two before getting a long look.

ESHELMAN, VAUGHN - TL - Age 27
Eshelman hasn't been the same since falling out of the Red Sox' rotation early in the 1995 season. He doesn't have overpowering stuff and has to get by on locating his fastball, then coming back with a changeup. He couldn't locate the fastball very well in 1996 and opponents hit over .300 against him. He was mediocre in seven Triple-A starts and poor in 39 big-league relief appearances. Being lefthanded will help, but Eshelman will still have to pitch much, better before he gets a regular big-league role.

	W	SV	ERA	IP	H	BB	SO	B/I	$
1995 Boston AL	6	0	4.85	81	86	36	41	1.49	1
1996 Boston AL	6	0	7.08	87	112	58	59	1.95	-

ESTAVIL, MAURICIO - TL - Age 24
The Phils' 1994 11th round draftee's main selling point is that he throws lefthanded. He has a decent fastball but unspectacular breaking stuff, and doesn't have particularly good command of any of his pitches. He is somewhat effective at retiring lefties, but is an easy mark for righties.

ESTES, SHAWN - TL - Age 24
This Seattle reclamation project may be the closest thing the Giants have to a real staff ace. He lacks some in durability, and is injury prone, but he has a fastball in the low 90's and a great overhand curve. He pitched well at both Phoenix and with the Giants, and if he stays healthy should be a solid starter.

	W	SV	ERA	IP	H	BB	SO	B/I	$
1995 San Francisco NL	0	0	6.75	17	16	5	14	1.21	-
1996 San Francisco NL	3	0	3.60	70	63	39	60	1.46	0

ETHERIDGE, ROGER - TL - Age 25
In two seasons at Double-A Greenville, Etheridge has combined for a 6-12 record, a 6.15 ERA and more walks than strikeouts. He's lefthanded, but he'll have to have much better results to get any farther up the Braves' chain.

EVANS, BART - TR - Age 26
When scouts talk about a pitcher having control problems, Evans' line at Class A Wilmington is what they are talking about: 36 walks in 24 innings, plus twelve wild pitches. The 1994 Carolina League Pitcher of the Year has gone in reverse the last two years and was removed from the Royals' 40-man roster. Evans' season ended early due to surgery to remove elbow bone spurs.

EVANS, DAVE - TR - Age 29
Evans spent four years in the Seattle system before signing a minor league contract with the Astros in 1995. He has been used as both a starter and reliever. With a 6-12, 5.32 mark at Triple-A in 1996, he is not on a track that is leading to a major league opportunity.

EVERSGERD, BRYAN - TL - Age 28
Eversgerd had a fine season as a lefty swingman for Oklahoma City. Basically a finesse pitcher, Eversgerd could have a decent career as an extra lefty in someone's major league pen, but is behind three other lefties in the Texas organization.

EYRE, SCOTT - TL - Age 24
Going farther than expected in 1996, Eyre jumped from low A-ball to Double-A on the White Sox farm. He produced a 12-7 record with a 4.38 ERA. Eyre is still improving and was ticketed to start 1997 at Triple-A.

FALTEISEK, STEVE - TR - Age 24
Falteisek is a sinker/slider hurler who got off to a weak start in 1996 at Triple-A, then righted himself while helping lead Double-A Harrisburg to the Eastern League championship in 1996.

FARMER, MIKE - TL - Age 28
A former All-American outfielder, Farmer almost beat Tom Glavine and the World Champion Braves in Atlanta in his major league debut. His 1996 season was otherwise disappointing and short-lived due to arm problems. If Farmer is healthy in 1997, he could challenge for a starting spot.

FARRELL, JOHN - TR - Age 34
In the late 1980's, Farrell used to take a regular turn in Cleveland's rotation. Arm trouble cost him much of two seasons and when he returned he could no longer throw his best stuff past major league hitters. His comeback attempt has probably come to an end after six bad starts at Triple-A Toledo and six poor innings in Detroit.

FARSON, BRYAN - TL - Age 24
A decent pitching prospect in the Pirates' system, Farson was limited to four games at Double-A Carolina because of arm problems. It's hard to say what his future is until he proves he is healthy in 1997.

FASSERO, JEFF - TL - Age 34
Fassero had a fine season in 1996 for the Expos as he continued to be one of the most underrated lefthanded starters in the major leagues. Fassero is good for 15 wins a year, though it will be interesting to see where he winds up in 1997. He is becoming too expensive for the cost-conscious Expos and should be in a great demand.

	W	SV	ERA	IP	H	BB	SO	B / I	$
1995 Montreal NL	13	0	4.33	189	207	74	164	1.49	2
1996 Montreal NL	15	0	3.30	231	217	55	222	1.18	18

FERMIN, RAMON - TR - Age 24
It took Fermin four years to get out of A-ball, but he quickly made the jump to the majors with Oakland in 1995. Now with the Tigers, Fermin is being used in a swingman role, with disappointing results. His fastball isn't enough for him to succeed in the majors.

FERNANDEZ, ALEX - TR - Age 27
After years of showing his potential, Fernandez finally showed what that potential can translate into, in terms of wins and ERA, in 1996. And there is more good news: he is still improving as a pitcher, now that he has learned not to try and throw his fastball past the batter on every pitch.

	W	SV	ERA	IP	H	BB	SO	B / I	$
1995 Chicago AL	12	0	3.80	203	200	65	159	1.30	15
1996 Chicago AL	16	0	3.45	258	248	72	200	1.24	26

FERNANDEZ, JARED - TR - Age 25
Fernandez worked on his knuckleball in the Australian winter leagues before leading Double-A Trenton with 29 games started. Spotty results mean more minor league seasoning for Fernandez in 1997.

FERNANDEZ, OSVALDO - TR - Age 28
The Cuban refugee suffered a lot from culture shock in 1996. Fernandez' family was able to join him towards the end of the season, and as Osvaldo got acculturated, his pitching did improve. He could get a lot better in 1997.

	W	SV	ERA	IP	H	BB	SO	B / I	$
1996 San Francisco NL	7	0	4.61	171	193	57	106	1.46	0

FERNANDEZ, SID - TL - Age 34
Fernandez is a darn near unhittable hurler when healthy. He gave the Phils 11 dominant starts in 1996 before his body again failed him. He has 156 strikeouts in 128 innings as a Phil over two seasons, allowing but 145 baserunners. His 90 MPH rising fastball and mound savvy have made him one of the toughest pitchers to hit in baseball history.

	W	SV	ERA	IP	H	BB	SO	B / I	$
1995 Baltimore AL	0	0	7.39	28	36	17	31	1.89	
1995 Philadelphia NL	6	0	3.34	64	48	21	79	1.07	2
1996 Philadelphia NL	3	0	3.43	63	50	26	77	1.21	2

FESH, SEAN - TL - Age 24
Fesh had a good year in 1994 as a setup man and middle reliever for the Padres Triple-A club. He had elbow surgery in 1996, missing much of the season.

FETTERS, MIKE - TR - Age 32
Fetters finally cracked the 30 save mark and pitched well all year. Ron Villone is not ready to take over. Fetters could have been a free agent but was quickly re-signed by the Brewers.

	W	SV	ERA	IP	H	BB	SO	B/I	$
1995 Milwaukee AL	0	22	3.38	34	40	20	33	1.73	20
1996 Milwaukee AL	3	32	3.38	61	65	26	53	1.49	32

FIGUEROA, NELSON - TR - Age 22
The man with the most strikeouts (200) in the minors in 1996, the Sally League's Pitcher of the Year and ERA leader dominated hitters, finishing with a 14-7 mark and a 2.04 ERA. The strikeouts don't reveal that his strength is control more than velocity. Figueroa has an average fastball, a curve, change and a good splitter.

FINLEY, CHUCK - TL - Age 34
Angel ace Chuck Finley's 4.16 ERA of last season looks good in a rabbit-ball year. For the past four years, Finley has settled into being a .500 pitcher, and that's about what one can expect for 1997. The below-4.00 ERA's are also a thing of the past, as he last posted a below-4.00 ERA in 1993 at 3.15.

	W	SV	ERA	IP	H	BB	SO	B/I	$
1995 California AL	15	0	4.21	203	192	93	195	1.40	12
1996 California AL	15	0	4.16	238	241	94	215	1.41	15

FINNVOLD, GAR - TR - Age 29
A control pitcher, Finnvold has lost most of the last two years to a right shoulder injury. Since making eight starts for Boston in 1994, Finnvold has suffered a precipitous drop. A full recovery is necessary for Finnvold to have a remote hope of returning to the majors.

FLENER, HUCK - TL - Age 28
Flener started well but collapsed late and eventually was moved out of the starting rotation. His fastball is nothing to write home about and he needs work on keeping the ball down in the strike zone. He enters this spring training as a candidate to start.

	W	SV	ERA	IP	H	BB	SO	B/I	$
1996 Toronto AL	3	0	4.58	70	68	33	44	1.44	0

FLETCHER, PAUL - TR - Age 30
Acquired from the Phils, he had a good season at Edmonton in 1996, but not good enough.

FLORENCE, DON - TL - Age 30
Reliever Don Florence is a veteran of nine years in the minors, but he did get into 14 games with the Mets in 1995. He was even pressed into starting eight games with the Orioles Triple-A club in 1996. Overall he had a rough year, surprising because he's had some outstanding years in the top minors. Florence was involved in one of 1996's baseball oddities: the Phillies agreed to take him from the Orioles as part of the Todd Zeile trade, only to discover that the Orioles Triple-A club had released him several days before.

FLORIE, BRYCE - TR - Age 26
Florie was a starter in the minors until converted to relief in 1994. He's a slider-sinker type of pitcher looking to get ground balls.

	W	SV	ERA	IP	H	BB	SO	B/I	$
1995 San Diego NL	2	1	3.01	68	49	38	68	1.28	4
1996 San Diego NL	2	0	4.01	49	45	27	51	1.47	-
1996 Milwaukee AL	0	0	6.63	19	20	13	12	1.74	-

FLYNT, WILL - TL - Age 29
The Orioles signed Flynt out of the Mexican League to a Triple-A contract in July, 1996. He's a tall lefty who has pitched almost everywhere except in the majors, making stops in Mexico, Canada, the Netherlands and Taiwan; and before

1996, he last pitched in the United States in 1991. Flynt was released by the Triple-A team in August, but as a true baseball vagabond he'll probably surface in a baseball league somewhere in 1997.

FORDHAM, TOM - TL - Age 23
Fordham got a midseason promotion in 1995 for going 9-0 with 2.04 ERA in A-ball, and he continued doing well at Double-A. In 1996 he was a success at Triple-A, giving Nashville 10 wins against eight losses and producing a 3.45 ERA. He is not far from the White Sox rotation at this rate.

FORSTER, SCOTT - TL - Age 25
The Expos' 1994 sixth round pick places the ball well within the strike zone despite not having a predominant strikeout pitch. He allowed less than a hit per inning with only three walks per nine innings in 1996.

FORTUGNO, TIMOTHY - TL - Age 34
A hard throwing and wild lefty, Fortugno occasionally gets a chance in the majors as a mop up and lefty setup man. He's hanging on for one more shot.

FOSSAS, TONY - TL - Age 39
Yes, he's something like 76 years old now. But Fossas' job is to get lefthanded hitters out and he does it as well as anyone. At the rate he's going, he might just pitch until he is 76.

	W	SV	ERA	IP	H	BB	SO	B/I	$
1995 St. Louis NL	3	0	1.47	36	28	10	40	1.05	5
1996 St. Louis NL	0	2	2.68	47	43	21	36	1.36	2

FOSTER, KEVIN - TR - Age 28
Despite a ballooning ERA in Chicago, the Cubs expect Foster to be in the starting rotation next season. He spent much of his time at Triple-A Iowa working on keeping the ball down (he's a notorious flyball pitcher). Foster likes to throw his fastball up in the strike zone, but his best pitch is his changeup. Despite his work, Foster surrendered 16 home runs in just 87 big league innings.

	W	SV	ERA	IP	H	BB	SO	B/I	$
1995 Chicago NL	12	0	4.51	167	149	65	146	1.28	6
1996 Chicago NL	7	0	6.21	87	98	35	53	1.53	-

FOSTER, MARK - TL - Age 25
Foster, the Phils' 23th round draftee in 1993, has a mediocre fastball, average breaking pitches and below average command. He has not posted an ERA below 4.00 in his four-year pro career, but as if by reflex, his managers continue to call on him when they need a key out against a lefthanded hitter late in the game.

FOULKE, KEITH - TR - Age 24
Foulke finished up a good sophomore year as a pro with Shreveport. He again showed excellent control and essentially dominated hitters. He'll advance another level to Triple-A in 1997, and the Giants will probably be patient with him, but he looks like he very well could be the real deal.

FOX, CHAD - TR - Age 26
Acquired from the Reds for Mike Kelly, Fox owns a hard, sinking fastball and sharp curve, but has yet to perform up to expectations above Class A. Adding a slider to his repertoire helped Fox strikeout nearly a batter per inning at Triple-A Richmond. He finished the season on the disabled list with a 4.73 ERA and a 3-10 record. Fox was on the Braves' 40-man roster, so he'll get a shot at a long-relief role in the spring.

FRANCO, JOHN - TL - Age 36
With a career total well over 300 saves, the most by any lefty ever, Franco doesn't look back. He says he wants to pitch another five years and reach 400 saves. We think he can do it. His strengths are location (low) and changing speeds (his changeup flutters so much, hitters call it a screwball).

	W	SV	ERA	IP	H	BB	SO	B/I	$
1995 New York NL	5	29	2.44	51	48	17	41	1.27	29
1996 New York NL	4	28	1.83	54	54	21	48	1.39	25

FRANKLIN, RYAN - TR - Age 24
Franklin led Double-A Port City in starts, innings, strikeouts - and losses. He has good control, having consistently walked fewer than three batters per nine innings during his four years as a pro. Franklin is getting some attention from the Mariners and should start 1997 at Triple-A Tacoma with a midseason callup being a distinct possibility.

FRASCATORE, JOHN - TR - Age 27
After being drafted from C.W. Post University, Frascatore dropped some weight and added 10 MPH to his fastball. Baseball America called his fastball the best in the Cardinals' organization. Frascatore has good movement on the fastball and uses a cutter and occasional slider. He can suffer from streaks of wildness. A former starter, Frascatore moved to the pen for long relief. There was some talk that Frascatore would be the closer of the future, but after a disappointing season at Triple-A Louisville, he looks best suited for long relief.

FRASER, WILLIE - TR - Age 32
Fraser was mostly unsuccessful with a number of major league teams in parts of eight seasons. Now in Japan, he had a good record, 9-2 with a 3.15 ERA, starting with the Orix Blue Wave in the Pacific League in 1996.

FRAZIER, RON - TR - Age 28
His dream of reaching the majors as a starter gone, Frazier spent his second season as a mediocre long reliever in 1996 with the Reds' chain.

FREEHILL, MIKE - TR - Age 25
Freehill is an Angels minor league closer who had a good year in Double-A in 1996, was promoted to Triple-A, but was hammered in nine games. He strikes out lots of hitters, but doesn't have closer-type velocity. Freehill could adjust to the higher level in 1997, even getting promoted to the Angels.

FREEMAN, CHRIS - TR - Age 24
One of the better prospects in the organization, Freeman improved dramatically in his second season at Double-A. Apparently, he has settled in as a reliever. The strikeouts are nice and he might deserve a look as closer material.

FREEMAN, MARVIN - TR - Age 33
Colorado's love affair with "Mahvin" ended in 1996, as the Rockies released him in August following a number of lackluster starts. Freemen has the physical skills to be an effective pitcher, but his mental toughness is often questioned. He'll get a try with his hometown White Sox in 1997.

	W	SV	ERA	IP	H	BB	SO	B/I	$
1995 Colorado NL	3	0	5.89	94	122	41	61	1.73	-
1996 Colorado NL	7	0	6.04	129	151	57	71	1.61	-
1996 Chicago AL	0	0	13.50	2	4	1	1	2.50	-

FREY, STEVE - TL - Age 33
A well-traveled journeyman reliever who has been able to hang around the major leagues on the strength of a left arm that can throw strikes, Frey got a string of saves with the Expos a few years ago. Now he is strictly a lefty-lefty matchup specialist.

	W	SV	ERA	IP	H	BB	SO	B/I	$
1995 Seattle AL	0	0	4.76	11	16	6	7	2.34	
1995 Two NL Teams	0	1	2.12	17	10	4	7	0.82	1
1996 Philadelphia NL	0	0	4.72	34	38	18	12	1.64	-

FRIETAS, MIKE - TR - Age 27
Last year was Frietas' second in the Double-A Southern League, but he took a step backwards and had a much worse year. He's a middle reliever and setup man.

FROHWIRTH, TODD - TR - Age 34
Submariner Frohwirth is a veteran of eight major league seasons for three teams, but has recently been Triple-A roster filler. He's still a decent pitcher and would have been opportunities in a less-well-stocked farm system. Frohwirth could compete for a setup or middle relief role in the right major league situation.

FUSSELL, CHRIS - TR - Age 20
Orioles Manager Davey Johnson prides himself that when he was managing the Mets and Reds, he jumped young hard-throwing pitchers from Single-A to the majors. Fussell fits that profile, and thus he has a chance, especially if he continues to dominate minor leagues. Fussell's total minor league record is 16-6 with an eye-popping 257 strikeouts in 208 innings.

FYHRIE, MIKE - TR - Age 27
This long-time Royals farmhand came to the Mets organization in March 1996. Featuring good control and the ability to change speeds, Fyhrie went on to lead the International League in wins and was named the IL Most Valuable Pitcher. Due to modest velocity, he is still just a longshot for major league success.

GAILLARD, EDDY - TR - Age 26
Galliard's first full year in Double-A was reasonably good. He served as Jacksonville's long-relief righthander and was second on the club with nine victories. Galliard has earned a shot at Triple-A for 1997.

GALLAHER, KEVIN - TR - Age 28
After six seasons in the Astro organization, Gallaher was traded to Detroit in the Gregg Olson deal. Formerly a starter, he was relegated to middle relief in 1996, where he compiled a mediocre 4-2, 4.66 record at Triple-A Tucson. He failed in a couple of spring opportunities with the Astros but should have another chance with the Tigers.

GAMBOA, JAVIER - TR - Age 23
A sore arm sidelined Gamboa for the first part of the year, but he got a quick promotion after just six starts at Class A Wilmington. He pitched well early for Wichita, then got hit hard down the stretch. Gamboa has an above-average fastball, but needs to develop his other pitches. He may put up a few poor pitching lines while that development takes place, but you can count on Gamboa's rapid advancement once he starts showing consistency with his off-speed stuff.

GANDARILLAS, GUS - TR - Age 25
Gandarillas missed almost all of the '96 season with a broken arm. The righthander has marginal big league potential.

GARAGOZZO, KEITH - TL - Age 27
The former Yankee farmhand once pitched seven major league games for the Twins, and spent the 1996 season on the Triple-A disabled list in the Marlins' system after sitting out the entire 1995 season. The only reason anyone even calls him anymore is because he's lefthanded.

GARCES, RICH - TR - Age 25
Since his long-ago anointment as the Twins' future closer (never happened), Garces has travelled a long, winding road to reach the Red Sox' bullpen in 1996. With his fourth team in three years, Garces had his best season in years. Getting his weight under control and throwing his plus fastball for strikes earned Garces a quick promotion from Triple-A Pawtucket and he served as one of Boston's more reliable relievers over the second half. He's still a bit too heavy, but it won't matter if he keeps striking out more than eleven hitters per nine innings like he did in 1996.

	W	SV	ERA	IP	H	BB	SO	B/I	$
1995 Two Teams	0	0	4.44	24	25	11	22	1.48	-
1996 Boston AL	3	0	4.91	44	42	33	55	1.70	-

GARCIA, AL - TR - Age 22
Garcia, a solidly built righthander, followed up a 1995 season when he pitched 177 innings and finished 14-9 with a 6-7 season that found him working out of the bullpen from time to time. Garcia is just 22, but he has pitched a lot of innings for a young pitcher. He may need another year of seasoning in the minors before getting a look at the big leagues.

GARCIA, JOSE - TR - Age 24
Garcia is a side-arming, two-inning relief specialist. He had a much better year at Triple-A in 1996, his second season spent partly in Albuquerque. Garcia doesn't throw hard, so he'll have to hit spots to succeed.

GARCIA, RAMON - TR - Age 27
The White Sox liked Garcia so much in 1991, they brought him up before Wilson Alvarez. The enchantment wore off, however. Garcia was not recalled again and was released at the end of 1993. He's still young enough to succeed somewhere in the majors.

	W	SV	ERA	IP	H	BB	SO	B/I	$
1996 Milwaukee AL	4	4	6.66	75	84	21	40	1.40	2

GARDINER, MIKE - TR - Age 31
Eastern League pitcher of the year in 1990, Gardiner got a lengthy trial with the Red Sox in 1991-1992 but didn't have enough velocity or location to make it in the majors. He bounced around with the Expos and Tigers briefly and looked like a career minor leaguer until his unusually strong 1996 performance made him worthy of more consideration for the majors. He still has the full repertoire: fastball, slider, curve and change.

GARDNER, MARK - TR - Age 35
A last minute addition to the pitching staff, Gardner started 28 games for the Giants and pitched especially well before the All-Star break and his appendectomy. He was given a one-year extension on his contract as a result of his contribution.

	W	SV	ERA	IP	H	BB	SO	B/I	$
1995 Florida NL	5	1	4.49	102	109	43	87	1.49	0
1996 San Francisco NL	12	0	4.42	179	200	57	145	1.43	4

GASPAR, CADE - TR - Age 23
Out of Pepperdine University, Cade Gaspar was the Tigers top draft pick in 1994. Their best hopes where that, as a mature college pitcher, he could move into the Tigers rotation after a year in the minors. He took his lumps in Class A in 1995, and was traded to the Padres by the new Tigers management who didn't value him so highly. He was in the Single-A California League in 1996, a tough place to pitch, but he had a decent record. But Gaspar isn't making much progress towards the majors.

GENTILE, SCOTT - TR - Age 26
Thought to be on the fast track prior to 1996, Gentile lost a decent chunk of the 1996 season to injury, and was no better than the number three righty in the Expos' Double-A bullpen upon his return. The stocky Gentile throws a heavy fastball and usually records about a strikeout per inning, but no longer appears to be in the hunt for a major league bullpen role.

GIBSON, PAUL - TL - Age 37
A lefty-lefty matchup specialist who had some success with the Tigers in 1988-1991, Gibson has become the classic example of a short relief southpaw who can hang around forever.

GIVENS, BRIAN - TL - Age 31
This veteran minor leaguer was the ace of the Brewers Triple-A New Orleans franchise in 1996, collecting ten wins with a 3.02 ERA. In four starts for Milwaukee he struggled, but another chance remains possible.

GLAVINE, TOM - TL - Age 31
The majors' winningest pitcher over the last six years (1991-6 record: 106-51), Glavine was again one of baseball's top lefty starters in 1996. He throws an excellent slider that induces ground balls and requires fine infield defense behind him. He threw a few more fastballs in on hitters' hands in 1996, helping him record more strikeouts than usual. A model of consistency, Glavine will continue 1997 as the top lefty on baseball's top pitching staff.

	W	SV	ERA	IP	H	BB	SO	B/I	$
1995 Atlanta NL	16	0	3.08	198	182	66	127	1.25	17
1996 Atlanta NL	15	0	2.98	235	222	85	181	1.31	17

GOHR, GREG - TR - Age 29
Gohr was once a top Tigers prospect, but he never developed into the winning starter they hoped. He has below average stuff and command. Last year, he was a struggling starter and middle reliever with the Angels. Batters hit him for a .330 average.

	W	SV	ERA	IP	H	BB	SO	B/I	$
1995 Detroit AL	1	0	0.87	10	9	3	12	1.16	1
1996 California AL	5	1	7.24	115	163	44	75	1.80	-

GOLDEN, MATT - TR - Age 25
The Double-A Arkansas closer got 18 saves, but his 4.14 ERA in relief is a better measure of his abilities. Golden lacks a big league fastball and has to rely on off-speed stuff to get by; he's not a good prospect.

GOMES, WAYNE - TR - Age 24
The Phils have brought their 1993 first round pick along slowly, using him as a starter in 1994 and 1995 to build up arm strength, and then using him as the Double-A closer in 1996. His main attraction is a deadly curve ball, rated as the best in the Eastern League by its managers. He also has a 90-plus MPH fastball, but has trouble throwing either consistently for strike one. He has the raw ability to be a closer, but he must consistently improve his career ratio of seven walks per nine innings.

GONZALEZ, JEREMI - TR - Age 22
Gonzalez finished the 1995 season strong after a promotion to Daytona. He finished 5-1 pitching mostly out of the bullpen, and owned a 1.22 ERA. He's not a strikeout pitcher, but he can get the K when he needs it. The 22-year old was moved into a starting role with Double-A Orlando and posted good numbers in 17 games (14 starts); Gonzalez finished 6-3 with a 3.34 ERA. He's not considered a blue chip prospect, but he is young, and has been productive. The Cubs will be patient with him.

GOOCH, ARNOLD - TR - Age 19
Any teenager with success attracts attention in the pro ranks, and Gooch did that on the Mets' farm with a 2.58 ERA at Class A St. Lucie. He has a dominant curve but will need to add velocity to his mid-80's fastball to move up. At his age, there is time.

GOODEN, DWIGHT - TR - Age 32
Like we foresaw here a year ago, Gooden surprised a lot of people who thought he was washed up after off-field problems took him out of the game for all of 1995. His comeback, built on a 94-MPH fastball, that big old curveball, and a slider that he added in 1996, peaked with a no-hitter. Gooden hadn't worked a full year since 1993, however, and he was really tired by August.

	W	SV	ERA	IP	H	BB	SO	B/I	$
1995			Did Not Play						
1996 New York AL	11	0	5.01	170	169	88	126	1.51	4

GORDON, TOM - TR - Age 29
In his first year with Boston, Gordon got terrific run support on his way to a 12-9 record. He needed every bit of help he could get as he led the majors with 134 earned runs allowed and 354 baserunners. He was among the top ten in hits, runs and walks allowed in 1996. When Gordon can get his sparkling curveball over the plate he can be tough. When the first-pitch curve is called ball one, Gordon lacks the fastball necessary to get back ahead of the hitter.

	W	SV	ERA	IP	H	BB	SO	B/I	$
1995 Kansas City AL	12	0	4.43	189	204	89	119	1.55	5
1996 Boston AL	12	0	5.59	215	249	105	171	1.64	-

GRACE, MIKE - TR - Age 26
Grace has been little short of spectacular in his 14 major league starts, going 8-3 while walking only 20 hitters in 91 innings. However, the Phils are fully aware that they have a risk with his right elbow and shoulder each time he takes the mound. He has an upper-80's fastball, varies speeds and locations well, and has an excellent idea of how to pitch. He is expected to be healthy to start 1997, but remains a major injury risk.

	W	SV	ERA	IP	H	BB	SO	B/I	$
1995 Philadelphia NL	1	0	3.18	11	10	4	7	1.26	0
1996 Philadelphia NL	7	0	3.49	80	72	16	49	1.10	6

GRANGER, JEFF - TL - Age 25
In his first full year in relief, Granger finally began to look like the guy who the Royals drafted in the first round in 1993. He had both the fastball and slider working effectively at Triple-A Omaha, but was spotty in his infrequent big-league appearances. The lefty setup job appeared open in Kansas City and Granger could have it if he can only show more consistency.

GRAVES, DANNY - TR - Age 23
Graves was dominant at Triple-A Buffalo, averaging well under a hit allowed per inning, and sometimes lasting two or three innings as a closer. He was voted the best closer in the league by its managers. However, he is not your prototypical hard throwing closer. He relies on breaking stuff and location to get the job done.

GRAY, DENNIS - TL - Age 27
With 51 walks in 46 innings at Double-A Greenville, Gray has obviously not overcome the control problems that have plagued him for the last six years.

GREEN, TYLER - TR - Age 27
His confidence abandoned him during the second half of 1995, as he pitched his way out of the Phils' not-so-deep rotation. He then underwent surgery on his pitching shoulder, costing him all of 1996. Green is expected to be healthy to begin 1997, but major concerns persist. Though he might be better suited for a relief role, he just doesn't have the necessary bounce-back arm.

GREENE, RICH - TR - Age 26
A member of Team USA in 1992, Greene was the Tigers' first-round draft pick in 1992. Except for two spot starts in A-ball in 1994, he has been used exclusively in relief. Greene led Double-A Jacksonville with 30 saves in 1996, but his other numbers were not indicative of a closer: 4.98 ERA, 39 walks and 42 strikeouts in 56 innings. The Tigers will push him up the ladder, but 1997 is a make-or-break year for Greene.

GREENE, TOMMY - TR - Age 29
Greene has now been injured for most of the last three seasons, and no longer has an above average fastball. After his extended rest period, he toured the Phils' minor league system in 1996 as more of a finesse pitcher. He surprised many in the Phils' chain with his success, combining a mid-80's heater and a solid curve with career-best control.

GREER, KEN - TR - Age 29
Greer had a decent season (5-4, 3.97 in 46 games) as a setup reliever at Triple-A Calgary and the Pirates thought of calling him up. Then, they wised up. He has had trials with the New York Mets and San Francisco, proving both times he isn't a big-league pitcher.

GRIGSBY, BENJI - TR - Age 26
The Indians took a chance on the A's 1990 first round pick after he was released early in 1996. He has been plagued with arm injuries throughout his career, and he no longer has overpowering velocity. However, he threw better than he had in years as a setup man and part-time closer for Double-A Canton-Akron in 1996. Grigsby must first prove that it wasn't a mirage, and even then, could only hope for an eventual middle relief role in the majors.

GRIMSLEY, JASON - TR - Age 29
Grimsley is a former Phillie and Indian who got another chance in the majors with the Angels in 1996. He was a reliever and starter, and although he was hit pretty hard overall, he pitched two complete games including a shutout. Grimsley's a below average pitcher, and his best major league role is as a reliever or fifth starter.

	W	SV	ERA	IP	H	BB	SO	B/I	$
1995 Cleveland AL	0	1	6.09	34	37	32	25	2.03	-
1996 California AL	5	0	6.84	130	150	74	82	1.72	-

GROOM, BUDDY - TL - Age 31
Appearing in 72 games, Groom was more effective than not, especially over the first part of the season. He can no longer cut it as even a spot starter, and he lost steam towards the last couple of months of the season.

	W	SV	ERA	IP	H	BB	SO	B/I	$
1995 Detroit AL	1	1	7.52	40	55	26	23	1.99	
1995 Florida NL	1	0	7.20	15	26	6	12	2.13	-
1996 Oakland AL	5	2	3.84	77	85	34	57	1.54	4

GROSS, KEVIN - TR - Age 35
Gross began the season as the number three starter for Texas, was dropped from the rotation in midsummer, resurfaced as a successful reliever and then finished on the DL with a herniated disc in his back. For the second straight year, Gross posted bad numbers, and that, plus the back injury, casts doubt upon his future. At this point in his career, Gross is hittable, walks too many and has trouble keeping the ball in the park.

	W	SV	ERA	IP	H	BB	SO	B/I	$
1995 Texas AL	9	0	5.54	183	200	89	106	1.57	-
1996 Texas AL	11	0	5.22	129	151	50	78	1.56	2

GROSS, KIP - TR - Age 32
Gross became the first American pitcher to lead the Japanese Pacific League in victories as he won sixteen for the Nippon Ham Fighters while posting a 3.04 ERA in 1995. He had appeared briefly for the Reds and Dodgers from 1990 to 1993. Gross would be a fringe major leaguer in the States, but has apparently become a reliable starting pitcher in Japan.

GROTT, MATT - TL - Age 29
Grott spent most of his eight-year pro career in the minors, making the show for two games with the 1995 Reds. He was a starter and reliever for the Orioles Triple-A club in 1996. It's significant that the Orioles didn't call him up last summer when they badly needed bullpen help. Grott looks like a career minor leaguer.

GRUNDT, KEN - TL - Age 27
Lefty Grundt earned his big-league debut in 1996 by posting a 9-4 record in long relief at Triple-A Pawtucket. He can get a strikeout when required and can be a useful major league lefty. Grundt's one game in the bigs in 1996 won't be his last.

GRZANICH, MIKE - TR - Age 24
Grzanich has completed two full seasons as a middle reliever at the Double-A level with modest success. He was 5-4, 3.98 ERA with six saves and 80 strikeouts in 72 innings in 1996. He needs to make a strong showing in the Arizona Fall League and at Triple-A in 1997 to earn a major league opportunity.

GUARDADO, EDDIE - TL - Age 26
Last year the A-Z book recommended you keep an eye on Guardado, who led the Twins' relievers in appearances in '96. He has made steps toward being as solid a lefty reliever as you'll find.

	W	SV	ERA	IP	H	BB	SO	B/I	$
1995 Minnesota AL	4	2	5.12	91	99	45	71	1.58	1
1996 Minnesota AL	6	4	5.25	73	61	33	74	1.28	6

GUBICZA, MARK - TR - Age 34
A liner off of Paul Molitor's bat broke Gubicza's left leg and ended his season in July. It ended Gubicza's worst professional season and may signal the final round for this 13-year major league veteran. He lacks a good fastball and his breaking stuff just isn't as sharp as it needs to be. Gubicza would like to come back - and the Royals want him back.

	W	SV	ERA	IP	H	BB	SO	B/I	$
1995 Kansas City AL	12	0	3.75	213	222	62	81	1.33	15
1996 Kansas City AL	4	0	5.13	119	132	34	55	1.39	2

GUERRA, MARK - TR - Age 25
A finesse pitcher with a fastball, curve, slider and change, Guerra worked his way from the bullpen into the starting rotation on the Mets farm in 1996. He is still some distance from the majors.

GUETTERMAN, LEE - TL - Age 38
A veteran lefty who is brought in to face one or two left handed hitters, or mop up in a blowout. He relies on a sinkerball and gets into serious problems when he leaves his pitches high in the strike zone. Guetterman must have sharp control to succeed.

GUILFOYLE, MICHAEL - TL - Age 28
Advancing to Triple-A after a good '95 season at Double-A Jacksonville, Guilfoyle led Toledo with 54 appearances, all in relief. His other numbers were equally high: 5.14 ERA and 90 baserunners allowed in 49 innings. At the age of 28, Guilfoyle is a distant hope for the majors.

GUNDERSON, ERIC - TL - Age 31
Gunderson's frequent Triple-A successes and major league failures help to point out the difference between the majors and high minors. His fastball just isn't fast enough and his breaking pitches aren't sharp enough.

GUTHRIE, MARK - TL - Age 31
Guthrie posted a fine year in 1996 and expanded his role beyond that of a lefty specialist. The 73 innings pitched were

his most since 1992. He is likely to remain a set up man in 1997, with almost no chance to accumulate any saves.

	W	SV	ERA	IP	H	BB	SO	B/I	$
1995 Minnesota AL	5	0	4.46	42	47	16	48	1.49	
1995 Los Angeles NL	0	0	3.66	19	19	9	19	1.42	1
1996 Los Angeles NL	2	1	2.22	73	65	22	56	1.19	5

GUTIERREZ, JIM - TR - Age 26
Gutierrez has spent eight years in the minors and has never pitched above Double-A. His 3.76 ERA as a swingman for Jacksonville in 1996 provided no evidence that he's finally on his way up the Tigers' minor league ladder.

GUZMAN, JOSE - TR - Age 33
Guzman's second stint on the DL has probably finished him for good. He came back pretty well after missing most of two seasons after arthroscopic surgery in 1989. He had the same procedure in 1994 and just last year returned to active duty. It was a disappointing return as Guzman went 1-6 with a 8.45 ERA at Double-A Orlando, earning his release from the Cubs. He's lost a lot off his fastball.

GUZMAN, JUAN - TR - Age 30
An emergency appendectomy ended his comeback season in late August but he won the American League ERA title anyway. Guzman's fastball is back to where it was when he first came up with the Blue Jays and his control has never been better. Whether it was new pitching coach Mel Queen or the fact that Guzman realized that his stuff is dominating enough to throw down the middle, he is back.

	W	SV	ERA	IP	H	BB	SO	B/I	$
1995 Toronto AL	4	0	6.32	135	151	73	94	1.66	-
1996 Toronto AL	11	0	2.93	187	158	53	165	1.13	22

HABYAN, JOHN - TR - Age 33
Signed as a minor league free agent by the Rockies during the off-season, Habyan was lit up in limited early 1996 action, then released. He caught on with the Expos, but this middle reliever has become increasingly erratic as the years pass by.

	W	SV	ERA	IP	H	BB	SO	B/I	$
1995 St. Louis NL	3	0	2.88	40	32	15	35	1.16	
1995 California AL	1	0	4.13	32	36	12	25	1.47	5
1996 Colorado NL	1	0	7.13	24	34	14	25	2.00	-

HALAMA, JOHN - TL - Age 25
Halama was the workhorse of the Double-A Jackson staff with a 9-10 record and a 3.21 ERA. He made a successful transition to a starting role after being used as a middle reliever at the low Class-A level in 1995. He needs an impressive year at Triple-A in 1997 to get a major league opportunity.

HALE, SHANE - TL - Age 28
Orioles minor league starter Shane Hale pitched in Double-A in 1996 at age 27, somewhat old for Double-A, but he missed virtually all of 1992 and 1993 due to a serious elbow problem requiring reconstructive surgery. Hale had a poor year in Double-A in 1996, and he needs to improve quickly.

HALLADAY, ROY - TR - Age 20
With a fastball clocked in the low 90's and a knuckle-curve that has a mind of its own, Halladay is turning some heads quickly. He dominated at Single-A Dunedin with a 15-7 record and a 2.73 ERA. The Jays' first round pick from 1995, he is farther along than originally expected and could be in Toronto soon.

HALL, DARREN - TR - Age 32
After being a surprise closer in 1994, Hall was disappointing in 1996, spending a lot of time on the disabled list. He wasn't throwing hard and was wild high. He pitched only 12 innings for the Dodgers.

HALPERIN, MIKE - TL - Age 23
Making the logical progression to Double-A, he enjoyed perhaps the best season of any Knoxville pitcher. A 13-7 mark combined with a 3.48 ERA might force him to move up the ladder more quickly than expected. He's one to watch in the spring.

HAMILTON, JOEY - TR - Age 26
Hamilton has a great arm, excellent stuff and good pitching smarts, and with all that, he was expected to win big in 1996, as many as 18 or even 20 games. But shoulder soreness limited him to 15 wins, and it caused some erratic outings derailing him on the road to becoming one of the best pitchers in baseball. He pitched with an inflamed shoulder for more than a month.

	W	SV	ERA	IP	H	BB	SO	B/I	$
1995 San Diego NL	6	0	3.08	204	189	56	123	1.20	14
1996 San Diego NL	15	0	4.17	211	206	83	184	1.37	8

HAMMOND, CHRIS - TL - Age 31
A finesse pitcher who requires extreme precision to succeed, Hammond hit the wall in 1996, as his average stuff consistently caught too much of the plate. When Hammond got off to a poor start in 1996, it was obvious he was in trouble, as he has always been one of baseball's best April/May hurlers. He also has battled a succession of nagging injuries in recent seasons.

	W	SV	ERA	IP	H	BB	SO	B/I	$
1995 Florida NL	9	0	3.80	161	157	47	126	1.27	8
1996 Florida NL	5	0	6.56	81	104	27	50	1.62	-

HAMPTON, MIKE - TL - Age 24
Hampton has had two productive seasons in the Astro rotation, but was hampered by shoulder problems in 1996. Hampton is not overpowering but he throws hard enough to set up his other pitches, all of which are of major league quality. He has a promising major league career ahead of him if he can overcome his shoulder problems.

	W	SV	ERA	IP	H	BB	SO	B/I	$
1995 Houston NL	9	0	3.35	150	141	49	115	1.26	10
1996 Houston NL	10	0	3.59	160	175	49	101	1.40	6

HANCOCK, RYAN - TR - Age 25
Hancock is a former quarterback for Brigham Young University who opted for a baseball career. He is a soft tosser, much like Bob Tewksbury, and he throws lots of strikes. He showed great improvement in Triple-A in 1996, earning a promotion where he moved into Jim Abbott's rotation spot. He had some good starts and some bad ones, pitching like a typical erratic rookie. Nevertheless, Hancock could be the fifth starter for the Angels, or he may be a middle reliever.

HANEY, CHRIS - TL - Age 28
In Haney's first full year in the majors, he returned from back surgery that cut short his 1995 season to have a roller coaster campaign. The positives were career highs in nearly all pitching categories. The negatives: 29 homers and a major league leading 267 hits allowed. Haney has great control, but must get better command within the strike zone. He's a young lefty, just coming into his own, so don't be surprised if he emerges as one of the American League's best lefthanded starters in 1997 or 1998.

	W	SV	ERA	IP	H	BB	SO	B/I	$
1995 Kansas City AL	3	0	3.65	81	78	33	31	1.37	4
1996 Kansas City AL	10	0	4.70	228	267	51	115	1.39	10

HANSELL, GREG - TR - Age 26
Hansell started '96 well before fading badly in the second half. He has a major league arm but is going through an adjustment period, and as a rookie his 74 innings in '96 were probably too much.

	W	SV	ERA	IP	H	BB	SO	B/I	$
1995 Los Angeles NL	0	0	7.45	19	29	6	13	1.81	-
1996 Minnesota AL	3	3	5.69	74	83	31	46	1.54	1

HANSEN, BRENT - TR - Age 26
Hansen fought injuries and his control while splitting time between Triple-A Pawtucket and Class A Sarasota. He lost on both counts and doesn't look like a major league prospect at this point.

HANSON, ERIK - TR - Age 31
The biggest disappointment of the Toronto pitching staff, Hanson is a better pitcher than his numbers showed. The curveball was everything it needs to be and if anything betrayed Hanson, it was his lack of control. Not only were his

102 walks a career high, he had never walked seventy batters in a season and that was as far back as 1990. Expect the overall pitching line to improve and he could come back strong.

	W	SV	ERA	IP	H	BB	SO	B/I	$
1995 Boston AL	15	0	4.24	186	187	59	139	1.32	13
1996 Toronto AL	13	0	5.41	214	243	102	156	1.61	1

HARIKKALA, TIM - TR - Age 25
The soft throwing Harikkala has encountered problems with each promotion. A good season in Tacoma would have moved him into contention for a shot at the majors in 1997, but he was roughed up instead, going 8-12 with a 4.83 ERA and a 1.59 ratio.

HARKEY, MIKE - TR - Age 30
The one time Cubs starter has entered the journeyman phase of his career. The Dodgers are his fourth organization in three years, and he split his time at Albuquerque between starting and relieving. He still has the big fastball, with 90 strikeouts in 118 innings, but not much else as Triple-A hitters tagged him for a 5.38 ERA. His best year was 1990.

HARNISCH, PETE - TR - Age 30
Harnisch has great stuff: a fastball over 90 MPH and an assortment of breaking pitches. Shoulder trouble has put him on the DL and made him inconsistent since 1994, but when he has a good game it can still be spectacular.

	W	SV	ERA	IP	H	BB	SO	B/I	$
1995 New York NL	2	0	3.68	110	111	24	82	1.23	4
1996 New York NL	8	0	4.21	194	195	61	114	1.32	6

HARRIGER, DENNY - TR - Age 27
Although Harriger spent some time with the parent Padres in 1996, he spent most of the season in Triple-A where he had a so-so year as a starter. The bad news is that it was his third year in Triple-A, and he hasn't shown much improvement. Harriger was waived off the Padres 40-man roster in July, but there were no claims.

HARRIS, DOUG - TR - Age 27
Harris is a righty who filled the middle innings at Double and Triple-A in the Marlins' chain in 1996. He has great control, averaging just over two walks per nine innings over his seven year pro career, but is eminently hittable, has mediocre stuff, and has never filled a key role on any of his minor league clubs. He might linger a little longer.

HARRIS, GENE - TR - Age 32
The Pirates became something like the 21st team to give this righthanded reliever a chance to pitch in the minor leagues last season. Like so many other teams before, they learned he's really not very good. He has just about exhausted his chances.

HARRIS, GREG W. - TR - Age 33
Harris has a career 45-64 major league record with the Twins, Padres and Rockies. He signed a Padres minor league contract last season, hoping to make a comeback, but he didn't succeed.

HARRIS, PEP - TR - Age 24
Harris was formerly in the Indians farm system where he had some good years as a reliever. The Angels acquired him in the Brian Anderson contract-snafu trade, and used him as a starter in the minors. He wasn't effective in Triple-A despite having a winning 9-3 record. Harris doesn't throw hard, but could earn a bullpen job in the majors if he can continue to finesse hitters.

	W	SV	ERA	IP	H	BB	SO	B/I	$
1996 California AL	2	0	3.90	32	31	17	20	1.50	-

HARRIS, REGGIE - TR - Age 28
An extremely hard thrower, Harris led Double-A Trenton with 17 saves and fanned more than a batter per inning. However, he still walks far too many hitters and is now 28 years old. It's been the same story for his entire career: If he can harness the control of his heater, Harris can go far. Every succeeding year makes that "if" grow bigger.

HARRISON, BRIAN - TR - Age 28
Harrison had a surprisingly good year for Wichita in 1996, going 9-2 with a 3.66 ERA while serving as a swingman.

It was the best of his three seasons spent largely at Double-A. As always, Harrison had excellent control; he has walked just 62 in 371 innings over the last three years. But, in 1996 he added a strikeout dimension, fanning 80 in 118 innings. Harrison is an organizational hurler who just might get to the big leagues for a cup of coffee one day.

HARRISON, TOMMY - TR - Age 25
After advancing through three levels in 1995, Harrison went the opposite direction in 1996, getting demoted to Greenville after ten relief appearances at Richmond. He had more success, pitching primarily in the rotation at Greenville. Harrison walks too many batters for a pitcher lacking overpowering stuff; his midseason demotion marks him as less than a top prospect.

HART, JASON - TR - Age 25
A 25-year-old relief specialist, Hart appeared in 51 games for the Double-A Orlando Cubs. His 78 strikeout, 28 walk totals are impressive. He's always been around a strikeout per inning throughout his career. He was drafted out of junior college so the Cubs put him on a slow schedule but he's a tad old to be pitching in Double-A.

HARTGRAVES, DEAN - TL - Age 30
Astros manager Terry Collins took a liking to Hartgraves early in 1995 and made the long-time farmhand an integral part of his late-inning relief corps. Hartgraves proved himself capable of handling situational setup work. However, the Astros tried to sneak him back to the minors via the waiver wire and he was snatched by the Braves for their pennant drive. Hartgraves isn't great talent, but can be a useful lefty in a major league bullpen.

	W	SV	ERA	IP	H	BB	SO	B/I	$
1995 Houston NL	2	0	3.22	36	30	16	24	1.27	1
1996 Atlanta NL	1	0	4.78	37	34	23	30	1.53	-

HARVEY, BRYAN - TR - Age 33
The Angels signed Harvey, but he didn't pitch in 1996 because of an elbow problem. Harvey was one of the top closers in the game back in 1988-93, but elbow injuries have been a major problem for the past three years limiting him to 13 games over that span. Even if he comes back for the Angels, he will be a setup man for ace closer Troy Percival.

HATHAWAY, HILLY - TL - Age 27
Ex-Angel Hathaway tried to make a comeback in the Padres minors in 1996, but had elbow surgery and missed two months.

HAWBLITZEL, RYAN - TR - Age 25
Hawblitzel finally made it to the majors in 1996 - the Rockies' last expansion draft pick to do so. Unfortunately, this finesse pitcher left too many balls up in the strike zone, and he was cut loose by the Rocks at season's end.

HAWKINS, LaTROY - TR - Age 24
Hawkins tried the majors in the first half of '96 but was shelled back to Triple-A. He then pitched well the rest of the year (9-8, 3.92).

	W	SV	ERA	IP	H	BB	SO	B/I	$
1995 Minnesota AL	2	0	8.67	27	39	12	9	1.89	-
1996 Minnesota AL	1	0	8.20	26	42	9	24	1.95	-

HAYNES, JIMMY - TR - Age 24
Expected to be a junior version of Mike Mussina, Haynes was the fifth starter in the rotation when the 1996 season began. But he was a major disappointment to the Orioles. His mechanics were messed up, and he lost his confidence was sent home in September at a time when clubs were expanding their rosters with call-ups.

	W	SV	ERA	IP	H	BB	SO	B/I	$
1995 Baltimore AL	2	0	2.25	24	11	12	22	0.96	3
1996 Baltimore AL	3	1	8.29	89	122	58	65	2.02	-

HEATHCOTT, MIKE - TR - Age 27
Heathcott did much better in his second try at the Double-A level. The White Sox had given him some time at Birmingham in 1994 with bad results, but after regrouping at Class A in 1995, Heathcott returned and won 11 games for Birmingham in 1996, with a 4.02 ERA and less than a hit per inning.

HECKER, DOUG - TR - Age 26
Hecker couldn't hit enough to make it as an outfielder, so he turned to pitching in 1995. In his first full season on the mound, Hecker pitched well enough to earn a promotion to Double-A Trenton. He has a good fastball and showed a strikeout knack while posting a 3:1 strikeout-to-walk ratio. Hecker is a longshot, but his 1996 results are encouraging.

HEFLIN, BRONSON - TR - Age 25
The Phils' 1994 37th round draftee became one of the first in his draft class to make it to the majors in 1996. Heflin's success has been totally dependent on his role thus far in his pro career; when used as a closer, he is confident, and spots his average fastball on the corners at will. When used in other roles, he has pitched timidly, catching too much of the plate with his strikes and then overcompensating by nibbling around the edges of the plate. Unfortunately, his average stuff won't allow him to close in the bigs.

HELLING, RICH - TR - Age 26
Helling went to Florida in the Burkett deal. A change of scenery could do him a lot of good.

	W	SV	ERA	IP	H	BB	SO	B/I	$
1995 Texas AL	0	0	6.57	12	17	8	5	2.03	-
1996 Texas AL	1	0	7.52	20	23	9	16	1.59	-
1996 Florida NL	2	0	1.95	27	14	7	26	0.77	2

HENDERSON, KENNY - TR - Age 24
Milwaukee's number one pick in 1991, Henderson rejected the Brewers offer and instead took a scholarship to play for the Hurricanes. He did surface in Class-A in 1996.

HENDERSON, ROD - TR - Age 26
Just when it appeared that the Expos' 1992 first round pick was climbing back on the track to the majors, he suffered through a difficult Triple-A season (4-11, 5.19) in 1996. Despite his once impressive fastball/curve combination, Henderson no longer has the bite on his pitches to get the ball past higher level hitters. When he's hitting his spots precisely, Henderson can still be a difficult matchup. He just doesn't do it often enough.

HENDERSON, RYAN - TR - Age 27
Henderson had a good year at San Antonio, but is far too old to be just tasting Double-A success. He's no prospect.

HENNEMAN, MIKE - TR - Age 35
The good news: Henneman posted a career high in saves. The bad news: a bum right shoulder turned a fast start into a nightmarish finish that saw Henneman vanish from Johnny Oates' radar screen. How many closers have had 30 saves with an ERA of 5.79 for a season? Throw in an 0-7 record and you have one difficult season. Henneman was contemplating retirement at the end of the season. If he does return, setup work may be the new assignment.

	W	SV	ERA	IP	H	BB	SO	B/I	$
1995 Detroit AL	0	18	1.53	29	24	9	24	1.13	
1995 Houston NL	0	8	3.00	21	21	4	19	1.19	26
1996 Texas AL	0	31	5.79	42	41	17	34	1.38	27

HENRY, BUTCH - TL - Age 28
A promising lefty starter, Henry lost the last part of 1995 and all of 1996 to elbow surgery. Before the surgery he had control of three good pitches. If his arm is sound in 1997, Henry could be a pleasant surprise for Boston.

HENRY, DOUG - TR - Age 33
Despite getting a handful of saves and spending most of the year as the Mets' top righty reliever, Henry ended the year with mixed results. He gave new manager Bobby Valentine his first victory with a two-inning save, but on other occasions he faltered. Henry has added an assortment of pitches to his good fastball, and he could hang around the majors for years if he can just show consistency.

	W	SV	ERA	IP	H	BB	SO	B/I	$
1995 New York NL	3	4	2.96	67	48	25	62	1.09	9
1996 New York NL	2	9	4.68	75	82	36	58	1.57	4

HENRY, DWAYNE - TR - Age 35
Henry was shelled repeatedly at Triple-A in '96 in what was likely his last chance to get back to the majors.

HENTGEN, PAT - TR - Age 28
His numbers were better than Andy Pettitte in every category but wins, where he fell short by just one. After allowing the most hits and runs in the American League in 1995, Hentgen took over as the ace of the Blue Jays' staff, becoming just the second Blue Jay to win twenty games in a season (Jack Morris being the other). He opens 1997 as one of the best starting pitchers in the American League and will be hard-pressed to repeat his great season.

	W	SV	ERA	IP	H	BB	SO	B / I	$
1995 Toronto AL	10	0	5.11	200	236	90	135	1.62	-
1996 Toronto AL	20	0	3.22	265	238	94	177	1.25	29

HENTHORNE, KEVIN - TR - Age 27
One of many mature arms on the Yankee farm, Henthorne worked his way into a major league system via the Independent Texas-Louisiana League in 1995. He was successful at Double-A in 1996 (2.26 ERA)

HEREDIA, FELIX - TL - Age 20
Heredia is a wiry (6'0", 160 pounds) lefthander who got a late season trial with the Marlins last year. He has always had excellent control in the minors, and is particularly tough on lefthanded hitters. He must learn to paint the corners better. He nibbled around the edges in the majors and had to come in with his average fastball, which was hit hard. He will do battle with Yorkis Perez and Vic Darensbourg, among others, for the lefty reliever role In South Florida. He is still a baby and could mature into a top setup man.

HEREDIA, GIL - TR - Age 31
Heredia had the worst year of his career in 1996, as American League hitters hit everything he threw at them. Heredia pitched a bit better after a trip to the minors, but never found a groove all year. He'll probably get another shot to make somebody's staff.

	W	SV	ERA	IP	H	BB	SO	B / I	$
1995 Montreal NL	5	1	4.31	119	137	21	74	1.33	3
1996 Texas AL	2	1	5.89	73	91	14	43	1.44	-

HEREDIA, JULIAN - TR - Age 27
He throws hard, but Heredia had a woeful 1996 and was passed on the closer chart by the likes of Rickey Picket and Shawn Purdy. He could be make it as a setup man, but is a long shot as a closer.

HEREDIA, WILSON - TR - Age 25
Heredia was acquired by the Marlins from the Rangers late in 1995, and then spent the entire 1996 season on the major league disabled list. He has always tantalized scouts with his fastball, which is hard but straight. He also has had bouts of control trouble. Losing the season might have been a fatal blow to his career - the Marlins were in the process of converting him into a starter, and those precious innings can never be replaced. If he regains full velocity, he could crack the majors as a swingman in 1998.

HERMANSON, DUSTIN - TR - Age 24
Padre prospect Dustin Hermanson is a flame-throwing reliever with a 94-MPH fastball, a good slider and changeup. He has the stuff and mental make-up to be a top closer, but his opportunities are limited with the Padres because of incumbent closer Trevor Hoffman. Hermanson could become another Mariano Rivera, a dominating and valuable setup man.

	W	SV	ERA	IP	H	BB	SO	B / I	$
1995 San Diego NL	3	0	6.82	31	35	22	19	1.80	-
1996 San Diego NL	1	0	8.56	13	18	4	11	1.67	-

HERNANDEZ, FERNANDO - TR - Age 25
Padres starting prospect Hernandez has had two consecutive good years in the minors. Last year in Double-A, his ERA was a 4.64, but he gave up only 161 hits in 178 innings while striking out 163 and walking 85.

HERNANDEZ, JEREMY - TR - Age 30
This righthanded workhorse was a Marlins' lifesaver in early 1994, after an injury to Bryan Harvey and before the emergence of Robb Nen, before he lost a full calendar year due to a bulging disk in his neck. He showed layers of rust in his brief comeback in late 1995. He was last seen playing in Class-A in 1996 trying to make it back.

HERNANDEZ, LIVAN - TR - Age 22
The highly touted Cuban expatriate battled through an uneven first pro season in the Marlins' chain. He was racked at Triple-A, but got his mechanics and conditioning in order at Double-A Portland, and settled down to strike out better than a batter per inning. He has a mid-90's fastball and the makings of a solid breaking ball repertoire. He might need only another half season in the minors before crashing the big league rotation.

HERNANDEZ, ROBERTO - TR - Age 32
With a mid-90's fastball and a drop-off splitter, Hernandez is exactly the type of pitcher who can succeed as a major league closer. He has a resilient arm and the right mentality, too.

	W	SV	ERA	IP	H	BB	SO	B/I	$
1995 Chicago AL	3	32	3.92	59	63	28	84	1.54	32
1996 Chicago AL	6	38	1.91	84	65	38	85	1.22	46

HERNANDEZ, XAVIER - TR - Age 31
Hernandez returned to Houston in May after being released by Cincinnati. In his career, he has generally pitched well for the Astros but has done poorly with other teams. His best pitch is a forkball and if he keeps it down, he can make batters look bad. He is most effective as a setup man who gets occasional save opportunities. He should fill that role again in 1997.

	W	SV	ERA	IP	H	BB	SO	B/I	$
1995 Cincinnati NL	7	3	4.60	90	95	31	84	1.40	4
1996 Houston NL	5	6	4.62	78	77	28	81	1.35	5

HERRMANN, GARY - TL - Age 27
Herrmann didn't make it to Double-A until his fifth pro season at age 26. Herrmann is a lefthander with marginal stuff and relatively poor control who was used mainly in mop-up situations during the 1996 season. It was unlikely that Herrmann would be brought back by the Phils in 1997.

HERSHISER, OREL - TR - Age 38
Hershiser has excellent command, but his stuff is gradually fading. Hershiser has become a rather easy mark for lefthanded hitters, as he was lit up to the tune of a .314 batting average by southpaws last season. However, his penchant for escaping jams coupled with the luxury of playing for an offensive juggernaut has smoothed his decline phase considerably.

	W	SV	ERA	IP	H	BB	SO	B/I	$
1995 Cleveland AL	16	0	3.87	167	151	51	111	1.21	17
1996 Cleveland AL	15	0	4.24	206	238	58	125	1.44	12

HILJUS, ERIK - TR - Age 24
Mets' ex-prospect Hiljus lost the better par of the last two years to elbow problems. His ten starts at Double-A Arkansas featured poor control and a hittable fastball. Hiljus needs to fully recover before his progress can be measured.

HILL, KEN - TR - Age 31
Hill had a remarkably successful season as the Rangers' number one starter, posting career highs in innings, starts and strikeouts. Free of the leg woes that have plagued him in previous seasons, Hill completed seven starts, more than twice his previous high. The heavy workload, combined with Hill's tenuous control, gives cause for concern about his ability to continue to perform at this level. Hill credits an adjustment he made in late 1995 while with Cleveland for his recent resurgence.

	W	SV	ERA	IP	H	BB	SO	B/I	$
1995 St. Louis NL	6	0	5.06	110	125	45	50	1.54	
1995 Cleveland AL	4	0	3.98	74	77	32	48	1.46	4
1996 Texas AL	16	0	3.63	250	250	95	170	1.38	20

HILL, MILT - TR - Age 31
Hill attempted a comeback in Double-A in 1996 with the Orioles Double-A club where he was hittable. He's a veteran of four major league seasons, relieving for the Reds, Mariners and Braves in 1991-94. His comeback hit a setback because of his poor season.

HILLMAN, ERIC - TL - Age 30
Hillman is a tall lefty like Randy Johnson, but the resemblance ends there. Hillman is a sinker/slider pitcher who needs to keep the ball down, which he didn't do well in 1994 and then took his stuff to Japan for a workout in 1995 and 1996.

HITCHCOCK, STERLING - TL - Age 25
Despite the high ERA he managed a team high 13 wins. In 1995 as a Yankee, righthanded batters hit only .233 against him. There is a mini lesson in park effects here. Despite that, he's a potential 16-18 game winner. If Randy Johnson can come back, he'll carry Hitchcock along.

	W	SV	ERA	IP	H	BB	SO	B/I	$
1995 New York AL	11	0	4.70	168	155	68	121	1.33	9
1996 Seattle AL	13	0	5.35	196	245	73	132	1.62	2

HOFFMAN, TREVOR - TR - Age 29
Relying on a fastball with good movement, Trevor Hoffman is one of the top closers in the National League. He held opposing hitters to a .161 batting average in 1996.

	W	SV	ERA	IP	H	BB	SO	B/I	$
1995 San Diego NL	7	31	3.88	53	48	14	52	1.17	31
1996 San Diego NL	9	42	2.25	88	50	31	111	0.92	45

HOLDRIDGE, DAVID - TR - Age 28
Holdridge was a middle reliever for the Angels Triple-A club in 1996, posting a modest record.

HOLLINGER, ADRIAN - TR - Age 26
Hollinger is an Angels minor league middle reliever who had a good record in Single-A in 1996, but he found the going a little tougher in Double-A. He appeared in only 13 games in Double-A, with a so-so record, and he should be back in Double-A in 1997.

HOLLINS, STACY - TR - Age 24
After progressing well over the first four years of his career, Hollins took a step back in 1996, returning to Huntsville for an up-and-down year. Time is getting short.

HOLLIS, RON - TR - Age 23
By midseason in 1996, Hollis had jumped to Double-A and established himself as a reliable setup man in the bullpen. While Hollis isn't considered a top prospect, he'll get a long look this spring for a major league relief role.

HOLMAN, CRAIG - TR - Age 28
Casual minor league observers might take note of Holman's 6-1, 3.50, mark at Double-A Reading and conclude that he is a real major league prospect. In reality, Holman is a six-year pro journeyman with a Single-A fastball who had not pitched in a major role since 1993.

HOLMAN, SHAWN - TR - Age 32
Holman has kicked around the minor leagues and the Mexican League for 12 seasons while making only five major league appearances in relief with Detroit in 1989. He is actually a good pitcher who was usually in the wrong place at the wrong time. Now, he is content to finish up his career pitching under contract to the Pirates in the Mexican League for the Mexico City Reds.

HOLMES, DARREN - TR - Age 30
This former Rockies save leader alternated as a middle reliever and setup man in 1996. He has a devastating overhand curve, but when he leaves it up in the strike zone at high altitude, prodigious blasts often result. Holmes wants a shot at the starting rotation in 1997.

	W	SV	ERA	IP	H	BB	SO	B/I	$
1995 Colorado NL	6	14	3.24	66	59	28	61	1.31	16
1996 Colorado NL	5	1	3.97	77	78	28	73	1.38	2

HOLT, CHRIS - TR - Age 25
Holt is a big righthander who has moved steadily up through the Astro system in his five year career. His strong point is control, maintaining a strikeout to walk ratio over 3.35 for his career. In the 1996 Baseball America poll, he was

named the best control pitcher in the Pacific Coast League. After a 9-6, 3.62 season at Triple-A, he was called up to Houston for the final month where he appeared in only four games, all in relief. He should be a candidate for a spot in the starting rotation in 1997.

HOLTZ, MIKE - TL - Age 24
Holtz is a small lefty one would not think is a strikeout pitcher. Nevertheless, he has always struck out an average of more than one hitter per inning. With the Angels, he held opponents to a .204 batting average in 1996, and he should be a steady setup man in the bullpen for years to come.

	W	SV	ERA	IP	H	BB	SO	B/I	$
1996 California AL	3	0	2.45	29	21	19	31	1.37	1

HOLZEMER, MARK - TL - Age 27
Holzemer is a southpaw reliever who spent some time with the Angels over the past three years with a poor record.

HONEYCUTT, RICK - TL - Age 42
Honeycutt was the oldest player in the major leagues last season but he had a fine season in his first year with the Cardinals. He can still get lefties out. As long as he does that, he can pitch until he's 60. A thought: Do Honeycutt and Tony Fossas sit in the Cardinals' bullpen and think back to pitching at the Polo Grounds?

	W	SV	ERA	IP	H	BB	SO	B/I	$
1995 Two Teams	5	2	2.96	45	39	10	21	1.08	8
1996 St. Louis NL	2	4	2.85	47	42	7	30	1.04	5

HOOK, CHRIS - TR - Age 28
A righthander bullpen specialist who held lefties to a .210 average and managed five wins, but righties clubbed him, suggesting he will never rise above the specialist stage of his career.

HOPE, JOHN - TR - Age 26
Hope got his third crack at the major leagues early last season. The Pirates put him into the starting rotation and he bombed again. He once was a fine prospect but shoulder and elbow operations have taken his ability.

HORSMAN, VINCE - TL - Age 30
He will be thirty on Opening Day and is now just hanging on. After a disappointing 1995 season with the Twins (and with Triple-A Salt Lake), Horsman caught on with the organization from which he was originally developed. His fastball is ordinary and his Triple-A numbers in 1996 could have been even worse. He might be better off with an organization that lacks lefthanded pitching prospects.

HOSTETLER, MARCUS - TR - Age 27
Hostetler is a submarining reliever in the Orioles farm system. He spent 1993-95 in the Braves system. He switched to throwing submarine last June, and became much more effective, especially against right handed batters.

HOSTETLER, MIKE - TR - Age 26
Overcoming elbow ligament replacement in his right arm, Hostetler has made steady progress, reaching Triple-A Richmond in 1996, where he went 11-9 with a 4.38 ERA and a 2-to-1 strikeout-to-walk ratio. Hostetler still has some work to do before he's ready for Atlanta's rotation.

HOWE, STEVE - TL - Age 39
It is unlikely that Howe will ever pitch in the majors again. His poor record in 1996 was a circular problem: he wasn't sharp because he didn't get enough work, and he wasn't used frequently because his performances were erratic.

HOWRY, BOBBY - TR - Age 23
Howry got good run support and as a result sniffed out ten wins for Double-A Shreveport in 1996. He is not a strikeout pitcher so he has to be in total command. He is only 23, and could become a big league starter, but there are a lot of other youngsters ahead of him. He's worth keeping an eye on.

HUBBS, DAN - TR - Age 27
As expected, Hubbs moved up to Triple-A Albuquerque in a setup role. He's an older prospect, but has had pretty good results as a hard-throwing control pitcher. Hubbs will have a shot at a major league bullpen job in 1997.

HUDEK, JOHN - TR - Age 30
With a high-velocity fastball -- and not much else -- Hudek went from Triple-A Tucson to the top of the Astros bullpen corps in just a few weeks. But the fastball eventually deserted him, and then a rib injury put Hudek on the comeback trail.

	W	SV	ERA	IP	H	BB	SO	B/I	$
1995 Houston NL	2	7	5.40	20	19	5	29	1.20	6
1996 Houston NL	2	2	2.81	16	12	5	14	1.06	1

HUDSON, JOE - TR - Age 26
Hudson's command wasn't as good in 1996, although he managed to spend a significant amount of time in Boston's bullpen. A steady long-reliever who doesn't throw hard, Hudson is a tenth or eleventh man on a major league staff.

	W	SV	ERA	IP	H	BB	SO	B/I	$
1995 Boston AL	0	1	4.11	46	53	23	29	1.65	-
1996 Boston AL	3	1	5.40	45	57	32	19	1.98	-

HUISMAN, RICK - TR - Age 27
Huisman split 1996 between Triple-A Omaha and Kansas City, being used similarly at both sites. He's a middle-innings guy with a good fastball that's just too straight to throw past big-league hitters. Huisman will be in the hunt for a bullpen job in 1997.

	W	SV	ERA	IP	H	BB	SO	B/I	$
1996 Kansas City AL	2	1	4.60	29	25	18	23	1.48	-

HUMPHREY, RICH - TR - Age 25
Humphrey, who has never started a game in his four year career, pitched at three levels in 1996. He pitched well at Double-A but was hit hard at Triple-A. A 57th round draft choice in 1993, he has not established credentials as a prospect.

HUNTER, RICH - TR - Age 22
The worst thing that this top Phils' starting pitcher prospect could have done was pitch extremely well in spring training and make the Phils' rotation at the outset of the 1996 season. He was not ready. With a fastball topping out in the mid-80's plus a curveball and an excellent changeup, Hunter needs pinpoint precision to be effective.

	W	SV	ERA	IP	H	BB	SO	B/I	$
1996 Philadelphia NL	3	0	6.49	69	84	33	32	1.69	-

HURST, BILL - TR - Age 26
Hurst was the Marlins' Double-A closer, but he was not as effective as his save total might indicate. He is an imposing 6'7", 215 pound presence who is tough on righties, but his control is poor. He is likely to remain a minor league closer in the short term, but has little chance of cracking the major league fraternity.

HURTADO, EDWIN - TR - Age 27
Hurtado started four games with the Mariners, and also appeared in relief. One of the players acquired from Toronto for Bill Risley, Hurtado may stick in middle relief in 1997. He features a fair cut fastball, curve, slider and splitter.

	W	SV	ERA	IP	H	BB	SO	B/I	$
1995 Toronto AL	5	0	5.45	77	81	40	33	1.56	-
1996 Seattle AL	2	2	7.74	47	61	30	36	1.93	-

HURTADO, VICTOR - TL - Age 19
Hurtado had an extremely promising initial full season in the minors at Low-A Kane County in 1996, ranking among Midwest League leaders in wins, innings and complete games. He is rail-thin at 6'2", 170 pounds and should add more power to his repertoire as he physically develops. His standing as one of the youngest full season pitchers in the pros last season also works in his favor. Hurtado is a candidate for a major breakout season, beginning at High-A Brevard County, in 1997.

HUTCHESON, DAVID - TR - Age 25
Hutcheson can be dominating when he's on. The University of South Florida graduate led the Florida State League with a 13-5 record and three shutouts with Daytona in 1994, including a no-hitter that season. Since then, he has been inconsistent. He went 8-10 with an ERA over four in 1995 with Double-A Orlando and pitched just 19 games, 13 starts,

with Orlando in 1996. He's not a true power pitcher, but he is not Bob Tewksbury either. His promising season of 1994 is now three years removed, Hutcheson needs to put together a healthy, productive 1997.

HUTTON, MARK - TR - Age 27
After years of rumor and innuendo, the Yankees finally traded Hutton, dealing him to the Marlins in exchange for David Weathers. Though Hutton possesses above average velocity on his fastball, its lack of movement prevents him from being classified as a true power pitcher. He had not been an effective minor league starter since 1993, but fared well in his one trip around the National League in 1996.

	W	SV	ERA	IP	H	BB	SO	B/I	$
1996 New York AL	0	0	5.04	30	32	18	25	1.66	-
1996 Florida NL	5	0	3.67	56	47	18	31	1.16	3

HYDE, RICH - TR - Age 27
He'll be 28 on Christmas Eve and he is still struggling to master Double-A pitching.

ILSLEY, BLAISE - TL - Age 32
This 12-year minor league vet has now pitched 1462 minor league innings, but only ten in the majors. There is a reason for this - Ilsely has not allowed less than a hit per inning since the 1987 season, when Reagan was President and Larry Sheets hit 30 homers. His style has always been simple - throw low strikes and hope the ball gets hit at someone.

INGRAM, TODD - TR - Age 29
Ingram had a rough year pitching for the Angels Double-A club in 1996. Previously, he was in the Oakland system where he also struggled in Double-A. Obviously, he has some things to overcome if he is to move up. At age 28 in 1996, Ingram was older than his Double-A peers, and time is about to run out on him.

ISRINGHAUSEN, JASON - TR - Age 24
With a sharp curve that he can throw to precise spots, Isringhausen burst onto the major league scene in 1995 with surprising success. It was natural that batters would do better after getting a long look at him, but high expectations made Isringhausen's season were disappointing. With less preseason pressure, he should do better in 1997 than he did in '96.

	W	SV	ERA	IP	H	BB	SO	B/I	$
1995 New York NL	9	0	2.81	93	88	31	55	1.28	8
1996 New York NL	6	0	4.77	171	190	73	114	1.54	-

STATS, INC.
Minor League Handbook - 1997

The most complete career minor league statistics

Bill James' major league equivalencies

Minor league leader board

Stadium pitching and hitting data

See order form inside the back cover for more details

JACKSON, DANNY - TL - Age 35
The move the Cardinals made in signing Jackson to a three-year contract prior to the 1995 has turned out to be a disaster. First, Jackson had to overcome thyroid cancer at the start of '95 then had his season curtailed by a severe ankle sprain. The ankle still bothered him through much of '96 and left him as a high-paid long reliever. Jackson has as much courage as anyone in the game, though, and will likely come back to have a solid season as a starter in 1997.

	W	SV	ERA	IP	H	BB	SO	B/I	$
1995 St. Louis NL	2	0	5.90	100	120	48	52	1.68	-
1996 St. Louis NL	1	0	4.46	36	33	16	27	1.36	-

JACKSON, MIKE - TR - Age 32
Jackson is always on the verge of becoming a closer. He's slightly fragile but has an excellent fastball and hard slider. He did get six saves in 1996 and picked up the slack when Charlton faltered.

	W	SV	ERA	IP	H	BB	SO	B/I	$
1995 Cincinnati NL	6	2	2.39	49	38	19	41	1.16	7
1996 Seattle AL	1	6	3.63	72	61	24	70	1.18	9

JACOBS, RYAN - TL - Age 23
Adding a slider and a curve to his fastball/changeup repertoire earned Jacobs a place on Atlanta's 40-man roster last spring. He might lose that spot after a 3-9, 6.68 showing in 1996, however. Jacobs never had command of any pitch and was routinely roughed up in 21 starts at Greenville. At age 22, this lefthander will have to fully recover all of his pitches to continue his climb to Atlanta.

JACOBSEN, JOE - TR - Age 25
Jacobsen was lost by the Dodgers in the Rule Five draft but later returned. He had a reasonably good year at Double-A San Antonio in 1996, collecting five saves as a righthanded setup man. Jacobsen has a chance to reach the majors as a bullpen righty.

JACOME, JASON - TL - Age 26
As expected, Jacome's sub-par fastball was not enough for him to remain in the starting rotation. But, once shifted to the bullpen, Jacome was reborn as a situational lefty reliever. His 2.47 relief ERA in 1996 gives Jacome the edge as the Royals' lefty setup reliever in 1997. The question remains, however: How long can Jacome get by with just an 83-MPH fastball?

	W	SV	ERA	IP	H	BB	SO	B/I	$
1995 New York NL	0	0	10.29	21	33	15	11	2.29	-
1995 Kansas City AL	4	0	5.36	84	101	21	39	1.45	-
1996 Kansas City AL	0	1	4.72	47	67	22	32	1.89	-

JAMES, MIKE - TR - Age 29
After toiling in the minors for seven years, Angels setup reliever Mike James finally got his chance in 1995, and he came through with an excellent season. In 1996, he showed that 1995 wasn't a fluke. James' best pitch is a fastball with good movement.

	W	SV	ERA	IP	H	BB	SO	B/I	$
1995 California AL	3	1	3.88	55	49	26	36	1.36	3
1996 California AL	5	1	2.67	81	62	42	65	1.28	8

JANICKI, PETE - TR - Age 26
Janicki was the Angels' first round pick in 1992, selected 8th overall. He's had elbow ailments for several years slowing his progress. He has a good arm and excellent stuff, but he had a rough year in Triple-A in 1996, and was demoted to Double-A in July. Nevertheless, Janicki could put things together quickly to become an effective major league pitcher.

JANZEN, MARTY - TR - Age 23
Janzen, like Huck Flener, started exceptionally well and then fizzled after being inserted into the Blue Jays' rotation. He has a decent fastball but needs more time in the minor leagues. The key player in the deal that sent David Cone to the Yankees in 1995, Janzen goes into spring training trying to land a spot as either a fifth starter or long reliever.

	W	SV	ERA	IP	H	BB	SO	B/I	$
1996 Toronto AL	4	0	7.33	73	95	38	47	1.82	-

Benson's Baseball Player Guide: 1997

JARVIS, KEVIN - TR - Age 27
After racing through the minors in three years, Jarvis has struggled at the major league level the last three seasons. He pitched well in spots in 1996, but his performance deteriorated to such an extent that the Reds were talking of trading him at the end of the season. He features the standard four pitches and has shown good control in the minors, but 17 home runs allowed in 120 innings and a low strikeout rate suggest he is not much of a prospect at this time. He should be back for the fifth starter battle for 1997.

	W	SV	ERA	IP	H	BB	SO	B/I	$
1995 Cincinnati NL	3	0	5.70	79	91	32	33	1.56	-
1996 Cincinnati NL	8	0	5.98	120	152	43	63	1.62	-

JARVIS, MATT - TL - Age 25
Jarvis is a starter in the Orioles minor league system. He didn't pitch much for them in 1996.

JEAN, DOMINGO - TR - Age 28
This former Yankee phenom was converted to a closer by the Reds, and he led the Southern League in saves with 33. However, his peripheral stats were not that impressive (17 walks in 39.2 innings, 4.08 ERA) and he was pounded in a brief stint at Triple-A.

JIMINEZ, MIGUEL - TR - Age 27
Jimenez is too old to be pitching in Single-A, which is where he started the year. He was promoted to Huntsville in 1996, but got hammered there.

JOHNS, DOUG - TL - Age 29
Johns began the season as the most effective Oakland starter, but that dissipated and he struggled, finally landing in the bull pen. He is not overpowering and his control is also suspect.

	W	SV	ERA	IP	H	BB	SO	B/I	$
1995 Oakland AL	5	0	4.61	54	44	26	25	1.29	3
1996 Oakland AL	6	1	5.98	158	187	69	71	1.62	-

JOHNSON, DANE - TR - Age 34
A minor league journeyman, Johnson pitched in the Toronto bullpen in September, hoping to make a lasting impression for 1997. Immediately after the season ended, he was placed on waivers and claimed by Oakland. A hard thrower at times, Johnson is competing for a spot in the major league bullpen.

JOHNSON, JONATHAN - TR - Age 22
The seventh pick overall in the 1995 draft, Johnson looks like the real thing. After only 33 professional starts, it's wise not to get too carried away, but Johnson has good control of his fastball and a first-rate curve. Johnson is not overpowering and doesn't have eye-popping K/BB ratios, but he really knows how to pitch.

JOHNSON, RANDY - TL - Age 33
Let's hope he can make it all the way back. A gangly 6'10" guy with a bad back is a real concern. Keep your fingers crossed.

	W	SV	ERA	IP	H	BB	SO	B/I	$
1995 Seattle AL	18	0	2.48	214	159	65	294	1.05	33
1996 Seattle AL	5	1	3.67	61	48	25	85	1.19	5

JOHNSTONE, JOHN - TR - Age 28
Johnstone is a hard thrower who had a chance with the Astros in 1996 but didn't deliver. He pitched well at Triple-A Tucson (3-3, 3.42 ERA, five saves, 70 strikeouts in 55 innings). He also failed in three previous years with Florida before missing most of the 1995 season with an injury. He could get another major league opportunity as a middle reliever.

JONES, BARRY - TR - Age 34
Jones got thrashed in the bigs a few years back, although he continues to impress whenever demoted to the minors. Last seen in independent ball in 1996.

JONES, BOBBY - TL - Age 24
Not to be confused with the Mets starter of the same name, this former starter spent all of 1996 at Triple-A Colorado Springs, primarily as a middle reliever. He led the team in appearances, but sported a ratio of almost 1.7.

JONES, BOBBY - TR - Age 27
The Mets continue to get good work out of Jones, who began the 1996 season without sharp command but settled down as the season wore on. Jones is a good pitcher, just not a great one. His main asset is poise on the mound; when he has good command his smarts and large repertoire can work wonders.

	W	SV	ERA	IP	H	BB	SO	B / I	$
1995 New York NL	10	0	4.19	195	209	53	127	1.33	6
1996 New York NL	12	0	4.42	195	219	46	116	1.36	6

JONES, DOUG - TR - Age 39
Jones wasn't a closer for the Brewers, but he's not washed up. Phil Garner realizes Jones needs frequent work to stay sharp. If he goes to another team he could close, or he could sit, get rusty and become ineffective. He's still worth watching.

	W	SV	ERA	IP	H	BB	SO	B / I	$
1995 Baltimore AL	0	22	5.01	46	55	16	42	1.52	19
1996 Chicago NL	2	2	5.01	32	41	7	26	1.50	-
1996 Milwaukee AL	5	1	3.41	31	31	13	34	1.41	2

JONES, STACY - TR - Age 29
Jones had some fun with the kids, in 27 games at Double-A Birmingham on the White Sox farm in 1996. Jones recorded 14 saves and a 2.57 ERA, and had a five to one strikeout/walk ratio.

JONES, TODD - TR - Age 28
With a mid nineties fastball and the menacing look of a closer, Jones has had numerous opportunities to establish himself in this role but has failed to do so. Part of his problem in 1996 was due to a shoulder which put him on the disabled list on two occasions. The problem is not believed to be serious and Jones has a good chance to be physically sound in 1997. However, a question remains as to whether he has the mental makeup required for a closer.

	W	SV	ERA	IP	H	BB	SO	B / I	$
1995 Houston NL	6	15	3.07	99	89	52	96	1.41	17
1996 Houston NL	6	17	4.40	57	61	32	44	1.63	12

JORDAN, RICARDO - TL - Age 26
Jordan was one of the Phillies' few bright spots in 1996, as he rose from the minors to become the Phils' top lefthanded setup man during the second half. Jordan's best pitch is clearly his 90 MPH fastball, which is particularly tough on lefties, whom he held to a .152 average in 1996. Jordan's Achilles heel has always been control.

	W	SV	ERA	IP	H	BB	SO	B / I	$
1995 Toronto AL	1	1	6.60	15	18	13	10	2.02	-
1996 Philadelphia NL	2	0	1.80	25	18	12	17	1.20	0

JUDEN, JEFF - TR - Age 26
The big righthander has been a major disappointment with Houston, Philadelphia and San Francisco. However, Montreal has been known to be a haven for guys on their last chance. The Expos took a liking to Juden after acquiring him from San Francisco late last July. They sent him to winter ball to be a closer and he could be first in line for the job if the Expos don't re-sign Mel Rojas. The conditions are ripe for Juden to finally blossom.

	W	SV	ERA	IP	H	BB	SO	B / I	$
1995 Philadelphia NL	2	0	4.02	62	53	31	47	1.34	1
1996 Montreal NL	5	0	3.27	74	61	34	61	1.28	3

JUELSGAARD, JAROD - TR - Age 29
Juelsgaard has now spent six years in the no-man's land of minor league pitching staffs - middle relief. He is a breaking ball pitcher with below average power and control, who is useful only because of his ability to eat up two to three innings out of the bullpen, sometimes on consecutive days.

KAMIENIECKI, SCOTT - TR - Age 32
For years Kamieniecki got by with his standard four-pitch repertoire, often beginning a season in the bullpen and then joining the starting rotation when someone else got hurt. In 1996 he never got on track and lost his hold on a major league roster spot.

	W	SV	ERA	IP	H	BB	SO	B/I	$
1995 New York AL	7	0	4.01	89	83	49	43	1.48	4
1996 New York AL	1	0	11.12	22	36	19	15	2.48	-

KARCHNER, MATT - TR - Age 29
A sinker slider pitcher who simply throws strikes to get the ball in play, Karchner collected his seven wins all in relief in 1996. He was better during the first half of the year when he kept his pitches down more consistently.

	W	SV	ERA	IP	H	BB	SO	B/I	$
1995 Chicago AL	4	0	1.69	32	33	12	24	1.41	3
1996 Chicago AL	7	1	5.76	59	61	41	46	1.73	-

KARL, SCOTT - TL - Age 25
Karl is ready for a spot in the rotation. The Brewers have eased him along in middle relief and spot starting for a couple years, but he was a starter in the minors and one of the Brewers Arizona Fall League candidates in 1994. He's not overpowering, but has a veteran's poise.

	W	SV	ERA	IP	H	BB	SO	B/I	$
1995 Milwaukee AL	6	0	4.14	124	141	50	59	1.54	3
1996 Milwaukee AL	13	0	4.86	207	220	72	121	1.41	9

KARP, RYAN - TL - Age 26
Karp is a curveballing lefty who spent the bulk of the 1996 season on the disabled list with arm trouble. He knows how to pitch. He varies speed and location well, and posts decent strikeout totals for a hurler without a single overpowering pitch.

KARSAY, STEVE - TR - Age 25
Karsay missed the entire 1995 season due to injury. He was a good pitcher before the injuries. He went to Class-A in 1996 to start his comeback, after he failed to fully recover from elbow surgery. He started 1996 in spring training, but his recovery was slower than expected.

KAUFMAN, BRAD - TR - Age 24
Kaufman had an excellent year in the Double-A Southern League in 1996, but it was his second season in the league. His ERA and other key pitching statistics were good, and he could be in the Padres rotation in 1997 or '98.

KEAGLE, GREG - TR - Age 25
A Rule Five draftee from the Mariners, Keagle was hit hard with the Tigers in 1996. His marginal stuff has been routinely bashed by hitters above A-ball. Keagle is not likely to remain in the majors for long.

	W	SV	ERA	IP	H	BB	SO	B/I	$
1996 Detroit AL	3	0	7.39	87	104	68	70	1.97	-

KELING, KOREY - TR - Age 28
Last year was Keling's third year in Double-A, but it was his worst, a major setback in his progress, and he was even sent back to Class-A in June. Older than his minor league peers, Keling is no prospect.

KELLY, JOHN - TR - Age 29
Before being tried in a starting role for Double-A Jacksonville in 1996, Kelly had wracked up 153 saves in six pro seasons in the Cardinals' and Tigers' farm systems. He lacks the velocity necessary to advance to the majors.

KERSHNER, JASON - TL - Age 20
The Phils' 1995 12th round pick came out of nowhere to strike out nearly a batter per inning with solid control as one of the youngest pitchers in the Low-A South Atlantic League. He relies heavily on his 90 MPH heater which has the sharp movement typical of a lefty. He could really be scary once his 6'2", 160-pound body develops. His location within the strike zone could be better, and he tends to struggle with runners on base.

KESTER, TIM - TR - Age 25
Kester spent most of the 1996 season as a middle reliever at Double-A (2-4, 3.73, one save). He was hit hard in one start at Triple-A. Kester has had remarkable control in his four year career (86 walks and 321 strikeouts in 497 innings). However, he does not appear to have enough in his arsenal to retire major league hitters.

KEY, JIMMY - TL - Age 35
Still the master craftsman at changing speeds with fine control, Key pitched some magnificent games in 1996. He also had recurring trouble with his shoulder early in the season (when no one but Key thought he should have been pitching, anyway). By year-end he looked fine and poised for a good 1997 season.

	W	SV	ERA	IP	H	BB	SO	B/I	$
1995 New York AL	1	0	5.64	30	40	6	14	1.53	-
1996 New York AL	12	0	4.68	169	171	58	116	1.35	9

KEYSER, BRIAN - TR - Age 30
Once given ten starts when the White Sox were desperate for rotation help, Keyser was back in the pen, where he belongs, in 1996. Lacking big velocity, he needs to hit precise locations and move the ball around to be successful. The walks indicate his failure.

	W	SV	ERA	IP	H	BB	SO	B/I	$
1995 Chicago AL	5	0	4.97	92	114	27	48	1.53	1
1996 Chicago AL	1	1	4.98	59	78	28	19	1.79	-

KIEFER, MARK - TR - Age 28
Once a highly regarded prospect with the Brewers, Kiefer never really developed to a major league level and was released by the Brewers. He finished the year as a swingman at Triple-A Omaha and his chances of returning to the majors are dimmer than ever.

KILE, DARRYL - TR - Age 28
Kile made a strong comeback in 1996 after two disappointing seasons. Possessor of one of the best curve balls in the major leagues, Kile had good command of it through most of the 1996 season. He also has a mid-nineties fastball and with these tools he has the potential for putting together a monster season. His biggest problems in the past have been with control and a loss of self confidence. However, these lapses were less frequent in 1996 and he could be on the verge of moving his career to another level.

	W	SV	ERA	IP	H	BB	SO	B/I	$
1995 Houston NL	4	0	4.96	127	114	73	113	1.47	-
1996 Houston NL	12	0	4.19	219	233	97	219	1.51	4

KILGO, RUSTY - TL - Age 30
Southpaw reliever Rusty Kilgo pitched in Double-A and Triple-A in 1994-95, but he took a step backwards in 1996 pitching in Double-A again, this time for the Padres. He had a decent year, but at age 30, he's much older than his peers, and he has little chance of making the majors.

KIRKREIT, DARON - TR - Age 24
The Indians' 1993 number one pick took some baby steps back from serious arm problems with six highly professional starts late in 1996 for High-A Kinston. Formerly a hard thrower, Kirkreit will now need to rely more on control and location to advance. He does have a diverse repertoire, and a 6'6", 225-pound frame, so there is still hope.

KLINE, STEVE - TL - Age 24
The Indians' 1993 eighth-round pick has not been the same pitcher since missing a healthy chunk of the 1995 season with elbow trouble. The southpaw's velocity is poor, and his strikes catch too much of the plate. Kline is getting a little old for a prospect yet to taste Double-A success. He is a lefty, so he could have a chance for advancement as a situational reliever if he improves his command.

KLINGENBECK, SCOTT - TR - Age 26
Klingenbeck complained about his lack of use during his time in Minnesota this summer, desiring to start despite repeatedly being shelled. He is a fringe major leaguer.

Benson's Baseball Player Guide: 1997

	W	SV	ERA	IP	H	BB	SO	B/I	$
1995 Baltimore-Minnesota AL	2	0	7.12	79	101	42	42	1.79	-
1996 Minnesota AL	1	0	7.85	28	42	10	15	1.84	-

KLINK, JOE - TL - Age 35
Klink made a cameo appearance with Seattle in 1996. He can still be tough on lefty batters.

KNACKERT, BRENT - TR - Age 27
Ten years as a pro have produced just 34 major league innings for Knackert. Repeated elbow injuries took their toll early in his career and now he has below-average stuff. The Red Sox have much better prospects for all pitching roles; Knackert will have to change organizations again to get back to the big leagues.

KNOLL, RANDY - TR - Age 20
He throws an upper-80's fastball plus an assortment of offspeed stuff, and locates all of his pitches precisely. South Atlantic League managers recognized him as the having the circuit's best control. The 6'4", 190-pound righty should add velocity as he matures. He has jumped on the fast track to the majors, and could show up in Philly late in 1998.

KNUDSEN, KURT - TR - Age 30
Knudsen has below average stuff and hasn't been effective in his brief major league appearances, despite seven saves for the Tigers from 1992 to 1994. He can get Triple-A hitters out, but can't get his pitches past big league hitters. It's unlikely that he'll get another chance in the majors. He was playing out the string in independent ball.

KOLB, DANNY - TR - Age 22
Kolb is an imposing figure on the mound at 6'4" 185 pounds. He needs to cut down on the walks and avoid the injuries, and will start the year at A Charlotte. He's a hard throwing righthander who will be a good major league pitcher if he can learn to throw strikes.

KOLLER, JERRY - TR - Age 24
Koller's third straight season in Double-A was his worst. He went 2-10 with a 5.50 ERA in 13 starts at Greenville before being placed on the temporary inactive list. After seven pro seasons, Koller's future as a pitcher is in serious jeopardy.

KONIECZKI, DOM - TL - Age 27
Every club needs a few lefthanders in the bullpen and Konieczki is a lefty. But that's about his only qualification for pro ball. He lacks major league stuff or control. Konieczki is minor league roster filler.

KONUSZEWSKI, DENNIS - TR - Age 26
This guy actually pitched in a major league game for the Pirates in 1995. Konuszewski, who had a 6.30 ERA in 32 games at Double-A Carolina in 1996, is living proof of the old adage of how some things in life can't be explained.

KOPPE, CLINT - TR - Age 23
The Reds' 1994 sixth round draftee has the look of a power pitcher at 6'4", 220, but instead relies on pinpoint control, ranked the best in the High-A Carolina League in 1996. A major red flag was his ability to strike out only 46 batters in 1996.

KRAMER, TOM - TR - Age 29
Kramer joined the Rockies from the Cincinnati organization, and divided his time between starting and long/middle relief at Triple-A Colorado Springs. He has a better than average fastball, but needs stronger breaking and off-speed stuff to improve.

KRIVDA, RICK - TL - Age 27
Krivda's 1996 season was an up-and-down year between the majors and minors, but he gained a great deal of respect by pitching the Orioles to a crucial victory at the end of the year. Pencil him in as the fifth starter for 1997, but if he's ineffective, he could lose the job. Krivda is basically a finesse pitcher with average stuff.

	W	SV	ERA	IP	H	BB	SO	B/I	$
1995 Baltimore AL	2	0	4.54	75	76	25	53	1.34	2
1996 Baltimore AL	3	0	4.96	81	89	39	54	1.58	-

KROON, MARC - TR - Age 23
Kroon is a top Padres pitching prospect who was converted to a closer in 1996 in Double-A. He has an outstanding 95-MPH fastball, and he's added a breaking ball and a changeup. He could be in the Padres bullpen some time in 1997, but his progress to the majors was slowed in 1996 by tearing ligaments in his thumb in July.

KUBINSKI, TIM - TL - Age 25
A big hard thrower, Kublinski pitched well after a promotion to Double-A. Not a real high profile guy, but Kublinski could surprise.

KUSIEWICZ, MIKE - TL - Age 20
The Rockies consider Kusiewicz a crafty lefty who gets a lot of ground ball outs. In only his second season of pro ball, he spent most of 1996 at Double-A New Haven, where he further refined his impressive curveball. He'll remain at the Double-A level for most of 1997.

LACY, KERRY - TR - Age 24
One of several marginal righthanders tried by the Red Sox in September, Lacy has a brighter future than most. Starting with the Rangers' Triple-A club at Oklahoma City, Lacy was overshadowed by Danny Patterson and dealt to Boston. He continued to pitch well in Triple-A and finished the season with his major league debut. A one-pitch righthander, Lacy can earn a righthanded relief role with the Red Sox in 1997.

LaGARDE, JOE - TR - Age 22
So far, LaGarde has made his below-average stuff go a long way. He rode a 1.74 ERA in 24 games at Double-A San Antonio to get his first Triple-A chance in 1996. LaGarde isn't likely to make it to the majors, but he's been successful thus far.

LANCASTER, LES - TR - Age 34
Another of the aging, veteran relievers playing it out in independent ball in 1996.

LANE, AARON - TL - Age 25
Normally a reliever, Lane was used as a starter in Double-A in 1996, pitching a no-hitter in the process. The Orioles demoted him from Triple-A to get better command of his pitches, and it looks like he succeeded.

LANGSTON, MARK - TL - Age 36
Langston was on the disabled list three times in 1996, with right knee and calf injuries. But his arm is sound, and he could come back with a good year in 1997, possibly coming close to what he did in 1995, when he went 15-7. Langston was once a below-3.00 ERA pitcher, but not since 1993.

	W	SV	ERA	IP	H	BB	SO	B/I	$
1995 California AL	15	0	4.63	200	212	64	142	1.38	10
1996 California AL	6	0	4.82	123	116	45	83	1.31	5

LANKFORD, FRANK - TR - Age 26
It took three years for this University of Virginia alumnus to work his way up to Double-A on the Yankees farm, but he succeeded when he got there in 1996: a 2.66 ERA and less than a hit per inning. He needs to improve his control to advance further.

LARKIN, ANDY - TR - Age 22
Larkin has been limited to 89 innings over the past two Double-A seasons by elbow troubles. When healthy, Larkin has been a force. He has a 90 MPH heater and varies speeds well with excellent control. He was a surprise September callup, and the Marlins will give him every consideration for the 1997 rotation if he can prove his health. He projects as a future mid-rotation starter in the majors.

LARSON, TOBY - TR - Age 24
Larson pitched at four levels on the Mets farm in 1996: low A, high A, Double-A and Triple-A. His one-day tenure in the Sally League came when the Mets noticed that he would be driving past a stadium where they needed a starter for that day's game, and they asked him to stop and do the job (seven innings, one run). Larson's odyssey ended with elbow surgery, and he was a question mark for 1997.

LAWRENCE, SEAN - TL - Age 26
Lawrence split time between the rotation and bullpen at Double-A Carolina in 1996 and intrigued the Pirates enough that they sent him to the Arizona Fall League. He was 3-5, 3.95 in 37 games for the Mudcats. The Pirates love lefties so he is a sleeper candidate to eventually get to the major leagues.

LEE, JEREMY - TR - Age 22
The third of four Toronto first-round draft picks in '93, and the second of three pitchers, Lee also was the only one who signed early enough to pitch in the minors in 1994 because he accepted a relatively meager $165,000 bonus. Another big one, at 6'7" still working out his skills in 1996 in A-ball.

LEE, MARK - TL - Age 32
Lefty situational reliever Lee had a good year in setup relief for Triple-A Richmond in 1996, showing remarkably good control. The Braves have plenty of lefthanders, but don't be surprised to see Lee turn up in a major league bullpen in 1997. It'll be as a situational lefty reliever, of course; Lee is not a closer candidate.

LEFTWICH, PHIL - TR - Age 27
Leftwich started 32 games for the Angels in 1993 and '94, and was their third starter at the onset of 1994. Since then, he's been ineffective and had some shoulder problems requiring arthroscopic surgery in March 1995. He had a lengthy rehab period finally making a major league start last April, his first start since August 1994. Leftwich has been working hard to make a comeback and win a job in the Angels rotation.

LEGAULT, KEVIN - TR - Age 26
In his first year at Triple-A, Legault led Salt Lake City with fifty appearances out of the bullpen. Batters ripped him for 100 hits in 81 innings and he was prone to the home run, contributing to his 5.36 ERA.

LEHMAN, TOBY - TR - Age 25
Lehman is an Orioles minor league reliever struggling to get things together to move upwards in the minors. Thus far, he's spent most of his time in A-ball.

LEIPER, DAVE - TL - Age 34
Leiper was a huge disappointment for Philadelphia but then headed back to the familiar surroundings of the Montreal organization after being released in June. He had a bad year in 1996 but the Expos will give him a chance to right his career. He can be effective reliever against lefties.

	W	SV	ERA	IP	H	BB	SO	B/I	$
1995 Oakland AL	1	0	3.57	22	23	13	10	1.59	-
1995 Montreal NL	0	2	2.86	22	16	6	12	1.00	3
1996 Montreal NL	2	0	7.20	25	40	9	13	1.96	-

LEITER, AL - TL - Age 31
Leiter was one of the most difficult pitchers to hit in all of baseball in 1996, allowing only 6.39 hits per nine innings and holding hitters to a .202 average in his first National League season. The hard-throwing southpaw still has trouble consistently finding the plate, however. The high pitch counts he tends to run make him a six or seven inning hurler most nights.

	W	SV	ERA	IP	H	BB	SO	B/I	$
1995 Toronto AL	11	0	3.64	183	162	108	153	1.48	10
1996 Florida NL	16	0	2.93	215	153	119	200	1.26	17

LEITER, MARK - TR - Age 33
Leiter had a decent year for the Giants in 1995. San Francisco anointed him as their top starter to begin 1996. Leiter wilted under the pressure and was dealt to Montreal in late July where he somewhat righted himself. Leiter is a fourth or fifth starter not an ace.

	W	SV	ERA	IP	H	BB	SO	B/I	$
1995 San Francisco NL	10	0	3.82	195	185	55	129	1.23	11
1996 SF-Montreal NL	8	0	4.92	205	219	69	164	1.40	1

LEMP, CHRIS - TR - Age 25
Lemp has been a closer for the Orioles' low minor league teams, moving to middle relief and setup in Double-A in 1996 where he had a so-so year. It looks like more Double-A in 1997.

LeROY, JOHN - TR - Age 21
LeRoy earned a midseason promotion to Double-A Greenville, where he continued to impress. He may lack the stamina to be a successful major league starter; LeRoy has completed just one of 58 starts since joining the rotation permanently in 1994. Overall it was a good year for LeRoy and he'll get a longer look in the high minors in 1997 on the Braves farm.

LESKANIC, CURT - TR - Age 28
Leskanic could have had the closer role to himself in 1996, but after a poor start, his primary role was that of setup man. He maintained his ability to strike batters out, but he also seemed to walk batters or give up base hits in critical situations too frequently. Leskanic's consistency needs improvement in 1997.

	W	SV	ERA	IP	H	BB	SO	B / I	$
1995 Colorado NL	6	10	3.40	98	83	33	107	1.18	16
1996 Colorado NL	7	6	6.23	73	82	38	76	1.64	1

LEVINE, ALAN - TR - Age 27
Levine recorded 12 saves with Triple-A Nashville on the White Sox farm in 1996. He was a starter until the second half of 1995, and he has been much better as a reliever.

LEWIS, JIM - TR - Age 27
Lewis is a finesse pitcher whose control abandoned him for the first time in his career at Triple-A Buffalo in the Indians' chain in 1996. Lewis is one of the many experienced minor leaguers - Casey Candaele, Ryan Thompson, Geronimo Pena and Tom Marsh played for this bunch - kept around by the Indians as Triple-A insurance policies. Lewis' window of opportunity to reach the majors has likely closed.

LEWIS, RICHIE - TR - Age 31
Lewis was the best Tiger reliever in '96, which was a little like being the best navigator on the Titanic. He worked too many innings and walked an unacceptable six men per nine innings.

	W	SV	ERA	IP	H	BB	SO	B / I	$
1995 Florida NL	0	0	3.75	36	30	15	32	1.25	0
1996 Detroit AL	4	2	4.18	90	78	65	78	1.59	3

LEWIS, SCOTT - TR - Age 31
Lewis got into 74 games with the Angels in 1990-94, pitching 178 innings giving up 210 hits with a 5.01 ERA. He had a rough year with the Padres Triple-A club in 1996. Lewis has below average stuff and command, thus limiting him to Triple-A on the fringes of the majors.

LIDLE, CORY - TR - Age 25
Lidle features a good curve which he will throw on any count, to complement his fastball and changeup. He had the second highest win total in the Eastern League in 1996, and remains a lukewarm prospect.

LIEBER, JON - TR - Age 26
Lieber regained his status as a future anchor of a young Pirates' rotation after being switched from reliever to starting at midseason. He had a good year, bringing back memories of his solid rookie season of 1994 instead of his poor 1995. He has added a changeup which only enhances his chances of becoming an above-average major league starter.

	W	SV	ERA	IP	H	BB	SO	B / I	$
1995 Pittsburgh NL	4	0	6.32	72	103	14	45	1.62	-
1996 Pittsburgh NL	9	1	3.99	142	156	28	94	1.30	7

LILLIQUIST, DEREK - TL - Age 31
The former Brave and Indian pitched extremely well for Triple-A Indianapolis as a lefty situational pitcher (a strikeout per inning and 7:1 strikeout to walk ratio) and given the shortage of lefty setup men, should get another chance in the bigs in that role. His last good year in the majors was 1993 with the Indians.

LIMA, JOSE - TR - Age 24
Young Dominican Jose Lima was hit hard at Triple-A and in Detroit in '96. He has good control and might eventually develop into a reliable reliever.

	W	SV	ERA	IP	H	BB	SO	B/I	$
1995 Detroit AL	3	0	6.11	73	85	18	37	1.41	-
1996 Detroit AL	5	3	5.70	72	87	22	59	1.51	2

LINEBARGER, KEITH - TR - Age 25
Linebarger's first year in Double-A was a success. He pitched mostly in long relief, made a few spot starts, and even collected four saves. Linebarger lacks an outstanding pitch, though, so he's not considered a good prospect.

LINTON, DOUG - TR - Age 31
His pitching line looks much worse than he pitched. Because Linton is barely a six inning hurler pitching for a weak offensive team, his won/loss record wasn't good. His ERA looks bad only because of a couple of bad outings. Mostly, Linton was a reliable spot starter for the Royals in 1996. He has finally regained the 93-MPH fastball that was lost to shoulder surgery years ago. Linton probably won't be back in Kansas City in 1997; if he winds up on a club with an offense and a decent bullpen, Linton could be a winner.

	W	SV	ERA	IP	H	BB	SO	B/I	$
1995 Kansas City AL	0	0	7.25	22	22	10	13	1.45	-
1996 Kansas City AL	7	0	5.02	104	111	26	87	1.32	4

LIRA, FELIPE - TR - Age 24
Lira led the Tigers in innings and strikeouts in '96 and turned in an ERA only a bit above the league average (5.00). If he were a Los Angeles Dodger Lira could pitch fifty good innings in '97, but as a member of Detroit's rotation he'll continue to give up a lot of runs.

	W	SV	ERA	IP	H	BB	SO	B/I	$
1995 Detroit AL	9	1	4.31	146	151	56	89	1.42	8
1996 Detroit AL	6	0	5.22	194	204	66	113	1.39	5

LLOYD, GRAEME - TL - Age 29
Lloyd appeared to be injured when he first arrived in New York, but he showed in September and in the World Series that he is still a top lefty setup man.

	W	SV	ERA	IP	H	BB	SO	B/I	$
1995 Milwaukee AL	0	4	4.50	32	28	8	13	1.13	4
1996 Milw-New York AL	2	0	4.29	56	61	22	30	1.48	-

LOAIZA, ESTEBAN - TR - Age 25
After tying for the National League lead in starts with 31 as a Pirates' rookie in 1995, Loaiza appeared headed to oblivion in 1996. He began the season at Triple-A Calgary, was bombed in two June starts with the Pirates then banished to the Mexican League. He came back in late August and pitched pretty well at times down the stretch. He has the ability to become a big winner.

	W	SV	ERA	IP	H	BB	SO	B/I	$
1995 Pittsburgh NL	8	0	5.16	172	205	55	85	1.51	-
1996 Pittsburgh NL	2	0	4.96	52	65	19	32	1.61	-

LOEWER, CARLTON - TR - Age 23
The Phils' 1994 first round pick has all of the pitches - an above average fastball, plus a developing curve and changeup, all of which he throws for strikes. However, he doesn't change speeds or locations well, and sometimes insists on throwing a pitch that is obviously wrong for the situation, with often disastrous results. Also, his strikes tend to catch a whole lot of the plate.

LOISELLE, RICH - TR - Age 25
The Pirates acquired the big righthander from the Houston organization last July in a trade for Danny Darwin. He was considered a middle-of-the-road prospect by Houston but was impressive during three late-season starts with the Pirates. He is definitely a candidate for the Pirates' rotation in 1997 and could be a fixture in their youth movement.

	W	SV	ERA	IP	H	BB	SO	B/I	$
1996 Pittsburgh NL	1	0	3.05	20	22	8	9	1.49	-

LOMON, KEVIN - TR - Age 25
For the second consecutive year, Lomon used a decent year at Triple-A Richmond to get exactly six major league

appearances, this time with the Braves. Lomon made it to the bigs with the Mets in 1995, then wasn't offered a contract over the winter and he returned to Atlanta as a minor league free agent. Lomon could be a big beneficiary of major league expansion, advancing from fringe status to a more regular role.

LONG, JOEY - TL - Age 26
Long was a middle reliever and setup man for the Padres Triple-A club in 1996. He's a lefty, and because southpaws are always in demand, he could make the majors as a situational pitcher and setup man.

LOONEY, BRIAN - TL - Age 27
An underachiever with a wide assortment of breaking pitches, Looney is unable to find any consistency. He has pitched in the majors for both Montreal and Boston, but those days are becoming a distant memory with each passing game. Being lefthanded will extend Looney's chances; he'll need it to get another big league chance.

LOOPER, BRADEN - TR - Age 21
The Cardinals used the third overall pick in the 1996 draft to take Looper, a flame throwing righthander from Wichita State. Looper throws harder than anyone else in the draft. His fastball routinely topped 95 and registered 97 and 98 on the fast gun. There has been some talk that Looper may be moved to the starting rotation to get him more work in the minors, but chances are Looper will find himself in the majors as a reliever.

LOPEZ, ALBIE - TR - Age 25
Lopez had his best opportunity yet to secure a spot in the Indians' rotation in 1996, but failed due to his poor command within the strike zone and his vulnerability to the home run ball (28 in 152 career major league innings). Lopez has an upper-80's fastball and a biting curve at the forefront of his diversified four-pitch repertoire, but he tends to fall behind hitters and groove his fastball down the middle in the bigs, with disastrous results.

	W	SV	ERA	IP	H	BB	SO	B/I	$
1995 Cleveland AL	0	0	3.13	23	17	7	22	1.04	1
1996 Cleveland AL	5	0	6.39	62	80	22	45	1.65	-

LORRAINE, ANDREW - TL - Age 24
Lorraine's numbers have fallen off a lot since his 12-4 season in Vancouver during 1994. He has suffered control problems. He has great stuff when he is on. Remember fellow Stanford alum Jack McDowell took a few years to get it together.

LOVINGIER, KEVIN - TR - Age 24
As a one-inning righthanded setup specialist at Double-A Arkansas, Lovingier fanned 73 batters in 64 innings, but he also walked 48. He's not a great prospect, but if he can find the plate a little more often he'll advance.

LOWE, DEREK - TR - Age 23
Lowe is a big (6'6") righthander with good stuff. He doesn't have a dominant fastball, but has pretty good stuff, nonetheless. Lowe used ten good starts at Double-A Port City (5-3, 3.05 ERA) to reach Triple-A for the first time in 1996. He doesn't look like the kind of pitcher who will be overpowering right from the start, but he should eventually develop into a guy who can take a regular turn in the majors.

LOWE, SEAN - TR - Age 26
Lowe was the Cardinals' top draft pick in 1992, but appears to have stalled in the high minors. He made six starts at Double-A Arkansas, then was just marginal in Triple-A Louisville's rotation. Lowe finished the year in the bullpen and that may be his long range future.

LUDWICK, ERIC - TR - Age 25
Acquired from the New York Mets as part of the Bernard Gilkey trade prior to 1996, Ludwick had mixed reviews in the Cardinals' organization. He was 3-4 with a 2.83 ERA at Triple-A Louisville but was overmatched in six September appearances with the big-league club. He needs a full year at Triple-A and then we'll know where he stands as a potential big-league starter.

LUEBBERS, LARRY - TR - Age 27
Luebbers improved in 1996 after two terrible years, but he should not be regarded as a prospect due to his low strikeout rate. He had a cup of coffee with the Reds in 1993.

LUKASIEWICZ, MARK - TL - Age 24
The 6'7" Lukasiewicz, a 1993 supplemental first-round draft pick by the Blue Jays, made his pro debut in 1995 and played in Class-A in 1996. He didn't throw his mid-90s fastball for strikes often enough.

LYONS, CURT - TR - Age 22
A sixth round pick in 1992, Lyons went from roster filler to best pitching prospect in the Reds organization in a year. A huge (6'5", 240 pounds) righthander, Lyons dominated at Double-A Chattanooga, leading the Southern League in strikeouts and displaying much better control (3.4:1 strikeout to walk ratio) than could be expected from a hard thrower. His performance earned a late season look with the Reds and a strong spring could give him a chance as a number five starter.

MACCA, CHRIS - TR - Age 22
This impressive closer has a better than average moving fastball and an excellent slider, both delivered from the side. He recorded a total of 30 saves in 1996, half with Low-A Asheville, and the other half with Double-A New Haven. He's only in his second year as a pro, but the Rockies desperately need bullpen help, and Macca could get a shot as early as 1997.

MacDONALD, BOB - TL - Age 31
Lefties who can throw strikes seem to hang around forever, and that was what MacDonald was doing in 1996 (4-1 with a 3.13 ERA at Triple-A Norfolk).

MACEY, FAUSTO - TR - Age 21
Macey is a major bean pole at 185 pounds and 6'4". Surprisingly, he is neither overpowering nor is he wild. He is young and held his own against older more experienced hitters in the South Atlantic League. Keep a sharp eye on his development.

MADDUX, GREG - TR - Age 30
Because he didn't get very good run support, Maddux went just 15-11 despite having a better ERA than Cy Young winning teammate John Smoltz. Otherwise, Maddux is every bit as dominating a pitcher as he was while winning four straight Cy Young awards. He still uses his smarts as well as his great stuff to get hitters to get themselves out. A six-time Gold Glove winner who has never missed a start due to injury, Maddux is still the best pitcher in the game.

	W	SV	ERA	IP	H	BB	SO	B/I	$
1995 Atlanta NL	19	0	1.63	209	147	23	181	0.81	41
1996 Atlanta NL	15	0	2.72	245	225	28	172	1.03	26

MADDUX, MIKE - TR - Age 35
Elder brother of repeat Cy Young winner Greg, Maddux doesn't have his brother's command. Mike spent the year shuttling between the Red Sox' bullpen, rotation and the DL. He saved the worst for September; his numbers look worse than he actually pitched. Maddux can serve a useful long-relief/ spot-start role in the majors.

	W	SV	ERA	IP	H	BB	SO	B/I	$
1995 Pittsburgh NL	1	0	9.00	9	14	3	4	1.89	-
1995 Boston AL	4	1	3.61	89	86	15	65	1.13	8
1996 Boston AL	3	0	4.48	64	76	27	32	1.61	-

MADURO, CALVIN - TR - Age 22
Maduro was acquired by the Phils from the O's in the Todd Zeile stretch-run rental deal. He is a finesse pitcher with an 85 MPH fastball and pinpoint control who acquitted himself well in his major league trial. However, he has needed a second tour to dominate at each level - this progression suggests that he needs a half-season at Triple-A before arriving in the majors to stay. He'll be a productive mid-rotation major league starter by 1998.

MAEDA, KATSUHIRO - TR - Age 25
Not exactly Hideo Nomo, Maeda spent 1996 at Class A and Double-A on the Yankee farm, with an ERA slightly over 4.00 at both levels. He needs better control to move up.

MAGNANTE, MIKE - TL - Age 31
Formerly the Royals' lefty long reliever, Magnante fairly disappeared down the stretch. He wasn't pitching especially

well before he got hurt. When he returned, his name was written on the Royals' roster in invisible ink; he pitched just five times over the last month of the season. Magnante doesn't throw especially hard and has almost no platoon differential, so he's not likely to win a situational relief role. Still, he can pitch and should have a job some place in the majors in 1997.

	W	SV	ERA	IP	H	BB	SO	B / I	$
1995 Kansas City AL	1	0	4.23	44	45	16	28	1.38	1
1996 Kansas City AL	2	0	5.67	54	58	24	32	1.52	-

MAGRANE, JOE - TL - Age 32
Magrane continued his long fade-put with the White Sox in 1996. He worked in 27 games Triple-A with a 5.47 ERA before the season ended.

	W	SV	ERA	IP	H	BB	SO	B / I	$
1996 Chicago AL	1	0	6.88	53	70	25	21	1.79	-

MAHAY, RON - TR - Age 25
1995's first replacement player in the majors (as an outfielder) has put away his bats and taken to the mound. He has a low-90s fastball but it's too straight and he has nothing to go with it.

MAHOMES, PAT - TR - Age 26
The Twins gave up on Mahomes in '96 after tiring of his lack of development. Boston picked him up for their stretch run and he posted mixed results for them. He will not be effective in the majors in '97.

	W	SV	ERA	IP	H	BB	SO	B / I	$
1995 Minnesota AL	4	3	6.37	94	100	47	67	1.56	-
1996 Boston AL	3	2	6.91	57	72	33	36	1.84	-

MAINE, DALTON - TR - Age 25
Maine is an Orioles minor league reliever. He had a good 1996 season in Single-A, getting promoted to Double-A for a few games. He has good control, walks few, and has a good strike out rate. 1997 sees him getting tested more in Double-A and Triple-A, and if he continues to pitch well, he could be in Camden Yards soon.

MALONEY, SEAN - TR - Age 25
Maloney has been collecting minor league saves on his way up the Brewers farm ladder, He got 22 in 1994 at Class A Beloit, 15 at Double-A El Paso in 1995, and then 38 in his second year at Double-A in 1996.

MANTEI, MATT - TR - Age 23
The Marlins envisioned Mantei as a future closer candidate because of his fastball and bulldog mentality, but he went down in mid-1996 with a torn rotator cuff. Prior to the injury he featured a low-90's fastball, but had struggled with his location at the major league level. Even if he fully recovers and regains his former velocity - an iffy proposition. He must get behind Robb Nen and Jay Powell in line. All bets are off until a radar gun reading is available.

MANUEL, BARRY - TR - Age 31
This one-time Texas prospect returned from oblivion to have a fine 1996 season with Montreal as a setup reliever. How the Expos continue to resurrect guys like this is incredible. Manuel could wind up closing in 1997 if the Expos don't re-sign Mel Rojas.

	W	SV	ERA	IP	H	BB	SO	B / I	$
1996 Montreal NL	4	0	3.24	86	70	26	62	1.12	5

MARSHALL, RANDY - TL - Age 30
This guy went 20-2 in 1990, but hasn't been a good pitcher above A-ball. He was used as a swingman at Triple-A Toledo in 1996, where he was 3-5 with a 4.15 ERA. Marshall will compete for a long relief role in a major league bullpen in 1997, but is a long shot.

MARTIN, JEFF - TR - Age 24
Martin hasn't pitched above Class A in four seasons, but has pitched well at that level since converting to the bullpen and is a fading, marginal prospect.

MARTIN, TOM - TL - Age 26
Martin has spent eight years in the minor leagues. In his first year in the Astro system in 1996, he compiled a 6-2 record with a 3.24 ERA and three saves at Double-A Jackson as a setup man. He also appeared in five games with Triple-A Tucson in only his second career opportunity at that level. Martin was a surprise selection for the Arizona Fall League which finally provided a chance for him to get noticed.

MARTINEZ, DENNIS - TR - Age 41
Age has seemingly caught up with El Presidente. His strikeout rate had long been in decline, but it fell off of a cliff in 1996, due in part to a series of nagging injuries. He had little chance of returning with the Indians.

	W	SV	ERA	IP	H	BB	SO	B/I	$
1995 Cleveland AL	12	0	3.08	187	174	46	99	1.18	21
1996 Cleveland AL	9	0	4.50	112	122	37	48	1.42	5

MARTINEZ, JESUS - TL - Age 23
This Martinez brother (Pedro J. and Ramon are siblings) is a lefty. He's a highly-regarded hard-thrower who has been brought along slowly. Last year he was the leading starter at Double-A San Antonio, going 10-13 with a 4.40 ERA in 27 starts. Martinez should advance to Triple-A in 1997, with a major league appearance shortly thereafter.

MARTINEZ, JOHNNY - TR - Age 24
Martinez is a slender righty (6'3", 168 pounds) with decent velocity, a deceptive motion and solid control. However, he lost the vast majority of his 1996 season to injury, and has never pitched enough innings in a pro season to truly get into a rhythm.

MARTINEZ, PEDRO A - TL - Age 28
The "other" Pedro Martinez, this reliever had some success as a lefty-lefty matchup specialist and general setup man, but his control has been off the last two years.

MARTINEZ, PEDRO J - TR - Age 25
He's answered all the questions about his stamina. He has proven he is more than just a head hunter. Though he doesn't receive proper credit, Martinez is the Expos' best starting pitcher and one of the better righthanders in the National League. He is the real deal and good for 15 wins a year for many years to come.

	W	SV	ERA	IP	H	BB	SO	B/I	$
1995 Montreal NL	14	0	3.51	194	158	66	174	1.15	17
1996 Montreal NL	13	0	3.70	216	189	70	222	1.20	14

MARTINEZ, RAMON - TR - Age 29
Martinez pitched fairly well in 1996 despite missing five starts to injury, but not as well as his record. He is still rather wild (4.6 walks per game) but survives by giving up relatively few hits and keeping the ball in the park (and by getting 6.0 runs/game in support). One positive sign was that his strikeout rate was the best since his outstanding 1990 season.

	W	SV	ERA	IP	H	BB	SO	B/I	$
1995 Los Angeles NL	17	0	3.66	206	176	81	138	1.25	15
1996 Los Angeles NL	15	0	3.42	168	153	86	133	1.42	9

MASON, ROGER - TR - Age 38
After missing most of 1995 following surgery shoulder, the veteran righthanded reliever tried a comeback with the Pirates in 1996. Mason never made it out of extended spring training, though, and retired. He was a class individual and an unsung hero as a middle reliever on the Pirates' National League East championship team in 1991 and 1992.

MATHEWS, T.J. - TR - Age 27
He is the closer-in-waiting for the Cardinals, ready to move into the role whenever Dennis Eckersley decides to retire. Converted to short relief in 1995, Mathews was outstanding in '96, his first full season in the major leagues. He throws hard, has good movement on his pitches and outstanding poise. No less an expert than Eckersley said Mathews will be a first-rate closer in the big leagues.

	W	SV	ERA	IP	H	BB	SO	B/I	$
1995 St. Louis NL	1	2	1.52	29	21	11	28	1.08	4
1996 St. Louis NL	2	6	3.01	83	62	32	80	1.13	9

MATHEWS, TERRY - TR - Age 32
Veteran setup reliever Terry Mathews was acquired by the Orioles from the Marlins in late August in a waiver-wire trade after the normal trading deadline. The Orioles bullpen was decimated at the time, and Mathews did an adequate job shoring it up. He throws a good 90-MPH fastball and a breaking pitch, but he has been known for his inconsistency. He continued to have his ups and downs for the Orioles, but it was tolerable. The inconsistency will prevent Mathews from becoming a top reliever.

	W	SV	ERA	IP	H	BB	SO	B/I	$
1995 Florida NL	4	3	3.38	82	70	27	72	1.17	8
1996 Florida NL	2	4	4.91	55	59	27	49	1.56	0

MATRANGA, JEFF - TR - Age 26
A strikeout per inning and a 2.15 ERA at Double-A Arkansas have helped Matranga attract some attention despite his marginal stuff. He led the club in appearances (62) in his second year pitching exclusively from the bullpen. Matranga isn't a good prospect, but can't be ignored after his 1996 performance.

MATTHEWS, MIKE - TL - Age 23
The Indians' 1992 number two draftee has seemingly fully recovered physically from 1993 rotator cuff surgery, but has been largely ineffective in his two Double-A seasons. However, his velocity did increase in 1996, though his control was relatively poor and his strikes caught too much of the plate. He is a lefty, and is still young, so the Indians will be exceedingly patient with him. A breakthrough to true prospect status still would be a surprise.

MATTES, TROY - TR - Age 21
Mattes posted a 151/50 strikeout/walk ratio at Low-A Delmarva in his first year in a full-season league. He doesn't throw all that hard, but often overpowers righties with his whiplike delivery. He made major mechanical strides in 1996 after walking more hitters than he struck out in Rookie ball in 1995.

MATTSON, ROB - TR - Age 30
Mattson pitched in Double-A at the age of 29 in 1996, much older than his peers. He had a good year, but not good enough to propel him to the majors in the near future.

MATULEVICH, JEFF - TR - Age 26
The Cardinals' Double-A pitching staff at Arkansas is loaded with righthanders in their mid-20s and Matulevich is just one more guy who served as a middle-innings guy there in 1996. He's just a minor league roster filler.

MAURER, MIKE - TR - Age 24
Maurer isn't overpowering, but he does seem to be effective. He could make it as a setup pitcher. He has pitched well with each new level.

MAXCY, BRIAN - TR - Age 25
Acquired from Detroit in a midseason trade for Tom Urbani in 1996, this righthanded reliever was sent to Triple-A Louisville and was never called to the big club. He went 4-2 with a 4.79 ERA in 36 games with Louisville.

MAY, DARRELL - TL - Age 24
The Pirates hoped they had found something when they claimed May off waivers in early April. However, the lefthander was bombed in two brief trials with the Pirates then lost to California on waivers in early September. He has some ability but hasn't been able to get his feet on the ground in the big leagues.

McCARTHY, GREG - TL - Age 28
McCarthy is a work in progress who fanned 79, but walked 48 in 61 innings at Triple-A Tacoma in 1996.

McCASKILL, KIRK - TR - Age 35
McCaskill can still throw a good curve, but that's about it. He made four starts in 1996 as his career wound down.

	W	SV	ERA	IP	H	BB	SO	B/I	$
1995 Chicago AL	6	2	4.89	81	97	33	50	1.60	2
1996 Chicago AL	5	0	6.97	51	72	31	28	2.01	-

McCOMMOM, JASON - TR - Age 25
The Expos' 1994 10th round pick is a finesse hurler whose control held up impressively from 1995 at High-A (38 walks in 156 innings) to 1996 at Double-A (44 walks in 153 innings). He is a steady journeyman who will linger a while in the upper minors.

McCREADY, JIM - TR - Age 27
A useful reliever working his way up the Mets' farm system, McCready had major shoulder surgery and was still on the comeback trail in 1996.

McCURRY, JEFF - TR - Age 27
McCurry washed out of the Pirates' system after reaching the majors for the first time in 1995. He has below-average stuff, and is a fringe major leaguer, at best.

McDERMOTT, RYAN - TR - Age 18
While many other clubs shied away from the 6'10", 230 pound McDermott because of their belief that he would opt to play basketball at Arizona State, the Indians invested a second round pick, and paid him handsomely. McDermott is just a baby and has the poor mechanics often found in a prospect his size, but has a low-90's fastball with the potential for much more. If McDermott earns a spot in a full-season minor league rotation in 1997 and pitches well, watch out.

McDILL, ALLEN - TL - Age 25
A move to the bullpen by this former Mets' farmhand helped him post great numbers in the second half of 1995 and in winter ball. However, it didn't carry over to 1996; McDill was hittable at Double-A Wichita despite a number of mechanical changes designed to have the opposite effect. McDill will need a far better season in 1997 to regain prospect status.

McDONALD, BEN - TR - Age 29
McDonald pitched well for the Brewers, and finally stayed healthy all year. He has had a history of arm trouble, which is a red flag, and while pitching in County Stadium didn't seem to bother him as much as you'd think, it is still a tough place to pitch.

	W	SV	ERA	IP	H	BB	SO	B/I	$
1995 Baltimore AL	3	0	4.16	80	67	38	62	1.31	4
1996 Milwaukee AL	12	0	3.90	221	228	67	146	1.33	16

McDOWELL, JACK - TR - Age 31
McDowell ranks right up there as one of the biggest disappointments in the American League in 1996. Expected to take charge of the aging Indians' rotation, McDowell was no better than their number three starter in a campaign riddled by inconsistency and nagging injuries. McDowell still possesses well above average command, and tended to allow baserunners in bunches in 1996, a trend that shouldn't continue in 1997.

	W	SV	ERA	IP	H	BB	SO	B/I	$
1995 New York AL	15	0	3.93	217	211	78	157	1.33	16
1996 Cleveland AL	13	0	5.11	192	214	67	141	1.46	6

McDOWELL, ROGER - TR - Age 36
Veteran reliever Roger McDowell was having a good season when he came down with a shoulder problem serious enough to require surgery. He was used heavily early in the season, and that may have had something to do with his shoulder problem. He had the surgery in August, and he might need a year of rehab. McDowell was a very important part of the Orioles bullpen, and it was a serious blow when he went down with the injury.

	W	SV	ERA	IP	H	BB	SO	B/I	$
1995 Texas AL	7	4	4.02	85	86	34	49	1.41	8
1996 Baltimore AL	1	4	4.25	59	69	23	20	1.56	3

McELROY, CHUCK - TL - Age 29
Ex-National League reliever Chuck McElroy had a good year with the Angels, holding opposing hitters to a .239 batting average. He was an inconsistent reliever with the Cubs and Reds, having streaks of good pitching followed by periods where he was hittable. He's the Angels only veteran lefty in the bullpen, and that distinction solidifies his standing with the Angels.

	W	SV	ERA	IP	H	BB	SO	B/I	$
1995 Cincinnati NL	3	0	6.02	40	46	15	27	1.51	-
1996 Cincinnati NL	2	0	6.57	12	13	10	13	1.90	-
1996 California AL	5	0	2.95	36	32	13	32	1.24	2

McENTIRE, ETHAN - TL - Age 21
To some observers, McEntire might have been overlooked on the Class A Columbia pitching staff, because they had so many good arms in 1996. Being a southpaw, and a young one, McEntire won't be overlooked by the Mets front office. He was 9-6 with a 2.22 ERA and 190 strikeouts for Columbia.

McKENZIE, SCOTT - TR - Age 26
Here's a case study on why one should never become too enamored with minor league closers' save totals. McKenzie nailed down 20 saves at High-A Winston-Salem in 1995, where he displayed nondescript power and control. Upon graduation to Double-A in 1996, he struggled.

McMICHAEL, GREG - TR - Age 30
After a year as Braves closer (1994), McMichael has settled into an important setup role in the bullpen. His breaking stuff works well to complement the 95-MPH-plus fastball that closer Mark Wohlers throws. McMichael throws strikes and can still get an occasional save, if necessary.

	W	SV	ERA	IP	H	BB	SO	B/I	$
1995 Atlanta NL	7	2	2.79	80	64	32	74	1.19	9
1996 Atlanta NL	5	2	3.22	86	84	27	78	1.29	5

MEACHAM, RUSTY - TR - Age 29
Meacham started five games in 1996. His opponents left/right splits; .383 / .280.

	W	SV	ERA	IP	H	BB	SO	B/I	$
1995 Kansas City AL	4	2	4.98	59	72	19	30	1.54	2
1996 Seattle AL	1	1	5.74	42	57	13	25	1.66	-

MEADOWS, BRIAN - TR - Age 21
Once considered one of the top prospects in the Marlins' chain, Meadows has evolved into one of the largest (6'4", 210 pounds) finesse pitchers, walking about one and a half batters per nine innings at Low-A Brevard County in 1996. Unfortunately, he struck out only four per nine innings. The 1994 number three pick cannot be disregarded, as he has always been one of his leagues' younger starters, and could squeeze out a couple more MPH by refining his mechanics.

MECIR, JIM - TR - Age 26
An experienced minor league closer, Mecir got some work in setup and middle relief with the Yankees in 1996. He doesn't have closer stuff for the big leagues, but he is a fearless direct worker, and he is as good as the average reliever in the majors today.

	W	SV	ERA	IP	H	BB	SO	B/I	$
1996 New York AL	1	0	5.13	40	42	23	38	1.62	-

MEDINA, RAFAEL - TR - Age 22
A hard-throwing Panamanian, Medina can hit a little, too. He won the Triple Crown in the Panama Metro League. At Double-A in 1996 he had a 3.06 ERA with better than a strikeout per inning.

MENDOZA, RAMIRO - TR - Age 24
When he first came up and pitched one good start, Yankee beat writers were calling Mendoza the new Mariano Rivera. One difference: Mendoza throws a fastball around 89 MPH while Rivera is in the mid-90's. Still, when he keeps that fastball down, he can be effective.

	W	SV	ERA	IP	H	BB	SO	B/I	$
1996 New York AL	4	0	6.79	53	80	10	34	1.70	-

MENDOZA, REYNOL - TR - Age 26
Not to be confused with Ramiro Mendoza, the extremely similar Yankees' prospect, this Mendoza is Marlin property. He is a finesse pitcher with average stuff who requires the finest precision to be successful. He had it at Double-A, but pitched batting practice at Triple-A in 1996.

MENHART, PAUL - TR - Age 28
Menhart is another candidate for the Seattle rotation or setup work. When he's wild, he misses high and inside to lefthanded hitters.

	W	SV	ERA	IP	H	BB	SO	B / I	$
1995 Toronto AL	1	0	4.92	78	72	47	50	1.51	-
1996 Seattle AL	2	0	7.29	42	55	25	18	1.90	-

MERCADO, HECTOR - TL - Age 22
Mercado is a big lefthander who has shown some promise at times in his four years in the Astro system, but needs more consistency. He is still young and needs a breakthrough year.

MERCEDES, JOSE - TR - Age 27
Although he had some major league success in 31 innings in 1994, Mercedes is looking more like a career minor leaguer as the years go by. Other than his brief appearance with the Brewers in 1996, he spent the summer at Triple-A New Orleans, going 3-7 with a 3.56 ERA.

MERCKER, KENT - TL - Age 29
Mercker's mechanics were all fouled up in a wasted 1996 season which marked him as the offseason's biggest free agent bust. His stints with the Orioles and Indians were both characterized by poor control and subpar velocity, leading to a strikeout frequency barely better than half of his career rate. The Indians hope that the life returns to his fastball, enabling him to be a fifth starter option or a bullpen specialist.

	W	SV	ERA	IP	H	BB	SO	B / I	$
1995 Atlanta NL	7	0	4.15	143	140	61	102	1.41	2
1996 Balt-Cleveland AL	4	0	6.98	69	83	38	29	1.75	-

MERRILL, ETHAN - TR - Age 24
Merrill earned a midseason promotion by going 5-6 with a 4.31 ERA in 14 starts for Class A Sarasota. He found the going tougher in Trenton, where his 7.05 ERA was easily the highest on the club. Merrill has little chance of reaching the majors.

MESA, JOSE - TR - Age 30
As predicted in this space in 1996, Mesa's performance declined markedly in 1996, though you couldn't tell from his save total. Mesa isn't ready for the scrap heap by any means, but his position among elite major league closers is becoming precarious. Pencil him in for another 30-plus save season, with possible further deterioration.

	W	SV	ERA	IP	H	BB	SO	B / I	$
1995 Cleveland AL	3	46	1.13	64	49	17	58	1.03	54
1996 Cleveland AL	2	39	3.73	72	69	28	64	1.35	39

METHENEY, NELSON - TR - Age 25
Metheney brings little to the table. He does have a bounce-back arm that allows him to pitch often on back-to-back days, but his stuff, location and consistency are less than remarkable.

MEYER, DAVID - TL - Age 25
In his third try at Class A, Meyer produced a 2.11 ERA although he gave up more than a hit per inning and walked almost as many as he struck out. The 1994 Big Eight Athlete of the Year (University of Kansas) moved up to Double-A anyway.

MICELI, DANNY - TR - Age 26
God has blessed Miceli with an incredible right arm. However, Miceli still hasn't figured out how to use it. He saved 21 games for the Pirates in 1995, his first full season in the majors but lost the closer's job early in 1996. The Pirates then experimented with Miceli as a starter but he fizzled in the rotation after a decent start. He still has the makings of a good closer but needs to step forward pretty soon.

	W	SV	ERA	IP	H	BB	SO	B / I	$
1995 Pittsburgh NL	4	21	4.66	58	61	28	56	1.53	17
1996 Pittsburgh NL	2	1	5.78	85	99	45	66	1.69	-

MILACKI, BOB - TR - Age 32
Soft-tosser Milacki continues to fool Triple-A batters but hasn't been a good major league pitcher for years. He'll hang around the major league fringe waiting for a call. In the meantime, Milacki is just a minor league roster filler.

	W	SV	ERA	IP	H	BB	SO	B/I	$
1996 Seattle AL	1	0	6.86	21	30	15	13	2.14	-

MILCHIN, MIKE - TL - Age 29
The lefthanded Milchin bounced from Triple-A to the Minnesota and Baltimore bullpens in '96. AL batters hit .336 against him and his ERA was 7.44. You get the idea.

	W	SV	ERA	IP	H	BB	SO	B/I	$
1996 Baltimore AL	3	0	7.44	32	44	17	29	1.89	-

MILITELLO, SAM - TR - Age 27
The Sporting News once rated him the top prospect in the minors. Baseball America named him the number one prospect in the International League. In the minors, he just toyed with the opposition without a dominating fastball. But then he developed arm problems and he has gone nowhere (he was in Class-A in 1996).

MILLER, KURT - TR - Age 24
Onetime phenom Miller made it back to the majors with the Marlins in 1996, but did not show the mid-90's velocity that once made him the most prized prospect in the Pirates' and Rangers' systems. Miller lost it when he first visited the Pacific Coast League in late 1993. He messed with his mechanics, and lost his control along with a few inches on his heater. Though he has become a craftier pitcher since, he has never fully regained his stuff or his confidence.

	W	SV	ERA	IP	H	BB	SO	B/I	$
1996 Florida NL	1	0	6.80	46	57	33	30	1.95	-

MILLER, TRAVIS - TL - Age 24
Miller is a genuine prospect with good control. He keeps the ball in play and benefits from a good defense behind him. He has climbed straight up the Twins ladder, a level per year, since coming into the organization. In 1996 at Triple-A Salt Lake he made 27 starts and had a better than two-to-one strikeout/walk ratio.

MILLER, TREVER - TL - Age 23
The Tigers have had high hopes for Miller since drafting him in the second round in 1991. He has made steady progress through the Tigers' farm system, reaching Triple-A in 1996. He led Toledo in starts, wins, innings and strikeouts, but his 4.90 ERA was a disappointment.

MILLION, DOUG - TL - Age 21
If this kid can consistently control his pitches, his raw talent will carry him far. With a 90+ MPH moving fastball and a sharply-breaking curve, Million throws a lot of ground ball outs. He needs to spend at least one more full year in the minors, but as one of the Rockies only lefty starter prospects, he could conceivably get the call in mid-to-late 1997.

MILLS, ALAN - TR - Age 30
Mills was a very effective setup reliever back in 1992 and '93. But he then lost something, and even underwent surgery in 1995. A new and strong Mills emerged in July of in 1996, with a 96-MPH fastball, a sinking fastball, and a good slider. But even with the good stuff, his main problem was wildness in the strike zone, leading to his being home run prone.

	W	SV	ERA	IP	H	BB	SO	B/I	$
1995 Baltimore AL	3	0	7.43	23	30	18	16	2.09	-
1996 Baltimore AL	3	3	4.28	54	40	35	50	1.38	4

MIMBS, MARK - TL - Age 28
After a great 1995 season at Albuquerque, Mimb's chance at cracking the majors was blocked when the Dodgers used Mark Guthrie and Scott Radinsky to fill the lefty bullpen roles. His overall Triple-A performance in 1996 as a starter/reliever was not impressive, but 136 strikeouts in 151 innings suggests some potential. As a lefty who throws hard, he will get a chance with someone eventually.

MIMBS, MIKE - TL - Age 28
Mimbs is a breaking ball pitcher who tends to nibble around the edges of he plate, fall behind hitters, and then have to groove mediocre fastballs down the middle, with often poor results. He has retired lefties in the past, and could well

do so again in the future if he gets his mechanics squared away. Look for him to contend for a middle relief role in 1997.

	W	SV	ERA	IP	H	BB	SO	B / I	$
1995 Philadelphia NL	9	1	4.15	136	127	75	93	1.48	3
1996 Philadelphia NL	3	0	5.53	99	116	41	56	1.58	-

MINCHEY, NATE - TR - Age 27
Another of the many righthanders who were tried and found wanting by the Red Sox down the stretch, Minchey is a distant prospect who gets by on guile alone. He was one of Triple-A Pawtucket's better starters in 1996, but he doesn't really have big-league stuff.

MINOR, BLAS - TR - Age 31
Going from spacious Shea Stadium to the claustrophobic Kingdome, Minor did OK. He's a capable middle relief workhorse, Minor features a fastball, curve, and splitter. His skills are solid, but righty relievers can fall into obscurity rather easily.

	W	SV	ERA	IP	H	BB	SO	B / I	$
1995 New York NL	4	1	3.66	46	44	13	43	1.22	3
1996 New York NL	0	0	3.51	25	23	6	20	1.15	-
1996 Seattle AL	0	0	4.97	25	27	11	14	1.51	-

MINTZ, STEVE - TR - Age 28
Mintz turned in a respectable 1995 season at Triple-A Phoenix, but it all fell apart in 1996.

MIRANDA, ANGEL - TL - Age 27
He was either brilliant, or awful in 1996. If Scott Karl is in the rotation, Miranda will resume his situational "lefty vs lefty" mop up role. He's still talented, but just doesn't appear to be able move his game up to the next level.

	W	SV	ERA	IP	H	BB	SO	B / I	$
1995 Milwaukee AL	4	1	5.23	74	83	49	45	1.78	-
1996 Milwaukee AL	7	1	4.94	109	116	69	78	1.70	0

MITCHELL, LARRY - TR - Age 25
The Phils' 1992 fifth round pick has always possessed above average stuff, including a good fastball and a hard curve, delivered from a deceptive straight overhand motion. However, his concentration has always wavered, from batter to batter, and from pitch to pitch. He can blow away the meat of the order, and then walk the bottom. However, the higher he rose through the ranks in 1996, the better he pitched.

MIX, GREG - TR - Age 25
Mix has now bounced through the Marlins' chain for four years without ever being entrusted with a regular starting rotation spot or primary relief role. He has always possessed solid control, but has become increasingly hittable as time has passed.

MLICKI, DAVE - TR - Age 28
Mlicki began the 1996 season with two spot starts to help an ailing Mets rotation, but he soon found himself in the bullpen. Overall he had a successful year. Mlicki throws only a mediocre fastball, but he has an assortment of pitches. His curve is above average, and he isn't afraid to throw it on any count.

	W	SV	ERA	IP	H	BB	SO	B / I	$
1995 New York NL	9	0	4.26	160	160	54	123	1.33	5
1996 New York NL	6	1	3.30	90	95	33	83	1.42	4

MLICKI, DOUG - TR - Age 25
Mlicki, the younger brother of Dave Mlicki of the Mets, pitched consistently well in his first four years in the Astro system. However, since being promoted to the Triple-A level in mid-1995, he has been hit hard. He has an excellent curveball and an average fastball and change. He needs to keep his pitches down to be effective. Mlicki must show he can succeed at Triple-A in 1997 to rate a major league opportunity.

MOEHLER, BRIAN - TR - Age 25
Moehler revived his big league chances in his second try at Double-A in '96, going 15-6, 3.48. He could develop into a reliever with another solid season or two.

MOHLER, MIKE - TL - Age 28
Mohler was effective over the first portion of the season in the setup role, and then during his turn as the closer. He then couldn't get anyone out. Mohler is a good relief pitcher, but he is not a closer and suffers when overused.

	W	SV	ERA	IP	H	BB	SO	B/I	$
1995 Oakland AL	1	1	3.04	23	16	18	15	1.44	1
1996 Oakland AL	6	7	3.67	81	79	41	64	1.48	10

MONTANE, IVAN - TR - Age 23
Montane's control difficulties continued in 1996. Over the last two years he has walked 146 batters in 193 innings. It has led to an ERA over five each year although Montane did advance to Double-A Port City last year. Montane will only go as far as his control lets him.

MONTELEONE, RICH - TR - Age 34
Monteleone was once a good middle reliever and setup man with the Yankees and Giants. Last year, he got into a dozen games with the Angels, but spent most of the season in Triple-A with the Yankees where he had an excellent record.

MONTGOMERY, JEFF - TR - Age 35
Montgomery complained of shoulder pain and weakness for most of the year before succumbing to September surgery. It was his worst year as a closer. Surgery was deemed successful and Montgomery should again be among the American League's elite closers in 1997.

	W	SV	ERA	IP	H	BB	SO	B/I	$
1995 Kansas City AL	2	31	3.43	65	60	25	49	1.29	33
1996 Kansas City AL	4	24	4.26	63	59	19	45	1.24	26

MONTGOMERY, STEVE - TR - Age 26
The Cardinals knew something when they traded Montgomery to Oakland. He is a classic minor league closer, able to pick up a chunk of saves and a future relief ace. But Triple-A is his element.

MONTOYA, WILMER - TR - Age 23
Montoya jumped over a level to Double-A Canton-Akron and was generally impressive as their closer. He is not a major league closer candidate, however, due to his small stature (5'10", 165 pounds) and reliance on his curve as an out pitch. He must refine his control further to move into contention for a major league role by 1998. He projects as a future big league setup man or middle reliever.

MOODY, ERIC - TR - Age 26
Moody had a fine season as the closer for Double-A Tulsa. Like a lot of minor league closers, he needs to repeat that success at Triple-A before anyone gets too excited. The organization thought enough of his potential to send him to the Arizona Fall League.

MOODY, RITCHIE - TL - Age 26
Moody had a so-so season in his comeback from rotator cuff problems.

MOORE, MARCUS - TR - Age 26
Moore recorded a couple of early season saves for the Reds while Jeff Brantley was injured, but was as erratic as ever. After he was sent to Indianapolis, the Reds tried him as a starter, where his strikeout rate, walk rate, and ERA all dropped. Pitchers with Moore's stuff get about a thousand chances to succeed and he is still young enough to do so.

	W	SV	ERA	IP	H	BB	SO	B/I	$
1996 Cincinnati NL	3	2	5.81	26	26	22	27	1.84	-

MOORE, MIKE - TR - Age 37
Moore's career continued its rapid decline in '95 as his ERA ascended to become an all-time major league record (!) and earned him a release from the Tigers. He was last seen in Double-A in 1996.

MOORE, TREY - TL - Age 24
Moore got a spring invite to the major league camp last spring but probably won't be back after his poor showing in eleven Double-A starts last year. He went 1-6 with a 7.71 ERA for Port City after a 7-5, 4.10 ERA performance in A-ball. Moore was imminently hittable at both stops.

MORAGA, DAVID - TL - Age 21
He is a control pitcher who will not likely develop above average velocity. Moraga has the savvy to go as far as his abilities will carry him.

MOREL, RAMON - TR - Age 22
Morel had a so-so season for the Pirates in middle relief in 1996 after beginning the season at Double-A Carolina. He was rushed to the majors and his niche will eventually be as a starter where he can take advantage of his excellent control and command of four pitches. Discount last year's numbers, he's better than that.

	W	SV	ERA	IP	H	BB	SO	B/I	$
1996 Pittsburgh NL	2	0	5.36	42	57	19	22	1.81	-

MORGAN, MIKE - TR - Age 37
Morgan has never been a dominant pitcher, but he has decent control, keeps the ball in the park, and is a typical crafty veteran. He was released by the Cardinals after a poor season, and signed by the Reds for what amounted to a September tryout. He pitched well enough to receive a contract for 1997. Given Morgan's age, extensive injury history the last three years, and recent performance, 10 wins with a league average ERA is about as much as one could hope for in 1997. There is an equal chance of a career ending 6.00 ERA.

	W	SV	ERA	IP	H	BB	SO	B/I	$
1995 St. Louis NL	7	0	3.56	131	133	34	61	1.27	7
1996 Cincinnati NL	6	0	4.63	130	146	47	74	1.48	-

MORMAN, ALVIN - TL - Age 28
After posting a 17-2 record in his first three professional seasons, Morman was considered one of the brightest prospects in the Astro organization. He stalled at Triple-A level for two years before reaching the majors for the first time in 1996. He spent the entire season in the Houston bullpen as a limited-role reliever. He achieved modest success and is likely to be in the same role in 1997.

	W	SV	ERA	IP	H	BB	SO	B/I	$
1996 Houston NL	4	0	4.93	42	43	24	31	1.60	-

MORONES, GENO - TR - Age 26
Morones earned a midseason promotion from Class A Wilmington with the best ERA among Blue Rocks' starters (3.09) but had difficulty with Double-A hitters, allowing 50 hits in just 38 innings. Morones was obtained from the Cubs in the Brian McRae deal. He looks like a minor league roster filler at this stage.

MORRIS, JACK - TR - Age 41
The old veteran Morris pitched for Mike Veeck's St. Paul Saints in the independent Northern League in 1996. Several major league teams were looking for starters, and Morris's name popped up in a number of major league cities, but he wasn't signed.

MORRIS, MATT - TR - Age 22
The Cards' first-round pick from Seton Hall in '95, Morris has been a durable starter. He tossed four complete game shutouts and posted a 120/48 strikeout-to-walk ratio. The righthander works off the fastball. He's not a flame-thrower, but has above-average velocity on a straight fastball. His skills are polished and could get a shot at the majors soon.

MORSE, PAUL - TR - Age 24
A hard-thrower, Morse had a disappointing season at Double-A New Britain; it was his first year above A-ball. He can throw the ball past Double-A hitters and now must prove he can throw it over the plate. Morse will need another dose of Double-A.

MOSS, DAMIAN - TL - Age 20
Considered by many as one of the Braves top pitching prospects, Moss dominated the Carolina League, going 9-1 with a 2.25 ERA and more than a strikeout per inning before his midseason promotion to Double-A Greenville. He found the going more difficult there, but still had some impressive outings - all before the age of 20. Yet another of the Braves' many international finds, Australian Moss has a plus fastball and a good curve. He just needs a little better command of the curve and he'll be ready for a big step up.

MOTEN, SCOTT - TR - Age 24
The Cubs picked up Moten after the Twins put him on waivers following the 1995 season. He spent most of 1996 trying to get healthy. Moten finished the year at Orlando but didn't pitch well at any stop. He's still young, so he's not finished yet, but he needs to learn to pitch down in the strike zone to have a chance.

MOUNCE, TONY - TL - Age 22
Mounce was Houston's seventh round draft choice out of high school in 1994 and has been the surprise of the draft. He has had two strong seasons and outperformed the more highly touted Scott Elarton at Class-A Quad Cities in 1995. He had the lowest ERA in the Astro minor league system in 1995 and was second in both wins and strikeouts. He is on track for a shot at a major league job in two or three years.

MOYER, JAMIE - TL - Age 34
Relegated to relief work in Boston, Moyer came to Seattle in the stretch and was amazingly effective. He didn't develop a new pitch or bulk up, he simply got a chance to pitch, and honed his control, his major strength. Moyer has to be precise with his pitches to be effective. He's always been surprisingly tough on righthanded batters.

	W	SV	ERA	IP	H	BB	SO	B/I	$
1995 Baltimore AL	8	0	5.21	115	117	30	65	1.27	5
1996 Boston-Seattle AL	13	0	3.98	160	177	46	79	1.39	11

MULHOLLAND, TERRY - TL - Age 34
Mulholland arrived in Seattle about the same time as Moyer. He didn't set the world on fire. Never a huge strikeout pitcher and thus unlikely to have a long career in any event, Mulholland will likely show up again on someone's roster.

	W	SV	ERA	IP	H	BB	SO	B/I	$
1995 San Francisco NL	5	0	5.80	149	190	38	65	1.53	-
1996 Philadelphia NL	8	0	4.66	133	157	21	52	1.34	2
1996 Seattle AL	5	0	4.67	69	75	28	34	1.49	1

MULL, BLAINE - TR - Age 20
One of the Royals better prospects in the low minors, Mull was impressive for Lansing, going 15-8 in 28 starts and striking out three times as many batters as he walked. He's just 20 years old; the Royals will develop him slowly.

MUNOZ, BOBBY - TR - Age 29
Munoz appears to be a dominant major league starter on the basis of one solid trip around the league in early 1994. He has suffered through injuries and bad mechanics ever since. Munoz' fastball is not yet back to peak velocity.

	W	SV	ERA	IP	H	BB	SO	B/I	$
1995 Philadelphia NL	0	0	5.74	15	15	9	6	1.53	-
1996 Philadelphia NL	0	0	7.82	25	42	7	8	1.95	-

MUNOZ, MIKE - TL - Age 31
This finesse reliever was largely ineffective for the Rockies in early 1996, injured during the middle part of the season, but came on stronger near season's end. He is so much more effective against lefties than righties that he often faces only a single batter in an appearance.

	W	SV	ERA	IP	H	BB	SO	B/I	$
1995 Colorado NL	2	2	7.42	43	54	27	37	1.85	-
1996 Colorado NL	2	0	6.65	44	55	16	45	1.61	-

MUNOZ, OSCAR - TR - Age 27
Munoz was a starter and reliever in Triple-A in the Orioles organization in 1996, after spending five years in the minors with the Indians and Twins. The Orioles claimed him off waivers in 1995. He's had some rough years in Triple-A, but he was having a good year in 1996 when he had the bad luck of coming down with an elbow injury missing a month at the time that the Orioles were desperate for bullpen help.

MUNRO, PETER - TR - Age 21
Another of the talented, young Red Sox righthanders, Munro is far from the majors due to an injury in 1995. He rebounded well in 1996, leading Class A Sarasota in victories, games started and innings. Munro has a good fastball and an improving slider. Look for him at Double-A Trenton in 1997.

MURRAY, HEATH - TL - Age 23
Murray was part of the 1995 trade that sent Mike Stanton to Boston. He was re-acquired by the Braves late in 1996 when the Phillies placed him on waivers after a difficult year at Triple-A Scranton/Wilkes-Barre. Murray just doesn't throw hard, so he'll have to have much better control than he showed in 1996 when he walked almost a batter per inning.

MURRAY, MATT - TR - Age 26
Murray returned to the Braves after short stints with Boston and Philadelphia. In 1995, Murray ran up a 17-3 minor league record; the tables were turned on him in 1996, though, as he stumbled to a 2-10 record with an awful 7.38 ERA. The difference was control. In 1995 he walked 42 in 152 minor league innings. A year later, he walked almost a batter per inning, 63 in 68 innings. Murray isn't a strikeout pitcher, so his control has to be sharp for him to succeed.

MUSSELWHITE, JAMES - TR - Age 25
In his second try at Double-A in 1996, Musselwhite gave up less than a hit per inning and produced a 2.25 ERA in five starts. He has flirted with no-hitters a few times in his young career.

MUSSINA, MIKE - TR - Age 28
Mussina had a good season, but he was not the dominant ace the Orioles expected. Overall he was hit much harder than in past years, and like many others, he found hitter-friendly Camden Yards a tough place to pitch. He had his usual midseason funk, going 3-6 in one stretch. In the "Baseball America" poll of managers, Mussina was rated as having the best control, the second best curveball, the best changeup, and overall as the best pitcher in the American League. There is a big Cy Young-year somewhere in his future, maybe it will come in 1997.

	W	SV	ERA	IP	H	BB	SO	B/I	$
1995 Baltimore AL	19	0	3.29	221	187	50	158	1.07	30
1996 Baltimore AL	19	0	4.81	243	264	69	204	1.37	15

MYERS, JASON - TL - Age 23
San Francisco's 10th-round draft choice in 1993 became a prospect and has been pitching well in Class-A.

MYERS, JIMMY - TR - Age 27
Orioles reliever Jimmy Myers was formerly in the Giants organization for whom he pitched for eight years, spending the last two in the Orioles system. He was with the parent Orioles club early in 1996 where he had a rough time, but pitched most of the year in Triple-A where he had a good year. It's significant that Myers was passed over when the Orioles were desperate for bullpen help at mid-year.

MYERS, MIKE - TL - Age 27
Myers did his job in '96, appearing in 83 games and holding lefthanders to a .229 average. He is about as close to a reliable Tiger reliever as one will find.

	W	SV	ERA	IP	H	BB	SO	B/I	$
1995 Two Teams	1	0	9.95	8	11	7	4	2.25	-
1996 Detroit AL	1	6	5.01	64	70	34	69	1.62	3

MYERS, RANDY - TL - Age 34
Myers was the Orioles closer in 1996, but he was inconsistent at times, leading to seven blown saves. He held lefthanded hitters to a .208 average, but righthanded hitters clipped him at .281, poor for an ace closer. Manager Davey Johnson used other relievers as closers at times, and he may continue the practice in 1997.

	W	SV	ERA	IP	H	BB	SO	B/I	$
1995 Chicago NL	1	38	3.88	55	49	28	59	1.39	32
1996 Baltimore AL	4	31	3.53	58	60	29	74	1.53	31

MYERS, ROD - TR - Age 27
A sore right shoulder through much of his minor league career prompted a move to the bullpen by Myers in 1994. He finally got to the majors in 1996.

	W	SV	ERA	IP	H	BB	SO	B/I	$
1996 Chicago NL	2	0	4.68	67	61	38	50	1.48	-

NAGY, CHARLES - TR - Age 29
Nagy continued to evolve into one of the most reliable major league starting pitchers in 1996. Nagy was not overpowering in 1996, but he varied speeds well and pitched to the corners more consistently than he had at any point in his career. Nagy conserves pitches well, throwing strike one and letting hitters retire themselves.

	W	SV	ERA	IP	H	BB	SO	B/I	$
1995 Cleveland AL	16	0	4.55	178	194	61	139	1.43	9
1996 Cleveland AL	17	0	3.41	222	217	61	167	1.25	23

NARCISSE, TYRONE - TR - Age 25
Narcisse failed to progress in his second full season at Double-A. He has compiled a 30-54 won-loss record in his seven year career and will have trouble reaching the Triple-A level.

NAULTY, DAN - TR - Age 27
Naulty was enjoying a good rookie season and was even picking up some saves when a shoulder problem ended his season in July. He's a good pitcher if he's healthy, but that's a big if.

	W	SV	ERA	IP	H	BB	SO	B/I	$
1996 Minnesota AL	3	4	3.79	57	43	35	56	1.37	5

NAVARRO, JAIME - TR - Age 29
In the last season of a two-year contract, Navarro was the one of two reliable starters for the Cubs (along with Steve Trachsel). Navarro has good control and works the corners well. He has an above-average sinker, and throws a slider as his breaking ball. He will also use a forkball to lefthanders. Whether or not the Cubs re-sign him, Navarro will be a middle of the staff, innings eater who will give any team reliable if unspectacular pitching.

	W	SV	ERA	IP	H	BB	SO	B/I	$
1995 Chicago NL	14	0	3.28	200	194	56	128	1.25	15
1996 Chicago NL	15	0	3.92	236	244	72	158	1.34	11

NEAGLE, DENNY - TL - Age 28
It really doesn't seem fair that the Braves could add this guy to their staff late in 1996. Neagle has a fine changeup and knows how to spot his other pitches; it's a devastating combination that has helped him move to the forefront of major league lefties. Although he wasn't especially good after joining Atlanta for the stretch drive, he is expected to re-sign with the Braves and be their fourth starter in 1997.

	W	SV	ERA	IP	H	BB	SO	B/I	$
1995 Pittsburgh NL	13	0	3.43	209	221	45	150	1.27	14
1996 Pitt-Atlanta NL	16	0	3.50	221	226	48	149	1.24	15

NEAL, BLAINE - TR - Age 19
The Marlins' 1996 fourth round pick battled elbow troubles throughout his high school career, but has a 6'4", 185 pound body and a near 90 MPH fastball. He signed late and pitched sparingly in Rookie ball, but could be a candidate for the full season Low-A Kane County rotation in 1997. They could always move him to shortstop if pitching doesn't work out.

NELSON, JEFF - TR - Age 30
After a terrific year as a setup man for the Mariners in 1995, Nelson struggled early in 1996 with the Yankees. Eventually the sidearmer settled down, stopped trying to blow away every batter, and finished the year as a productive contributor on a championship team.

	W	SV	ERA	IP	H	BB	SO	B/I	$
1995 Seattle AL	7	2	2.17	78	58	27	96	1.08	14
1996 New York AL	4	2	4.36	74	75	36	91	1.50	3

NEN, ROBB - TR - Age 27
Very quietly, Nen has settled in as one of the most dominant closers in all of baseball. He brings it at 95 MPH. Righties don't have a chance against him (.218 average in 1995, .210 in 1996), and he improved upon his most serious weakness from earlier seasons, as only two bases were stolen against him. Nen is a throwback who actually enjoys being brought into a game with runners on base.

	W	SV	ERA	IP	H	BB	SO	B/I	$
1995 Florida NL	0	23	3.29	65	62	23	68	1.29	21
1996 Florida NL	5	35	1.95	83	67	21	92	1.06	36

NEWTON, GERONIMO - TL - Age 23
Newton was one of Double-A Port City's more reliable long-relief righthanders in 1996. He was 4-1 with a 2.76 ERA in 33 games, although he doesn't really have dominant stuff. Newton gets by on finesse. He's not a well-regarded prospect, but any lefthander who posts good numbers in the high minors has to be taken seriously.

NICHOLS, ROD - TR - Age 32
This guy has been around a while, collecting over 400 major league innings, but he has pitched almost exclusively at the Triple-A level over the last four seasons, with three different clubs. Nichols has found great success as a short reliever, collecting 45 saves for Richmond the last two years while posting low ERAs. It's a testament to the Braves' pitching depth that he has gotten just 6.2 innings in the majors the last two seasons. For the Braves, he's injury insurance; for another team Nichols might have a more important role.

NICHTING, CHRIS - TR - Age 30
Nichting managed to draw a major league salary for almost the entire season by landing on the DL in spring training. He's one of those pitchers who's above average for Triple-A but not good enough for the majors.

NIED, DAVE - TR - Age 28
Nied was the first overall pick in the 1992 expansion draft, and has traveled a tough road the last two years. After losing most of 1995 to injuries, he began 1996 at Double-A Colorado Springs with little confidence in his ability, and he was torched in one appearance after another. He finally regrouped at Class A Salem, but may have ended his career as a Rockie following a late season start in which he couldn't get out of the second inning.

NITKOWSKI, C.J. - TL - Age 24
It's hard to tell whether Nitkowski will be better than a fourth or fifth starter in the majors, since he has only been pitching professionally for two full years. A lefthander who came from Cincinnati to Detroit, he was wild in the AL in '96 after pitching decently at Triple-A (4-6, 4.46).

	W	SV	ERA	IP	H	BB	SO	B/I	$
1995 Cincinnati NL	1	0	6.12	32	41	15	18	1.74	
1995 Detroit AL	1	0	7.09	39	53	20	13	1.87	-
1996 Detroit AL	2	0	8.08	45	62	38	36	2.21	-

NIX, JAMES - TR - Age 26
For the second straight year, Nix pitched well in relief at Double-A Chattanooga, with 11 saves, a strikeout per inning and 3.34 ERA. Nix was a 19th round draft pick in 1992 and has posted good strikeout totals throughout his minor league career.

NORMAN, SCOTT - TR - Age 24
For a control pitcher, Norman gave up an awful lot of hits in 1995 (122 in 97 innings). He also walked more batters than he struck out, making him a distant prospect for major league duty.

NOMO, HIDEO - TR - Age 28
The only thing that makes Nomo's 1996 performance look bad is the comparison to his brilliant 1995 season. Nomo was fourth in the league in wins, seventh in ERA, third in opponents batting average, and second in strikeouts and strikeout rate. Nomo is vulnerable to the gopher ball, particularly when he falls behind in the count and has to come in with a fastball, but the combination of his outstanding stuff and Dodger Stadium (Nomo posted a 2.75 ERA at home vs. a 3.82 ERA on the road) make him one of the best starters in the National League.

	W	SV	ERA	IP	H	BB	SO	B/I	$
1995 Los Angeles NL	13	0	2.54	191	124	78	236	1.06	23
1996 Los Angeles NL	16	0	3.19	228	180	85	234	1.16	19

NORRIS, JOE - TR - Age 26
After a promising season in the bullpen at Double-A New Britain in 1995, Norris stumbled a bit in 1996, before finishing the year on the DL. He's a big guy (6'4", 216 pounds.) who can get a strikeout when he needs it. Norris will challenge for a bullpen job with the Twins in 1997.

NOVOA, RAFAEL - TL - Age 29
Novoa has been in the majors in 1990 and 1993 as a starter and reliever with the Giants and Brewers pitching 75

innings with a 5.06 ERA. In 1996, he pitched for the Angels Double-A and Triple-A clubs trying to get back into the big time. He was hit hard in both leagues, so his upward climb will be difficult.

NUNEZ, CLEMENTE - TR - Age 22
He had been a durable starter in A-ball for the Marlins, walking less than two batters per nine innings and lasting deep into ball games, but the 5'11", 181 pounds righty couldn't even crack the Double-A rotation because of his average stuff. Double-A hitters sat on his fat fastball, easy pickings when he threw it over the middle of the plate. He's still young, and could develop into a passable middle reliever if he learns to pitch to the corners. 1997 is his make or break season.

Do You Surf The NET?

Visit John Benson's Web Site:

hhtp://www.johnbenson.com

For the latest news on products and services.

Download Benson's
Draft Software DEMO - FREE !!

View a FREE copy of the on-line magazine
John Benson on Baseball

O'DONOGHUE, JOHN - TL - Age 27
Once on the fast track to the majors, O'Donoghue never developed the necessary ability to get lefthanders out. He's been in the Dodgers' and Rangers' farms systems over the last two years and is now back with the Orioles. He's not a good prospect and is beginning to look like a minor league roster filler.

OGEA, CHAD - TR - Age 26
The curveballing righty proved to be one of the Indians' most reliable starters for a second consecutive season. Ogea has impeccable control and is greatly improved at holding baserunners on first, but the Tribe is constantly tempted to bypass him because of his lack of raw velocity.

	W	SV	ERA	IP	H	BB	SO	B/I	$
1995 Cleveland AL	8	0	3.05	106	95	29	57	1.17	12
1996 Cleveland AL	10	0	4.79	146	151	42	101	1.32	8

OHME, KEVIN - TL - Age 25
A finesse pitcher by nature, Ohme has done little to explain why the Twins have been so enamored with him. Last year was his first exclusively in the bullpen. He'll need a better showing to advance.

OJALA, KIRT - TL - Age 28
Ojala is a precise innings-gobbler who has been a serviceable Triple-A starter for three seasons now, most recently in the Reds' chain, where he walked 31 hitters in 134 innings in 1996.

OLIVARES, OMAR - TR - Age 29
Olivares was the Tigers' most reliable starting pitcher for most of 1996. Without his 160 innings and 4.89 ERA, the Tigers may have set a major league record for highest team ERA. Olivares led the staff with just seven wins. He's really not a staff ace, but Olivares can give a major league staff some useful innings either as a starter or in his more familiar role as a long-reliever and spot starter.

	W	SV	ERA	IP	H	BB	SO	B/I	$
1996 Detroit AL	7	0	4.89	160	169	75	81	1.52	3

OLIVER, DARREN - TL - Age 26
This talented lefthander managed to stay healthy for the entire season, and proved that he could be a major league starter. Oliver has a good fastball, and a nasty breaking pitch that held lefthanded hitters to a .226 average. He needs to improve his control and must develop a pitch to get righties out to move to the next level. Oliver was used carefully in 1996, frequently pitching on five days rest or more, and his durability is a significant question mark, but the ability is there.

	W	SV	ERA	IP	H	BB	SO	B/I	$
1995 Texas AL	4	0	4.22	49	47	32	39	1.61	1
1996 Texas AL	14	0	4.66	173	190	76	112	1.54	7

OLSEN, STEVE - TR - Age 27
Veteran Olsen joined the Royals as a minor league Rule Five selection. His results in Double-A and Triple-A were as different as night and day. He went 6-0 with a 2.77 ERA for Wichita, earning a midseason promotion to Omaha, where he posted a 5.07 ERA. Olsen is a big guy who doesn't throw especially hard; he gets by on good control.

OLSON, GREGG - TR - Age 30
Once one of the premier closers in the major leagues, Olson has bounced around for the last three years after suffering arm problems. Traded by Detroit to Houston in late August, Olson was strictly a one-inning pitcher in 1996. He can still reach 90 MPH with his fastball but he no longer has the command of his curve ball which was the key to his earlier success. Olson might have enough left to be a setup man in the major leagues but is not likely to get an opportunity as a closer.

	W	SV	ERA	IP	H	BB	SO	B/I	$
1995 Cleveland/Kansas City AL	3	3	4.09	33	28	19	21	1.42	4
1996 Houston NL	1	0	4.82	9	12	7	8	2.09	-
1996 Detroit AL	3	8	5.02	43	43	28	29	1.65	6

ONTIVEROS, STEVE - TR - Age 36
Ontiveros went on the Angels' 60-day disabled list in March with arthritis in his elbow. He's returned from the dead before.

	W	SV	ERA	IP	H	BB	SO	B/I	$
1995 Oakland AL	9	0	4.37	129	144	38	77	1.40	6
1996 Oakland AL			Did Not Play - Injured						

OQUIST, MIKE - TR - Age 28
After several failed trials with the Orioles, Oquist was released in 1995. He eventually caught on with the Padres, and in 1996, he pitched well in the tough Triple-A Pacific Coast League, posting the second best ERA in the league. Oquist has below average stuff, so he has to rely on finesse, and his best chance of getting a major league job is as a middle reliever.

ORELLANO, RAFAEL - TL - Age 23
Orellano's breakthrough season in 1995 landed him on the Red Sox 40-man roster and many "top prospects" lists, then he fell just as fast in 1996. The "fosh" changeup that Orellano relies upon so heavily just wasn't working and he has little to go with that pitch. The results - 4-11, 7.88 ERA - were telling. Orellano simply must have another pitch to succeed.

OROSCO, JESSE - TL - Age 39
Orosco's ERA ballooned in 1996 when he allowed eight earned runs in one-third of an inning and a total 12 earned runs in 2 1/3 innings against Texas in two days in April. Other than that he was a effective lefty setup man. They say Jesse is as old as dirt, but he can still get his slider in there.

	W	SV	ERA	IP	H	BB	SO	B/I	$
1995 Baltimore AL	2	3	3.26	49	28	27	58	1.11	7
1996 Baltimore AL	3	0	3.40	55	42	28	52	1.27	3

ORTIZ, RUSS - TR - Age 22
Ortiz is a hard throwing closer who pitched well in Single-A (23 saves over 37 innings, 63:20 strikeout-to-walk ratio and 0.25 ERA) and had a little more trouble when promoted to Double A. He did finish the year with 36 saves and is certainly worth watching.

OSBORNE, DONOVAN - TL - Age 27
The lefthander finally recovered from his '94 shoulder surgery to have a fine year for the Cardinals. Few hurlers in the National League have a better feel for pitching than Osborne. Now that he's healthy, he should be good for 12-15 wins a year for many summers to come.

	W	SV	ERA	IP	H	BB	SO	B/I	$
1995 St. Louis NL	4	0	3.81	113	112	34	82	1.29	4
1996 St. Louis NL	13	0	3.53	198	191	57	134	1.25	13

OSUNA, AL - TL - Age 31
Osuna is a veteran of five major league seasons with the Astros and Dodgers with a career 3.86 ERA in 189 innings, yielding 151 hits. He has a good mix of pitches and good command except that he walks a few too many. Osuna got into 11 games with the Padres Triple-A club in 1996, trying to make a comeback.

OSUNA, ANTONIO - TR - Age 23
With half the teams in the National League, Osuna would already be the closer. With the Dodgers, he is the heir apparent thanks to Todd Worrell's unlikely comeback (with 76 saves in the past two years). Osuna features a great fastball (striking out a hitter per inning throughout his career) with decent control. Young flamethrowers, no matter how good their stuff is, do not usually take the closer role from a veteran who is still effective. Osuna is the Dodgers closer of the future in 1997 or 1998.

	W	SV	ERA	IP	H	BB	SO	B/I	$
1996 Los Angeles NL	9	4	3.00	84	65	32	85	1.15	10

PACE, SCOTTY - TL - Age 24
His quick rise through the ranks of the farm system continued as Pace began his conversion to reliever. He needs to improve his control and get better velocity out of his pitches. He gets good movement but must overcome his problems with the home run ball.

PACHECO, ALEX - TR - Age 23
The 23-year-old righthander is said to have a great arm. You would not know it by looking at his minor league ERAs, which have been consistently high. Yet, he still got a five-game trial with the Expos last season and probably will get more.

PAINTER, LANCE - TL - Age 29
Painter spent much of 1996 on the disabled list after working middle relief and getting a couple of spot starts. He's not consistent enough to start on a regular basis, even for the Rockies.

	W	SV	ERA	IP	H	BB	SO	B/I	$
1995 Colorado NL	3	1	4.37	45	55	10	36	1.44	1
1996 Colorado NL	4	0	5.86	50	56	25	48	1.61	-

PALL, DONN - TR - Age 35
The veteran soft tosser has excellent control and can give you two or three innings per appearance. If his location is not letter perfect, he gets hit hard.

	W	SV	ERA	IP	H	BB	SO	B/I	$
1996 Florida NL	1	0	5.79	18	16	9	9	1.37	-

PANIAGUA, JOSE - TR - Age 23
This young Expos righthander has ""big winner" written all over him. He has a great arm, outstanding poise and throws his killer changeup like a 35-year-old veteran. Small market or not, Montreal will continue to win by developing guys like Paniagua.

	W	SV	ERA	IP	H	BB	SO	B/I	$
1996 Montreal NL	2	0	3.53	51	55	23	27	1.53	-

PARK, CHAN-HO - TR - Age 23
1994's Grapefruit league sensation stayed on the major league roster for the entire season, where he demonstrated strong velocity with weak command. He struck out nearly 10 batters per nine innings and walked nearly six per nine innings while holding hitters to a .209 batting average. If he shows any command at all in spring training, he is a good candidate for the fourth or fifth starter role. The question about Park is not if he will develop, but when.

	W	SV	ERA	IP	H	BB	SO	B/I	$
1996 Los Angeles NL	5	0	3.64	108	82	71	119	1.41	2

PARRA, JOSE - TR - Age 24
Parra was called up before the All Star break despite not pitching well at Triple-A (5-3, 5.11) and was generally pounded in middle relief. The slender Dominican will need a few more years to start hitting the corners.

	W	SV	ERA	IP	H	BB	SO	B/I	$
1995 Los Angeles NL	0	0	4.35	10	10	6	7	1.55	
1995 Minnesota AL	1	0	7.59	61	83	22	29	1.70	-
1996 Minnesota AL	5	0	6.04	70	88	27	50	1.64	-

PARRETT, JEFF - TR - Age 35
Parrett clearly possesses major league ability, and has a durable arm that allows him to pitch several times a week without a noticeable dropoff in velocity.

	W	SV	ERA	IP	H	BB	SO	B/I	$
1995 St. Louis NL	4	0	3.64	76	71	28	71	1.29	3
1996 Philadelphia NL	3	0	3.39	66	64	31	64	1.44	1

PARRIS, STEVE - TR - Age 29
Parris showed promise as a rookie in 1995 but lost most of in 1996 to injuries. He had arthroscopic shoulder surgery in spring training then missed the last six weeks of the season with a strained muscle in his side. He was passed by many younger pitchers last season and is no longer in the Pirates' plans.

	W	SV	ERA	IP	H	BB	SO	B/I	$
1995 Pittsburgh NL	6	0	5.38	82	89	33	61	1.49	-
1996 Pittsburgh NL	0	0	7.18	26	35	11	27	1.76	-

PATRICK, BRONSWELL - TR - Age 26
Patrick has spent nine years in the minor leagues but only two in the Houston system. In 1996, he was used as both a starter and reliever at Triple-A Tucson and had one of his best years (7-3, 3.51 ERA).

PATTERSON, BOB - TL - Age 37
Like teammate Larry Casian, Patterson is a veteran situational lefthander. He doesn't possess much of a fastball, but his slider is death to lefthanded hitters. Patterson has played 15 professional seasons and has earned the label of "crafty lefthander."

	W	SV	ERA	IP	H	BB	SO	B / I	$
1995 California AL	5	0	3.04	53	48	13	41	1.14	6
1996 Chicago NL	3	8	3.13	54	46	22	53	1.25	8

PATTERSON, DANNY - TR - Age 26
Patterson's good control has helped him get promoted in midseason during each of the last three seasons, most recently to the Ballpark in Arlington. He led Oklahoma City with 10 saves in 1996 and will soon get a shot at the Rangers' closer job.

PAVANO, CARL - TR - Age 21
Already one of the Red Sox' brightest pitching prospects, Pavano added an improved changeup and a slider while increasing his fastball into the mid-90s in 1996. The young righthander finished the year 16-5 with a 2.63 ERA for Double-A Trenton, leading the staff in strikeouts and winning the Eastern League ERA crown. Pavano was named pitcher of the year for the Eastern League by Baseball America. He has all the pitches and now just needs some refinement before he'll be in Fenway.

PAVLAS, DAVE - TR - Age 34
A non-roster spring training invitee with the Yankees in 1996, Pavlas produced excellent work while hanging around at Triple-A (8-2 with a 1.99 ERA and 26 saves). He was proof of the Yankee depth stored in the minors.

	W	SV	ERA	IP	H	BB	SO	B / I	$
1995 New York AL	0	0	3.18	5	8	0	3	1.41	-
1996 New York AL	0	1	2.35	23	23	7	18	1.30	-

PAVLIK, ROGER - TR - Age 29
Pavlik won 12 games in the first half of 1996 and was named to the All-Star team despite an ERA that hovered around 5.00. The phenomenal run support that he had enjoyed over the first half subsided somewhat, and Pavlik ended the season as the fifth man in the rotation. Pavlik's control has always been suspect, but he has thrived on working out of trouble.

	W	SV	ERA	IP	H	BB	SO	B / I	$
1995 Texas AL	10	0	4.37	191	174	90	149	1.38	9
1996 Texas AL	15	0	5.19	201	216	81	127	1.48	7

PEDRAZA, ROD - TR - Age 27
After not pitching an inning in 1995 due to rotator cuff surgery, Pedraza came back strong, pitching effectively in 18 starts at Double-A New Haven and in five starts at Triple-A Colorado Springs. Not overpowering, Pedraza earns his pay on the edges of the strike zone. He's likely to see some playing time with the Rockies in 1997.

PENA, ALEJANDRO - TR - Age 37
After returning for a second tour of duty with the Marlins in 1996, Pena quickly tore his rotator cuff. It has now been 13 years since he won the NL ERA title and then blew out his elbow. Amazingly, he has always regained full velocity after each of his injuries. He'll be invited to someone's spring training camp in 1997, and could stick as the tenth man on a staff. He isn't capable of much more than one-inning setup detail.

	W	SV	ERA	IP	H	BB	SO	B / I	$
1995 Boston AL	1	0	7.40	24	33	12	25	1.85	-
1995 Florida - Atlanta NL	2	0	2.61	31	22	7	39	0.94	0

PENA, JUAN - TR - Age 19
With super control for a strikeout pitcher, Pena was among Midwest League leaders in victories, innings pitched, strikeouts and ERA. He's just 20 years old and will be at higher Class A Sarasota in 1997.

PENNINGTON, BRAD - TL - Age 27
Pennington throws hard, but he's hittable. He needs to develop a better breaking ball and get better command, and become a smarter pitcher. Throwing a 90 plus MPH fastball down the middle just doesn't get many hitters out anymore, which is what he does when in a jam.

	W	SV	ERA	IP	H	BB	SO	B/I	$
1996 California AL	0	0	6.20	20	11	31	20	2.09	-

PERCIBAL, WILLIAM - TR - Age 23
Orioles minor league starter Billy Percibal was considered to be one of their better pitching prospects. In 1992-1995, his minor league record was 80-63 with a 3.68 ERA and excellent strikeout numbers while giving up less than one hit per inning. But due to serious elbow problems, he didn't pitch at all in 1996, and twice underwent surgery.

PERCIVAL, TROY - TR - Age 27
Percival won the Angels battle for the closer's job over future Hall-of-Famer Lee Smith who was sent to the Reds. Percival throws heat, and he's one of the most intimidating closers in baseball.

	W	SV	ERA	IP	H	BB	SO	B/I	$
1995 California AL	3	3	1.95	74	37	26	94	0.85	15
1996 California AL	0	36	2.31	74	38	31	100	0.93	42

PEREZ, CARLOS - TL - Age 26
Perez had major shoulder surgery in early April and missed the entire season for the Expos. He pitched in the All-Star Game in 1995 and looked like a quality young lefthander How he responds from his operation will determine how bright his future remains.

	W	SV	ERA	IP	H	BB	SO	B/I	$
1995 Montreal NL	10	0	3.69	141	142	28	106	1.20	10
1996 Montreal NL			Did Not Play - Injured						

PEREZ, MELIDO - TR - Age 31
Perez never came back from the sore shoulder that ruined his 1995 season. He hasn't had a really good year since 1992, but if he ever does get healthy, his highly effective fastball/forkball repertoire can make him a winner again.

	W	SV	ERA	IP	H	BB	SO	B/I	$
1995 New York AL	5	0	5.58	69	70	31	44	1.46	0
1996 New York AL			Did Not Play - Injured						

PEREZ, MIKE - TR - Age 32
Once considered a future closer, Perez lost the hop on his fastball. The effects of a shoulder injury may be lingering. If he doesn't really show better stuff in the spring, Perez may be looking for a job elsewhere.

	W	SV	ERA	IP	H	BB	SO	B/I	$
1995 Chicago NL	2	2	3.66	71	72	27	49	1.39	3
1996 Chicago NL	1	0	4.67	27	29	13	22	1.56	-

PEREZ, YORKIS - TL - Age 29
Perez is a bullpen specialist, toiling only 94 innings in his 133 appearances over the past two seasons. He struggled with his control in 1996, and for the first time in his career was knocked around somewhat by lefthanded hitters (.299 average). He is a hard thrower, but his lack of control makes him unsuitable for a role which usually finds him entering games with runners on base.

	W	SV	ERA	IP	H	BB	SO	B/I	$
1995 Florida NL	2	1	5.21	46	35	28	47	1.35	0
1996 Florida NL	3	0	5.29	47	51	31	47	1.74	-

PERISHO, MATT - TL - Age 21
Perisho is a young Angels prospect who had an excellent season in the tough California League in 1996. Promoted to Double-A, he continued to impress people. In the tough Double-A Texas League, he struck out 50 in 53 innings while walking 20, both good indicators of his future success at higher levels. Perisho's 3.21 ERA in the hitter-friendly Texas League.

PERSON, ROBERT - TR - Age 27
Once sent to the Arizona Fall League to be groomed as a setup man and possible closer, Person was held back by arm trouble. He eventually worked his way to the majors as a swing man, starting 11 games for the Mets in 1996. His straightforward fastball/slider style has been enhanced with the addition of a curve and a straight change.

	W	SV	ERA	IP	H	BB	SO	B/I	$
1995 New York NL	1	0	0.75	12	5	2	10	0.58	2
1996 New York NL	4	0	4.52	89	86	35	76	1.36	0

PETERS, CHRIS - TL - Age 25
The little lefthander was rushed to the majors in mid-July last season and immediately took his lumps. However, Peters showed some promise as the year wore on both as a starter and reliever. He was 7-3, 2.64 ERA in 14 starts at Double-A Carolina and 1-1, 0.98 ERA in four starts with Triple-A Calgary, proving he has some ability. He could well wind up in the bullpen, though, because he is a small man and the Pirates question his durability.

	W	SV	ERA	IP	H	BB	SO	B/I	$
1996 Pittsburgh NL	2	0	5.63	64	72	25	28	1.52	-

PETERSON, JAYSON - TR - Age 21
Peterson's reward for an undefeated season at Denver's East High School was being drafted in the first round by the Cubs in 1995. He's had a lot of trouble throwing strikes as a pro, never getting out of A-ball in 1996.

PETERSON, MARK - TL - Age 26
Peterson spent a second year at Double-A in 1996 learning the set up/situational trade. He had a fabulous 4:1 strikeout-to-walk ratio over 56 innings and should appear in Triple-A in 1997.

PETKOVSEK, MARK - TR - Age 31
Many things have to go right for a club to win its division. Case in point: Petkovsek going 11-2 for the Cardinals last season. That's not to say Petkovsek is a bad pitcher because he's not. But he's not a guy capable of going 11-2 again either, though he has some value with his ability to both start and pitch in various relief roles.

	W	SV	ERA	IP	H	BB	SO	B/I	$
1995 St. Louis NL	6	0	4.00	137	136	35	71	1.25	6
1996 St. Louis NL	11	0	3.55	88	83	35	45	1.34	5

PETT, JOSE - TR - Age 21
Pett has an overpowering fastball and decent changeup. He could land a spot in the major league bullpen soon but would be best served with another year at Triple-A to work on using his fastball more.

PETTITTE, ANDY - TL - Age 24
A major success at a young age, Pettitte became the true ace of the Yankee staff when injuries affected all the veteran starters at some time during the year. Pettitte has a high velocity fastball and an assortment of breaking stuff that should make him effective for years to come.

	W	SV	ERA	IP	H	BB	SO	B/I	$
1995 New York AL	12	0	4.17	175	183	63	114	1.41	9
1996 New York AL	21	0	3.87	221	229	72	162	1.36	19

PHELPS, TOM - TL - Age 25
The Expos' 1992 eighth round pick made major strides in 1996, pitching extremely well at High-A West Palm Beach before making a major contribution to Double-A Harrisburg's championship drive. The lanky lefty is a sinker/slider pitcher with excellent control who makes a habit of getting ahead in the count, enabling him to pitch deeply into ballgames. He could be dangerous if he adds a little juice to his fastball.

PHILLIPS, RANDY - TR - Age 25
Phillips put in a good season at Shreveport coaxing ground outs out of batters. Though his numbers are certainly not bad, based upon the number of pitchers who have passed him, the Giants must and like him where he is.

PHILLIPS, TONY - TR - Age 27
Phillips made progress at Triple-A in 1996, working 52 innings of middle relief with a 2.92 ERA at New Orleans. A shot with the Brewers wouldn't be surprising.

PHOENIX, STEVE - TR - Age 29
The one-time Oakland prospect pitched well in relief for the Pirates in 1996 at Triple-A Calgary (1-1, 1.69 in 10 games) and not so well at Double-A Carolina (2-2, 4.98 in 20 games). He showed just enough to give hope he could pitch again for somebody in the majors.

PICHARDO, HIPOLITO -TR - Age 27
Given the role of primary setup man in the Royals' bullpen, Pichardo had a horrible season, blowing leads and getting rocked on a regular basis. He lost the confidence of Manager Bob Boone, who turned to Jaime Bluma instead of Pichardo when closer Jeff Montgomery was lost for the season in September. Pichardo couldn't throw strikes early in the count, had to come inside with his fastball, and got ripped. Pichardo is destined for a long relief role in 1997.

	W	SV	ERA	IP	H	BB	SO	B/I	$
1995 Kansas City AL	8	1	4.36	64	66	30	43	1.50	4
1996 Kansas City AL	3	3	5.43	68	74	26	43	1.47	2

PIERCE, JEFF - TR - Age 27
Pierce is a long-relief specialist who has been on the major league fringe for a few years; he first made it to the majors with Boston in 1995. Pierce can get a strikeout when necessary. He's no better or worse than you'll find as the tenth or eleventh man in many major league bullpens.

PIERSON, JASON - TL - Age 26
Pierson is a crafty southpaw with good control and an improving changeup. In 1996, in his second try at Double-A, this time with the Mets system, he had a good year and remains upward bound.

PISCIOTTA, MARC - TR - Age 26
The big righthander lost a lot of his luster as a prospect last season at Triple-A Calgary by going 2-7 with a 4.11 ERA in 57 games as a setup man. The Pirates no longer think he will turn into a major league closer but sent him to the Arizona Fall League at the end of last season to prove he could be useful as a middle reliever.

PISCIOTTA, SCOTT - TR - Age 24
The Expos' 1991 second round pick has been a disappointment, not even making it to Double-A until 1996. The 6'7", 225, righty has lost velocity, and has struggled with his mechanics. His control has been poor and he has not been entrusted with an important staff role in years.

PITTSLEY, JIM - TR - Age 22
The Royals resisted the temptation to call up their top pitching prospect in 1996. He lost almost a year due to elbow surgery and was being brought along slowly, not that the hitters he faced in Triple-A noticed; Pittsley was 7-1 with a 3.97 ERA at Omaha. A big (6'7"), hard-throwing (90 MPH fastball) righthander, Pittsley has two good breaking balls and a changeup and an intimidating presence on the mound. Expected to spend time in the Kansas City rotation in 1997, Pittsley has the makings of top-flight major league starting pitcher.

PIVARAL, HUGO - TR - Age 20
The Dodgers must be scouting junior high schools all over the world. Their latest international rising star is the Guatemalan Pivaral. Stay tuned on this youngster.

PLANTENBERG, ERIK - TL - Age 28
Plantenberg owns one of the worst career major league strikeout/walk ratio among active players - with four whiffs to 19 walks. He has lingered because he throws with his left arm. He produces best when used in small doses versus lefthanded hitters - as he was at Double-A Canton-Akron in the Indians chain in 1996.

PLASTER, ALAN - TR - Age 26
Minor league reliever Alan Plaster was formerly in the Oakland farm system where he reached Double-A and had a good season in 1995. His strike out rate was impressive enough to indicate that he could be successful at higher levels of competition. Last year Plaster got into a few games with the Orioles Double-A club.

PLESAC, DAN - TL - Age 35
Plesac had a solid year as the lone veteran in the Pirates' bullpen and even picked up 11 saves along the way. He is no longer the dominant closer he was with Milwaukee at the end of the last decade but is still a top-flight lefty reliever.

The Pirates had him under contract for 1997 but have promised to trade him as they are in a major rebuilding mode.

	W	SV	ERA	IP	H	BB	SO	B / I	$
1995 Pittsburgh NL	4	3	3.58	60	53	27	57	1.33	5
1996 Pittsburgh NL	6	11	4.09	70	67	24	76	1.30	11

PLUNK, ERIC - TR - Age 33
Plunk has established himself as one of the most fearsome righthanded setup men in baseball over the past four seasons, and was clearly the most valuable member of the Tribe's bullpen in 1996, his playoff struggles notwithstanding. He still brings heat at over 90 MPH, and has held lefties to averages of .171, .200 and .170 over the past three seasons, sustaining strikeout rates of well over a batter per inning, despite mediocre control.

	W	SV	ERA	IP	H	BB	SO	B / I	$
1995 Cleveland AL	6	2	2.67	64	48	27	71	1.17	10
1996 Cleveland AL	3	2	2.43	77	56	34	85	1.17	9

POLLEY, DALE - TL - Age 32
A non-roster invitee to spring training with the Yankees, Polley became the next-best alternative to a struggling Steve Howe for lefty relief work. Not fully satisfied, the Yankees obtained Graham Lloyd from the Brewers.

	W	SV	ERA	IP	H	BB	SO	B / I	$
1996 New York AL	1	0	7.89	21	23	11	14	1.60	-

PONSON, SIDNEY - TR - Age 20
Ponson had off-season knee surgery and spent the early part of 1996 rehabbing. He was later overpowering in Single-A where the fastballer showed good control, walking only 28 in 107 innings with 110 strikeouts. He faced tougher competition in the Arizona Fall League, and he could move up quickly.

PONTBRIANT, MATT - TL - Age 25
Often prospects are separated from the suspects at the Double-A level. Pontbriant went 2-2, 5.95 in 45 relief appearances for the Pirates' Double-A Carolina farm club last season. We suspect that makes him a suspect.

POOLE, JIM - TL - Age 30
Poole did a great job after his acquisition from Cleveland in 1996. He is murder against lefties, holding them to a .154 average. Righties only hit .211 against Poole, for that matter. He is the perfect one inning lefty.
An unobtrusive journeyman whose sole major league mission is to retire key lefties, Poole was an excellent #3 lefty out of the Indians' pen in 1995. His role will never expand - a solid indicator of his one-dimensional nature is his ratio of games to innings pitched - in 186 career outings, he has pitched only 177 innings. It was only fitting that Poole pitched 1995 in the same pen as Paul Assenmacher, an older version of himself. Poole should age similarly.

	W	SV	ERA	IP	H	BB	SO	B / I	$
1995 Cleveland AL	3	0	3.75	50	40	17	41	1.13	4
1996 Cleveland AL	4	0	3.04	26	29	14	19	1.64	-
1996 San Francisco NL	2	0	2.66	23	15	13	19	1.21	-

PORTUGAL, MARK - TR - Age 34
After a slow start, Portugal turned in his typical performance despite missing three weeks with a hamstring injury. Portugal mixes his pitches well, usually posts a league average or better ERA, wins about as many as he loses, is vulnerable to the longball, and has good control. A free agent, Portugal is a perfectly acceptable number four starter.

	W	SV	ERA	IP	H	BB	SO	B / I	$
1995 Two Teams	11	0	4.01	181	185	56	96	1.33	7
1996 Cincinnati NL	8	0	3.98	156	146	42	93	1.21	8

POTE, LOU - TR - Age 25
Pote has never been the same pitcher since missing most of 1994 with arm trouble when he was in the Giants' system. A Double-A starter in the Expos' chain in 1996, he is no better than a five-inning starter who must try to outsmart virtually every hitter due to his lack of stuff.

POTTS, MICHAEL - TL - Age 26
Potts did better in the major leagues than he did in the minors. He's an ex-Braves farmhand who walks too many batters for a soft-tosser.

	W	SV	ERA	IP	H	BB	SO	B/I	$
1996 Milwaukee AL	1	1	7.15	45	58	30	21	1.95	-

POWELL, DENNIS - TL - Age 33
Powell is a fading vet playing in Triple-A in 1996 after a disappointing season in Japan.

POWELL, JAY - TR - Age 25
The hard throwing Powell's mechanics weren't quite right in 1996, causing his fastball to be fairly straight, holding his strikeout totals down. Powell also was much more timid than he had been in the minors, as he nibbled around the edges of the plate and failed to pitch inside often enough.

	W	SV	ERA	IP	H	BB	SO	B/I	$
1996 Florida NL	4	2	4.54	71	71	36	52	1.50	0

POWELL, JEREMY - TR - Age 21
The Expos' 1994 fourth round pick dominated over short stretches thus far in his pro career. Mechanical fine tuning might allow him to improve upon his 1996 109/66 strikeout/walk ratio at Low-A Delmarva, but at this point he might be most effective out of the pen, where he could throw fastballs once around the order.

POWELL, ROSS - TL - Age 29
Powell has pitched poorly in three cameo major league appearances, but as a lefthander with pretty decent stuff, he might be kept in the wings for years to come.

	W	SV	ERA	IP	H	BB	SO	B/I	$
1995 Pittsburgh NL	0	0	6.98	29	36	21	20	1.92	-

PRATT, RICH - TL - Age 25
Pratt was the ace of the staff at Double-A Birmingham on the White Sox farm in 1996. He won 13 games, a career high, with a 3.86 ERA and a three to one strikeout/walk ratio.

PRESLEY, KIRK - TR - Age 22
Until 1995, he was known only as Elvis Presley's third cousin and the Mets' 1993 first-round draft pick. Minor league fans finally got a chance to see his 90 MPH fastball and near-major league curve. He needs to prove himself above Class-A batters in order to get more major league attention.

PRIETO, ARIEL - TR - Age 27
Prieto was ineffective at the beginning of the season and injured his arm. That might have been the best thing for him, as Oakland sent him to Edmonton for three starts after he completed his rehab in Modesto. Prieto responded, pitching well for both the Trappers and the Athletics down the stretch. With an improving club, Prieto could step forward and establish himself.

	W	SV	ERA	IP	H	BB	SO	B/I	$
1995 Oakland AL	2	0	4.97	58	57	32	37	1.53	-
1996 Oakland AL	6	0	4.15	125	130	54	75	1.47	4

PUGH, TIM - TR - Age 30
In a rather comical sequence of events (unless you are Tim Pugh), Pugh was shuttled between Cincinnati, Kansas City, and Indianapolis at almost every opportunity in 1997. His performance makes one wonder what all the fuss was about. Pugh actually pitched well at Indianapolis but he struggled again at the major league level. Pugh relies on a sinker and guile to be effective.

	W	SV	ERA	IP	H	BB	SO	B/I	$
1995 Cincinnati NL	6	0	3.84	98	100	32	38	1.34	3
1996 Cincinnati NL	1	0	11.49	15	24	11	9	2.30	-
1996 Kansas City AL	0	0	5.45	36	42	12	27	1.50	-

PULIDO, CARLOS - TL - Age 25
Pulido is a screwballing lefthander (referring to his stuff, not his personality). Pulido looks nothing like the pitcher who baffled the Kansas City Royals in 1994 as a member of the Twins.

PULSIPHER, BILL - TL - Age 23
A minor league standout with huge strikeout totals with his 90+ fastball, Pulsipher has been less impressive in the majors. He is younger than most fans realize, and as he learns more about pitching, and if he can stay healthy, his performance will improve markedly.

	W	SV	ERA	IP	H	BB	SO	B / I	$
1995 New York NL	5	0	3.98	126	122	45	81	1.32	4
1996 New York NL			Did Not Play - Injured						

PURDY, SHAWN - TR - Age 28
Purdy followed his 1995 27 save year with 16 more saves in 1996. That's two straight years mired at Double-A for a 28 year old.

PYC, DAVE - TL - Age 26
Pyc has a good fastball and had a good year at Double-A San Antonio in 1996, going 7-5 with a 2.98 ERA, despite allowing 106 hits in 97 innings. He's the most developed lefty starter in the Dodgers' farm system, but not a good prospect for extended major league time.

QUANTRILL, PAUL - TR - Age 28
Quantrill gives up far too many homers to be a starter and his fastball isn't special enough for him to work in the late innings either. His best role is probably as a middle reliever and spot starter and that's probably where he'll be in 1997.

	W	SV	ERA	IP	H	BB	SO	B / I	$
1995 Philadelphia NL	11	0	4.67	179	212	44	103	1.43	1
1996 Toronto AL	5	0	5.43	134	172	51	86	1.66	-

RADINSKY, SCOTT - TL - Age 29
The Dodgers comeback player pitched extremely well in 1996 in the lefty specialist role, posting 48 strikeouts in 52 innings and allowing only two home runs during the season. Radinsky and Mark Guthrie give the Dodgers two excellent lefty setup relievers - most teams don't have one. Despite his fine season, Radinsky is not likely to expand his role in 1997.

	W	SV	ERA	IP	H	BB	SO	B / I	$
1995 Chicago AL	2	1	5.45	38	46	17	14	1.66	-
1996 Los Angeles NL	5	1	2.41	52	52	17	48	1.32	4

RADKE, BRAD - TR - Age 24
Radke is the only reliable young pitcher Minnesota has entering '97. Radke was one of the most improved players in the AL in '96 as he hiked his strikeout rate dramatically while keeping his fine control. His mechanics are sound.

	W	SV	ERA	IP	H	BB	SO	B / I	$
1995 Minnesota AL	11	0	5.32	181	195	47	75	1.34	6
1996 Minnesota AL	11	0	4.46	232	231	57	148	1.24	16

RAGGIO, BRADY - TR - Age 24
Injuries early in Raggio's career stalled his progress, but he was healthy in 1996 and had a good year at Double-A Arkansas. He went 9-10 with a 3.22 ERA while striking out three times as many batters as he walked. Look for a promotion to Triple-A Arkansas for Raggio in 1997.

RAIN, STEVE - TR - Age 21
Rain is a young closer prospect for the Cubs. His delivery is herky-jerky, and is similar to the Royals' Rick Huisman's. His stuff is similar to Huisman, too. Rain throws a heavy fastball and a tremendous slider. Rain will most likely start the season at Triple-A Iowa.

RALSTON, KRIS - TR - Age 25
A rotator cuff tear sidelined Ralston after just one game at Triple-A Omaha in 1996. He had used his good fastball to move steadily through the Royals' farm system. Give Ralston a year to fully recover.

RAMIREZ, HECTOR - TR - Age 25
With velocity in the low to mid 90's, Ramirez often has flashes of brilliance working in relief. He collected six saves on the Mets farm in 1996. His control has been only fair, however, and will need to improve for him to move up.

RAMOS, EDGAR - TR - Age 22
Signed at the age of 16 in Venezuela, Ramos finally attracted some attention in 1996 in his fourth minor league season. At Class-A Kissimmee, he was 9-0, with a 1.51 ERA and 15 walks and 81 strikeouts in 78 innings. After a promotion to Double-A Jackson, he was injured and started slowly before recovering to post a 4-5, 4.88 record including a no-hitter. Ramos is not a hard thrower and needs to show he can get batters out in the high minors to stay on track for a chance in the majors.

RANDOLPH, STEPHEN - TL - Age 22
A hard-throwing lefty always bears watching. Randolph has excellent velocity but needs better control. There is still time for him to become an exciting prospect.

RAPP, PAT - TR - Age 29
Rapp had been one of baseball's more fortunate hurlers in 1995, dancing out of trouble often and receiving excellent run support. No such luck in 1996 - Rapp's average stuff never came together, as he struggled with his control and couldn't get the ball past hitters to escape tight spots. Rapp is a battler who keeps the ball down and in the ballpark.

	W	SV	ERA	IP	H	BB	SO	B/I	$
1995 Florida NL	14	0	3.44	167	158	76	102	1.40	9
1996 Florida NL	8	0	5.10	162	184	91	86	1.70	-

RATH, GARY - TL - Age 24
A second round draft pick by the Dodgers in 1994, Rath is not a particularly hard thrower and he has struggled with his control at the Triple-A level. The Dodgers could use a left handed starter, but it appears that Rath may still be a couple of years away.

RATLIFF, JON - TR - Age 25
Ratliff showed average Triple-A stuff. Without a scorecard, you would be hard pressed to tell Ratliff from several other Cubs minor league pitchers.

RAWITZER, KEVIN - TL - Age 26
A control specialist, Rawitzer was a lefty longman for Double-A Wichita, doing nothing to change the notion that he is not headed to the big leagues any time soon.

RAY, KEN - TR - Age 22
Ray's second shot at Double-A was even more forgettable than the first. He led Wichita with 12 losses in 22 starts to go with a 6.12 ERA. Ray needs another pitch; he can't survive on his fastball alone.

REDMAN, MARK - TL - Age 23
Redman was the Twins' first round pick from the U. of Oklahoma in the '95 draft. He shined in '96 between Class A (3-4, 1.85) and Double-A (7-7, 3.81) and is on the fast track to the majors. The lefthanded Redman can pitch 200 innings a year in the big leagues.

REED, BRANDON - TR - Age 22
Reed was named the Tigers' minor league player of the year after leading Fayetteville with 41 saves and a 0.97 ERA in 1995, then lost nearly all of 1996 to arm trouble. He threw hard, and with good control, before the injury. See if Reed can rebound in 1997.

REED, CHRIS - TR - Age 23
An erratic (4.5 walks per game in the minors) starting pitching prospect, Reed was a seventh round draft pick in 1991. He isn't much of a prospect until his control improves.

REED, RICK - TR - Age 32
Yes, that Rick Reed, who has pitched with the Pirates, Royals, Rangers and Reds. For the Mets at Triple-A in 1996, Reed had a 3.16 ERA, gave up much less than a hit per inning, and held a strikeout/walk ratio near four, keeping his career very much alive.

REED, STEVE - TR - Age 31
Reeder was once again a workhorse in the Rockies' pen, albeit somewhat less effective than in 1995. His sidearm

sliders terrorize righthanded hitters, and an improving changeup is to freeze many lefties. Reed should have no trouble finding work as a setup man should the Rockies fail to re-sign him in 1997.

	W	SV	ERA	IP	H	BB	SO	B/I	$
1995 Colorado NL	5	3	2.14	84	61	21	79	0.98	14
1996 Colorado NL	4	0	3.96	75	66	19	51	1.13	3

REKAR, BRYAN - TR - Age 24
Rekar came out of spring training in 1996 with a starting job for the Rockies, and promptly pitched his way down to Triple-A Colorado Springs. He's got plenty of raw talent, but he seemed to get frustrated too easily at the major league level when the pressure was on. Maturity and perhaps some more seasoning in the high minors should help Rekar's chances in 1997.

	W	SV	ERA	IP	H	BB	SO	B/I	$
1995 Colorado NL	4	0	4.98	85	95	24	60	1.40	-
1996 Colorado NL	2	0	8.95	58	87	26	25	1.94	-

REMLINGER, MIKE - TL - Age 31
This lefty journeyman shows signs of getting over the hump in 1996, with 97 strikeouts in 89 innings in Triple-A. He struggled with his control at the major league level, but surrendered few hits and should be in line for a lefty situational role in 1997.

	W	SV	ERA	IP	H	BB	SO	B/I	$
1995 Two Teams	0	0	6.75	6	9	5	7	2.10	-
1996 Cincinnati NL	0	0	5.60	27	24	19	19	1.59	-

RESZ, GREG - TR - Age 25
A save artist in the low minors, Resz moved up to Double-A in 1996 and produced a 2.52 ERA while striking out more than a batter per inning. Overall he has done well for a 15th-round pick, but the Yankees' depth in minor league pitching has been a factor minimizing opportunity for advancement so far.

REVENIG, TODD - TR - Age 27
Reliever Revenig pitched five years in the Athletics organization reaching Triple-A in 1995 where he had a good years as a setup man. He pitched for the Orioles Double-A and Triple-A clubs in 1996. Revenig could be a middle reliever and setup man in a major league bullpen.

REYES, CARLOS - TR - Age 27
Reyes, who just got hammered as a starter is well suited to middle relief. He can confuse hitters the first time through, but give them a second look and it is trouble. He gives up a lot of homers.

	W	SV	ERA	IP	H	BB	SO	B/I	$
1995 Oakland AL	4	0	5.09	69	71	28	48	1.43	1
1996 Oakland AL	7	0	4.78	122	134	61	78	1.60	1

REYNOLDS, SHANE - TR - Age 29
Reynolds has clearly established himself as the ace of the Astros' staff and as one of the top starting pitchers in the National League. His primary assets are excellent control and an outstanding split fingered fastball. His repertoire also features a 90 MPH fastball and a curve. He has ranked among the league leaders in strikeout to walk ratio in his three years as a starter. Reynolds is a hard worker and should have what it takes to be a consistent winner in the major leagues for many years.

	W	SV	ERA	IP	H	BB	SO	B/I	$
1995 Houston NL	10	0	3.47	189	196	37	175	1.23	12
1996 Houston NL	16	0	3.65	239	227	44	204	1.13	18

REYNOSO, ARMANDO - TR - Age 30
The crafty Rockie had his first season free of serious injury problems in three years, but the results were mixed. He remained a stalwart in the starting rotation all season, but seemed to lack the command of his pitches he has displayed in the past. Reynoso still has one of the most wicked pick-off moves in the game.

	W	SV	ERA	IP	H	BB	SO	B/I	$
1995 Colorado NL	7	0	5.32	93	116	36	40	1.63	-
1996 Colorado NL	8	0	4.96	168	195	49	88	1.45	

RHINE, KENDALL - TR - Age 26
Rhine rose to Double-A by midseason in 1996 and was shaky as a setup man and occasional closer. His control abandoned him and he's probably no more than a minor league setup man for now.

RHODES, ARTHUR - TL - Age 27
With a great arm, Arthur Rhodes carried the great prospect label for a number of years, only to come up short every time. After pitching erratically as a starter, Manager Phil Regan moved him to the bullpen in mid-1995. Rhodes pitched effectively as a long and middle reliever, but pain in the top of his shoulder caused him to miss nearly two months of last season.

	W	SV	ERA	IP	H	BB	SO	B / I	$
1995 Baltimore AL	2	0	6.21	75	68	48	77	1.54	-
1996 Baltimore AL	9	1	4.08	53	48	23	62	1.34	5

RICCI, CHUCK - TR - Age 28
Ricci was given new life by the Red Sox, who brought him to their spring camp. A sinker/slider pitcher, Ricci wound up at Triple-A Pawtucket, where he led the staff with 13 saves and 60 appearances. It was the second straight season that he had led a Triple-A club in saves. Often discounted because he doesn't throw particularly hard, Ricci could be useful in a major league bullpen.

RICKEN, RAYMOND - TR - Age 23
An All-Big-Ten pitcher at the University of Michigan, this big hard thrower did well enough in his third pro season, going 9-7 with an ERA in the mid fours at Double-A and Triple-A. The Yankees will bring him along patiently.

RIGBY, BRAD - TR - Age 23
A hard thrower, Rigby adjusted to life in Hunstville well. He is durable, and though his control suffered just a little after his promotion, he pitched well. Probably needs some more time at Double-A, but definitely is worth watching.

RIJO, JOSE - TR - Age 31
The Reds were counting on a return by Rijo by June in 1996, and he was reportedly throwing in the 90's in spring training. However, he reinjured the elbow and required additional surgery, missing the entire season. In a post season interview, Jim Bowden was not optimistic that Rijo would ever be able to pitch again. Healthy, he was the best starter in the National League not named Maddux.

	W	SV	ERA	IP	H	BB	SO	B / I	$
1995 Cincinnati NL	5	0	4.17	69	76	22	62	1.42	1
1996				Did Not Play - Injured					

RIOS, DANNY - TR - Age 24
An undrafted free agent out of Seminole Junior College and the University of Miami, Rios has done well on the Yankee farm. He worked as a closer at Double-A in 1996 and got 17 saves; at Triple-A he had a 1.95 ERA doing middle relief and setup work.

RISLEY, BILL - TR - Age 29
A year ago, he looked like the Blue Jays' closer. Weakness in his right shoulder in June combined with the emergence of Mike Timlin mean that Risley is now looking to bounce back. His fastball was off in 1996 and his control was inconsistent.

	W	SV	ERA	IP	H	BB	SO	B / I	$
1995 Seattle AL	2	1	3.13	60	55	18	65	1.21	6
1996 Toronto AL	0	0	3.89	41	33	25	29	1.41	-

RITCHIE, TODD - TR - Age 25
Once a top prospect, Ritchie simply hasn't been the same pitcher since he lost part of 1993 and 1994 to shoulder surgery. He doesn't throw nearly as hard as he used to and now has to work the corners. The Twins' top draft pick of 1990, Ritchie is probably not going to make it in the majors.

RITZ, KEVIN - TR - Age 31
Crackerman was once again the most reliable workhorse among Rockies starters, but his effectiveness diminished somewhat from a year earlier. The powerful fastball and grounder-inducing slider did their usual magic for Ritz, but

he also left too many breaking balls up in the strike zone and issued too many bases on balls.

	W	SV	ERA	IP	H	BB	SO	B / I	$
1995 Colorado NL	11	2	4.21	173	171	65	120	1.36	7
1996 Colorado NL	17	0	5.28	213	236	105	105	1.60	-

RIVERA, BEN - TR - Age 29
Poor conditioning has led to arm trouble, and in 1996 he was a sorry sight, posting a 6.46 ERA as a Triple-A starter in the Expos' system.

RIVERA, MARIANO - TR - Age 27
A rising fastball that commonly reaches 96 MPH was the key factor in Rivera's emergence as one of the best setup men anywhere. He could be a closer for any team and filled that role for the Yankees in 1996 when John Wetteland wasn't available. Rivera has a good slider and has tinkered with a splitter, but that big heater is really enough.

	W	SV	ERA	IP	H	BB	SO	B / I	$
1995 New York AL	5	0	5.51	67	71	30	51	1.51	0
1996 New York AL	8	5	2.09	107	73	34	130	1.00	21

RIVERA, ROBERTO - TL - Age 28
A sturdy minor league lefthander, Rivera pitched well for the Cubs Triple-A affiliate. Unfortunately for Rivera, the Cubs are stocked with situational lefthanders. If he can show he can get major league hitters out, he could find his way into the bullpen in the big leagues. He's not young, he turned 28 in January, but he has very few innings on his arm. Rivera has logged just 225 total innings over the past four seasons.

RIZZO, TODD - TL - Age 25
Released by the Dodgers during spring training in 1993, Rizzo eventually worked his way back into pro ball with the independent Texas-Louisiana league in 1994. The White Sox signed him in 1995 and got a good season of relief work, sporting a 2.78 ERA at Class A. In 1996 he got 10 saves with a 2.75 ERA at Double-A Birmingham.

ROA, JOE - TR - Age 25
How good is his Roa's control? Well, his 37 walks in 1996 were the highest figure in his eight year pro career. Unfortunately, he has never struck out more than 96 hitters in a season. Despite all of the injuries endured by the Tribe's major league rotation in 1996, Roa was never given a material shot. That's all you need to know about his major league future.

ROACH, PETIE - TL - Age 26
Upon reaching Double-A San Antonio in 1996 Roach began working exclusively in a rotation. He had good results, going 6-3 with a 3.82 ERA. But, Roach lacks a big-league repertoire. He'll probably end up in long relief before he gets to the majors.

ROBBINS, JASON - TR - Age 24
Robbins appears to be the latest in the line of Reds' pitching prospects to fizzle when making the quantum leap from High-A to Double-A opposition. Robbins possesses a decent fastball but struggled with his control.

ROBERSON, SID - TL - Age 25
Although he got a brief trial with the Brewers in 1995 and was almost major league material, Roberson's mixture of offspeed and breaking junk hasn't retired many batters since then. He was at Triple-A New Orleans in 1996.

ROBERTS, BRETT - TR - Age 27
Roberts led Triple-A Salt Lake City with 30 starts and 168 innings, but also led in hits allowed - 211 - one of the highest totals in the minors. Roberts dabbled with a pro basketball career and may have to go back to it if he has another year like 1996.

ROBERTS, CHRIS - TL - Age 25
Roberts had labrum surgery early in 1996 and spent the summer on the rehab trail. He improved late in the year, including a strong playoff performance, showing that his 7.24 ERA for the Mets' Double-A Binghamton team was not an accurate indication of his future ability.

ROBERTSON, RICH - TL - Age 28
One perplexing question of '96 is why Tom Kelly left Rich Robertson in his starts long enough to lead the AL in walks. It's one thing to allow Clemens, Alvarez, or Finley to walk four men a game.

	W	SV	ERA	IP	H	BB	SO	B/I	$
1995 Minnesota AL	2	0	3.83	51	48	31	38	1.53	1
1996 Minnesota AL	7	0	5.12	186	197	116	114	1.68	-

ROBINSON, KEN - TR - Age 27
He spent the early part of the season with the Kansas City Royals before being reacquired on waivers by Toronto in early May. Robinson, who is usually listed at 5'9" but who looks two inches shorter, has one of the best fastballs in the organization. If he could overcome his problems with the home run, he'd be back in the majors.

RODRIGUEZ, FELIX - TR - Age 24
Last year was Rodriguez's worst as a pitcher; he went 3-9 with a 5.53 ERA at Triple-A Albuquerque. He was formerly a catcher and was converted to pitching in 1993. He's going to have to be more consistent in 1997.

RODRIGUEZ, FRANK - TR - Age 24
Rodriguez held down his spot in the rotation in '96 and pitched decently, winning 13 games. His control is still below average, and he lacks a strikeout pitch. Expect him to come over the plate more and be hit hard for the next couple of years.

	W	SV	ERA	IP	H	BB	SO	B/I	$
1995 Boston - Minnesota AL	5	0	6.13	105	114	57	59	1.62	-
1996 Minnesota AL	13	2	5.05	206	218	78	110	1.44	10

RODRIGUEZ, JOSEPH FRANK - TR - Age 24
Known as "Frankie" but not to be confused with the Twins pitcher Frank Rodriguez, this one is a Brewers farmhand. He had a good year in 1994 at Double-A El Paso but hasn't been very effective since then. He spent 1996 partly at Double-A and partly at Triple-A, with an ERA over 6.00 at both levels.

RODRIGUEZ, NERIO - TR - Age 24
It's a remarkable story that Nerio Rodriguez pitched for the Orioles in 1996, actually starting a game in the last week of the season. It's an amazing story because up until mid-1995, he was a poor hitting catcher struggling in Single-A when the Orioles coaches converted him to a pitcher because of his great arm. He began 1996 as a pitcher dominating in Single-A ball, earning a promotion to Triple-A, and then to the Orioles where he impressed a lot of people. The Orioles drafted him out of the White Sox farm system in the 1994 Triple-A Rule 5 draft for $12,000, a move that looks like a real steal. He's 6'0" and 165 pounds., but he throws hard with a smooth, easy delivery.

RODRIGUEZ, RICH - TL - Age 34
Veteran lefthander Rodriguez tried to rebound from serious arm and shoulder trouble with a good year at Triple-A Omaha. He struck out nearly a batter per inning and was the O-Royals most reliable lefty reliever. Can Rodriguez still pitch in the majors? He has certainly earned the chance to try.

ROGERS, BRYAN - TR - Age 29
Rogers had back surgery and missed the first of 1996, but he later had good results as a reliever (1.54 ERA at Class A St. Lucie and a 3.38 ERA for Triple-A) on the Mets farm. He is a basic sinker/slider groundball pitcher.

ROGERS, JIMMY - TR - Age 30
He'll be thirty on Opening Day and getting rocked at Triple-A didn't help. Rogers' control is better than any minor leaguer in the Toronto organization but when he puts it over, there hasn't been much to stop batters from hitting it. He's hoping for another year somewhere.

ROGERS, KENNY - TL - Age 32
Rogers emerged as one of the premier lefthanders in the American League in 1995. He has a good enough fastball to challenge hitters and an outstanding curve. Pitching for the Yankees in 1997, he should win more.

	W	SV	ERA	IP	H	BB	SO	B/I	$
1995 Texas AL	17	0	3.38	208	192	76	140	1.29	20
1996 New York AL	12	0	4.68	179	179	83	92	1.46	7

ROGERS, KEVIN - TL - Age 28
After an outstanding rookie season in the San Francisco bullpen in 1993, the lefthander has yet to recover from the blood clot that developed in his pitching arm in 1994. The Pirates claimed Rogers off waivers from the Giants following the 1995 season but he spent all of in 1996 on the disabled list at Triple-A Calgary.

ROJAS, EUCLIDES - TR - Age 29
The Marlins thought it would be a great idea to give a pro opportunity to Rojas, then a 27-year-old Miami native playing in the independent Western League. Barely a year later they pulled the plug.

ROJAS, MEL - TR - Age 30
Perhaps still stung by former Expos GM Kevin Malone dubbing him "The Excuse Man" a year earlier, Rojas showed more maturity in 1996 and went on to have his best season. He finally blossomed into a top-flight closer and Montreal, seriously changing its tune, went into the offseason saying they would do whatever it takes to re-sign the potential free agent.

	W	SV	ERA	IP	H	BB	SO	B/I	$
1995 Montreal NL	1	30	4.12	67	69	29	61	1.45	25
1996 Montreal NL	7	36	3.22	81	56	28	92	1.04	35

ROMANO, MICHAEL - TR - Age 25
He gives up too many home runs and lacks control. He may be beginning a transition to relief pitching but shouldn't count on anything more than another year at Knoxville.

ROPER, JOHN - TR - Age 25
Roper did not pitch at all in 1996 after battling injuries most of the last three seasons. A comeback is always possible, but Roper has not pitched really well since 1991 in A ball.

ROQUE, RAFAEL - TL - Age 25
Roque looked ready for Double-A competition in 1996, but the Dominican native had some bad starts (too often in cold weather) in the Eastern League, and the Mets sent him back to Class A St. Lucie, where Roque had a 2.12 ERA. He will start 1997 at Double-A, hoping for warm weather. The last name rhymes with OK.

ROSADO, JOSE - TL - Age 22
Everyone was wondering: who is this kid? Pitching in A-ball in 1995 and not considered one of the Royals' top five minor league pitchers, Rosado had two scoreless starts for Double-A Wichita, ripped through Triple-A at Omaha (8-3, 3.17 ERA) and wound up in the Royals rotation where he quickly made his mark by earning pitcher-of-the-month awards in July and August. Rosado has a marvelous changeup and great poise on the mound. A word of caution: Rosado has only been around once in the AL and may not see the same level of success the next time through.

	W	SV	ERA	IP	H	BB	SO	B/I	$
1996 Kansas City AL	8	0	3.21	106	101	26	64	1.20	10

ROSE, BRIAN - TR - Age 21
Outstanding control and a low-90s fastball made Rose one of the best pitchers in Double-A in 1996. Shoulder tendinitis slowed him early in the year, but he rebounded to go 12-7 with a 4.01 ERA. Rose has great stuff and just needs a little polish before reaching the majors.

ROSE, SCOTT - TR - Age 26
He doesn't seem like much, but his numbers and effectiveness keep improving. Rose isn't overpowering by a long shot, but he seems to get the job done. He doesn't seem like a big league reliever, but he could surprise.

ROSENGREN, JOHN - TL - Age 24
Lefty Rosengren has a good fastball, but poor location. He led Double-A Jacksonville with 60 appearances in 1996, but walked 37 batters in 55 innings. He'll have to find the plate to find his way farther up the Tigers' farm system.

ROSSELLI, JOE - TL - Age 24
Lefty Angel minor league reliever Joe Rosselli had a good season in Triple-A in 1996 as a setup man and middle reliever. He was injured in 1993, and he has struggled trying to recapture his effective winning form. Judging from his performance in 1996, he's made it back.

Benson's Baseball Player Guide: 1997

RUEBEL, MATT - TL - Age 27
Ruebel was called up in May by the Pirates and was knocked around as a starter. He came back in mid-July and pitched pretty well out of the bullpen. His major league future is most likely as a lefthanded relief specialist who can get tough lefthanded hitters with a good curveball. However, the Pirates still haven't given up of him being a starter if he can regain the five MPH he mysteriously lost on his fastball last season.

	W	SV	ERA	IP	H	BB	SO	B / I	$
1996 Pittsburgh NL	1	1	4.60	58	64	25	22	1.53	-

RUETER, KIRK - TL - Age 26
Rueter gave the Giants three good starts after the deadline deal which sent him west. Since his amazing nine straight win debut in '94, he has struggled. Like his new teammate William Van Landinghan, Reuter jumped from Double-A to the majors. He is not overpowering, and is just really learning to pitch at the major league level. If he can stay healthy he is certainly worth looking at (though maybe not for long).

	W	SV	ERA	IP	H	BB	SO	B / I	$
1995 Montreal NL	5	0	3.23	47	38	9	28	0.99	5
1996 San Francisco NL	6	0	3.97	102	109	27	46	1.33	3

RUFFCORN, SCOTT - TR - Age 27
A first round pick in 1991, Ruffcorn has been held back by injuries and has struggled in his brief major league opportunities. He was 13-4 with a 3.87 ERA yielding less than a hit per inning at Triple-A Nashville in 1996.

RUFFIN, BRUCE - TL - Age 33
Ruffin emerged as the number one closer for the Rockies following a series of blown saves by contenders Curt Leskanic and Darren Holmes early in the year. Ruff's slider is one of the best in the game, which makes it doubly tough for hitters to catch up to his above-average heater.

	W	SV	ERA	IP	H	BB	SO	B / I	$
1995 Colorado NL	0	11	2.12	34	26	19	23	1.32	11
1996 Colorado NL	7	24	4.00	69	55	29	74	1.21	22

RUFFIN, JOHNNY - TR - Age 25
Ruffin found himself in Ray Knight's doghouse in spring training (when his manager described his pitching as "pukey") and never really got out. Ruffin has great stuff (69 strikeouts in 62 innings) featuring a moving fastball and slider, but his command was lacking (10 homers). Ruffin has pitched well at the major league level in trials from 1993-1995, so he may just need to upgrade his role in 1997.

	W	SV	ERA	IP	H	BB	SO	B / I	$
1995 Cincinnati NL	0	0	1.35	13	4	11	11	1.13	0
1996 Cincinnati NL	1	0	5.49	62	71	37	69	1.74	-

RUMER, TIM - TL - Age 27
This veteran minor leaguer moved from starting to relief in 1996 and had good results, producing a 2.25 ERA at Double-A and a 2.72 ERA at Triple-A. The Yankees are not the only team looking for lefty relief help, so stay tuned.

RUSCH, GLENDON - TL - Age 22
Skipping over Double-A and going straight to Triple-A in 1996, Rusch didn't miss a beat. Second only to Jim Pittsley among Royals minor league pitching prospects, Rusch has pinpoint control of a fastball, curve and changeup. He can get strikeouts despite not throwing hard simply because of great command and working against hitters timing. Rusch's strikeout-to-walk ratio is better than 3.5-to-1 over the last three years. It's not a question of if, but when will Rusch reach the majors.

RUSSELL, JEFF - TR - Age 35
Russell served as the primary righthanded setup man for Texas, and was tough on righthanded hitters (.229). Lefties ate his lunch (.329). In what is becoming an annual ritual, Russell was contemplating retirement at season's end. If he returns, he will pitch in middle or late relief. His closer days are over.

	W	SV	ERA	IP	H	BB	SO	B / I	$
1995 Texas AL	1	20	3.03	32	36	9	21	1.38	20
1996 Texas AL	3	3	3.38	56	58	22	23	1.43	4

RUSSELL, LaGRANDE - TR - Age 26
Russell spent his second straight season at Double-A Port City, this time as a swingman. His performance was poor; opponents hit nearly .300 against him and his ERA was more than a run worse than the previous year. Russell lacks major league stuff.

RYAN, JAY - TR - Age 21
Ryan struggled at Double-A Orlando and was demoted to Daytona in 1996, where he finished the season. He didn't fare any better there. He's a three-pitch pitcher but he doesn't handle pressure well. The Cubs think of him as one of their top pitching prospects, especially after a solid 11-5 mark in 1995. But he really struggled in 1996. He needs to rebound with a solid season in 1997.

RYAN, KEN - TR - Age 28
Ryan showed he could be a closer in 1994. Then completely lost it in 1995, first losing his closer role, then getting demoted to the minors. A fresh start with a new team did him a world of good in 1996. With confidence restored, he is a top setup man and closer-in-waiting.

	W	SV	ERA	IP	H	BB	SO	B/I	$
1995 Boston AL	0	7	4.96	32	34	24	34	1.78	4
1996 Philadelphia NL	3	8	2.43	89	71	45	71	1.30	11

RYAN, MATT - TR - Age 25
Ryan's 20 saves at Triple-A Calgary looked good in 1996, but his 2-6 record and 5.30 ERA in 51 games didn't. The Pirates did not recall him in September, a sign that they are not convinced about him. He isn't the classic hard-throwing closer, relying more on a sinker. If he gets to the major leagues, it will most likely be as a middle reliever or setup man.

RYCHEL, KEVIN - TR - Age 25
Rychel is a little hard-throwing righthanded reliever in the Pirates' farm system who had a poor 1996, going 2-0 with an 8.18 ERA in 11 games with Triple-A Calgary and 1-1 with a 4.46 ERA in 26 games with Double-A Carolina. He is a borderline prospect who has never been regarded highly enough to be put on the 40-man roster.

GOT A QUESTION?
CALL JOHN BENSON LIVE

Your Question - Your Roster - Your Situation

Let the top analyst in the business help you!!

1-900-773-7526

$2.49/minute

1 pm to 11 pm Eastern Time - 7 days a Week

SABERHAGEN, BRET - TR - Age 32
Sabes had reconstructive shoulder surgery and didn't throw a pitch in 1996. He's offered to sign an incentive-laden minor league contract to prove himself fit for 1997, but it remains to be seen whether the arm strength is there. Saberhagen has vowed to retire rather than became a finesse pitcher.

	W	SV	ERA	IP	H	BB	SO	B / I	$
1995 Two Teams	7	0	4.18	153	165	33	100	1.29	5
1996				Did Not Play					

SACKINSKY, BRIAN - TR - Age 25
Sackinsky's 1996 season was limited due to elbow problems and later, shoulder problems. It was his second consecutive injury-filled year. He has outstanding control but only average stuff and posted a good record in Triple-A in 1996. Considering that Sackinsky breaks down physically, most likely from pitching lots of innings, he may be better off as reliever.

SAGER, A.J. - TR - Age 32
Sager worked in long relief for Detroit after his mid season call up. He has spent his entire career with the Padres and could not break in, yet he will have a decent year or two in the majors.

	W	SV	ERA	IP	H	BB	SO	B / I	$
1995 Colorado NL	0	0	7.36	14	19	7	10	1.77	-
1996 Detroit AL	4	0	5.01	79	91	29	52	1.52	-

SAIPE, MIKE - TR - Age 23
Saipe was the staff ace at Colorado's Double-A New Haven franchise, the only starter there to get 10 wins in 1996. He sported a 3.07 ERA with less than a hit per inning and a three to one strikeout/walk ratio. Saipe has both velocity and control. He will advance in 1997, though he is likely to be a reliever by the time he reaches the majors.

SALAZAR, MIKE - TL - Age 25
A long-reliever and spot starter for Double-A Jacksonville, Salazar doesn't have major league stuff. He has to have good control to succeed since he can't throw the ball past hitters. Salazar is a marginal prospect.

SALKELD, ROGER - TR - Age 26
Salkeld took over the fifth starter role early in the season and pitched pretty well in the first half (3.63 ERA). However, he collapsed in the second half (7.35 ERA) and was dropped from the rotation in September. Salkeld has a decent fastball and slider, but will need better command to hold a major league roster spot. He will be part of the fifth starter derby in 1997.

	W	SV	ERA	IP	H	BB	SO	B / I	$
1996 Cincinnati NL	8	0	5.20	116	114	54	82	1.45	-

SAMPSON, BENJI - TL - Age 21
Sampson isn't a highly-regarded prospect, but impressed scouts with his durability and command. His inability to get righthanded hitters out may lead to a bullpen role as a situational lefty.

SANDERS, FRANKIE - TR - Age 21
Drafted in the 13th round in 1995 out of noted baseball factory Pasco Hernandez (Fla.) Community College, Sanders is an undersized (5'11", 165 pounds) curveball specialist. He had the best breaking pitch in the Low-A South Atlantic League, according to its managers, and exhibited excellent command and mound presence. He averaged less than six innings per start, and has only an average fastball, two factors that could work against him at Double-A and above.

SANDERS, SCOTT - TR - Age 28
Big seasons have been expected from the talented Sanders in the past, but he's often come down with elbow ailments. The Padres used him carefully in 1996, breaking him in slowly in relief in his first 30 appearances. He held up well and was moved to the rotation, and overall he had a good 9-5 record with a nice 3.38 ERA while giving up only 117 hits in 144 innings.

	W	SV	ERA	IP	H	BB	SO	B / I	$
1995 San Diego NL	5	0	4.30	90	79	31	88	1.22	4
1996 San Diego NL	9	0	3.38	144	117	48	157	1.15	10

SANDERSON, SCOTT - TR - Age 40
Sanderson was on the DL early in 1996 with a strained groin muscle, and had difficulty coming back. He was in the majors for all or parts of 20 years, with excellent years for the Cubs, Athletics, Yankees and White Sox winning 163 games overall.

SANFORD, MO - TR - Age 30
Sanford put together a nice Triple-A season as a starter for Oklahoma City, and may have given himself one more chance at a major league job. At age 30, it'll be an uphill battle. Sanford's control did improve markedly in 1996.

SANTANA, JULIO - TR - Age 24
He's listed at 6'0" 175 pounds, but looks heavier than that. A converted shortstop, he hasn't struck out more than a batter an inning since 1994. He's not likely to be the big impact starter the Rangers had once envisioned.

SAUERBECK, SCOTT - TL - Age 25
Sauerbeck's breaking pitches got him to Double-A after two and half years at Class A. Basically, he is a lefty who can throw strikes, and that is why the Mets are keeping him around patiently.

SAUNDERS, TONY - TL - Age 22
Seemingly recovered from the arm trouble that had cost him sizeable chunks of the previous two seasons, Saunders was one of the most dominant starters in the Double-A Eastern League in 1996. He features an upper-80's fastball with sharp movement, plus a curve and changeup. He showed excellent stamina and mound presence, and has the added feature of being a lefty.

SAUVER, RICH - TL - Age 33
The veteran minor leaguer pitched well at Triple-A and got a brief appearance with the White Sox in 1996.

SCANLAN, BOB - TR - Age 30
Scanlan wore out his welcome in Milwaukee and joined the Royals near the end of the year. Once a potential closer, Scanlan is now just barely hanging on to a major league job.

	W	SV	ERA	IP	H	BB	SO	B/I	$
1995 Milwaukee AL	4	0	6.59	83	101	44	29	1.74	-
1996 Kansas City AL	0	0	6.85	22	29	12	6	1.86	-

SCHILLING, CURT - TR - Age 30
Though it went unnoticed by many, Schilling was clearly one of the most dominant major league starters in 1996. Despite missing the first month and a half of the season, Schilling led the NL in complete games (8), and allowed about a baserunner per inning while striking out a batter per inning. He still throws a mid-90's heater, and complements it with a biting slider and deadly split-fingered fastball.

	W	SV	ERA	IP	H	BB	SO	B/I	$
1995 Philadelphia NL	7	0	3.57	116	96	26	114	1.05	10
1996 Philadelphia NL	9	0	3.19	183	149	50	182	1.09	15

SCHMIDT, CURT - TR - Age 27
Schmidt is a lanky sidearming righty who has tasted consistent minor league success, largely due to his ability to consistently throw low strikes. Schmidt was flustered in his early 1995 audition in the majors, uncharacteristically walking nine in 10 innings.

SCHMIDT, JASON - TR - Age 24
Anointed as the newest member of baseball's best pitching staff, Schmidt quickly proceeded to go into the tank. He posted a 6.75 ERA to earn a trip back to Triple-A Richmond. Schmidt turned it around (going 3-0 with a 2.56 ERA in seven starts) before he was included in the waiver-wire trade to the Pirates for Denny Neagle. Schmidt quickly becomes one of the best and brightest prospects with the Bucs. He'll be in the Pittsburgh rotation in 1997.

	W	SV	ERA	IP	H	BB	SO	B/I	$
1995 Atlanta NL	2	0	5.76	25	27	18	19	1.80	-
1996 Pittsburgh NL	5	0	5.70	96	108	53	74	1.68	-

SCHMIDT, JEFF - TR - Age 26
Middle reliever and setup man Jeff Schmidt pitched poorly for the Angels last season, but got two lucky wins by being in the right place at the right time. Rookie nervousness could have caused the shaky debut because he's a better pitcher than his 7.88 ERA indicates. He had a good record in Triple-A before being called up, and in a Baseball America poll of managers, he was rated the top reliever in the Pacific Coast League. Schmidt has a good fastball and slider, and the Angels see him as one of the two setup men for Troy Percival.

SCHMITT, TODD - TR - Age 27
Schmitt is a reliever in the Padres farm system where he's been a closer in Double-A for the past two years. He's struggled in two short stints in Triple-A, not the type of performance that gets one to the majors. Schmitt struck out 47 in 39 Double-A innings, a good rate that catches scouts' attention.

SCHOENEWEIS, SCOTT - TR - Age 22
Angel farmhand Scott Schoeneweis posted a good record as a starter in the hitter-friendly California League in 1996 showing good control with an excellent strikeout rate. It's amazing because he was only drafted in 1996, and he's shown good talent and poise thus far. He's an experienced college pitcher from Duke. The Angels sent Schoeneweis to the Arizona Fall League, where top prospects are usually sent. He could move up quickly.

SCHOUREK, PETE - TL - Age 27
Ray Knight gave him a 137 pitch start in an April game, and Schourek was never the same. He was shut down in July and underwent successful elbow surgery, and was throwing by the end of the season. Unlike Jose Rijo, Schourek is a decent bet to return in 1997, although there is some question whether it will be with the Reds. Healthy, Schourek features a good fastball and sharp breaking curveball and is a good comeback/sleeper candidate for 1997.

	W	SV	ERA	IP	H	BB	SO	B/I	$
1995 Cincinnati NL	18	0	3.22	190	158	45	160	1.07	22
1996 Cincinnati NL	4	0	6.01	67	79	24	54	1.54	-

SCHUERMANN, LANCE - TL - Age 27
Southpaw minor league reliever Lance Schuermann got into a few games for the Orioles Double-A club in 1996. He was formerly in the Ranger organization where he was a reliever and starter getting as high as Triple-A with a so-so record.

SCHULLSTROM, ERIK - TR - Age 28
Once considered a closer candidate for the Twins, Schullstrom dropped back to Double-A with the Red Sox in 1996. He earned a midseason promotion to Triple-A Pawtucket but was ineffective as a starter. Now with his third organization in two years, Schullstrom will have to regain his control to return to the majors.

SCHUTZ, CARL - TL - Age 25
Leading his team in saves each of the past two years earned Schutz a spot on the Braves' 40-man roster and a promotion to Richmond. In Triple-A for the first time, Schutz struggled for much of the year and was inserted into the rotation to help him get some consistency. Schutz's star has dimmed a little but the Braves still think highly of him; he'll get another chance at Richmond in 1997.

SCHWARZ, JEFF - TR - Age 32
A thirteen year pro, Schwarz spent nine years in the minors before getting his first major league chance with the White Sox in 1993. He's a marginal major league finesse artist who will fight for a bullpen role.

SCOTT, DARRYL - TR - Age 28
Scott is a journeyman minor leaguer who might already have enough major league time to qualify for a pension if he were lefthanded. He has averaged better than a strikeout per inning with a better than three to one strikeout to walk ratio for his career, generally as his clubs' closer or top setup man. Maybe the next round of expansion will do the trick. He is currently one of the Indians' many minor league insurance policies.

SCOTT, TIM - TR - Age 30
Hampered by injuries, Scott struggled to gain command of his pitches; his body; his psyche, in 1996 with little ability to master any. He has played well in the past and does throw hard. He was also released by the Giants.

	W	SV	ERA	IP	H	BB	SO	B / I	$
1995 Montreal NL	2	2	3.98	63	52	23	57	1.18	4
1996 San Francisco NL	5	1	4.64	66	65	30	47	1.44	0

SEANEZ, RUDY - TR - Age 28
His career has consisted of time on the DL (mostly back and arm problems) and brief flashes of a great fastball. The last time he threw more than 60 innings in a year was 1989. Any chance of him becoming the Dodgers closer was ended by the development of Antonio Osuna.

SEBACH, KYLE - TR - Age 25
Angels' farmhand Kyle Sebach had a good record as starter/reliever in the hitter-friendly Single-A California League in 1996. He also got into four games in Double-A, where he will likely begin the 1997 season. His high strike-out rate in Single-A looks good, but he will be tested at higher competitive levels.

SEELBACH, CHRIS - TR - Age 24
Seelbach has dominated at all other minor league levels, but has been lit up at a 13-24, 5.33 clip at the Triple-A level in three stints, culminating in his 1996 debacle. Seelbach has lacked the confidence to throw his fastball for a quality strike one at Triple-A, and has paid the price. He has now slid down from the prospect to the suspect category - only a full season of much improved performance will edge him back onto the Marlins' major league radar screen.

SELE, AARON - TR - Age 26
Sele wasn't quite back to full strength in 1996 after losing most of 1995 to a shoulder injury. His fastball wasn't as strong as it used to be and he didn't have much bite on the breaking pitches. But Sele was improving as 1996 wound to a close. He can still pitch and should be in the Red Sox' rotation again in 1997; don't write him off yet.

	W	SV	ERA	IP	H	BB	SO	B / I	$
1995 Boston AL	3	0	3.06	32	32	14	21	1.42	2
1996 Boston AL	7	2	5.32	157	195	67	137	1.65	-

SENIOR, SHAWN - TR - Age 25
Personal difficulties drove Senior off the Double-A Trenton club late in the season. Senior is not a great prospect, but has some talent and could move up to Triple-A in 1997.

SERAFINI, DAN - TL - Age 23
Big things are expected of Serafini, the Twins' top draft pick of 1992. He had a difficult year in his first extended Triple-A experience. The Pacific Coast League can produce some bad pitching lines and Serafini had his share in 1996. Still, he's considered one of the top lefthanded prospects in the organization.

SERVICE, SCOTT- TR - Age 30
For the second straight year, Service pitched well for Indianapolis (15 saves, 58 strikeouts and 10 walks in 48 innings). He was called up for a cup of coffee with the Reds and pitched well enough to earn a shot at a setup role in 1997. A typical journeyman middle reliever, his career high in innings is 46 with the Reds and Rockies in 1993.

	W	SV	ERA	IP	H	BB	SO	B / I	$
1995 San Francisco NL	3	0	3.19	31	18	20	30	1.23	2
1996 Cincinnati NL	1	0	3.94	48	51	18	46	1.44	-

SEXTON, JEFF - TR - Age 25
Sexton learned the difference between Single-A and Double-A hitters the hard way in 1996. He was able to get away with his average velocity and above average command at lower levels, but he became a nibbler after he learned that the higher level hitters could hammer his mediocre fastball.

SHAW, CURTIS - TL - Age 27
A workhorse reliever spent most of the year at Single-A and didn't dominate. Strikes out a lot, walks a lot, and doesn't have much of a chance to do much more.

SHAW, JEFF - TR - Age 30
This former Expo was signed by the Reds as a free agent and posted the best year of his career. Starting the season as the long man, Shaw worked his way up to the number two man in the bullpen. Signed to a two year deal after the

season, Shaw will be the primary setup man and the closer if anything happens to Jeff Brantley.

	W	SV	ERA	IP	H	BB	SO	B / I	$
1995 Montreal NL	1	3	4.62	62	58	26	45	1.35	3
1995 Chicago AL	0	0	6.52	9	12	1	6	1.34	-
1996 Cincinnati NL	8	4	2.49	104	99	29	69	1.23	12

SHEPHERD, ALVIE - TR - Age 22
Hard throwing Alvie Shepherd was the Orioles top pick in the 1995 draft. He began his career in 1996 in the Double-A Carolina League where he pitched well striking out 104 in 97 innings as a reliever and occasional starter. Baseball America rated his fastball as having the best velocity in the 1995 amateur draft.

SHEPHERD, KEITH - TR - Age 29
The well-travelled Shepard spent 10 years in the minors with the Phillies, Rockies, Red Sox, Indians, Royals, and Marlins. He was signed by the Orioles in early 1996 on the recommendation of Bobby Bonilla and Roberto Alomar who saw that he was almost unhittable in the Puerto Rican winter league. But there's a big difference between the winter league and the show. The Orioles gave him numerous chances as a reliever in 1996, but he was ineffective, cleared waivers, and assigned to their Triple-A team.

	W	SV	ERA	IP	H	BB	SO	B / I	$
1996 Baltimore AL	0	0	8.71	20	31	18	17	2.43	-

SHOUSE, BRIAN - TL - Age 28
Shouse had a good season in 1996 as a middle reliever and setup man for the Orioles Triple-A club, his third year in Triple-A. He didn't get called up in 1996 when the Orioles needed bullpen help, and he has also been passed over by other major league teams in prior years, all indicating that he's good enough for Triple-A, but not good enough for the show.

SHUEY, PAUL - TR - Age 26
Shuey made impressive strides towards becoming the next Indians' closer during the 1996 season. He possesses a heavy 90 MPH fastball and a drop-dead forkball. He is darn near unhittable when he has both pitches working. Throwing strike one is his biggest hurdle; doing so enables him to throw the forkball at will.

	W	SV	ERA	IP	H	BB	SO	B / I	$
1996 Cleveland AL	5	4	2.85	53	45	26	44	1.33	7

SHUMATE, JACOB - TR - Age 21
Shumate, the Braves' number one draft choice in 1994 continued in Class-A in 1996. Control may continue to be a problem; he walked 55 in 65 innings for his high school team.

SIEVERT, MARK - TR - Age 24
Sievert dominated Single-A and Double-A batters before getting knocked around at Syracuse late last season. If his control returns to where it was in the lower minors, he's going to compete for a starting job in Toronto soon.

SIKORSKI, BRIAN - TR - Age 23
Sikorski was a fourth round draft choice by the Astros in 1995 from Western Michigan University. He has had two successful seasons, one as a closer and one as a starter. He was the ace of the low Class-A Quad Cities staff in 1996 with an 11-8 record and an ERA of 3.13. He led the Astro minor league system in strike-outs with 150. Sikorski has a 90 MPH fastball but needs to sharpen his control as he moves up. He needs another strong showing at a higher level in 1997 to stay on track.

SILVA, JOSE - TR - Age 23
Silva has a good fastball, but lost part of the year to should problems. He was brought along slowly at Double-A Knoxville in 1996, going 2-3 with a 4.91 ERA. His strikeouts were down, but that can be attributed to less velocity from the shoulder problem. If he can return healthy in 1997 then he might pick up where he left off in 1993 when his fastball was voted the best in the South Atlantic League.

SILVA, TED - TR - Age 22
A 17-4 record and an ERA under 3.00 with a midseason promotion will generally get a pitcher noticed, and Silva is no exception. His strikeout rate fell noticeably after being promoted to Double-A, but he continued to post good numbers. He doesn't have dominating stuff, but he knows how to pitch.

SIMAS, BILL - TR - Age 25
Acquired from California in the Jim Abbott trade, Simas did setup and long relief work in 1996. A hard thrower, Simas was a closer in the low minors.

	W	SV	ERA	IP	H	BB	SO	B/I	$
1995 Chicago AL	1	0	2.57	14	15	10	16	1.79	-
1996 Chicago AL	2	2	4.58	72	75	39	65	1.58	1

SIMMONS, SCOTT - TL - Age 27
As one of the few lefty prospects high in the Cardinals' minor league system, Simmons has gotten by on an off-speed repertoire. Simmons was among league ERA leaders in Double-A in 1995 and went 5-6 with a 4.15 ERA at Triple-A Louisville in 1996. He's such a soft tosser that he has to be precise.

SIMONS, DOUG - TL - Age 30
Simons is a journeyman who began his professional career in 1988. He appeared in the major leagues briefly in 1991 and 1992. He was signed to a minor league contract by the Astros in 1996 and pitched well at Double-A but was less successful at Triple-A. His marginal stuff is not likely to get him back to the majors.

SIROTKA, MIKE - TL - Age 25
Sirotka is a lefty finesse pitcher who gets into trouble when he tries to get too fine with his breaking pitches, leaving them out over the plate.

	W	SV	ERA	IP	H	BB	SO	B/I	$
1995 Chicago AL	1	0	4.19	34	39	17	19	1.63	-
1996 Chicago AL	1	0	7.18	26	34	12	11	1.76	-

SLOCUMB, HEATHCLIFF - TR - Age 30
Acquired from the Phillies in a winter deal, Slocumb was given the Red Sox' closer job from the outset. His early struggles caused all kinds of wild speculation, but Slocumb righted himself and made a big contribution to Boston's late pennant drive. He's not one of the league's better closers; Slocumb is best used as a one-inning closer. Slocumb's save totals are more a function of how well the setup relievers do to give him a good situation than his own abilities.

	W	SV	ERA	IP	H	BB	SO	B/I	$
1995 Philadelphia NL	5	32	2.89	65	64	35	63	1.52	30
1996 Boston AL	5	31	3.02	83	68	55	88	1.48	34

SLUSARSKI, JOE - TR - Age 30
Still trying to find some offspeed and breaking stuff to go with his major league quality fastball, Slusarski worked 40 games as a reliever at Triple-A New Orleans in 1996, with a 4.95 ERA and more than a hit per inning.

SMALL, AARON - TR - Age 25
Former Jay and Marlin, Small showed good stuff in Edmonton and was then lit up in Oakland over three starts and 28.2 innings. Just doesn't seem to have it.

	W	SV	ERA	IP	H	BB	SO	B/I	$
1995 Florida NL	1	0	1.42	6	7	6	5	2.05	-
1996 Oakland AL	1	0	8.16	28	37	22	17	2.09	-

SMALL, MARK - TR - Age 29
Small reached the major leagues for the first time in 1996 in his eighth year in the Astro system. He split the season between Triple-A, where he pitched well, and Houston, where he was not effective. He appears to be a borderline major leaguer.

	W	SV	ERA	IP	H	BB	SO	B/I	$
1996 Houston NL	0	0	5.92	24	33	13	16	1.91	-

SMILEY, JOHN - TL - Age 32
The veteran lefthander quietly posted another excellent season, and would have won more games with better run support (getting only 4.3 runs per game). Smiley has excellent command of four pitches and signed a new three year deal with the Reds at the end of the season (at considerably below his market value). His only bad years in the majors occurred when he tried to pitch hurt.

	W	SV	ERA	IP	H	BB	SO	B/I	$
1995 Cincinnati NL	12	0	3.46	176	173	39	124	1.20	14
1996 Cincinnati NL	13	0	3.64	217	207	54	171	1.20	14

SMITH, BRIAN - TR - Age 24
After a spectacular season at Single-A Hagerstown in 1995, Smith became the closer at Double-A Knoxville and looked just as comfortable. He's still a while from the majors but could get a look by September.

SMITH, LEE - TR - Age 39
The Reds traded for Lee Smith to prevent the Astros from acquiring him to be their closer. The Astros were forced to settle for Billy Wagner. Smith wasn't awful for the Reds, but by the end of the season he was strictly a mop up man. Given the shortage of pitching in the majors, he could catch on with another team as a setup man if he wants to pitch for a minimal salary plus incentives, but his days as a closer are over.

	W	SV	ERA	IP	H	BB	SO	B/I	$
1995 California AL	0	37	3.47	49	42	25	43	1.36	37
1996 California AL	0	0	2.45	11	8	3	6	1.00	-
1996 Cincinnati NL	3	2	4.06	44	49	23	35	1.63	-

SMITH, OTTIS - TL - Age 26
The Cubs got Smith as a toss-in in the Jose Vizcaino-Anthony Young trade with the Mets. Smith is not intimidating physically and he has fought arm problems recently. He doesn't throw hard at all and must get his curve and changeup over to be effective. He was hurt late in 1995 and didn't pitch in 1996.

SMITH, PETE - TR - Age 31
Major league veteran starter Pete Smith was on the comeback trail in 1996 pitching for the Padres Triple-A club. He spent nine years in the majors with the Braves, Mets and Reds, making 136 starts with a career 35-60 record and a 4.40 ERA. He was "high-potential" for years but didn't quite live up to it. Smith isn't old, and he could make it back as a fourth or fifth starter.

SMITH, RYAN - TR - Age 25
In his first year above A-ball, Smith became a righthanded setup man for Port City. It was a decent year for Smith, but his stuff is ordinary. He'll continue in a similar role for a few years, toiling in the high minors with little chance of making a major league contribution.

SMITH, TOBY - TR - Age 25
The righthanded half of the save duo at Double-A Wichita, Smith had a decent season in his first year above A-ball. A Wichita State University product, Smith was a late-round draft pick in 1993. He hasn't done anything to attract attention yet and is not a highly regarded prospect. Still, Smith has had nothing but success so far.

SMITH, WILLIE - TR - Age 29
The Indians were prepared to give journeyman reliever Smith a Triple-A opportunity after he missed the entire 1995 season, but it was prevented by injury. Once a flamethrower often compared to Lee Smith, Smith is now a merely a former flamethrower. His pro career is likely over.

SMITH, ZANE - TL - Age 36
Smith got off to a good start in his return to the Pirates last season but was released just before the All-Star break after four poor starts. No one picked him up, though a lot of that was by Smith's choice. He still has enough left to be a decent fourth or fifth starter but it doesn't look like he wants to play anymore.

	W	SV	ERA	IP	H	BB	SO	B/I	$
1995 Boston AL	8	0	5.61	110	144	23	47	1.51	0
1996 Pittsburgh NL	4	0	5.08	83	104	21	47	1.50	-

SMOLTZ, JOHN - TR - Age 29
Combining a good fastball, hard slider and surprisingly good changeup, Smoltz led baseball with 276 strikeouts and 24 victories on the way to his first Cy Young award, giving pitchers in the Braves' starting rotation the last six awards. He was especially tough in the early going, running off a long string of victories to prevent the Braves from ever having a lengthy losing streak. Smoltz isn't as good as his 1996 record, but he's still one of the NL's best pitchers.

	W	SV	ERA	IP	H	BB	SO	B/I	$
1995 Atlanta NL	12	0	3.18	192	166	72	193	1.24	15
1996 Atlanta NL	24	0	2.94	253	199	55	276	1.00	30

SODERSTROM, STEVE - TR - Age 24
Completing a second consecutive injury-free season, Soderstrom started 29 games, though he didn't complete any of them. Soderstrom will start another year at Phoenix but he could appear with the big club sometime in '97.

SODOWSKY, CLINT - TR - Age 24
In 1996, Sodowsky couldn't build on the success he had in 1995 which saw him jump all the way from A-ball to the majors. He's not a strikeout pitcher and spent all season at Triple-A Toledo refining his off-speed repertoire. Sodowsky was 6-8 with a 3.94 ERA and should compete for a rotation job with the Tigers in 1997.

	W	SV	ERA	IP	H	BB	SO	B/I	$
1995 Detroit AL	2	0	5.01	23	24	18	14	1.80	-
1996 Detroit AL	1	0	11.84	24	40	20	9	2.49	-

SPARKS, STEVE - TR - Age 31
The knuckleballer who had some modest major league success in 1995, Sparks really struggled in 1996, even in the minors. He was 2-6 with more than a hit per inning and more walks than strikeouts at Triple-A New Orleans.

	W	SV	ERA	IP	H	BB	SO	B/I	$
1995 Milwaukee AL	9	0	4.63	202	210	86	96	1.47	5
1996 Milwaukee AL	4	0	6.60	88	103	52	21	1.76	-

SPEIER, JUSTIN - TR - Age 24
Speier is a classic overachiever. Selected by the Cubs in the 55th round of the 1995 draft, Speier has put together back-to-back strong seasons as a reliever. In 1996 he lead Double-A Orlando with a 2.05 ERA and walked just five batters in 26.1 innings. He's the son of former major league infielder Chris Speier.

SPOLJARIC, PAUL - TL - Age 26
After becoming a reliever with Syracuse a couple of years ago, Spoljaric has arrived in the majors to stay. His fastball continues to improve and his control is coming around. Spoljaric's effectiveness enabled the Blue Jays to deal Tony Castillo to the White Sox and he enters 1997 as a key lefty out of the bullpen.

	W	SV	ERA	IP	H	BB	SO	B/I	$
1996 Toronto AL	2	1	3.08	38	30	19	38	1.29	2

SPRADLIN, JERRY - TR - Age 29
A 6' 7", 240 pound soft thrower, Spradlin has been at the fringes of the majors since 1992, pitching well in the minors (career minor league ERA of 2.96) but rarely getting much of a chance in the majors. Pitchers like Spradlin need luck (and a manager that likes them) to establish more than a mop up role in the majors.

SPRINGER, DENNIS - TR - Age 32
Springer is a veteran of 10 minor league seasons, and at age 31, 1996 was his best shot at any lengthy time in the majors. He's a knuckleballer, and as Tim Wakefield has shown, a knuckle ball pitcher can have a big season at any time. He held opponents to a .251 batting average in 1996.

	W	SV	ERA	IP	H	BB	SO	B/I	$
1995 Philadelphia NL	0	0	4.84	22	21	9	15	1.34	-
1996 California AL	5	0	5.51	94	91	43	64	1.42	0

SPRINGER, RUSS - TR - Age 28
Springer really does have good stuff, and still could be a productive major league hurler. Springer possesses an above average fastball and a sometimes unhittable curve, and is tough on lefties (.240 average in 1996). However, he has trouble throwing strike one and is vulnerable to the longball. Springer got off to an excellent start out of the bullpen in 1996, but imploded shortly after being thrust into the rotation.

	W	SV	ERA	IP	H	BB	SO	B/I	$
1995 California AL	1	1	6.10	51	60	25	38	1.65	-
1995 Philadelphia NL	0	0	3.71	26	22	10	32	1.20	-
1996 Philadelphia NL	3	0	4.66	96	106	38	94	1.50	-

STANTON, MIKE - TL - Age 29
Stanton is not the same pitcher who saved 27 games with the Braves in 1993. Since that time, he appears to have lost some velocity, and was a dismal 1-for-6 in save opportunities with Boston and Texas. Stanton was not particularly effective against lefthanded hitters (.263), and that may negatively affect his appeal as a lefty setup man; as we know, however, lefthanded pitchers with decent stuff can always get work.

	W	SV	ERA	IP	H	BB	SO	B/I	$
1995 Atlanta NL	1	1	5.59	19	31	6	13	1.91	1
1995 Boston AL	1	0	3.00	21	17	8	10	1.19	1
1996 Boston AL	4	1	3.66	78	78	27	60	1.34	5

STEED, RICK - TR - Age 26
Formerly a Blue Jays' farmhand, Steed bounced from Class A co-op Bakersfield to the Mexican League to Double-A Greenville in 1996. He did a creditable job in a long relief/spot starter role, but doesn't appear to be in the Braves' long-range plans.

STEENSTRA, KENNIE - TR - Age 26
Steenstra may frustrate more hitters than any pitcher in the Cubs chain. He doesn't throw hard, leaves balls up in the zone and gives up lots of hits. But, Steenstra is a workhorse who gets hitters out despite his stuff. As a collegian at Wichita State, Steenstra collected an NCAA record 65 wins. Although he went 8-12 in 1996, Steenstra was, for the most part, a reliable starter who averaged over six innings per outing.

STEPH, ROD - TR - Age 27
Ex-Indians' farmhand Steph spent most of the 1996 season at Richmond in a setup role. He was relatively effective, using his experience and control to baffle Triple-A hitters. But, his lack of velocity is a barrier to his advancement to the majors.

STEPHENSON, BRIAN - TR - Age 23
The Orlando Cubs kept throwing Stephenson out on the mound. At least he was tenacious. Rated as one of the top five pitchers in Cubs chain before 1996, Stephenson finished with a 5-13 record for the O-Cubs. He's a power pitcher; Stephenson's fastball has been clocked in the mid-90's and he throws a hard curve. His deceptive delivery makes his pitches tough to pickup, but is has also caused him problems with his release point.

STEPHENSON, GARRET - TR - Age 25
Ex-Orioles prospect Garret Stephenson was swapped to the Phillies as part of the Todd Zeile and Pete Incaviglia deal. He matured as a pitcher in 1996, learning how to use all of the plate, especially pitching inside. He doesn't throw hard and is a finesse pitcher with below average stuff. Stephenson has to rely on pitching smarts to get batters out, and has been successful so far in the minors, but it remains to be seen if he can slip by major league hitters.

STEVENS, DAVE - TR - Age 27
Ineffective as a closer, Stevens went on the disabled list after punching a wall following yet another blown save. When he returned, it was as a setup man for the new closer. Stevens will probably not get a full-time closer job again, but could do the job briefly in a pinch. He should have a much steadier - and calmer - year in 1997.

	W	SV	ERA	IP	H	BB	SO	B/I	$
1995 Minnesota AL	5	10	5.07	65	74	32	47	1.61	9
1996 Minnesota AL	3	11	4.66	58	58	25	29	1.43	10

STEVENS, KRIS - TL - Age 19
The Phils' 1996 third round pick is a lefthanded curveball specialist who struggled in Rookie ball as he left his pitches over the middle of the plate. Location is paramount, as he is unlikely to fill out 6'2", 185 pound, frame much further, leaving him with mid-80's peak velocity.

STEWART, RACHAAD - TL - Age 22
Two trips to the DL slowed this big (6'4") lefty in his first year with the Braves; Stewart was obtained from Baltimore in the Kent Mercker trade. Stewart is a strikeout pitcher who will need another year at Double-A before he can truly be called a prospect.

STIDHAM, PHIL - TR - Age 28
A Rule Five pick out of the Mets' farm system, Stidham led Triple-A Salt Lake City with ten victories in 1996 despite an abysmal 6.78 ERA and 140 baserunners allowed in just 78 innings. Stidham's career has been in reverse since he made five appearances for the Tigers in 1994. He won't stand in the way of the Twins' better prospects.

STOTTLEMYRE, TODD - TR - Age 31
Stottlemyre had his best season yet in 1996 when he switched leagues, coming over to the Cardinals in a trade with Oakland. Stottlemyre has finally learned to harness his outstanding ability - and once-uncontrollable emotions. Stottlemyre has thrived under pitching coach Dave Duncan's tutelage. As long as Duncan is at his side, Stottlemyre will be a quality major league starter.

	W	SV	ERA	IP	H	BB	SO	B/I	$
1995 Oakland AL	14	0	4.55	209	228	80	205	1.47	-
1996 St. Louis NL	14	0	3.87	223	191	93	194	1.27	12

STULL, EVERETT - TR - Age 25
Stull throws a mid-90's fastball and a biting curve. Strike one has been his problem. He throws too many pitches as a result, rarely pitching deeply into ball games. Also, he throws from a straight overhand motion, causing his fastball to be pitching-machine straight at times. It has taken him a second season to dominate at each successive minor league level, meaning he should rule Triple-A in 1997.

STUMPF, BRIAN - TL - Age 24
The Phils' 1994 45th round draft pick defied his low draft status to become a dominant closer. He is not a flamethrower, but he has good movement on his pitches and has extremely good control.

STURTZE, TANYON - TR - Age 26
Sturtze inherited the closer role at Triple-A Iowa for a few weeks when Kent Bottenfield was called up. The willowy righthander responded with four saves, but never seemed comfortable in that role. After starting 17 games for Iowa in 1995, Sturtze started just one in 1996. The 26-year old didn't tear up the league in 1996, but he clocked in with some good innings out of the pen. Sturtze doesn't throw particularly hard and isn't deceptive, despite his 6'5" frame.

SULLIVAN, SCOTT - TR - Age 26
A 1993 second round pick out of Auburn, Sullivan pitched fairly well at Indianapolis and earned a brief look from the Reds. He features a fastball and slider and is one of about a dozen candidates for a setup role with the Reds in 1997.

SUPPAN, JEFF - TR - Age 22
The crown jewel of a good set of young pitching prospects in the Red Sox' high minors, Suppan enjoyed a successful year at Triple-A Pawtucket, leading the club in most pitching categories before joining the Red Sox in September.

	W	SV	ERA	IP	H	BB	SO	B/I	$
1995 Boston AL	1	0	5.96	22	29	5	19	1.50	-
1996 Boston AL	1	0	7.54	22	29	13	13	1.89	-

SUTHERLAND, JOHN - TR - Age 28
This veteran minor leaguer and alumnus of the Hawaiian Winter League got into 26 games for the Yankees Triple-A Columbus team in 1996, producing a 2.74 ERA from the bullpen. In an organization with less pitching depth, he could have been given a better shot at a major league trial.

SUZUKI, MAKATO - TR - Age 21
Suzuki was called up in 1996, got in one game and allowed three runs in 1.33 innings. In the minors at Tacoma, the "future closer" had relatively poor results.

SWAN, RUSS - TL - Age 33
Swan was a starter and reliever in the majors for the Giants, Mariners and Indians in 1989-94 posting a 14-22 record with a career 4.83 ERA. The Giants and Mariners had high expectations, but he never quite lived up to them. The Mariners even tried him as a closer. Swan pitched for the Padres Triple-A team last season, attempting to make a comeback, but he had a rough year.

SWARTZBAUGH, DAVE - TR - Age 29
Swartzbaugh found new life late in the season when he was forced into the starting rotation due to injuries. Swartzbaugh had started just one game since 1993, but he pitched well enough to warrant a September callup. He impressed the Cubs more than his numbers might indicate. Swartzbaugh's fastball is barely average but he does a good job of working both sides of the plate. When he changes speeds and keeps his fastball down, he can be a decent pitcher.

	W	SV	ERA	IP	H	BB	SO	B/I	$
1996 Chicago NL	0	0	6.38	24	26	14	13	1.67	-

SWIFT, BILL - TR - Age 35
After having arthroscopic shoulder surgery twice in eight months, Swifty pitched in just six games for the Rockies in 1996, three of them in a relief role. He's convinced he'll be completely healthy for 1997, but Swift isn't known for staying injury free for complete seasons at a time. He's an upper-crust starter with a nifty sinker nevertheless.

	W	SV	ERA	IP	H	BB	SO	B/I	$
1995 Colorado NL	9	0	4.94	105	122	43	68	1.56	-
1996 Colorado NL	1	2	5.40	18	23	5	5	1.55	-

SWINDELL, GREG - TL - Age 32
Swindell has been throwing batting practice for four seasons now, but he's lefthanded and has solid control, so you've got to figure he has some chances left.

	W	SV	ERA	IP	H	BB	SO	B/I	$
1995 Houston NL	10	0	4.47	153	180	39	96	1.43	2
1996 Houston NL	0	0	7.83	23	35	11	15	2.00	-
1996 Cleveland AL	1	0	6.59	28	31	8	21	1.38	-

SWINGLE, PAUL - TR - Age 30
The Angels signed reliever Swingle to a minor league contract in late June, 1996. He relieved in 15 games in Triple-A and looked good. He's had his ups-and-downs in the past in the minors, but he may get another major league shot if he continues to pitch well.

TABAKA, JEFF - TL - Age 33
Tabaka had some success as a lefthanded reliever in the Astro bullpen in 1995 but he failed to repeat in 1996. He was demoted to Triple-A where he spent most of the season. Tabaka throws hard but he has control problems which get him in trouble. He will have trouble holding a major league job.

	W	SV	ERA	IP	H	BB	SO	B/I	$
1995 Two Teams	1	0	3.23	30	27	17	25	1.43	0
1996 Houston NL	0	1	6.64	20	28	14	18	2.09	-

TAM, JEFF - TR - Age 26
Tam had knee surgery in 1995 but came back in '96 to work a healthy season in a setup role, finishing with a 2.44 ERA and six wins. The Mets sent him to Venezuelan winter ball after the '96 season.

TAPANI, KEVIN - TR - Age 33
Tapani has good breaking pitches plus the ability to change speeds. He was an above-average performer in 1996, and his stats reflect it. Tapani could be a big winner with a stronger team behind him. He isn't the type to carry a team himself.

	W	SV	ERA	IP	H	BB	SO	B/I	$
1995 Minnesota AL	6	0	4.92	133	155	34	88	1.41	-
1995 Los Angeles NL	4	0	5.05	57	72	14	43	1.51	-
1996 Chicago AL	13	0	4.59	225	236	76	150	1.39	12

TAULBEE, ANDY - TR - Age 24
Taulbee is a big (6'4", 215 pounds) guy but he isn't overpowering. His strikeouts are low for a guy of his size and he must either increase his velocity or his command to go anywhere.

TAVAREZ, JULIAN - TR - Age 23
Tavarez has not been the same pitcher since struggling in the 1995 post season. He seemed to have lost confidence

in his fastball and was reluctant to pitch inside during the 1996 season. He grooved fastballs down the middle, was hit by lefties at a .371 clip, and was reduced to mopup detail by the end of the season.

	W	SV	ERA	IP	H	BB	SO	B/I	$
1995 Cleveland AL	10	0	2.44	85	76	21	68	1.14	13
1996 Cleveland AL	4	0	5.36	80	101	22	46	1.53	-

TAYLOR, BILL - TR - Age 35
The long-time Braves farmhand finally got his major league shot at age 30 and fit nicely into the Oakland pen. Although he found himself back in the minors for a while, Taylor worked hard to stay sharp and remained in the Athletics' future plans.

	W	SV	ERA	IP	H	BB	SO	B/I	$
1996 Oakland AL	6	17	4.33	60	52	25	67	1.28	19

TAYLOR, BRIEN - TL - Age 25
The former number one overall draft pick never recovered from reconstructive surgery on his pitching shoulder before the 1994 season, following an offseason scuffle. He tried nine starts at Class A in 1996, with bad results (18.76 ERA).

TAYLOR, RODNEY SCOTT - TL - Age 29
Taylor began the season 7-0 for the Pirates' Double-A Carolina farm club but tailed off to 11-7, 4.61 in 29 games. He started three games for Texas in 1995 and that's likely to be his one and only taste of the big leagues.

TELEMACO, AMAURY - TR - Age 23
Telemaco put in only eight starts at Iowa before getting the call to Chicago. He struggled, giving up 20 homers in 97.1 innings. However, Telemaco is young, just 23, and his slider is already one of the best on the staff. Telemaco is a strikeout pitcher by makeup, but he didn't show it in the majors. His fastball is above average but has good movement. In the big leagues, Telemaco should be a third or fourth starter or better.

	W	SV	ERA	IP	H	BB	SO	B/I	$
1996 Chicago NL	5	0	5.46	97	108	31	64	1.43	-

TELFORD, ANTHONY - TR - Age 31
It has been three years since his last major league appearance, and he has not held down a regular rotation spot in the minors since. He has pitched for four organizations in the last three seasons, most recently at Triple-A Ottawa in the Expos' chain.

TELGHEDER, DAVE - TR - Age 30
The former Mets prospect can be highly effective when he gets his split-finger pitch over the plate, but he has never done that consistently enough to stick around the major leagues for long. If experience counts, he has plenty of that now from his minor league travels.

	W	SV	ERA	IP	H	BB	SO	B/I	$
1995 New York NL	1	0	5.61	25	34	7	16	1.60	-
1996 Oakland AL	4	0	4.65	79	92	26	43	1.49	1

TESSMER, JAY - TR - Age 25
After pitching in the College World Series for the University of Miami (Florida) Tessmer began his pro career in 1995 with a 0.95 ERA while being groomed as a closer. His progress in 1996 merits consideration for a double promotion some time in 1997.

TEWKSBURY, BOB - TR - Age 36
Tewksbury still walks few hitters, and 1996 was his first year to go over 200 innings since 1993. The past three years have shown that Tewksbury is a .500 pitcher, and if he holds up in 1997, his record will probably be around 11-11. Tewksbury has always been the ultimate control pitcher - hittable, but few walks. The walks are still few, but the hits are getting more frequent every year. Tewksbury is still an acceptable fourth starter on most teams, but he is clearly on the decline. Tewksbury was slowed toward the end of the season by a pulled muscle.

	W	SV	ERA	IP	H	BB	SO	B/I	$
1995 Texas AL	8	0	4.58	129	169	20	53	1.46	4
1996 San Diego NL	10	0	4.31	206	224	43	126	1.29	7

THOBE, TOM - TL - Age 27
Out of baseball for four years (1989-92) while he chased waves around the world, this surfer has spent the last two years in a setup role at Triple-A Richmond. He got his major league cup of coffee in 1995 and was back for another sip in 1996. Thobe was often terrible in his spot starts at Richmond and is better suited to his accustomed relief role; he's a marginal major leaguer.

THOMAS, LARRY -TL - Age 27
Thomas became a top setup man in 1996. He is not a hard thrower, but he has a good slider and can baffle hitters by changing speeds.

	W	SV	ERA	IP	H	BB	SO	B/I	$
1995 Chicago AL	0	0	1.32	13	8	6	12	1.02	1
1996 Chicago AL	2	0	3.23	30	32	14	20	1.52	-

THOMAS, ROYAL - TR - Age 27
Thomas has been on the fringe as a professional pitcher for the last two years. He began the year in the Mexican League, then joined the Braves Double-A club before finishing the year at Orlando. He relies on a fastball that is merely average and has little of major league quality to go with it. Thomas is a distant hope for the big leagues.

THOMPSON, JUSTIN - TL - Age 24
The Tigers' first-round draft pick in 1991, Thompson is the most advanced of their good pitching prospects. In thirteen starts for Triple-A Toledo he went 6-3 with a 3.42 ERA, then made his major league debut for Detroit. He suffered through some uncharacteristic control problems, but righted himself before the season wound to a close. Thompson should start 1997 in the Tigers' rotation and is one of their better young pitching prospects.

	W	SV	ERA	IP	H	BB	SO	B/I	$
1996 Detroit AL	1	0	4.58	59	62	31	44	1.58	-

THOMPSON, MARK - TR - Age 25
Thompson was a pleasant surprise in the starting rotation in 1996, showing consistency and getting the Rockies' first complete game shutout in Coors Field history. His weakness of going deep into counts improved somewhat, but his SO/BB ratio could still use some improvement.

	W	SV	ERA	IP	H	BB	SO	B/I	$
1995 Colorado NL	2	0	6.53	51	73	22	30	1.86	-
1996 Colorado NL	9	0	5.30	169	189	74	99	1.55	-

THOMSON, JOHN - TR - Age 23
Thomson knocked 'em dead in 16 starts at pitcher-friendly Double-A New Haven, but got knocked around in 11 starts at hitter-friendly Triple-A Colorado Springs. In only his fourth year of pro ball, Thomson has an excellent SO/BB ratio and may soon get a shot with the parent Rockies if he can get comfortable pitching at altitude.

THORNTON, PAUL - TR - Age 27
The Marlins 1993 number six draftee didn't reach Double-A until age 26, hardly a harbinger of future major league success. Thornton was the Marlins' primary Double-A setup man last season, and he showed a slightly above average fastball and suspect control. He has a sturdy two-inning arm which should prolong his pro career.

THURMOND, TRAVIS - TR - Age 23
Angels minor league starter Travis Thurmond put it together in 1996. That's after he went AWOL after hearing he was assigned to Class-A for the third consecutive year. He's got good control and a good strikeout rate, indications of success at higher levels. He was slated for the Arizona Fall League where he will face tougher competition.

TILTON, IRA - TR - Age 22
The Phils' 1996 fifth round draftee was selected based on raw tools. His 90 MPH fastball and his prototype 6'3", 185 pound body. Tilton has been unable to parlay his repertoire into big strikeout totals in college or in his first pro season. He needs to modify his mechanics in order to pick up a touch of speed and allow him to locate the ball on the corners with consistency.

TIMLIN, MIKE - TR - Age 31
The Blue Jays entered the winter trying to sign Timlin to a long-term deal as he has become the team's closer. His

sinker and fastball are what they need to be and his poise makes him more than adequate. He has all the tools to remain a stopper for a few years.

	W	SV	ERA	IP	H	BB	SO	B/I	$
1995 Toronto AL	4	5	2.14	42	38	17	36	1.31	9
1996 Toronto AL	1	31	3.65	56	47	18	52	1.16	32

TOLAR, KEVIN - TL - Age 26
Tolar, as the consummate specialist, has logged only 76 innings pitched in his 80 appearances over the past two seasons, most recently at Double-A Canton-Akron in the Indians' chain. However, his lack of an out pitch and his iffy control will prevent him from further advancement.

TOLLBERG, BRIAN - TR - Age 24
Tollberg was one of the better starters at Double-A El Paso on the Brewers farm in 1996. His strength is fine control. He lets the opposition put the ball in play and depends on a good defense behind him.

TOMKO, BRETT - TR - Age 24
Tomko is ray of hope in the Reds' largely moribund minor league system. Their 1995 second round pick has a low-90's fastball and an arsenal of sharp breaking pitches, all of which he throws for strikes consistently.

TOMLIN, RANDY - TL - Age 30
The erstwhile Pirates' starter lost all of 1995 and most of 1996 to elbow surgery, then went 0-2 with a 8.31 ERA in five games for Triple-A Pawtucket in 1996. If he can recover fully, Tomlin could again pitch in the majors, although he's unlikely to return to a regular role in the rotation.

TORRES, DILSON - TR - Age 26
Torres got into Bob Boone's doghouse early on and has yet to resurface. He was demoted from Omaha to Wichita in midseason and is now a long way from the majors after making 24 appearances for Kansas City in 1995. Torres has a better chance with another organization where he might be able to get a fresh start.

TORRES, SALOMON - TR - Age 25
He's still young and may be ready for a breakthrough. He was 6-9 in Tacoma but fanned 99 in only 109 IP. Called up to Seattle, Torres showed flashes of the form that made him so highly regarded. For Seattle, he went 3-3 in seven starts and had one complete game. True it was September, but the fact that he didn't fold under pennant pressure is encouraging.

	W	SV	ERA	IP	H	BB	SO	B/I	$
1995 Two Teams	3	0	6.30	80	100	49	47	1.86	-
1996 Seattle AL	3	0	4.59	49	44	23	36	1.37	0

TOTH, ROBERT - TR - Age 24
The last pitcher cut in spring training, Toth spiraled downward, posting a 7.04 ERA at Triple-A Omaha before getting demoted to Wichita where he was more effective. Toth is a control pitcher with a great changeup. He needs to improve his fastball to make the changeup more effective.

TRACHSEL, STEVE - TR - Age 26
Despite some nagging injuries, Trachsel delivered the best season by a Cubs pitcher in 1996, although he gave up a staff high 30 home runs. If 1995 was an aberration, then Trachsel could be on his way to becoming a good pitcher for many years. He sports a hard fastball, although it doesn't move much. Trachsel also relies on the splitter and an occasional sinker. He started 1996 as a question mark and finished as the ace of the staff.

	W	SV	ERA	IP	H	BB	SO	B/I	$
1995 Chicago NL	7	0	5.15	160	174	76	117	1.56	-
1996 Chicago NL	13	0	3.03	205	181	62	132	1.19	17

TRANBARGER, MARK - TL - Age 27
Oriole southpaw reliever Mark Tranberger had a rough year in Double-A in 1996, and he gained a reputation as a flake by dying his hair red when he wanted it to be blond. He was then known as "Little Orphan Trannie."

TRINIDAD, HECTOR - TR - Age 23
Trinidad came to the Twins as compensation for the loss of General Manager Andy MacPhail to the Cubs. He has since spent two years at Double-A New Britain where he has displayed fine control. Trinidad has earned a shot at the majors, but will probably spend at least one more year in the high minors.

TRLICEK, RICK - TR - Age 27
Trlicek has been released or waived by the Phillies, Braves, Dodgers, Red Sox, Giants, and Indians. He couldn't stick with the Tigers in spring training 1996. When we wrote this, he hadn't yet been released by the Mets, and was in fact in the majors on a September callup after crafting a 1.87 ERA and leading the International League in game appearances for Norfolk. He may yet find a major league role as a rubber-armed middle reliever, but it's getting late.

TROMBLEY, MIKE - TR - Age 29
Trombley finally broke through at the major league level in '96 and was the Twins' most effective reliever in the second half. He made the turnaround with the help of a split fingered fastball, which takes a toll on a pitcher's arm but seems to have made a difference here.

	W	SV	ERA	IP	H	BB	SO	B/I	$
1995 Minnesota AL	4	0	5.62	97	107	42	68	1.53	-
1996 Minnesota AL	5	6	3.01	68	61	25	57	1.26	11

TROUTMAN, KEITH - TR - Age 23
This former Dodgers' prospect moved to the Phils' chain in 1996. Troutman is a workhorse middle reliever who always wants the ball, and who can eat up two to three innings at a time. He has above average velocity and a deceptive delivery, and is actually more effective against lefties, a good sign.

TURRENTINE, RICH - TR - Age 25
A converted infielder with a strong arm (he throws well over 90 MPH) Turrentine was a Rule Five draftee by the Mets two years ago. In 1996 he got 21 saves with a 2.28 ERA as the closer for Class A St. Lucie and then worked eight games at Double-A with a 2.89 ERA and three more saves. With improved control and consistency he can keep moving up.

TWIGGS, GARY - TL - Age 25
Twiggs posted fine numbers in 1995 at Class A Daytona. His 8-3 record and 1.41 ERA came while starting all but five of his 18 appearances. The lefthander has good control, walking about three batters per nine innings in his pro career. He pitched exclusively out of the pen in 1996 at Double-A.

URBANI, TOM - TL - Age 29
Obtained from the Cardinals in midseason, Urbani was hammered in his AL debut. He is a finesse pitcher who tries to work the corners with off-speed stuff. It didn't work and Urbani posted a career high ERA for the year. He is a much better pitcher than he showed last year and should get another major league chance in 1997.

	W	SV	ERA	IP	H	BB	SO	B/I	$
1995 St. Louis NL	3	0	3.70	82	99	21	52	1.45	1
1996 Detroit AL	2	0	8.37	23	31	14	20	1.94	-

URBINA, UGUETH - TR - Age 23
Urbina split time between the Expos' rotation and bullpen last season and seemed to find a home in relief. Montreal manager Felipe Alou says Urbina could become a dominant closer. That chance could come as early as this season if Mel Rojas isn't re-signed as a free agent.

	W	SV	ERA	IP	H	BB	SO	B/I	$
1995 Montreal NL	2	0	6.17	23	26	14	15	1.71	-
1996 Montreal NL	10	0	3.71	114	102	44	108	1.28	6

URSO, SAL - TL - Age 24
Urso is being groomed as a lefty situational specialist. He advanced to Triple-A Tacoma in 1996 and had a fine season. He was 6-2 in 46 appearances, posting a 2.35 ERA. Since Urso doesn't throw particularly hard, he won't be a big strikeout pitcher or get a chance to close many games. He'll get a shot in the Mariners bullpen in 1997.

VALDES, ISMAEL - TR - Age 23
Valdes is only the best young pitcher in the game, but he is easily overlooked on the Dodger staff, which features the charismatic Nomo, the flashy won-loss record of Martinez, and interesting youngsters like Park and Osuna. Valdes features everything you could possibly want in a pitcher - a good strikeout rate, excellent control, durability, an extremely smooth motion, and Dodger Stadium (a 2.60 ERA at home vs. a 4.07 ERA on the road). Valdes will continue to be an excellent starter, and with Lasorda out of the picture, he has the chance to turn in a long, in addition to productive, career.

	W	SV	ERA	IP	H	BB	SO	B / I	$
1995 Los Angeles NL	13	1	3.05	197	168	51	150	1.11	21
1996 Los Angeles NL	15	0	3.32	225	219	54	173	1.21	17

VALDES, MARC - TR - Age 25
The Marlins' 1993 first round pick has not been the same pitcher since first being called up to the majors in 1995, getting launched, and then admitting that he was awed by the experience. The sinker/slider specialist has not aggressively attacked hitters at any level since. Valdes clearly has the raw ability to pitch in the majors, but as his 15/32 strikeout/walk ratio in 56 major league innings suggests, he is simply not ready.

	W	SV	ERA	IP	H	BB	SO	B / I	$
1996 Florida NL	1	0	4.81	48	63	23	13	1.78	-

VALDEZ, CARLOS - TR - Age 25
During his second season at Triple-A, Valdez dropped a notch in his effectiveness in 1996. His rise was mercurial, so he may get it together as a set up pitcher, but right now it doesn't look like he is going anywhere fast anymore.

VALDEZ, SERGIO - TR - Age 31
Valdez didn't pitch in 1996, and probably won't in San Francisco in 1997. He's been around forever, mostly as a reliever when in the majors. He has good control and is not a bad pitcher.

VALENZUELA, FERNANDO - TL - Age 36
Valenzuela had a surprising rebirth with the Padres in 1996, especially to those of us who wrote him off after a poor 1995. He held up well and made 31 starts, and he may do it all again in 1997.

	W	SV	ERA	IP	H	BB	SO	B / I	$
1995 San Diego NL	8	0	4.98	90	101	34	57	1.49	-
1996 San Diego NL	13	0	3.62	171	177	67	95	1.43	7

VALERA, JULIO - TR - Age 28
Finally fully recovered from Tommy John surgery, Valera impressed the Royals with a strong winter ball showing. He earned the last spot in the pen and proceeded to fall apart. Each outing was successively worse; he'd miss with his first pitch, then throw a high fastball that batters would rip. He was eventually demoted to Triple-A Omaha where he pitched no better before earning an outright release.

	W	SV	ERA	IP	H	BB	SO	B / I	$
1996 Kansas City AL	3	1	6.46	61	75	27	31	1.67	-

VANDERWEELE, DOUG - TR - Age 27
After his 1995, he was considered good, but undistinguished. After his 1996, he lost both of those modifiers.

VAN DE WEG, RYAN - TR - Age 23
Van De Weg is a Padres prospect who is making good progress. His minor league record is excellent, but he needs to be tested in the tougher leagues to be sure that he has what it takes to be a winner in the majors.

VANEGMOND, TIM - TR - Age 27
Not a particularly hot prospect, VanEgmond moved to the Brewers' midway through 1996. He's got a good enough repertoire to succeed as a fourth or fifth starter, although he lacks any special out pitch. VanEgmond lost part of 1995 due to a groin injury, then missed part of last year due to a freak accident in which he burned his pitching hand. VanEgmond will compete for a major league job in 1997.

	W	SV	ERA	IP	H	BB	SO	B / I	$
1996 Milwaukee AL	3	0	5.27	54	58	23	33	1.49	-

Benson's Baseball Player Guide: 1997

VANLANDINGHAM, WILLIAM - TR - Age 26
No Giant struggled through 1996 any more than VanLandinham did. He went 2-9 over his first dozen starts, but finished off at 7-7 over the remainder of his decisions. He had some good performances, but a lot of bad ones. He has good stuff and the confidence of his manager. 1997 will tell if he can put it all together.

	W	SV	ERA	IP	H	BB	SO	B/I	$
1995 San Francisco NL	6	0	3.67	122	124	40	95	1.34	5
1996 San Francisco NL	9	0	5.40	181	196	78	97	1.51	-

VAN POPPEL, TODD - TR - Age 25
Van Poppel was released by Oakland after he appeared to be on the right track in '95. Detroit then gave him a few starts, a strange decision since he wasn't getting anybody out. Van Poppel could succeed as a reliever, but he won't turn everything around in '97.

	W	SV	ERA	IP	H	BB	SO	B/I	$
1995 Oakland AL	4	0	4.88	138	125	56	122	1.31	4
1996 Detroit AL	3	1	9.06	99	139	62	53	2.03	-

VANRYN, BEN - TL - Age 25
Van Ryn had a brief major league trial with California last season then was traded to St. Louis for Pat Borders. The Cardinals sent him to Triple-A Louisville where he was an uninspiring 4-6 with a 4.88 ERA in 19 games, 10 starts.

VARDIJAN, DAN - TR - Age 20
The Marlins' 1994 25th round pick was a productive part of a young, effective Low-A Kane County rotation in 1996. Vardijan has a 6'5", 193 pound body, plus solid control for a youngster. The Marlins hope that the physical maturation process will add more hop to his heater, a necessity for success at Double-A and above. He's just a baby, and has about two years to stamp himself as a prospect.

VAZQUEZ, JAVIER - TR - Age 21
The Expos' 1994 fifth round pick emerged as arguably the Expos' best pitching prospect with a rousing 14-3, 2.68, campaign at Low-A Delmarva in 1996. At present, his fastball is only slightly above average, though that will likely change as his 6'2", 175, body matures. He posted an impressive 173/57 strikeout/walk ratio in 164 innings in 1996, largely due to the exceptional movement on his pitches and his impeccable control. One can't get too excited about a hurler who dominates in his second Low-A season, but Vazquez has a chance to be special. He should make Double-A by the end of 1997.

VAUGHT, JAY - TR - Age 25
The Indians' 1994 10th round draftee was an effective Class A starter as a finesse pitcher, but his lack of velocity and a true out pitch doomed him to middle relief detail at Double-A Canton-Akron in 1996. Even if he extends his career by throwing higher quality strikes to the corners of the strike zone, it won't be enough to get him to the bigs.

VERAS, DARIO - TR - Age 24
The Padres obtained reliever Dario Veras from the Dodgers in the 1993 minor league draft. Last year, he was promoted from Double-A to the majors where he pitched well. Manager Bruce Bochy didn't hesitate to use him in critical situations. "He's fearless," said Bochy.

	W	SV	ERA	IP	H	BB	SO	B/I	$
1996 San Diego NL	3	0	2.79	29	24	10	23	1.17	1

VERES, DAVE - TR - Age 30
Veres had a decent season for the Expos in 1996 after being acquired from Houston in the offseason in the Sean Berry trade. Montreal, though, expected more. Veres is durable reliever who is capable of a better year than '96.

	W	SV	ERA	IP	H	BB	SO	B/I	$
1995 Houston NL	5	1	2.26	103	89	30	94	1.15	11
1996 Montreal NL	6	4	4.17	77	85	32	81	1.52	3

VERES, RANDY - TR - Age 31
A middle-reliever lacking any outstanding pitch, Veres has gotten by on guile. He did poorly for the Tigers in 1996, but it was really not a true measure of his abilities. Veres should get another major league shot in 1997.

VIANO, JACOB - TR - Age 23
This guy appeared to be the Rockies' closer of the (not-so-distant) future a year ago, but high ERA's and ratios at both Double-A New Haven and Triple-A Colorado Springs didn't help his cause in 1996. Perhaps it was several spot starts that made Viano wonder where his future really lies, but the fireballer needs to improve in 1997.

VILLANO, MIKE - TR - Age 25
A real flame thrower, Villano was effective at Single-A San Jose, but had a tougher time when pushed up to Double-A. He is prone to wildness. Over one inning during a May game against Bakersfield, he walked one, struck out one, gave up three wild pitches one of which was so wild that a runner scored from second base. He also struck out 133 over 88 innings at San Jose.

VILLONE, RON - TL - Age 27
Coming back to the AL, Villone had some rocky moments, but will benefit from the experience. Villone has an excellent fastball which he can move in on righthanded batters, a must if he's going to be a closer. His best pitch; a sinking change up, is at times very effective. Once he gains control of all his pitches, (he also has a decent slider) he'll be ready to close. Should Villone find his groove, the Brewers could consider moving Fetters to a contender for the stretch.

	W	SV	ERA	IP	H	BB	SO	B/I	$
1995 Seattle AL	0	0	7.91	19	20	23	26	2.22	
1995 San Diego NL	2	1	4.21	25	24	11	37	1.36	-
1996 San Diego NL	1	0	2.95	18	17	7	19	1.33	-
1996 Milwaukee AL	0	2	3.28	24	14	18	19	1.32	0

VIOLA, FRANK - TL - Age 36
After dominating minor league batters, Viola got one more shot in the big leagues. He couldn't perform after being recalled from the minors and after a minor disagreement over his role with the Blue Jays, he was given his release. No one picked him up and Viola's excellent career appears to be over.

	W	SV	ERA	IP	H	BB	SO	B/I	$
1995 Cincinnati NL	0	0	6.28	14	20	3	4	1.60	-
1996 Toronto AL	1	0	7.71	30	43	21	18	2.13	-

VOSBERG, ED - TL - Age 35
Vosberg seems to have found his niche as a one-out lefty, but was quite effective when asked to close games (eight saves in nine chances). He pitched better when used more frequently. Vosberg has one of the best pickoff moves in baseball; hardly anyone runs on him. His out pitch is the slider.

	W	SV	ERA	IP	H	BB	SO	B/I	$
1995 Texas AL	5	4	3.00	36	32	16	36	1.33	7
1996 Texas AL	1	8	3.27	44	51	21	32	1.64	7

WADE, TERRELL - TL - Age 24
In his first full major league season, Wade was successful in a long relief role, especially early in the season. He throws extremely hard, occasionally getting into trouble by trying to overthrow his fastball. Wade doesn't have great control of his other pitches, though, so a relief role might best suit his talents.

	W	SV	ERA	IP	H	BB	SO	B/I	$
1996 Atlanta NL	5	1	2.97	69	57	47	79	1.50	2

WAGNER, BILLY - TL - Age 25
Wagner was promoted to Houston in early June and achieved instant success. He became the team's primary closer although he had never pitched even one game in relief in his four year minor league career. Wagner was Houston's first round draft choice in 1993 and has been their top pitching prospect throughout his career. He has an overpowering fastball and has made progress in developing his off speed and breaking pitches. Wagner will be an important part of the Astro staff in 1997, probably as a starter, since the club appears to have other options for the closer role. He has the tools and the makeup for an outstanding career if he stays healthy.

	W	SV	ERA	IP	H	BB	SO	B/I	$
1996 Houston NL	2	9	2.44	51	28	30	67	1.13	10

WAGNER, BRET - TL - Age 23
Wagner throws a "sneaky-quick" fastball with a good curve, a hard slider and a decent change. Wagner, a lefthander, was the Cardinals' first-round pick in 1994 out of Wake Forest. There have been some concerns about the durability of his arm. He may find himself in the bullpen if he gets to the majors, but that won't happen until at least 1998.

WAGNER, MATT - TR - Age 24
A hard thrower (mid-90s fastball), Wagner blew away Pacific Coast League hitters on his way to a 9-2 mark with a 2.41 ERA in fifteen starts for Tacoma. He fanned 82 in 93 innings and earned a promotion to Seattle. Wagner had a couple of good starts for the Mariners, but was mostly treated to an early shower in his fifteen appearances. Wagner should be a good pitcher in the bigs, but he needs to have better command than he showed in 1996.

	W	SV	ERA	IP	H	BB	SO	B/I	$
1996 Seattle AL	3	0	6.86	80	91	38	41	1.61	-

WAGNER, PAUL - TR - Age 29
Wagner finally began to fulfill his vast potential at the start of last season with the Pirates. However, his shoulder began to hurt and then he blew out his elbow in July and underwent reconstructive surgery. Wagner vows he will be back better than ever but only time will tell. It's doubtful he will be ready by opening day. He had the makings of a fine power pitcher before the injury but who knows what he'll be like now.

	W	SV	ERA	IP	H	BB	SO	B/I	$
1995 Pittsburgh NL	5	1	4.80	165	174	72	120	1.49	-
1996 Pittsburgh NL	4	0	5.40	81	86	39	81	1.54	-

WAINHOUSE, DAVE - TR - Age 29
Wainhouse, a top pick of Montreal in 1988, battled back from major back surgery to post 25 saves for the Pirates' Double-A Carolina farm club. That got him a chance to spend the final two months of the season in Pittsburgh. He pitched better in the major leagues than his number indicate. Though he won't live up the promise he showed as a collegian at Washington State, he still has a chance to stick around the big leagues as a middle reliever.

	W	SV	ERA	IP	H	BB	SO	B/I	$
1996 Pittsburgh NL	1	0	5.70	23	22	10	16	1.38	-

WAKEFIELD, TIM - TR - Age 30
Knuckleballer Wakefield managed to surrender sixteen hits in one 1996 contest; it was indicative of the kind of rollercoaster year Wakefield had. He was much better over the second half, but that doesn't mean as much for a knuckleball pitcher as it might for anybody else. Wakefield will be as good - or as bad - as his knuckler from one start to the next.

	W	SV	ERA	IP	H	BB	SO	B/I	$
1995 Boston AL	16	0	2.95	195	163	68	119	1.18	24
1996 Boston AL	14	0	5.14	211	238	90	140	1.55	5

WALKER, JAMIE - TL - Age 25
Walker has made some progress in his five years in the Astro system. He was 5-1 with a 2.50 ERA as a middle reliever and spot starter in his second year at Double-A. He needs to have a big year at Triple-A to get noticed.

WALKER, MIKE - TR - Age 30
Journeyman junkballer Walker was extremely hittable in 1996. His only successful major league campaign was with the Cubs in 1995, but he has always walked more batters than he has struck out and has always allowed more than a hit per inning pitched in the majors.

	W	SV	ERA	IP	H	BB	SO	B/I	$
1995 Chicago NL	1	1	3.22	44	45	24	20	1.54	1
1996 Detroit AL	0	1	8.46	27	40	17	13	2.10	-

WALKER, PETE - TR - Age 27
Reliever Pete Walker came to the Padres from the Mets in 1996 in the Roberto Petagine trade. He had a rough year in Triple-A last season, dropping his status considerably. The Padres thought enough of him to tab him for the Arizona Fall League where most top prospects play.

WALKER, WADE - TR - Age 25
Walker was the workhorse for the Orlando Cubs, logging 187.2 innings and absorbing an 8-14 record. He led the Cubs

organization in wins in 1994. He doesn't have great velocity on his fastball but it has good sinking movement. He compliments the sinker with a slider. The questions about his durability were dispelled in 1996. He should eat up innings wherever he pitches.

WALL, DONNIE - TR - Age 29
Wall had a breakthrough season in 1995, leading the Pacific Coast League with 17 wins, 119 strikeouts and an ERA of 3.30 while being named the league's most valuable player. However, he failed to make the Houston staff in spring training in 1996. He was recalled in mid-May and the Astros won the first 10 games he started. Wall has excellent control, but he has marginal major league stuff. His best pitch is his changeup and he must vary speeds and have pinpoint control to be effective. He had less success in the second half as hitters saw him for the second and third time. Wall has earned a chance to compete for a major league job again in 1997 but success is not assured.

	W	SV	ERA	IP	H	BB	SO	B/I	$
1995 Houston NL	3	0	5.55	24	33	5	16	1.56	-
1996 Houston NL	9	0	4.56	150	170	34	99	1.36	3

WALLACE, B. J. - TL - Age 25
The Expos' 1992 first round pick was claimed by the Phils' in the 1995 minor league Rule Five draft. He has missed significant time due to chronic shoulder problems, and the Phils attempted to test his arm by using him as a starter at High-A Clearwater in 1996. It was not a successful experiment, as Wallace's fastball was nowhere near peak velocity and his command was quite poor.

WALLACE, DEREK - TR - Age 25
Wallace was tied for the International League lead in saves when the Mets called him up on August 13th. He features a fastball, slider and split-finger pitch, but his biggest asset is the trust of Bobby Valentine which he earned at Norfolk. Wallace can expect a 1997 role that includes at least a few saves.

	W	SV	ERA	IP	H	BB	SO	B/I	$
1996 New York NL	2	3	4.01	24	29	14	15	1.78	-

WARD, BRYAN - TL - Age 25
This 1993 20th round pick has a slightly above average fastball and excellent control, though his pitches caught too much of the plate at Double-A Portland last season. He has been used as a starter and reliever, but appears to be a better relief prospect, as he is particularly effective the first time around the lineup.

WARD, DUANE - TR - Age 32
This longtime major league reliever barely made it out of Florida last March thanks to a shoulder that hasn't recovered fully from surgery. Ward gave up four hits and four runs in his inning and a third. That was his full season.

WARE, JEFF - TR - Age 26
Most felt that he would be the fifth starter in 1996 but he was worse than anyone could have expected. Ware had no control and little, if anything, on his pitches. He needs a comeback season and most feel that it will come at Triple-A, not in the majors.

	W	SV	ERA	IP	H	BB	SO	B/I	$
1995 Toronto AL	2	0	5.47	26	28	21	18	1.86	-
1996 Toronto AL	1	0	9.09	32	35	31	11	2.05	-

WARREN, BRIAN - TR - Age 29
Warren is a junkballing reliever who has endured seven minor league seasons on the strength of his usually pinpoint control.

WARREN, DESHAWN - TL - Age 22
Because of poor control, Warren threw so many pitches he often went less than five innings per start. The young, hard-throwing lefthander will get plenty of chances to improve.

WASDIN, JOHN - TR - Age 24
Wasdin started the season at Edmonton, then moved to Oakland where he finished the season. He had some good starts, and he had some bad ones. He has a good slider and a good curve. With a lot of potential, and in the majors at age 24, the Athletics will be patient with him.

	W	SV	ERA	IP	H	BB	SO	B/I	$
1995 Oakland AL	1	0	4.67	17	14	3	6	0.98	1
1996 Oakland AL	8	0	5.96	131	145	50	75	1.49	0

WASHBURN, JARROD - TL - Age 22
The Angels promoted lefty starter Jarrod Washburn from Single-A to Double-A Midland in the Texas League in July. Midland and the Texas League are tough places for pitchers, but he held his own with a relatively good 4.40 ERA. He gave up 77 hits in 85 innings, less than one hit per inning on the average, a good sign, and especially good considering that it was in the Texas League. Washburn is the Angels top lefty pitching prospect. He has good stuff including a 93-MPH fastball with good movement, and he could be in the Angels rotation sometime in 1997.

WATKINS, SCOTT - TL - Age 26
The Pacific Coast League can produce some scary ERAs, but you really have to pitch pretty badly to run up a 7.69 ERA in relief the way that Watkins did for Salt Lake City in 1996. Watkins was among the league's best closers in 1995, saving 20 games, but was lucky to save his skin after 1996. He'll need a far, far better year to get back to the majors.

WATSON, ALLEN - TL - Age 26
Watson was probably the closest thing to a staff ace the Giants had in 1996. He still throws in the low 90's and has a good curve. He is tenacious and when he pitches aggressively he is hard to hit. He'll be better in 1997.

	W	SV	ERA	IP	H	BB	SO	B/I	$
1995 St. Louis NL	7	0	4.96	114	126	41	49	1.46	-
1996 San Francisco NL	8	0	4.61	185	189	69	128	1.39	2

WATTS, BRANDON - TL - Age 24
Watts' first year above A-ball was a success, despite the 6-10 record. He had a 4.50 ERA, which is good in the Texas League as one of San Antonio's more solid starters. However, Watts is walking too many batters to be a success at higher levels. His real test will be in Triple-A where walks turn into runs in the offense-happy Pacific Coast League.

WEATHERS, DAVE - TR - Age 27
Weathers had some success early in 1994 with the Marlins, but hitters learned to sit on his fastball, and he doesn't have any reliable breaking pitch. The Marlins finally gave up on their 29th expansion pick, sending him to the Yankees. Post season exposure couldn't have hurt his confidence any.

	W	SV	ERA	IP	H	BB	SO	B/I	$
1995 Florida NL	4	0	5.98	90	104	52	60	1.73	-
1996 Florida NL	2	0	4.54	71	85	28	40	1.59	-
1996 New York AL	0	0	9.35	17	23	14	13	2.16	-

WEAVER, ERIC - TR - Age 23
Weaver has been erratic in his five pro seasons. He throws pretty hard, but hasn't consistently had control of the hard stuff. His fine start at Double-A San Antonio (10-5 with a 3.30 ERA in 18 starts) helped him advance to Triple-A Albuquerque for the first time. Weaver can be a winner if he can just show a little more consistency from one start to the next.

WEBER, NEIL - TL - Age 24
The Expos' 1993 eighth round draftee was at Double-A Harrisburg in the Expos' chain for the full 1996 season despite his emergence as one of the Eastern League's more reliable hurlers. He has a slightly above average fastball which he spotted consistently for the first time in his pro career.

WEBER, WESTON - TR - Age 33
At age 32, Weber relieved in seven games for the Padres Triple-A club. He's now a veteran of 11 minor league years, spending a lot of time in Triple-A, but never getting the call to the big time.

WEGMAN, BILL - TR - Age 34
Wegman appears to have fulfilled all of his potential as he continues to fade.

WEGMANN, TOM - TR - Age 28
Orioles minor leaguer Tom Wegmann had some good years relieving in Triple-A, but his stuff just isn't good enough

to take him any higher. Last year, he got into a few games with the Orioles Single-A and rookie leagues, and unless he gets another minor league contract, his career may be over.

WELCH, MIKE - TR - Age 24
Welch was the closer for the Mets Double-A Binghamton team in 1996, getting 27 saves there before he moved up to Triple-A when Norfolk closer Derek Wallace got promoted to New York. Welch is a direct worker in the style of, "Here it is; try to hit it."

WELLS, BOB - TR - Age 30
Wells, a 1996 first half surprise, was often brilliant in a starting role. Late in the first half he began to run out of gas and lost the bite on his slider. By August he was back in the pen.

	W	SV	ERA	IP	H	BB	SO	B/I	$
1995 Seattle AL	4	0	5.75	76	88	39	38	1.66	-
1996 Seattle AL	12	0	5.30	130	141	46	94	1.44	5

WELLS, DAVID - TL - Age 33
Wells showed his streakiness again in 1996, although his good streaks were not as good as the Koufax-like streaks he's had in the past. He's a fiery competitor who could conceivably have a good streak for an entire season.

	W	SV	ERA	IP	H	BB	SO	B/I	$
1995 Detroit AL	10	0	3.04	130	120	37	83	1.20	17
1995 Cincinnati NL	6	0	3.59	72	74	16	50	1.24	17
1996 Baltimore AL	11	0	5.14	224	247	51	130	1.33	10

WENDELL, TURK - TR - Age 29
The quirky Wendell is a fan favorite thanks to his odd rituals. He also became the Cubs closer in 1996. He performed well in that role, leading the team in saves. However, the Cubs are grooming Terry Adams and Steve Rain as closers of the future. Wendell will start the season as the Cubs' closer, but most likely, he won't finish it in the same role.

	W	SV	ERA	IP	H	BB	SO	B/I	$
1995 Chicago NL	3	0	4.92	60	71	24	50	1.57	-
1996 Chicago NL	4	18	2.84	79	58	44	75	1.29	18

WENGERT, DON - TR - Age 27
Wengert was able to return to his starter role, and responded well enough. Since he is not a hard thrower, he needs to spot those pitches. He can be too fine and the results are less than pretty. Wengert is probably not much of a long term solution to anything, but he is a good competitor.

	W	SV	ERA	IP	H	BB	SO	B/I	$
1995 Oakland AL	1	0	3.34	29	30	12	16	1.42	1
1996 Oakland AL	7	0	5.58	161	200	60	75	1.61	-

WEST, DAVID - TL - Age 32
West has used his above average fastball and a decent breaking ball arsenal to more than hold his own. He has routinely devoured lefties throughout his career (.200 average in 1996), and his control struggles have caused him to run up high pitch counts and rarely last longer than six innings.

	W	SV	ERA	IP	H	BB	SO	B/I	$
1995 Philadelphia NL	3	0	3.79	38	34	19	25	1.39	1
1996 Philadelphia NL	2	0	4.76	28	31	11	22	1.49	-

WESTBROOK, DESTRY - TR - Age 26
The Phils snatched this former Astros' farmhand to complete their High-A Clearwater bullpen in 1996, and he went on to debut at Double-A at the ripe age of 25 by season's end. Westbrook throws strikes, but doesn't have high velocity or location within the strike zone.

WESTON, MICKEY - TR - Age 36
The ultimate finesse pitcher has never struck out 100 batters in any of his 13 pro seasons, and is easy to hit if he has anything less than ideal location. Weston will likely catch on somewhere for his ninth consecutive Triple-A season, but won't likely ever earn his sixth major league trial.

WETTELAND, JOHN - TR - Age 30
With a big high-velocity fastball, and a curve that he used more in 1996, Wetteland remains at the top of the relief pitcher profession. There may be two or three who are as good as Wetteland, but no one is better.

	W	SV	ERA	IP	H	BB	SO	B/I	$
1995 New York AL	1	31	2.93	61	40	14	66	0.88	37
1996 New York AL	2	43	2.83	63	54	21	69	1.19	45

WHISENANT, MATT - TL - Age 26
Whisenant is a hard-throwing lefty who has always intrigued scouts with his raw stuff. However, his career-long control problems intensified at Triple-A in 1996, as he ranked among minor league leaders in walks.

WHITE, GABE - TL - Age 25
The Reds acquired this former Expo prospect (and disappointment) prior to the season and White had earned a promotion to Cincinnati after an excellent stint at Indianapolis. However, in his last start before being called up, he blew out his shoulder and missed the rest of the season. White is young and talented enough to make a comeback, but the injury sets him back at least a year.

WHITE, RICK - TR - Age 28
White had reconstructive elbow surgery in December, 1995 and recovered enough to pitch two games for Double-A Carolina at the end of 1996. He claims he has made a total recovery but the Pirates didn't feel he was ready for the big leagues in September. He was a decent pitcher before the surgery but no one can know for sure what he'll be like now.

WHITEHURST, WALLY - TR - Age 32
The former Mets and Padres starter did well enough at Triple-A (6-3 with a 2.47 ERA) to merit a callup when the Yankees needed pitching help in 1996, but Whitehurst soon found himself back in the minors. He's a sinker/slider pitcher long past his prime for the majors.

WHITESIDE, MATT - TR - Age 29
Whiteside had a tough April and found himself at Triple-A for most of the season. Never an overpowering pitcher, Whiteside has to be very fine with his control. He pitched well at Triple-A but is now on the major league fringe.

	W	SV	ERA	IP	H	BB	SO	B/I	$
1996 Texas AL	0	0	6.68	32	43	11	15	1.68	-

WHITTEN, CASEY - TL - Age 24
The Indians' 1993 number two dominated hitters with a slightly above average heater and solid offspeed repertoire in 1996. The season will go down as a disappointment, however, as he imploded at Triple-A. The southpaw needs to throw high quality strikes consistently, at the risk of exposing his average fastball on hitters' counts.

WICKANDER, KEVIN - TL - Age 32
Being a lefty, Wickander should have a role somewhere. Possessing below average stuff, Wickander survives by changing speeds and rarely throws a strike. If he can nick the corners or get a friendly umpire, he can succeed. Smart hitters know he won't throw it over the plate, so they try to take him deep in the count and then drive the ball or take the walk.

	W	SV	ERA	IP	H	BB	SO	B/I	$
1995 Two Teams	0	1	1.93	23	19	12	11	1.33	2
1996 Milwaukee AL	2	0	4.97	25	26	17	19	1.71	-

WICKMAN, BOB - TR - Age 28
A good resilient worker, Wickman was more prominent as the Yankees' top righty setup man before the emergence of Mariano Rivera. Although he's less visible, Wickman remains a useful talent.

	W	SV	ERA	IP	H	BB	SO	B/I	$
1995 New York AL	2	1	4.05	80	77	33	51	1.38	3
1996 NY-Milwaukee AL	7	0	4.42	95	106	44	75	1.58	2

WIEGANT, SCOTT - TL - Age 29
He has toiled at Double-A or higher for the pitching-poor Phillies for six seasons now - usually faring quite well, as his career ERA is under 3.00 - and has never gotten the call to the majors. He is a finesse, one-batter lefty who will get one major league appearance if there is any justice.

WILKINS, MARC - TR - Age 26
Wilkins, who is built like Barney Rubble, might have been the Pirates' most pleasant surprise in an otherwise dismal season. The untouted righthander was called up from Double-A Carolina in early May and pitched consistently well in middle and setup relief. He has an outstanding curveball and good movement on his fastball. The Pirates think he might turn into a starter but he seemed more comfortable in the bullpen where he can go all out for one or two innings at a time.

	W	SV	ERA	IP	H	BB	SO	B / I	$
1996 Pittsburgh NL	4	1	3.84	75	75	36	62	1.48	1

WILLIAMS, BRIAN - TR - Age 28
The Tigers announced before the 1996 season started that Williams would be their ace reliever. He ended up collecting only two saves and went back to starting and long relief, proving that it takes more than managerial blessing to make an ace reliever.

	W	SV	ERA	IP	H	BB	SO	B / I	$
1995 San Diego NL	3	0	6.00	72	79	38	75	1.63	-
1996 Detroit AL	3	2	6.77	121	145	85	72	1.90	-

WILLIAMS, JIMMY - TL - Age 32
Williams is a 13-year minor vet who has bounced through the Dodgers, Twins, Giants, Cubs, Expos, Mets, Orioles, and most recently, Indians organizations. He is a lefty with a decent fastball but spotty control who has always been effective once around the order.

WILLIAMS, MIKE - TR - Age 28
Williams doesn't get his fastball above the mid-80's on the gun, and relies on keeping the ball down and in varying speed and location to achieve success. He did none of the above in 1996. He frustrated his team with such exciting feats as walking the pitcher, and grooving fastballs down the middle on 0-2 pitches throughout the 1996 season.

	W	SV	ERA	IP	H	BB	SO	B / I	$
1995 Philadelphia NL	3	0	3.29	87	78	29	57	1.22	5
1996 Philadelphia NL	6	0	5.44	167	188	67	103	1.53	-

WILLIAMS, MITCH - TL - Age 32
After sitting out almost a year, Williams attempted a comeback with the Phillies in 1996 and failed.

WILLIAMS, SHAD - TR - Age 26
Williams is a finesse pitcher with an excellent curveball and good control. He has pitched well in two seasons in Triple-A, but was hit hard in a short stint with the Angels in 1996. He could win a job in the Angels rotation as a fifth starter or in the bullpen as a middle reliever. Finesse pitchers usually take longer to develop.

	W	SV	ERA	IP	H	BB	SO	B / I	$
1996 California AL	0	0	8.89	28	42	21	26	2.24	-

WILLIAMS, TODD - TR - Age 26
A submariner with good control but not much else, Williams got his first chance at the majors in 1995, and was not effective. His 1996 numbers are worse; four more walks than strikeouts. Williams could be an effective set up man for a team that put a good defense behind him.

WILLIAMS, WOODY - TR - Age 30
Williams has silently been an effective pitcher when given the chance. He'll try to solidify a spot in the starting rotation but needs to stay healthy for a full year. He had arthroscopic surgery on his right shoulder in September, 1995 and experienced some pain there again last June.

	W	SV	ERA	IP	H	BB	SO	B / I	$
1995 Toronto AL	1	0	3.69	53	44	28	41	1.34	2
1996 Toronto AL	4	0	4.73	59	64	21	43	1.44	0

WILSON, GARY - TR - Age 27
Though he was their minor league pitcher of the year in 1994, the Pirates don't mention Wilson's name anymore. The righthander went 6-9, 5.08 in 27 starts for Triple-A Calgary last season and will likely wind up in another organization. The change of scenery might do him good.

WILSON, PAUL - TR - Age 24
Much was expected from Wilson in 1996 - too much. Wilson has great stuff but hasn't yet produced great results. Making just a few bad pitches here and there has made his numbers worse than they ought to be. Wilson also needs to prove that his arm is OK, but the future looks bright for him.

	W	SV	ERA	IP	H	BB	SO	B/I	$
1996 New York NL	5	0	5.38	149	157	71	109	1.53	-

WILSON, TREVOR - TL - Age 30
The often injured lefty sat out all of 1996 and his future looked bleak. At best, he might come back as a fifth starter candidate. When he is healthy, Wilson has a decent fastball and curve, but suffers from erratic control.

WITASICK, JAY - TR - Age 24
Witasick, pitched well at Double-A, but not so well over short stints in Edmonton and Oakland. Witasick is big and strong, throws hard, and could probably use a full year at Triple-A.

WITHEM, SHANNON - TR - Age 24
Withem gets along with good breaking stuff, not high velocity. He pitched at three levels for the Mets in 1996: Class St. Lucie (1-0, 1.29 ERA), Double-A Binghamton (6-3, 3.24 ERA) and Triple-A Norfolk (3-3, 4.64 ERA) all as a starter.

WITT, BOBBY - TR - Age 32
Blessed with superb physical health and an above-average fastball, Witt nonetheless is a mediocre pitcher. He gives up baserunners at an alarming rate, and has trouble keeping the ball in the park (one homer every 7 innings). Witt is durable, and will give a team a lot of innings, and has just enough decent outings to stay in the big leagues.

	W	SV	ERA	IP	H	BB	SO	B/I	$
1995 Florida NL	2	0	3.90	110	104	47	95	1.36	5
1995 Texas AL	3	0	4.55	61	81	21	46	1.66	5
1996 Texas AL	16	0	5.41	199	235	96	157	1.66	2

WITTE, TREY - TR - Age 24
Witte was one of the righthanders to get saves after Scott Davison was promoted to the big leagues. He's a control specialist without any outstanding pitch. Witte had a 2.15 ERA in 35 appearances at Triple-A Tacoma; he's not a good prospect.

WOHLERS, MARK - TR - Age 27
Good control of an upper-90s fastball makes Wohlers the most feared closer in the game. He has converted 73 of his last 80 save chances and fanned 12 batters per nine innings over the last two years. Wohlers is your prototypical closer: a hard-thrower with good control and no fear. He should continue to dominate NL hitters for the next few years.

	W	SV	ERA	IP	H	BB	SO	B/I	$
1995 Atlanta NL	7	25	2.09	64	51	24	90	1.16	29
1996 Atlanta NL	2	39	3.03	77	71	21	100	1.19	34

WOJCIECHOWSKI, STEVE - TL - Age 26
Another Athletics starter who was in command for a spell, then fell on hard times. Pitched well when he went back down to Triple-A, and could use more time there.

	W	SV	ERA	IP	H	BB	SO	B/I	$
1995 Oakland AL	2	0	5.18	48	51	28	13	1.62	-
1996 Oakland AL	5	0	5.65	79	97	28	30	1.58	-

WOLCOTT, BOB - TR - Age 23
In 1995 Wolcott did well in the glare of a pennant race and pitched a strong game against the Yankees in the playoffs. Many felt he was already a good pitcher despite having under 40 innings of major league experience. Wolcott struggled in 1996 in Seattle's rotation, but completed an invaluable 150 innings of work.

	W	SV	ERA	IP	H	BB	SO	B/I	$
1995 Seattle AL	3	0	4.42	36	43	14	19	1.55	
1996 Seattle AL	7	0	5.73	149	179	54	78	1.56	-

WOODALL, BRAD - TL - Age 27
Control specialist Woodall missed his chance to gain a foothold in the Braves' stellar rotation when he stumbled out of the gate in 1995. His 1996 campaign was more in line with his career numbers, but he's now no better than fourth in the lefty starter pecking order. Barring serious and numerous injuries in Atlanta, Woodall's only hope for a major league future is with another team.

WOOD, KERRY - TR - Age 20
Wood is a young, polished flame-throwing righthander whose fastball can hit 98. He complements his heat with a good breaking ball. Wood is tall and has an easy delivery. Like most power pitchers, Wood doesn't hold runners on well and he doesn't have much of an off-speed pitch, but he can flat out bring it. Wood posted a 10-2 record and struck out an organizational best 136 batters in 114 innings at High-A Daytona. He gave up just 72 hits, but he walked 70, so he'll have to refine his control a bit.

WORLEY, ROBERT - TR - Age 26
For a guy who doesn't throw hard, Worley also doesn't have particularly good control. He has consistently walked as many batters as he has struck out. Worley is no longer a starting pitcher, having made the transition to a relief role in 1996. He's an unremarkable middle-innings guy now.

WORRELL, TIM - TR - Age 29
Tim Worrell had a torn elbow ligament a few years ago, and it's taken him a few years to come back. He was a reliever and starter last season, and he had an outstanding year. He held up well, and could win a starter's job in 1997.

	W	SV	ERA	IP	H	BB	SO	B/I	$
1995 San Diego NL	1	0	4.73	13	16	6	13	1.65	-
1996 San Diego NL	9	1	3.05	121	109	39	99	1.22	10

WORRELL, TODD - TR - Age 37
Worrell followed up his unlikely comeback in 1995 with a tremendous 1996 season, breaking his own team record for saves with 44, while posting a strikeout an inning with excellent control. As long as he pitches like this, he obviously will hold the closers job, but Antonio Osuna is waiting in the wings. The Dodgers will be tempted to give Osuna a chance in the event of another injury (which would seem likely given Worrell's past injury history) or a bout of ineffectiveness.

	W	SV	ERA	IP	H	BB	SO	B/I	$
1995 Los Angeles NL	4	32	2.02	62	50	19	61	1.11	34
1996 Los Angeles NL	4	44	3.03	65	70	15	66	1.31	37

WRIGHT, JAMEY - TR - Age 22
Wright made the big jump from Double-A New Haven to the parent Rockies in 1996, much the way Bryan Rekar did a year earlier. The results were similar as well - more success in early appearances than more recent ones. Wright has been primarily a control pitcher, but at 6'5", he is developing an intimidating fastball that he's willing to throw inside. The rookie could use more seasoning at the Triple-A level, but the helter-skelter Rockie pitching staff made that impossible in 1996.

	W	SV	ERA	IP	H	BB	SO	B/I	$
1996 Colorado NL	4	0	4.93	91	105	41	45	1.60	-

WRIGHT, JARET - TR - Age 21
The Indians' number one pick in 1994 remains right on schedule, as he located his dominant 95 MPH fastball much more precisely at High-A Kinston in 1996. He lost a third of 1996 to a broken jaw, suffered in a freak batting practice incident by the bat of then-Braves' prospect Ron Wright. His breaking pitches are improving, and will fill out an arsenal befitting of a future major league number one starter or closer.

YAN, ESTEBAN - TR - Age 22
Yan is only 22, but the Orioles are his third organization. He began 1996 in Single-A in the Expos system, was waived in May, and claimed by the Orioles. He has a good arm and good control, and with some pitch improvements and additional experience, he could become a good major league pitcher.

YOUNG, ANTHONY - TR - Age 31
Young began the 1996 season in the Astro bullpen but he was too inconsistent to hold the job. After a demotion to Tucson, he was injured and missed most of the season after arm surgery. Young has never had a winning season in his five years in the major leagues and may not get another chance.

	W	SV	ERA	IP	H	BB	SO	B/I	$
1995 Chicago NL	3	2	3.70	41	47	14	15	1.48	2
1996 Houston NL	3	0	4.59	33	36	22	19	1.75	-

ZANCANERO, DAVE - TL - Age 28
Former first round pick, Zancanero, who has had injury problems over the years, has hung around more because of potential than anything else. That is not a good enough reason to justify much of anything.

ZERBE, CHAD - TL - Age 24
Zerbe doesn't have a strikeout repertoire, so he'll need to refine his stuff and stop walking batters if he hopes to advance past Double-A. Zerbe was 4-6 with a 4.50 ERA as a swingman at San Antonio in 1996.

ZIMMERMAN, MIKE - TR - Age 28
Zimmerman has spent the bulk of the last four years in Triple-A for three different clubs. In 1996 it was the Mariners and he was awful. His combined ERA for the last two full seasons is near 7.00 and he continues to walk a lot of hitters. He's a swingman and long reliever, and he's almost finished as a professional pitcher.

GOT A QUESTION?
CALL JOHN BENSON LIVE

Your Question - Your Roster - Your Situation

Let the top analyst in the business help you!!

1-900-773-7526

$2.49/minute

1 pm to 11 pm Eastern Time - 7 days a Week

Top 100 Prospects Now and for the Future

By Lary Bump

For a long time, I have contended that it takes LOTS for a young player to make it in the majors leagues. That acronym stands for Luck, Opportunity, Talent and Skill.

It's not possible to combine all those factors on a two-dimensional piece of paper, but we can represent three of them here on the lists of the top 100 prospects for this season and of the top 100 for the two following years.

The way to think of it is to place the lists side by side, with the '97 list on the left and the future list on the right.

Like cream, Talent will rise to the top of each list. Two other factors separate the players into the left and right groupings. Opportunity can push a player to the left. A pitching prospect for a team short of arms (listen up, Rockies fans) would be likely to be rushed somewhat to the majors. Thus, that opportunity would slide him across that invisible line from down-the-road prospect to prospect now. But, because his talent isn't as mature as for most of those on the '97 list, he wouldn't be as high on the talent totem pole in that grouping.

Maturity is the other key factor. For purposes of this listing, the word Maturity replaces Skill, which is in essence the refinement of talent as a player ages - at least in terms of baseball wisdom. Maturity just doesn't fit as well in the talent acronym - a prospect needs LOTS, not LOTM.

That means that the Maturity axis, like the Opportunity scale, slides a player from right to left. Maturity can mean both physical aging and the kind of baseball precociousness that causes a player such as Chipper Jones or Alex Rodriguez seemingly to arrive in the majors full grown at a young age.
The very best prospects on these lists, then, will be in the upper left hand corner, at the top of the 1997 list. Talent converges at the top with Maturity and Opportunity on the left. The riskiest bets for stardom are in the lower right, where players have less physical Talent as well as less immediate Opportunity and the Maturity to cope in major league ball.

That accounts for three of the factors in the prospect equation. The wild card, the X factor, is luck. There is no way to measure the impact of that factor six months before the next season begins. (As I write this, the major league postseason is in full swing.) For example, a year ago, we had no way of knowing that players on our Top 100 for 1996 list such as Jay Payton or Antone Williamson would be held back because of injuries. Luck had nothing to do with their Talent or Maturity, but did diminish their opportunity. Nor could we have projected that the Tigers would have traded for Mark Lewis. Tough Luck for Steve Rodriguez, and therefore no opportunity.

Keep in mind that these lists contain not technical rookies, essentially those with 130 or fewer at bats and 50 or fewer innings pitched, but prospects. I draw the line at players who had more at bats or innings pitched in the minors than in the majors a year ago. Thus, the 1997 list doesn't include Alex Ochoa or Mike Sweeney or Jose Rosado, but Billy Wagner sneaks onto the list.

A year ago, 80 players on my '96 Top 100 list played in the majors. In a nice symmetrical touch, 20 from the '97-98 list also reached the big leagues.

The highest-rated player on the '96 list who didn't compete in the majors last year was Payton (No. 9). Everyone else in the top 30 made it. As we would expect, most of those who didn't play in the majors came from the less-talented lower half of the list. For the record, the top 10 were Alan Benes, Karim Garcia, Derek Jeter, Carlos Delgado, Paul Wilson, Nomar Garciaparra, Todd Walker, Ochoa, Payton and Alan Embree. Number 11 on the list, Mariano Rivera, didn't have a bad year, either.

The top four players from last year's list of future prospects all arrived in the majors a year early: Trot Nixon, Darin Erstad, Andruw Jones and Scott Rolen. Two others from the top 10 (No. 7 Calvin Maduro and No. 8 Raul Casanova) also became big leaguers, aided by the Luck - or Opportunity - provided by being traded. The biggest overachiever may have been No. 91 Jacob Cruz who was propelled into the Giants outfield by a series of injuries. Opportunity, or Luck?

You will see those players, and some of the those from the '96 Top 100, repeated in this year's Top 100 list. And by definition, many players from last year's list of the top 100 for '97-'98 will appear on one or the other of this year's lists.

As a very rough rule of thumb, you can expect the players in the top half of the '98-'99 list to arrive in the majors in 1998, and the lower half to become big-leaguers in 1999. The numbers in parentheses are the players' reported ages as of April 1, 1997.

In any event, by the time our calendars begin with the number 2, we should see all 200 of the players on these lists in the major leagues. Barring bad luck, of course.

1. Andruw Jones, Braves OF (19) -- A minor league player of the year twice while in his teens, Jones is the best power/speed talent coming along. The biggest limiting factor is Opportunity. David Justice, Ryan Klesko and Jermaine Dye (who also jumped from the '97-'98 top 100 to the majors) stand in Jones' way, but free agency and trades could shove them aside.

2. Nomar Garciaparra, Red Sox SS (23) -- A knee injury held him back last year, but the slightly built Garciaparra came back with surprising power. He's an absolute wizard with the glove. Like Jones, he was trusted with a key role for a contender down last year's stretch.

3. Billy Wagner, Astros LHP (25) -- This one is so easy it almost feels like cheating. Wagner was Houston's closer until the team fell apart and he had nothing left to close. He could even be a solid rotation starter this season.

4. Scott Rolen, Phillies 3B (21) -- No problem with Opportunity. The broken wrist that ended his major league debut could be a more serious limiting factor.

5. Vladimir Guerrero, Expos OF (21) -- The talent well dug by Dave Dombrowski in Montreal is beginning to dry up, but hit a gusher in Guerrero. Like Jones, he advanced from A ball to the majors. Guerrero stopped in the Eastern League long enough to pick up a batting title and MVP award.

6. Jay Payton, Mets OF (24) -- Because of two elbow surgeries, he didn't play an inning in the field last year. But even if he has to move from center field to left, he'll do far better than most people expect. His injury has made him a bit of a forgotten man. I've seen him play since his days in short-season ball and, OK, I saw the greatest night he'll probably ever have as a pro.

7. Todd Walker, Twins 3B (23) -- Even if his statistics were inflated by playing at Salt Lake City, Walker has shown enough to indicate he will hit no matter where he plays. He'll fill the third base hole that has existed since Gary Gaetti left Minnesota.

8. Calvin Maduro, Phillies RHP (22) -- His track record indicates he will struggle at a higher level, go back down a step, then come back and dominate with the more advanced club. His control is so good it's a good thing he got out of Baltimore, where batters would have swung at pitches always around the plate and lifted them for cheap homers.

9. Dmitri Young, Cardinals 1B (23) -- He turned his attitude and his game around to win the American Association batting title. St. Louis thought enough of him to promote in time to be eligible for postseason play. The only concern is his weight.

10. Jeff Suppan, Red Sox RHP (22) -- Boston's new manager will have some excellent young talent - even on the mound with Aaron Sele and Suppan.

11. Darin Erstad, Angels OF (22) -- The Anaheim club was talking of trading Garret Anderson to make room for Erstad. That should be a sufficient endorsement.

12. Luis Castillo, Marlins 2B (21) -- He's another who essentially earned a job last season. He doesn't have to win it this spring, and isn't likely to lose it. He has pushed aside Quilvio Veras and Ralph Milliard. Castillo's base-stealing ability can make him far more valuable in fantasy baseball than in the real thing.

13. Ruben Rivera, Yankees OF (23) -- The raw talent is there; the production hasn't been. I'm not as high as most people on Rivera, who has little concept of the strike zone. Lately, we haven't heard any comparisons to Mickey Mantle. At Columbus last year, Rivera played more like Bubba Carpenter.

14. Bubba Trammell, Tigers OF (25) -- On the other hand, you might never have heard of Trammell if you didn't buy "Future Stars" last year. I wrote that he is a "hitting machine," and he was in high gear in 1996.

15. Justin Thompson, Tigers LHP (24) -- While everyone seemed to be lamenting the Tigers' pitching woes last season, they were quietly building up a strong young pitching staff at Toledo. Thompson was the Mud Hens' best.

16. Todd Greene, Angels C (25) -- All he has to do is stick his glove in front of most of the pitches that come his way. Greene's bat will do the rest for him. Injuries held him back last year; don't be fooled.

17. Jaime Bluma, Royals RHP (24) -- By the end of last season, Kansas City fans looked at the Royals bullpen and said "Jeff Who?"

18. Jamey Wright, Rockies RHP (22) -- Wright's rise in '96 was reminiscent of Bryan Rekar's a year earlier. Wright, who improved his strikeout ratio, should have better staying power than Rekar.

19. Jorge Posada, Yankees C (25) -- Posada is a dream: a switch-hitting catcher with some pop in his bat and a strong throwing arm. He's frequently on base because he draws lots of walks. Joe Girardi stands in Posada's way, but if he is traded, his rating in this top 100 would shoot up about 10 places.

20. Brian Sackinsky, Orioles RHP (25) -- In one respect, he's a poor man's Calvin Maduro, throwing a lot of strikes and giving up fly balls that end up as home runs. But

Sackinsky is a much more consistent pitcher who must be seen over a long period to be appreciated. The downside is that elbow problems have kept anyone from seeing him very long during the past two seasons.

21. Jeff Abbott, White Sox OF (24) -- He doesn't have speed or an arm or a lot of power. But, oh my, can he hit line drives. Chicago will have to find a place for him in its lineup.

22. Jay Witasick, Athletics RHP (24) -- Witasick should provide the biggest return from the Todd Stottlemyre trade. Somewhat fragile as a starter, Witasick went to the bullpen at Huntsville and could emerge as Oakland's stopper sometime this year. He throws heat.

23. Jeff D'Amico, Brewers RHP (21) -- There's plenty of opportunity in Milwaukee, and D'Amico is a former Brewers first-round draft pick. The hulking D'Amico showed a lot as a major league rookie. Injuries have kept him from pitching much in the minors, so he's still learning.

24. Glendon Rusch, Royals LHP (22) -- The express train carrying all those KC pitching prospects from Wilmington has been sidetracked. Now Rusch appears to be the best - healthiest, at least - coming up through the organization. Being lefthanded won't hurt him.

25. Rich Hunter, Phillies RHP (22) -- Like so many other youngsters, Hunter arrived in Philadelphia prematurely last season. The most important factor for Phillies prospects may be whether Lee Thomas and the new manager can get on the same page in dealing with prospects. Hunter may begin this season in Scranton, but expect him to come down the Turnpike by mid-season.

26. Wilson Delgado, Giants SS (21) -- Delgado is another player who arrived in the majors ahead of our timetable. He's a good defensive player and a maturing hitter who could contend for playing time this season.

27. Todd Helton, Rockies 1B (23) -- Helton has one big problem; the guy in front of him drove in 150 runs in the majors a year ago. But the former Tennessee quarterback has a picture-perfect swing, and should develop more power -- even if he is traded away from Colorado.

28. Trever Miller, Tigers LHP (23) -- Miller didn't pitch as well as Thompson in the majors, but he was right behind him with Corporal Klinger's favorite team. Miller is a former number one draft pick who outsmarts hitters instead of overpowering them.

29. Wendell Magee, Phillies OF (24) -- He shot through a Philadelphia farm system that didn't have a whole lot of talent blocking his path. Don't expect to see a lot more from him than an outfielder with some speed who can hit for average. Who is Wendell Magee Sr., and what does he do?

30. Antone Williamson, Brewers 3B-1B (23) -- Another former Milwaukee number one pick (the Brewers are doing some good scouting), Williamson missed nearly half of last season, when he was supposed to reach the majors. Make that this year, and watch his power increase as he matures.

31. Ramiro Mendoza, Yankees RHP (24) -- Those scrambling to find information on Mendoza when the Yanks called him up last season could have looked on page 297 of "Future Stars." He was a much better pitcher, with excellent control, after being returned to Columbus. Last year's aution remains: "His best career move could be to the bullpen."

32. Shannon Stewart, Blue Jays OF (23) -- Stewart's improvement over the course of last season was palpable. He can play center field, he can run, he can get on base and he can drive the ball to the gaps. He should be even better on artificial turf.

33. Curt Lyons, Reds RHP (22) -- Lyons is another 1996 success story. Cincinnati is holding a place for the Southern League Pitcher of the Year in its rotation.

34. Robin Jennings, Cubs OF (24) -- I liked him long before the world discovered him in the 1995 Arizona Fall League. After all, the world didn't follow the Geneva Cubs. The question is whether the Chicago Cubs will recognize Jennings' talent or will continue to believe that Luis Gonzalez is a productive major league corner outfielder.

35. Raul Casanova, Tigers C (24) -- Casanova is an excellent power hitter and a young catcher who could develop along with Detroit's young pitchers. He should share time with Brad Ausmus this season.

36. Travis Miller, Twins LHP (24) -- After a miserable start to his major league career, Miller settled down somewhat. Fantasy players' biggest problem will be keeping him and Trever Miller straight.

37. Pokey Reese, Reds SS (23) -- Two problems: last year's injury setback, and having Barry Larkin playing in front of him. Reese's value increases if he's traded. He's a good defensive player who is more valuable to a major league team than to a fantasy team.

38. Karim Garcia, Dodgers OF (21) -- He has slipped, especially in the eyes of the Dodgers organization. He received a punitive demotion to San Antonio. So did Raul Mondesi. So did Braulio Castillo. Let's wait and see which player Garcia approaches more closely.

39. Darren Dreifort, Dodgers RHP (24) -- He has been up before -- before surgery cost him all of 1995, that is. Dreifort came back last year throwing well enough that he could be considered an alternative to Todd Worrell.

40. Yamil Benitez, Expos OF (24) -- On a truly awful Ottawa team in 1996, Benitez was one of the few players who showed improvement. He made strike-zone adjustments similar to those by Butch Huskey in '95. Benitez is a strong-armed outfielder whose biggest potential problem is being leap-frogged by Vladimir Guerrero.

41. Ricky Ledee, Yankees OF (23) -- Ledee comes with a warning label: Death to righthanded pitchers. Against lefties, and in the outfield - well, that's a different story. He made great strides last year, and could help the Bronx Bombers in '97.

42. Carl Pavano, Red Sox RHP (21) -- It's shocking, isn't it, seeing all these good young pitchers coming through the Boston organization? And they're mostly righthanders well suited for Fenway Park. Pawtucket's McCoy Stadium provide the first test for Pavano.

43. Paul Konerko, Dodgers 1B (21) -- Like Todd Helton, Konerko faces an established incumbent at first base. And this is after he switched from catching to avoid being trapped behind Mike Piazza, who might move to . . . first base.

44. Derrek Lee, Padres 1B (21) -- San Diego's patience with its number one draft choice is about to pay off. Wally Joyner's job is in jeopardy.

45. Jose Cruz Jr., Mariners OF (22) -- It took a long time for the baseball world to recognize Cruz Sr.'s hitting talent. That won't be the case with his son.

46. Brett Tomko, Reds RHP (23) -- Tomko combined with Lyons to give Chattanooga a devastating one-two starting punch. Tomko can reach the majors by midseason.

47. Shawn Estes, Giants LHP (24) -- Any healthy warm body would be a good addition to San Francisco's staff. Estes is sizzling.

48. Bob Abreu, Astros OF (23) -- The only limiting factor is the crowded condition of the Houston outfield. However, the Astros are a team ripe for trading away some underachievers.

49. Rick Helling, Marlins RHP (26) -- For some reason, Helling and the Rangers never got together. He'll be part of an exceptional pitching staff in Florida, where Jim Leyland will think he died and went to heaven.

50. Billy McMillon, Marlins OF (25) -- The International League batting champ didn't receive regular duty in Florida. He's a hustling overachiever who could provide a steady boost to the Marlins' offense.

51. LaTroy Hawkins, Twins RHP (24) -- After rising rapidly through the Minnesota system, Hawkins stalled and was somewhat disappointing -- until last year, when he pitched well in tough ballpark.

52. Elieser Marrero, Cardinals C (23) -- In 1996, he added some power to his exceptional defense. And Tom Pagnozzi is slowing down.

53. Edgard Velazquez, Rockies OF (21) -- Velazquez hasn't been a power hitter -- at least not until he gets to Colorado -- but he can hit and throw the ball hard, and wait out pitchers for walks.

54. Nerio Rodriguez, Orioles RHP (24) -- About a year after converting from catching in A ball, Rodriguez reached the majors as a pitcher. He throws hard, and has seemed undaunted by performing at higher levels.

55. Scott Klingenbeck, Twins RHP (26) -- Klingenbeck has had several trials with the Orioles and Twins. He appears to be ready this time.

56. Derek Wallace, Mets RHP (25) -- One evening last season, Norfolk manager Bobby Valentine decided to try Wallace, newly acquired from the Kansas City organization, as his closer. Valentine now manages in New York, where he may reward Wallace's success by making him a righthanded complement to closer John Franco.

57. Kevin Brown, Rangers C (23) -- Brown emerged with a big year in 1996. The only problem is that Pudge Rodriguez is ahead of him.

58. Ron Belliard, Brewers 2B (21) -- Belliard projects as a leadoff hitter because of his speed and batting eye. He has some extra-base pop as well.

59. Enrique Wilson, Indians SS (21) -- Wilson simply can do it all at bat, on the bases and in the field.

60. Richard Hidalgo, Astros OF (21) -- In time, Hidalgo may be an even better prospect than Abreu. Hidalgo has one of baseball's best arms and gap power that could convert to more home runs in a new ballpark.

61. Arquimedez Pozo, Red Sox 2B-3B (23) -- Heretofore, "Quime" Pozo was known more for his offense than his defense. But after the Sox acquired him from Seattle, he was more impressive with his glove. The problem is the sudden glut of infield talent in Boston.

62. Jim Pittsley, Royals RHP (22) -- The only limiting factor for the big righthander has been arm trouble. He totaled a 10-2 record in the minors last year.

63. Jason Dickson, Angels RHP (24) -- California has been looking for a righthanded starter. For Dickson to fill that role, he'll need to pitch with a bit more power.

64. Einar Diaz, Indians C (24) -- Cleveland called up Diaz before the Sept. 1 deadline for establishing the postseason roster, because of his defense.

65. Jason Hardtke, Mets 2B (25) -- Hardtke became another Bobby Valentine favorite at Norfolk, and that popularity could carry over in New York. Hardtke's biggest problem has been playing so hard that he has injured himself.

66. Scott Spiezio, Athletics 3B (24) -- The son of ex-major leaguer Ed Spiezio showed power in a September callup, and appears to be a better all-around player than his old man.

67. Jermaine Allensworth, Pirates OF (25) -- Pittsburgh thought enough of Allensworth, who was having a good year in the Pacific Coast League, that they all but gave Jacob Brumfield to the Blue Jays. The Bucs expect Allensworth to be their leadoff batter and center fielder for years to come, as well as their best former Purdue player since Bob Friend.

68. Dustin Hermanson, Padres RHP (24) -- With Trevor Hoffman in San Diego, the Padres haven't needed to rush Hermanson. He hasn't really been ready, but he may be now. He could combine with Hoffman to provide a setup/closer combo similar to the Yankees'.

69. Jacob Cruz, Giants OF (24) -- San Francisco's outfielders caught the injury bug that usually afflicts its pitchers. In his injury-induced trial, Cruz showed he can play right field. His hitting should come around as well.

70. Robert Smith, Braves 3B (22) -- Smith had a disappointing season with his bat, but played defense well enough that the organization tried him at shortstop while Jeff Blauser was injured.

71. Ralph Milliard, Marlins 2B (23) -- It was a difficult 1996 for Milliard, who had an elbow injury and was demoted because he allegedly couldn't get along with the other kids at Charlotte. If he isn't traded, perhaps Milliard's former manager at Portland, Carlos Tosca, can straighten him out.

72. Matt Morris, Cardinals RHP (22) -- Morris was a Texas League all-star, but his strikeout totals have been disappointing for a pitcher who throws as hard as he does.

73. Livan Hernandez, Marlins RHP (22) -- Hernandez survived early-season inactivity and an eating binge brought on by The Big Chill at the beginning of season. Back in Double-A, he showed the dominance that attracted Florida and other teams to the Cuban expatriate.

74. Bartolo Colon, Indians RHP (21) -- Arm trouble the last two seasons has raised serious doubts about Colon's durability, if not his long-range future. He may be best served by moving to the bullpen.

75. Luis Andujar, Blue Jays RHP (24) -- The Jays obtained Andujar from the White Sox for Tony Castillo and Domingo Cedeno. Before long, the operative verb may be that they stole Andujar from Chicago.

76. Shane Dennis, Padres LHP (25) -- Dennis not only led the Southern League in ERA, he also struck out better than a batter an inning.

77. Heath Murray, Padres LHP (23) -- Dennis had the better statistical line at Memphis, but Murray was voted to the Southern League all-star team.

78. Bill Mueller, Giants 3B (26) -- Mueller (pronounced Miller) received a promotion to San Francisco only because Matt Williams and Kim Batiste were injured. Once Mueller arrived, no one could get him out of the lineup. He has no power, but gets on base with frequent walks. The Giants also tried him at second base.

79. Homer Bush, Padres 2B (24) -- Bush has been injured so much, and has come back so often, that he resembles nothing so much as the Black Knight, who wanted to continue fighting after all his limbs were cut off in "Monty Python and the Holy Grail." Bush is a much better hitter.

80. Felipe Crespo, Blue Jays 2B (24) -- An early-season injury stalled Crespo's progress, but he picked up another skill by playing right field at Syracuse, then drove in the winning runs in Pat Hentgen's 20th win.

81. Pedro Valdes, Cubs OF (23) -- Valdes is a good offensive outfielder whose playing time would increase if he was traded away from Chicago.

82. Aaron Boone, Reds 3B (24) -- It's in the genes. Aaron turned in a solid performance in the Southern League.

83. Dan Serafini, Twins LHP (23) -- Serafini has two things going for him: He's lefthanded, and the Twins always need pitching. The downside is that Minnesota plays its home games in the Metrodome.

84. Tony Saunders, Marlins LHP (22) -- As the ace with first-place Portland, Saunders was an Eastern League all-star. He picked up his strikeout pace in '96.

85. Angelo Encarnacion, Pirates C (23) -- Encarnacion was displaced by two rookies last season, but he is still Pittsburgh's best defensive backstop. He went back to Triple-A and had a big offensive year. There's a good chance the Bucs will move Jason Kendall out from behind the plate, reopening that job for the flamboyant Encarnacion.

86. Scott McClain, Orioles 3B (24) -- The best defensive third baseman in the International League also came on with his bat during the latter part of last season.

87. Tom Fordham, White Sox LHP (23) -- All that stands between Fordham and the Chicago rotation is a little better control.

88. Manny Aybar, Cardinals RHP (22) -- The slender Aybar had success with a poor team after an in-season promotion.

89. Jonathan Johnson, Rangers RHP (22) -- Little more than a year out of Florida State, Texas' 1995 first-round draft pick pitched a complete-game win in his Triple-A debut.

90. Bruce Aven, Indians OF (25) -- Aven took a step ahead of more spectacular slugger Rich Sexson by hitting with power throughout last season.

91. Neifi Perez, Rockies SS (21) -- Along his path to the majors, the slick-fielding, switch-hitting Perez also picked up an effective bat.

92. Chris Widger, Mariners C (25) -- Widger used to have an offensive advantage over Seattle's incumbent catcher, until Dan Wilson turned in his career year in 1996. Widger could be a viable target in a trade.

93. Brent Brede, Twins OF (25) -- Brede became a candidate for Minnesota's leadoff job with a pleasantly surprising big season in his Triple-A debut.

94. Fausto Cruz, Tigers SS-2B (25) -- With Alan Trammell finally out the door, it is open for Cruz, who was obtained from the Oakland organization. He needs better strike-zone judgment.

95. Rafael Orellano, Red Sox LHP (23) -- The statistics say Orellano had a terrible season in 1996. However, he recovered well after some lengthy initial shellshock at Pawtucket. He could blossom, especially if he's moved to the bullpen.

96. Todd Dunwoody, Marlins OF (21) -- Dunwoody has mastered every part of the game except making contact. He has time to improve that and become a strong major league candidate by late this season.

97. Damian Jackson, Indians SS (23) -- Wilson is a better prospect, but Jackson came of age last season when he shouldered the responsibility of batting leadoff for Buffalo and kept the Bisons from falling out of the American Association lead.

98. Dante Powell, Giants OF (23) -- Powell came of age last season. He's a good power/speed prospect.

99. Julio Mosquera, Blue Jays C (25) -- Mosquera is kind of the opposite of Carlos Delgado -- a weak hitter who plays exceptional defense. Toronto needs Mosquera behind the plate, but he's of little use to a fantasy team.

100. Mike Cameron, White Sox OF (24) -- An excellent right fielder, Cameron added power hitting to his arsenal last year.

Top 100 Prospects for 1998-1999

1. Chad Hermansen, Pirates SS (19) -- Hermansen is a power-hitting shortstop who also plays excellent defense. He succeeded while playing at two Class A levels in 1996, just a year after Pittsburgh made him its first draft pick out of high school. There's plenty of upward mobility in the Pirates system.

2. Miguel Tejada, Athletics SS (19) -- Tejada showed more speed than Hermansen, but not as much power in a better hitting environment.

3. Jaret Wright, Indians RHP (21) -- The son of former Angels lefty Clyde Wright has been earmarked as a strong prospect since the Tribe drafted him in the first round in 1994.

4. Ron Wright, Pirates 1B (21) -- Pittsburgh didn't come up entirely empty in the Denny Neagle trade. The Pirates landed one of the minors' best power hitters.

5. Juan Melo, Padres SS (20) -- Melo, a high-average hitter, was overshadowed by Tejada in the California League.

6. Mike Drumright, Tigers RHP (22) -- Detroit's 1995 first-round draft pick is a power pitcher who should benefit this season at Toledo from the organization's new-found patience with its pitchers.

7. Jose Guillen, Pirates OF (20) -- The comparisons to Roberto Clemente are unfortunate, but inevitable, for the Carolina League's most valuable player. While we weren't looking, the Pirates have been replenishing their farm system.

8. Kevin Witt, Blue Jays SS (21) -- Witt follows a couple of trends on this list. He's a former first-round draft pick, and he's a shortstop. He may move to third base before his career is very old.

9. Mario Valdez, White Sox 1B (22) -- Valdez tore apart the Midwest League, then survived a jump to the Southern League.

10. Nelson Figueroa, Mets RHP (22) -- Figueroa, the Sally League Pitcher of the Year, is on the crest of the next wave of pitching prospects heading for Shea Stadium.

11. Aaron Boone, Reds 3B (24) -- It's in the genes. Aaron had a solid year in the Southern League.

12. Hiram Bocachica, Expos SS (21) -- Because of a bad arm, Bocachica couldn't play in the field, but he spent last season working on his hitting.

13. Ben Grieve, Athletics OF (20) -- Grieve struggled a bit after his promotion to the Southern League, but the former number one pick is on target to follow his father to the majors.

14. Kelvim Escobar, Blue Jays RHP (20) -- Escobar is a strikeout-an-inning pitcher who can move into Toronto's rotation by 1999.

15. Damian Moss, Braves LHP (20) -- Moss is another power pitcher, and another of the Australians making their mark in the majors.

16. Wes Helms, Braves 3B (20) -- With Ron Wright gone, Helms represents Atlanta's best long-range power hope.

17. Kerry Wood, Cubs RHP (19) -- Get used to this combination on this list -- first-round draft pick (1995), power pitcher, precocious.

18. Elvin Hernandez, Pirates (19) -- Hernandez is a tall, thin strikeout pitcher who has dominated competition in the lower minors.

19. Jay Tessmer, Yankees RHP (24) -- On the other hand, Tessmer an exception to the rule. He's older, a 19th-round draft choice (U. of Miami) and is being groomed as a closer. If he can skip Double-A, or move up to Triple-A during this season, he can catch up with his contemporaries.

20. Blake Stein, Cardinals RHP (23) -- Stein, the Florida State League ERA leader, is the kind of power pitcher you'd expect a 6-7, 210-pounder to be.

21. Darin Blood, Giants RHP (22) -- Blood dominated California League hitters, which isn't easy to do. He struck out more than a batter an inning and led the league in ERA.

22. Ken Cloude, Mariners RHP (22) -- Cloude is another young power pitcher, in an organization where he can move up fast.

23. Dan Kolb, Rangers RHP (22) -- Kolb advanced as far as Double-A last season, his second as a pro. He has strikeout-an-inning stuff, but hasn't yet translated that into being a consistent winner.

24. Marlon Anderson, Phillies 2B (23) -- Players were flying through the Philadelphia organization last year, and Anderson reached Double-A. The speedy lefthander held his own at Reading, but may need to return there to start '97.

25. Adrian Beltre, Dodgers 3B (19) -- Beltre hit well in adverse conditions in the Sally League to earn a promotion. Even if LA is measuring his age in dog years, he's a prospect.

26. Ethan McEntire, Mets LHP (21) -- A finesse pitcher in 1995, McEntire turned on the power last year to give Columbia one of the minors' best righty-lefty combinations in Figueroa and McEntire.

27. Britt Reames, Cardinals RHP (23) -- Reames is following right behind Stein, who is 16 days older. Reames led the Midwest League in ERA while striking out more than a batter an inning.

28. Edwin Diaz, Rangers 2B (22) -- Diaz slipped behind Kevin Brown in the Rangers' prospect order. Diaz will need a whole season in Triple-A, if not even starting this year back in Double-A, to learn the strike zone.

29. Tony Mounce, Astros LHP (22) -- Mounce's strikeout ratio fell in the Midwest League, but he is a durable pitcher who is hard to hit.

30. Kris Benson, Pirates RHP (22) -- Pittsburgh gave its 1995 number one draft choice a record $2-million bonus. After he spent a long season pitching at Clemson and on the Olympic team, they kept him out of pro ball. They didn't want him to be overworked the way college stars such as John Hoover, Ben McDonald and Paul Wilson have been.

31. Daryle Ward, Tigers 1B (21) -- Ward's Florida State League season was interrupted by an emergency callup to Triple-A. He didn't show as much home run power as the Tigers had hoped.

32. Geoff Jenkins, Brewers OF (22) -- Jenkins is another former number one pick. He can hit for average, but without much power.

33. Lindsey Gulin, Mets LHP (20) -- The real strikeout machine on a loaded staff at Columbia was Gulin, a stringbean lefty.

34. Doug Million, Rockies LHP (21) -- Million is a former first-round draft pick who did better in his second trip through the Carolina League.

35. Brad Fullmer, Expos OF (22) -- Fullmer, a former first and third baseman, is a high-average hitter who was promoted to Double-A during last season.

36. Dwight Maness, Mets OF (22) -- Maness is a gifted outfielder whose best offensive weapon is his speed. He could develop enough patience at the plate to become a leadoff batter.

37. Anton French, Tigers OF (21) -- The lightning-quick, switch-hitting French has bounced from organization to organization the last two years. The Braves traded him to the Detroit organization during last season. The half-empty explanation is that the teams that have him don't want him. The half-full reason is that lots of teams want his skills.

38. Richard Almanzar, Tigers 2B (20) -- Almanzar showed greatly improved base-stealing ability and a .300 bat in his second tour of the Florida State League.

39. Roy Halladay, Blue Jays RHP (19) -- The 6-6 Halladay was a Florida State League all-star. He had a better won-lost record than Escobar, his Dunedin teammate.

40. Keith Luuloa, Angels 2B (22) -- The Hawaiian Luuloa may need another season in the Texas League before he can say "Aloha!" to the majors.

41. Jose Valentin, Twins C (21) -- There must be a limit on the number of home runs guys named Jose Valentin can total in a season. While the Brewers' shortstop was having a career year for power, the Twins' catcher saw his home run total drop from 19 to 10. He reached the Eastern League last season.

42. Jose Vidro, Expos 3B (22) -- The switch-hitter moved from second base last season. He was able to move from the middle infield because he showed surprising power.

43. Deivi Cruz, Giants SS (21) -- Cruz showed enough on offense and on defense to make the Midwest League all-star team.

44. Juan Encarnacion, Tigers OF (21) -- Encarnacion had a much better 1995 season, then struggled in the pitching-rich Florida State League. He still led Lakeland in home runs. His future will depend on how well he can cut down his strikeouts.

45. Charles Peterson, Pirates OF (21) -- Peterson can run and play the outfield, but he hasn't yet developed the power Pittsburgh expects from the ex-football player.

46. David Dellucci, Orioles OF (23) -- A 10th-round draft choice out of the U. of Mississippi, Dellucci is a hustling outfielder who has earned in-season promotions in both of his years as a pro.

47. David Arias, Mariners 1B (21) -- In the Midwest League, Arias showed the potential to become a big-time power hitter.

48. Arnold Gooch, Mets RHP (20) -- The Mets obtained Gooch from Colorado in the Bret Saberhagen trade. Gooch was one step ahead of Figueroa et al., but not as dominant as the trio of pitchers at Columbia.

49. Anthony Sanders, Blue Jays OF (23) -- Sanders is a power/speed prospect, as long as he can cut down his strikeouts.

50. Rob Burger, Phillies RHP (21) -- Burger was the most dominant of this year's crop of strong Philadelphia pitching prospects at Piedmont.

51. Heath Bost, Rockies RHP (22) -- Bost is a burly 18th-round draft pick who has advanced from the small-college ranks at Catawba to success in last year's bullpens at Asheville and New Haven.

52. Michael Barrett, Expos C (20) -- Barrett's hitting suffered as he was switching from shortstop to catcher. He can drive the ball to the gaps when he's right.

53. Dean Crow, Mariners RHP (24) -- Crow, a closer, is not a big strikeout pitcher, but he throws strikes and fools batters.

54. Mark Raynor, Phillies SS (24) -- Raynor had a very good year in the South Atlantic League. He didn't hit for average in his brief time in the Florida State League, but he got on base with his exceptional plate discipline

55. Kurt Bierek, Yankees OF (24) -- Bierek hit for average, tied for his team's lead in home runs and walked more than he struck out.

56. Mike Villano, Giants RHP (25) -- The former catcher has been sometimes a starter, sometimes a reliever, but always effective.

57. David Coggin, Phillies RHP (20) -- Coggin didn't pitch as well as Burger in the Sally League, but Coggin is seven months younger.

58. Vladimir Nunez, Diamondbacks RHP (21) -- Nunez is another in the line of Cuban pitchers defecting to the U.S., and he is the Arizona organization's first best prospect. The 6-5 Nunez throws hard, but he may be several years older than his listed age.

59. George Lombard, Braves OF (21) -- Lombard is a lefthanded power hitter. Like most of his ilk, he needs to be more selective at the plate.

60. Don Denbow, Giants OF (23) -- Denbow is one of the best power prospects in the lower minors because he began to master the art of patience. He can run a bit, too.

61. Andy Hall, Cardinals 2B (22) -- Hall can run, he can draw walks and he has been a consistent .300 hitter in his two pro seasons.

62. Nick Bierbrodt, Diamondbacks LHP (19) -- The first draft pick in Arizona history pitched just 11 games as a pro. The 6-4 Bierbrodt showed few effects from the foot injury that bothered him as a high schooler.

63. Alejandro Freire, Astros OF (22) -- Moving from first base to the outfield seemed to increase Freire's base-stealing speed. Moving from the Midwest League to the Florida State League took a bite out of his offense output.

64. Hernando Arredondo, Devil Rays 3B (19) -- For now, the Pioneer League all-star is baseball's equivalent of Roseanne Roseannadanna. Before Tampa Bay has played many games, he may be its third baseman, with a good combination of on-base ability and gap power.

65. Kevin Sweeney, Diamondbacks OF (22) -- Sweeney was the Pioneer League batting champ and MVP. It remains to be seen whether that was a result of superior talent or of greater age than most players in the league.

66. Russ Ortiz, Giants RHP (22) -- San Francisco eventually would like Ortiz to replace Rod Beck. He was a bullpen ace even after being promoted to Double-A.

67. Ben Davis, Padres C (20) -- San Diego's first-round draft pick in 1995 has been much better behind the plate than at it.

68. Ramon Castro, Astros C (21) -- Castro remains a otential power threat with a rifle arm. He still needs work on making contact at the plate and handling pitchers better behind it.

69. Sean Casey, Indians 1B (22) -- Casey hit for average last season, but not much power for a 6-4, 215-pounder. The Indians believe it's a matter of time before he starts turning doubles into home runs.

70. Shea Morenz, Yankees OF (23) -- Morenz didn't increase his power output as expected, and had trouble making contact in '96. His upside could approach Ricky Ledee's. Give Morenz a couple of years to find out.

71. Valerio de los Santos, Brewers LHP (21) -- The flamethrowing de los Santos, who has reached 95 MPH, switched from starter to closer late in the 1996 Midwest League season.

72. Jeff Liefer, White Sox 3B (23) -- Liefer's biggest problem will be finding a position. He's barely adequate at third base, but has played both first and the outfield.

73. Larry Barnes, Angels 1B (22) -- Barnes went undrafted out of Fresno State, but developed into the Midwest League's top power hitter.

74. A.J. Pierzynski, Twins C (20) -- Every team would like to have a good catcher. Minnesota has two in Valentin and Pierzynski. The youngest's greatest strength is defense, but he also was a good run-producer in the Midwest League.

75. Brian Simmons, White Sox OF (23) -- Simmons was Chicago's second pick in the 1995 draft, after Liefer, who has greater power.

76. Ramon Hernandez, Athletics C (20) -- Hernandez is a good defensive catcher with a strong arm. He also projects as a strong power hitter.

77. Ben Petrick, Rockies C (20) -- Petrick has good power and speed for a catcher. He needs work on defense, but appears to have the physical tools to become a good receiver.

78. Ruben Mateo, Rangers OF (19) -- Mateo is a speedy outfielder with an arm considered the best in the Sally League. He can convert his gap power to home runs as he grows.

79. Willis Roberts, Tigers RHP (21) -- In his fifth pro season, the Dominican Roberts continued to develop in the Florida State League. His greatest need is to put some weight on his 6-3, 175-pound bones to develop strikeout power.

80. Carlos Febles, Royals 2B (20) -- Febles can be a good leadoff hitter because of his base-stealing speed and ability to get on base.

81. David Newhan, Athletics OF (23) -- The son of long-time sports columnist Ross Newhan exploded at bat last season in the California League. If Oakland should ever need another power source, the younger Newhan could be the man.

82. Stephen Randolph, Yankees LHP (22) -- Randolph is a power pitcher. He also is a wild pitcher. He has to improve the latter without losing the former.

83. Brent Iddon, Mariners RHP (21) -- The Australian Iddon made a successful transition to the bullpen and blew away Midwest League batters last year.

84. Brett Hinchliffe, Mariners RHP (22) -- Hinchliffe improved dramatically in his second California League season.

85. Mike Kinkade, Brewers 3B (23) -- Kinkade was a 100-RBI man and a successful base-stealer in the Midwest League.

86. Josh Booty, Marlins 3B (21) -- One of the nation's top high school quarterbacks before the Marlins drafted him in the first round, Booty has treated baseball like a non-contact sport at bat. When he does hit the ball, it can go a long way.

87. Russell Branyan, Indians 3B (21) -- Branyan went back to the Sally League for the second year, and destroyed its pitching early on. He wasn't promoted, and his power-hitting game cooled off as the season wore on.

88. Bryan Corey, Tigers RHP (23) -- Corey was Fayetteville's closer in '96, and he's the among those least likely to succeed in the majors -- closers groomed from their earliest days in the minors.

89. Dan Perkins, Twins RHP (22) -- Perkins' performance really improved after a shaky '95 season at Fort Wayne. Last year he was a sometime-starter, sometime-reliever in the Florida State League.

90. Matt Perisho, Angels LHP (21) -- After an in-season promotion to Double-A, Perisho performed even better than he had in the California League.

91. John LeRoy, Braves RHP (21) -- Atlanta's prospect express has slowed somewhat, but LeRoy was effective in both the Carolina and Southern leagues.

92. Scott Hunter, Mets OF (21) -- Hunter is a base-stealing outfielder obtained from the Dodgers for Brett Butler. The question with Hunter is whether he will hit big-league pitching.

93. Decomba Conner, Reds OF (23) -- Conner improved his batting average, home run power and base-stealing in his first Carolina League season.

94. Edgar Ramos, Astros RHP (22) -- Undefeated in 11 Florida State League starts, Ramos cooled considerably in the Texas League.

95. Mitch Meluskey, Astros C (23) -- Meluskey is many teams' favorite kind of catcher -- a switch hitter. With Castro, he gives Houston a couple of future catching options.

96. Mendy Lopez, Royals 3B (22) -- Lopez hit for average and stole some bases, but struck out too often in the 1996 Texas League.

97. Damian Sapp, Red Sox C (20) -- Sapp is part of a wave of promising catchers about to hit the high minors. In moving up to the Midwest League, he improved his batting average 124 points, in a tough park for hitters.

98. Russ Herbert, White Sox RHP (24) -- Herbert didn't have a winning record with a weak team at Prince William, but he mowed down more than one Carolina League batter per inning.

99. Bret Hemphill, Angels C (25) -- Another catcher, another switch hitter. Hemphill turned on pitches to turn on his power in the California League.

100. Eric Stuckenschneider, Dodgers OF (25) -- Stuckenschneider is a very late bloomer who can steal bases and hit with power and extreme patience. If the Dodgers don't challenge him at least in Double-A this season, it's probably too late for him.

101. Terrence Long, Mets OF (21) -- I'm hedging my bets with this one. I'm not convinced Long is a prospect, but I'm willing to accept the multitude of opinions from those who think he is. But I can't go lower than number 101.

1997 Projections

This book launches an annual process that doesn't end until Opening Day. Projecting player performance requires careful attention to the individual situation of every player. Obviously a player's situation can change. During spring training, these changes occur rapidly. During March, projections will change due to managerial decision or physical condition (to name just two variables) for twenty to forty players every day. The more important changes will be reported in the Benson Baseball Monthly, which appears three times during the final six weeks before Opening Day. All changes are recorded in the bi-weekly player databases for John Benson's Draft Software.

Players are presented here within the context of a league, because without a context there cannot be real accuracy. Players are shown within the league where they finished the 1996 season, or their new team if they were traded or signed across leagues before the free agency signing date.

Dollar values in these tables are standard eight category RLBA values, uninflated and unadjusted for position.

1997 Projections for American League Batters

NAME	AB	RUN	HR	RBI	SB	AVG	$VAL	NAME	AB	RUN	HR	RBI	SB	AVG	$VAL
Mike Aldrete	83	11	4	14	0	.238	-$2	Tony Clark	540	77	30	98	0	.269	$13
Manny Alexander	63	8	1	5	3	.220	-$2	Will Clark	469	80	15	85	2	.285	$11
Roberto Alomar	582	114	19	84	23	.318	$30	Ron Coomer	174	25	9	31	2	.270	$2
Sandy Alomar	390	53	13	52	3	.273	$7	Joey Cora	506	83	5	44	10	.291	$11
Rich Amaral	311	64	2	27	24	.286	$14	Wil Cordero	400	55	8	55	7	.288	$10
Brady Anderson	580	114	29	83	25	.282	$27	Marty Cordova	514	85	18	95	13	.300	$21
Garret Anderson	552	72	15	75	7	.295	$16	Felipe Crespo	102	15	2	10	2	.242	-$2
George Arias	402	60	8	70	3	.250	$4	Fausto Cruz	77	7	0	5	0	.222	-$4
Brad Ausmus	398	51	6	38	8	.245	$3	Milt Cuyler	52	9	0	5	3	.207	-$3
Harold Baines	442	69	22	81	2	.306	$16	Johnny Damon	525	66	9	53	24	.285	$19
Kim Bartee	347	51	4	38	21	.256	$11	Chili Davis	516	81	27	98	4	.272	$15
Tony Batista	303	49	9	39	8	.270	$7	Russ Davis	255	36	9	35	2	.253	$2
Allen Battle	145	20	1	11	9	.249	$1	Carlos Delgado	500	70	27	91	0	.274	$13
Rich Becker	530	83	9	63	17	.292	$18	Mike Devereaux	253	37	7	32	6	.251	$3
Albert Belle	603	128	45	135	10	.310	$33	Alex Diaz	165	24	2	14	10	.246	$2
Esteban Beltre	54	5	0	5	1	.248	-$3	Gary Disarcina	550	72	6	52	4	.269	$6
Geronimo Berroa	583	98	31	102	3	.288	$19	Mariano Duncan	338	50	7	47	4	.318	$10
Wade Boggs	457	74	4	49	1	.310	$9	Todd Dunn	157	33	8	35	1	.296	$3
Bobby Bonilla	600	105	29	112	1	.280	$17	Mike Durant	54	7	1	7	1	.219	-$3
Pat Borders	233	17	5	19	0	.254	-$1	Ray Durham	552	78	12	63	27	.280	$22
Mike Bordick	514	48	6	52	8	.248	$4	Damion Easley	222	25	5	25	4	.231	$0
Rafael Bournigal	167	20	0	12	2	.240	-$3	Jim Edmonds	487	89	28	81	3	.296	$17
Darren Bragg	302	52	7	33	11	.256	$6	Kevin Elster	501	76	19	93	3	.245	$8
Tilson Brito	94	12	1	11	3	.240	-$2	Darin Erstad	408	65	7	44	8	.284	$9
Scott Brosius	433	71	21	65	6	.284	$13	Jorge Fabregas	247	21	2	25	0	.274	$0
Jacob Brumfield	234	39	6	28	10	.263	$5	Sal Fasano	188	33	6	36	1	.251	$0
Damon Buford	144	28	5	17	8	.252	$3	Cecil Fielder	551	80	36	104	1	.250	$13
Jay Buhner	547	104	43	133	0	.269	$19	Andy Fox	149	21	3	11	8	.220	$0
Jeromy Burnitz	283	56	12	52	6	.266	$7	Julio Franco	308	51	11	55	6	.292	$9
Mike Cameron	89	15	2	14	2	.234	-$2	Lou Frazier	104	15	0	9	10	.233	$1
Casey Candaele	55	11	2	4	0	.229	-$4	Jeff Frye	351	56	4	34	12	.287	$9
Jose Canseco	380	70	27	82	5	.270	$13	Travis Fryman	620	89	21	98	4	.270	$13
Chuck Carr	228	38	2	18	16	.250	$6	Carlos Garcia	415	60	7	47	12	.287	$11
Mark Carreon	308	40	10	48	2	.287	$6	Nomar Garciaparra	513	75	14	70	16	.270	$15
Joe Carter	574	77	26	96	9	.255	$14	Brent Gates	357	40	3	40	2	.260	$1
Raul Casanova	105	13	3	14	1	.241	-$2	Jason Giambi	507	79	21	75	1	.286	$12
Domingo Cedeno	143	21	2	10	2	.254	-$2	Benji Gil	143	12	3	16	1	.233	-$2
Jeff Cirillo	533	93	14	74	6	.310	$17	Brian Giles	107	25	4	24	5	.303	$2

Benson's Baseball Player Guide: 1997

NAME	AB	RUN	HR	RBI	SB	AVG	$VAL	NAME	AB	RUN	HR	RBI	SB	AVG	$VAL
Joe Girardi	424	57	4	47	8	.281	$8	Edgar Martinez	517	120	27	107	4	.333	$25
Rene Gonzales	75	15	1	4	0	.206	-$4	Sandy Martinez	202	14	2	19	0	.231	-$4
Alex Gonzalez	530	68	14	63	13	.245	$9	Tino Martinez	578	86	28	116	1	.290	$18
Juan Gonzalez	555	90	44	139	2	.305	$27	John Marzano	96	7	0	6	0	.241	-$4
Tom Goodwin	514	78	2	32	60	.284	$34	Damon Mashore	203	26	3	14	17	.229	$5
Shawn Green	425	54	13	50	3	.292	$10	Mike Matheny	294	28	6	42	2	.230	-$1
Todd Greene	287	51	15	52	1	.284	$7	Mark McGwire	420	98	40	100	0	.298	$19
Mike Greenwell	345	47	10	52	5	.293	$9	Mark McLemore	516	81	5	45	26	.278	$17
Rusty Greer	505	82	17	87	6	.314	$19	Pat Meares	506	67	10	64	10	.267	$10
Ken Griffey	544	121	47	127	14	.297	$32	Orlando Merced	490	73	17	83	7	.295	$16
Ozzie Guillen	476	58	3	45	6	.261	$4	Matt Mieske	351	47	14	60	2	.269	$7
Chip Hale	103	10	1	17	0	.269	-$2	Izzy Molina	50	4	1	6	0	.195	-$4
Bob Hamelin	257	34	11	42	4	.236	$2	Paul Molitor	636	93	12	99	18	.321	$28
Darryl Hamilton	530	78	5	47	13	.286	$13	Kerwin Moore	101	20	1	7	6	.219	-$1
Jeffrey Hammonds	244	35	8	28	4	.260	$3	Lyle Mouton	189	23	6	32	2	.287	$3
Bill Haselman	205	29	7	29	3	.262	$2	Pedro Munoz	303	39	14	46	0	.286	$6
Charlie Hayes	303	33	7	44	3	.264	$3	Eddie Murray	527	69	22	83	5	.276	$14
Jose Herrera	345	46	6	30	8	.266	$5	Greg Myers	307	35	7	42	0	.276	$3
Phil Hiatt	77	9	2	8	0	.202	-$4	Rod Myers	104	15	1	13	3	.267	-$1
Bob Higginson	472	78	24	74	7	.279	$15	Tim Naehring	326	53	11	47	1	.293	$7
Denny Hocking	109	13	1	9	2	.244	-$2	Phil Nevin	303	32	10	39	2	.254	$2
Chris Hoiles	409	63	24	71	1	.254	$8	Marc Newfield	473	58	15	72	2	.280	$10
Dave Hollins	404	73	13	59	4	.253	$5	Warren Newson	208	34	8	25	3	.257	$2
Dwayne Hosey	87	15	2	9	6	.257	$0	Melvin Nieves	482	77	27	69	1	.259	$9
Dave Howard	334	38	3	35	5	.225	-$1	Dave Nilsson	506	85	19	95	2	.312	$18
Jack Howell	106	17	4	18	0	.233	-$2	Otis Nixon	479	78	1	31	48	.288	$28
Rex Hudler	274	48	10	36	13	.298	$12	Trot Nixon	59	7	1	6	1	.221	-$3
David Hulse	148	22	1	14	6	.243	$0	Greg Norton	83	12	1	11	1	.224	-$3
Brianr Hunter	181	20	7	28	1	.253	$0	Jonathan Nunnally	196	34	10	30	3	.243	$2
Pete Incaviglia	205	25	12	32	1	.240	$1	Charlie O'Brien	302	31	13	41	0	.227	$0
Damian Jackson	51	8	1	4	2	.242	-$3	Troy O'Leary	442	62	13	66	4	.275	$9
John Jaha	503	97	31	104	3	.298	$20	Paul O'Neill	534	91	22	99	1	.307	$18
Reggie Jefferson	295	51	15	58	0	.310	$9	Jose Offerman	515	78	4	43	15	.292	$14
Derek Jeter	580	102	10	78	13	.311	$21	John Olerud	458	66	15	64	1	.283	$9
Ron Karkovice	351	46	12	44	1	.218	-$1	Orlando Palmeiro	89	8	0	6	0	.274	-$3
Pat Kelly	144	18	2	17	4	.241	-$1	Rafael Palmeiro	623	107	40	131	7	.298	$28
Roberto Kelly	330	42	6	42	12	.301	$11	Dean Palmer	551	96	35	102	3	.281	$19
Chuck Knoblauch	590	132	12	72	47	.335	$43	Craig Paquette	410	58	20	65	6	.248	$8
Chad Kreuter	102	13	2	14	0	.222	-$3	Mark Parent	122	14	8	19	0	.221	-$2
Matt Lawton	262	37	8	44	7	.272	$6	Rudy Pemberton	81	14	2	11	5	.284	$1
Brian Lesher	101	17	4	15	1	.235	-$2	Tony Pena	167	15	2	22	0	.202	-$5
Jessie Levis	176	20	2	17	0	.260	-$2	Shannon Penn	95	15	0	7	4	.234	-$2
Darren Lewis	424	65	3	44	28	.241	$12	Danny Perez	52	7	1	6	0	.275	-$3
Mark Lewis	505	65	10	56	5	.278	$9	Robert Perez	202	28	3	20	3	.290	$2
Jim Leyritz	205	24	6	33	1	.263	$1	Tomas Perez	298	26	1	20	1	.251	-$2
Pat Listach	250	35	1	23	16	.234	$4	Herbert Perry	92	12	2	12	1	.284	-$1
Keith Lockhart	368	45	7	46	9	.284	$9	Tony Phillips	557	118	18	64	13	.273	$15
Kenny Lofton	624	125	12	66	72	.318	$52	Phil Plantier	190	26	7	26	1	.226	-$1
Mark Loretta	190	28	2	16	3	.276	$1	Arquimedez Pozo	105	9	2	15	3	.260	-$1
Torey Lovullo	58	11	2	6	1	.222	-$3	Curtis Pride	251	49	10	26	11	.272	$8
Mike Macfarlane	334	48	15	47	3	.257	$5	Tim Raines	344	65	11	50	12	.282	$11
Jose Malave	112	19	5	20	0	.269	-$1	Manny Ramirez	534	92	33	112	7	.306	$25
Jeff Manto	147	19	8	19	0	.231	-$2	Joe Randa	346	37	6	46	9	.279	$8
Norberto Martin	166	28	2	17	7	.280	$3	Jeff Reboulet	220	27	2	23	3	.244	-$1
Dave Martinez	339	60	7	41	10	.309	$12	Billy Ripken	98	14	2	9	0	.250	-$3

NAME	AB	RUN	HR	RBI	SB	AVG	$VAL
Cal Ripken	632	90	23	101	1	.277	$14
Ruben Rivera	123	23	2	23	8	.270	$3
Bip Roberts	360	44	1	44	17	.295	$12
Alex Rodriguez	600	137	36	130	16	.323	$35
Ivan Rodriguez	600	96	18	82	4	.301	$17
Tony Rodriguez	104	10	0	9	1	.205	-$4
Tim Salmon	582	101	33	104	4	.300	$22
Juan Samuel	180	31	6	29	7	.253	$3
Kevin Seitzer	553	76	10	77	5	.321	$18
Andy Sheets	152	17	1	12	2	.231	-$3
Duane Singleton	96	11	0	13	3	.207	-$3
Don Slaught	177	18	3	24	0	.288	$0
Mark Smith	91	10	3	12	1	.237	-$2
Chris Snopek	124	22	5	19	0	.277	$0
JT Snow	560	71	19	79	1	.265	$9
Luis Sojo	162	18	2	15	2	.250	-$2
Paul Sorrento	451	65	25	94	0	.275	$12
Scott Spiezio	88	13	2	14	1	.254	-$2
Ed Sprague	587	84	29	92	0	.245	$9
Scott Stahoviak	395	63	11	52	4	.279	$8
Matt Stairs	161	22	9	29	1	.273	$2
Mike Stanley	390	69	22	73	2	.272	$10
Terry Steinbach	500	69	28	91	1	.275	$14
Lee Stevens	57	5	2	8	0	.226	-$3
Kurt Stillwell	56	7	1	6	0	.257	-$3
Kelly Stinnett	133	14	3	10	1	.204	-$4
Doug Strange	134	14	2	17	1	.241	-$2
Darryl Strawberry	163	28	8	28	4	.243	-$2
Chris Stynes	107	11	1	6	3	.272	$1
BJ Surhoff	520	77	19	83	2	.299	$15
Mike Sweeney	235	33	6	33	2	.269	$2
Tony Tarasco	216	32	6	22	9	.258	$4
Danny Tartabull	433	56	22	82	1	.250	$7
Mickey Tettleton	453	74	26	77	1	.244	$7
Frank Thomas	538	115	43	132	2	.337	$31
Jim Thome	500	112	34	101	3	.308	$22
Ryan Thompson	61	7	2	8	1	.249	-$2
Lee Tinsley	247	37	4	22	11	.247	$4
Michael Tucker	369	58	13	53	8	.268	$9
John Valentin	534	94	18	77	13	.298	$20
Jose Valentin	530	89	22	87	19	.248	$16
Dave Valle	90	13	2	13	0	.273	-$2
Mo Vaughn	622	113	43	140	5	.317	$32
Randy Velarde	501	79	12	55	6	.283	$11
Robin Ventura	574	92	32	105	2	.289	$19
Fernando Vina	510	86	6	43	14	.276	$11
Joe Vitiello	270	30	10	42	1	.265	$3
Omar Vizquel	548	94	8	62	33	.285	$24
Matt Walbeck	309	33	2	34	3	.235	-$1
Todd Walker	506	86	23	91	12	.281	$19
Turner Ward	135	18	4	18	5	.227	$0
Mark Whiten	402	71	19	66	14	.260	$13
Bernie Williams	577	107	25	97	15	.304	$26
Eddie Williams	173	20	6	25	0	.236	-$2
George Williams	126	18	4	13	0	.238	-$3

NAME	AB	R	HR	RBI	SB	AVG	$VAL
Gerald Williams	268	40	6	32	7	.253	$3
Matt Williams	400	70	27	86	1	.310	$17
Dan Wilson	490	49	15	74	1	.277	$9
Ernie Young	404	64	16	56	5	.247	$6
Kevin Young	160	18	7	23	2	.250	$0
Todd Zeile	572	72	22	87	1	.259	$9

Unlisted players are projected to have under 50 at-bats in 1997.

1997 Projections for National League Batters

NAME	AB	R	HR	RBI	SB	AVG	$VAL
Kurt Abbott	309	39	10	36	3	.253	$4
Bob Abreu	427	61	10	75	10	.264	$11
Edgardo Alfonzo	408	41	10	54	3	.280	$9
Luis Alicea	222	32	3	25	7	.254	$3
J. Allensworth	502	70	6	56	12	.267	$10
Moises Alou	525	84	21	93	8	.286	$19
Ruben Amaro	114	13	2	15	1	.245	-$1
Shane Andrews	345	40	16	57	2	.230	$4
Eric Anthony	183	28	9	24	2	.248	$2
Alex Arias	192	21	3	22	2	.272	$2
Billy Ashley	191	23	11	33	0	.241	$2
Rich Aude	106	7	2	16	1	.248	-$1
Rich Aurilia	353	33	5	30	5	.247	$2
Carlos Baerga	407	56	11	60	4	.281	$10
Jeff Bagwell	548	111	31	118	19	.314	$33
Jason Bates	205	26	4	21	2	.258	$1
Kim Batiste	107	13	2	8	2	.215	-$2
Howard Battle	51	7	1	7	1	.249	-$2
Danny Bautista	136	17	3	15	2	.233	-$1
Trey Beamon	461	73	5	50	13	.291	$13
Tim Belk	85	13	2	18	1	.257	$0
David Bell	136	12	1	12	1	.240	-$2
Derek Bell	589	79	15	104	30	.286	$26
Jay Bell	524	71	12	63	5	.257	$8
Rafael Belliard	163	11	0	5	2	.196	-$5
Marvin Benard	384	62	4	31	18	.263	$9
Mike Benjamin	133	15	4	13	6	.224	$0
Sean Berry	440	56	17	87	11	.290	$18
Dante Bichette	643	113	36	141	26	.305	$38
Craig Biggio	611	122	17	79	32	.286	$26
Jeff Blauser	357	57	11	38	6	.239	$4
Mike Blowers	206	24	7	34	1	.264	$3
Tim Bogar	100	15	1	10	1	.221	-$2
Barry Bonds	535	122	42	124	39	.304	$42
Bret Boone	518	61	13	71	4	.270	$11
Brent Bowers	98	11	1	7	2	.223	-$2
Jeff Branson	247	29	8	32	2	.252	$3
Rico Brogna	408	51	18	63	0	.280	$11
Brant Brown	110	13	2	10	1	.252	-$1
Scott Bullett	150	22	3	17	7	.233	$1
Ellis Burks	514	111	33	103	23	.328	$36
Mike Busch	110	14	4	12	1	.237	-$1
Brett Butler	310	51	1	22	19	.270	$8
Ken Caminiti	562	99	35	120	11	.314	$31

Benson's Baseball Player Guide: 1997

NAME	AB	R	HR	RBI	SB	AVG	$VAL	NAME	AB	R	HR	RBI	SB	AVG	$VAL
John Cangelosi	185	36	1	12	14	.240	$3	Willie Greene	404	66	20	83	1	.256	$10
Jay Canizaro	370	68	7	50	7	.264	$7	Marquis Grissom	655	104	19	65	32	.292	$28
Vinny Castilla	573	88	35	101	5	.299	$25	Mark Grudzielanek	621	87	5	46	28	.295	$21
Alberto Castillo	104	11	2	14	0	.223	-$2	Vladimir Guerrero	330	61	12	61	9	.298	$13
Luis Castillo	430	70	2	30	31	.270	$14	Wilton Guerrero	395	63	1	32	16	.280	$9
Juan Castro	89	11	0	3	1	.198	-$4	Ricky Gutierrez	222	28	1	17	6	.274	$3
Andujar Cedeno	291	28	7	31	4	.218	$0	Chris Gwynn	70	7	1	8	0	.212	-$3
Roger Cedeno	200	26	1	17	5	.255	$1	Tony Gwynn	510	79	7	69	13	.363	$28
Archi Cianfrocco	175	21	3	31	1	.270	$2	Todd Haney	64	9	1	3	1	.226	-$2
Dave Clark	183	25	6	28	2	.260	$2	Dave Hansen	130	11	0	9	0	.278	-$1
Royce Clayton	520	63	6	45	31	.282	$19	Jason Hardtke	128	14	2	16	0	.225	-$2
Greg Colbrunn	506	62	18	76	6	.290	$16	Lenny Harris	222	27	3	23	11	.267	$5
Jeff Conine	584	83	27	104	1	.298	$22	Rickey Henderson	458	98	9	38	36	.260	$17
Jake Cruz	157	30	4	26	2	.267	$2	Jose Hernandez	290	44	11	38	3	.243	$3
Midre Cummings	306	35	8	30	2	.252	$2	Glenallen Hill	433	64	21	75	15	.275	$17
Chad Curtis	493	81	14	50	20	.258	$13	Todd Hollandsworth	505	69	17	63	20	.285	$20
Eric Davis	266	51	16	52	15	.252	$11	Tyler Houston	204	20	3	23	2	.252	$1
Steve Decker	133	18	2	16	1	.242	-$1	Thomas Howard	266	38	4	29	8	.280	$6
Rob Deer	65	10	3	10	0	.198	-$2	Trent Hubbard	78	14	2	12	2	.239	-$1
Wilson Delgado	51	7	0	4	2	.240	-$2	Todd Hundley	510	78	33	100	1	.261	$16
Delino Deshields	517	71	8	40	44	.235	$16	Brian L Hunter	427	62	4	30	29	.282	$15
David Doster	104	16	4	14	2	.239	$0	Butch Huskey	366	37	13	52	1	.268	$7
Shawon Dunston	379	41	9	43	9	.296	$12	Stan Javier	372	64	5	38	24	.274	$13
Jermaine Dye	292	32	11	37	2	.270	$6	Gregg Jefferies	480	69	10	59	18	.301	$19
Lenny Dykstra	210	35	3	17	7	.265	$3	Robin Jennings	105	16	2	16	1	.266	$0
Angel Echevarria	185	22	5	29	1	.270	$2	Marcus Jensen	145	22	2	22	0	.255	$0
Jim Eisenreich	300	39	5	40	9	.339	$13	Brian Johnson	229	19	6	33	0	.264	$2
Angelo Encarnacion	94	10	1	7	0	.244	-$2	Charles Johnson	388	40	14	41	1	.239	$3
Alvaro Espinoza	163	19	4	18	1	.260	$1	Lance Johnson	656	109	9	66	46	.320	$36
Bobby Estalella	209	25	9	30	1	.224	$0	Mark Johnson	280	44	12	38	5	.256	$6
Tony Eusebio	207	24	3	31	0	.288	$3	Andruw Jones	505	84	25	85	16	.290	$23
Carl Everett	220	35	5	29	5	.270	$4	Chipper Jones	535	109	30	102	12	.310	$28
Steve Finley	635	120	23	76	27	.296	$28	Chris Jones	130	21	4	18	1	.233	-$1
John Flaherty	374	37	12	52	2	.269	$7	Dax Jones	116	15	1	10	1	.255	-$1
Darrin Fletcher	394	43	12	57	0	.271	$7	Brian Jordan	520	82	19	96	23	.303	$27
Cliff Floyd	334	41	10	39	11	.270	$9	Kevin Jordan	97	11	2	9	1	.264	-$1
Chad Fonville	198	30	0	11	10	.239	$1	Wally Joyner	467	66	10	75	4	.292	$13
Matt Franco	54	7	2	4	0	.228	-$2	David Justice	420	73	22	77	3	.285	$15
Gary Gaetti	532	76	24	88	2	.271	$15	Eric Karros	607	86	33	108	6	.272	$21
Greg Gagne	427	51	8	54	5	.256	$6	Mike Kelly	54	8	1	8	3	.206	-$2
Andres Galarraga	621	112	43	138	16	.298	$35	Jason Kendall	413	53	3	42	5	.301	$10
Mike Gallego	120	11	1	8	0	.203	-$4	Jeff Kent	440	61	15	59	5	.283	$12
Ron Gant	390	71	28	79	16	.257	$18	Brooks Kieschnick	121	15	3	14	0	.254	-$1
Karim Garcia	255	34	8	36	3	.252	$3	Jeff King	552	80	25	102	12	.269	$19
Steve Gibralter	270	31	6	33	2	.242	$1	Mike Kingery	270	41	4	28	5	.256	$3
Bernard Gilkey	558	97	25	100	16	.305	$27	Wayne Kirby	187	26	2	13	6	.252	$1
Ed Giovanola	133	19	2	15	1	.243	-$1	Ryan Klesko	525	86	35	98	6	.288	$23
Doug Glanville	205	26	4	25	5	.248	$2	Randy Knorr	104	12	3	11	0	.209	-$3
Chris Gomez	460	53	7	51	4	.246	$3	Tom Lampkin	132	18	4	20	1	.241	$0
Leo Gomez	256	32	12	38	1	.243	$3	Ray Lankford	548	100	24	87	31	.275	$26
Luis Gonzalez	493	72	15	78	10	.273	$14	Mike Lansing	597	81	11	58	25	.275	$18
Curtis Goodwin	259	36	1	16	20	.255	$6	Barry Larkin	537	114	26	83	42	.302	$35
Mark Grace	571	93	12	82	3	.326	$22	Mark Lemke	482	58	5	39	4	.258	$4
Tony Graffanino	88	13	1	10	3	.270	$0	Mike Lieberthal	170	19	5	22	0	.254	$0
Craig Grebeck	100	11	1	10	0	.243	-$2	Nelson Liriano	211	24	3	29	2	.272	$2

NAME	AB	R	HR	RBI	SB	AVG	$VAL	NAME	AB	R	HR	RBI	SB	AVG	$VAL
Scott Livingstone	137	15	2	17	1	.286	$1	Scott Rolen	502	65	18	80	9	.290	$18
Javier Lopez	470	53	21	67	1	.287	$14	Rey Sanchez	358	40	2	20	7	.246	$1
Luis Lopez	104	8	1	9	0	.210	-$3	Ryne Sandberg	540	80	21	86	11	.250	$13
John Mabry	460	50	9	59	2	.300	$12	Reggie Sanders	480	85	25	76	36	.276	$27
Dave Magadan	199	26	2	24	1	.280	$2	FP Santangelo	269	36	5	37	3	.259	$3
Wendell Magee	270	16	5	27	5	.264	$4	Benito Santiago	405	58	22	69	2	.266	$11
Kirt Manwaring	298	19	2	26	0	.241	-$1	Steve Scarsone	203	24	5	19	2	.236	$0
Al Martin	565	91	16	62	32	.294	$26	Gene Schall	84	7	1	11	0	.258	-$1
Manny Martinez	93	13	2	10	2	.230	-$1	Kevin Sefcik	158	24	1	15	4	.245	$0
Derrick May	311	35	7	44	3	.267	$5	David Segui	450	71	12	64	3	.289	$12
Brent Mayne	183	16	1	15	0	.256	-$1	Scott Servais	391	42	12	59	1	.259	$6
David McCarty	149	16	4	18	2	.244	$0	Danny Sheaffer	204	16	3	24	2	.228	-$1
Quinton McCracken	223	39	4	31	13	.289	$8	Gary Sheffield	515	114	41	118	22	.312	$36
Willie McGee	208	34	4	25	4	.280	$4	Craig Shipley	122	15	1	12	5	.294	$2
Fred McGriff	607	89	31	109	6	.293	$24	Terry Shumpert	52	8	2	7	3	.234	-$1
Billy McMillon	104	18	3	18	2	.280	$1	Joe Siddall	63	2	0	4	0	.211	-$3
Brian McRae	631	108	15	61	35	.279	$24	Ruben Sierra	502	67	16	80	5	.254	$10
Miguel Mejia	111	31	1	22	7	.268	$2	Dave Silvestri	111	13	2	12	2	.212	-$2
Orlando Miller	396	38	11	48	3	.259	$6	Mike Simms	54	5	3	9	1	.216	-$1
Ralph Milliard	111	24	3	12	3	.241	$0	Dwight Smith	133	16	3	17	1	.229	-$1
Kevin Mitchell	227	33	11	46	0	.309	$8	Sammy Sosa	549	89	40	110	25	.274	$30
Raul Mondesi	622	98	25	90	19	.294	$26	Bill Spiers	185	22	4	22	5	.246	$1
Mickey Morandini	528	66	4	39	20	.263	$10	Andy Stankiewicz	55	9	0	6	2	.241	-$2
Mike Mordecai	128	16	2	16	2	.235	-$1	Kevin Stocker	403	46	4	38	6	.244	$2
Hal Morris	499	75	15	76	5	.307	$18	Dale Sveum	202	41	10	42	0	.252	$3
Chad Mottola	102	11	2	11	1	.217	-$2	Mark Sweeney	128	21	2	18	2	.267	$1
James Mouton	304	41	3	30	23	.263	$10	Eddie Taubensee	316	45	12	50	3	.289	$9
Bill Mueller	466	74	2	49	1	.290	$7	Jesus Tavarez	138	19	1	9	5	.251	0
Glenn Murray	103	16	5	18	3	.223	$0	Robby Thompson	237	36	5	19	2	.216	-$2
Rob Natal	113	7	2	7	0	.203	-$3	Ozzie Timmons	142	21	6	19	2	.240	$1
Sherman Obando	180	27	7	21	2	.269	$3	Andy Tomberlin	103	17	4	14	1	.236	-$1
Alex Ochoa	380	52	6	42	8	.290	$10	Pedro Valdes	92	10	0	9	0	.254	-$2
Joe Oliver	290	33	8	45	2	.254	$4	Greg Vaughn	505	92	34	100	10	.250	$18
Rey Ordonez	505	52	2	39	2	.248	$1	Quilvio Veras	300	53	4	19	24	.257	$9
Joe Orsulak	209	26	2	23	1	.249	$0	Jose Vizcaino	394	51	1	36	9	.290	$8
Keith Osik	161	14	2	16	1	.240	-$1	Larry Walker	476	96	32	100	22	.296	$29
Ricky Otero	264	34	1	20	10	.264	$4	Tim Wallach	153	16	5	20	0	.239	$0
Eric Owens	124	17	1	10	9	.226	$1	Lenny Webster	175	19	3	18	0	.246	-$1
Jayhawk Owens	205	36	7	23	3	.265	$3	John Wehner	205	27	2	17	3	.264	$1
Tom Pagnozzi	352	37	9	44	2	.259	$5	Walt Weiss	513	83	5	42	13	.272	$10
Dan Peltier	55	4	0	7	0	.259	-$2	Devon White	532	76	15	75	18	.276	$18
Terry Pendleton	287	30	6	39	1	.255	$2	Rondell White	509	72	11	63	23	.293	$20
Eddie Perez	160	20	4	20	0	.238	-$1	Chris Widger	299	33	9	34	3	.254	$4
Eduardo Perez	67	9	2	8	0	.232	-$2	Rick Wilkins	358	48	12	47	1	.233	$2
Neifi Perez	334	45	6	34	3	.260	$3	Desi Wilson	178	15	2	18	6	.258	$2
Roberto Petagine	102	11	3	16	0	.251	-$1	Tony Womack	59	9	0	6	2	.270	-$1
JR Phillips	146	16	7	19	0	.202	-$2	Dmitri Young	308	36	5	37	2	.255	$2
Mike Piazza	531	89	36	107	0	.337	$30	Eric Young	556	108	9	68	52	.319	$36
Luis Polonia	180	27	1	13	9	.273	$3	Gregg Zaun	118	18	2	14	1	.249	-$1
Tom Prince	53	5	1	8	0	.233	-$2	Jon Zuber	165	24	3	21	1	.264	$1
Jeff Reed	257	26	5	26	1	.270	$2								
Jody Reed	404	43	2	39	3	.251	$1								
Desi Relaford	202	21	3	20	4	.220	-$1								
Edgar Renteria	580	84	8	58	20	.296	$19								
Henry Rodriguez	439	62	25	79	1	.271	$13								

Unlisted players are projected to have under 50 at-bats in 1997.

1997 Projections for American League Pitchers

NAME	W	SV	ERA	IP	H	BB	K	B/I	$VAL
Jim Abbott	6	0	6.04	174	204	83	76	1.65	-$11
Mark Acre	1	0	5.57	30	35	14	21	1.65	-$3
Willie Adams	9	0	3.92	152	151	46	135	1.30	$11
Rick Aguilera	8	0	5.19	136	151	37	109	1.38	$2
Jose Alberro	1	0	4.57	41	47	21	30	1.67	-$2
Scott Aldred	6	0	5.62	187	205	74	126	1.49	-$4
Wilson Alvarez	14	0	4.16	212	209	98	163	1.45	$9
Brian Anderson	5	0	4.88	110	122	29	48	1.37	$2
Luis Andujar	3	0	5.83	81	90	35	24	1.55	-$4
Kevin Appier	14	0	3.72	216	191	82	207	1.26	$20
P. Assenmacher	4	1	3.35	46	42	14	44	1.23	$5
Bobby Ayala	5	6	5.07	72	69	29	73	1.36	$7
James Baldwin	7	0	4.68	170	171	57	127	1.34	$6
Tim Belcher	13	0	4.27	226	247	81	111	1.45	$9
Stan Belinda	2	3	4.47	48	40	23	35	1.33	$4
A. Benitez	2	9	3.83	56	38	34	60	1.29	$11
Erik Bennett	1	0	5.04	73	78	37	53	1.58	-$3
Jason Bere	8	0	5.14	152	156	102	132	1.70	-$6
Mike Bertotti	1	0	5.25	53	56	30	28	1.62	-$3
Brian Bevil	2	0	4.82	67	67	23	42	1.34	$1
Jaime Bluma	2	6	3.52	57	53	19	40	1.26	$9
Brian Boehringer	1	0	4.00	44	44	18	36	1.42	$0
Ricky Bones	3	0	5.26	113	133	48	44	1.60	-$4
Chris Bosio	3	0	5.15	60	69	22	33	1.52	-$1
Shawn Boskie	10	0	5.54	171	210	57	110	1.56	-$4
Marshall Boze	0	0	5.19	38	39	24	25	1.67	-$3
M. Brandenburg	3	0	3.84	55	58	22	47	1.45	$2
Scott Brow	2	0	5.40	76	94	31	47	1.65	-$4
John Burkett	12	0	4.25	219	232	57	147	1.32	$13
R. Carmona	5	1	4.60	70	73	43	47	1.65	$0
G. Carrara	1	0	5.56	39	49	22	23	1.82	-$4
Tony Castillo	4	3	3.38	91	88	26	53	1.25	$11
Norm Charlton	4	17	4.44	69	63	35	67	1.42	$17
B. Chouinard	1	0	5.21	65	69	25	31	1.44	-$2
Roger Clemens	13	0	3.66	217	189	91	222	1.29	$19
David Cone	16	0	3.14	188	148	74	163	1.18	$25
Dennis Cook	3	1	4.32	66	59	32	60	1.38	$3
R. Coppinger	10	0	4.98	193	187	91	161	1.44	$3
Archie Corbin	1	0	4.94	33	27	26	24	1.58	-$2
Jim Corsi	4	2	4.08	62	55	30	36	1.38	$4
Tim Crabtree	3	2	3.07	51	46	18	41	1.24	$6
John Cummings	3	0	4.98	46	54	24	30	1.68	-$2
Jeff D'Amico	8	0	5.26	167	168	57	103	1.35	$3
Jeff Darwin	1	0	3.64	39	36	12	19	1.23	$2
Tim Davis	2	0	3.98	41	43	17	31	1.49	$0
Jason Dickson	3	0	4.40	90	103	37	42	1.56	$0
Joey Eischen	1	0	4.07	48	52	24	36	1.58	-$1
Cal Eldred	8	0	4.42	168	159	76	100	1.40	$6
Scott Erickson	13	0	4.99	220	253	70	110	1.47	$3
V. Eshelman	6	0	6.31	80	96	47	49	1.78	-$7
Jeff Fassero	15	0	4.36	222	230	65	205	1.33	$13
Alex Fernandez	17	0	3.48	247	239	70	191	1.25	$26
Mike Fetters	2	29	3.65	55	58	26	47	1.53	$27
Chuck Finley	15	0	4.19	237	234	97	215	1.40	$12
Huck Flener	5	0	5.08	136	137	70	85	1.52	-$2
Bryce Florie	2	0	4.37	65	59	38	62	1.48	$0
Marvin Freeman	6	0	5.66	127	155	54	73	1.65	-$6
Rich Garces	2	0	4.46	49	48	33	57	1.64	-$1
Ramon Garcia	2	2	6.15	45	50	12	24	1.38	$0
Greg Gohr	4	1	6.77	78	106	30	52	1.75	-$8
Dwight Gooden	11	0	4.90	170	167	85	128	1.48	$2
Tom Gordon	12	0	5.12	215	237	104	160	1.59	-$3
Jeff Granger	1	0	5.44	41	49	18	26	1.64	-$3
Danny Graves	2	0	4.74	38	39	15	28	1.43	$0
Jason Grimsley	4	0	6.49	96	110	58	62	1.75	-$10
Buddy Groom	4	1	4.81	70	83	33	50	1.66	-$1
Kevin Gross	4	0	5.12	102	114	41	63	1.52	-$2
Eddie Guardado	5	4	5.30	77	74	34	69	1.39	$4
Mark Gubicza	5	0	4.44	110	120	30	47	1.36	$4
Juan Guzman	10	0	3.46	179	162	62	148	1.25	$17
Chris Haney	8	0	4.74	188	216	49	92	1.41	$4
Greg Hansell	1	1	5.42	45	50	18	28	1.51	-$1
Erik Hanson	12	0	4.95	209	228	83	155	1.49	$2
Pep Harris	1	0	4.17	38	37	18	24	1.46	$0
Jimmy Haynes	2	0	6.55	62	70	35	46	1.70	-$6
Mike Henneman	1	22	4.41	47	46	17	39	1.33	$20
Pat Hentgen	18	0	3.74	252	244	93	172	1.34	$20
Gil Heredia	3	1	4.95	80	95	14	50	1.37	$2
R. Hernandez	5	36	2.68	78	66	35	86	1.30	$40
Orel Hershiser	15	0	4.09	199	218	60	122	1.40	$12
Ken Hill	15	0	3.86	234	238	87	147	1.39	$15
S. Hitchcock	12	0	5.10	190	215	73	131	1.52	$0
Mike Holtz	2	0	4.16	33	24	22	35	1.39	$0
Joe Hudson	2	1	4.92	43	52	27	21	1.85	-$3
Rick Huisman	1	1	5.05	33	31	18	28	1.48	$0
Edwin Hurtado	2	1	5.90	36	41	20	21	1.70	-$2
Mike Jackson	3	5	3.12	66	53	22	63	1.14	$12
Jason Jacome	2	1	4.85	72	93	27	40	1.68	-$2
Mike James	4	1	3.00	67	54	33	51	1.29	$7
Marty Janzen	2	0	6.34	63	77	31	40	1.72	-$6
Doug Johns	4	1	5.75	125	140	55	56	1.56	-$5
Randy Johnson	10	0	2.93	149	113	58	200	1.15	$20
Doug Jones	4	2	4.17	62	69	18	55	1.42	$4
S. Kamieniecki	3	0	5.54	60	66	33	33	1.63	-$3
Matt Karchner	4	1	4.82	66	68	40	51	1.64	-$1
Scott Karl	10	0	4.90	190	205	68	106	1.44	$3
Greg Keagle	2	0	5.34	3	54	36	42	1.71	-$4
Jimmy Key	15	0	4.50	176	183	56	114	1.36	$10
Brian Keyser	2	1	5.04	67	85	26	28	1.66	-$2
S. Klingenbeck	1	0	6.94	45	60	20	24	1.78	-$7
Rick Krivda	4	0	4.81	94	100	40	64	1.49	$0
Mark Langston	10	0	4.90	158	158	56	113	1.35	$6
Richie Lewis	3	1	4.26	82	73	54	71	1.55	$1
Jose Lima	4	2	5.35	69	82	20	49	1.47	$1
Doug Linton	8	0	4.97	128	140	36	101	1.38	$3
Felipe Lira	8	0	4.94	194	199	65	114	1.36	$5
Graeme Lloyd	1	2	4.44	51	53	18	27	1.37	$2
Albie Lopez	6	0	5.33	127	152	44	99	1.54	-$3

NAME	W	SV	ERA	IP	H	BB	K	B/I	$VAL	NAME	W	SV	ERA	IP	H	BB	K	B/I	$VAL
Mike Maddux	4	1	4.36	78	86	26	47	1.43	$3	Jeff Russell	2	4	3.49	50	55	19	25	1.48	$5
Mike Magnante	2	0	5.13	54	58	23	32	1.50	-$1	AJ Sager	5	0	5.12	137	159	52	90	1.54	-$2
Pat Mahomes	4	2	6.26	83	94	44	52	1.66	-$5	Bob Scanlan	2	0	5.14	40	49	18	16	1.67	-$2
Dennis Martinez	9	0	3.76	110	118	35	53	1.39	$7	Aaron Sele	6	0	4.88	152	177	65	126	1.59	-$2
Terry Mathews	4	3	4.21	78	77	31	64	1.38	$6	Paul Shuey	3	3	2.74	56	46	27	47	1.31	$8
Ben McDonald	11	0	3.95	201	200	66	135	1.32	$14	Bill Simas	2	1	4.38	48	50	27	44	1.59	$0
Jack McDowell	14	0	4.54	214	231	77	155	1.44	$7	Mike Sirotka	1	0	5.92	30	37	14	14	1.69	-$3
Roger McDowell	1	1	4.43	49	57	19	23	1.56	$0	Heath Slocumb	5	31	2.97	82	73	49	82	1.48	$33
Chuck McElroy	3	0	4.10	51	50	22	41	1.40	$2	Steve Sparks	3	0	5.49	80	87	40	30	1.59	-$4
Rusty Meacham	2	2	5.17	53	66	15	30	1.54	$0	Paul Spoljaric	2	0	3.68	48	38	24	48	1.29	$3
Jim Mecir	1	0	5.20	32	33	17	30	1.58	-$2	Dennis Springer	3	0	5.43	64	62	29	43	1.41	-$1
R. Mendoza	2	0	5.52	58	78	11	37	1.53	-$3	Mike Stanton	3	1	3.76	67	69	24	49	1.38	$4
Kent Mercker	6	0	5.16	106	110	49	67	1.50	-$1	Dave Stevens	4	5	5.01	63	67	29	37	1.52	$4
Jose Mesa	3	35	2.99	75	70	26	67	1.28	$38	Jeff Suppan	3	0	5.33	60	69	22	40	1.52	-$2
Danny Miceli	3	10	5.49	75	84	37	62	1.62	$5	Kevin Tapani	12	0	4.90	221	243	66	147	1.40	$6
Mike Milchin	1	0	6.56	32	39	17	28	1.76	-$4	Julian Tavarez	5	0	4.32	77	87	20	51	1.38	$3
Travis Miller	1	0	7.27	41	61	14	23	1.84	-$7	Billy Taylor	4	16	4.41	54	48	24	60	1.33	$17
Alan Mills	3	2	4.61	56	48	36	50	1.50	$2	Dave Telgheder	4	0	5.10	97	113	33	53	1.50	-$1
Blas Minor	1	0	4.26	49	49	16	37	1.31	$1	J. Thompson	5	0	4.67	142	149	77	106	1.59	-$2
Angel Miranda	4	1	5.03	80	85	51	54	1.70	-$3	Mike Timlin	2	30	3.78	54	47	19	49	1.23	$30
Mike Mohler	4	3	3.70	73	68	39	56	1.47	$6	Salomon Torres	4	0	4.41	90	90	40	57	1.44	$2
J. Montgomery	3	29	3.96	66	62	21	51	1.26	$30	Mike Trombley	5	5	4.01	81	80	31	62	1.38	$8
Jamie Moyer	13	0	4.39	164	176	45	86	1.35	$10	Tom Urbani	3	0	5.53	60	75	22	36	1.60	-$3
T. Mulholland	11	0	4.88	195	232	49	86	1.44	$4	Julio Valera	2	0	5.94	35	43	14	18	1.63	-$3
Mike Mussina	19	0	4.34	245	252	67	190	1.30	$18	Tim Vanegmond	2	0	5.64	40	43	19	25	1.53	-$2
Mike Myers	1	6	4.80	64	76	17	68	1.46	$4	Todd Vanpoppel	3	0	6.37	106	126	55	73	1.70	-$10
Randy Myers	3	30	3.87	55	54	27	60	1.46	$28	Ron Villone	1	4	4.12	41	29	26	44	1.34	$4
Charles Nagy	17	0	3.73	217	220	62	162	1.30	$20	Ed Vosberg	2	6	3.47	39	41	18	31	1.54	$6
Dan Naulty	2	6	4.12	44	33	26	43	1.34	$7	Tim Wakefield	14	0	4.39	193	198	76	124	1.42	$9
Jeff Nelson	4	2	3.48	77	69	33	93	1.33	$7	John Wasdin	7	0	5.87	140	152	51	78	1.45	-$3
CJ Nitkowski	3	0	6.24	93	108	60	73	1.81	-$10	Dave Weathers	3	0	5.58	78	94	39	47	1.70	-$5
Chad Ogea	9	0	4.31	126	126	36	81	1.28	$8	Bob Wells	9	0	5.37	106	115	41	70	1.48	$0
Omar Olivares	7	0	5.19	162	177	77	80	1.57	-$3	David Wells	13	0	4.54	219	233	52	133	1.30	$12
Darren Oliver	11	0	4.53	171	181	82	117	1.54	$3	Don Wengert	7	0	5.36	147	179	55	69	1.59	-$4
Jesse Orosco	3	1	3.38	56	39	29	56	1.23	$5	John Wetteland	2	40	2.76	68	53	23	73	1.12	$44
Jose Parra	3	0	5.94	66	84	25	42	1.65	-$5	Matt Whiteside	2	0	5.36	46	52	18	30	1.51	-$2
Roger Pavlik	13	0	5.00	192	201	83	131	1.48	$3	Bob Wickman	4	1	4.17	94	99	42	70	1.50	$3
Troy Percival	1	33	2.45	69	41	28	92	1.00	$39	Brian Williams	5	0	6.49	138	165	88	96	1.84	-$16
Andy Pettitte	18	0	3.96	200	208	66	142	1.37	$15	Woody Williams	6	0	4.27	139	134	60	107	1.39	$5
H. Pichardo	5	3	5.04	72	78	29	45	1.49	$3	Bobby Witt	13	0	4.99	197	225	90	157	1.60	-$2
Dan Plesac	3	5	4.40	70	69	28	72	1.38	$6	Steve Wojc'ski	4	0	5.52	64	75	26	22	1.58	-$2
Eric Plunk	5	2	2.51	78	58	35	85	1.19	$12	Bob Wolcott	5	0	4.98	111	133	39	58	1.55	-$1
Ariel Prieto	8	0	3.83	169	161	71	102	1.37	$10										
Tim Pugh	1	0	5.55	40	46	16	21	1.54	-$2										
Paul Quantrill	4	0	5.09	148	184	46	90	1.55	-$3										

Unlisted pitchers are projected to have under 30 innings in 1997.

1997 Projections for National League Pitchers

NAME	W	SV	ERA	IP	H	BB	K	B/I	$VAL
Brad Radke	10	0	4.72	200	204	50	114	1.27	$11
Carlos Reyes	4	0	4.65	90	96	43	59	1.54	$0
Arthur Rhodes	4	1	5.11	65	59	34	70	1.44	$1
Bill Risley	2	0	3.52	53	43	24	48	1.26	$3
Mariano Rivera	6	4	2.56	87	68	30	95	1.12	$16
Rich Robertson	7	0	5.08	180	188	111	113	1.66	-$6
F. Rodriguez	10	0	5.29	199	218	63	107	1.41	$2
Nerio Rodriguez	1	0	4.60	32	34	13	26	1.49	-$1
Kenny Rogers	14	0	4.20	201	196	82	119	1.38	$11
Jose Rosado	10	0	3.77	164	158	42	98	1.22	$15

NAME	W	SV	ERA	IP	H	BB	K	B/I	$VAL
Terry Adams	3	8	3.36	67	58	33	52	1.36	$9
Tavo Alvarez	2	0	4.87	35	36	14	20	1.44	-$1
Andy Ashby	10	0	3.30	178	169	47	119	1.21	$15
Pedro Astacio	12	0	3.46	208	200	60	137	1.25	$15
Steve Avery	8	0	4.70	158	169	51	116	1.39	$1
Cory Bailey	3	0	3.30	36	37	16	25	1.46	$1
Roger Bailey	4	0	5.79	90	100	51	44	1.67	-$7
Miguel Batista	0	0	5.40	36	40	15	26	1.54	-$3

Benson's Baseball Player Guide: 1997

NAME	W	SV	ERA	IP	H	BB	K	B/I	$VAL	NAME	W	SV	ERA	IP	H	BB	K	B/I	$VAL
Jose Bautista	3	0	3.90	86	91	20	38	1.29	$3	Mike Grace	6	0	3.87	98	98	24	60	1.24	$6
Rod Beck	2	35	3.62	64	62	15	48	1.21	$31	Mark Guthrie	3	1	3.19	72	68	23	62	1.27	$5
Matt Beech	4	0	5.18	82	87	29	60	1.42	-$1	Joey Hamilton	14	0	3.72	211	203	76	160	1.32	$12
Alan Benes	11	0	4.85	180	181	71	128	1.40	$2	Chris Hammond	4	0	5.67	83	99	28	57	1.53	-$4
Andy Benes	17	0	4.08	224	213	75	180	1.29	$12	Mike Hampton	9	0	3.60	153	162	49	103	1.38	$7
Sean Bergman	5	0	4.25	86	92	32	61	1.44	$1	Pete Harnisch	8	0	4.18	191	192	56	120	1.30	$7
Mike Bielecki	4	1	3.33	74	69	31	60	1.34	$4	Dean Hartgraves	1	0	4.80	39	34	21	29	1.42	-$1
Willie Blair	2	1	4.62	70	68	26	53	1.34	$1	Rick Helling	2	0	4.42	40	37	14	30	1.27	$1
Ron Blazier	0	0	5.38	40	45	18	24	1.57	-$3	Doug Henry	2	5	4.72	72	73	34	59	1.49	$2
Doug Bochtler	3	2	3.36	55	40	29	56	1.26	$5	X. Hernandez	5	5	4.41	83	85	30	82	1.39	$5
Joe Boever	1	1	5.70	30	34	12	19	1.55	-$2	Trevor Hoffman	5	39	2.65	83	56	27	99	1.00	$41
Pedro Borbon	2	1	2.86	37	29	11	34	1.09	$4	Darren Holmes	5	4	3.77	73	72	28	69	1.37	$6
Toby Borland	5	1	3.88	84	81	40	69	1.44	$3	Rick Honeycutt	3	3	3.20	47	44	8	28	1.10	$7
Joe Borowski	1	0	4.45	56	59	31	32	1.60	-$2	John Hudek	2	6	3.88	40	36	14	39	1.26	$6
Ricky Bottalico	4	35	2.86	71	45	28	74	1.04	$35	Rich Hunter	5	0	4.94	135	151	60	62	1.57	-$5
Kent Bottenfeld	2	1	3.20	70	70	22	37	1.31	$4	Mark Hutton	4	0	4.08	96	88	39	62	1.32	$3
Steve Bourgeois	1	0	5.12	59	68	35	32	1.74	-$5	J. Isringhausen	8	0	4.60	155	160	60	100	1.42	$1
Jeff Brantley	2	39	2.54	75	57	27	75	1.11	$38	Danny Jackson	3	0	4.69	81	86	32	52	1.46	-$1
Doug Brocail	3	0	4.46	55	61	20	32	1.47	$0	Kevin Jarvis	6	0	5.94	127	157	47	63	1.60	-$8
Kevin Brown	15	0	3.30	222	211	42	152	1.14	$22	Bobby Jones	12	0	4.19	206	224	52	124	1.34	$7
Jim Bullinger	6	1	5.39	132	146	65	89	1.60	-$6	Todd Jones	4	5	4.66	78	77	40	68	1.50	$3
Dave Burba	10	0	3.89	187	167	93	152	1.39	$6	Ricardo Jordan	2	1	3.00	45	38	22	30	1.33	$3
John Burke	1	0	5.90	63	75	31	54	1.68	-$6	Jeff Juden	4	0	3.65	70	59	30	56	1.27	$4
Mike Busby	1	0	5.60	37	42	19	20	1.65	-$3	Daryl Kile	11	0	4.39	195	200	93	184	1.50	$1
Paul Byrd	1	0	3.78	49	48	20	38	1.40	$0	Al Leiter	14	0	3.30	207	164	115	186	1.35	$13
Tom Candiotti	9	0	4.44	177	194	54	109	1.40	$3	Mark Leiter	9	0	4.54	202	218	69	152	1.42	$2
Dan Carlson	1	0	4.45	34	39	12	18	1.51	-$1	Curt Leskanic	6	3	5.04	80	81	35	84	1.44	$2
Hector Carrasco	4	3	3.74	82	70	47	63	1.42	$4	Jon Lieber	11	0	4.11	179	207	36	117	1.36	$6
Larry Casian	1	0	3.18	35	32	17	22	1.38	$1	Esteban Loaiza	6	0	5.08	164	194	52	87	1.50	-$4
Frank Castillo	8	0	4.51	176	191	47	132	1.35	$3	Rich Loiselle	1	0	4.08	33	36	12	16	1.47	-$1
J. Christiansen	2	0	5.64	46	49	20	41	1.52	-$3	Greg Maddux	20	0	2.62	246	216	30	186	1.00	$36
Mark Clark	13	0	3.88	195	207	52	121	1.33	$10	Barry Manuel	2	0	3.46	52	45	18	37	1.23	$3
Brad Clontz	6	1	5.02	72	71	27	48	1.37	$1	Pedroj Martinez	14	0	3.60	216	188	73	212	1.21	$17
F. Cordova	4	4	4.14	98	102	20	94	1.24	$7	R. Martinez	16	0	3.56	195	173	87	143	1.34	$12
Rheal Cormier	7	0	4.19	140	149	35	87	1.31	$5	Tj Mathews	2	4	3.06	60	44	24	57	1.14	$8
Doug Creek	0	0	6.04	31	28	19	26	1.48	-$3	Greg McMichael	5	2	3.14	87	81	29	78	1.26	$8
Omar Daal	4	0	4.34	61	56	28	54	1.37	$1	Kurt Miller	2	0	5.56	46	57	22	30	1.72	-$4
Danny Darwin	5	0	4.81	103	111	22	61	1.29	$2	Mike Mimbs	5	0	4.92	136	145	63	84	1.53	-$3
Rich Delucia	3	0	5.77	66	63	32	61	1.43	-$3	Dave Mlicki	6	0	3.78	108	111	38	91	1.38	$4
Mark Dewey	4	0	4.33	68	66	32	49	1.45	$0	Ramon Morel	2	0	5.16	49	65	21	25	1.76	-$4
Jerry Dipoto	6	1	4.15	75	84	38	49	1.63	$0	Mike Morgan	6	0	4.71	134	152	45	73	1.47	-$1
Doug Drabek	9	0	4.60	191	212	60	147	1.43	$1	Alvin Morman	2	0	4.82	37	38	20	27	1.57	-$2
Darren Dreifort	2	1	4.83	40	40	19	38	1.47	$0	Bobby Munoz	1	0	5.36	40	51	14	17	1.61	-$3
Mike Dyer	4	1	4.47	73	77	32	50	1.49	$0	Mike Munoz	2	0	6.18	48	56	23	44	1.65	-$5
D. Eckersley	2	31	3.53	59	64	8	49	1.22	$27	Rod Myers	1	0	4.78	40	37	24	30	1.49	-$1
John Ericks	3	12	3.88	64	70	28	55	1.54	$9	Jaime Navarro	14	0	3.87	222	231	71	147	1.36	$10
Shawn Estes	6	0	3.98	148	134	77	126	1.42	$3	Denny Neagle	17	0	3.61	223	229	49	157	1.25	$17
O. Fernandez	8	0	4.42	174	193	56	107	1.43	$2	Robb Nen	4	36	2.42	80	68	22	87	1.12	$37
Sid Fernandez	6	0	3.70	135	117	55	153	1.27	$7	Hideo Nomo	14	0	2.98	201	150	76	220	1.12	$23
Tony Fossas	1	1	2.56	45	40	18	39	1.28	$3	Gregg Olson	3	6	5.26	45	45	29	31	1.66	$2
Kevin Foster	8	0	5.09	120	119	48	92	1.39	$0	D. Osborne	11	0	3.59	190	184	54	130	1.25	$13
John Franco	4	26	2.55	53	51	20	45	1.34	$24	Antonio Osuna	5	3	3.32	66	52	25	67	1.18	$8
Steve Frey	0	0	5.45	30	37	13	13	1.67	-$3	Lance Painter	3	0	5.28	46	53	18	38	1.55	-$2
Mark Gardner	10	0	4.47	160	182	55	128	1.48	$1	Jose Paniagua	4	0	3.43	76	81	31	40	1.47	$2
Tom Glavine	16	0	3.10	231	219	82	171	1.30	$18	Chanho Park	6	0	3.72	111	83	67	123	1.35	$5

NAME	W	SV	ERA	IP	H	BB	K	B/I	$VAL	NAME	W	SV	ERA	IP	H	BB	K	B/I	$VAL
Jeff Parrett	3	0	3.48	66	63	29	62	1.40	$2	John Smoltz	20	0	3.10	236	194	68	246	1.11	$28
Steve Parris	2	0	6.03	43	51	18	37	1.58	-$3	Russ Springer	2	0	4.89	91	99	36	84	1.48	-$2
Bob Patterson	4	6	3.46	57	51	20	50	1.25	$8	T. Stottlemyre	14	0	4.11	224	212	88	200	1.34	$9
Mike Perez	2	2	4.51	45	49	18	33	1.51	$0	D. Swartzbaugh	0	0	4.90	34	37	17	18	1.59	-$2
Yorkis Perez	3	0	5.05	50	47	30	50	1.53	-$2	Bill Swift	4	0	4.97	62	70	21	35	1.48	-$1
Robert Person	4	0	4.33	97	91	38	82	1.33	$2	A. Telemaco	3	0	5.16	58	65	19	38	1.43	-$1
Chris Peters	1	0	4.43	62	70	23	27	1.49	-$1	Bob Tewksbury	10	0	4.48	190	218	34	104	1.33	$5
Mark Petkovsek	9	0	3.53	88	85	29	45	1.29	$6	Mark Thompson	8	0	5.25	171	199	74	100	1.60	-$7
Jim Poole	3	0	3.38	50	45	25	39	1.39	$2	Steve Trachsel	12	0	3.62	198	186	71	134	1.30	$12
Mark Portugal	9	0	3.98	174	169	50	100	1.26	$9	Ugueth Urbina	7	0	3.54	88	81	35	81	1.32	$5
Jay Powell	2	1	4.27	70	70	33	51	1.47	$0	Ismael Valdes	14	0	3.22	206	191	50	158	1.17	$20
Scott Radinsky	3	1	3.22	44	44	15	34	1.33	$3	Marc Valdes	1	0	4.86	50	69	25	13	1.87	-$5
Pat Rapp	8	0	5.05	155	177	86	87	1.70	-$8	F. Valenzuela	11	0	3.88	155	162	58	87	1.42	$6
Steve Reed	5	1	3.33	82	71	22	64	1.13	$8	W. Vanland'ham	10	0	4.49	178	186	72	108	1.45	$2
Bryan Rekar	3	0	6.96	64	84	23	35	1.69	-$7	Dario Veras	2	0	3.36	47	44	18	37	1.31	$2
Mike Remlinger	1	0	5.40	48	46	30	34	1.59	-$3	Dave Veres	4	3	2.98	80	79	28	77	1.34	$7
S. Reynolds	16	0	3.55	225	220	40	197	1.16	$20	Terrell Wade	3	1	3.31	43	35	29	48	1.49	$2
A. Reynoso	8	0	5.03	140	164	45	70	1.49	-$2	Billy Wagner	5	6	2.43	88	51	50	114	1.15	$14
Kevin Ritz	15	0	4.97	197	215	90	111	1.55	-$3	Matt Wagner	5	0	5.87	118	130	53	60	1.55	-$7
Mel Rojas	5	37	3.08	83	64	29	88	1.12	$37	Paul Wagner	4	0	5.01	121	129	54	101	1.51	-$3
Matt Ruebel	2	1	4.49	58	61	24	22	1.47	$0	D. Wainhouse	1	0	5.27	34	35	15	23	1.46	-$2
Kirk Rueter	6	0	4.01	100	103	24	49	1.27	$5	Donne Wall	7	0	4.98	166	191	36	110	1.37	$0
Bruce Ruffin	5	20	3.65	61	49	27	61	1.25	$19	Derek Wallace	2	2	4.44	55	65	23	33	1.60	$0
Johnny Ruffin	2	0	4.67	52	50	28	51	1.51	-$1	Allen Watson	8	0	4.77	166	174	62	104	1.42	$0
Ken Ryan	2	6	2.82	71	60	37	59	1.37	$8	Turk Wendell	3	14	3.70	70	64	29	63	1.33	$13
Roger Salkeld	5	0	5.36	115	114	55	81	1.47	-$3	David West	3	0	4.09	56	52	27	43	1.41	$1
Scott Sanders	12	0	3.63	170	140	57	179	1.16	$15	Marc Wilkins	2	1	4.04	73	73	35	60	1.48	$1
Curt Schilling	11	0	3.37	181	151	48	176	1.10	$18	Mike Williams	6	0	5.06	161	174	61	100	1.46	-$3
Jason Schmidt	6	0	5.70	136	152	77	104	1.68	-$10	Paul Wilson	9	0	4.60	160	161	60	117	1.38	$3
Pete Schourek	9	0	4.28	136	133	38	113	1.26	$6	Mark Wohlers	4	40	2.90	75	65	25	98	1.20	$37
Tim Scott	3	0	5.52	68	71	31	53	1.49	-$3	Brad Woodall	2	0	6.83	36	45	12	31	1.58	-$4
Scott Service	2	0	3.83	40	38	18	38	1.38	$1	Tim Worrell	8	0	3.16	125	114	40	104	1.23	$10
Jeff Shaw	5	2	3.22	97	92	28	65	1.25	$8	Todd Worrell	3	39	3.10	66	67	20	66	1.31	$34
John Smiley	13	0	3.52	212	203	49	160	1.19	$17	Jamey Wright	7	0	5.02	180	206	80	89	1.59	-$7
Lee Smith	2	2	4.04	55	57	27	45	1.52	$1										

Unlisted pitchers are projected to have under 30 innings in 1997.

Got a Question?   Ask John Benson

1-900-773-7526
(900-PRE-PLAN)
Just $2.49 per minute

Latest News Analysis, Updates, Revised Projections

Your Question - Ask the Top Analyst - LIVE!

1PM - 11PM Eastern Time

Benson's Baseball Player Guide: 1997

**HOURLY / DAILY / WEEKLY UPDATES
BY PHONE**

BOX SCORES - INJURIES - ALL SPORTS

YEAR ROUND STATS & ANALYSIS

Football - Basketball - Baseball

JOHN BENSON offers you................

PUSH-BUTTON access from any touchtone phone:

900-737-1234

**UP-TO-DATE INFORMATION
ON ALL SPORTS
JUST 99 CENTS/MINUTE**

John Benson's Draft Software

SIXTH YEAR!

"The First... The Best..."
"The only program with a proven track record"
Available for Windows® 3.1 / Windows '95®

Includes **1997** Forecast Stats

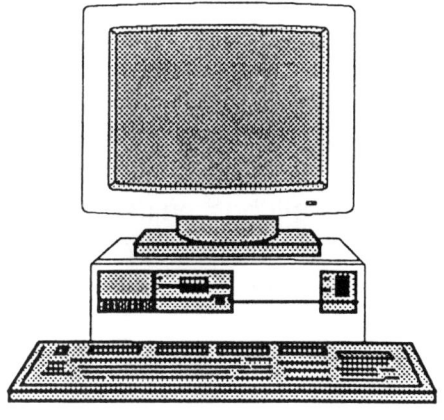

Requires 486 + 1 MEG HD

BEFORE THE DRAFT

- View and modify John Benson's 1997 Forecast
- View and Compare 1996 and 3 year average stats
- View Major League winter rosters and depth charts
- Analyze trades, enter freeze lists, toppers
- Customize program to suit your league!

- any roster, any dollar amounts
- select AL/NL, mixed or any group of teams
- choose from over 30 stat categories

INSTANT PLAYER VALUATION to fit YOUR LEAGUE and forecasts

FROM JOHN BENSON, THE GAME'S TOP EXPERT

DURING THE DRAFT

- One keystroke operation! Fast!!
- Assign players to rosters
- See instantly, at every moment:

    - rosters for every team
    - players taken and remaining: money spent and left
    - projected league standings
    - potential standings impact of every player on every team
    - draft inflation rates & adjusted values, updated continuously
    - John Benson's forecast stats & values

Only $49.95 plus $2 shipping, please specify disk size
Mail to: Diamond Library
15 Cannon Road, Wilton, CT 06897
1-800-707-9090 for VISA/Mastercard orders
for questions and Canadian orders, call 203-834-1231

Diamond Library Proudly Presents:

"This year" in baseball now begins in November! Don't wait until spring to get ready. STATS Inc books -- now available from Diamond Library -- come out very early compared to the rest of the book population. STATS does a wonderful service for baseball readers, by not waiting for the annual ceremonial blessing of statistics in December. STATS is printing and distributing books while others are waiting, and waiting, and waiting. You get the idea: this is the first and best source for the numbers you need. I use them myself. What else can I say by way of endorsement?

> ***Bill James presents the STATS Major League Handbook 1997*** - complete career line-by-line performance for every player who was in the majors in 1996. Rookies will have their career picture filled out with minor league year-by-year track record, so you get a complete picture. This book includes the harder-to-find numbers like On Base Percentage and Slugging Percentage, times hit by pitch, sacrifice bunts and sacrifice flies, wild pitches, balks, intentional walks, everything. The most complete and the earliest-issued book available anywhere at any price. Baseball writers call it "the red book," and you see it in every press box.

> ***Bill James presents the STATS Minor League Handbook 1997*** - same as the major league book, for those who haven't yet made it to the majors. Complete career numbers, year-by-year. Known as "the green book."

> ***STATS Player Profiles 1997*** - every noteworthy split, breakdown, and percentage you might want to use. For pitchers, get home/away, left/right, performance by days of rest, separate starter and reliever stats, before and after the All-Star break, and for last five years also get performance breakdown by months, by inning, by pitch count, and more. For hitters, get performance by place in batting order, with runners in scoring position and close/late situations, day/night, first half and second half ... the numbers just go on and on. I would find it hard to be a baseball journalist without this book at my fingertips. I use the blue book extensively to answer all kinds of questions. Does Pedro Martinez maintain his effectiveness after 105 pitches into a start? (No.) Is Pedro Astacio much better at home than on the road? (Yes.) Has Cecil Fielder show signs of tiring in September? (Yes.) Does Pat Hentgen perform well in September? (Yes.) Can Bill Risley pitch well when he pitched the day before? (No.) This book answers literally thousands and thousands of questions like these, quickly and easily, Also you can see the raw data behind the answers, and draw your own conclusions, too.

> ***The Scouting Notebook 1997*** - A guy named John Benson writes the Mets and Yankees reports, so you know the book is geared toward serious insight. Get a full page report on the strengths, weaknesses, critical factors and 1997 outlook for every major league regular and backup, from an authoritative source who covers each team. Also includes pieces on bit-part players and farmhands in each organization. There is simply no other book like it.

> ***The Minor League Scouting Notebook*** - alphabetical presentation of all the top prospects and best-known suspects, with a combination of sabermetrics and first-hand scouting reports. Every prospect gets rated A, B, C, on down, with the reasons behind the ratings clearly presented for your consideration.

AND ALL THE DIAMOND LIBRARY BOOKS ARE ALSO AVAILABLE EARLIER
(see order form inside back cover)

* * * * * * * * * * * * * * *

Stay Current All Year

You asked for it ... you got it:

JOHN BENSON'S WEEKLY Baseball Analysis Message On Tape

During the baseball season including spring training
Updates **EVERY SUNDAY**

During the winter: updates monthly

900-737-3707
Just $1.49 / minute

Choose from American League or National League

Who's coming, who's going
Impacts of free agent signings
Who's hurt - and what it means
Winners and losers in trades and other deals

FUTURE STARS -
The Minor League Abstract

<u>NOT</u> just a Pre-Season Guide
This book is an in-season resource

The one book that remains valuable all year long !!!

John Benson presents: FUTURE STARS - The Minor League Abstract. Knowing tomorrow's great players BEFORE they become famous -- that is the essence of FUTURE STARS. This book is packed full of vital information and insightful tips for minor league enthusiasts, Rotisserie leaguers, card collectors, and all baseball fans interested in the future of their favorite team.

FUTURE STARS combines two separate approaches to every player: statistical analysis and eyewitness scouting. John Benson expertly blends two approaches from two top analysts: Tony Blengino, pioneer on the frontiers of statistical analysis and forecasting player performance, and Lary Bump, baseball journalist who travels the country scouting minor league talent.

With these combined talents using different methods, FUTURE STARS gives you the most comprehensive look at the minor leagues today....and for tomorrow

Call Toll free, 24 hours a day **1-800-707-9090** for Mastercard and Visa orders.
For customer service, questions or Canadian orders, call **203-834-1231**
Or see the last page of this book for an order form.

Do You Surf The NET?

Visit **John Benson's** Web Site:

hhtp://www.johnbenson.com

For the latest news on products and services.

Download Benson's Draft Software DEMO - FREE !!

View a FREE copy of the on-line magazine - *John Benson on Baseball*

The Benson Baseball Monthly

25 to 40+ PAGES EVERY MONTH, YEAR ROUND

- The ultimate publication for insider tips, news before it happens, and analysis of unfolding events.

- The first, best, largest periodical for serious fans including scouts, management personnel, and Rotisserie league enthusiasts. Benson and his network of beat writers cover the major and minor leagues like no one else. Not just who's going to be traded, but who else gets affected and why and not just who's hurt or slumping or streaking, but who gets to play more, for how long, and why.

- The focus is always on the future. Benson's monthly features EXCLUSIVE QUOTES AND INTERVIEWS with players, coaches, managers, GM's and agents -- everyone with the most inside information and the power to make decisions. John Benson talks to GM's, front office executives, scouts, coaches, players and managers in their homes, offices, dugouts and clubhouses, for REAL, FIRST-HAND INFORMATION AND GENUINE SCOOPS!

- The Benson Monthly is featured in the book TOTAL BASEBALL, by John Thorn and Pete Palmer, as the pace-setter for the future in baseball analysis. Much too big to be called a "newsletter" the Benson Baseball Monthly packs every issue with 26 to 40+ pages of tips, commentary, letters, and insights from fifty writers and analysts nationwide.

- The Monthly offers both preseason forecast stats and values for all players, and in-season changes in forecasts and values -- always forward-looking.

Subscriptions are just $59 per year for FIRST CLASS MAIL. Or choose six months for $35, or the most popular option: two years for $99. A sample issue is $7.

Call Toll free, 24 hours a day **1-800-707-9090** for Mastercard and Visa orders.
For customer service, questions or Canadian orders, call **203-834-1231**
Or see the last page of this book for an order form.

GET READY FOR 1997

John Benson's
Rotisserie Baseball Annual - 1997
Ninth Annual Edition - A Proven Winner
Reserve your copy now.

- The most complete, in-depth preview of the coming season
- The most accurate forecast stats and values of any publication
- The last two editions both SOLD OUT, so order early!!

Now with a vastly expanded section on strategies, the Rotisserie Baseball Annual is the first, best, largest book for serious competitors, viewing every major league roster from the manager's and GM's viewpoint: who's going to play and how well they will do in the coming year, and why. In-depth analysis of every position on every team: which rookies are rising, and which veterans are fading. The best track record and most accurate forecasts of any publication -- and over a hundred tips on how to get the right players in drafts and auctions. Available February 25th.

Get an early edge on your competitors!
The sooner you have it, the more
you will benefit from it.

NOW With More New Strategies!!!

Call Toll free, 24 hours a day **1-800-707-9090** for Mastercard and Visa orders.
For customer service, questions or Canadian orders, call **203-834-1231**
Or see the enclosed order form.

AVAILABLE FROM DIAMOND LIBRARY FOR 1997

Title:	Quantity	Price	Total
The Rotisserie Baseball Annual 1997, Available February 25, 1997	_____	$22.95	_____
Future Stars - The Minor League Abstract, Available Feb. 25, 1997	_____	$19.95	_____
Rotisserie Baseball - Volume I, Available NOW	_____	$12.95	_____
Rotisserie Baseball - Volume II, Available NOW	_____	$12.95	_____
Baseball's Top 100, Available NOW	_____	$19.95	_____
Fantasy Football - Playing for Blood. - 1996, Available NOW	_____	$19.95	_____
Draft Software - - Specify Windows or Dos	_____	$49.95	_____

call 203-834-1231 for more details or try the demo at www.johnbenson.com

---

Diamond Library proudly offers: **STATS Inc. books** for 1997:

	Quantity	Price	Total
Bill James presents the STATS 1997 Major League Handbook (the "red book") - available NOW	_____	$19.95	_____
Bill James presents the STATS 1997 Minor League Handbook (the "green book") - available NOW	_____	$19.95	_____
STATS Player Profiles 1997 (the "blue book") - available NOW	_____	$19.95	_____
The Scouting Notebook 1997 - available February 1997	_____	$18.95	_____
The Minor League Scouting Notebook - available February 1997	_____	$18.95	_____
The STATS Pro Football Handbook - available NOW	_____	$17.95	_____

John Benson's **Baseball Monthly** -- exclusive news, quotes, interviews, latest developments in player valuation and performance forecasting, periodic review and update of entire player population. Single issues see below -- Six months $35 -- One year $59 -- Two years $99 (Canada add 10%) _____
March - April - May issues each $15, all other months $7

Shipping: $3 per book, $10 maximum for one order on one form
(Canada $7.50 per book $30 maximum.) _____

Order Total _____

Call Toll free, 24 hours a day **1-800-707-9090** for Mastercard and Visa orders.
For customer service, questions or Canadian orders, call **203-834-1231**
Diamond Library, 15 Cannon Road, Wilton, CT 06897

Please print your name _____ Address _____

City _____ State _____ Zip _____ Phone _____

Mastercard/Visa # _____ - _____ - _____ - _____ Exp _____ Signature _____

Please make check or M.O. payable to Diamond Library -- U.S. funds drawn on U.S. dollar accounts.
Rotisserie League Baseball is a registered trademark of R.L.B.A., Inc.